MULTI-LEVEL ISSUES IN CREATIVITY AND INNOVATION

RESEARCH IN MULTI-LEVEL ISSUES

Series Editors: Francis J. Yammarino and
Fred Dansereau

Volume 1:   The Many Faces of Multi-Level Issues
Volume 2:   Multi-Level Issues in Organizational Behavior and Strategy
Volume 3:   Multi-Level Issues in Organizational Behavior and Processes
Volume 4:   Multi-Level Issues in Strategy and Methods
Volume 5:   Multi-Level Issues in Social Systems
Volume 6:   Multi-Level Issues in Organizations and Time

RESEARCH IN MULTI-LEVEL ISSUES   VOLUME 7

MULTI-LEVEL ISSUES IN CREATIVITY AND INNOVATION

EDITED BY

MICHAEL D. MUMFORD

University of Oklahoma, USA

SAMUEL T. HUNTER

Pennsylvania State University, USA

KATRINA E. BEDELL-AVERS

University of Oklahoma, USA

ELSEVIER
JAI

Amsterdam – Boston – Heidelberg – London – New York – Oxford – Paris
San Diego – San Francisco – Singapore – Sydney – Tokyo

JAI Press is an imprint of Elsevier

JAI Press is an imprint of Elsevier
Linacre House, Jordan Hill, Oxford OX2 8DP, UK
Radarweg 29, PO Box 211, 1000 AE Amsterdam, The Netherlands
525 B Street, Suite 1900, San Diego, CA 92101-4495, USA

First edition 2008

Notice
No responsibility is assumed by the publisher for any injury and/or damage to persons
or property as a matter of products liability, negligence or otherwise, or from any use
or operation of any methods, products, instructions or ideas contained in the material
herein. Because of rapid advances in the medical sciences, in particular, independent
verification of diagnoses and drug dosages should be made

British Library Cataloguing in Publication Data
A catalogue record for this book is available from the British Library

ISBN: 978-0-7623-1476-8
ISSN: 1475-9144 (Series)

For information on all JAI Press publications
visit our website at books.elsevier.com

Printed and bound in the United Kingdom

08 09 10 11 12 10 9 8 7 6 5 4 3 2 1

Working together to grow
libraries in developing countries

www.elsevier.com | www.bookaid.org | www.sabre.org

ELSEVIER   BOOK AID International   Sabre Foundation

CONTENTS

ABOUT THE EDITORS   *ix*

LIST OF CONTRIBUTORS   *xi*

OVERVIEW: MULTI-LEVEL ISSUES IN CREATIVITY
AND INNOVATION
Francis J. Yammarino and Fred Dansereau   *xiii*

PART I: CREATIVITY AND SOCIAL INFLUENCE

SOCIAL INFLUENCE AND CREATIVITY IN
ORGANIZATIONS: A MULTI-LEVEL LENS FOR
THEORY, RESEARCH, AND PRACTICE
Mark D. Agars, James C. Kaufman and   *3*
Tiffany R. Locke

SOCIAL INFLUENCE, CREATIVITY, AND
INNOVATION: BOUNDARIES, BRACKETS,
AND NON-LINEARITY
Shelley D. Dionne   *63*

CREATIVITY RESEARCH SHOULD BE A SOCIAL
SCIENCE
Mark A. Runco   *75*

FACING AMBIGUITY IN ORGANIZATIONAL
CREATIVITY RESEARCH: CHOICES MADE IN
THE MUD
Mark D. Agars and James C. Kaufman   *95*

PART II: INNOVATION AND PLANNING

PLANNING FOR INNOVATION:
A MULTI-LEVEL PERSPECTIVE
  Michael D. Mumford, Katrina E. Bedell-Avers and   *107*
  Samuel T. Hunter

TEMPLATES FOR INNOVATION
  John E. Ettlie   *155*

INNOVATION AS A CONTESTED TERRAIN:
PLANNED CREATIVITY AND INNOVATION VERSUS
EMERGENT CREATIVITY AND INNOVATION
  Christine Miller and Richard N. Osborn   *169*

CONSTRAINTS ON INNOVATION: PLANNING AS
A CONTEXT FOR CREATIVITY
  Michael D. Mumford, Samuel T. Hunter and   *191*
  Katrina E. Bedell-Avers

PART III: CREATIVITY AND COGNITIVE PROCESSES

CREATIVITY AND COGNITIVE PROCESSES:
MULTI-LEVEL LINKAGES BETWEEN INDIVIDUAL
AND TEAM COGNITION
  Roni Reiter-Palmon, Anne E. Herman and   *203*
  Francis J. Yammarino

TEAM CREATIVITY: MORE THAN THE SUM OF
ITS PARTS?
  Claudia A. Sacramento, Jeremy F. Dawson and   *269*
  Michael A. West

TEAM COGNITION: THE IMPORTANCE OF TEAM
PROCESS AND COMPOSITION FOR THE CREATIVE
PROBLEM-SOLVING PROCESS
Christina E. Shalley 289

BEYOND COGNITIVE PROCESSES: ANTECEDENTS
AND INFLUENCES ON TEAM COGNITION
Roni Reiter-Palmon, Anne E. Herman and 305
Francis J. Yammarino

PART IV: SUBSYSTEM CONFIGURATION

SUBSYSTEM CONFIGURATION: A MODEL OF
STRATEGY, CONTEXT, AND HUMAN RESOURCES
MANAGEMENT ALIGNMENT
Simon Taggar, Lorne Sulsky and Heather MacDonald 317

LINKING INNOVATION AND CREATIVITY
WITH HUMAN RESOURCES STRATEGIES
AND PRACTICES: A MATTER OF FIT
OR FLEXIBILITY?
James L. Farr and Veronique Tran 377

MULTI-LEVEL STRATEGIC HRM: FACILITATING
COMPETITIVE ADVANTAGE THROUGH SOCIAL
NETWORKS AND SUPPLY CHAINS
Anthony R. Wheeler, Jonathon R. B. Halbesleben and 393
M. Ronald Buckley

A MODEL OF STRATEGY, CONTEXT, AND HUMAN
RESOURCE MANAGEMENT ALIGNMENT
Simon Taggar, Heather MacDonald and Lorne Sulsky 411

PART V: NEW VENTURE EMERGENCE

A MULTI-LEVEL PROCESS VIEW
OF NEW VENTURE EMERGENCE
    Cameron M. Ford and Diane M. Sullivan   *423*

A MULTI-LEVEL PROCESS VIEW OF NEW-VENTURE
EMERGENCE: IMPRESSIVE FIRST STEP TOWARD
A MODEL
    Claudia C. Cogliser and Jeffrey E. Stambaugh   *471*

DO LEVELS AND PHASES ALWAYS HAPPEN
TOGETHER? QUESTIONS FOR CONSIDERING
THE CASE OF NEW-VENTURE EMERGENCE
    Kimberly S. Jaussi   *479*

RECURSIVE LINKS AFFECTING THE DYNAMICS
OF NEW-VENTURE EMERGENCE
    Cameron M. Ford and Diane M. Sullivan   *493*

PART VI: ABOUT THE AUTHORS

ABOUT THE AUTHORS   *503*

ABOUT THE EDITORS

Michael D. Mumford is the George Lynn Cross Distinguished Professor of industrial and organizational psychology at the University of Oklahoma where he directs the Center for Applied Social Research. Dr. Mumford received his Ph.D. from the University of Georgia in 1983. He has held faculty positions at the Georgia Institute of Technology and George Mason University. Dr. Mumford has written more than 150 articles focusing on leadership, creativity, planning, and integrity. In addition, he has received more than 25 million in grant and contract funding. He is currently the senior editor of the *Leadership Quarterly* and serves on the editorial board of the *Creativity Research Journal, The Journal of Creative Behavior*, and *IEEE Transactions on Engineering Management*. He is a fellow of the American Psychological Association (Divisions 3, 5, and 14), the American Psychological Society, and the Society for Industrial and Organizational Psychology. He is a recipient of the M. Scott Myers Award for applied research in the workplace.

Samuel T. Hunter is an assistant professor in the industrial and organizational psychology program at Pennsylvania State University. He received his Ph.D. in industrial and organizational psychology from the University of Oklahoma. Dr. Hunter has notable research experience in the areas of leadership, creativity, and innovation with emphasis on multi-level investigation. Within these areas of research, he has published over 20 articles and book chapters. He is a member of the Society of Industrial and Organizational Psychology and the Academy of Management. Dr. Hunter has worked over four years with the Department of Defense.

Katrina E. Bedell-Avers is a research scientist at the University of Oklahoma's Center for Applied Social Research (CASR). She received her Ph.D. in industrial and organizational psychology from the University of Oklahoma. Dr. Bedell-Avers has published over 20 articles and book chapters in the areas of outstanding leadership, planning, innovation management, and leader errors. She is a member of the Society of Industrial and Organizational Psychology and the Academy of Management. Dr. Bedell-Avers has worked on multiple government contracts including those funded by the State of Oklahoma and the Department of Defense. She also serves as the editorial liaison for the *Leadership Quarterly*.

ABOUT THE SERIES EDITORS

Francis J. Yammarino is SUNY Distinguished Professor of Management and director and fellow of the Center for Leadership Studies at the State University of New York at Binghamton. He received his Ph.D. in organizational behavior (management) from the State University of New York at Buffalo. Dr. Yammarino has extensive research experience in the areas of superior–subordinate relationships, leadership, self–other agreement processes, and multiple levels of analysis issues. He has served on the editorial review boards of seven scholarly journals, including the *Academy of Management Journal, Journal of Applied Psychology,* and the *Leadership Quarterly*. Dr. Yammarino is a fellow of the American Psychological Society and the Society for Industrial and Organizational Psychology. He is the author of 12 books and has published over 100 articles. Dr. Yammarino has served as a consultant to numerous organizations, including IBM, Textron, TRW, Lockheed Martin, Medtronic, United Way, Skills Net, and the US Army, Navy, Air Force, and Department of Education.

Fred Dansereau is a professor of organization and human resources and associate dean for research in the School of Management at the State University of New York at Buffalo. He received his Ph.D. from the Labor and Industrial Relations Institute at the University of Illinois with a specialization in organizational behavior. Dr. Dansereau has extensive research experience in the areas of leadership and managing at the individual, dyad, group, and collective levels of analysis. Along with others, he has developed a theoretical and empirical approach to theorizing and testing at multiple levels of analysis. He has served on the editorial review boards of the *Academy of Management Review, Group and Organization Management,* and *Leadership Quarterly*. Dr. Dansereau is a fellow of the American Psychological Association and the American Psychological Society. He has authored 11 books and over 80 articles and is a consultant to numerous organizations, including the Bank of Chicago, Occidental, St. Joe Corp., Sears, TRW, the US Army and Navy, Worthington Industries, and various educational institutions.

LIST OF CONTRIBUTORS

Mark D. Agars	California State University, San Bernardino, USA
Katrina E. Bedell-Avers	University of Oklahoma, USA
M. Ronald Buckley	University of Oklahoma, USA
Claudia C. Cogliser	Texas Tech University, USA
Fred Dansereau	State University of New York at Buffalo, USA
Jeremy F. Dawson	University of Aston, United Kingdom
Shelley D. Dionne	State University of New York at Binghamton, USA
John E. Ettlie	Rochester Institute of Technology, USA
James L. Farr	Pennsylvania State University, USA
Cameron M. Ford	University of Central Florida, USA
Jonathon R. B. Halbesleben	University of Wisconsin–Eau Claire, USA
Anne E. Herman	University of Nebraska at Omaha, USA
Samuel T. Hunter	Pennsylvania State University, USA
Kimberly S. Jaussi	State University of New York at Binghamton, USA
James C. Kaufman	California State University, San Bernardino, USA
Tiffany R. Locke	California State University, San Bernardino, USA
Heather MacDonald	University of Waterloo, Canada

Christine Miller	Wayne State University, USA
Michael D. Mumford	University of Oklahoma, USA
Richard N. Osborn	Wayne State University, USA
Roni Reiter-Palmon	University of Nebraska at Omaha, USA
Mark A. Runco	California State University, Fullerton, USA
Claudia A. Sacramento	University of Aston, United Kingdom
Christina E. Shalley	Georgia Institute of Technology, USA
Jeffrey E. Stambaugh	Texas Tech University, USA
Diane M. Sullivan	University of Dayton, USA
Lorne Sulsky	Wilfrid Laurier University, Canada
Simon Taggar	Wilfrid Laurier University, Canada
Veronique Tran	ESCP-EAP, France
Michael A. West	University of Aston, United Kingdom
Anthony R. Wheeler	Bradley University, USA
Francis J. Yammarino	State University of New York at Binghamton, USA

OVERVIEW: MULTI-LEVEL ISSUES IN CREATIVITY AND INNOVATION

INTRODUCTION

"Multi-Level Issues in Creativity and Innovation" is Volume 7 of *Research in Multi-Level Issues*, an annual series that provides an outlet for the discussion of multi-level problems and solutions across a variety of fields of study. Using a scientific debate format of a key scholarly essay followed by two commentaries and a rebuttal, we present, in this series, theoretical work, significant empirical studies, methodological developments, analytical techniques, and philosophical treatments to advance the field of multi-level studies, regardless of disciplinary perspective.

Similar to Volumes 1 through 6 (Yammarino & Dansereau, 2002, 2004, 2006; Dansereau & Yammarino, 2003, 2005, 2007), this volume, Volume 7, edited by Mumford, Hunter, and Bedell-Avers, contains five major essays with commentaries and rebuttals that cover a range of topics, but in the realms of creativity and innovation. In particular, the five "critical essays" offer extensive literature reviews, new model developments, methodological advancements, and some data for the study of creativity and social influence, innovation and planning, creativity and cognitive processes, subsystem configuration, and new venture emergence. While each of the major essays, and associated commentaries and rebuttals, is unique in orientation, they show a common bond in raising and addressing multi-level issues or discussing problems and solutions that involve multiple levels of analysis in creativity and innovation.

CREATIVITY AND SOCIAL INFLUENCE

In the first essay, Agars, Kaufman, and Locke focus on organizational creativity and innovation. They examine the linkages between innovation *and* organizational effectiveness and survival through a multi-level lens, focusing particularly on the fundamental construct definitions of creativity and innovation from a multi-level perspective. In addition, two social influence areas, leadership and group factors, are considered as predictors of creativity and innovation to enhance multi-level understanding of the relevant issues. Agars et al. identify several multi-level models and advances in the creativity and innovation realms, but also several substantial limitations of prior work that can be addressed through a more comprehensive multi-level approach to creativity and organizational innovation.

In her commentary, Dionne notes a key contribution of the work of Agars et al.; i.e., a multi-level approach to creativity highlights that relevant social influences may differ by level, relevant domain characteristics may not hold across other domains, and creativity may be influenced differently than innovation. She then extends this work by considering several new research directions. These include levels-based boundaries for theoretical construct development, the use of bracketing to review construct implications at levels above and below the focal construct, and the use of simulation in multi-level modeling of social influence and creative processes to capture nonlinear dynamics.

In his commentary, Runco agrees with Agars et al. that innovation is an important part of business and can be informed by studies of creativity. He cautions creativity researchers to avoid "originality bias" and remember the older and larger body of social science scholarship that is relevant to work on creativity and innovation. Runco notes this is a complex subject matter with many diverse perspectives on it; and stresses the importance of individual differences, that creativity is not entirely a social process, and that aesthetics has a role in this realm of research.

In their reply, Agars and Kaufman note that the field of organizational creativity and innovation is complex and multifaceted, with core constructs that are ambiguously defined and levels issues that are confounded. They then provide an alternative perspective on the commentaries of Dionne and Runco, using levels of analysis issues to push theory development of the field. In particular, Agars and Kaufman highlight their disagreements with the commentaries, attempt to clarify some issues, and offer a multi-level solution to address several issues in future work.

INNOVATION AND PLANNING

In the second essay, Mumford, Bedell-Avers, and Hunter employ a multi-level perspective on planning to understand the contributions to creativity and innovation. They argue that effective planning, based on an incremental approach involving a viable portfolio of projects, is critical to innovation and will contribute to the generation of viable new ideas. Mumford et al. assert that planning for innovation must be based on fundamentals and missions derived from the project development cycle; and they discuss organizational-, group/team-, and individual-level influences on the planning process. Their multi-level model of innovation planning has implications for the management of innovation and creative ventures at the individual, team/group, and organizational levels of analysis.

In his commentary, Ettlie focuses on templates for innovation. He first notes the important contributions in the work of Mumford et al. Then he discusses underdeveloped or missing issues that would fit well into the Mumford et al. framework for future research on planning for innovation. Lastly, Ettlie presents conclusions and implications of these issues for innovation in general and the role of information technology and knowledge management for innovation planning in particular.

In their commentary, Miller and Osborn view the approach of Mumford et al. as a sophisticated incremental planning process across multiple levels of analysis. In contrast, they consider an emergent approach to innovation and creativity using grounded social processes, complexity theory, and an interpretive perspective. Miller and Osborn examine some emergent dynamics of the process and focus on both the middle of the innovation process and middle levels of management. They call on researchers to consider managerial mindsets and explicitly recognize differences in types of innovations and technological discontinuities.

In their reply, Mumford, Hunter, and Bedell-Avers note the differing perspectives taken by Ettlie and Miller and Osborn on the need for planning in the innovation process. Perhaps somewhat different from the commentators, Mumford et al. believe that innovation is inherently constrained, and such constraints both induce risk factors that merit attention and create other conditions for sustained innovation. In particular, they focus on over-systemization, complexity, and social systems at multiple levels of analysis that impact the innovation process.

CREATIVITY AND COGNITIVE PROCESSES

In the third essay, Reiter-Palmon, Herman, and Yammarino focus on the cognitive processes that facilitate creativity, specifically the multi-level linkages among individual and team cognition. Their work on team- and group-level cognition and creative problem-solving is built on the vast literature regarding various cognitive processes involved in creative production at the individual level and the factors that may facilitate or hinder the successful application of these processes. Specifically, for team-level creative problem-solving, they address problem identification and construction, information search and encoding, idea and solution generation, idea evaluation and selection, and implementation planning and monitoring. In all, Reiter-Palmon et al. generate over 50 propositions about team- and cross-level cognition and cognitive processes for future multi-level testing in the realm of creative problem-solving.

In their commentary, Sacramento, Dawson, and West develop the conceptualization of Reiter-Palmon et al. with an in-depth consideration of the emergence of team creativity. They apply multi-level theory and measurement ideas to the area of team creativity, concluding that there is no single way to treat team creativity and that the antecedents and definitions of the construct may change from situation to situation. Sacramento et al. view team creativity as a collective and emergent construct that has different practical implications across contexts.

In her commentary, Shalley extends the work of Reiter-Palmon et al. to the areas of team process and team composition. She indicates the importance of these issues when moving from the individual to the team level of analysis. In particular, Shalley examines how team process and composition influence team cognition and team creative problem solving. She also considers the dynamic nature of team membership and potential interventions to enhance team creative problem solving in organizations.

In their reply, Reiter-Palmon, Herman, and Yammarino acknowledge the extensions to their work provided in the commentaries of Sacramento et al. and Shalley. They then clarify some issues raised by the commentators and offer further multi-level extensions beyond the ideas of Sacramento et al. and Shalley. In particular, Reiter-Palmon et al. focus on leadership and context in terms of multiple levels of analysis to further develop their notions regarding team cognition.

SUB-SYSTEM CONFIGURATION

In the fourth essay, Taggar, Sulsky, and MacDonald focus on organizational sub-system configuration in a multi-level model of strategy, context, and human resource management alignment. Their model incorporates the following notions: the most advantageous human resources practices will vary based on strategic considerations; organizations have multiple sub-strategies, each of which should be aligned with a unique bundle of human resources practices; and the innovation sub-system and sub-strategy (rather than quality improvement and cost reduction sub-systems and sub-strategies) are the most valuable to organizations for contributing to sustainable competitive advantage. Taggar et al. provide numerous examples and data from a variety of organizations to illustrate their multi-level model and the implications for strategy-context-human resources management alignment and practices.

In their commentary, Farr and Tran question whether linking innovation and creativity with human resources strategies and practices is a matter of fit or flexibility. Taggar et al., who focus on fit, assert that the inner core is most critical to the attainment of an innovative sub-strategy goal and specific human resources bundles should be designed to encourage creative and innovative behaviors among inner-core employees. In contrast, Farr and Tran argue that innovation, an inherent part of the overall strategy, should be an important goal for all employee sectors, although the nature of needed innovative behaviors may differ. They indicate that integrating the work of Taggar et al. with their multi-level model of organizational innovation and creativity will enhance innovation in complex organizations.

In their commentary, Wheeler, Halbesleben, and Buckley analyze the model of Taggar et al. and note a number of "missed opportunities" that are not adequately integrated in the original work. In particular, Wheeler et al. question the top-down and vertical integration nature of the model as well as the lack of consideration of some human resources legal issues and best practices. They then expand the model with a multiple-level consideration of social network theory and the global supply chain. In this way, they hope to better capture the complexities of modern organizations and extend the work of Taggar et al.

In their reply, Taggar, MacDonald, and Sulsky attempt to clarify several issues raised in the commentaries of Wheeler et al. and Farr and Tran. Specifically, Taggar et al. note that their work is based on systems theory and, using this background, explicate the distinction between core and other employee groups, the importance of horizontal fit among the human resources management practices, and the critical nature of job analysis when considering innovative activities throughout firms.

NEW VENTURE EMERGENCE

In the fifth essay, Ford and Sullivan focus on new venture emergence via a multi-level process view to enhance our theoretical and empirical understanding of entrepreneurship. In particular, they use enactment theory and evolutionary theorizing, within and across multiple levels of analysis, to explain how ideas become organized into a new venture. They illustrate how organizing unfolds across multiple levels of analysis and multiple phases of development. Ford and Sullivan also explore implications of applying this multi-level perspective for new research directions and interpretations of prior work on new venture emergence. In all, their multi-level approach, which focuses on the founder, the founding team, and the venture, can serve as the basis for more comprehensive and testable explanations in the entrepreneurship realm.

In their commentary, Cogliser and Stambaugh first acknowledge the multi-level contribution of Ford and Sullivan to the new venture emergence area. They then note that, to be consistent with enactment theory, the recursive nature between the micro (individual) and macro (team and venture) levels should be addressed throughout each phase of the entrepreneurship process. As such, they highlight the importance of the individual level throughout the new venture process. Cogliser and Stambaugh also discuss three mechanisms–situational, action-formation, and transformation–to link the micro and macro levels in new venture emergence.

In her commentary, Jaussi raises questions about whether levels of analysis and phases of new-venture emergence occur concurrently. She agrees with Ford and Sullivan's call for a process approach to the study of entrepreneurial ventures. In this regard, Jaussi focuses on the potential processes associated with different levels of analysis that might underlie the enactment and effectuation processes in their model. Her primary concern is to explore if levels of analysis and phases of new-venture emergence always co-exist.

In their reply, Ford and Sullivan focus on two key themes that cut across the commentaries of Cogliser and Stambaugh and Jaussi. First, Ford and Sullivan explore recursive links between the micro and macro levels of analysis during the new-venture emergence process. Second, they highlight the underlying processes that may recursively affect new ventures at each level of analysis. Ford and Sullivan also emphasize the value of studying new-venture emergence as an evolutionary process involving multiple levels of analysis.

CONCLUSIONS

The essays, commentaries, and replies in this book illustrate the kind of issues that arise in dealing with multiple levels of analysis in creativity and innovation. The definitions of concepts (albeit creativity and social influence, innovation and planning, creativity and cognitive processes, sub-system configuration, and new venture emergence) change depending on what combination of levels of analysis are involved and added to them. The nuances of analytical methods (albeit, multi-level quantitative or qualitative in nature) change when one moves from one level of analysis to multiple levels of analysis. Moreover, although different paradigms may guide different scholars' theories and research methods and techniques, levels of analysis issues must be resolved to have a viable paradigm (albeit, traditional or novel). We believe that the demonstration of these issues in creativity and innovation, show that these insights, applications, and advances will apply to numerous areas of scholarly investigation.

The authors in this volume have challenged theorists, researchers, and methodologists to raise and address multi-level issues in all their disciplinary and interdisciplinary work. If you would like to be a part of contributing ideas to this scholarly endeavor, please contact us directly or visit our website at: www.levelsofanalysis.com

ACKNOWLEDGMENTS

We particularly thank Mike Mumford, Sam Hunter, and Katrina Bedell-Avers for editing this volume of the series. We believe that it has turned out very well, and we enjoyed greatly working with them. The publication of the *Research in Multi-Level Issues* annual series and this volume have been greatly facilitated by Julie Walker, Joanna Scott, Mary Malin, Zoe La Roche at Elsevier in the United Kingdom, and the production team of Macmillan India Limited. Closer to home, we thank our Schools of Management, the Center for Leadership Studies at Binghamton, the Jacobs Management Center at Buffalo, our secretaries, Marie Iobst, and Cheryl Tubisz, as well as our copy-editor, Jill Hobbs, for their help in preparing this book for publication. Finally and perhaps most importantly, we offer our sincere thanks to our contributors. The editors and the authors of the essays, commentaries, and rebuttals in this volume have provided new ideas and insights for unraveling the challenges of dealing with multiple levels of analysis and multi-level issues in a wide variety of areas. Thank you all.

REFERENCES

Dansereau, F., & Yammarino, F. J. (Eds). (2003). *Multi-level issues in organizational behavior and strategy* (Vol. 2 of *Research in Multi-Level Issues*). Oxford, UK: Elsevier.

Dansereau, F., & Yammarino, F. J. (Eds). (2005). *Multi-level issues in strategy and methods* (Vol. 4 of *Research in Multi-Level Issues*). Oxford, UK: Elsevier.

Dansereau, F., & Yammarino, F. J. (Eds). (2007). *Multi-level issues in organizations and time* (Vol. 6 of *Research in Multi-Level Issues*). Oxford, UK: Elsevier.

Yammarino, F. J., & Dansereau, F. (Eds). (2002). *The many faces of multi-level issues* (Vol. 1 of *Research in Multi-Level Issues*). Oxford, UK: Elsevier.

Yammarino, F. J., & Dansereau, F. (Eds). (2004). *Multi-level issues in organizational behavior and processes* (Vol. 3 of *Research in Multi-Level Issues*). Oxford, UK: Elsevier.

Yammarino, F. J., & Dansereau, F. (Eds). (2006). *Multi-level issues in social systems* (Vol. 5 of *Research in Multi-Level Issues*). Oxford, UK: Elsevier.

Francis J. Yammarino
Fred Dansereau
Series Editors

PART I:
CREATIVITY AND SOCIAL INFLUENCE

SOCIAL INFLUENCE AND CREATIVITY IN ORGANIZATIONS: A MULTI-LEVEL LENS FOR THEORY, RESEARCH, AND PRACTICE

Mark D. Agars, James C. Kaufman and Tiffany R. Locke

ABSTRACT

Organizational creativity and innovation are inherently complex phenomena, and subject to a myriad of broad contextual and social influences. As the evidence grows for the link between innovation and organizational effectiveness and, ultimately, organizational survival, there is no doubting the need for theoretical and practical advances in our understanding. The complex nature of these constructs, however, requires that such efforts utilize a multi-level lens. This chapter discusses key aspects of creativity and innovation in organizations, including fundamental construct definition issues, which underscore the need for a multi-level perspective. It also reviews extant theoretical perspectives for their contributions to a multi-level understanding, and the research in two key areas of social influence – group factors and leadership – that have received substantial attention in

Multi-Level Issues in Creativity and Innovation
Research in Multi-Level Issues, Volume 7, 3–61
Copyright © 2008 by Elsevier Ltd.
ISSN: 1475-9144/doi:10.1016/S1475-9144(07)00001-X

the organizational literature. The review and discussion of these areas reveal not only numerous advances, but also substantial limitations that must be resolved through more complex and comprehensive (i.e., multi-level) approaches. The chapter concludes with several recommendations intended to guide and inform future work in the organizational creativity and innovation field.

INTRODUCTION

A growing body of evidence indicates that creativity and innovation in organizations can have a substantial and positive impact on desired individual and organizational outcomes (Amabile, 1996; Cardozo, McLaughlin, Harmon, Reynolds, & Miller, 1993; Ford & Gioia, 1995; Nonaka, 1991; Shalley & Gilson, 2004). Indeed, some have argued that innovation has become an organizational necessity in the current age of international business and constant change in the world of work. As a consequence, understanding of the occurrence of creative processes within organizations and of the emergence of organizational innovations is a necessary and anxiously awaited development.

Despite the growing recognition of their importance, many aspects of organizational creativity and innovation remain to be elucidated. Perhaps, most responsible for this lack of understanding is the fact that organizational creativity and innovation are inherently complex phenomena. There is no doubting the substantial advances afforded by the last several decades of research and theory on creativity and innovation. At the same time, however, this work has revealed substantial limitations in our knowledge as it incrementally illuminates the complexities in the study of creativity and innovation. Significant questions remain about how to define creativity and innovation, the impact of contextual factors including the myriad of structural and social influences, and the absence of well-integrated and accepted theoretical models that capture the complexity of the topic. This is not to say that outstanding models of organizational creativity and innovation do not exist – in fact, they do (see e.g., Amabile, 1988, 1996; Drazin, Glynn, & Kazanjian, 1999; Farmer, Tierney, & Kung-McIntyre, 2003; Ford, 1996; Glynn, 1996; Hung, 2004; James, Clark, & Cropanzano, 1999; Meyer & Goes, 1988; Paulus & Dzindolet, 1993; Tagger, 2002; West, 2002; Woodman, Sawyer, & Griffin, 1993). Great voids in our understanding of organizational creativity and innovation remain not for lack of effort, we argue, but rather because of the inherent difficult and elusive nature of the subject matter.

Few topics are more deserving, or even requiring, of a multi-level lens than organizational creativity and innovation. For our contribution, we will focus in large part on a heavily researched issue – the role of social influence. We begin by discussing how to define creativity and innovation, a task that is a ubiquitous concern in innovation research. We then provide a brief overview of key theoretical advancements, followed by a discussion of two central areas of social influence in organizations, leadership and group influence. We end the chapter with a discussion of directions and recommendations for continued work in the field, with the goal of inspiring the continued pursuit of comprehensive approaches to understanding organizational innovation.

DEFINING ORGANIZATIONAL CREATIVITY AND INNOVATION

Despite repeated attention from scholars, defining creativity has remained an elusive accomplishment. Creativity has even been described as defying basic definition and, indeed, it is often *not* defined. Plucker, Beghetto, and Dow (2004) selected 90 articles that appeared in either of the two top creativity journals or that appeared in a different peer-reviewed journal with the word "creativity" in the title. Of these papers, only 38% explicitly defined creativity. Interestingly, although one might expect someone not to define the construct in a creativity journal – it is a reasonable assumption that the audience already knows the definition of this term – Plucker et al. point out that the rate at which the non-creativity journals defined creativity (33%) was actually lower than the overall average. Such uncertainty around construct definition merely serves to exacerbate the already formidable challenge of understanding and explaining creativity and innovation in organizations.

One early and prominent perspective on the definition of creativity comes from a researcher who is often referred to as the father of creativity, J. P. Guilford. Guilford (1956, 1967) placed creativity into a larger framework of intelligence in his "structure of intellect" model. He attempted to organize all of human cognition along three dimensions. The first dimension, "operations," simply means the mental gymnastics needed for any kind of task. The second dimension, "content," refers to the general subject area.

The third dimension, "product," represents the actual products that might result from different kinds of thinking in different kinds of subject matters.

One of the operations of Guilford's model (or thought processes) was that of divergent thinking – analyzing responses to questions with no obvious, singular answer (e.g., "What would happen if we did not need sleep?"). Guilford outlined four ways of examining divergent production: fluency, flexibility, originality, and elaboration. These four factors have shaped much of how creativity is conceptualized and measured. Fluency represents quantity – that is, the number of ideas you have. For example, if a person is asked to list possible uses of a shoelace, how many different responses are given? Flexibility looks at how many different categories a person can name, or how many different types of ideas a person has. Originality is being able to produce the most unusual ideas; it is an indication of uniqueness. If fluency is the ability to produce a great number of ideas, flexibility is the ability to produce many different types of ideas, and originality is the ability to produce the most unusual ideas, then elaboration – the final component of Guilford's model – is the ability to develop these ideas. One way to conceptualize this ability is the level of detail provided in a creative outcome.

Many critical challenges for defining the construct of creativity and innovation are specific to the realm of organizational studies. These include accounting for the multifaceted nature of creativity, incorporating issues related to domain specificity, recognizing the isomorphic (or non-isomorphic) nature of creativity and innovation as one transcends levels with organization, and differentiating between creativity and innovation. Sorting out these issues is not the purpose of this chapter; indeed, it may be a quixotic task in itself. However, most of these issues are relevant – if not fundamental – to developing a multi-level approach to organizational creativity and to understanding the role of social influences within such an approach. Consequently, we will discuss several of these issues and their importance to our pursuit.

Most early definitions implied that creativity was a singular entity. Specifically, creativity was often described as the production of novel ideas that are also appropriate and useful (Mumford & Gustafson, 1988). These initial conceptualizations, although meaningful, were somewhat limited in their application. Identical behaviors that may be considered "creative" in one organizational context may be unsettling or disruptive in another context. Ideas that are novel in one organization may be old or uninteresting in another setting. Similarly, creative acts carried out by an individual may be impossible or impractical for a group or organization. Ultimately, a singular conceptualization of creativity is lacking both theoretically and when one considers real outcomes in the business world.

Subsequent efforts to expand our understanding of the construct include the development of more complex typologies of creative outcomes (e.g., Sternberg, 1999; Sternberg, Kaufman, & Pretz, 2002, 2003a, 2003b), the identification and exploration of both positive and negative aspects of creativity (e.g., James et al., 1999), and the proposition that creativity is domain specific (Baer & Kaufman, 2005; Ford, 1996; Kaufman & Baer, 2004). Central to many of these efforts is the recognition (whether explicit or implicit) of the need to define and, ultimately, understand creativity through a multi-level lens.

Although it is certainly important to explore antecedents, correlates, and consequences of creativity and the creative process with a context-based lens, recognition of multi-level relationships is insufficient. Our understanding of what creativity *is* must be viewed from a more complex perspective.

Plucker et al. (2004) offer a definition of creativity that takes into account the concepts of person, place, process, and product: "Creativity is the interaction among aptitude, process, and environment by which an individual or group produces a perceptible product that is both novel and useful as defined within a social context" (p. 90). In other words, creativity is the how (ability and process) and the where and when (environment) made by the who (individual or group) making the what (a specific product both new and useful). Although perhaps too general to provide precise guidance to researchers and practitioners, such a definition magnificently articulates the complex and comprehensive nature of creativity and the multi-level considerations inherent in the construct itself.

In the realm of organizational studies, many (cf. Unsworth, 2001) have recognized the limitation of this definition and called for expanded consideration of the creativity construct. As part of this more extensive consideration, a growing number of definitions have been formulated that consider context. Unsworth (2001), for example, makes the simple but meaningful distinction between the problem type (open versus closed) and the driver for engagement (internal versus external). Driver type refers to the motivation underlying engagement in the creative process. Internal drivers represent behaviors born of self-determination (Deci & Ryan, 1987), whereas external drivers refer to behaviors that are responses to some form of external demands such as a job description or a monetary reward.

Although the ideas are presented in a 2 by 2 matrix, Unsworth argues that drivers for engagement range on a continuum from internal to external. The cells in her matrix include *Expected Creativity* (open problem, external driver for engagement), for which she provides the examples of "creating [professional] artwork"; *Proactive Creativity* (open problem, internal driver), for which she provides the example of "unprompted suggestions"; *Responsive Creativity* (closed, external), for which she provides the example of "responses produced by think tank"; and *Contributory Creativity* (closed, internal), for which she provides the example "contribution by non-project member." Although clearly an extension of the ideas introduced by Amabile (1983a, 1983b, 1988), Unsworth's matrix highlights the need for capturing multiple-level influences even at the definitional stage of the study of creativity in organizations.

Another definitional issue that demonstrates the multi-level nature of the construct is the increasingly popular recognition that creativity should be defined within the context of a particular domain (Baer & Kaufman, 2005; Ford, 1996; Kaufman & Baer, 2002, 2004). An intense debate has arisen over a similar question in the intelligence field. Some researchers argue passionately for a general factor of intelligence, g, in which one factor is largely responsible for academic performance, among many other things (Jensen, 1998, 2002). Other researchers argue just as passionately against g, offering instead theories of multiple intelligences or theories that paint a broader and more complex picture of intellectual abilities (Gardner, 1983, 2000; Sternberg, 1985, 1996). Is there a c of creativity that is analogous to intelligence's g and that transcends domains and enhances the creativity of a person across many different areas (for a debate of these issues, see Baer, 1998; Kaufman & Baer, 2002; Plucker, 1998)? Regardless of the existence of c, there are many reasons to focus more on the domain-specific angle.

If the creative product is measured, then creativity often appears domain specific. John Baer has conducted much of the work in this area. In several studies (e.g., Baer, 1991, 1992, 1994), he tested students ranging from second graders to college students. These students produced creative work by writing poetry and short stories, telling stories out loud, creating mathematical equations and mathematical word problems, and making a collage. Baer consistently found low and usually non-significant correlations between creative ability in these different areas. In other words, a student who wrote a creative poem was *not* more likely to also tell a creative story or write a creative mathematical equation. Several other studies (e.g., Han, 2003; Runco, 1989) have found similar results. In contrast, if the study focuses on the creative *person*, then creativity often appears general. Many of these studies rely on people describing or answering questions about their own creativity (e.g., Hocevar, 1976; Plucker, 1999).

Baer (1996, 1997, 1998) has argued that, regardless of where one falls theoretically along the generality–specificity spectrum, the practical outcomes would lead a smart manager to follow a domain-specific model. If one chooses creativity training activities based on a domain-general model (in which any choice of content for a creativity training exercise would, according to the generality hypothesis, be equally useful and valid), one might reasonably select only activities in a limited range of domains. In fact, unless one takes pains to avoid it, such a narrow selection is highly likely, because it is much easier to design creativity training activities in some domains than in others (which may explain why so many divergent-thinking exercises begin with the words "Think of many different uses for a ... ").

If domain generality were true, then creativity would be enhanced equally across all domains, even if all the exercises came from a single domain. According to a strict interpretation of this view, exercising poetic creativity should, therefore, increase creativity in personnel selection. But if creativity is, in fact, domain specific, then such a choice of creativity training exercises would result in increased creativity only in the domains chosen for training exercises and have little or no impact on creativity in other domains. Therefore, if domain specificity plays a significant role in creativity, then it matters greatly for creativity training. Conversely, if domain specificity does not play a significant role, then no harm has been done. If an organization does choose to emphasize creativity and try to train its employees to be more creative, why run the risk that the training will work only in a non-relevant area? Arts-based creativity institutes have seen a rise in popularity in recent years and are often highly recommended as ways to enhance organizational creativity (Katz-Buoincontro, 2005). Yet, until definitive evidence emerges that these institutes produce long-term improvement in areas relevant to an organization, a cautious supervisor may reasonably be skeptical of the benefits from such programs.

Similar ideas have also been presented more whimsically in the amusement park theoretical model (APT model) of creativity (Kaufman & Baer, 2004). The APT model suggests that although initial requirements such as intelligence, motivation, and an appropriate environment are necessary for creative performance, they do not present the full picture. What ultimately leads to creativity will be a function of the intersection of individual characteristics with general thematic areas, domains, and micro-domains within which an individual performs.

For example, Ruscio, Whitney, and Amabile (1998) studied factors that predicted creativity by domain (problem solving, art, and writing). Some factors were found to be important to all domains, but important differences were also identified. For example, in the domain of writing, which was measured with a haiku poem-writing task, the other central indicator of creativity was a factor called "striving." Striving was composed of difficulty, transitions, questioning how to do something, repeating something, and positive and negative exclamations. It is easy to see how striving might influence creativity in the writing task more than creativity in the art task of making a collage.

The ideas presented in the APT model have also been applied to creativity in organizations (Agars, Baer, & Kaufman, 2005). This extension of the concept argues that organizational practices related to the management of human resources would benefit from an expanded consideration of what creativity is and how individual and contextual factors matter. Similarly, in their substantive review of personal and contextual factors related to creativity, Shalley, Zhou, and Oldham (2004) discuss the importance of the person–context interaction in defining creativity. Among their many insights, they illustrate the need for domain specificity in their review of the cross-cultural creativity literature, suggesting that differences in creativity and the creative process manifest in different forms across cultures.

In presenting his "theory of individual creative action in multiple social domains" Ford (1996) defines creativity as "a domain-specific, subjective judgment of the novelty and value of an outcome of a particular action" (p. 1115). Ford says that because individuals within (and outside of) a particular domain identify or define creativity through their subjective judgments, what we consider to be creative in a particular domain (i.e., how we define creativity) is not independent of social-construction processes operating within that domain. Ford's definition makes clear that not only must we consider multi-level influences in our understanding of creativity, but we must also begin with the recognition that how we define this concept is also influenced by factors at higher levels. In his work, many of these are social factors, such as group socialization practices and organizational absorption.

Csikszentmihalyi (1996, 1999) devised a systems model that presents one way of looking at creative products. Creativity, he argued, is an interaction between the domain, the field, and the person. The domain could be as broad as mathematics or science, or it could be as specific as game theory or particle physics. The field is defined as the "gate keepers" – teachers, editors, critics, and others. Essentially, these are individuals whom you need to impress if you want to be successful. The third component is the person – the one who creates an idea, theory, or piece of art that the field enjoys and the domain accepts.

In Csikszentmihalyi's theory, the domain, field, and person work interactively. If the field did not believe that the later work of Bach was creative in the domain of music when he was still alive, it means that his work was not creative at the time. Only later, when more modern critics, professors, and musicians recognized his talent, can Bach's work be called creative. What Csikszentmihalyi's ideas imply for organizations is that social influence does not simply influence creativity but may actually determine what is or is not creative. If society does not accept a new product or service as creative, then (according to Csikszentmihalyi) it is not. Twenty years later, if society decides that the product is creative, then it becomes creative (albeit with little benefit likely to accrue to the organization).

In addition to the objective domain being important, some research suggests that *perceptions* of what we define as creative may differ within a given domain. In a study of 170 managers from top Egyptian companies, Mostafa (2005) found that managers provided different perceptions of what was and was not creative and innovative based on the functional area in which they worked, their own education level, their gender, and even their tendency to be (or not be) risk averse. In addition to the effects associated with the functional area, Mostafa found that temporal factors such as time pressure influenced perceptions of creativity and innovation. Clearly, our definitions of creativity and innovation are functions of perceptions, which are influenced by the social context in which we reside at the time.

Similar issues arise when we consider individual self-assessment of creativity. Kaufman and Baer (2002) found that, when asked to assess their own creativity in different domains, students tended to be consistent. If they viewed themselves as generally creative, then they also viewed themselves as creative in different areas. The only area that was not correlated with general creativity ratings was mathematics (and, for females, science). The only factor that was not correlated with self-reported general creativity and a creative personality score was a math and science factor. Why might this be the case? Mathematics and science may not fall into people's conceptions of creativity – they simply may not consider math an area in which to be creative.

This idea would be consistent with Paulos's (1988) idea of innumeracy, the inability to accurately use numbers and chance. "Romantic misconceptions about the nature of mathematics," Paulos wrote, "lead to an intellectual environment hospitable to and even encouraging of poor mathematical education and psychological distaste for the subject and lie at the base of much innumeracy" (p. 120). Perhaps we should not be surprised to find that individuals who are members of a society that does not value mathematical ability also do not perceive mathematics to be a field that affords opportunities for creativity.

Other attempts to provide more elaborate definitions of creativity have focused on the identification of unique creative outcomes, such as the propulsion model of creativity presented by Sternberg and his colleagues (Sternberg, 1999; Sternberg, Kaufman, & Pretz, 2001; Sternberg et al., 2002). The propulsion model focuses exclusively on creative products and has been applied to both business innovation and leadership (Sternberg, 1999; Sternberg et al., 2001, 2002, 2003a, 2003b; Sternberg, Pretz, & Kaufman, 2003). This theory describes eight different ways that a person or a company can make a creative contribution, each of which is based in one of three broad approaches:

- The first approach comprises types of outcomes that accept current paradigms and attempt to extend them.
- The second approach comprises types that reject the current paradigms and are intended to replace them.
- The third approach comprises types that attempt to create new paradigms through the integration of existing ones.

According to propulsion theory, the kind of creative contribution a product or campaign makes does not necessarily predict the quality of that work. The propulsion model (which will be described in more detail when we explore models of creativity later in this chapter) provides further illustration that defining creativity requires a multifaceted approach and is, to some extent, defined by the domain in which a creative product is introduced.

Regardless of the domain of interest, most research and theory-based definitions of "creativity" boil down to two components. First, creativity must represent something different, new, or innovative (Baer, 1997; Sternberg et al., 2002). Second, for something to be creative, it must be appropriate to the task at hand. In other words, a creative response is useful and relevant. A certain level of high quality is often linked with appropriateness – you not only fulfill task demands, but also do it well (Sternberg et al., 2002). This distinction has emerged in a number of forms.

One way of expressing the innovative–appropriate distinction is found in the Geneplore model (Finke, Ward, & Smith, 1992). This framework defines creativity as having two phases – generative and exploratory. Generation, the "novel" part, entails generating many different ideas. Exploration refers to evaluating these possible options and choosing the best one (or ones). Guilford (1967, 1988) was also interested in the concept of exploration; in his structure of intellect model, he presented a variation of the idea called "evaluation," which was included as one of the operations. The exploratory or evaluative aspect of creativity is often overlooked; indeed, when one thinks of a creative person, the image is not often one of an individual pondering and selecting the best alternative.

Another conception of creativity that makes a similar distinction is the recognition of functional creativity (Cropley & Cropley, 2005). This approach emphasizes the "evaluation" and "exploration" aspects of creativity discussed earlier. Functional creativity argues that most definitions and measurements of creativity overemphasize the aesthetic aspects of creativity. Indeed, most creativity tests or measured products involve wordplay, collages, poetry, and similar exercises. Yet for domains that must create a workable product (as in organizations), the relevance and effectiveness of a product are key considerations. This concept may seem obvious, but many non-organizational assessments and models of creativity do not emphasize it.

In addition to being novel, relevant, and effective, functional creativity may incorporate aspects of elegance and generalizability (Cropley, Kaufman, & Cropley, in press). Elegance captures how well a product feels complete and appears to be a good solution. Some products *feel* right – the consumer sees them and instantly grasps why they work and why they would make his or her life better. In contrast, generalizability taps into how broadly the product can be applied. Just as in the propulsion model, redefinition allows products to be marketed and promoted for alternative uses, so, too, does the generalizability of a product allow it to be more broadly applied.

In the organizational literature, the distinction between idea generation and implementation is now most commonly characterized by the differentiation of creativity and innovation. Shalley et al. (2004) state, "Creativity refers to the development of novel, potentially useful ideas. Although employees might share these ideas with others, only when the ideas are successfully implemented at the organization or unit level would they be considered innovation (Amabile, 1996; Mumford & Gustafson, 1988)" (p. 934). This distinction, however, is not simply a function of providing alternative names for an isomorphic construct. Innovation, when considered as an organizational outcome, is *not* simply a higher level of creativity, nor is it restricted to a collective. Innovation merely indicates the intentional implementation of a creative outcome, product, or process (e.g., novel, useful), which may occur at the individual, group, or organizational levels (West & Farr, 1990). Although innovation may more commonly occur at a higher level and creativity at the individual or group levels, they are not inherently limited in that way.

A further argument for creativity and innovation being independent constructs can be found in the different predictors of each. The components that lead to successful creativity are not the same as – and, indeed, can be opposite to – the components that lead to successful innovation. West (2002), as one example, suggests that the environmental condition of threat has not just differing, but also opposing effects on individual creativity and organizational innovation. Specifically, he argues that during the creative process, individuals produce fewer ideas (i.e., are less creative) under conditions of threat than when they are under non-threatening conditions.

Conversely, the likelihood that a new but existing idea is implemented (i.e., innovation) increases under conditions of threat. Rank, Pace, and Frese (2004) propose that certain individual characteristics (such as extroversion and action orientation) and certain contextual factors (such as external demands and charismatic leadership) will differentially influence creativity and innovation. This distinction is critical to the continued development of theoretical models of creativity and innovation.

In certain specific bodies of literature (e.g., marketing), a general definition of innovation as the "implementation" of a novel product or process is less helpful because concerns surrounding innovations are more precise. For example, Frambach and Schillewaert (2002) present a multi-level framework for understanding organizational innovation *adoption*, which is defined not as the implementation of a novel idea, but rather as the success or use of the innovation. Furthermore, they propose a two-level decision process that identifies both an organizational adoption and an individual adoption as unique outcomes. In other words, differences are evident not just between innovating and adopting, but also between adopting at different levels within the same organization. Such specific consideration of innovation is beyond the scope of the current chapter, however. Nevertheless, it is important to note that as we continue to expand our understanding of creativity and innovation in organizations, many frontiers remain to be explored.

Summary

Evident in the myriad of considerations in defining creativity is that how we define creativity affects the contextual factors of relevance. Relevant social influences at the individual level often differ from relevant social influences at the organizational level, for example. Meaningful domain characteristics such as social, structural, and other environmental influences differ across domains. Creativity – defined as the production of novel, useful ideas – may be influenced differently than innovation – defined as the implementation of novel ideas. Concomitantly, these issues underscore that theoretical and practical developments focusing on creativity and innovation in organizations *must* be clear in their construct definition so as to advance our field (Bacharach, 1989; Whetton, 1989). To that end, a number of multi-level models of creativity and innovation have been developed over the last 15 years, and we continue with an examination of several such contributions.

PREDICTING CREATIVITY: AN INITIAL LOOK AT SOCIAL FACTORS

Early efforts to understand creativity focused nearly exclusively on characteristics of the individual (Barron & Harrington, 1981; Galton, 1869; Goertzel, Goertzel, & Goertzel, 1978; Martindale, 1989; Reuter et al., 2005; Schaefer & Anastasi, 1968). Through these efforts we have learned much about individual creativity. One frequent topic of investigation, for example, is the relationship between intelligence and creativity. Creativity has been found to be associated with measures of intelligence (especially verbal intelligence), but this relationship is not particularly strong (see Barron & Harrington, 1981). Another commonly considered characteristic is personality, with the strongest relationship being found between creativity and openness to experience (Furnham, 1999; McCrae, 1987). Other individual traits that have been studied in relationship with creativity include mental illness (Jamison, 1989; Kaufman, 2001; Ludwig, 1995), productivity (Simonton, 1977, 1985), and social support (Bargar & Duncan, 1990; Cole, Sugioka, & Yamagata-Lynch, 1999; Miell & MacDonald, 2000). Early research on creativity in organizations followed a similar path. Although our understanding of individual-level creativity and individual-level antecedents was substantial, this early work provided virtually no consideration of the environment in which an individual acted.

It was not until the work of Amabile and her colleagues that the importance of contextual factors in creativity was more readily considered. Amabile's initial componential theory of creativity (1983a, 1983b) and her later componential model of organizational innovation (1988, 1997) are not true multi-level theories by commonly accepted standards (cf. Bacharach,

1989; Klein & Kozlowski, 2000; Rousseau, 1985; Whetton, 1989). However, these theories transformed the way we thought about creativity by moving the theoretical and research focus away from an exclusive consideration of the creative person and toward a more expanded vision emphasizing the potential influence that contextual factors might have on creative outcomes. Ultimately, the production of creative products and processes requires support from the environment (West, 1995), and Amabile's work represents an initial pursuit into the influence exerted by environmental factors.

In what represents the earliest theory of creativity to include social factors, Amabile, in her componential theory of creativity (1983a, 1983b), proposed that three components are required for individual creativity: intrinsic motivation to complete the task, skills in the task domain, and skills in creative thinking. Although a straightforward consideration of context is evident in the second component (i.e., one must have skills that match the requirements of the domain in which he or she is performing), context has received the most attention in this line of research for its potential effects on motivation. More specifically, the influence of social context on experiences of intrinsic and/or extrinsic motivation has been the focus of numerous studies. Next, we examine the extensive literature on motivation and creativity. Given the extent that this topic dominates the area of contextual factors, we believe that this in-depth look is warranted.

Motivation and Creativity

Teresa Amabile and her colleagues (Amabile, 1979, 1982, 1983a, 1983b, 1996; Amabile & Gitomer, 1984; Amabile, Hennessey, & Grossman, 1986; Amabile, Hill, Hennessey, & Tighe, 1994) have conducted many of the studies on the relationship between motivation and creativity. Amabile's work builds on what is sometimes called "hidden cost of reward" or "over justification" research (Bem, 1972; de Charms, 1968; Kelley, 1967, 1973; Lepper & Greene, 1975, 1978; Lepper, Greene, & Nisbett, 1973); such research shows that offering subjects a reward to perform a task they already find interesting will often decrease their intrinsic motivation. Indeed, according to this theory, offering extensive praise, rewards, or performance incentives may backfire when dealing with already dedicated and passionate workers (see e.g., Kohn, 1993). The seemingly simple insight that intrinsic motivation leads to higher levels of creativity than does extrinsic motivation and the not-as-obvious corollary that increasing extrinsic motivation (via rewards such as grades, payment, or the prospect of evaluation) actually *decreases* creativity have produced a significant quantity of interesting and increasingly refined research and experimental hypotheses.

Amabile (1985) studied the effects of an intrinsic versus extrinsic motivational orientation on creative-writing graduate and undergraduate students. Participants in this study first had to write a poem to establish a baseline of creative writing. Amabile then gave them a list of reasons for writing. One group received lists that stressed extrinsic motivation (i.e., "You want your writing teachers to be favorably impressed with your writing talent," "You know that many of the best jobs available require good writing skills"), while another group received lists that emphasized intrinsic motivation (i.e., "You enjoy the opportunity for self expression," "You like to play with words"). Amabile had the students rank-order these reasons and then write a second poem. Outside raters evaluated both poems. The students who were given the list of intrinsic reasons to rank, as well as members of a control group who received no lists, showed no significant difference in the ratings of creativity. The students given the extrinsic list, however, were rated significantly lower on their second poem.

Another contextual factor incorporated into Amabile's work is the domain of interest. For example, as discussed earlier, Ruscio et al. (1998) examined which task behaviors best predicted creativity in three domains (problem solving, art, and writing). The most important indicator was found to be a participant's involvement in the task, as measured through behavioral coding and think-aloud protocol analysis. Involvement in a task is a crucial component of intrinsic motivation.

In addition, Amabile et al. (1986) looked at the effect of rewards on students' creative performance. Their study included a "reward"/"no reward" condition and a second condition regarding how the task was presented – "work," "play," or no label. In the "reward" condition, the children were offered the use of a Polaroid camera – a desirable activity for these children – if they would promise to tell a story later. In the "no reward" condition, the children were allowed the use of a Polaroid camera, but its use was presented as merely another task, not as a reward for future activity. After the children in all conditions took photographs, they were asked to tell a story, based on a picture book. In the "work" condition, the storytelling task was labeled "work"; in the "play" task, it was labeled "play"; in the no-label condition, the storytelling activity was not assigned a label. These stories were then judged by outside raters. Amabile et al. (1986) found that children told more creative stories if they were in the "no reward" condition, while no significant effect was found for the task labeling condition.

The effect of rewards on creativity may be more complex, however, as some researchers have demonstrated that the harm to creativity from rewards may be minimized. In one study, individuals who received intrinsic motivation training (such as directed discussion sessions that focused on intrinsic reasons for performing the task in question) before performing a task and receiving a reward showed less negative effects on creativity (Hennessey, Amabile, & Martinage, 1989). Other researchers, however, have found that even with tasks set in an intrinsically motivating context, rewards have a negative effect on performance (Cooper, Clasen, Silva-Jalonen, & Butler, 1999).

Although extrinsic motivation can impair creativity, intrinsic motivation can specifically enhance creativity: Greer and Levine (1991) found that students given an intrinsic motivation introduction wrote poems that were judged to be more creative than those produced by a control group. One explanation for why intrinsic motivation may be so beneficial is that it frees people from concerns about the context of a situation (Amabile, Goldfarb, & Brackfield, 1990). This freedom then allows individuals to focus on the primary task at hand – whether writing a poem or developing a new product.

Recently, some reviews of the motivation research have challenged the assertion that intrinsic motivation is linked to higher performance (and increased creativity). Cameron and Pierce (1994), for example, conducted a meta-analysis of 96 experimental studies involving the effects of reward on intrinsic motivation, and found that the only negative effect came from a reward being tangible, expected, and given for the performance of a simple task. Eisenberger and Cameron (1996) have argued that rewards (which result in extrinsic motivation) are not necessarily detrimental to performance. They state that the detrimental effects occur under restricted and avoidable conditions and that reward can often have a positive effect on creativity.

Further studies have shown that intrinsic motivation and creativity are not negatively affected by a reward (particularly a verbal reward), and can actually be improved, if the reward is presented in a less salient manner, especially in tasks requiring divergent thinking (Eisenberger & Selbst, 1994). Eisenberger, Armeli, and Pretz (1998) found that a promised reward increased creativity if individuals received training in divergent thinking, or if instructions emphasized the need for creativity. Eisenberger, Haskins, and Gambleton (1999) found that rewards increased creativity if the students had prior experience with creative acts. Eisenberger and Rhoades (2001) found that employees offered more creative suggestions at work with the promise of a reward – if an intrinsic interest in the activity was already present. Eisenberger and Shanock (2003), in reviewing the many studies on the harm or benefits of reward, conclude that much of the debate relates to methodological issues. Rewarding creative performance, they argue, increases both intrinsic motivation and creativity, whereas rewarding conventional performance decreases both intrinsic motivation and creativity.

There may be a gender-related effect in the role of extrinsic motivation, although studies in this area have been conducted only on school-age children to date. Baer (1997) asked eighth-grade subjects (66 girls, 62 boys) to write original poems and stories under conditions favoring both intrinsic and extrinsic motivation. In the intrinsic motivation conditions, subjects were told that their poems and stories would not be evaluated; in the extrinsic condition, subjects were led to expect evaluation, and the importance of the evaluation was made highly salient. When the poems and stories were then judged for creativity by experts, the researchers found a significant gender by motivational interaction effect. For the boys, there was virtually no difference in creativity ratings under intrinsic and extrinsic conditions; in contrast, for the girls, these differences were quite large. This finding was confirmed in a follow-up study (Baer, 1998) using students of the same age, in which the negative impact of both rewards and anticipated evaluation were shown to be largely confined to female subjects. More recently, Conti, Collins, and Picariello (2001) found that girls were less creative in competitive situations while boys were more creative in it.

An extensive body of research has attempted to ascertain the actual benefits of intrinsic motivation, and the actual harmful effects of extrinsic motivation, on creativity. The prevalence of studies by Eisenberger and his colleagues makes it clear that this issue is a nuanced and complicated one. Clearly, rewards and extrinsic motivation may benefit creative output in some situations. Nevertheless, the overall trend seems to indicate that intrinsic motivation is still the best avenue to pursue, particularly in situations where employee interest may not be strong.

Applying Amabile's Work to Organizations

With the development of her model of creativity and innovation in organizations, Amabile (1988, 1997) further extended her ideas to incorporate both individual- and organizational-level components, processes, and outcomes. In this model, she argues that the three components – later called resources, techniques, and motivation – are similar in definition and in their relationship to creativity (at the individual level) and innovation (at the organizational level).

Skills in the task domain at the individual level are represented by "resources" at the organizational level. According to Amabile, resources should be defined broadly, and should essentially include all forms that may be required to produce novel work, including people, material, information, training, and time.

A second component, called "management practices," maps loosely onto what Amabile refers to as creative skills at the individual level. Management practices are demonstrated by leaders throughout the organizational hierarchy and represent actions that facilitate individual creativity. These actions may include clear setting of goals and objectives that support autonomy, open communication and feedback that focuses on the task, and the development of a diverse skill set within groups.

At the organizational level, Amabile (1997) defines motivation as the "basic orientation of the organization toward innovation, as well as supports for creativity and innovation throughout the organization" (p. 52). These factors would be representative of an organizational value for innovation, a future orientation, and a climate that was not risk averse.

Although this model focuses on organizational creativity, Amabile argues that the production of organizational innovation is a function of individual and group creative processes, which are actually influenced by organizational and other environmental factors. As such, the aforementioned research on the effects of contextual factors on individual creativity represents much of the research testing Amabile's ideas.

As the initial effort to consider contextual factors, the componential model of creativity and innovation encouraged the abundance of work that examined context-based influences on creativity – most commonly, the effects of context on intrinsic and extrinsic motivation. Subsequent to her ideas, a number of other models emerged as attempts were made to address creativity from a multi-level perspective.

MULTI-LEVEL MODELS OF CREATIVTY AND INNOVATION

Subsequent to Amabile's initial work, several theoretical approaches have been developed that aim to explain and describe some aspects of creativity or innovation in organizations. This section provides a brief overview of five of these advances, focusing on the multi-level nature of each and its inclusion of social influence factors. Although we do not provide a comprehensive explication of theoretical advances in the area of organizational creativity, this brief review does provide a perspective on the complexity of the area, and it reveals several key areas in which further theoretical and empirical work is warranted. The works are discussed here in chronological order, though – as with scientific growth in any field – the development from one to the other is not necessarily linear. In addition, other relevant but perhaps smaller theoretical advances have occurred during this time period. To the extent that they are relevant to our goals here, several of these advances are discussed in the sections on leadership or group influence. This section limits its coverage to the more comprehensive models that share a multi-level focus.

Theory of Organizational Creativity

Following the work of Amabile, the first comprehensive multi-level model of organizational creativity was presented by Woodman et al. (1993). Woodman et al. developed a theoretical framework for understanding creativity in complex social settings, identifying both social influences and contextual factors. These authors take an interactionist approach, integrating process, product, person, and place (e.g., environment) factors in developing a comprehensive, multi-level model of organizational creativity. Although they recognize the importance of individual differences in predicting creative behaviors, their efforts offer additional ideas for considering the group and organizational context in which creative behavior takes place.

In their model, Woodman et al. (1993) discuss the importance of group norms, group cohesiveness, social roles, and problem-solving approaches. At the organizational level, these authors indicate the importance of culture, resources, rewards, strategy, structure, and technology. Consistent with Amabile's work, they argue that these contextual factors interact both with one another and with individual factors by directly influencing creative behavior and by creating situational enhancers and inhibiters of creativity.

Woodman et al. present three propositions that underscore their model and that are intended to guide the development of testable hypotheses (several of which they introduce). These propositions explicate the prediction of creativity at the individual, group, and organizational levels in complex social settings. As one transcends levels, each higher-level proposition incorporates the predictions of the preceding propositions and adds contextual influences. Specifically, the first (individual-level) proposition suggests that individual creativity is a function of individual characteristics, social influences, and contextual influences. The second (group-level) proposition suggests that creativity is a function of individual creativity of group members, and of group and contextual characteristics. The third (organizational-level) proposition suggests that creativity is a function of group creativity and organizational characteristics. Although Woodman et al.'s proposed model suggests social influences operate primarily at the individual level, it is clear from their hypotheses that both social and contextual influences affect creativity at each level.

In predicting individual creativity, Woodman et al. propose that group norms for conformity will inhibit individual creativity, whereas group norms that support open sharing will enhance creativity. Organizational-level influences include reward systems and rigorous evaluation systems that are closely linked to extrinsic rewards and will decrease creativity, whereas the presence of a risk-taking culture will increase creativity. In the prediction of group-level creativity, Woodman et al. argue for the importance of diversity and non-autocratic leadership styles as creativity enhancers, although they suggest that the relationship between group cohesiveness and creativity will be curvilinear (group creativity may be inhibited at very low and very high levels of cohesiveness). They also suggest that organizational cultures and structures that encourage participation will likewise encourage group creativity. Finally, in predicting organizational-level creativity, Woodman et al. propose that organizational creativity will be facilitated by resource availability and through organizational designs, whereas restrictions on information exchanges with the environment will inhibit creativity. These authors also suggest that creativity at the organizational level is partly a function of the creativity demonstrated by the numerous groups that constitute the organization.

The hypotheses offered by Woodman et al. are meant to be illustrative (not exhaustive), but they are nevertheless representative of the ideas put forth in these authors' interactionist model. Although the propositions offered by Woodman et al. include a broad discussion of contextual factors and lay the foundation for numerous hypotheses, their lack of specificity somewhat limits the guidance offered by the theory. Social influence is included, although more complex considerations would not be integrated until later models. Little mention is made of leadership issues, for example, or of the effects of culture on group outcomes. Furthermore, in this model, the impact of social influence is restricted primarily to individual-level creativity. Consequently, social influences on group-level creativity are said to be a function of the extent to which social influences affect individuals within the group at earlier stages, and little consideration is given to how groups or organizations as a collective might be directly affected by social influence.

Despite these limitations, the substantial contribution of Woodman et al.'s work is to present organizational creativity from a true multi-level perspective. As the authors suggest, they were the first to acknowledge that systematic and comprehensive research on organizational creativity cannot be conducted without thinking about multiple levels. In addition, their work is more specific than previous theoretical developments in the identification of specific social influences and contextual factors. As one example, Woodman et al. articulate the important distinction between social influence from formal group membership and that from informal group membership. Finally, consistent with proponents of meso approaches (cf. Capelli & Sherer, 1991; House, Rousseau, & Thomas-Hunt, 1995), they argue for, and ultimately set the stage for, integrating macro-level innovation research with micro-level creativity work.

The work of Woodman et al. laid the groundwork for later theoretical developments and the inclusion of social influence factors. Yet despite these important advances, a few shortcomings in their work are worth noting. Although these authors differentiate between creativity and innovation in name, they do not really address the difference between the two in any real way. As later research has identified, the effects of social factors (such as environmental uncertainty) are not the same for both concepts. Although Woodman et al. distinguish between creativity and innovation at the organizational level (similar to the distinction described in the definitional section), their model focuses on organizational creativity as the outcome, with little discussion of real predictors of innovations. This is a problem common to other models as well.

Theory of Creative Action in Multiple Social Domains

In another effort to further research in organizational creativity and innovation, Ford (1996) presented his theory of creative action in multiple social domains. Ford's theory was based on the premise that creative and habitual actions are competing behavior alternatives, each being influenced by the interdependent force of the variety of social domains within which an individual is embedded: "Fields and domains represent the situation or context that influences individuals' actions" (p. 1114). Ford argues that situational antecedents may lead to either habitual actions or creative actions that are conceptually independent and essentially in competition with one another. Because they are independent, the restriction of one does not *necessarily* elicit the other. Like other models, Ford's work focuses on key individual processes that jointly influence the production of creative action, including sense-making motivation, knowledge, and ability (cf. Amabile, 1982, 1983a, 1983b, 1988, 1997; Drazin et al., 1999; Mumford, Scott, Gaddis, & Strange, 2002; Mumford, Strange, Scott, & Gaddis, 2003). Ford also suggests that the relationship among these processes is interactive and nonlinear.

According to Ford, what makes organizational contexts unique (in terms of their relationship to creativity) is that certain frames (also known as organizational culture) are held by organizational actors. Such a frame narrows the range of possible actions thought about and, ultimately, undertaken by an individual within the organization. Flaws in previous theory, Ford points out, ignore this inhibitive effect on creativity. Ford argues that "creative actions must hold a *relative advantage* to habitual actions in terms of personal consequences before creative pursuits will be intentionally undertaken" (1996, p. 1125). He also contends that four levels of social domain have been examined in the literature – group, organization, institutional environment, and external market – and have implications for the demonstration of creative action. Consequently, the key question to understand is, how do social influences affect these outcomes?

At the group level, Ford (1996) observes that selection and socialization processes operate in a manner consistent with Schneider's (1987) attraction–selection–attrition model, through which groups become more homogenous over time (Tsui & O'Reilly, 1989; O'Reilly, Caldwell, & Barnett, 1989). Consequently, social pressure in the form of group norms for individual behaviors and group operations (i.e., habitual behaviors) becomes strong. Creative behaviors, which are discouraged in such a context, are more likely to be rejected if displayed, and individuals who demonstrate creativity are likely to soon be dispelled. Consequently, both individual- and group-level forms of creativity are likely to be restricted under typical group conditions. Ford does suggest, however, that group processes that emphasize the diversity of individual skills can be developed and may serve as a form of group influence that supports creativity. Less well understood, Ford notes, is how a single "strong" individual may affect both other individuals in the group and the group as a whole.

At the organizational level, Ford discusses two processes relevant to creativity and innovation: (1) absorptive capacity, which is the capability of an organization to value, assimilate, and effectively use new information (Cohen & Levinthal, 1990) and (2) disposition toward risk, which reflects an organization's willingness to embrace actions that may fail (Shapira, 1995). Organizations with greater absorptive capacity and disposition toward risks encourage individual-, group-, and organizational-level creativity through the effects of other organizational characteristics such as strategy, reward systems, and resources. The most powerful effects, Ford notes, result from these characteristics' impact on knowledge production, exchange, and social incentives that reward (or reject) creativity and innovation.

At the institutional environment level, Ford suggests that creative or habitual action will be influenced by the three processes used to determine organizational action, suggested by DiMaggio and Powell (1983): "mimetic (imitation based on standard responses to uncertainty), coercive (conformity stemming from political pressures and legitimization problems), and normative (conformity associated with professionalization) forces that lead to organizational isomorphism" (Ford, 1996, p. 1130). Although these decision processes seem destined to restrict creativity and innovation, Ford suggests that in the typical situation, multiple and conflicting constraints act across institutional domains, which may support creative actions and innovation.

At the market level, Ford (1996) argues that organizational decisions for creativity are influenced by market preferences. Some markets create forces for habituation, such as stable markets or those that emphasize cost containment. Other markets encourage creativity, such as dynamic markets or those that encourage product differentiation. Although the immediate effects are felt at the organizational level, one reasonable implication is that market forces ultimately influence group- and individual-level actions through their impact on organizational-level policies and practices.

Ford also describes how the multiple-domain theory advances theories presented by Amabile (1983a, 1983b, 1988) and Woodman et al. (1993). He argues that the multiple-domain theory suggests limits to the generalizability of Amabile's work. Specifically, the saliency of goals and standards may vary across social domains. Further, Ford notes that individual creativity will be influenced by goals and standards from multiple domains simultaneously. With regard to Woodman et al.'s interactionist model, he suggests that multiple-domain theory builds on this work through the articulation of creative processes that produce creative action, such as the interaction between domain-specific goals and individual interests, and through the specification of the four levels of social domains that simultaneously influence individual creative action.

A Sense-Making Theory of Creativity in Organizations

Drazin et al. (1999), building on earlier expressed concerns (Drazin & Schoonhoven, 1996) about the lack of theoretical development in the organizational innovation arena, developed a multi-level model of how creativity progresses in multifaceted and long-term organizational projects. Their work came in response to previous creativity research that had almost exclusively focused on the individual level of analysis and ignored a more comprehensive explanation of creativity. These authors noted that one consequence of early theoretical work and subsequent research on creativity is that defining creativity only in terms of individual, small group, or project-based outcomes neglects organizational-level outcomes and the consideration of larger creative processes. To overcome this shortcoming, they introduce a sense-making perspective, which points to "cross-level, systematic, and embedded effects that may arise from idiosyncratic and/or communal interpretations of what it means to be creative" (Drazin et al., 1999, p. 287). Furthermore, this perspective "implies that conflict, political influence, and negotiated order may operate at more macro-organizational levels (Walsh & Fahey, 1986; Weick, 1995) and over time in organizations to influence creative processes" (p. 287). This theory illustrates, for the first time, important social influences at the organizational level. Drazin et al. further extend the multi-level approach by taking a process-based orientation, which considers time-based influences on organizational creativity.

In their presentation of the sense-making perspective on creativity, Drazin et al. (1999) make a distinction between different levels of analysis that become apparent as "individuals develop and maintain subjective inter-pretations of their roles in organizations" to address the question of how creativity unfolds over time. Their model examines how intra-subjective (individual), inter-subjective (two or more individuals), and collective (across inter-subjective levels) levels of analysis affect the creative processes in long-term and complex organizational projects, while considering how power shifts to preferentially promote creativity in some groups rather than in others.

An important contribution of the Drazin et al. (1999) approach is the shift in focus away from thinking exclusively about creative outcomes and toward thinking about the creative process as it evolves over time. Of particular interest is the influence of two types of crises – the crisis of functionality and the crisis of time/budget – on competing organizational constituents (i.e., project management staff and technical staff). According to Drazin et al., at the beginning of a project, a period of negotiation occurs during which individual sense-making frames emerge, as do shared frames of reference within communities. Following this period of negotiation, a negotiated order emerges in which levels of creative activity for each group are established.

At this point, shifts in the creative activity of each group will be inversely affected by each type of crisis. In case of a crisis of functionality, which represents problems specific to the task itself, power shifts to the technical staff, who function as problem solvers. Thus, creativity among technical staff members is encouraged and will increase. Once the crisis is addressed, Drazin et al. argue, norms for creative behavior return to their negotiated state. Conversely, a crisis of time and/or budget will shift power to management and result in increased creativity among management. Again, once the crisis has been addressed, balance is restored. The authors also note that repeated crises of either type may lead to a renegotiation of order. For example, multiple crises of functionality may cause more power to accrue to the technical staff, thereby leading to higher levels of creative activity among members of that group.

The distinction in *process* made in Drazin et al.'s model is consistent with the distinction in *outcome* often made between creativity and innovation when creativity is defined as the generation of solutions (technical staff creativity) and innovation is defined as the implementation of a solution (management staff creativity). In agreement with ideas put forth in Ford's (1996) multiple-domain theory, Drazin et al.'s theory suggests that different environment events affect each concept differently, such that what predicts creativity may limit innovation, and vice versa.

Propulsion Model of Creativity

Another recent model of organizational creativity is that presented by Sternberg and his colleagues (Sternberg, 1999; Sternberg et al., 2003a, 2003b). Their propulsion model of creativity attempts to explain elaborate definitions of creativity through the development of a typology of creativity. These authors emphasize differentiating among the various intended differences in the outcomes of the creative process. The propulsion model of creativity focuses exclusively on creative products and has been applied to both business innovation and leadership (Sternberg, 1999; Sternberg et al., 2001, 2002, 2003a, 2003b; Sternberg, Pretz, & Kaufman, 2003). This theory describes eight ways in which a leader or an organization can make a creative contribution, and it categorizes these contributions based on their relationship to the domain (which could range from advertising to soap production). The first four types of creative contributions stay within the existing definitions and framework of a particular domain. The latter four result in rejection or replacement of the current paradigm. Although not explicitly described by the model, one important factor to keep in mind is how social influence and other factors may lead to the selection of one path over another.

According to Sternberg (1999) and Sternberg et al. (2002), four types of contributions maintain the existing paradigm: replication, redefinition, forward incrementation, and advanced forward incrementation.

Of these four, the most basic creative contribution that can be made is *replication*. Replication efforts are intended to maintain current activities or success be reproducing past successes. As one example, Sternberg et al. cite consumer-goods companies such as supermarket chains that offer their own store-brand products, which are designed to mirror popular brand-name items – such as cold medicine "NightTime" being offered as an alternative to the brand-name product Nyquil. These replications are usually significantly less expensive than the brand-name product, and these products exist for the sole purpose of replicating other companies' success at a lower cost (Sternberg et al., 2002).

The second type of creative contribution, *redefinition*, is an attempt to present the domain in a different or new light so as to show that "the field or organization is in the right place, but not for the reason(s) that leaders of the field think it is" (Sternberg et al., 2003a, 2003b). The example provided by the authors is the now widespread use of aspirin to prevent heart attacks. By redefining this product's purpose from simple pain relief to preventive heart medicine, companies that produce aspirin have substantially expanded the market and added to their overall success through one form of creative action.

With the third type of contribution, *forward incrementation*, organizations or individual leaders choose products or paths that remain consistent with the current domain, but push the domain forward in small increments. Sternberg et al. (2003a, 2003b) suggest that one example of forward incrementation is the online company Amazon.com, which became successful when it was able to advance the book industry by offering a nearly infinite selection of books, because Amazon.com did not require a centrally located warehouse.

The final approach that maintains the existing domain is *advance forward incrementation*. According to Sternberg et al. (2003a, 2003b), these creative efforts advance an individual leader, organization, or product well beyond where the field currently resides. Although such efforts are consistent with the existing domain, such examples are often viewed as bold and can meet with criticism or resistance because of the extent (or pace) of the change. Sternberg et al. suggest that some of Leonardo DaVinci's ideas and inventions, such as the flying machine, are examples of advance forward incrementation. Not only did such ideas meet with resistance, but also they were so advanced as to be beyond the capability of the then-current engineering knowledge. One interesting aspect of this creativity type is that it breaks away from the assumption that for something to be creative, it must also be useful. Clearly, such an innovation, although useful in the long run, would not have been viewed as such during its inception.

The remaining four types of creative contributions consist of redirection, reconstruction/redirection, reinitiation, and integration (or synthesis). Each of these four types represents a creative effort that is intended to reject and replace the current paradigm.

Redirection represents an attempt by the individual, leader, or organization to change the direction of a product or process. As one example, Sternberg et al. (2003a, 2003b) suggest that Mattel engaged in redirection when the company introduced the new advertising strategy of targeting children for its toy products instead of parents.

Reconstruction/redirection is a creative effort that requires a change in the direction of a domain by returning it to an earlier state (i.e., a reconstruction of prior success). According to Sternberg et al. (2003a, 2003b), one example of a product that represents reconstruction/redirection is the sale of wristwatches that include mechanical movements, including those made by Rolex, even though the watches are actually battery operated.

The most radical type of creative effort, according to Sternberg et al. (2003a, 2003b), is *reinitiation*. Individuals, leaders, or organizations that engage in reinitiation attempt to move the domain to a new foundation or starting point, so that future progress will be based on a new beginning point. According to Sternberg et al., new products that can be viewed as forms of reinitiations include modern electric and gas appliances that have replaced mechanical or hand-based systems (e.g., the gas stove instead of fire). Reinitiations do not just build on the mechanisms employed by their predecessors, but rather rely on entirely different mechanisms. They conceive of a process or service that is fundamentally different from its predecessor (Sternberg et al., 2003a, 2003b). It is worth noting that just as advanced forward incrementations may be *too* advanced to reap rewards during the innovator's lifetime, so, too, are many reinitiation contributions ahead of their time.

The last creative contribution is *integration* (also referred to as *synthesis*), in which two diverse domains are merged to create a new idea. According to Sternberg et al. (2003a, 2003b), examples of products that represent integration include office suite software, which combines multiple independent products into a single package, and e-books, which combine computer software and electronic video display with what were formerly printed books.

Sternberg et al. (2003a, 2003b) suggest that the type of creativity that emerges in an organization, or from a leader, will be a function of organizational characteristics that facilitate or inhibit the various types. Change-resistant organizations (Sternberg et al., 2002), for example, may have structural characteristics (e.g., high centralization, low formalization) that inhibit creativity. As a consequence, organizational- or leader-based creative outcomes in such contexts are likely to be of the type that accept existing paradigms (e.g., replication) rather than the type that rejects the existing paradigms (e.g., redirection). Structure is, however, merely one organizational-level characteristic. Others, such as climate for safety, reward structure, and current economic state (i.e., success versus failure in a market), will also affect creativity. Indeed, a successful organization may be more likely to reproduce (e.g., replicate) existing products, services, and processes than to challenge the existing paradigm through redirection, reconstruction/redirection, or reinitiation.

The propulsion model of creativity provides a useful starting point for a multi-level consideration of organizational creativity. By focusing on the possible creative outcomes, rather than on individual and/or group characteristics of the creative processes, the model draws our attention to recognized endogenous choices for creativity and encourages us to advance our understanding through the identification of exogenous factors and processes. What is particularly appealing about this model is its inclusion of organizational-level creative outcomes – a facet that is somewhat lacking in theoretical approaches to creativity. Obviously, this model serves primarily as a starting point for future research and theoretical development taking a multi-level approach to organizational creativity. Further development in this area will require greater explication of the specific individual, group, organizational, and external factors that facilitate or hinder each type of creative outcome. In addition, a clearer distinction between creativity and innovation among the outcomes is needed that will be consistent with or clarify how the two are currently represented in the field.

Integrative Model of Creativity and Innovation Implementation in Work Groups

In 2002, West introduced a model of group creativity and innovation implementation that is multi-level in design and is process oriented. West (2002) argues that innovation is a nonlinear process that "may be conceived of as cyclical with periods of innovation initiation, implementation, adaptation, and stabilisation" (p. 358). According to West, creative thinking and behavior occur as part of the innovation process – most commonly at early stages, but also during times of change or adaptation. An important assertion of West's model is that the distinction between creativity and innovation is critical because environmental characteristics (i.e., external demands and threat) have opposite effects on each one.

In developing his model, West (2002) builds on early work by Amabile (1983a, 1983b) and Amabile & Conti (1999) and other previous theoretical works (e.g., Drazin & Schoonhoven, 1996). West argues that four groups of factors – task characteristics, group knowledge diversity and skills, external demands, and integrating group processes – determine group creativity and innovation. Specifically, he identifies eight integrating group processes that sit at the center of a model that predicts group innovation. These processes are directly affected by group task characteristics, group knowledge diversity and skills, and external demands, and, in turn, they affect creativity and innovation. External demands are also predicted to directly affect creativity and innovation.

In describing the role of group task characteristics, West builds on sociotechnical systems theory (STST) (cf. Cooper & Foster, 1971), which argues that "autonomous work groups provide a structure through which the demands of social and technical subsystems of an organization can be jointly optimized" (West, 2002, p. 360). Accordingly, when joint optimism occurs, groups are independent and responsible for a whole task, group members are required to work interdependently, and the group has a sense of identity with its work. West refers to this state as "task orientation," which includes such specific characteristics as varying demands, autonomy, and opportunity for social interaction, among others. These characteristics are quite similar to the task characteristics identified in the job characteristics theory (JCT) literature (Hackman & Oldham, 1975), which were also predicted to lead to core psychological states, which in turn were predicted to lead to intrinsic motivation, among other positive outcomes. Indeed, West (2002) suggests that group "task orientation" is much like the intrinsic motivation described in Amabile's (1982, 1983a, 1983b, 1996) componential theory of creativity. Consequently, both group creativity and innovation are predicted to be positively influenced by the development of these group task characteristics.

The second set of factors, group knowledge and skill diversity, is also expected to generally increase group innovation, although West (2002) predicts a nonlinear relationship. Specifically, he suggests that extremely low and extremely high levels of knowledge and skill diversity may prove problematic for diversity. Low levels of diversity may create pressures for conformity (rather than innovativeness), whereas high levels of diversity may lead to communication difficulties, excessive conflict, and lack of shared frames. Outside of these exceptions, increased group knowledge diversity and skills should, according to West, encourage innovation.

West identifies multiple external demands, time demands, environmental uncertainty, competition, and organizational climate. External factors can derive from the organizational context as well as the external environment. Regardless of their source, the key influence of these factors stems from the extent to which they contribute to conditions of threat or safety. West argues that external demands that create perceptions of threat (e.g., competition) are likely to enhance innovation implementation, but will adversely affect creativity. Conversely, the creation of a safe climate encourages creativity, but minimizes the need for innovations. West (2002) puts it succinctly: "Creativity requires an undemanding environment, while implementation requires precisely the opposite" (p. 366).

The eight integrating group processes identified by West (2002) include clarifying and ensuring commitment to group objectives, participation in decision making, managing conflict, minority influence, supporting innovation, intra-group safety, reflexivity, and developing member integration skills. The task, group, and external factors influence these processes in both positive and negative ways, thereby affecting both creativity and innovation. For some of these factors (e.g., supporting innovation), their relationship to innovation is fairly straightforward and has been demonstrated in the literature (Carter & West, 1998; West & Anderson, 1996). For others (e.g., intra-group safety), relationships are more complex. For example, West suggests that although the lack of external threats (i.e., the perception of safety) will increase creativity and decrease innovation, perceptions of intra-group safety will encourage both creativity and innovation. Finally, for some factors (e.g., effective conflict management), much remains to be understood. Despite the recognition that managing conflict is necessary for creativity and innovation (Mumford & Gustafson, 1988), the impact of varying types of conflict on the varying group processes is less clear and awaits further study.

West's (2002) model of creativity and innovation implementation represents a substantial theoretical advance in several respects. First, it incorporates the strengths of several other models, including those developed by Amabile, Drazin et al., and Ford, by describing the important prerequisite group *and* task characteristics, the importance and influence of environmental factors (including critical forms of social influence), and the group processes that mediate the relationship between the factors and the production of creativity and innovation. In addition, by incorporating the distinction between and interrelatedness of creativity and innovation, West's model provides a strong foundation for further consideration of these constructs.

SOCIAL INFLUENCE AND CREATIVITY

As is evidenced in the foregoing discussion of creativity, there has been increasing consideration of social context in theoretical models of creativity. Many aspects of that context contribute to forms of social influence that affect individual, group, and organizational outcomes. Social influence in organizations refers to the "social" nature of influence – specifically, the influence that comes from having to deal with human beings who are living together (Ferris et al., 2002). Understanding the role of social influence on creativity and innovation in organizations is complicated, however, and much remains to be elucidated despite its increased inclusion in extant theoretical models.

Concurrent with the development of these theoretical models, two forms of social influence – group and leadership – have received substantial attention in the organizational literature. The remainder of this chapter explores the literature dealing with three primary sources of social influence: groups, leaders, and culture. Of course, these are not the only forms of social influence worth discussing, nor will this chapter attempt to provide a complete review of each area. The goal here is simply to highlight key findings in each area, particularly as they relate to that area's potential as a social influence in the context of a multi-level consideration of creativity and innovation.

CREATIVITY, INNOVATION, AND GROUP INFLUENCE

To date, much organizational research has focused on providing organizations with the knowledge they need to survive in a competitive and consistently changing business world. Given the strong arguments that innovation (Cummings & Oldham, 1997) and team-based work (Sundstrom & Associates, 1999) are key assets in maintaining a competitive edge, it is not surprising that theory and research have focused on group-level creativity and innovation. Indeed, several of the aforementioned theoretical advances have considered group influences in either a specific (West, 2002) or a more general (Ford, 1996) fashion. In addition to these comprehensive theories, several other authors (e.g., Gilson & Shalley, 2004; Madjar, 2005; Oldham & Cummings, 1996; Tagger, 2002) have developed meaningful theoretical advances for considering group creativity. Nevertheless, much remains to be understood about group factors, and particularly the social influences they bring forth.

As mentioned earlier, the group creativity literature conceptualizes innovation as encompassing both creativity and innovation implementation. "Creativity is the development of ideas, while innovation implementation is the application of ideas" (West, 2002, p. 356–347). This distinction is necessary because current research has indicated that creativity may be more readily evident in the early stages of innovation processes, when teams are required to develop ideas in response to a perceived need for innovation. As this innovation is tailored to the organizational need and is stabilized, however, less creativity is required (West, 2002). In addition, Ford and Sullivan (2004) have suggested that idea generation is vital to teams that are still attempting to meet the requirements of the project; later, after the team's attention changes to executing an innovation, introduction of novel ideas may disrupt the team's efforts and lead to negative consequences, such as lower project quality, decreased team member satisfaction, and reduced team member learning.

Researchers have also identified many social and contextual variables that affect a group's innovation capacity, at multiple levels in an organization. At the individual level, researchers have considered group composition and its effects on creativity; that is, they have identified characteristics that enhance creativity when group members possess these characteristics. One such area is diversity, defined in terms of race, gender, ethnicity, age, disability, education, expertise, department where employed, rank in organization, personality, or abilities (Egan, 2005). The diverse character-istics that a group possesses may either inhibit or enhance creative outcomes, depending on the type of conflict that results (Kurtzberg & Amabile, 2000–2001; Shalley, 2002). After integrating the diversity, conflict, and creativity research, Kurtzberg and Amabile (2000–2001) proposed that a moderate amount of task conflict will lead to more creative outcomes in a group setting, but that other types of conflict (relationship and process) will prove detrimental to a group's creative outcomes. However, much research is needed to more completely establish the relationship between group conflict and creativity.

Tagger (2002) identified other characteristics such as task motivation, domain-relevant skills, and creativity-relevant group processes as important to the individual level of creative outputs of individuals who are participating in groups. Creativity-relevant group processes include goal setting, preparation, participation in group problem solving, and synthesis of ideas, all of which influence an individual's creativity within a group. Although considering that individual-level contextual factors' effects on group creativity and innovation is certainly useful, it is also crucial to look at social influences on group creativity at other levels.

At the group level, a variety of components operate to affect group creativity: group conflict (Beersma & De Dreu, 2005; Kurtzberg & Amabile, 2000–2001; Shalley, 2002), group autonomy, task requirements, reflexivity (West, 2002), participation in decision making (West, 2002; De Dreu & West, 2001), psychological safety (Edmondson, 1999; Ford & Sullivan, 2004), minority dissent (De Dreu & West, 2001; De Dreu, 2002), and reflexivity (De Dreu, 2002). Psychological safety has been defined as "a shared belief that the team is safe for interpersonal risk taking" (Edmondson, 1999, p. 354). Edmondson's (1999) research examining the effects of psychological safety and learning behavior on work teams has revealed that learning behavior – including seeking feedback, sharing information, asking for help, talking about errors, and experimenting – mediates the relationship between team psychological safety and team performance. Ford and Sullivan (2004) assert that psychological safety can also influence the creative process in work groups; more specifically, they claim that psychological safety moderates the relationship between novel contributions and team member satisfaction. Although empirical research is limited on how psychological safety plays an intervening role relative to creativity and innovation, this is certainly a promising avenue for further exploration.

Other studies have looked at minority dissent and reflexivity as important social and contextual factors at the group level of team creativity and innovation (De Dreu & West, 2001; De Dreu, 2002). For example, De Dreu (2002) found that high levels of minority dissent, which emerges when a minority in a group publicly disagrees with the ideas held by the majority of the group, result in more innovation and greater team effectiveness as compared with low levels of minority dissent in groups, but only when there is a high level of team reflexivity. West (1996) defines team reflexivity as "the extent to which team members overtly reflect upon the group's objectives, strategies, and processes and adapt them to current or anticipated endogenous or environmental circumstances" (p. 559). This research further illustrates the importance of context – specifically, social influence factors – for group-level creativity and innovation.

Finally, at the organizational level, several other contextual influences affect creativity within groups: organizational climate, support systems, market environment, environmental uncertainty (West, 2002), the influence of others inside and outside the organization (Egan, 2005), slack (Nohria & Gulati, 1996), job complexity (Oldham & Cummings, 1996), and a supportive environment (Janssen, van de Vliert, & West, 2004).

West (2002) illustrated that in organizational settings that are supportive of team innovation, it is important to group outcomes so that a team perceives a task as significant to the organization as well as to society. Additionally, West elucidates the importance of environmental pressures at different stages of the innovation process. At the early stages of the innovation process, a lack of pressure will stimulate creative ideas. At later stages, however, perceived pressure and demand will increase the likelihood of innovation implementation.

The concept of organizational slack is also relevant to group creativity and innovation at the organizational level of analysis. Although organizations often strive to eliminate forms of organizational slack, research has indicated that some degree of slack may be essential for innovation. Nohria and Gulati (1996) found that moderate amounts of organizational slack encourage greater experimentation and are beneficial to a group's innovation, but that either too much or too little slack is detrimental to the group's success. Their research also highlighted the importance of conducting research on the effects of social influence and contextual factors on group-level creativity and innovation at multiple levels of the organization.

Other researchers have looked at a team's innovation process and the issue of individual versus team creativity. Laboratory research has suggested that individuals may be more creative, but that groups may be more innovative (Nijstad & De Dreu, 2002). This line of research suggests that an effective innovation process may require an alternation between individual and group work to maximize the innovative outcome. Not surprisingly, as Nijstad and De Dreu (2002) have pointed out, fully elucidating the effects of individual versus individual creativity in the group innovation process will require field research in conjunction with the existing laboratory research.

A strong source of social influence within a group context is the encouragement of a creative climate. In theory, this development has been identified as creative support (West, 2002), but climate issues have also been examined based on the need for a "safe climate." As with most of these areas of interest, the effects of climate are not simple. As one part of their study examining creativity, climate, and team effectiveness, Gilson, Mathieu, Shalley, and Ruddy (2005) examined how a creative environment influences group performance as measured by customer satisfaction. They found that creative environments (compared with standardized environments) can lead to enhanced performance when the workforce is highly skilled and well trained, but may otherwise be less positively viewed by customers than the less ambiguous standardized environments.

Madjar (2005) has proposed a group-based theory of creativity in which she identifies three general groups (work and non-work) that influence individual creativity in the workplace: (1) coworkers within one's primary workgroup, (2) coworkers with whom one interacts but who are external to one's primary workgroup, and (3) non-work individuals such as family and friends. Unlike much of the traditional research on creativity and group influence, which has looked more directly at how social factors influence motivation, Madjar's works (Madjar, 2005; Madjar, Oldham, & Pratt, 2002) consider the more indirect impact of group influence through support and information, both of which are expected to enhance creative performance. Although uniquely explicated in the group-based model, such ideas are consistent with Amabile's (1988, 1997) inclusion of environmental resources in the componential model of creativity.

Madjar's model is also supported by the broader motivation theory of means efficacy (Agars, Kottke, & Unckless, 2006; Eden, 2001), which argues that the perceived presence of resources in the environment (including information and social support) will enhance motivation. Although creativity researchers have yet to explore means efficacy in depth, the available resources have been presented as important (Amabile, 1988, 1997).

Studies considering individual perceptions of resources are likely to reveal similarly important relationships. In addition, social influences from both groups and leaders are likely to affect means-efficacy perceptions.

To date, most research on group influence has considered primary workgroups, such that very little attention has been given to other collectives within organizations. This is clearly a shortcoming in the study of group influence on creativity and innovation. In actual organizations, individuals are members of, and are influenced by, multiple groups – some of which are fully or partially nested, others that are largely independent of each other. Furthermore, identified group memberships may include both formally defined groups (e.g., project teams) and informal groups (e.g., the new employees). Whether the group memberships are formal or informal, nested or independent, the social influence exercised through such entities cannot be captured in a study of single group influence. Madjar's work highlights one important piece of this distinction – namely, that group influences on work creativity need not come from workgroups only.

Although much research has focused on increasing our understanding of group-level creativity and innovation, the true complexity of group influence on creativity is underexplored and not well understood. Evident in what we do know about group creativity and innovation, however, is the importance of exploring contextual and social influence factors on the creativity and innovation process through a multi-level lens. Additional efforts that take into consideration the multi-level nature of group influence are clearly needed, because relevant social influences are obviously different at each level in the organization. In addition, subsequent research must continue to draw a distinction between idea generation and innovation implementation, as distinguished by West (2002), and to consider collective groups other than primary workgroups (Madjar, 2005).

CREATIVITY, INNOVATION, AND LEADERSHIP

As a powerful form of social influence in organizations, the topic of leadership as it affects creativity and innovation has received a great deal of attention in the literature during the last 5–10 years. Much of this work has examined leaders' influence on the creative processes and has studied the outcomes of their subordinates. There has also been a clear recognition that the domain of leadership and creativity is multi-level in nature and should be studied as such (Drazin et al., 1999). Redmond, Mumford, and Teach (1993) argue that leadership represents a key environmental variable because of its influence on group goals, rewards, and resource control. Specifically, leaders play a major role in defining organizational culture, climate, and norms. In support of these ideas, several articles from special issues of *Leadership Quarterly* have demonstrated the important impact of leaders on creativity and innovation (Elkins & Keller, 2003; Hunt, Stelluto, & Hooijberg, 2004; West et al., 2003).

Much of the past literature, however, has looked primarily at how leaders can directly affect their subordinates through traits and behaviors. Leaders of creative people must have a complex and varied expertise to effectively lead individual subordinates or groups so that they produce innovative and novel outcomes. There are several key differences between undertaking a creative task versus completing a normal task: Success is far less likely; there is natural tension between production demands and innovation needs; creativity requires substantial resources, and innovation requires the creation of something that has not yet been established or fit into the organization As a consequence, individuals who lead a group or organization in creative pursuits face many obstacles (Mumford et al., 2002).

Other research on leader characteristics reveals that leader skills and expertise in a given domain are strong predictors of creative behavior among subordinates (Andrews & Farris, 1967; Tierney, Farmer, & Graen, 1999). In addition to general skill and expertise, a leader's level of creative problem-solving skills has shown to be a critical predictor of creativity among individuals and groups under their supervision (Mouly & Sankaran, 1999).

Leader behaviors represent a meaningful component of work context. Consequently, although this topic has not traditionally received a great deal of attention as a precursor to creativity (Mumford et al., 2002), a great deal of attention has recently focused on how leaders affect creativity and innovation. Much of the initial research on leader behaviors was based on the work of Amabile (1982, 1983a, 1983b, 1988, 1996) and targeted the importance of intrinsic motivation to creativity. As Amabile has indicated, contextual factors have a direct and powerful impact on the level of intrinsic motivation felt by individuals in the workplace, and leadership is an important aspect of context.

In addition, much of leaders' effectiveness can be explained through social influence (Mumford et al., 2002). For example, research examining the effects of leader behaviors on creativity has revealed that while close monitoring inhibits creativity, providing developmental feedback promotes creative outcomes (Zhou, 2003). Leaders who engage in stress reduction, clear communication, and active goal setting also enhance the likelihood of creativity. Furthermore, by encouraging or facilitating collaboration, intellectual stimulation, discussion facilitation, and conflict resolution, leaders enhance creativity (Mumford et al., 2002).

Scott and Bruce (1994) found that leader behaviors influenced innovative behavior through a direct effect of leader role expectations and leader–member exchange behaviors, as well as through an indirect effect of leader–member exchange behavior on the creation of perceived support for innovation (a climate phenomena). These researchers did not find an effect of role expectations on climate (which was expected). More importantly, they found that the type of task (technicians versus engineers and scientists) moderated the relationship of role expectations with innovation – specifically, it was significant for technicians, but was not significant for scientists and engineers.

Mumford et al. (2002) also described how leader behaviors could have an indirect effect on subordinate creativity. These behaviors alter the working environment, meaning that the work environment can be a tool that is well within a leader's influence. Social and contextual factors within the work environment include individual-level factors, job characteristics, role expectations and goals, sufficient resources, rewards, supervisory support, external evaluation of work, social context, group composition, organizational climate, and organizational-level human resources practices. Leaders can manipulate these factors to enhance group creativity (Shalley & Gilson, 2004).

Successfully navigating the appropriate leader behaviors is not a simple matter, however. Shalley and Gilson (2004) note that behaviors that imply close supervision from a leader have negative effects on creativity, whereas behaviors that convey leader support have positive effects. Research on feedback and evaluation, as described earlier in this chapter, has also yielded somewhat conflicting results. There are clearly some instances in which feedback and evaluation diminish creativity, but there are also specific situations in which these activities will produce either no effect or even a mild benefit. Interestingly, Baer, Oldham, and Cummings (2003) reported that on complex jobs, extrinsic rewards are less beneficial. As Zhou's (2003) study implies, differentiating between "monitoring" and "providing support" may be critical to understanding these effects. Clearly, these relationships are complex and require a more meaningful consideration of the context in which leaders are behaving.

Reiter-Palmon and Illies (2004) explain that leaders must create an environment conducive to problem identification, information gathering and analysis, solution generation, and solution evaluation. This task is not an easy one, and the successful leader must balance the needs of the group and the needs of the organization – which are usually in conflict. The leader is the group's connection to the broader goals and systems of the organization and must effectively guide the group's creative efforts to produce an organizationally viable creative outcome while allowing the group creative freedom.

Leaders serve as role models for employees who regularly observe their behavior. The research on how creative role models influence observer creativity, however, has produced inconsistent results (Amabile, 1996). Recognizing the complexities inherent in studying role model effects (namely, how the context in which a role model behaves affects the outcome), Zhou (2003) designed a study to examine workgroup effects – specifically, the presence of creative coworkers – on observer creativity. It is worth noting that the Zhou study is actually a more comprehensive examination of supervisor behaviors and individual characteristics. It is a powerful example of the importance of examining the interaction between leader and group characteristics in the facilitation of creative outcomes, and it exemplifies the need for taking a multi-level perspective in the study of organizational creativity and innovation.

Mohamed (2002) examined the effects of a number of supervisor, group, and organizational characteristics on group-level innovation (as measured by supervisor ratings of group outcomes) in a study of 902 public employees and supervisors representing 150 individual departments at the federal level in the United Arab Emirates. In his study, Mohamed found managerial attitudes toward change and supervisory support to be two of the strongest predictors of innovation among these groups. Also of note, albeit not explored in depth, was the finding that group diversity (measured as percentage of expatriates within a group) was a strong predictor of innovation.

Another interesting effect that occurs in many creative group projects, and that has implications for understanding bottom-up multi-level influences on group creativity and innovation, is the emergence of a champion of the creative vision. This person could be the leader, but may also be a subordinate. This individual assumes the responsibility of ensuring the perseverance of the creative process and rallying others to get involved with the process (Howell & Boies, 2004). A champion usually has expertise in the area of creative focus, as he or she must fluently convey the meaning and ideas of the innovation to other entities. What is unknown, however, is which combination of factors makes the success of such a champion more or less likely. Certainly research from the general literature on minority influence is useful. As we have noted in other areas of creativity, however, this is a unique domain, so existing relationships do not always transfer from other areas.

In describing the research on leader behavior and creativity, we must also consider the abundance of research examining transformational leadership. Being a leader of creativity in an organization is a creative process in itself. Problem solving, vision, planning, plan implementation, accruing support, and engagement are all different facets of creativity in leaders. Although creativity is crucial for leaders, its form may vary depending on leadership styles (Mumford et al., 2003). The research on formal types of leadership (rather than fundamental leader characteristics and behaviors) and creativity further illustrates this complexity (and the need for employing a multi-level lens).

Bass and Avolio (1994) argue that transformational leaders display behaviors that encourage intellectual stimulation and provide individualized consideration and inspirational motivation. These characteristics, it is argued, are consistent with those identified in the creativity literature as behaviors that are conducive to creativity (Sosik, Kahai, & Avolio, 1998). In their review of leadership and creativity, Mumford et al. (2002) also proposed that transformational leadership should enhance creativity. Empirical results related to this question, however, have been mixed.

When Jung (2001) conducted a study to examine how leadership type affects group performance (creativity), he found that transformational leadership led to the production of more creative ideas than transactional leadership did. He argues that this finding is consistent with the work of Amabile (1998), who suggested that creativity can be enhanced by creating a culture/climate in which individuals fell free to share ideas; transformational leadership can achieve exactly that goal. Essentially, transformational leaders create norms that enhance intrinsic motivation. From a multi-level perspective, this scenario is somewhat complex – the phenomenon of interest includes an individual (leader) who is influencing an organization's characteristics (culture/climate), which in turn are affecting a group-level behavior (sharing of ideas) that is functional for creativity because it fosters an individual-level characteristic (intrinsic motivation).

This issue certainly poses a wonderful challenge for multi-level researchers, but tremendous obstacles readily present themselves. That said, these ideas are supported by the componential theory of creativity (Amabile, 1988, 1997), theory on transformational leadership (Avolio & Bass, 1988; Bass, 1985), transactional leadership theory (Waldman, Bass, &

Yammarino, 1990), general leadership theory (Redmond et al., 1993), and other general ideas presented by Amabile (1996, 1997).

In a lab study of 159 undergraduate students placed into 36 groups, Sosik et al. (1998) examined how transformational leadership influenced group creativity by using a computer-mediated brainstorming task. These researchers examined Guilford's (1967, 1988; see also Torrance, 1974) four components of divergent thinking: fluency, flexibility, originality, and elaboration. Although groups working under high-transformational leadership conditions were found to be more creative in terms of originality and elaboration than those working under low-transformational conditions, no significant effects of leadership on fluency and flexibility were observed. In addition, the effects on originality were only marginal. Sosik et al. (1998) found that group perceptions of transformational *and* transactional leadership related to creative outcomes. Overall, creative and innovative outcomes appear to derive from a complex interaction between the leader's style and traits, his or her interaction with followers, effective direction of activities, and interaction with the organization (Mumford & Licuanan, 2004).

The complexity involved in how leadership influences creativity is further evidenced through the recognition that creative leadership differs from leadership in other domains. Mumford et al. (2002) identify three unique aspects of creative leadership to illustrate this problem:

- The nature of creative work is fundamentally different than most other forms of work that leaders are often accountable for, in that creative work is ill defined and does not often conform to predefined structures.
- Typical forms of influence exercised by a leader – such as that wielded through position power, extrinsic rewards, and other forms of persuasion – may actually prove detrimental to the creative process.
- There is an inherent conflict between innovation and the organization, such that change brought by any innovation brings natural conflict.

Consequently, our understanding of effective leadership in the creativity domain may require different paradigms than traditionally considered. At the very least, the individual, group, and organizational factors affected by leaders must be reexamined for their differential importance in a creativity domain.

As Mumford et al. (2002) articulate, the importance of expertise and problem-solving skills may be critical for leaders in creative domains because traditional forms of social influence are less effective in producing creativity. As discussed earlier, the use of power and extrinsic rewards often undermine the intrinsic motivation of individuals, making creativity less likely (Amabile, 1988). Ultimately, Mumford et al. argue that as the complexity of the task increases and the demand for novel (i.e., creative) outcomes increases, leader expertise becomes a more important characteristic.

A review of the literature on leadership and creativity reveals critical findings related to individual leader characteristics and specific leader behaviors, leadership styles (e.g., transformational leadership), consideration of both direct and indirect influences, and other approaches to leadership. Running through each of these research streams, however, is its ability to alter the organizational or group climate for creativity, and the powerful social influence that this capability represents.

Perhaps the most critical lesson regarding the role of leadership in the creative process is how a variety of approaches, styles, attitudes, and behaviors might combine to produce a climate or context that is supportive of creativity. The literature on transformational leadership, for example, suggests that transformational leaders facilitate and enhance the likelihood of creativity because they create an environment where individual sharing of ideas is rewarded, where individuals are intellectually stimulated, and where workers are intrinsically motivated (to care about their jobs). Conversely, leaders who create a risk-averse or unsafe climate, such as those who engage in close monitoring, are likely to hinder and inhibit creativity (Zhou, 2003). Numerous studies have demonstrated that many forms of reward-based leadership can inhibit creativity (see Amabile, 1996, for a review), in part because they create an environment that focuses on evaluation of the person, rather than an emphasis on the creative task (cf. Kluger & DeNisi, 1996). Finally, when leaders create a climate of support, creativity is enhanced (Amabile, Schatzel, Moneta, & Kramer, 2004).

In short, leadership influences on creativity have been well documented, and demonstrate powerful effects of social influence factors operating in both cross-level and multi-level relationships to impact creativity.

CONCLUSIONS

Starting with some of the earliest work on creativity and innovation in organizations, researchers have recognized the important role played by social influence factors. Based on Amabile's (1983a, 1983b, 1996) recognition of the importance of intrinsic motivation in producing creative outcomes, a myriad of studies have examined contextual factors – especially social influence factors such as leadership practices and group norms – and provide evidence of their substantial influence. Subsequent theoretical developments have increasingly considered context in general, and social influence in particular, as critical precursors to creativity and innovation. Most recent models such as those presented by West (2002), Amabile (1997), Sternberg (1999), Sternberg et al. (2003a, 2003b), and Drazin et al. (1999), among others, and smaller incremental theoretical advances such as those provided by Tagger (2002), Glynn (1996), and Elenkov and Manev (2005), have stressed the increased importance of social influence factors and underscored the need to think about context and examine creativity and innovation with a multi-level lens.

Despite this outstanding work, much remains to be elucidated about the impact of social influence factors on creativity and on innovation. Clearly, creativity and innovation within an organization are complicated and comprehensive phenomena that feature a complex array of relationships among their elements. We are certainly much closer to the beginning than to the end, especially given that we have just begun to apply a true multi-level analytical lens to our approach. Consequently, we end this chapter with recommendations for key areas to address as we continue to move forward. Although not meant to be all-inclusive, this section draws on the reviewed theory and research to present seven areas that offer ripe prospects for future work. They range in level of specificity and are not presented in any particular order of importance. What each shares in common, however, is the need for a multi-level lens.

Construct Definition Advances

Despite the acknowledgment by most researchers in the organizational creativity and innovation literature that defining the construct is critical, inconsistency in definitions abounds. In particular, two key issues must be resolved. First, what is the nature of creativity and innovation as one transcends levels? Second, what is the distinction between creativity and innovation? Although these are separate issues, they become intertwined when we examine how these constructs have been defined in the theories put forth to date.

Too often, theorists or researchers speak of organizational creativity in their work as though there were clear and accepted organizational-level and group-level manifestations of what we define as creativity at the individual level. Because so much of the creativity research has been conducted at the individual level (and more recently at the group level), much is left to be understood about organizational-level creativity. The theoretical models discussed in this chapter have evinced conflicting thoughts on this issue.

For example, in the propulsion model of creativity (Sternberg, 1999; Sternberg et al., 2003a, 2003b), its authors imply that creative outcomes at the organizational level are similar to those at the individual level: An individual looking to improve his or her status in an organization by taking a new path is just as capable of engaging in the redirection strategy as is an organization looking to improve its status in the market.

Other authors, such as Amabile (1988, 1997) in her componential theory of organizational creativity and innovation, suggest that organizational-level creativity is really the implementation of creative products – in other words, innovation. West (2002) goes even further, by making a distinction between creativity and innovation and differences at the organizational level. He suggests that organizational-level factors, such as time demands, environmental uncertainty, competition, and organizational climate, create threat perceptions that affect innovation and creativity in different, and sometimes opposite, ways.

Certainly, a clear understanding of what creativity *is* at each level and what innovation *is* at each level requires a clear construct definition of each. Although we are closer to that point today, we are not quite there yet, as evidenced by these concepts' treatment in our models. Many researchers now define creativity as the generation of useful and novel ideas, and suggest that it is a necessary component of innovation (Amabile, 1997; Cummings & Oldham, 1997; Mumford, Connelly, & Gaddis, 2003). Although the popularity of this perspective is increasing, it is not a uniformly held view, nor has it been emphatically demonstrated in the empirical literature. Although West and Farr (1990) noted this omission from the literature more than 15 years ago, the gap caused by the independence of creativity and innovation research streams is just beginning to be addressed.

We believe that there is ample evidence to suggest each construct exists independently and interdependently at each level within an organization, but that this point must be demonstrated through empirical work. If we are to understand how social influence factors affect creativity and innovation in organizations, multi-level theorists and researchers must first undertake a fundamental task (Klein & Kozlowski, 2000): We must begin by establishing clear and testable definitions of the creativity and innovation constructs at each relevant level of analysis.

Differential Effects of Social Factors on Creativity and Innovation

In addition to establishing clear definitions of the creativity and innovation constructs, it is important to look at the differential effects of social factors on creativity and innovation. Given the issues related to defining creativity and innovation, there is clearly a need to more explicitly articulate how social factors (and other antecedents) differentially impact each outcome.

Ideas articulated by West (2002) provide ample support for the expectation that social influence factors will have differential effects on creativity and innovation. These relationships must be further developed and explored, however. As West (2002) articulated, the role of threat may be a social factor that acts as a differential influence on creativity and innovation. Given the relationship between external evaluation, perceived threat, and extrinsic motivation (Baer, 1997), we might expect similar differential effects of motivation on creativity versus innovation. Indeed, some of the seemingly incompatible results regarding the potentially harmful or helpful effects of extrinsic motivation on creativity may be due to a lack of distinction between creativity and innovation.

Social Influence and Factors Other Than Intrinsic Motivation

As described in this chapter, researchers have thoroughly investigated social influence factors as related to creativity and innovation in the workplace. Much of that empirical work on social influence has been built on or is consistent with the ideas presented in Amabile's componential model. Specifically, much of it considers social influence factors only in terms of their impact on intrinsic and extrinsic motivation. Theoretical developments incorporating more complex considerations of social influence factors, such as those proposed in some other models (e.g., Ford, 1996; Sternberg et al., 2002, 2003a, 2003b; West, 2002), have been largely untested, and even they stray only marginally from the focus on motivation orientation.

For example, West's (2002) model of group creativity and innovation examines how contextual factors (including social influence) affect group integration processes. Many of these factors, however, are similar – if not identical – to group-level manifestations of intrinsic motivation (i.e., task orientation). Similarly, Amabile's (1988, 1997) componential theory of organizational innovation presents an organizational condition critical to creativity that closely resembles an aggregation of intrinsic motivation. Finally, the work on groups and leadership discussed in this chapter has only modest connections to extant multi-level theory, instead focusing on more specific relationships that often emphasize motivation.

Clearly, there remains great need for comprehensive, multi-level, theoretical developments in the area of creativity and innovation that incorporate social influence factors on a more complex level. This is not to say we should exclude motivation from such research – quite the contrary, in fact. Instead, we simply argue for an expanded consideration of social influence factors.

The Social Impact of Diversity in Organizational Creativity and Innovation

One possible area for expansion beyond social influence and motivation is the study of social influence factors from diversity as predictors of creativity in groups and in organizations. To date, much of the research examining diversity and creativity in organizations has focused on the direct impact of having a diverse group of individuals. Many authors have suggested, for example, that the presence of a diverse workforce increases the overall talent pool, thereby expanding the available knowledge, skills, and perspectives, which in turn results in increased creativity (Milliken & Martins, 1996). Researchers in this area have examined such demographic differences and diversity and found that they are meaningful predictors of creativity and innovation (Ancona & Caldwell, 1992; Lattimer, 1998; Simons, Pelled, & Smith, 1999).

The increase in individual resources brought about by a diverse workforce, however, is merely one manifestation of how diversity might alter organizational creativity and innovation. Clearly, more complex considerations of the relevant diversity-based social factors are warranted.

In addition to representing the breadth and depth of individual characteristics and indicating the resources required for creativity and organization, the presence of diversity within a group or organization has the potential to create powerful social influences that may, in turn, either hinder or enhance creativity. In addressing this concern, more recent efforts have begun to consider social factors that emerge from diversity for their relationship with creativity. A primary focus of these efforts has been to consider the potential for group conflict that diversity may bring (Pelled, Eisenhardt, & Xin, 1999). As Bassett-Jones (2005) notes, diversity can cause misunderstandings and conflict, and group influences such as low morale, which can result in negative outcomes such as inhibition of creativity. Other researchers have demonstrated that the interactive effects between diversity and creativity may affect motivation (Kickul & Gundry, 2001).

In short, the resource-based influences of diversity on creativity, though meaningful, are limiting. The presence of diverse groups can create powerful social influences that ultimately determine the organization's creativity. These social factors need to be incorporated into our theories and more fully explored in our research. In addition, this is yet another area where the distinction between creativity and innovation needs to be examined.

Further Development of the Role of Domains

How one defines creativity, and the processes that facilitate or inhibit creativity and innovation, likely differ as a function of the domain of interest. Although domains have often been considered quite broadly when thinking about creativity (e.g., comparing the domain of music to that of business or science), Ford's (1996) theory of multiple social domains highlights how organizations, and the individuals and groups that constitute an organization, operate within a multi-level nest of social domains and suggests that social influences and other contextual factors within these domains may have facilitating or inhibiting effects on creativity. His theory emphasizes the importance of considering domain specificity, and it provides a well-developed argument regarding the importance of considering domain factors, including social influences, in the study of creativity. The propulsion model (Sternberg, 1999; Sternberg et al., 2002, 2003a, 2003b) also presents conditions where domains are relevant. Finally, although not explicitly described as domains in researchers' work, leadership decisions about which creative outcome to pursue (e.g., redirection versus replication) will certainly be a function of industry or market type, which is one form of a domain.

One recent and somewhat whimsical model, the amusement park theory of creativity (Baer & Kaufman, 2005; Kaufman & Baer, 2004), is also relevant to our discussion of domains. The APT model advances the importance of considering domains, albeit on a more micro-level than Ford's work would suggest. In recognizing the existence of domains and micro-domains within which creativity and innovative acts may occur, the APT model illustrates interesting possibilities for developing a more detailed understanding of domain-based influences. Just as the APT model applies to different domains on a broad level, so its relevance to organizational creativity has been discussed (Agars et al., 2005), it can also be meaningfully applied to the different structural and functional areas within organizations.

Many of the creative theories focus on leadership – which qualities make for a strong leader of creativity or how a leader influences the creativity of subordinate individuals and groups. In truth, each area within an organization can be thought of as a unique domain. Within each domain, there is the possibility of creativity and innovation, and the requirements for these outcomes may vary based on the particular area of interest. Under support services, for example, there may exist many different domains – technical support, administrative support, custodial support, and so on. Within each of these domains, creativity and innovation are likely to be defined somewhat differently. Furthermore, each area may require its own pattern of motivations, personality, thinking styles, intellectual ability, emotional intelligence, and other individual-level determinants, as well as the contextual and social influence factors associated with creativity.

Within these areas (domains), micro-domains may reveal similar distinctions. Custodial support, for example, may include some positions in which individuals clean offices and other positions designated for individuals who fix broken equipment. Within each of these position types, we may define creativity differently. Likewise, the determinants of creativity are likely to be different with the various micro-domains.

Incorporating this level of detail into our theoretical models and our research is a necessary step if we hope to fully capture the importance of domains and to determine how the social influences within particular domains affect organizational creativity and innovation.

General Summary of Theory/Model Development Issues

Although representing a unique need in its own right, each of the aforementioned recommendations represents one piece of a larger need – specifically, the need for a more comprehensive theoretical approach that accomplishes two goals:

- It captures a greater level of complexity and clarity in the construct definitions of creativity and innovation.
- It incorporates additional relationships between underexamined factors and intrinsic motivation, addresses how social influence factors affect factors other than intrinsic motivation, and represents the interactive effects of social influence factors at different levels within the organization.

In short, more comprehensive models, in the true spirit of meso-level research, are needed. Perhaps, an ambitious scholar could integrate many of the theories presented in this chapter. This new theory might be both complex and multi-level and encompass such issues as cross-domain differences, the creativity–innovation distinction, and the interaction among social influences at different levels.

Capturing the Applied Context

Unraveling the complex nature of creativity and innovation in organizations – in particular, the impact of social influence factors – will inevitably require applied data. Enhanced efforts to examine creativity and innovation in real organizations are therefore needed. As Amabile (1997) notes, much of the research on creativity has been conducted with individuals and in a lab setting. This limitation has also plagued the research specific to organizational creativity. A more complete understanding of social influences on creativity and innovation in organizations, however, requires us to place a greater emphasis on theory and methodology that allows us to capture phenomena in real organizations. Although a fairly substantial amount of research has been carried out in the groups and leadership arenas, these represent only parts of the much larger picture to be explored.

As one example of the importance of considering applied issues, we note that the actual value of pursuing creativity and innovation in organizations, though seemingly obvious, may not be so straightforward for many organizations. The general assumptions held by many creativity theorists and researchers, as well as by many practitioners and organizational leaders, is that creativity and innovation are important or even critical organizational outcomes. Nevertheless, some authors suggest that there is reason to question the ubiquitous nature of such beliefs. Evidence from the general creativity literature, for example, indicates that creative people are often thought to be different, mentally unbalanced, or difficult to work with (see e.g., Bromley & Kaufman, 2006; Plucker et al., 2004). In the organizational literature, Janssen (2003) found that innovative employees run the risk of entering into conflict with others who are not open to change.

In a more comprehensive consideration of potential harmful effects of creativity, James et al. (1999) suggested that creativity, if applied to the wrong ends, may cause harm (i.e., creativity is not just a desired outcome.).

They provide a multi-level model of outcomes of creativity that proposes individual and environmental (organizational) factors that may produce both positive outcomes (e.g., product creation, marketing ideas, and employee morale) and negative outcomes (e.g., theft, sabotage, social attacks, and undermining of goals and policies). Although these negative manifestations of creativity are not often identified, their mere existence makes this area fertile ground for future theory and research.

Finally, when one considers the growing recognition that the domain of interest plays a critical role in defining the construct of creativity (i.e., novel and *useful* outcomes) in a given context (Ford, 1996; Baer & Kaufman, 2005), it is not unreasonable to extrapolate to certain contexts in which the domain reveals no positive useful outcome. In other words, if the domain helps define what is creative, might we identify certain domains in which all efforts to engage in creativity result in outcomes that not only fail to be creative but are also ultimately negative for the organization? Although this is an extreme expansion of current domain theories, efforts to consider such possibilities are not without merit.

Although use of the multi-level paradigm that currently drives so much theory and research in the organizational behavior field is spearheaded largely by the efforts of academicians, methodologists, and particularly savvy statisticians, the *need* for these efforts is driven by our desire as a field to more accurately capture the actual dynamics within real organizations. In a field such as organizational creativity and innovation, many aspects of the phenomena of interest simply cannot be captured or even simulated in controlled research settings. Particularly when it comes to understanding the myriad of social influences and multi-level relationships that may explain creativity and innovation, applied research contexts are needed. Consequently, to adequately address these issues, our efforts in the field of organizational creativity and innovation must lead us to think about applications as we develop and test our models.

REFERENCES

Agars, M. D., Baer, J., & Kaufman, J. C. (2005). The many creativities of business and the APT model of creativity. *Korean Journal of Thinking and Problem Solving, 15,* 133–142.

Agars, M.D., Kottke, J.L., & Unckless, A. (2006). Development and validation of the general means-efficacy scale. Unpublished manuscript.

Amabile, T. M. (1979). Effects of external evaluation on artistic creativity. *Journal of Personality and Social Psychology, 37,* 221–233.

Amabile, T. M. (1982). Social psychology of creativity: A consensual assessment technique. *Journal of Personality and Social Psychology, 43,* 997–1013.

Amabile, T. M. (1983a). *The social psychology of creativity.* New York: Springer-Verlag.

Amabile, T. M. (1983b). Social psychology of creativity: A componential conceptualization. *Journal of Personality and Social Psychology, 45,* 357–376.

Amabile, T. M. (1985). Motivation and creativity: Effects of motivational orientation in creative writers. *Journal of Personality and Social Psychology, 48,* 393–397.

Amabile, T. M. (1988). A model of creativity and innovation in organizations. In: B. M. Staw & L. L. Cummings (Eds), *Research in organizational behavior* (pp. 123–167). Greenwich, CT: JAI Press.

Amabile, T. M. (1996). *Creativity in context.* Boulder, CO: Westview.

Amabile, T. M. (1997). Motivating creativity in organizations: On doing what you love and loving what you do. *California Management Review, 40,* 39–58.

Amabile, T. M. (1998). How to kill creativity. *Harvard Business Review, 76,* 77–87.

Amabile, T. M., & Conti, R. (1999). Changes in the work environment for creativity during downsizing. *Academy of Management Journal, 42,* 630–640.

Amabile, T. M., & Gitomer, J. (1984). Children's artistic creativity: Effects of choice in task materials. *Personality and Social Psychology Bulletin, 10,* 209–215.

Amabile, T. M., Goldfarb, P., & Brackfield, S. C. (1990). Social influences on creativity: Evaluation, coaction, and surveillance. *Creativity Research Journal, 3,* 6–21.

Amabile, T. M., Hennessey, B. A., & Grossman, B. S. (1986). Social influences on creativity: The effects of contracted-for reward. *Journal of Personality and Social Psychology, 50,* 14–23.

Amabile, T. M., Hill, K. G., Hennessey, B. A., & Tighe, E. M. (1994). The work preference inventory: Assessing intrinsic and extrinsic motivational orientations. *Journal of Personality and Social Psychology, 66,* 950–967.

Amabile, T. M., Schatzel, E. A., Moneta, G. B., & Kramer, S. J. (2004). Leader behaviors and the work environment for creativity: Perceived leader support. *Leadership Quarterly, 15,* 5–32.

Ancona, D. L., & Caldwell, D. (1992). Demography and design: Predictors of new product team performance. *Organization Science, 3,* 321–341.

Andrews, F. M., & Farris, G. F. (1967). Supervisory practices and innovation in scientific teams. *Personnel Psychology, 20,* 497–515.

Avolio, B. J., & Bass, B. M. (1988). Transformational leadership, charisma, and beyond. In: J. G. Hunt, B. R. Baliga, H. P. Dachler & C. A. Schriesheim (Eds), *Emerging leadership vistas* (pp. 29–39). Lexington, MA: Lexington Books.

Bacharach, S. B. (1989). Organizational theories: Some criteria for evaluation. *Academy of Management Review, 14,* 496–515.

Baer, J. (1991). Generality of creativity across performance domains. *Creativity Research Journal, 4,* 23–39.

Baer, J. (1992, August). *Divergent thinking is not a general trait: A multi-domain training experiment.* Paper presented at the annual meeting of the American Psychological Association, Washington, DC.

Baer, J. (1994). Divergent thinking is not a general trait: A multi-domain training experiment. *Creativity Research Journal, 7,* 35–46.

Baer, J. (1996). The effects of task-specific divergent-thinking training. *Journal of Creative Behavior, 30,* 183–187.

Baer, J. (1997). Gender differences in the effects of anticipated evaluation on creativity. *Creativity Research Journal, 10,* 25–31.

Baer, J. (1998). The case for domain specificity in creativity. *Creativity Research Journal, 11*, 173–177.

Baer, J., & Kaufman, J. C. (2005). Bridging generality and specificity: The amusement park theoretical (APT) model of creativity. *Roeper Review, 27*, 158–163.

Baer, M., Oldham, G. R., & Cummings, A. (2003). Rewarding creativity: When does it really matter? *Leadership Quarterly, 14*, 569–586.

Bargar, R. R., & Duncan, J. K. (1990). Creative endeavor in Ph.D. research: Principles, contexts, and conceptions. *Journal of Creative Behavior, 24*, 59–71.

Barron, F. B., & Harrington, D. M. (1981). Creativity, intelligence, and personality. *Annual Review of Psychology, 32*, 439–476.

Bass, B. M. (1985). *Leadership and performance beyond expectations.* New York: Free Press.

Bass, B. M., & Avolio, B. J. (1994). *Improving organizational effectiveness through transformational leadership.* Thousand Oaks, CA: Sage.

Bassett-Jones, N. (2005). The paradox of diversity management, creativity, and innovation. *Creativity and Innovation Management, 14*, 169–175.

Beersma, B., & De Dreu, C. K. W. (2005). Conflict's consequences: Effects of social motives on postnegotiation creative and convergent group functioning and performance. *Journal of Personality and Social Psychology, 89*, 358–374.

Bem, D. J. (1972). Constructing cross-situational consistencies in behavior: Some thoughts on Alker's critique of Mischel. *Journal of Personality, 40*, 17–26.

Bromley, M.L., & Kaufman, J.C. (2006, August). *Have you heard voices? I've heard them calling my name: Creativity and endorsement of the Mad Genius stereotype.* Presentation at the American Psychological Association, New Orleans, LA.

Cameron, J., & Pierce, W. D. (1994). Reinforcement, reward, and intrinsic motivation: A meta-analysis. *Review of Educational Research, 64*, 363–423.

Capelli, P., & Sherer, P. (1991). The missing role of context in OB: The need for a meso-level approach. In: B. M. Staw & L. L. Cummings (Eds), *Research in organizational behavior* (pp. 55–110). Greenwich, CT: JAI.

Cardozo, R., McLaughlin, K., Harmon, B., Reynolds, P., & Miller, B. (1993). Product-market choices and growth of new business. *Journal of Product Innovation Management, 10*, 331–340.

Carter, S. M., & West, M. A. (1998). Reflexivity, effectiveness, and mental health in BBC-TV production teams. *Small Group Research, 29*, 583–601.

Cohen, W. M., & Levinthal, D. A. (1990). Absorptive capacity: A new perspective on learning and innovation. *Administrative Science Quarterly, 35*, 128–152.

Cole, D. G., Sugioka, H. L., & Yamagata-Lynch, L. C. (1999). Supportive classroom environments for creativity in higher education. *Journal of Creative Behavior, 33*, 277–293.

Conti, R., Collins, M. A., & Picariello, M. L. (2001). The impact of competition on intrinsic motivation and creativity: Considering gender, gender segregation, and gender role orientation. *Personality and Individual Differences, 31*, 1273–1289.

Cooper, B. L., Clasen, P., Silva-Jalonen, D. E., & Butler, M. C. (1999). Creative performance on an in-basket exercise: Effects of inoculation against extrinsic reward. *Journal of Managerial Psychology, 14*, 39–56.

Cooper, R., & Foster, M. (1971). Sociotechnical systems. *American Psychologist, 26*, 467–474.

Cropley, D., & Cropley, A. (2005). Engineering creativity: A systems concept of functional creativity. In: J. C. Kaufman & J. Baer (Eds), *Creativity across domains: Faces of the muse* (pp. 169–185). Mahwah, NJ: Erlbaum.

Cropley, D.H., Kaufman, J.C., & Cropley, A.J. (in press). Malevolent creativity: A functional model of creativity in terrorism and crime. *Creativity Research Journal*.

Csikszentmihalyi, M. (1996). *Creativity*. New York: Harper Collins.

Csikszentmihalyi, M. (1999). Implications of a systems perspective for the study of creativity. In: R. J. Sternberg (Ed.), *Handbook of human creativity* (pp. 313–338). New York: Cambridge University Press.

Cummings, A., & Oldham, G. R. (1997). Enhancing creativity: Managing work contexts for the high potential employee. *California Management Review, 40*, 22–38.

de Charms, R. (1968). *Personal causation: The internal affective determinants of behavior*. New York: Academic Press.

Deci, E. L., & Ryan, R. M. (1987). The support of autonomy and the control of behavior. *Journal of Personality and Social Psychology, 53*, 1024–1037.

De Dreu, C. K. W. (2002). Team innovation and team effectiveness: The importance of minority dissent and reflexivity. *European Journal of Work and Organizational Psychology, 11*, 285–298.

De Dreu, C. K. W., & West, M. A. (2001). Minority dissent and team innovation: The importance of participation in decision making. *Journal of Applied Psychology, 86*, 1191–1201.

DiMaggio, P. J., & Powell, W. W. (1983). The iron cage revisited: Institutional isomorphism and collective rationality in organizational fields. *American Sociological Review, 48*, 147–160.

Drazin, R., Glynn, M. A., & Kazanjian, R. K. (1999). Multilevel theorizing about creativity in organizations: A sensemaking perspective. *Academy of Management Review, 24*, 286–307.

Drazin, R., & Schoonhoven, C. B. (1996). Community, population, and organizational effects on innovation: A multilevel perspective. *Academy of Management Journal, 39*, 1065–1083.

Eden, D. (2001). Means efficacy: External sources of general and specific subjective efficacy. In: M. Erez, U. Kleinbeck & H. Thierry (Eds), *Work motivation in the context of a globalizing economy* (pp. 65–77). Hillsdale, NJ: Erlbaum.

Edmondson, A. (1999). Psychological safety and learning behavior in work teams. *Administrative Science Quarterly, 44*, 350–383.

Egan, T. M. (2005). Creativity in the context of team diversity: Team leader perspectives. *Advances in Developing Human Resources, 7*, 207–225.

Eisenberger, R., Armeli, S., & Pretz, J. (1998). Can the promise of reward increase creativity? *Journal of Personality and Social Psychology, 74*, 704–714.

Eisenberger, R., & Cameron, J. (1996). Detrimental effects of reward: Reality or myth? *American Psychologist, 51*, 1153–1166.

Eisenberger, R., Haskins, F., & Gambleton, P. (1999). Promised reward and creativity: Effects of prior experience. *Journal of Experimental Social Psychology, 35*, 308–325.

Eisenberger, R., & Rhoades, L. (2001). Incremental effects of reward on creativity. *Journal of Personality and Social Psychology, 81*, 728–741.

Eisenberger, R., & Selbst, M. (1994). Does reward increase or decrease creativity? *Journal of Personality and Social Psychology, 66*, 1116–1127.

Eisenberger, R., & Shanock, L. (2003). Rewards, intrinsic motivation, and creativity: A case study of conceptual and methodological isolation. *Creativity Research Journal, 15*, 121–130.

Elenkov, D. S., & Manev, I. M. (2005). Top management leadership and influence on innovation: The role of sociocultural context. *Journal of Management, 31*, 381–402.

Elkins, T., & Keller, R. T. (2003). Leadership in research and development organizations: A literature review and conceptual framework. *Leadership Quarterly, 14*, 587–606.

Farmer, S. M., Tierney, P., & Kung-McIntyre, K. (2003). Employee creativity in Taiwan: An application of role identity theory. *Academy of Management Journal, 46*, 618–630.

Ferris, G. R., Hochwarter, W. A., Douglas, C., Blass, F. R., Kolodinsky, R. W., & Treadway, D. C. (2002). Social influence processes in organizations and human resources systems. In: G. R. Ferris & J. J. Martocchio (Eds), *Research in personnel and human resources management* (pp. 65–128). Greenwich, CT: Elsevier/JAI.

Finke, R. A., Ward, T. B., & Smith, S. M. (1992). *Creative cognition: Theory, research, and applications.* Cambridge, MA: MIT Press.

Ford, C., & Sullivan, D. M. (2004). A time for everything: How the timing of novel contributions influences project team outcomes. *Journal of Organizational Behavior, 25*, 279–292.

Ford, C. M. (1996). A theory of individual creativity in multiple social domains. *Academy of Management Review, 21*, 1112–1134.

Ford, C. M., & Gioia, D. A. (1995). *Creative action in organizations.* Thousand Oaks, CA: Sage.

Frambach, R. T., & Schillewaert, N. (2002). Organizational innovation adoption: A multi-level framework for determinants and opportunities for future research. *Journal of Business Research, 55*, 163–176.

Furnham, A. (1999). Personality and creativity. *Perceptual and Motor Skills, 88*, 407–408.

Galton, F. (1869). *Hereditary genius.* London: Macmillan.

Gardner, H. (1983). *Frames of mind: The theory of multiple intelligences.* New York: Basic Books.

Gardner, H. (2000). *Intelligence reframed.* New York: Basic Books.

Gilson, L. L., Mathieu, J. E., Shalley, C. E., & Ruddy, T. M. (2005). Creativity and standardization: Complementary or conflicting drivers of team effectiveness? *Academy of Management Journal, 48*, 521–531.

Gilson, L. L., & Shalley, C. E. (2004). A little creativity goes a long way: An examination of teams' engagement in creative processes. *Journal of Management, 30*, 453–470.

Glynn, M. A. (1996). Innovative genius: A framework for relating individual and organizational intelligences to innovation. *Academy of Management Review, 21*, 1081–1111.

Goertzel, M. G., Goertzel, V., & Goertzel, T. G. (1978). *Three hundred eminent personalities.* San Francisco: Jossey-Bass.

Greer, M., & Levine, E. (1991). Enhancing creative performance in college students. *Journal of Creative Behavior, 25*, 250–255.

Guilford, J. P. (1956). The structure of intellect. *Psychological Bulletin, 53*, 267–293.

Guilford, J. P. (1967). *The nature of human intelligence.* New York: McGraw-Hill.

Guilford, J. P. (1988). Some changes in the structure-of-intellect model. *Educational and Psychological Measurement, 48*, 1–4.

Hackman, J. R., & Oldham, G. R. (1975). Development of the job diagnostic survey. *Journal of Applied Psychology, 60*, 159–170.

Han, K. (2003). Domain-specificity of creativity in young children: How quantitative and qualitative data support it. *Journal of Creative Behavior, 37*, 117–142.

Hennessey, B. A., Amabile, T. M., & Martinage, M. (1989). Immunizing children against the negative effects of reward. *Contemporary Educational Psychology, 14*, 212–227.

Hocevar, D. (1976). Dimensionality of creativity. *Psychological Reports, 39*, 869–870.

House, R., Rousseau, D. M., & Thomas-Hunt, M. (1995). The meso paradigm: A framework for the integration of micro and macro organizational behavior. *Research in Organizational Behavior, 17*, 71–114.

Howell, J. M., & Boies, K. (2004). Champions of technological innovation: The influence of contextual knowledge, role orientation, idea generation, and idea promotion on champion emergence. *Leadership Quarterly, 15*, 123–143.

Hung, S. C. (2004). Explaining the process of innovation: The dynamic reconciliation of action and structure. *Human Relations, 57*, 1479–1497.

Hunt, J. G., Stelluto, G. E., & Hooijberg, R. (2004). Toward new-wave organization creativity: Beyond romance and analogy in the relationship between orchestra-conductor leadership and musician creativity. *Leadership Quarterly, 15*, 145–162.

James, K., Clark, K., & Cropanzano, R. (1999). Positive and negative creativity in groups, institutions, and organizations: A model and theoretical extension. *Creativity Research Journal, 12*, 211–226.

Jamison, K. R. (1989). Mood disorders and patterns of creativity in British writers and artists. *Journal for the Study of Interpersonal Processes, 52*, 125–134.

Janssen, O. (2003). Innovative behaviors and job involvement at the price of conflict and less satisfactory relations with co-workers. *Journal of Occupational and Organizational Psychology, 76*, 347–364.

Janssen, O., van de Vliert, E., & West, M. (2004). The bright and dark sides of individual and group innovation: A special issue introduction. *Journal of Organizational Behavior, 25*, 129–145.

Jensen, A. R. (1998). *The g factor.* New York: Praeger.

Jensen, A. R. (2002). Psychometric *g*: Definition and substantiation. In: R. J. Sternberg & E. L. Grigorenko (Eds), *The general factor of intelligence: How general is it?* (pp. 39–53). Mahwah, NJ: Erlbaum.

Jung, D. I. (2001). Transformational and transactional leadership and their effects on creativity in groups. *Creativity Research Journal, 13*, 185–195.

Katz-Buoincontro, J. (2005, April). *Does arts-based learning enhance leadership? Case studies of creativity-oriented executive institutes.* Presentation at the American Educational Research Association, Montreal, Quebec.

Kaufman, J. C. (2001). The Sylvia Plath effect: Mental illness in eminent creative writers. *Journal of Creative Behavior, 35*(1), 37–50.

Kaufman, J. C., & Baer, J. (2002). Could Steven Spielberg manage the Yankees? Creative thinking in different domains. *Korean Journal of Thinking and Problem Solving, 12*(2), 5–15.

Kaufman, J. C., & Baer, J. (2004). The amusement park theoretical (APT) model of creativity. *Korean Journal of Thinking and Problem Solving, 14*(2), 15–25.

Kelley, H. H. (1967). Attribution theory in social psychology. *Nebraska Symposium on Motivation, 15*, 192–238.

Kelley, H. H. (1973). The processes of causal attribution. *American Psychologist, 28*, 107–128.

Kickul, J., & Gundry, L. K. (2001). Breaking through boundaries for organizational innovation: New managerial roles and practices in e-commerce firms. *Journal of Management, 27*, 347–361.

Klein, K. J., & Kozlowski, S. W. J. (2000). *Multilevel theory, research, and methods in organizations: Foundations, extensions, and new directions.* San Francisco, CA: Jossey-Bass.

Kluger, A. N., & DeNisi, A. (1996). Effects of feedback intervention on performance: A historical review, a meta-analysis, and a preliminary feedback intervention theory. *Psychological Bulletin, 119,* 254–284.

Kohn, A. (1993). *Punished by rewards.* Boston: Houghton Mifflin.

Kurtzberg, T. R., & Amabile, T. M. (2000–2001). From Guilford to creative synergy: Opening the black box of team-level creativity. *Creativity Research Journal, 13,* 285–294.

Lattimer, R. L. (1998). The case for diversity in global business, and the impact of diversity on team performance. *Competitiveness Review, 8,* 3–17.

Lepper, M. R., & Greene, D. (1975). Turning play into work: Effects of adult surveillance and extrinsic rewards on children's intrinsic motivation. *Journal of Personality and Social Psychology, 31,* 479–486.

Lepper, M. R., & Greene, D. (1978). *The hidden costs of reward: New perspectives on the psychology of human motivation.* Oxford, UK: Erlbaum.

Lepper, M. R., Greene, D., & Nisbett, R. E. (1973). Undermining children's intrinsic interest with extrinsic reward: A test of the "overjustification" hypothesis. *Journal of Personality and Social Psychology, 28,* 129–137.

Ludwig, A. M. (1995). *The price of greatness.* New York: Guilford Press.

Madjar, N. (2005). The contributions of different groups of individuals to employees' creativity. *Advances in Developing Human Resources, 7,* 182–206.

Madjar, N., Oldham, G. R., & Pratt, M. G. (2002). There's no place like home? The contributions of work and non-work creativity support to employees' creative performance. *Academy of Management Journal, 45,* 757–767.

Martindale, C. (1989). Personality, situation, creativity. In: J. A. Glover, R. R. Ronning & C. R. Reynolds (Eds), *Handbook of creativity* (pp. 211–232). New York: Plenum.

McCrae, R. R. (1987). Creativity, divergent thinking, and openness to experience. *Journal of Personality and Social Psychology, 52,* 1258–1265.

Meyer, A. D., & Goes, J. B. (1988). Organizational assimilation of innovations: A multilevel contextual analysis. *Academy of Management Journal, 31,* 897–923.

Miell, D., & MacDonald, R. (2000). Children's creative collaborations: The importance of friendship when working together on a musical composition. *Social Development, 9,* 348–369.

Milliken, F., & Martins, L. (1996). Searching for common threads: Understanding the multiple effects of diversity in organizational groups. *Academy of Management Review, 21,* 402–433.

Mohamed, M. A. K. (2002). Assessing determinants of departmental innovation: An exploratory multi-level approach. *Personnel Review, 31,* 620–641.

Mostafa, M. (2005). Factors affecting organizational creativity and innovativeness in Egyptian business organizations: An empirical investigation. *Journal of Management Development, 24,* 7–33.

Mouly, V., & Sankaran, J. K. (1999). Barriers to the cohesiveness and effectiveness of Indian R&D project groups: Insights from four federal R&D organizations. In: J. A. Wagner (Ed.), *Advances in qualitative organization research* (Vol. 2, pp. 221–244). Stamford, CT: Elsevier Science/JAI Press.

Mumford, M. D., Connelly, S., & Gaddis, B. (2003a). How creative leaders think. *Leadership Quarterly, 14,* 422–432.

Mumford, M. D., & Gustafson, S. B. (1988). Creativity syndrome: Integration, application, and innovation. *Psychological Bulletin, 103*, 27–43.

Mumford, M. D., & Licuanan, B. (2004). Leading for innovation: Conclusions, issues, and directions. *Leadership Quarterly, 15*, 163–171.

Mumford, M. D., Scott, G. M., Gaddis, B., & Strange, J. M. (2002). Leading creative people: Orchestrating expertise and relationships. *Leadership Quarterly, 13*, 705–750.

Mumford, M. D., Strange, J. M., Scott, G. M., & Gaddis, B. P. (2003b). Creative problem-solving skills in leadership: Direction, actions, and reactions. In: J. C. Kaufman & J. Baer (Eds), *Faces of the muse: How people think, work, and act creatively in diverse domains* (pp. 607–634). Mahwah, NJ: Erlbaum.

Nijstad, B. A., & De Dreu, C. K. W. (2002). Creativity and group innovation. *Applied Psychology: An International Review, 51*, 400–406.

Nohria, N., & Gulati, R. (1996). Is slack good or bad for innovation? *Academy of Management Journal, 39*, 1245–1264.

Nonaka, I. (1991). The knowledge-creating company. *Harvard Business Review, 69*, 96–104.

Oldham, G. R., & Cummings, A. (1996). Employee creativity: Personal and contextual factors at work. *Academy of Management Journal, 39*, 607–634.

O'Reilly, C. A., Caldwell, D. F., & Barnett, W. P. (1989). Work group demography, social integration, and turnover. *Administrative Science Quarterly, 34*, 21–37.

Paulos, J. A. (1988). *Innumeracy: Mathematical illiteracy and its social consequences*. New York: Hill and Wang.

Paulus, P. B., & Dzindolet, M. T. (1993). Social influence processes in group brainstorming. *Journal of Personality and Social Psychology, 64*, 575–586.

Pelled, L. H., Eisenhardt, K. M., & Xin, K. R. (1999). Exploring the black box: An analysis of work group diversity, conflict, and performance. *Administrative Science Quarterly, 44*, 1–28.

Plucker, J. A. (1998). Beware of simple conclusions: The case for the content generality of creativity. *Creativity Research Journal, 11*, 179–182.

Plucker, J. A. (1999). Reanalyses of student responses to creativity checklists: Evidence of content generality. *Journal of Creative Behavior, 33*, 126–137.

Plucker, J. A., Beghetto, R. A., & Dow, G. T. (2004). Why isn't creativity more important to educational psychologists? Potentials, pitfalls, and future directions in creativity research. *Educational Psychologist, 39*, 83–96.

Rank, J., Pace, V. L., & Frese, M. (2004). Three avenues for future research on creativity, innovation, and initiative. *Applied Psychology: An International Review, 53*, 518–528.

Redmond, M. R., Mumford, M. D., & Teach, R. (1993). Putting creativity to work: Effects of leader behavior on subordinate creativity. *Organizational Behavior and Human Decision Processes, 55*, 120–151.

Reiter-Palmon, R., & Illies, J. J. (2004). Leadership and creativity: Understanding leadership from a creative problem-solving perspective. *Leadership Quarterly, 15*, 55–77.

Reuter, M., Panksepp, J., Schnabel, N., Kellerhoff, N., Kemple, P., & Hennig, J. (2005). Personality and biological markers of creativity. *European Journal of Personality, 19*, 83–95.

Rousseau, D. M. (1985). Issues of level in organizational research. *Research in Organizational Behavior, 7*, 1–37.

Runco, M. A. (1989). The creativity of children's art. *Child Study Journal, 19*, 177–189.

Ruscio, J., Whitney, D. M., & Amabile, T. M. (1998). Looking inside the fishbowl of creativity: Verbal and behavioral predictors of creative performance. *Creativity Research Journal*, *11*, 243–263.

Schaefer, C. E., & Anastasi, A. (1968). A biographical inventory for identifying creativity in adolescent boys. *Journal of Applied Psychology*, *52*, 42–48.

Schneider, B. (1987). The people make the place. *Personnel Psychology*, *40*, 437–453.

Scott, S. G., & Bruce, R. A. (1994). Determinants of innovative behavior: A path model of individual innovation in the workplace. *Academy of Management Journal*, *37*, 580–607.

Shalley, C. E. (2002). How valid and useful is the integrative model for understanding work groups' creativity and innovation? *Applied Psychology: An International Review*, *51*, 406–410.

Shalley, C. E., & Gilson, L. L. (2004). What leaders need to know: A review of social and contextual factors that can foster or hinder creativity. *Leadership Quarterly*, *15*, 33–53.

Shalley, C. E., Zhou, J., & Oldham, G. R. (2004). The effects of personal and contextual characteristics on creativity: Where should we go from here? *Journal of Management*, *30*, 933–958.

Shapira, Z. (1995). *Risk-taking: A managerial perspective*. New York: Russell Sage Foundation.

Simons, T., Pelled, L. H., & Smith, K. A. (1999). Making use of difference: Diversity, debate, and decision comprehensiveness in top management teams. *Academy of Management Journal*, *42*, 662–673.

Simonton, D. K. (1977). Creative production, age, and stress: A biological time-series analysis of 10 classical composers. *Journal of Personality and Social Psychology*, *35*, 791–804.

Simonton, D. K. (1985). Quality, quantity, and age: The careers of ten distinguished psychologists. *International Journal of Aging and Human Development*, *21*, 241–254.

Sosik, J. J., Kahai, S. S., & Avolio, B. J. (1998). Transformational leadership and dimensions of creativity: Motivating idea generation in computer-mediated groups. *Creativity Research Journal*, *11*, 111–121.

Sternberg, R. J. (1985). *Beyond IQ: A triarchic theory of human intelligence*. Cambridge, MA: Cambridge University Press.

Sternberg, R. J. (1996). *Successful intelligence*. New York: Simon and Schuster.

Sternberg, R. J. (1999). A propulsion model of types of creative contributions. *Review of General Psychology*, *3*, 83–100.

Sternberg, R. J., Kaufman, J. C., & Pretz, J. E. (2001). The propulsion model of creative contributions applied to the arts and letters. *Journal of Creative Behavior*, *35*, 75–101.

Sternberg, R. J., Kaufman, J. C., & Pretz, J. E. (2002). *The creativity conundrum: A propulsion model of kinds of creative contributions*. New York: Psychology Press.

Sternberg, R. J., Kaufman, J. C., & Pretz, J. E. (2003a). A propulsion model of creative leadership. *Leadership Quarterly*, *14*, 455–473.

Sternberg, R. J., Kaufman, J. C., & Pretz, J. E. (2003b). A propulsion model of creative leadership. *Creativity and Innovation Management*, *13*, 125–153.

Sternberg, R. J., Pretz, J. E., & Kaufman, J. C. (2003c). Types of innovations. In: L. Shavinina (Ed.), *The international handbook of innovation* (pp. 158–169). Mahwah, NJ: Lawrence Erlbaum.

Sundstrom, E., & Associates. (1999). *Supporting work team effectiveness: Best management practices for fostering high performance*. San Francisco, CA: Jossey-Bass.

Tagger, S. (2002). Individual creativity and group ability to utilize individual creative resources: A multilevel model. *Academy of Management Journal, 45*, 315–330.

Tierney, P., Farmer, S. M., & Graen, G. B. (1999). An examination of leadership and employee creativity: The relevance of traits and relationships. *Personnel Psychology, 52*, 591–620.

Torrance, E. P. (1974). *Torrance tests of creative thinking*. Lexington, MA: Ginn.

Tsui, A. E., & O'Reilly, C. A. (1989). Beyond simple demographic effects: The importance of relational demography in superior subordinate dyads. *Academy of Management Journal, 32*, 402–423.

Unsworth, K. (2001). Unpacking creativity. *Academy of Management Review, 26*, 289–297.

Waldman, D. A., Bass, B. M., & Yammarino, F. J. (1990). Adding to contingent-reward behavior: The augmenting effect of charismatic leadership. *Group and Organization Studies, 15*, 381–394.

Walsh, J. P., & Fahey, L. (1986). The role of negotiated belief structures in strategy making. *Journal of Management, 12*, 325–338.

Weick, K. E. (1995). *Sensemaking in organizations*. London: Sage.

West, M. A. (1995). Creativity values and creativity visions in teams at work. In: C. Ford & D. A. Gioia (Eds), *Creative action in organizations: Ivory tower visions and real world voices* (pp. 71–77). Thousand Oaks, CA: Sage.

West, M. A. (1996). Reflexivity and work group effectiveness: A conceptual integration. In: M. A. West (Ed.), *Handbook of work group psychology* (pp. 555–579). Chichester, UK: Wiley.

West, M. A. (2002). Sparkling fountains or stagnant ponds: An integrative model of creativity and innovation implementation in work groups. *Applied Psychology: An International Review, 51*, 355–424.

West, M. A., & Anderson, N. R. (1996). Innovation in top management teams. *Journal of Applied Psychology, 81*, 680–693.

West, M. A., Borrill, C. S., Dawson, J. F., Brodbeck, F., Shapiro, D. A., & Haward, B. (2003). Leadership clarity and team innovation in health care. *Leadership Quarterly, 14*, 393–410.

West, M. A., & Farr, J. L. (1990). *Innovation and creativity at work*. Chichester, UK: Wiley.

Whetton, D. A. (1989). What constitutes a theoretical contribution? *Academy of Management Review, 14*, 490–495.

Woodman, R. W., Sawyer, J. E., & Griffin, R. W. (1993). Toward a theory of organizational creativity. *Academy of Management Review, 18*, 293–321.

Zhou, J. (2003). When the presence of creative coworkers is related to creativity: Role of supervisor close monitoring, developmental feedback, and creative personality. *Journal of Applied Psychology, 88*, 413–422.

SOCIAL INFLUENCE, CREATIVITY, AND INNOVATION: BOUNDARIES, BRACKETS, AND NON-LINEARITY

Shelley D. Dionne

ABSTRACT

Agars, Kaufman, and Locke's (this volume) review of social influence within the creativity and innovation literature provides an introduction to multi-level issues within creativity research. Their chapter reveals that relevant social influences may differ by level, relevant domain character-istics may not hold across other domains, and creativity may be influenced differently than innovation. Building on Agars et al.'s work, this com-mentary offers several suggestions pertaining to multi-level research as a means of advancing creativity research, specifically as it relates to social influence. Suggestions for future research include consideration of levels-based boundaries within theoretical construct development, employment of a bracketing technique to review construct implications at levels above and below the construct of interest, and improvement in multi-level modeling of particular social influence and/or creative processes that are non-linear in nature.

Multi-Level Issues in Creativity and Innovation
Research in Multi-Level Issues, Volume 7, 63–73
Copyright © 2008 by Elsevier Ltd.
ISSN: 1475-9144/doi:10.1016/S1475-9144(07)00002-1

INTRODUCTION

Agars, Kaufman, and Locke's (this volume) multi-level examination of social influence and creativity in organizations provides an excellent review of the state of creativity and innovation literature, with particular emphasis on social influence. As an introductory chapter related to levels of analysis issues within this social influence and creativity domain, their work reviews several levels of analysis issues present within the creativity and social influence literature. Unfortunately, as in other research domains such as diversity (cf. Dionne, Randel, Jaussi, & Chun, 2004) and leadership (cf. Yammarino, Dionne, Chun, & Dansereau, 2005), although levels of analysis within creativity and innovation relationships are inherent, often they are not explicitly addressed by researchers.

In their summary of definitions of creativity, Agars and colleagues (this volume) note that the definition of creativity may inherently affect the contextual factors of relevance, including the notions that social influences may differ by level, meaningful domain characteristics may differ across domains, and creativity may be influenced differently than innovation. All three of these conclusions provide an appropriate base for which to include a multi-level perspective and, as such, should serve as a call to creativity researchers to expand our understanding of the nature and influence of levels of analysis within the field.

SOCIAL INFLUENCE MAY DIFFER BY LEVEL

Addressing the first concern – that relevant social influences may differ by level of analysis – future creativity research has ample room for development surrounding the concept of social influence. While predominantly presented as forms of leadership, group influence, and/or cultural influence (Agars, Kaufman, & Locke, this volume) within the extant creativity literature, social influence represents an enormous domain under which to classify relationships between an individual's creativity and nearly anything that may influence that creativity or, likewise, influence a group's, leader's, or even organization's creativity. Without a specific, theoretical levels-based focus that is both explicitly noted and tested within these multi-level relationships, social influence is a paradox – too broad of a topic, yet not broad enough.

Social Influence as Too Broad

A common social influence factor noted within the creativity literature is leadership. Even though leadership is implicitly and/or explicitly addressed in its relationship with both creativity and innovation, the concept of leadership is often presented with a broad brushstroke. For example, the interactionist theory regarding creativity (Woodman, Sawyer, & Griffin, 1993) asserts that non-autocratic leadership is a creativity enhancer for groups. Sternberg and colleagues (Sternberg, 1999; Sternberg, Kaufman, & Pretz, 2001, 2002, 2004) describe several methods that a leader might use to make a creative contribution and further note that several organizational characteristics could potentially influence these leadership suggestions. Within these theories, the concept of leadership is defined broadly in that linkages between the influence process of leadership and creativity (or innovation) are offered generally, but without much detail on the specific leader behaviors and characteristics that subordinates are likely to encounter, or the method by which the leader asserts the influence.

Moreover, these leadership concepts are broad in that they often describe multi-level linkages without theoretically addressing the multi-level nature of leadership. For example, how does the non-autocratic behavior of the individual leader operate at the group level? Does the leader always meet with the entire group and never display autocratic behavior? Does the leader meet with individual subordinates and all subordinates notice that the leader is non-autocratic? Or is the leader not autocratic during particular phases of the creativity process, but as a deadline looms, exercises autocratic decision making to move the group toward progress? In such a case, most of the time the leader is non-autocratic, but on occasion he or she does exercise an autocratic action or decision.

An absence of carefully constructed, levels-based theory makes the social influence concept of leadership seem too broad, especially given that the boundary conditions explicitly addressed in appropriate multi-level theoretical development (cf. Dansereau & Yammarino, 2000; Dansereau, Alutto, & Yammarino, 1984) are absent. Crossing levels, or implying anything more than a single-level relationship, opens the door to a variety of options between relationships, including dyadic, group, and collective relationships. All of these possibilities have been addressed in prior leadership theories and, as such, may be plausible candidates for consideration, albeit not necessarily relevant ones.

And therein lies the paradox: The absence of specific multi-level linkages surrounding several inherently multi-level social influence factors has produced a broadness (or vagueness) about the topic as related to creativity, yet multi-level specifications are necessary components, given that many social influences inherently involve individuals, groups, and/or collectives. The vagueness surrounding social influence as being too broad presently may only be eradicated by *increasing* the broadness of our view of social influence. However, this increase in broadness is accomplished by *specificity* and careful examination of the relevance of social influence at multiple levels of analysis.

Social Influence as Not Broad Enough

To advance our understanding of social influence, researchers need to broaden how they construct the multi-level network surrounding social influence beyond considering the generic terms of "leadership," "group dynamics," and "culture." These simplified views of extremely complex multi-level phenomena may be too broad for organizations and practitioners to glean implementation suggestions and focus on the practicality of applications. By considering the broader implications of these complex phenomena through careful multi-level development, researchers can provide a more specific guide to leaders and organizations that may be struggling to enhance individual or group creativity, to manage conflict into a functional precursor for innovation, or to develop a culture of risk and acceptance of failure. What are the bounds of current creativity and social influence theory? If some creativity technique works for groups, will it necessarily work for an individual – or better yet, for an entire organization? If researchers broaden the multi-level lens of the relationship and consider the broader implications, if any, of their theories, both the research side and the practical side of understanding creativity will benefit.

To improve our understanding of the social influence of leadership on creativity, research needs to become more specific about the anticipated effect of the leadership influence, and specifically regarding which entities are affected. "Non-autocratic leadership" can mean many things (i.e., too broad); moreover, this term can mean many things to many people (i.e., not broad enough regarding our understanding for relevant entities). As noted earlier, both autocratic influence and non-autocratic influence probably have individual-, dyad-, and group-level implications, and delineating these differences and similarities is one way that researchers might respond to

Agars and colleague's (this volume) suggestion that relevant social influences may differ by level.

DOMAIN CHARACTERISTICS DIFFER ACROSS DOMAINS

The same multi-level theoretical framework can be applied to Agars and colleague's (this volume) second concern – namely, that domain character-istics differ across domains. This area could greatly benefit from specifying the level of the characteristic and the level of each domain. In particular, characteristics and domains need clear identification of the theoretical boundary conditions of the variables of interest, lest they too become too broad a concept or relation. Agars et al. (this volume) note that the concept and role of domains must be expanded to advance creativity theory, and they assert the likelihood that micro-domains exist within domains. That being the case, clearly delineating the relevant levels and entities within domains and micro-domains becomes even more imperative.

Hackman's (2003) description of bracketing as a means of examining the relevance of multi-level phenomena may serve the creativity literature well, considering the interplay between characteristics, domains, and micro-domains. Although bracketing – growth of understanding of a construct in both the downward and upward directions – is an accepted means of investigation in science and mathematics, its use has not been as prevalent in social science (Hackman, 2003). Given that much of the social influence within the creativity literature focuses on group issues (Agars et al., this volume), bracketing a group issue would require theoretical investigation of relationships to creativity at the group level in addition to moving down to the individual level to consider the implications for the focal phenomenon at an individual-level context (i.e., member characteristics or leadership). Likewise, bracketing a group issue would require moving up to the organizational level to consider contextual implications on the focal phenomenon.

Agars and colleagues (this volume) highlight the social effects of diversity on creativity, suggesting that consideration of social influences created by the breadth and depth of individual characteristics within a group be further developed. Using that suggestion as an example, group conflict caused by diversity (Pelled, Eisenhardt, & Xin, 1999), and operating at the group level of analysis, is an area where bracketing may be useful in elucidating the multi-level bounds of diversity and social influence. Bracketing at a lower level – for example, examining conflict at a dyadic level – may provide a richer understanding of group conflict, as it may pinpoint problematic dyads or dyads within groups that significantly influence group conflict. Bracketing at even lower level – for example, examining individual characteristics related to or contributing to group conflict – also may enhance our understanding of how to address group conflict within a diverse team.

Similarly, bracketing at a higher level – for example, examining organizational-level factors related to group diversity and its resultant conflict – may enrich our understanding of group conflict. How is group diversity part of the larger cultural context, and can diversity be mapped to this higher level? Bracketing diversity in this way helps researchers begin to understand that group conflict within a diverse team might stem from acrimonious dyadic relations; as such, leadership needs to address the dyadic conflict first and foremost. Alternatively, perhaps conflict is systemic within an organizational culture, and therefore senior leaders need to address a macro diversity and conflict issue to best resolve group conflict within diverse teams.

In assessing the integrity of group conflict, researchers need to be certain that "conflict" is not reducible to a lower level and that, in fact, group conflict resides solely at the group level and would not be more appropriately modeled as a dyadic or dyad-within-group level phenomenon. A group-level phenomenon is not relevant for consideration below the group level, meaning that "group conflict" is solely understood and interpreted by the group as an entity. As a consequence, examination of dyads and or individuals would produce no interpretive power for better understanding "group conflict."

Bracketing helps clarify a construct's integrity, in that entertaining the possibility of alternative or competing hypotheses helps researchers strengthen the focal construct's definition. The more specific and detailed the information related to the focal construct, the better the prediction of the construct's behavior when paired with other key areas, such as creativity and innovation. As noted by Hackman (2003), bracketing requires that constructs have conceptual integrity at their own level – not a novel idea, as it was one of the concepts in the early development of levels of analysis research within organizational behavior (cf. Dansereau et al., 1984). Despite more than 20 years of work exploring this field, scholars note a continued trend of blurring the micro and meso boundaries, particularly when individual characteristics and components are used to describe group and organizational dynamics (Hackman, 2003; Larson & Christensen, 1993). Unfortunately, it seems that levels of analysis within the social science field may be pigeon-holed as a methodological issue, rather than a theoretical issue with methodological implications (Yammarino et al., 2005). Well-developed multi-level theory needs to precede any concern for empirical tests, as blurring boundaries between theoretical levels cannot be saved by employing sophisticated multi-level analytic tools.

CREATIVITY AND INNOVATION INFLUENCES

Finally, Agars and colleagues (this volume) assert that creativity may be influenced differently than innovation. From a social influence perspective, this notion provides a particularly ripe area for investigation. Although some creativity researchers indicated the presence of non-linear relationships between creativity, innovation, and other variables (Woodman et al., 1993; West, 2002), most of the creativity research continues to hypothesize and test linear relationships. This narrow focus is unfortunate, because biographies and anecdotal evidence suggest many of the great scientific breakthroughs and innovations are the result of "ah-ha" moments: After tirelessly searching a problem space, the scientist moves on to other projects, pursuits, hobbies, and sleep, only to have the creative moment happen unexpectedly (Ghiselin, 1985). A key factor in many of these descriptions relates to the search of a problem space. This process often takes a very convoluted or exploratory form, especially given that the entire problem space may not even be defined. Moreover, the search could involve peaks and valleys, representing successes and failures within a problem space. As such, an individual creativity pattern, in addition to possibly being non-linear, may be non-monotonic.

What relevance does this exploration have to multi-level research? Differences in these creativity and innovation patterns at different levels might exist, such that an individual creative problem-solving process might proceed by searching a problem space, circling back to previous ideas, or having minor breakthroughs that unfortunately lead to failures. Nevertheless, this journey, through a process of learning, might eventually result in success. Implementing the novel outcome, defined as innovation (Agars et al., this volume), may be an equally difficult struggle for the individual and reflect non-linear or non-monotonic patterns.

At the dyadic level, the interaction of two creative individuals may provide some benefit for both parties – for example, exhausting the problem space more efficiently, and implementing the innovation more effectively. As such, the pattern assumes a different form, perhaps remaining non-linear, but possibly displaying more monotonic properties. At the group level, exhausting the problem space and implementing innovations may become even more efficient. Again we see the process taking a less chaotic path, and further easing away from non-monotonic properties of the individual creative process. Finally, at the organization level, we may see creativity and innovation that resemble a more linear process, as policies and procedures and vast support networks can enhance the efficiency of the process.

Although at this point the levels-based progression of creativity and innovation from non-monotonic to monotonic (either linear or non-linear) is purely speculative, given that creativity and innovation scholars have noted the processes are likely non-linear or curvilinear (Woodman et al., 1993; West, 2002), researchers need to begin to theoretically examine non-linear concepts. This exploration offers an opportunity for creativity scholars to move the entire social science field forward by being pioneers in testing non-linear social influence processes and their implications for creativity and innovation.

CONCLUSIONS

Both creativity and innovation may benefit from a better incorporation of levels of analysis. Creativity – defined as the production of novel, useful ideas (Agars et al., this volume) – seems easily conceived as an individual-level concept (i.e., artist/cartoonist). As the level of analysis becomes higher, however, the concept becomes a bit more blurred. For example, was the collaborative team producing the movie *Cars* for Disney/Pixar creative at the group level, meaning that creativity cannot be reduced to its individual components (i.e., artists/cartoonists), or was the production better captured as the sum of individual creativity? Maybe *Cars* represents group creativity; if so, can Disney/Pixar be considered creative at an organizational level, and not reduced to its component creative groups? As creativity researchers, we need to be particularly careful when incorporating levels of analysis into our concepts, so they can help point the appropriate influences within the appropriate domains.

Agars and colleagues (this volume) offer seven recommendations for moving creativity and innovation research forward. Both of their first two recommendations – construct definition advances and differential effects of social factors on creativity and innovation, respectively – may be advanced by considering the boundary conditions of the focal phenomenon more carefully. Conceptual integrity is critical, yet it is not possible without viewing the focal phenomenon within a complete levels-of-analysis framework. This framework provides relevance for the construct and directs all empirical tests. Bracketing may be one method for accomplishing this integrity. In any event, given the inherent multi-level nature of social influence presented in the creativity literature, a multi-level framework needs to accompany several social influence concepts.

Agars et al.'s third recommendation – expanding social influence's domain beyond its link with intrinsic motivation and creativity – is a timely one. Several opportunities exist for multi-level advancement of our understanding of social influence processes, including expansion of leadership's influence on creativity and innovation beyond motivation. First, multi-level views of leadership exist that might add considerable complexity and depth to our understanding of social influence, in that group-based, shared leadership may influence group properties (beyond motivation) such as decision making and norms. Similarly, dyadic leadership may influence decision making and norm development within a group in a completely different way. Although both leadership models may influence decision and norms, the effect may have a differential effect on creativity and innovation. For example, the suggestion that "supportive" leadership may enhance creativity in groups may be a level-specific phenomenon: At the group level, it may be highly effective; at the dyadic level, supportive leadership may not be as effective at influencing group creativity. Leadership, although remaining instrumental in subordinate motivation, contains multi-level intricacies and complexities that, when paired with creativity and/or innovation, possesses great potential to expand the domain of social influence beyond motivation.

Agars et al.'s fourth and fifth recommendations – studying the social impact of diversity and further developing the role of domains, respectively – also represent areas where multi-level boundaries can greatly enhance the understanding and use of diversity within appropriate domains. These are particularly tricky areas for consideration, as diversity may be one of those "blurred" concepts where individual characteristics define a group construct (Dionne et al., 2004), and domains may possess micro-domains that likewise blur the multi-level boundaries. Carefully considering relevant levels-based boundaries may illuminate exactly which concepts become most relevant in the pursuit of creative outcomes and innovations. For example, an outwardly diverse group produces creative products, but what are the relevant individual-level characteristics? Did age or functional diversity spur creative thinking? Or could gender diversity have provided a new perspective? At a higher level, does some aspect of culture relate to creative groups or diverse groups? Understanding the theoretical bounds of diversity or social influence enriches our understanding of creativity and innovation and its place within particular domains.

Agars et al.'s sixth recommendation – better capturing the complexity and clarity in the construct definitions of creativity and innovation – may be best served by taking a non-linear approach to investigating relationships, as suggested by prior creativity research (Woodman et al., 1993; West, 2002). Moreover, specific multi-level linkages within certain boundaries add to the complexity of the constructs, even as they clarify those constructs. The better researchers can capture and model creativity, the more helpful advice we can provide to individuals, leaders, and organizations regarding creativity and innovation.

One example of multi-level research examining a non-linear process can be found in the leadership literature. Dionne and Dionne (in press) investigated how various leadership models at the individual, dyad, and group levels of analysis related to decision optimization in hierarchical groups. Employing a Monte Carlo simulation technique, thousands of groups were examined under each leadership model. Of the four leadership models examined, shared leadership (i.e., group level of analysis) was a more effective leadership style, in that groups were able to optimize decisions more quickly. Although not specifically related to creativity, group decision making may play a role in creativity. As a consequence, a similar model might examine creativity variables while modeling non-linear relationships.

Agars et al.'s seventh recommendation highlights the need for applied research within the creativity and innovation field. Again, strong multi-level theory directs strong multi-level methodologies focused on relevant and appropriate entities of interest. If a construct is theorized to reduce to the individual level, then research (i.e., surveys, studies) should address and accommodate individual characteristics. If a construct is theorized to hold only at the group level, then research should address and accommodate group-level characteristics, not merely individual characteristics that would aggregate to a higher level.

Agars and colleagues have provided a road map for successful social influence research within the creativity and innovation domains. Ideally, future research will address the variety of multi-level issues on its way to building better theory, testing more sophisticated models, and interpreting results with stronger, more targeted, practical implications.

REFERENCES

Agars, M., Kaufman, J., & Locke, J. (this volume). Social influence and creativity in organizations: A multi-level lens for theory, research, and practice. In: M. D. Mumford, S. T. Hunter & K. E. Bedell-Avers (Eds), *Multi-level issues in creativity and innovation* (Vol. 7). Oxford: Elsevier.

Dansereau, F., Alutto, J. A., & Yammarino, F. J. (1984). *Theory testing in organizational behavior: The varient approach.* Englewood Cliffs, NJ: Prentice-Hall.

Dansereau, F., & Yammarino, F. J. (2000). The varient paradigm as an underlying approach to theory building and testing. In: K. J. Klein & S. W. J. Kozlowski (Eds), *Multilevel theory, research, and methods in organizations: Foundations, extensions, and new directions* (pp. 425–466). San Francisco, CA: Jossey-Bass.

Dionne, S. D., & Dionne, P. J. (in press). Levels-based leadership and hierarchical group decision optimization: A Monte Carlo simulation. *Leadership Quarterly.*

Dionne, S. D., Randel, A. E., Jaussi, K. S., & Chun, J. U. (2004). Diversity and demography in organizations: A levels of analysis review of the literature. *Research in Multi-Level Issues, 3*, 181–229.

Ghiselin, B. (1985). *The creative process: Reflections on the inventions in the arts and sciences.* Berkley, CA: University of California Press.

Hackman, J. R. (2003). Learning more by crossing levels: Evidence from airplanes, hospitals, and orchestras. *Journal of Organizational Behavior, 24*(8), 905–922.

Larson, J. R., & Christensen, C. (1993). Groups as problem-solving units: Toward a new meaning of social cognition. *British Journal of Social Psychology, 32*, 5–30.

Pelled, L. H., Eisenhardt, K. M., & Xin, K. R. (1999). Exploring the black box: An analysis of work group diversity, conflict, and performance. *Administrative Science Quarterly, 44*, 1–28.

Sternberg, R. J. (1999). A propulsion model of types of creative contributions. *Review of General Psychology, 3*, 83–100.

Sternberg, R. J., Kaufman, J. C., & Pretz, J. E. (2001). The propulsion model of creative contributions applied to arts and letters. *Journal of Creative Behavior, 35*, 75–101.

Sternberg, R. J., Kaufman, J. C., & Pretz, J. E. (2002). *The creativity conundrum: A propulsion model of kinds of creative contributions.* New York, NY: Psychological Press.

Sternberg, R. J., Kaufman, J. C., & Pretz, J. E. (2004). A propulsion model of creative leadership. *Leadership Quarterly, 14*, 455–473.

West, M. A. (2002). Sparkling fountains or stagnant ponds: An integrative model of creativity and innovation implementation in work groups. *Applied Psychology: An International Review, 51*, 355–424.

Woodman, R. W., Sawyer, J. E., & Griffin, R. W. (1993). Toward a theory of organizational creativity. *Academy of Management Review, 18*, 293–321.

Yammarino, F. J., Dionne, S. D., Chun, J. U., & Dansereau, F. (2005). Leadership and levels of analysis: A state-of-the-science review. *Leadership Quarterly, 16*(6), 879–919.

CREATIVITY RESEARCH SHOULD BE A SOCIAL SCIENCE

Mark A. Runco

ABSTRACT

This commentary is intended to complement the chapter written by Agars, Kaufman, and Locke (this volume). Agars et al. (this volume) are correct in stating that innovation is a vital part of business and that much can be learned about innovation from studies of creativity. This commentary underscores several of the more important points made by Agars et al., questions others, and fills in several gaps found in their chapter. Perhaps most important are the qualifications offered in the present commentary, which are intended to constrain some of the claims made in Agars et al.'s chapter. Related to this is the need to consider the larger picture of scholarship dealing with innovation and creativity. For example, there may be an originality bias among creativity researchers and an unfortunate tendency to ignore relevant but older research. This commentary does have a critical tone, but only because many of Agars et al.'s arguments are entirely tenable and need not be repeated. The gaps, however, should be filled, and some of the claims qualified. Nevertheless, some ambiguity is useful with a complex topic, such as creativity, and it is important to recognize that creativity is not entirely a social process.

Multi-Level Issues in Creativity and Innovation
Research in Multi-Level Issues, Volume 7, 75–94
Copyright © 2008 by Elsevier Ltd.
ISSN: 1475-9144/doi:10.1016/S1475-9144(07)00003-3

INTRODUCTION

At the risk of relying on a trite expression, it almost "goes without saying" these days that organizations need to invest in innovation, and that innovation depends a great deal on creative efforts. Agars, Kaufman, and Locke (this volume) are, then, absolutely correct when they state that there is growing evidence that creativity and innovation in organizations can have a substantial and positive impact on desired individual and organizational outcomes. These authors are also absolutely correct when they note that innovation has become an organizational necessity in the current age of international business and constant changing in the world of work. A third entirely tenable point made early on by Agars et al. is that the occurrences of creative processes within organizations, and ultimately the emergence of organizational innovations, are necessary and anxiously awaited developments. Obviously, I have no arguments with the basic premises laid out by Agars et al.; indeed, their chapter contains many highly useful ideas. A number of them are practical, and most are well connected to current research.

This commentary is intended to complement the chapter of Agars et al. It does not cover exactly the same ground, for that would be redundant. Instead, it highlights a few points, questions others, and fills in some gaps. Perhaps most important are the qualifications offered for several of the claims presented by Agars et al., as a few claims in their chapter are seriously in need of qualification. Related to this is the need to stand back and consider the larger picture of scholarship dealing with innovation and creativity. There is reason to be concerned about this scholarship (Runco, in press) and the chapter prepared by Agars et al. merely confirms the need to perform rigorous research in this area.

Let me reiterate, however, that Agars et al.'s chapter is an admirable overview of issues involved in social influence and creativity in organizations. One way to describe how my effort fits with theirs is as follows: They presented a nice overview, and the present commentary fills in some of the details.

This takes us directly to the "general concern" just mentioned. A huge amount of research is currently being produced on creativity and innovation. Put bluntly, however, a fair amount of it seems to have been prepared without adequate consultation of the existing literature. I am not referring specifically to the chapter prepared by Agars et al., though this omission is why I add citations and qualify a number of their claims. Rather, I am speaking more generally about the field of creative studies. It has become a legitimate science, which indicates that knowledge should be shared and that individuals producing the data should consult others. This research is not a competition. The goal is to gather and accumulate objective and reliable information. To that end, new findings should be thoroughly integrated into the existing field (Runco, 1988). Sadly, more and more research is being published that is inadequately tied to earlier research.

At one point I thought perhaps this failure reflected the "publish or perish" pressure placed on scholars, but I no longer think that is the case. Instead, I blame technology. Indeed, technological advances are creating problems in the sciences, and in particular in literature reviews. This is probably related to Tenner's (1996) concerns, presented in his engaging volume, *Why Things Bite Back: Technology and the Reverse of Unintended Consequences.* What is most relevant to the present discussion is the possibility that scholars are only searching online resources in their attempts to identify previous research. This strategy would be understandable given how easy it is to search online and how thorough the results might appear to be. Online searches often uncover a surprising number of sources – but they are not comprehensive. All too often I read a manuscript and wonder why the author is reinventing the wheel or ignoring directly relevant research. This almost always occurs when the earlier research is a bit older and may not be available online. It does not have to be that old, either: The *Creativity Research Journal*, for example, has articles dating back only to 1995. The point is that there is a lack of sufficient integration, and many authors fail to do their homework.

The problem is not just technological, however, and it is especially acute in the field of creative studies. I cannot be certain of its origins (nor of my explanation about online searches), but it appears as if those of us studying creativity appreciate creativity so much that originality becomes all-important. Originality is, of course, the key to creativity. Nevertheless, it is not sufficient as the sole indicator of creativity, but rather is a necessary part of it. Originality is the only aspect of creativity on which everyone agrees. Perhaps it should come as no surprise, then, that ties and important bridges are not explored as thoroughly as they should be. If I am correct about this point, this trend constitutes a systematic bias, an intentional act – and one that is especially problematic in studies of creativity. I will refer to it as the *originality bias* (Runco, 1995).

I explored this originality bias recently in an editorial for the *Creativity Research Journal* (Runco, in press); I also argued for integration (the bridges and ties just mentioned) in the premiere editorial of the same journal (Runco, 1988). These concerns explain why I offer additional citations and emphasize ties to existing research in the present commentary. This forum does allow me to underscore some of the more compelling ideas found in the chapter written by Agars et al. Indeed, this commentary covers many concepts, including the creativity complex and the benefits of ambiguity, domain differences in creativity, intrinsic motivation, the product bias, the role of interpretation, risk aversion, and aesthetics. It also raises several questions, also based on earlier research. What follows does have a critical emphasis, but that is because many of Agars et al.'s points need not be repeated and are entirely tenable.

THE CREATIVITY COMPLEX

Let us first consider the claim that it would be useful to have a "singular conceptualization of creativity." Such conceptualization strikes me as unrealistic and unnecessary. Creativity is expressed in many different ways and can be defined as a complex or syndrome (Albert & Runco, 1989; MacKinnon, 1965; Mumford & Gustafson, 1988). Any singular conceptualization of creativity could easily overemphasize one aspect of creativity (e.g., the person, the process, the product, or the environment). It may also oversimplify to the degree that the conceptualization becomes unrealistic. Of course, specificity can sometimes both help to clarify causality and ensure semantic precision, but then again this makes sense only when the phenomenon in question is, in fact, a simple one. Additionally, the social and behavioral sciences have other complexes and constructs that are quite useful and similar to creativity in terms of their level of complexity and abstraction. Morals, culture, and the cognitive unit called a *bit*, for instance, are all realistic only because they allow for individual differences and diversity and reflect a similar level of ambiguity. If they were defined in a singular or absolute fashion, they would lose their validity and explanatory power.

There are actually two intertwined issues here. One involves the complex nature of the subject matter, and the other the value of approaching it from different perspectives. They are intertwined because a complex subject matter probably requires diverse perspectives. Indeed, the creativity literature itself is replete with examples of the benefits of diversity. "Shift one's perspective" and "consult others" are both well-recognized tactics for creative problem solving. Surely we should practice what we preach and use these tactics when studying creativity! Along the same lines, given that creativity is associated with particular cognitive capacities, personality traits, and affective tendencies, it makes sense to appreciate diverse perspectives. These naturally lead to a non-singular conceptualization. This argument is essentially a restatement of what Barron (1995) and others have suggested with their ideas about being creative about creativity. We cannot use traditional science (e.g., reductionism) for creativity. Rogers (1970) referred to the technique that I am describing as a *holistic* approach to creativity.

Agars et al. may be assuming that ambiguity and complexity are undesirable in a definition of creativity. They refer to the lack of explicit definitions in the creativity research (citing Plucker, Beghetto, & Dow, 2004) and complain about uncertainty around the construct definition. Uncertainty does sound like a problem, but it may very well be that varied and flexible definitions of creativity are necessary, given that creativity is a complex subject. In fact, in this light, we have another example of creative studies influencing their own methods! Tolerance of ambiguity has previously been found to characterize creative persons and to allow highly divergent creative thinking (Barron, 1955), so perhaps this lesson has been taken to heart such that those studying creativity are themselves tolerant of the complex and the necessary ambiguity. Or perhaps it is a kind of postponement of closure, which has also been shown to support original thinking (Runco & Basadur, 1993). These conjectures are, of course, mere hypotheses, and the important point is that some ambiguity about creativity may be beneficial.

To the credit of Agars et al., there is ample discussion of domain differences. These differences, of course, imply that creativity is expressed in diverse ways. Nevertheless, thinking back on the need to consider the larger creativity literature, it seems unfortunate that all the attention is given to research in the 1980s and later (e.g., Baer, 1991, 1992, 1994). In fact, Albert (1969) was studying domain differences long before then, and many of the seminal studies conducted at the Institute of Personality Research and Assessment (IPAR) in the 1950s and 1960s compared architects, writers, and several other domains (e.g., Barron, 1995; Helson, 1966; MacKinnon, 1965). Going even further back, Patrick (1935, 1937) recognized the need to examine creativity within domains and looked within samples of artists, writers, and scientists as part of her investigation.

In the middle of their chapter, Agars et al. revisit the idea of domain specificity and acknowledge the possibility of a general creativity factor, which they call "*c*." It seems that, in their eyes, it is more important to focus on the domain-specific aspects of creativity. This conclusion is debatable. One specific problem arises when Agars et al. explore the general creativity factor. They refer to studies on the creative person and imply that generality on that level is possible. This leap shows what can happen when one ignores the larger (and older, pre-Internet) corpus of literature. Agars et al. write as if the level of personality and "the creative person" constitute a generality, but had they looked at a larger literature – some of which is older than the sources they consulted and cited – they would have found that this is not always true. Architects, for example, differ in significant ways from writers in their personalities (Barron, 1968). All writers, including both Agars et al. and myself, should, of course, avoid false dichotomies. I remain concerned that they relied on such a false assumption when discussing divergent thinking tests and their generality, but the same applies to personality. We need not choose between general and domain-specific personality traits; both may exist in creative samples.

Agars et al. mention intrinsic motivation a number of times but, again, they cite only work from the 1980s and 1990s. Some very good research – including the initial identification of the role of intrinsic motivation – occurred at least 20 years before then. The researchers at IPAR wrote many times about this issue (e.g., MacKinnon, 1965). This omission is not just a matter of giving credit where credit is due (although determining who initiated a breakthrough is often a question in the sciences). Earlier research should not be ignored, because good science is both collaborative and integrative. Also, why reinvent the wheel?

The seemingly simple insight that intrinsic motivation would lead to higher levels of creativity than extrinsic motivation was not first proposed in 1979, as Agars et al. (this volume) seem to believe. In fact, Sir Francis Galton was well aware of the importance of intrinsic motivation – in 1869 (i.e., *Hereditary Genius*; cf. Runco & Charles, 1993). Admittedly, his ideas were not tested in the laboratory (although he did have archival data). Galton did not, to my knowledge, use the exact phrase "intrinsic motivation," but instead wrote how there are vital "qualities of intellect and disposition," which act as an "inherent stimulus" in the work of eminent individuals. More recently (but still well before the research of the 1980s), Nicholls described the role of personal motives: "First...it maintains the activity needed to establish the necessary skills or information and to generate the necessary possible solutions...Second, it brings an attitude of mind that allows task requirements to come to the fore" (Nicholls, 1983, p. 270).

The field of creative studies certainly owes a large debt to Amabile (1983, 1990a, b) and Eisenberger and Masterson (1983) for developing such useful methodologies for the study of intrinsic motivation. These authors have also refined our understanding of how intrinsic and extrinsic factors sometimes work together. Amabile (1990a, b) took the additional step of identifying methods to immunize individuals against the potentially inhibitive effects of extrinsic incentives and rewards, and Amabile's work with Hennessey shows how the various factors can be best used in creative work on computers (Hennessey, 1989).

Sometimes both intrinsic and extrinsic factors can play a role in creative work (Eisenberger & Shanock, 2003; Runco & Charles, 1993). This is precisely why I mentioned avoiding the either/or fallacy and false dichotomies earlier. Classic personality theory is useful here, in that it describes "trait × state" interactions. An individual may, for example, be intrinsically motivated in some settings but not others. Commercial artists may enjoy their work, not only because they are creating art but also because they earn a salary. Clearly, creativity is not always entirely dependent on intrinsic motivation, and extrinsic factors do not always inhibit creative efforts.

Agars et al. seem to assume that creativity is necessarily a social process. This perspective is widely held (e.g., Csikszentmihalyi, 1990; Ford, 1996; Kasof, 1995; Montuori, 1998). Sometimes the process is social, in that judgments by experts (the "field") are necessary for something to be deemed "creative." Consider the claim of Agars et al. that, if the field did not believe that the later work of Bach was creative in the domain of music when he was still alive, this means that his work was not creative at that time. I disagree. The work itself is not changing: It is either creative or uncreative. It seems very clear that what *is* changing is not the work but rather the judgment of it. This is a confounding factor, then, for both the work and the judgment. If nothing else, it is contrary to a fundamental premise of the sciences – namely, parsimony. There is no reason to jilt the parsimonious and no reason to allow creative products to be confounded by social judgments. The two are extricable. Why not simply conclude that opinions vary in different contexts and eras? The products do not change; only the judgments change.

There are other reasons, in addition to parsimony, to avoid a reliance on expert judgment when defining creativity. One of them is that creativity is sometimes personal (Runco, 1996). There are numerous problems with science that relies on subjective judgments. For example, these judgments are often unreliable. Agars et al. (this volume) applied this thinking to the organization when they wrote that social influence does not impact creativity but may actually determine what is or is not creative. Their conclusion seems to be that social judgment may change the product. In truth, social judgment does not change the product; it merely changes the *judgments* about the product. Not to belabor the point, but the musical notes written by Bach are the same now as they were when he wrote them; it is simply the judgments about the music that have changed. Of course, Bach's own judgments about his music would also be subjective, as would the judgments of any creator, himself or herself.

Note that I am not suggesting that experts be ignored and creative persons themselves make all judgments. Indeed, both types of judgments are quite subjective. Misjudgments about creative works are extremely frequent (Runco, 1999a, b). Goethe, for example, apparently thought his best work was in optics, yet his work in this area is easily dismissed. Ben Franklin stated that his favorite invention was the armonica (a wonderful instrument that uses the vibrations of a series of crystal glasses) – not the lending library or the lightning rod. Of course, Franklin was referring to his *favorite* invention; if asked which of his many inventions was most significant on a social level, he may well have chosen electricity or the library.

A reliance on social judgments also leads directly to a reliance on creative products. Social judgments are typically offered for some product – an invention, a patent, a work of art or composition, and so on. As was the case with the logic of social judgments, the advantage of products is their objectivity. Products, for example, can be easily counted. Plucker, Beghetto, and Dow (2004) held a product view and defined creativity as "the interaction among aptitude, process, and environment by which an individual or group *produces a perceptible product* [emphasis added] that is both novel and useful as defined within a social context" (2004, p. 90). Agars et al. cite Ford's definition of creativity as "a domain-specific, subjective judgment of the novelty and value of an outcome of a particular action" (1996, p. 1115). Ford did not mention a product, however, but referred to outcomes. Outcomes, like products, do relate to the creative *process.* I have referred to the emphasis on outcomes as the *product bias* (Runco, 1995).

Studies of creative products tell us very little about the individual and little, if anything, about the process that leads to productivity. Although products can be studied objectively, in such a case the investigator is merely quantifying products. To make matters worse, as noted earlier, products need to be judged, and judgments are notoriously unreliable. Judgments vary from one historical period to another, for example, and they often change from one time to another. One need simply examine inter-judge reliability ratings to see statistical evidence of these tendencies. Essentially, judges attribute higher levels of creativity to some products and lower levels or lack of creativity to other products. What is important here is the fact that these judgments are attributions – and attributions are notoriously unreliable.

Agars et al. are aware of the product bias in much of the research they cite. They acknowledge that the propulsion model of creativity focuses exclusively on creative products. Then again, at certain points in their chapter they seem to favor a product view of creativity. For example, they suggest that "Creativity must represent something different, new, or innovative." Note the term "something" here.

Given the earlier mentions of social judgment, it is surprising that Agars et al. describe their work as an initial look at social factors. How is it "initial"? Social factors have been tied to creativity for many years (e.g., Albert, 1975; Galton, 1869; Goertzel & Goertzel, 1962). Along the same lines, Agars et al. come close to making a "straw man" argument when they suggest that early efforts to understand creativity focused exclusively on characteristics of the individual. The word "exclusively" is the problem here. In fact, if we take the long view, ample evidence indicates that the individual was actually considered unimportant in earlier research (Albert, 1975). In fact, the earliest descriptions of creative genius emphasized the roles played by "muses" and processes that were entirely beyond the individual. It was as if creative geniuses were merely inspired or acted as conduits for ideas and solutions. Admittedly, some of the most facile scientific efforts did emphasize the individual, but they did not focus exclusively on the individual.

I have already cited Galton (1869) twice in this commentary, but this is not some obscure source found in a dusty library. As a matter of fact, Agars et al. also cite Galton (1869)! He was the first cousin of Charles Darwin and was famous for bringing the normal distribution from mathematics to the social and the behavioral sciences. Galton's study of hereditary genius is a seminal work, and in it he acknowledged the need to consider the broader context, including society and the family. Indeed, Galton wrote about social attributions in such a way as to foreshadow modern consensual theories of creativity. Thus it is simply incorrect for Agars et al. to suggest that there has been, until lately, virtually no consideration of the environment in which an individual acted. Taylor (1972), Gordon (1972), Kay (1972), Owens (1969, 1972), and McPhearson (1972) presented environmental views of creativity 35 years ago, as did Harrington (1990) and McCoy (2005) much more recently. Then there is the work of Torrance (1965, 1972) on contextual factors, which are often environmental, and even the oft-cited idea from Rhodes (1961) that many "press" factors play into creativity. Thus it is clearly misleading to suggest that it was not until the work of Amabile and her colleagues that contextual factors were more readily considered for their importance in creativity. The idea of context influencing creativity has a rich and lengthy history.

The idea of "press" was taken from Murray's (1938) theory and simply implies pressures on behavior. Importantly, Murray distinguished between two kinds of presses: alpha and beta. Alpha press factors are primarily objective aspects of experience and the context. Beta press factors reflect an individual's interpretation of a particular contextual pressure. Thus the environment or immediate context is not all-important. Context contains or presents press factors, which individuals then interpret. I put it this way to yet again avoid an either/or position (e.g., either environment *or* the individual).

Consider next Agars et al.'s conclusion that the environmental conditions of threat have not just differing, but opposing, effects on individual creativity and organizational innovation (cf. Lust, 2002). This may be another simplification. Threats have an effect only when they are interpreted, and each individual interprets potential threats in an idiosyncratic fashion. As a consequence, individuals react in different ways to threats. It follows that not all creative effort will be inhibited by threat, nor necessarily enhanced by it. Very likely this holds true of any organizational innovation. This scenario is analogous to competition: some people are stimulated by competition, whereas others freeze (Runco, in press). It boils down to the interpretation and perception of the situation. This idea, of course, also applies to the specific processes involved in creative work, including ideation. I am thinking here of Agars et al.'s claim that during the creative process, individuals produce fewer ideas (i.e., are less creative) under conditions of threat than when they are under non-threatening conditions…conversely, the likelihood that a new but existing idea is implemented (i.e., innovation) increases under conditions of threat (cf. Lust, 2002; Rank, Pace, & Frese, 2004).

An interesting psycho-economic prediction has been made regarding threats – namely, that threats may be perceived *costs* and as such have differential effects on various ideational processes. Economic research has demonstrated, on the industrial level, that increased costs do not simply lower productivity but actually tend to increase quality. It is as if companies become more selective and more careful, and ensure that the few things they do produce are of high quality. Runco (2006) applied this concept to ideation, where the prediction is that when threats and other constraints are imposed, individuals and teams will produce fewer ideas but ideas of higher quality. Research in progress is testing this hypothesis with brainstorming groups. The expectation is that ideational fluency will decline in groups experiencing threats (e.g., interpersonal criticism) but that originality and other qualitative indicators will increase. This result seems to be in direct contrast with Agars et al.'s claim that individuals will produce fewer ideas and be less creative when threatened. If the psycho-economic prediction holds up, individuals may actually be more creative in such circumstances even though they are less productive and less fluent.

Actually, several investment and economic theories of creativity have been proposed (Runco, Lubart, & Goetz, 2007). Walberg and Stariha (1992) put forth an investment theory, and Sternberg and Lubart (1991) described creativity as a matter of "buying low and selling high." Viewed from this perspective, creativity may occur when an individual or organization invests in something that is unpopular – that is, when they buy low – only to reap the benefits and be attributed with creativity when the product or service later becomes more popular and they sell their ideas. This is somewhat metaphorical but a powerful idea.

Agars et al. recognize interpretations as being an important part of the creative process. In particular, they quote Drazin and Schoonhoven, who described "cross-level, systematic, and embedded effects that may arise from idiosyncratic and or communal interpretations of what it means to be creative" (Drazin & Schoonhoven, 1996, p. 287). In fact, "communal interpretations" of what it means to be creative might reflect organizational values. They might also reflect the current economic status or the particular organization. An organization's values may change when it experiences any sort of constraint or when costs are high, with the change most likely leading to lower production but increasing the premium placed on high-quality output (Rubenson & Runco, 1992). There is very good research on the role of values in the creative process (Helson, 1990; Dolinger, in press; Kasof, Chen, Himsel, & Greenberger, in press), which might help to explain interpretive tendencies.

INDIVIDUAL DIFFERENCES

Given the importance of the individual (e.g., in interpreting contextual press factors), I would have preferred some mention of individual differences in Agars et al.'s chapter. When they discuss threats, for example, they do not take into account individual differences in how threats are interpreted. This variation is especially pertinent to the discussion of the impact of crises. Agars et al. refer to two types of crises that may occur within organizations: one reflecting time and budgetary constraints, and the other involving what they call "functionality." These ideas seem to be entirely consistent with the research on tension (Runco, 1994), turbulence (Mumford, 1995), and conflict (Runco, 1999b), as well as much earlier work suggesting that creative talents may sometimes develop out of need – when the individual is faced with a crisis to which he or she needs to adapt in a creative fashion (e.g., Goertzel, Goertzel, & Goertzel, 1962). Recall here Murray's (1938) idea about the different kinds of presses. One person's crisis is another person's challenge. For some, a crisis may stimulate actions, whereas others may react to the same crisis by freezing or relying on routine. Surely a routine will not lead to creative work.

The fact that individual differences were often overlooked may explain why Agars et al.'s description of Guildford's (1968) structure of intellect model, and in particular divergent thinking, is superficial. What these authors did say is accurate. What they did not say was that divergent thinking is useful only in certain contexts. Divergent thinking does reflect a very useful model of creative thinking, and tests of divergent thinking are useful with many samples of subjects. All too often, however, the case for divergent thinking is overstated. Divergent thinking is not equivalent to creativity, nor is "divergent thinking" a synonym for "actual creative performance." Rather, divergent thinking is best viewed as an indicator or estimate of the potential for certain forms of creative problem solving (Runco, 1991, 1999a, in press). Agars et al. state that these four factors [fluency, flexibility, originality, and elaboration] have shaped how much of creativity is conceptualized and measured; that statement should read "the potential for creative problem solving" instead. There is an important difference between creativity and creative potential.

A related oversight involves the evaluative aspect of creativity. Agars et al. claim that the relevance of evaluation is often overlooked, when it has actually become one of the foci of contemporary research (Mumford, Baughman, & Sager, 2003; Runco, 2004; Simonton, 2003). Runco (1991, 2004) and Runco and Charles (1993) demonstrated that there is a unique skill that allows individuals to accurately evaluate the originality of ideas and that is distinct from other forms of critical thinking and convergent production. Runco and Basadur (1993) described the role of these evaluative skills in organizations, in particular for managers. Runco and Vega (1990) examined the evaluative skills of teachers and parents. Other approaches to the evaluative processes necessary for creative work are presented by Mumford et al. (2003), Simonton (2003), and Campbell (1960).

The discussion of sense making is one of the especially attractive aspects of Agars et al.'s chapter. I say that because there is a connection to the creative process and an admirable de-emphasis on outcomes and products. Agars et al. refer to shifting the focus away from thinking exclusively about creative outcomes and toward thinking about how creative processes evolve over time. In keeping with the idea of stepping back and considering all relevant research, here I wonder about the connection between sense making and what Heinzen (1994) and Richards (1997) described as proactive creativity.

Agars et al. present an interesting discussion of how competing behavioral alternatives may appear to be interdependent but instead are actually independent (cf. Ford, 1996). This is an extremely important idea because it suggests that people can simultaneously be both creative and conventional. That is, individuals could be original but also fit in socially. Approximately 10 years ago, I presented a parallel idea in a discussion of children and education (Runco, 1996). My conclusion was that discretion and decision making need to be encouraged so that students will be able to conform when such behavior is adaptive but also retain the capacity for non-conformity when it is adaptive and appropriate (i.e., in the service of creativity). These ideas may apply directly to an organization as well. Not long ago, I took this approach and explored parallels between schools and (business) organizations and similarities between teachers and managers (Runco, 2006). In education and business environments, individuals need to retain the capacity to think in a non-conforming and creative fashion, but they also need to recognize when such behavior is appropriate and when it is not. This can be viewed (and targeted) as a kind of *discretion* (Runco, 1996).

Agars et al. may have been aware of this kind of thing when they described the relative advantages of habitual versus creative actions. They again cite the fine work of Ford (1996) but might have enriched their discussion by looking at work carried out slightly earlier – in particular, at the economic and psycho-economic theories that were proposed a few years earlier. These theories are very useful for understanding habit and creativity and for explaining why individuals and organizations sometimes seem to prefer one or the other (Rubenson, 1991; Rubenson & Runco, 1992, 1995; Sternberg & Lubart, 1991). Many creative performances can, for example, be explained in terms of costs and benefits (to the individual) and in terms of supply and demand (in the organization or even culture) (Rubenson & Runco, 1992, 1995).

Additionally, as noted by both Agars et al. and Ford (1996), risk aversion is a critical factor for creative work that is often influenced by the organization – and is recognized in the aforementioned psycho-economic approach to creativity. An organization might have strict standards and inflexible expectations, in which case risk is relatively unlikely, especially for an individual who is risk averse. Conversely, another organization might be flexible and see the value of taking risks. The psycho-economic take on risk focuses on the investment strategies that characterize risk-averse individuals and organizations. Creative ideas and products typically require some sort of risk because they are always original and their benefits are sometimes difficult to predict. Yet if there is no investment because of risk aversion, ideas and products will not be explored and will rarely be original.

The same thing can be said about the market preferences noted by Agars et al. These are also frequently studied in the economic literature, and many of the results from this line of research can be applied to the actions of organizations. Clearly, a benefit would be realized from an interdisciplinary perspective of creativity; there is no reason not to use the extant psycho-economic and economic research. Recall here that Rubenson and Runco (1992) went into some detail about supply and demand as determinants of the market for creativity (also see Florida, 2004).

The discussion by Agars et al. of the positive and negative aspects of creativity is very useful (also see James, Clark, & Cropanzano, 1999). A recent article by Cropley, Cropley, and Kaufman (in press) extends this line of thought by defining *malevolent creativity* – which, of course, is another example of the negative aspects of creativity. McLaren's (1993) thinking on the "dark side of creativity" is also noteworthy. Applying this line of thought to organizational creativity and innovation, it should be recognized that it is not always easy to support creativity. Supervisors, managers, or clients may misjudge or misunderstand it, and sometimes it is simply difficult to accept. Supporting creativity and innovation very often requires a great deal of tolerance, for many reasons. In particular, creative people are not perfect and are sometimes not easy to get along with! This hypothesis is reinforced by many biographies, and even autobiographies, of creative people, but its veracity is also clear if one simply examines the personality traits that are correlated with creativity. Creative people are often non-conformists, for example, and at least as often are intrinsically motivated. These two characteristics help to support the creative process, but they can also make it difficult to coexist with the creative person.

Many of these ideas apply to both creativity and innovation, but it is important to distinguish between the two as well. Agars et al. cite a definition offered by Shalley, Zhou, and Oldham in which "creativity refers to the development of novel, potentially useful ideas. Although employees might share these ideas with others, only when the ideas are successfully implemented at the organization or unit level were they considered innovative" (Shalley, Zhou, and Oldham, 2004, p. 934). This particular definition intimates one reason why divergent thinking is often incorrectly equated with creativity (instead of being viewed as an estimate for the potential for creative problem solving, as described earlier) – that is, because of the emphasis on ideas. This result is exactly what is produced by the divergent thinking process: ideas. Note also that innovation in both this definition and the definition used by Agars et al. indicates the intentional implication of a creative outcome, product, or process. Given that both creativity and innovation are intentional, there certainly should be a great deal we can do about them!

Agars et al. are certainly correct when they state that innovation is not always a social and organizational phenomenon and creativity is not always an individual one. They also offer the useful idea that creativity and innovation can be contrasted with each other by examining their unique predictors. They write, that the components that lead to successful creativity are not the same and can be opposite of the components that lead to successful innovation.

AESTHETICS, INNOVATION, AND CREATIVITY

Agars et al. observe that many current operational definitions of creativity overemphasize the aesthetic aspects of creativity. They cite what I admit is an important article (Cropley et al., in press) that describes both functional creativity and elegance. "Elegance," somewhat surprisingly, is often tied to scientific creativity. This is, then, another example of domain specificity. The respect for elegance among scientists suggests that aesthetics are important in their work, just as in artistic endeavors. As Cole described it,

> In physics, truth and beauty often walk hand in hand. Physicists describe theories as "ugly" or "beautiful," talk about ideas that "smell" or "feel" right. Often, aesthetic judgments lead to discoveries, such as in Einstein's theory of gravity and Paul A. M. Dirac's discovery of antimatter. Aesthetics, French physicist Henri Poincaré said, is a "delicate sieve" that sorts the true from the misleading. Or as Dirac famously put it: "It is more important to have beauty in one's equations than to have them fit experiment." (Cole, 2006, p. R2)

I am not sure that either elegance or aesthetics is included often enough in studies of creativity and innovation. Most definitions of the former point to originality and fit or appropriateness, not aesthetic appeal (cf. Csikszentmihalyi & Getzels, 1971; Runco & Charles, 1993). In a sense the research on values, cited above, is also applicable here. Individuals sometimes have strong values which guide their interests and work (Helson, 1990).

CONCLUSIONS

It is likely that I have included more criticism than appreciation in the present commentary. That is probably because the best parts of Agars et al.'s chapter are, well, the best parts and there is little I could add to them. Agars et al. are to be applauded for their discussion of the role of motivation and creativity, for example, especially because they have captured a wide range of views on the topic. They do not merely acknowledge the role of intrinsic motivation but describe how in certain instances rewards can improve divergent thinking and creative work (see also Eisenberger & Shanock, 2003; Eisenberger & Rhoades, 2001; Rubenson & Runco, 1992, 1995).

At this juncture, it should be clear that we need to take a long view of creativity research and consider work that was done before the 1990s. Much of that extant research is very relevant to the concerns found in the Agars et al. chapter. There is no reason to reinvent the wheel simply because the initial invention is not available online. Individuals studying creativity need to do their homework, at least if they truly respect creativity and scientific research and hope for scientific advance. I am sure that is true of Agars et al., and I hope that my own commentary is taken primarily as an attempt to fill in the gaps in the Agars et al. chapter. The effort here is not meant simply to describe the mistakes they may have made, but rather to identify gaps and earlier research that might help to fill those gaps. In that way we should continue to make progress about creativity as a social, personal, and organizational phenomenon.

REFERENCES

Agars, M., Kaufman, J., & Locke, J. (this volume). Social influence and creativity in organizations: A multi-level lens for theory, research, and practice. In: M.D. Mumford, S.T. Hunter & K.E. Bedell-Avers (Eds), *Multi-level issues in creativity and innovation* (Vol. 7). Oxford: Elsevier.

Albert, R. S. (1969). The concept of genius and its implications for the study of creativity and giftedness. *American Psychologist, 24*, 743–753.

Albert, R. S. (1975). Toward a behavioral definition of genius. *American Psychologist, 30*, 140–151.

Albert, R. S., & Runco, M. A. (1989). Independence and the creative potential of gifted and exceptionally gifted boys. *Journal of Youth and Adolescence, 18*, 221–230.

Amabile, T. M. (1983). *The social psychology of creativity*. New York, NY: Springer-Verlag.

Amabile, T. M. (1990a). Within you, without you: Toward a social psychology of creativity and beyond. In: M. A. Runco & R. S. Albert (Eds), *Theories of creativity* (pp. 61–91). Newbury, CA: Sage.

Amabile, T. M. (1990b). Without you, without you: The social psychology of creativity and beyond. In: M. A. Runco & R. S. Albert (Eds), *Theories of creativity* (pp. 61–91). Thousand Oaks, CA: Sage.

Baer, J. (1991). Generality of creativity across performance domains. *Creativity Research Journal, 4*, 23–39.

Baer, J. (1992, August). *Divergent thinking is not a general trait: A multi-domain training experiment.* Paper presented at the annual meeting of the American Psychological Association, Washington, DC.

Baer, J. (1994). Divergent thinking is not a general trait: A multi-domain training experiment. *Creativity Research Journal, 7*, 35–46.

Barron, F. (1955). The disposition toward originality. *Journal of Abnormal and Social Psychology, 51*, 478–485.

Barron, F. (1968). *Creativity and personal freedom.* Mahwah, NJ: Van Nostrand.

Barron, F. (1995). *No rootless flower: An ecology of creativity.* Cresskill, NJ: Hampton.

Campbell, D. (1960). Blind variation and selective retention in creative thought as in other knowledge processes. *Psychological Review, 67*, 380–400.

Cole, K. C. (2006, October 8). Not even wrong: Review of P. Woit's The Failure of String Theory and the Search for Unity in Physical Law (Basic Books) and L. Smolin's The Trouble with Physics: The Rise of String Theory, the Fall of Science, and What Comes Next (Houghton Mifflin). Los Angeles Times Book Review, p. R2.

Cropley, D. H., & Kaufman, J. C., & Cropley, A. J. (in press). Malevolent creativity: A functional model of creativity in terrorism and crime. *Creativity Research Journal.*

Csikszentmihalyi, M. (1990). *Flow: The psychology of optimal experience.* San Francisco, CA: Harper & Row.

Csikszentmihalyi, M., & Getzels, J. W. (1971). Discovery-oriented behavior and the originality of creative products: A study with artists. *Journal of Personality and Social Psychology, 19*, 47–52.

Drazin, R., & Schoonhoven, C. B. (1996). Community, population, and organization effects on innovation: A multilevel perspective. *The Academy of Management Journal, 39*, 1065–1083.

Eisenberger, R., & Masterson, F. A. (1983). Required high effort increases subsequent persistence and reduces cheating. *Journal of Personality and Social Psychology, 44*, 593–599.

Eisenberger, R., & Rhoades, L. (2001). Incremental effects of reward on creativity. *Journal of Personality and Social Psychology, 81*, 728–741.

Eisenberger, R., & Shanock, L. (2003). Rewards, intrinsic motivation, and creativity: A case study of conceptual and methodological isolation. *Creativity Research Journal, 15*, 121–130.

Florida, R. (2004). America's looming creativity crisis. *Harvard Business Review, 82*, 122–136.

Ford, C. N. (1996). A theory of individual creativity and multiple social domains. *Academy of Management Review, 21*, 1112–1134.

Galton, F. (1869). *Hereditary genius.* New York, NY: Macmillan.

Goertzel, V., & Goertzel, M. G. (1962). *Cradles of eminence.* Boston, MA: Little Brown.

Gordon, G. (1972). The identification and use of creative abilities in scientific organizations. In: C. W. Taylor (Ed.), *Climate for creativity: Report of the seventh national research conference on creativity* (pp. 109–124). New York: Pergamon Press.

Guildford, J. P. (1968). *Creativity, intelligence, and their educational implications.* San Diego: EDITS/Robert Knapp.

Harrington, D. M. (1990). The ecology of human creativity: A psychological perspective. In: M. A. Runco & R. S. Albert (Eds), *Theories of creativity* (pp. 143–169). Thousand Oaks, CA: Sage.

Heinzen, T. (1994). Situational affect: Proactive and reactive creativity. In: M. P. Shaw & M. A. Runco (Eds), *Creativity and affect* (pp. 127–146). Norwood, NJ: Ablex.

Helson, R. (1966). Personality of women with imaginative and artistic interests: The role of masculinity, originality, and other characteristics in their creativity. *Journal of Personality, 34,* 1–25.

Helson, R. (1990). Creativity in women: Inner and outer views over time. In: M. A. Runco (Ed.), *Theories of creativity* (pp. 46–58). Newbury Park, CA: Sage.

Hennessey, B. A. (1989). The effect of extrinsic constraints on children's creativity while using a computer. *Creativity Research Journal, 2,* 151–168.

James, K., Clark, K., & Cropanzano, R. (1999). Positive and negative creativity in group, institutions, and organizations: A model and theoretical extension. *Creativity Research Journal, 12,* 211–226.

Kasof, J. (1995). Social determinants of creativity: Status expectations and the evaluation of original products. In: B. Markovsky, K. Heimer & J. O'Brien (Eds), *Advances in group processes* (pp. 167–220). Mahwah, NJ: Elsevier.

Kasof, J., Chen, C., Himsel, A., & Greenberger, E. (in press). Values and creativity. *Creativity Research Journal.*

Kay, A. (1972). Making organizational changes toward creativity. In: C. W. Taylor (Ed.), *Climate for creativity: Report of the seventh national research conference on creativity* (pp. 131–138). New York, NY: Pergamon Press.

Lust, J. A. (2002). Employee ownership: The new source of competitive advantage. *Personnel Psychology, 55,* 797–802.

MacKinnon, D. W. (1965). Personality and the realization of creative potential. *American Psychologist, 20,* 273–281.

McCoy, J. M. (2005). Linking the physical work environment to creative context. *Journal of Creative Behavior, 39,* 169–191.

McLaren, R. (1993). The dark side of creativity. *Creativity Research Journal, 6,* 137–144.

McPhearson, J. H. (1972). Assessing the relationship between the industrial climate and the creative process. In: C. W. Taylor (Ed.), *Climate for creativity: Report of the seventh national research conference on creativity* (pp. 97–108). New York, NY: Pergamon Press.

Montuori, A. (1998, August). Postmodern systems theory, epistemology, and environment: The challenge of reconceptualization. *Best papers of the proceedings of the academy of management conference,* Boston, MA.

Mumford, M. D. (1995). Situational influences on creative achievement: Attributions or interactions? *Creativity Research Journal, 8,* 405–412.

Mumford, M. D., Baughman, W. A., & Sager, C. E. (2003). Picking the right material: Cognitive processing skills and their role in creative thought. In: M. A. Runco (Ed.), *Critical creative processes* (pp. 19–68). Cresskill, NJ: Hampton Press.

Mumford, M. D., & Gustafson, S. B. (1988). Creativity syndrome: Integration, application, and innovation. *Psychological Bulletin, 103,* 27–43.

Murray, H. A. (1938). *Explorations in personality.* New York, NY: Oxford University Press.

Nicholls, J. C. (1983). Creativity in the person who will never produce anything original or useful. In: R. S. Albert (Ed.), *Genius and eminence: A social psychology of exceptional achievement* (pp. 265–279). New York, NY: Pergamon.

Owens, W. A. (1969). Cognitive, noncognitive and environmental correlates of mechanical ingenuity. *Journal of Applied Psychology*, *53*, 199–208.

Owens, W. A. (1972). Intellective, non-intellective, and environmental correlates of mechanical ingenuity. In: C. W. Taylor (Ed.), *Climate for creativity: Report of the seventh national research conference on creativity* (pp. 253–268). New York, NY: Pergamon Press.

Patrick, C. (1935). Creative thoughts in poets. *Archives of Psychology*, *178*, 35–73.

Patrick, C. (1937). Creative thoughts in artists. *Journal of Psychology*, *4*, 35–73.

Plucker, J. A., Beghetto, R. A., & Dow, G. T. (2004). Why isn't creativity more important to educational psychologists? Potentials, pitfalls, and future directions in creativity research. *Educational Psychologist*, *39*, 83–96.

Rank, J., Pace, V. L., & Frese, M. (2004). Three avenues for future research on creativity, innovation, and initiative. *Applied Psychology: An International Review*, *53*, 518–528.

Rhodes, M. (1961/1987). An analysis of creativity. In: S. G. Isaksen (Ed.), *Frontiers of creativity research: Beyond the basics* (pp. 216–222). Buffalo, NY: Bearly.

Richards, R. (1997). When illness yields creativity. In: M. Runco & R. Richards (Eds), *Eminent creativity, everyday creativity, and health* (pp. 485–540). Stanford, CT: Ablex.

Rogers, C. (1970). Toward a theory of creativity. In: P. E. Vernon (Ed.), *Creativity* (pp. 137–151). New York, NY: Penguin.

Rubenson, D. E. (1991). Creativity, economics, and baseball. *Creativity Research Journal*, *4*, 205–208.

Rubenson, D. L., & Runco, M. A. (1992). The psychoeconomic approach to creativity. *New Ideas in Psychology*, *10*, 131–147.

Rubenson, D. L., & Runco, M. A. (1995). The psycho-economic view of creative work in groups and organizations. *Creativity Innovation Management*, *4*, 232–241.

Runco, M. A. (1988). Creativity research: Originality, utility, and integration. *Creativity Research Journal*, *1*, 1–7.

Runco, M. A. (1991). *Divergent thinking*. Norwood, NJ: Ablex.

Runco, M. A. (Ed.) (1994). *Problem finding, problem solving, and creativity*. Norwood, NJ: Ablex.

Runco, M. A. (1995). Insight for creativity, expression for impact. *Creativity Research Journal*, *8*, 377–390.

Runco, M. A. (1996). Personal creativity: Definition and developmental issues. In: M. A. Runco (Ed.), *Creativity from childhood to adulthood: Developmental issues* (pp. 3–30). San Francisco, CA: Jossey-Bass.

Runco, M. A. (1999a). Divergent thinking. In: *Encyclopedia of creativity* (pp. 577–582). San Diego, CA: Academic Press.

Runco, M. A. (1999b). Tension, adaptability, and creativity. In: S. W. Russ (Ed.), *Affect, creative experience, and psychological adjustment* (pp. 165–194). Philadelphia, PA: Taylor & Francis.

Runco, M. A. (2004). Creativity. *Annual Review of Psychology*, *55*, 657–687.

Runco, M. A. (2006, January). *What the recent creativity research suggests about innovation and entrepreneurship*. Annual Norwegian Business Economics and Finance Conference, Bergen, Norway.

Runco, M. A. (in press). Creativity: Comments and corrections. *Creativity Research Journal*.

Runco, M. A., & Basadur, M. (1993). Assessing ideational and evaluative skills and creative styles and attitudes. *Creativity and Innovation Management, 2,* 166–173.

Runco, M. A., & Charles, R. (1993). Judgments of originality and appropriateness as predictors of creativity. *Personality and Individual Differences, 15,* 537–546.

Runco, M. A., Lubart, T., & Goetz, I. (2007). Creativity and economics. In: M. A. Runco (Ed.), *Creativity research handbook* (vol. 3, pp. 173–197). Cresskill, NJ: Hampton Press.

Runco, M. A., & Vega, L. (1990). Find more like this: Evaluating the creativity of children's ideas. *Journal of Social Behavior and Personality, 5,* 439–452.

Shalley, C. E., Zhou, J., & Oldham, G. R. (2004). The effects of personal and contextual characteristics on creativity: Where should we go from here? *Journal of Management, 30,* 933–958.

Simonton, D. (2003). Creativity as variation and selection: Some critical constraints. In: M. A. Runco (Ed.), *Critical creative processes* (pp. 3–18). Cresskill, NJ: Hampton Press.

Sternberg, R. J., & Lubart, T. (1991). Short selling investment theories of creativity? A reply to Runco. *Creativity Research Journal, 4,* 202–205.

Taylor, C. W. (1972). *Climate for creativity.* New York, NY: Pergamon.

Tenner, A. (1996). *Why things bite back: Technology and the revenge of unintended consequences.* New York, NY: Alfred A. Knopf.

Torrance, E. P. (1965). *Rewarding creative behavior: Experiments in classroom activity.* Englewood Cliffs, NJ: Prentice-Hall.

Torrance, E. P. (1972). Predictive validity of the torrance tests of creative thinking. *Journal of Creative Behavior, 6,* 236–252.

Walberg, H. J., & Stariha, W. E. (1992). Productive human capital: Learning, creativity, and eminence. *Creativity Research Journal, 5,* 323–340.

FACING AMBIGUITY IN ORGANIZATIONAL CREATIVITY RESEARCH: CHOICES MADE IN THE MUD

Mark D. Agars and James C. Kaufman

ABSTRACT

As the preceding chapter and commentaries reveal, the field of organizational creativity and innovation is both complex and multi-faceted. Many core constructs are ambiguously defined, and levels issues are often confounded within constructs and among proposed relationships. When attempting to advance the understanding of social influence factors and organizational creativity and innovation, multi-level perspectives are particularly well suited to address these complexities. The commentaries of Dionne and Runco represent alternative approaches to facing these challenges. This response to their commentaries discusses our perspective on their recommendations and presents some final thoughts on how multi-level approaches should form the basis for moving the field forward.

Multi-Level Issues in Creativity and Innovation
Research in Multi-Level Issues, Volume 7, 95–103
Copyright © 2008 by Elsevier Ltd.
ISSN: 1475-9144/doi:10.1016/S1475-9144(07)00004-5

INTRODUCTION

Addressing ambiguity in a field of research is a lot like dealing with a truck that has gotten stuck in the mud. You have only a few choices for how you respond to the crisis, and the right solution is not always readily apparent. It is also easy to become frustrated and make matters worse, not better. One of your choices is to sit where you are and step on the gas in the hope that the shock of the force may dislodge the truck. Although this technique works on rare occasions, most of the time it leads to spinning wheels, making the situation even more challenging. Your second choice is to look for ideas, tools, and other resources (e.g., tire chains, wood planks) that may help get the truck unstuck. Although neither solution eliminates the mud, both provide a means to deal with it and, ideally, move the truck forward.

As we described in our original chapter (Agars, Kaufman, & Locke, this volume), the field of creativity and innovation in organizations is filled with ambiguities (i.e., it is a murky area). After reviewing the commentaries by Dionne (this volume) and Runco (this volume), as well as the ideas presented in our original chapter, we find the mud metaphor a particularly useful guideline for considering ways to advance research on social influence on organizational creativity and innovation. We all have choices regarding how to deal with the ambiguity, but how can the multi-level perspective best serve us in this muddy area?

As researchers, we are all too familiar with ambiguity. Indeed, the scientific pursuit is predicated upon (among other things) the existence of ill-defined constructs, unknown or misunderstood relationships, and a lack of basic clarity around an explicit path to knowledge. If no such ambiguity existed, of course, we would all soon be searching for work. In our world, ambiguity represents opportunity; fortunately, we are not lacking for it. Within the field of organizational behavior, the topics of creativity and innovation are, for better and worse, rife with ambiguity. As we described in our initial chapter, this ambiguity presents challenges for researchers and practitioners alike, but these challenges are ones that multi-level approaches are well suited to address. A major point of emphasis in our chapter was illustrating how the application of a multi-level perspective could inform the development of new theories, assist us in integrating existing approaches, and more completely and clearly capture the complexities of creativity and innovation in an organizational context.

In their commentaries, Dionne (this volume) and Runco (this volume) reiterate the existence of complexities within creativity and innovation, and both present thoughts about ways to address these challenges. Consistent with the ideas we present, Dionne identifies a number of ways to move forward. Runco adds to our message by identifying other examples of the points we raise, but may misconstrue our central point: We see ambiguity and complexities within the field as *opportunities* for multi-level researchers, rather than as concerns. We do note, however, that ambiguity in the field is an issue worthy of address. Perhaps this is what Runco means when he emphasizes that many organizations value the individual characteristic "tolerance for ambiguity." Consistent with that interpretation, the call from the business world for developing such tolerance is clear (Oblinger & Verville, 1998; Rosen, 2006).

Tolerance for ambiguity, however, should not be equated with a *desire* for ambiguity. Indeed, what makes tolerance for ambiguity such a desirable individual characteristic is the expectation that those who have it are able to function effectively in the midst of such ambiguity and, ultimately, may reduce ambiguity while maintaining high levels of performance. In other words, even the value we place on tolerance for ambiguity depends in part on its relationship to the subsequent management and clarification of ambiguity.

PRESSING FORWARD THROUGH THE MUD

The most effective methods of dealing with ambiguity, we believe, lie in offering solutions and clarifying theory development. Consistent with the spirit of our review, Dionne identifies three broad suggestions for advancing the field, and provides specific examples of how each approach may by implemented in research and/or theory development.

One point noted by Dionne is that the consideration of social influence in the creativity/innovation literature is paradoxical. She notes, without a specific, theoretical levels-based focus explicitly noted and tested within these multi-level relationships, social influence is all at once a paradox – both too broad of a topic and yet not broad enough. Her example of how theories incorporating leadership concepts (e.g., Sternberg, 1999; Sternberg, Kaufman, & Pretz, 2001; Woodman, Sawyer, & Griffin, 1993) offer limited explication of specific leader behaviors and characteristics is an excellent representation of this concern. As evidenced in her illustration, even when we recognize that multi-level issues exist, we may nevertheless fail to *deal* with them in ways that capture their multi-level existence. As a consequence, we add further ambiguity rather than bringing new enlightenment to the field.

Dionne's point identifies a specific shortcoming in our theoretical efforts and works at expanding our scientific approaches to the field, in contrast to what we believe is Runco's suggestion that traditional scientific approaches cannot be applied to creativity. The shortcomings of using science to address creativity need not be fundamental to the scientific approach but rather may emerge as a result of limited specification of constructs, relationships, and contextual influences. Treating creativity from a multi-level perspective (i.e., incorporating levels issues into both our definitions and our relationships) offers the opportunity to benefit from scientific approaches. This is, perhaps, the greatest benefit of the multi-level perspective. As Dionne notes, adding specific linkages within boundaries does increase complexity, yet is a fruitful way to provide clarity. Although seemingly a paradox, the ensuing reduction in the ambiguity/vagueness that appears to be inherent in creativity theory and research may in part be simply a matter of careful specification. These ideas represent classic issues in theory development tied to comprehensiveness, parsimony, and utility (Bacharach, 1989; Whetton, 1989), with the added recognition that comprehensiveness is beneficial only when it provides greater clarity – a challenge as yet unmet in much organizational creativity work.

Dionne also suggests the use of bracketing (Hackman, 2003) as a means of advancing research in the organizational creativity domain. This suggestion is particularly well suited to the creativity/innovation field. As Hackman (2003) notes, bracketing not only helps us define constructs and relationships at the focal level of interest, but also serves to identify meaningful cross-level relationships (and eliminate others). Such bracketing increases our explanatory capacity. Indeed, we really can be "learning more by crossing levels" (p. 905). In addition to the group conflict (diversity) example provided by Dionne, comparable examples could exist in the creativity domain when looking at group composition effects on individual creativity.

Finally, Dionne encourages greater consideration of nonlinear relationships when assessing creativity. Unlike traditional approaches, multi-level models incorporating nonlinear processes afford us the opportunity to examine relationships in ways we might have otherwise missed. In contrast to what we believe is Runco's suggestion that traditional science may be unable to move the creativity field forward, Dionne's commentary recognizes that we need not stay stuck in the mud but rather need to think in more sophisticated ways. Nonlinear modeling represents one important way to achieve this goal. An example of where the exploration of nonlinear relationships may prove fruitful is when we examine the differential impact of social influence factors on different "levels" of creativity.

Most investigations of creativity, across a variety of cultures, tend to take one of two directions. The first direction focuses on eminent creativity, with the goals often being to learn about creative genius and discuss which creative works may last forever (Simonton, 1999). These types of studies and theories are typically referred to as studying "Big-C." The second predominant thrust of work in this field focuses on everyday creativity, such as those creative activities in which the non-expert may participate each day (e.g., Richards, Kinney, Benet, & Merzel, 1988). The theories and studies along this line of thinking are usually said to focus on "little-c." More recently, Beghetto and Kaufman (in press) have proposed a third direction for research into creativity. This new category, which they call "mini-c," was designed to encompass the creativity inherent in the learning process.

Runco makes an important point when he discusses the links between psychology, economics, and creativity. This line of analysis and thought is particularly exciting in our opinion. In addition to the fine work done by Sternberg (1999), Sternberg and Lubart (1995a, 1995b, 1996), Runco (1996, 2004, 2006), and others, we are intrigued by Florida's (2002, 2005) books that discuss the concept of the creative class (as opposed to the service class). We believe that "cross-pollination" across disciplines can, indeed, be fascinating. Notably, several of the early creativity researchers had backgrounds in art history or English literature. It will be interesting to observe the diversity of disciplines that ultimately weigh on the question of creativity and to learn which multi-level approaches are particularly well suited to multidisciplinary scholarship.

SPINNING WHEELS IN THE MUD

We confess to being surprised at the issues Runco drew into the discussion of creativity in his commentary. We are familiar with his important work on personal creativity (Runco, 1996) and his leadership in the field as the editor of *Creativity Research Journal*. We were excited to read his commentary, but disappointed to find that his approach did not seem to lend applicable suggestions to push our paper further along.

At several points in his commentary, Runco reiterates his concern that our discussion of the literature fails to incorporate older research specific to the field of creativity or creativity in non-organizational domains. Although his observation is correct, we believe that it misconstrues the goal of our original chapter. Our intention was not to provide a comprehensive review of research and theory in the broad field of creativity. Such a review – like the one found in Runco's (2006) own textbook on creativity – would likely run for several hundred pages. In the spirit of this series, our emphasis was directed toward research germane to social influence, creativity, and innovation in an organizational context. This review is, of course, informed by the larger literature, but merely identifying other research that addresses similar concerns, we believe, adds little to the discussion. Indeed, little of this work was conducted on the organizational population. In fact, Runco himself argues for the domain specificity of creativity, implying that studies that focus on artists or scientists may have poor application (if any) to the business world. We do, however, appreciate Runco's motivation to "fill in some of the gaps" through his own work (Runco, 2004), and several of his recommendations are informative if not directly applicable to the immediate topic.

Ultimately, the question becomes, what are the implications for multi-level work in organizational creativity and innovation? As Dionne notes, the failure to adequately articulate levels issues in our theory, even when such issues are implied in our ideas, is fundamental to the problem. By itself, noting that similar ideas and limitations are evident in creativity research in education, for example, does not especially further advance our ideas. To his credit, Runco states that he is not arguing with our overall premise, but rather filling in voids by seeking examples from other areas of creativity. For a more complete effort, we direct readers to his recent reviews of the creativity literature (Runco, 2004, 2006). We share Runco's concern that more and more research is being published that is inadequately tied to earlier research. In fact, a key point explicitly and implicitly addressed throughout our chapter is the need to integrate ideas (e.g., theory and research) from across both contextual and content domains. This effort is essential if we hope to move forward.

Although our general disagreement with Runco's premise is clear, such differences in perspective are not problematic. Two other pieces of Runco's commentary, however, we believe, represent a fundamental misunderstanding of key themes in our chapter that should be rectified. Both of these themes are tied to our beliefs about the role of multi-level modeling.

First, our chapter describes multiple examples of ideas or findings in the literature, which we believe, Runco incorrectly assumes we endorse. For example, he writes that we seem to assume that creativity is necessarily a social process, but his supporting evidence comes from our discussion of Csikszentmihalyi's (1997) systems model. We did not specifically advocate this model (and certainly did not claim to create it!), but rather sought to point out another scholar's views on this field. In many cases, we made the further point that other researchers' ideas by themselves were inadequate, but that by incorporating a multi-level perspective they might be more adequately addressed.

The second misunderstanding we believe relates to Runco's comments on our discussion of ways to define the creativity and innovation constructs. In our section on defining creativity (and in numerous places throughout the chapter), we discuss the complexity inherent in creativity and innovation in an organizational context. This complexity is a fundamental characteristic that necessitates multi-level efforts to further illuminate this field. In response to our discussion of this issue, Runco states that we claim it would be useful to have a singular conceptualization of creativity. This statement is, in fact, the direct opposite of our beliefs, as both implicitly and explicitly stated throughout the chapter. Indeed, early in our chapter we make precisely the opposite statement that, ultimately, a singular conceptualization of creativity is lacking both theoretically and when one considers real outcomes in the business world.

We are somewhat perplexed by the seemingly contradictory ideas presented by Runco. Although he purports to be an advocate of a "holistic" approach, we believe his critique often focuses on singular topics rather than on their integration – the latter point being something that our chapter actually emphasizes. Our message is that these advances do not stand alone, as singular and independent contributions that are unrelated to one another, but rather require integration. Multi-level theory and methodological approaches offer us exciting opportunities to study variables that exist at different levels (e.g., individual intrinsic motivation orientation and extrinsic reward systems), at different points in time, and in different forms (e.g., creative processes and creative products). By doing so, we become better able to understand the comprehensive nature of a phenomenon – in our case, creativity and innovation in organizations. These benefits are the fundamental rewards bestowed by multi-level efforts, and we encourage readers who may be less familiar with the ideas of multi-level perspectives to review any of the many outstanding introductory works in this area (e.g., Hoffman, 2002; House, Rousseau, & Thomas-Hunt, 1995; Klein & Kozlowski, 2000; Klein, Tosi, & Canella, 1999; Rousseau, 1985).

FINAL THOUGHTS ON MOVING ON

Runco (this volume) states that we should take a long view of creativity research. In this context, he means to emphasize the importance of looking backward and understanding the legacy of the great researchers in years past. We agree that doing one's homework and understanding the past is, indeed, a key component of understanding creativity. Yet we would argue that it is even more essential to take a long view of creativity research by looking *forward* – that is, at the approaches being used and the currently being done in relation to creativity and organizations. Further, as Dionne's commentary notes, by informing our theory with the incorporation of levels-based constructs and by using cross-level techniques such as bracketing, the challenges presented by ambiguity become eminently workable. If the ambiguity in the creativity literature is a mud pile in which it is easy to become bogged down, this obstacle need be merely one bump on a long road.

REFERENCES

Agars, M., Kaufman, J., & Locke, J. (this volume). Social influence and creativity in organizations: A multi-level lens for theory, research, and practice. In M. Mumford, S. Hunter & K.E. Bedell-Avers (Eds), *Multi-level issues in creativity and innovation* (Vol. 7). Oxford: Elsevier.

Bacharach, S. B. (1989). Organizational theories: Some criteria for evaluation. *Academy of Management Review, 14,* 496–515.

Beghetto, R.A., & Kaufman, J.C. (in press). Toward a broader conception of creativity: A case for "mini-c" creativity. *Psychology of Aesthetics, Creativity, and the Arts.*

Csikszentmihalyi, M. (1997). *Creativity: Flow and the psychology of discovery and invention.* New York: Harper.

Dionne, S. (this volume). Social influence, creativity, and innovation: Boundaries, brackets, and nonlinearity. In M. Mumford, S. Hunter & K.E. Bedell-Avers (Eds), *Multi-level issues in creativity and innovation* (Vol. 7). Oxford: Elsevier.

Florida, R. (2002). *The rise of the creative class.* New York: Basic Books.

Florida, R. (2005). *The flight of the creative class.* New York: HarperBusiness.

Hackman, J. R. (2003). Learning more by crossing levels: Evidence from airplanes, hospitals, and orchestras. *Journal of Organizational Behavior, 24,* 905–922.

Hoffman, D. A. (2002). Issues in level research: Theory development, measurement, and analysis. In: S. Rogelberg (Ed.), *Handbook of research methods in industrial and organizational psychology* (pp. 247–274). Oxford, UK: Blackwell.

House, R., Rousseau, D. M., & Thomas-Hunt, M. (1995). The meso paradigm: A framework for the integration of micro and macro organizational behavior. *Research in Organizational Behavior, 17,* 71–114.

Klein, K. J., & Kozlowski, S. W. J. (2000). *Multilevel theory, research, and methods in organizations: Foundations, extensions, and new directions.* San Francisco, CA: Jossey-Bass.

Klein, K. J., Tosi, H., & Canella, A. A., Jr. (1999). Multilevel theory building: Benefits, barriers, and new developments. *Academy of Management Review, 24,* 243–248.

Oblinger, D. G., & Verville, A. (1998). *What business wants from higher education.* Phoenix, AZ: Oryx Press.

Richards, R., Kinney, D. K., Benet, M., & Merzel, A. P. C. (1988). Assessing everyday creativity: Characteristics of the lifetime creativity scales and validation with three large samples. *Journal of Personality and Social Psychology, 54,* 476–485.

Rosen, R. (2006). *Global literacies: Lessons on business leadership and national cultures.* New York: Simon & Schuster.

Rousseau, D. M. (1985). Issues of level in organizational research. *Research in Organizational Behavior, 7,* 1–37.

Runco, M. (this volume). Creativity research should be a social science: Comment on "Social influence and creativity in organizations." In M. Mumford, S. Hunter & K.E. Bedell-Avers (Eds), *Multi-level issues in creativity and innovation* (Vol. 7). Oxford: Elsevier.

Runco, M. A. (1996). Personal creativity: Definition and developmental issues. *New Directions for Child Development, 72,* 3–30.

Runco, M. A. (2004). Creativity. *Annual Review of Psychology, 55,* 657–687.

Runco, M. A. (2006). *Creativity: Theories and themes: Research, development, and practice.* San Diego: Academic Press.

Simonton, D. K. (1999). Significant samples: The psychological study of eminent individuals. *Psychological Methods, 4,* 425–451.

Sternberg, R. J. (1999). A propulsion model of types of creative contributions. *Review of General Psychology, 3,* 83–100.

Sternberg, R. J., Kaufman, J. C., & Pretz, J. E. (2001). The propulsion model of creative contributions applied to the arts and letters. *Journal of Creative Behavior, 35,* 75–101.

Sternberg, R. J., & Lubart, T. (1995a). *Defying the crowd: Cultivating creativity in a culture of conformity.* New York: Free Press.

Sternberg, R. J., & Lubart, T. (1995b). An investment approach to creativity. In: S. M. Smith, T. B. Ward & R. A. Finke (Eds), *The creative cognition approach.* Cambridge: MIT Press.

Sternberg, R. J., & Lubart, T. (1996). Investing in creativity. *American Psychologist, 51*(7), 677–688.

Whetton, D. A. (1989). What constitutes a theoretical contribution? *Academy of Management Review, 14,* 490–495.

Woodman, R. W., Sawyer, J. E., & Griffin, R. W. (1993). Toward a theory of organizational creativity. *Academy of Management Review, 18,* 293–321.

PART II:
INNOVATION AND PLANNING

PLANNING FOR INNOVATION: A MULTI-LEVEL PERSPECTIVE

Michael D. Mumford, Katrina E. Bedell-Avers and Samuel T. Hunter

ABSTRACT

Scholars continue to debate whether planning, in fact, contributes to creativity and innovation. In this chapter, we argue that planning is critical to innovation and will contribute to the generation of viable new ideas. Effective planning, however, must be based on an incremental approach involving a viable portfolio of projects. The implications of this model for the management of innovation at the organizational, group, and individual levels are discussed. Potential new directions for research are considered, along with the model's implications for the management of creative ventures.

INTRODUCTION

In the past, the efficient production and delivery of products and services was the key to the sustained success of organizations (Chernow, 1998). In the future, however necessary efficient production of goods and efficient delivery of services may be, it is clear that the crucial determinant of long-term success will be the sustained development of innovative new products

Multi-Level Issues in Creativity and Innovation
Research in Multi-Level Issues, Volume 7, 107–154
Copyright © 2008 by Elsevier Ltd.
ISSN: 1475-9144/doi:10.1016/S1475-9144(07)00005-7

and services (Bullinger, Auernhammer, & Gomeringer, 2004; Dess & Pickens, 2000; Janssen, van de Vliert, & West, 2004). At present, organizations are operating at the cusp of this trend. Although globalization, new technology, and consumer expectations have obviously conspired to place a new premium on innovation (Florida, 2002; Halbesleben, Novicevic, Harvey, & Buckley, 2003), it is not clear how extant models and methods of management apply in an environment where success depends on innovation (Mumford & Hunter, 2005; Sternberg, 2005).

One can argue that the basis for management thought throughout much of the twentieth century has been planning – albeit planning with an eye toward efficiency (Kanigel, 1997). One fundamental problem confronting organizations as we move into the twenty-first century, as a result, is whether organizations can, or should, attempt to plan for innovation. The fundamental importance of planning to structure, strategy, and resource allocation seems to dictate the need for planning (Bluedorn, Johnson, Cartwright, & Barringer, 1994; Mumford, Schultz, & Osburn, 2002a). It is open to question whether planning, in fact, contributes to innovation (i.e., the development and fielding of new products and services) or creativity (i.e., generation of the ideas providing a basis for the development of these new products or services) (Amabile & Conti, 1999; Mumford & Gustafson, 1988).

In one study along these lines, Eisenhardt and Tabrizi (1995) examined 72 large and medium-size projects concerned with the development of innovative new products in the computer industry. People who had been involved in these projects were asked to describe the time spent in planning during the pre-development phase of the project along with other project attributes such as supplier involvement, use of manufacturing teams, and leader power. The researchers found that upfront planning increased project development time, whereas project leader power and use of multi-functional teams decreased project development time. Although project development time is only one of the many potential indicators of the effectiveness of creative efforts (Acs & Audretsch, 1988), other studies – notably those undertaken by Mintzberg and his colleagues (Mintzberg, 1991; Mintzberg, Raisinghani, & Theoret, 1976; Mintzberg & Waters, 1985) using project performance criteria – also suggest that planning may undermine innovation.

In contrast to the findings of Eisenhardt and Mintzberg, other studies suggest that planning may contribute to both creativity and innovation in organizational settings (Quinn, 1985). For example, Robinson and Pearce (1988) examined planning process quality across 609 firms employing various strategies, including a research and development (R&D), or innovation, strategy as well as brand, service, and efficiency strategies.

They found that the quality of planning processes contributes to the performance of firms following an R&D, or innovation, strategy as well as firms following a brand, service, or efficiency strategy. Along similar lines, Castrogiovanni (1991) has argued that planning may be crucial to the growth and survival of entrepreneurial firms, where innovation is at a premium.

Although other examples of this sort might be cited, the foregoing seem sufficient to make our point. Different scholars hold different views with regard to the influence of planning on creativity and innovation. Those scholars who believe that planning contributes to creativity and innovation hold that planning allows organizations to allocate resources, ensure the availability of requisite expertise, and establish a framework for effective collaborative exchange around critical issues (e.g., Andriopoulos, 2003; Cooper, 2000). Those scholars who believe that planning inhibits creativity and innovation hold that the production of new ideas is not predictable, nor is it possible to appraise the likely outcomes of idea development owing to the complexity of markets, competitor behavior, and the rate of technological change (e.g., Eisenhardt & Tabrizi, 1995; Kamoche & Cunha, 2001).

In this chapter, we argue that planning can, in fact, contribute to creativity and innovation. By virtue of the unique nature of creative and innovative efforts, however, the locus of planning – that is, the unit of analysis around which planning is oriented – and the processes applied in planning will differ from the loci and processes applied in more routine forms of planning. More specifically, we argue that planning for innovation must be based on fundamentals and missions derived from these fundamentals in a project development cycle. We then consider how actions occurring at the organizational, group, and individual levels influence the effective construction and execution of these plans across the project development cycle.

PROJECT PORTFOLIOS

Projects

In planning for creativity and innovation, it has been common practice to formulate planning models in terms of one of two key issues: (1) the actions to be taken in idea generation or (2) the actions to be taken in developing these ideas into useful products (e.g., Woods & Davies, 1973). What must be borne in mind in this regard, however, is that exactly the *who*, *when*, and *what* questions related to the ideas generated, and the paths that will be taken in idea development, are uncertain, and perhaps unknowable until after the fact (Simonton, 1999). Moreover, while we have a good understanding of the processes underlying creative achievement, processes such as problem construction, information gathering, concept selection, conceptual combination, idea evaluation, and revision, implementation planning, and monitoring (Brophy, 1998; Lonergan, Scott, & Mumford, 2004; Lubart, 2001; Mumford, Mobley, Uhlman, Reiter-Palmon, & Doares, 1991; Scott, Lonergan, & Mumford, 2005; Ward, Patterson, & Sifonis, 2004), execution of these processes is a demanding, resource-intensive activity that requires multiple interactive cycles of generation and exploration (Finke, Ward, & Smith, 1992). Thus our understanding of the creative process does not ensure certainty with regard to the outcomes of these processing activities.

Because both ideas and the outcomes of process execution in idea generation and idea development are uncertain, they do not provide an appropriate basis for planning. A more appropriate basis for planning, however, may be found in creative work. Creative work – that is, the pro-ducts to be produced as a result of idea generation and idea development – does appear to follow predictable patterns. Thus Simon and his colleagues (Simon, 1993; Langley, Simon, Bradshaw, & Zytkow, 1987) have shown that it is possible to develop software algorithms that will replicate major scientific discoveries. Other evidence for the predictability of creative work may be found in the simultaneous discovery phenomenon (Sharma, 1999) – for example, Newton's and Liebritz's simultaneous discovery of calculus.

One explanation for the apparent predictability of creative work may be found in Csikszentmihalyi's (1999) and Feldman's (1999) discussion of the "field." In their view, creative efforts occur within the context provided by a profession, or a group, that shares a common base of expertise. This shared expertise not only serves to define the standards to be pursued in appraising the work, as a function of prior work, available technology, and pragmatic need, but also defines the issues that must be, or might be, addressed at a given time. These consensually defined and created issues give rise to projects seeking to resolve critical issues and exploit the emerging potentialities. Thus the projects being pursued within a field provide a basis for predicting the content and direction of creative, or innovative, efforts.

Organizations, and the projects pursued in organizations, can also be argued to operate in a field. Although it appears feasible to extend the notions of fields and field-based projects to organizations, it is important to bear in mind how projects differ from simple idea generation or more routine forms of creative thought:

- Projects do not involve the generation of a single idea, but rather require the generation of multiple ideas and the synthesis of these ideas into an integrated model, theory, or product that resolves the issues evident in the field with respect to the phenomenon under consideration.
- Projects require scaffolding, where one idea, or effort, provides a basis for addressing other issues and generation of the next idea. As a result of this incremental scaffolding, projects unfold over relatively long periods of time (Gruber & Wallace, 1999).
- Because of the need for multiple ideas and innovations over time, projects require teamwork and collaboration (Abra, 1994; Dunbar, 1995; West, 2002).
- Because multiple ideas must be generated by multiple people working together for a substantial period of time, projects tend to be expensive and time-consuming ventures (Nohari & Gulatti, 1996).

Although creative idea generation and creative projects should not be arbitrarily equated, by virtue of their dependence on creative ideas – indeed, because of the need for multiple creative ideas over time – projects share a number of characteristics with other forms of creative work. To begin, projects require expertise or knowledge. Thus Thamhain (2003), in a study of 74 teams working on new-product development efforts, found that indices of expertise produced correlations in the high 0.30 s with managerial appraisals of product innovation and product performance. The findings of Olson, Walker, Ruekert, and Bonner (2001), however, have indicated that project performance requires not only expertise but also shifts in expertise as issues, ideas, and requirements unfold over time.

Not only do projects require expertise, and the information needed to apply expertise in problem solving (Brown & Eisenhardt, 1995; Troy, Szymanski, & Rajan, 2001), but they also appear to require many of the same processing activities evident in other forms of creative work. Thus problems must be defined, relevant approaches or concepts specified, new ideas and techniques generated through conceptual combination and exploration, and the feasibility of these ideas and techniques assessed. Projects differ with regard to the application of these processes, however, in two ways:

- Project work tends to be incremental, building on past work through interactive learning (Quinn, 1985).

• Work on any one issue must be integrated with prior work through an overall approach or general model. Thus Drazin, Glynn, and Kazanjian (1999), in a qualitative study of a new-product development effort, found that leader sense-making activity, by providing the integrative frameworks, was a critical influence on project performance and the eventual development of an innovative product.

Processes

Recently, Mumford and his colleagues (Mumford et al., 2002a; Mumford, Schultz, & Van Dorn, 2001) have proposed a model describing the processes involved in planning. Their model is based on the proposition that planning represents something more than the rote assembly and ordering of action scripts. In their view, planning is ultimately based on the mental simulation of future actions (Anzai, 1984; Hayes-Roth & Hayes-Roth, 1979; Patalano & Seifert, 1997; Xiao, Milgram, & Doyle, 1997) – simulations that provide the basis for script assembly and organization (Wilensky, 1983). These mental simulations not only direct action but also allow people to cope with change in two ways: (1) by calling attention to key causes, resources, contingencies, and restrictions, and (2) by ensuring the creation of backup plans that allow people to execute plans in an opportunistic, adaptive fashion.

The construction of these mental simulations is held to be a resource-intensive activity from a cognitive perspective. In keeping with this proposition, O'Hara and Payne (1998) found that people will stop planning unless the task is sufficiently difficult so that expected performance gains outweigh resource requirements. Difficulty, however, is not the only condition of task performance that appears to condition individuals' willingness to invest in plan construction. Planning is more likely to occur, and to be a more powerful influence on performance, when people are working in a turbulent environment, resources are scarce, interdependence is high, and external demands do not dictate a certain course of action (Bluedorn et al., 1994; Dean & Sharfman, 1996; Johannsen & Rouse, 1983; Weingart, 1992; Weldon, Jehn, & Pradhan, 1991). These conditions, of course, are virtually identical to the conditions that give rise to the need for, or possibility of, creativity. Thus there is reason to suspect that planning may be a critical determinant of performance in creative efforts.

Following earlier work by Berger and Jordan (1992), Hammond (1990), and Hershey, Walsh, Read, and Chulef (1990), Mumford et al. (2002a) argued that plans are constructed through the analysis and reconfiguration of experiential knowledge – specifically, case-based knowledge. Case-based knowledge represents schema abstracted from past experience in performing a goal-relevant task. These schematic representations are organized in a library that includes both prototypic cases and key exceptions, where the relevant cases include information about goals, positive and negative outcomes, causes of outcomes, contingencies, requisite resources, relevant restrictions, and major actions. Activation of these cases is based on perceived opportunities for goal attainment in relation to the environmental conditions at hand (Earley & Perry, 1987).

Once a set of relevant cases has been activated, people appear to search these cases to identify a limited number of critical causal operatives. These critical causes then provide the basis for construction of an initial template plan (Gaddis, 2005; Marcy & Mumford, in press). This template plan, along with relevant activated cases, supports an extended information search intended to identify the causes, resources, restrictions, contingencies, actions, and outcomes applicable in the setting at hand. Analysis of the information garnered in this extended search is next used to construct an initial plan. This initial plan provides the basis for forecasting the outcomes of plan execution within the setting at hand or variations on this setting. These forecasted outcomes enable plan refinement, the development of backup-plans, and the identification of markers for monitoring progress.

This model is of interest, in part, because it appears to provide a plausible description of how planning occurs across multiple levels of analysis in a variety of settings (Bluedorn, 2002). It is also of interest because it offers some clues as to why it has proven so difficult to plan for creativity and innovation. Specifically, five characteristics of creative projects appear to undermine planning processes: (1) lack of fully adequate case models, (2) the time frame over which planning must occur, (3) the potential for environmental change, (4) the uncertainty that characterizes creative work, and (5) ambiguity with respect to the markers to be applied in monitoring and appraising project performance.

By virtue of their novelty, a storehouse of multiple prior cases directly relevant to the situation at hand will not be available for most creative efforts. As a result, it will prove difficult to formulate systematic comprehensive plans, especially for radical innovations. In keeping with this observation, O'Connor (1998), in a qualitative study of eight radical product innovations, found that the lack of available case models often undermined effective project management. In fact, successful projects seemed to require technical visionaries who could not only envision significance but also project requirements.

As Scott et al. (2005) have pointed out, however, the synthesis of experience to generate new case models, or new technical visions, requires substantial skill and effort. Consequently, it is not surprising that people and organizations often fall back on more familiar, and more readily accessible, cases. Thus projects tend to be defined and evaluated based on their fit with prior efforts, their fit with current markets, and their fit with the organization's current strategy (Danneels & Kleinschmidt, 2001; Dougherty & Heller, 1994). This bias with regard to the application of familiar case models, while encouraging incrementalism, may lead people to lose sight of the unique needs and unique potentialities of a project – resulting in assumptions that inherently limit planning performance.

To complicate matters further, creative projects tend to unfold over substantial periods of time. Indeed, full-scale development of an initial idea occurs over a 20-year time frame (Hughes, 1989). The long time frames for creative efforts, however, imply that forecasting will become substantially more difficult (Makridakis, 1991). The difficulty entailed in long-term forecasting will not only limit the feasibility of constructing detailed plans, but also make it difficult to formulate backup plans and markers of plan performance. As a result, planning for creative efforts must necessarily proceed using broad general template plans (Simon, 1993). These broad general plans, by virtue of their lack of specificity, may not always provide adequate guidelines, thereby requiring planning to proceed in stages.

Because creative projects unfold over relatively long periods of time, the environmental conditions shaping initial assumptions about causes, resources, contingencies, restrictions, and actions may be obviated by unanticipated changes in the organization's operating environment. The effects of these changes on the planning of research and development projects can be seen in Dougherty and Hardy's (1996) study of 40 product development efforts. They found that changes in available resources, and priorities for resource allocation, frequently undermined both projects and project plans. What should be recognized in this regard, however, is that a host of other events – including competitor actions, new technological developments, legislation and regulatory changes, and changes in corporate strategy – may also act to undermine plans and projects. Thus ongoing environmental scanning and a willingness to revise and reconfigure initial plans may be integral to success in innovation planning.

Our forgoing observations with regard to environmental change point to another variable that undermines planning. Although projects provide a relatively stable basis for prediction and innovation planning, as noted earlier, they depend on the generation of ideas – often multiple ideas over the course of a project. Given the many uncertainties associated with creative work, there is no guarantee that creative ideas will either be generated or be generated when they are needed. Likewise, there is no guarantee that even when the requisite ideas are generated, they will prove workable within the context of ongoing project activities (Huber, 1998; Sharma, 1999). This inherent uncertainty makes it difficult to plan and ensures that planning creative efforts will involve working with, and working around, a host of unknowns.

Finally, creative efforts, by virtue of their uncertainty and novelty, typically prove difficult to evaluate. Licuanan, Dailey, and Mumford (in press) found that people typically underestimated the novelty of highly original new ideas unless they actively sought to identify original attributes of the ideas. Studies done by Blair (2005) and Kitchell (1995) reached similar conclusions, indicating that people often apply inappropriate standards (e.g., efficiency, acceptability) in evaluating new ideas, which limits the effectiveness of forecasting, plan revision, and backup planning. Moreover, even the assumptions underlying initial plan formation may prove faulty due to errors arising from ambiguity and uncertainty. Thus Dailey and Mumford (in press) found that people, in appraising new projects, tended to underestimate resource requirements and to overestimate outcomes – both tendencies that may lead to unrealistic assumptions in the formation of project plans.

Taken together, the lack of case models, long time frames, propensity for change, uncertainty of project work, and ambiguity in idea appraisal ensure that planning creative projects will prove unusually difficult. In fact, the difficulty involved in planning creative efforts, may account for the widespread application of default models in project planning – the ubiquitous "weed" and "seed" models (Keegan & Turner, 2002; Sharma, 1999). The "weed" model is reflected in the stage-gate approach. This model assumes that while ideas, progress, and success cannot be planned, control can be induced through staged evaluations associated with progressively more specific, and progressively more practical, evaluations that allow unworkable projects to be dropped (e.g., Cooper & Kleinschmidt, 2000). The "seed" model holds that we cannot evaluate new ideas; we can only test their potential. Accordingly, this model calls for multiple idea development efforts that proceed in an iterative experimental fashion, with market reactions providing guidance regarding which ideas are to be pursued and how these ideas are to be developed (e.g., Eisenhardt & Tabrizi, 1995). In the "weed" model, evaluation may lead to the premature, and perhaps inappropriate, rejection of ideas given relevant appraisal biases. In the "seed" model, enormous resources may be spent with little assurance of eventual success.

Although both the "weed" and "seed" models may have value under certain conditions, it is open to question whether they represent plans as much as ways of accruing evaluations. This point is of some importance because three considerations lead one to expect that planning is, in fact, critical to sustained innovation. First, plans, however difficult they may be to formulate, allow a viable response to uncertainty, long timeframes, interdependence, and resource scarcity – all conditions that characterize creative efforts. Second, lacking plans it becomes difficult to align innovative projects with broader business strategy and structure – leaving firms left asking that age old question "now what do we do with it?" Third, without plans, preferably overarching plans taking into account multiple projects, it is difficult to build the context needed to insure sustained, and sustainable, innovation.

Planning for Innovation

Although innovation is an inherently uncertain phenomenon, uncertainty decreases over time as information is acquired and the project proceeds toward implementation. This straightforward observation has an important – albeit oft-overlooked – implication. Planning for innovation is necessarily an incremental activity in which plans slowly unfold over time. This incremental approach, in fact, addresses many of the problems that arise in planning creative efforts. First, prior experience required as part of project development efforts provides the case-based knowledge needed for planning. Second, incremental approaches, by segmenting the work, allow planning to occur over shorter time frames. Third, shorter time frames, combined with periodic reviews, allow organizations to cope with environmental change. Fourth, as a project progresses, evaluative criteria become clearer, allowing different criteria – that is, those consistent with the nature of the work being done – to be applied in different segments.

Incrementalism, while capable of addressing many of the problems that plague attempts to plan for innovation, cannot address one problem. That is, innovative efforts depend on idea generation, and idea generation is an inherently uncertain phenomenon. One way organizations can reduce uncertainty with regard to a particular project is to pursue multiple projects (Kamoche & Cunha, 2001). This project portfolio approach has an inevitable problem (Cooper, 2000), however: The pursuit of multiple projects is expensive and potentially distracting (Van de Ven, 1986). Nevertheless, the expense entailed in pursuing multiple perspectives can be reduced if: (1) multiple projects are pursued only early on, when costs and commitments are relatively low, and (2) the projects pursued are developed around integrative themes that promote the emergence of cross-project synergies.

The concepts of incrementalism and the project portfolio provided the basis for development of the model presented in Fig. 1. This model

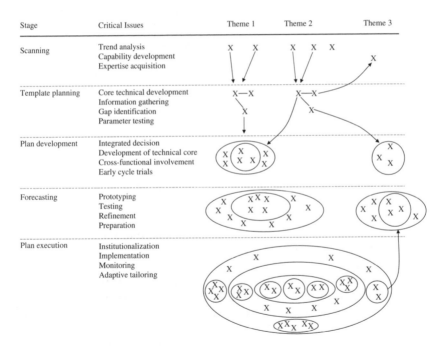

Note: X = Project elements

○ = Indicate more or less tightly integrated elements

→ = Indicate movement of or incorporation of elements

Fig. 1. Illustration of Planning Model.

represents a variation on the general model of planning processes developed by Mumford et al. (2002a). Within this framework, planning is assumed to occur simultaneously across a portfolio of projects organized around an integrated set of themes. For a given project, assuming the project moves through a complete cycle, planning is held to involve five stages: (1) scanning, (2) template planning, (3) plan development, (4) forecasting, and (5) plan execution. Each stage involves a qualitatively different form of planning, with different issues and requirements coming to the fore as projects move through each of the five stages.

Within this framework, planning is held to begin with scanning. Scanning involves two facets: (1) the identification of markets and market needs that might "pull" innovation, and (2) the identification of new technical capabilities that might "push" innovation (Pelz, 1983; Verhaeghe & Kfir, 2002). Identification of these push/pull forces should, in this early stage of planning, focus on broad general trends, as these trends will typically prove more stable and predictable than specific objectives (Simon, 1993). These trends, in turn, serve as the foundation for establishing the themes to be pursued. Organizations typically focus on a limited number of major themes that provide a basis for the generation of multiple innovations, where these themes are integrated and defined in terms of a broader business strategy.

Once themes have been identified, it becomes possible to initiate small-scale exploratory projects. These initial projects provide the basis for the firm to: (1) acquire requisite expertise, (2) develop the competencies needed to pursue work in the thematic area, and (3) provide an informed (albeit intuitive) evaluation of the promise of work in that area. In other words, these exploratory projects build absorbative capabilities (Cohen & Levinthal, 1990). These exploratory efforts, which ideally comprise a range of low-cost efforts, will in turn provide the basis for establishing projects.

Goal-oriented projects begin to emerge as efforts move from the scanning stage to the template planning phase. Template planning operations are not intended to result in a workable product. Instead, these efforts seek to define the framework around which one or more subsequent projects might be built. Thus, in template planning, the focus is on three types of activities: (1) the acquisition of relevant information, (2) the exploration and development of core technology, and (3) the identification of parameters (e.g., contingencies, resource requirements, alliance partners) that must be taken into account when framing projects (Kidder, 1981). Moreover, template planning efforts must identify gaps, or potential critical path problems, and initiate spin-off projects intended to close these gaps or provide solutions to critical path problems (Weingart, 1992). These spin-off efforts not only provide the information and techniques needed to resolve uncertainty but may also serve as an impetus for new exploratory efforts.

Initial development of a template plan, by virtue of the need for exploration and development along multiple avenues, will tend to be a prolonged, complex activity, in which a premium is placed on creative thought and idea generation. Moreover, marked shifts in direction can be expected in this phase as new issues come to the fore and new approaches are developed. This dynamic flexible exploration, of course, calls for an open structure. Nonetheless, template planning efforts must be sufficiently structured with respect to critical issues (Trevelyan, 2001) to allow key considerations impinging on feasibility and project direction – for example, core technology, experience requirements, expected time frame, and potential roadblocks – to be established. These observations, in turn, imply that the evaluation of template planning efforts should focus on the framing of feasibility assessments (e.g., what will be required) rather than concrete outcomes.

Assuming a viable template plan can be developed, it becomes possible to begin development of the project plan. In initial planning, the major components identified in template planning must be integrated and the socio-technical basis for project implementation developed. Moreover, early cycle trials of these integrated solutions must be conducted. The integration, assembly, and practical development of project components will require a strong technical core committed to the project. Conversely, to ensure cost-efficient development and consideration of multiple implementation issues, boundaries must be expanded to incorporate relevant forms of cross-functional expertise (Cooper & Kleinschmidt, 2000; Hull, 2003; Thamhain, 2003). Thus, during this stage, the project becomes a structured unique entity – one that, due to the need for integrated development, will establish strong boundaries and a clear agenda. Accordingly, evaluation focuses on project performance with respect to development requirements and progress toward fielding.

The forecasting stage involves an initial fielding of the product or service being developed by a project team. Because execution requirements and market reactions cannot be fully anticipated, forecasting must ultimately be based on development and fielding of a prototype or set of prototypes. The feedback from prototype fielding will, of course, provide a basis for refining initial offerings and building the knowledgebase needed for delivery and maintenance of the product. The need to prepare the organization for product delivery implies that a wider range and larger number of people, representing the various constituencies, must be involved in forecasting activities

(Mumford, 2000). As part of this effort, project staff serve as consultants and advocates for the product or service being developed. Even as project staff take on this knowledge dissemination role, however, they must resolve the crises and problems that invariably arise in initial field studies. Thus creative problem solving continues, albeit within a structure provided by prior project work and feedback from prototype fielding. Although the nature of this feedback, especially market reactions, will prove of singular importance in evaluating projects at this stage, broader organizational considerations, such as potential strategic outcomes and manufacturing capabilities, should also be taken into account (Stringer, 2000).

Assuming a positive evaluation with respect to these field-trial criteria, planning can then move to the execution stage. Although plan execution is often considered a routine activity, it may prove unusually demanding in the case of innovative projects. These extra demands arise from the need to institutionalize the innovation and to cope with the problems that arise as a new product or service is brought "online." Thus ongoing active monitoring, especially during the initial phases of plan execution, will be required, along with additive tailoring of plans to meet the unique challenges that emerge during the initial phases of plan execution. While evaluation can proceed using standard business models, it is important to bear in mind a notable exception to the general rule of thumb: The difficulties encountered in initial plan execution should not be over-weighted when appraising project performance.

In considering the stages involved in the incremental development of project plans, it is easy to lose sight of a broader issue – namely, the need for a balanced project portfolio. Of course, these stages, if effectively managed, will typically give rise to the kind of balanced project portfolio commonly held to be necessary to minimize risk and ensure sustained innovation. For example, the pursuit of projects in multiple thematic areas, with multiple projects being in different stages of development, will help maintain the requisite project mix (Topalian, 2000). Moreover, the availability of a mix of potential projects and multiple small-scale exploratory efforts allows organizations to select projects that vary in terms of their resource requirements and to engage in risk – juggling the projects pursued at different stages to optimize these criteria over time (Sharma, 1999). This point suggests that project evaluation cannot, and should not, be based solely on the project at hand, but rather should also consider the organization's project mix, timing, and opportunity costs.

Within this model, it becomes possible to manage projects in such a way that prior project work serves as a foundation for subsequent innovative efforts. One illustration of this point may be found in the spin-off projects that are used as an issue resolution strategy in initial template planning. Clearly, solutions developed and issues encountered as attempts are made to fill gaps in template plan generation may be used to "seed" new exploratory efforts. Moreover, adaptive tailoring and resolution of problems encountered in initial fielding will serve to identify new projects to be pursued.

Although this model points out a number of strategies that might be used to facilitate sustained innovation, it also implicitly acknowledges certain roadblocks that might inhibit innovation. For example, owing to their small size and relatively large number, exploratory efforts may not receive the attention needed to translate these initial efforts into viable projects (Van de Ven, 1986). Failure to create requisite linkages among themes and the various projects occurring within a given theme will tend to undermine the information exchange needed to stimulate innovation (Monge, Cozzens, & Contractor, 1992). Similarly, when greater structure is introduced in the planning stage, it may inhibit the search for solutions outside the project space (Allen & Cohen, 1969). Accordingly, in the following sections, we examine how various organizational-, group-, and individual-level variables contribute to effective planning and plan execution in organizations seeking innovation.

ORGANIZATIONAL-LEVEL INFLUENCES

Scanning and Monitoring

In the model of innovation planning presented in the preceding section, the definition of the themes to be pursued and the establishment of requisite exploratory efforts serve as the framework on which plans will be built. Thus organizations, by defining and legitimizing these fields of endeavor, can influence the nature and success of the innovative efforts being pursued. What should be recognized here, however, is that the definition of viable themes and the framing of requisite exploratory efforts require scanning of the external environment as well as monitoring of the organization's internal environment.

The importance of environmental scanning is nicely illustrated by a study undertaken by Souitaris (2001), which examined how the use of various information sources was related to new-product development and fielding in a sample of 105 manufacturing firms. Souitaris (2001) found that firms seeking viable sources of external information (e.g., customer feedback, supplier feedback, market research, competitor monitoring, and technology monitoring) were more likely to adopt and introduce new products. Some support for this conclusion may be found in Koberg, Uhlenbruck, and Sarason (1996). In their study of innovation among mature high-technology firms, they found that scanning and analysis of the external environment by senior managers was positively related to innovation.

Although it seems clear that environmental scanning is related to innovation, it also appears that scanning and analysis need not, and perhaps should not, focus solely on the external environment of the firm. In accordance with this observation, Ford and Gioia (2000), in a study of managerial decisions leading to innovation, found that problems encountered in day-to-day operations also served as a stimulus for innovation. These monitoring efforts may prove especially useful in theme identification and identification of requisite exploratory efforts when monitoring: (1) focuses on the outcomes of innovation efforts in the early stages of plan development and implementation and (2) capitalizes on the professional expertise of the workforce (Damanpour, 1991).

The effectiveness of scanning and monitoring, however, is contingent on a variety of factors. For example, the range (i.e., diversity) of the information sought in scanning and monitoring appears to contribute to innovation. A broad search strategy often proves necessary because emergent themes requiring early exploration often arise from technologies and competitors that are not directly tied to the organization's current operating environment; similarly, viable ideas often arise from units that are not considered integral to the organization's day-to-day operations. In keeping with this observation, Rodan (2002) found that senior managers who initiate innovative efforts evidence a diverse network of atypical contacts.

Of course, effective scanning and monitoring of a range of events depends on people's ability to identify trends and analyze anomalies (Mumford, Baughman, Supinski, & Maher, 1996). Kickul and Gundry (2001), for example, found that the creative abilities of senior managers moderated the effects of scanning and monitoring on firm innovation. Similarly, O'Connor (1998), in a qualitative study of eight radical technological innovations, found that effective scanning and monitoring required the involvement of senior managers who could envision the future implications of the information obtained.

Not only does effective scanning and monitoring require the capacity to see the downstream implications of relevant information, but it also requires the capacity to understand the implications of this information for current operations. Thus Bonnardel and Marmeche (2004) found that people's ability to apply diverse information in creative thought depends on their level of expertise. Because organizations are complex, multi-faceted entities, they may require multiple forms of expertise for scanning and monitoring activities. Accordingly, one would expect that scanning and monitoring would prove most effective with regard to initiation of innovative efforts when it occurs in senior management teams, where team members possess different forms of expertise (Bluedorn et al., 1994; Tushman & O'Reilly, 1997; West, 2002). Diverse scouting teams not only increase the amount of information available for decision making (Anacona & Caldwell, 1992), but also provide the multiple perspectives needed to stimulate the creative thought required for defining themes and establishing exploratory efforts (Georgsdottir & Getz, 2004).

Scanning and monitoring activities, however, are also contingent on certain organizational-level considerations. For example, scanning typically focuses on competitors, with competitor actions often serving as a stimulus to innovation – particularly when these actions represent a threat to extant markets and products (Debruyne et al., 2002; Majumdar & Venkataraman, 1993). This focus on current competitor actions, however, may undermine scanning with regard to future competitors, future competitor actions, and technological change.

Along related lines, scanning tends to occur within current networks – specifically, extant business networks. Clearly, strategic alliances and political networking are related to firm innovation (Li & Atuahene-Gima, 2001). Nonetheless, the tendency to rely on current network partners will limit the range of scanning activities, because the dependence on existing information may inhibit the formation of alliances with more distal, or peripheral, network members; these network members' contributions might, in turn, prove particularly useful as a stimulus for innovation (Perry-Smith & Shalley, 2003).

In addition, given the long time frames associated with the development of most innovations, effective scanning calls for the application of a long-term perspective that seeks to identify emerging trends (Simon, 1993). The problem here is that emerging trends are difficult to identify; because of their novelty and ambiguity, organizations tend to discount the significance of these trends, thereby undermining their scanning and monitoring efforts.

Not only will certain organizational variables diminish the effectiveness of external scanning, but the effectiveness of internal monitoring can also be limited by particular characteristics of the organization. For example, when internal monitoring acts as a stimulus for innovation, it is often problem-based (Ford & Gioia, 2000). This observation suggests that if problems are suppressed by the organization, owing to its climate or structure, and if senior managers do not seek to identify interrelationships among these problems, then innovation will suffer. Not surprisingly, a non-punitive culture that views problems as an opportunity for learning has been found to be positively related to firm innovation (Nyström, 1979).

In monitoring, it may not prove sufficient simply for senior managers to monitor outputs or problems encountered in production and marketing – a bias evident in many organizations. Instead, monitoring may need to consider both the problems and the opportunities revealed by initial exploratory and developmental efforts. Thus senior managers must "stay close" to the development process if monitoring is to provide a viable basis for innovation (Jelinek & Schoonhoven, 1990). Although this observation seems relatively straightforward, problems arise in organizations because senior managers often view innovative efforts as the province of "the techies."

Themes and Exploratory Efforts

In the case of most organizations, sustained scanning and monitoring of the sort called for in the preceding section will typically result in a number of potential themes that might be pursued in planning for innovation and a number of ideas that might be pursued in initial exploratory efforts. Thus the question arises as to which themes and exploratory efforts should be pursued and how these efforts should be managed. This question is of crucial importance because it is through the selection of themes, and the initiation of associated exploratory efforts, that organizations establish the framework in which innovation occurs.

Perhaps the first issue to emerge is the number, nature, and mix of themes to be pursued. With regard to the number of themes to be pursued, it should be recognized that the pursuit of a single theme based on a particular technology will, due to the various ambiguities inherent in innovative efforts, tend to place an organization at undue risk (Cooper, 2000; Kamoche & Cunha, 2001). By the same token, pursuit of a very large number of themes is expensive and will diffuse the organizational resources required for effective exploitation of any given theme (Nohari & Gulatti, 1996). Taken together, these observations suggest that organizations should pursue a limited number of themes, with the specific number selected varying as a function of available resources, broader organizational strategy, and the ability to effectively monitor the innovation process (Nutt, 1984).

If organizations can pursue only a limited number of themes, then the question arises as to which themes should be chosen. Scholars typically recommend that organizations select themes that: (1) fit with their extant strategy, (2) draw on their core competencies, (3) are consistent with current markets, (4) are sufficiently well formulated that practical development appears feasible, and (5) can be protected from ready imitation (Dougherty & Heller, 1994; Sharma, 1999). Although these recommendations seem reasonable, a hidden assumption undermines their value. Specifically, they require innovative efforts to be consistent with extant operations (Mumford & Hunter, 2005).

An alternative approach to theme identification has been suggested by Hughes (1989). In a historical analysis of laboratories evidencing sustained innovation, he found that innovation planning was often framed in terms of fundamentals, or broad conceptual infrastructure problems, relevant to a *number* of current organizational operations. Thus he attributes DuPont's success in the development of synthetic fibers to the company's decision to pursue polymer chemistry – a fundamental area of investigation that might contribute to a number of product areas in which DuPont already had an investment.

The definition and selection of themes with respect to these kinds of fundamental issues is advantageous for four reasons. First, fundamentals allow for the development of multiple products and increase the probability that spin-off efforts will prove useful in product development. Second, these fundamentals will tend to remain stable over time, thereby increasing the value of the knowledge acquired (Cohen & Levinthal, 1990). Third, fundamentals can be defined in terms of emerging, yet long-term trends (Simon, 1993). Fourth, definition of themes in terms of fundamentals allows for the emergence of synergies and will result in efforts that, at least in broad terms, are consistent with extant products, markets, and core competencies.

In selecting the fundamentals to be used in defining themes, however, a variety of considerations should be taken into account. To begin, fundamentals differ with regard to their generative potential. Clearly, the chance of innovation will increase if highly generative fundamentals are used as a basis for defining themes.

Fundamentals, moreover, differ with respect to prior development and thus their readiness for exploitation. When understanding of fundamentals has progressed to the point that project implications are obvious, fundamentals will prove of limited value in theme definition because they can be readily imitated by competitors. By contrast, fundamentals that require too much basic work will prove difficult to exploit in a timely fashion. Accordingly, fundamentals that have a background in basic concepts where knowledge and techniques remain fuzzy are most likely to provide a viable framework for defining themes.

Finally, in selecting fundamentals, it is important to bear in mind the need for a viable project portfolio (Cooper, 2000; Henderson, 1994). One implication of this observation is that the fundamentals selected for theme definition should cover a range of issues, allowing for the generation of multiple projects. Further, the fundamentals selected for investigation should involve some short-term and some long-term efforts, which differ with respect to the cost and difficulty of their exploration and exploitation.

Once organizations have identified relevant fundamentals and selected relevant themes on the basis of those fundamentals, it becomes possible to begin the initial exploratory efforts. Typically, these efforts will be low-cost initiatives intended to acquire requisite expertise, explore developmental parameters, and identify potentialities. As a result, it is both possible and desirable for organizations to initiate multiple independent exploratory efforts within the same theme. Thus Keegan and Turner (2002), in their study of project-based firms (i.e., firms where innovation is at a premium), found that managers often have a number of "boiling pots," or exploratory efforts, under way at any given time, which they could then blend and expand to define template projects.

Although there is apparently some value in initiating multiple exploratory efforts, management of these efforts presents organizations with a number of challenges. One noteworthy problem in this regard arises from project size. By virtue of their small size and exploratory nature, these initiatives may not be viewed as legitimate and, therefore, may not receive adequate attention from senior managers (Dougherty & Heller, 1994; Van de Ven, 1986). As a consequence, exploratory projects will need champions who can call senior managers' attention to the promise of the results emerging from these efforts (Howell & Boies, 2004).

Not only do exploratory efforts require attention and champions, but the small size and isolation of these efforts also place a premium on effective management. For example, although exploratory efforts appear to benefit from isolation (Cardinal & Hatfield, 2000), effective project planning requires organizations to draw "lessons learned" from multiple exploratory efforts. Thus senior managers must create conditions that promote effective exchange without placing undue constraints on exploration. Moreover, some consideration must be given to goals and objectives. Organizations value actionable knowledge. Exploratory efforts, however, can be deemed successful if they merely provide requisite framing information.

In fact, a successful exploratory effort may close off certain paths and bring up questions about the value of certain projects. This point is of some importance because it suggests that managers must carefully shape, and consistently reinforce, the unique objectives applying to exploratory efforts.

Evaluation

The foregoing observations with regard to the evaluation of exploratory efforts point to another way that organizations shape the nature of innovation. Here, of course, we refer to the standards and strategies applied by organizations in their evaluation of innovative efforts. Indeed, along with the definition of themes and exploratory efforts, the evaluation criteria applied by organizations represent one of the most powerful influences on innovation (Gailbraith, 1982). For example, when Kitchell (1995) examined the influence of different evaluation strategies (e.g., growth vs. efficiency) on innovation adoption in manufacturing firms, he found that the standards applied by firms had a marked impact on the adoption of new manufacturing processes. Along similar lines, Hitt, Hoskisson, Johnson, and Moesel (1996) found that the imposition of financial standards in appraising ideas tended to inhibit innovation at the organizational level.

Given the model of innovation planning presented earlier, however, the evaluation of creative efforts can be expected to be a rather complex process. The most straightforward, and perhaps most important, implication of this model of innovation planning is that organizations cannot apply a fixed set of evaluation standards to plans in different stages of development (Cooper & Kleinschmidt, 2000). Thus, as noted earlier, application of production or financial criteria in appraising exploratory efforts will generally prove ineffective. Instead, exploratory efforts should be appraised in terms of their capacity for generating the knowledge needed to explore a theme and provide the basis for establishing template projects. Similarly, template planning efforts, where the concern is elaboration and definition of parameters, should not be appraised in terms of specific goals, but rather in terms of issue resolution and development of the background knowledge needed to initiate projects. Criteria such as market potential, resource requirements, and time frame can also be applied in evaluating development efforts, although criteria such as schedule performance, market acceptance, and return on investment will prove less appropriate. Schedule performance, market acceptance, and return on investment will prove more valuable, however, in evaluating plans during the forecasting and execution stages.

Not only must different criteria be applied at different stages of plan development, but these criteria must also be applied in a flexible fashion. Traditionally, evaluation has been viewed as a form of decision making that results in a "go/no go" decision with regard to the project under consideration (Keegan & Turner, 2002). The problem here is that evaluation appears to be an inherently generative activity providing a basis for plan refinement. This point is nicely illustrated in a recent study by Lonergan et al. (2004). They asked undergraduates to assume the role of managers who were evaluating advertising campaigns for a new product, a three-dimensional holographic television. These authors found that the best advertising campaigns were obtained when evaluation was based on a compensatory revision strategy. More specifically, strong campaigns emerged when highly original ideas were evaluated using efficiency criteria and when high-quality ideas were evaluated using innovation criteria.

The implication of these findings, of course, is that evaluation should not be used simply to kill projects or permit progression to a later stage of development. Instead, it should be viewed as a developmental exercise, with multiple cycles of evaluation and revision occurring in any stage before planning moves on to the next stage. The question that arises here, however, is when an organization should act to protect its resources by ending a project. Perhaps the single most effective strategy for addressing this question is for organizations to evaluate projects, using appropriate criteria, relative to other projects at a similar stage of development within a thematic area, and to shift resources over time to the more promising projects being pursued within that area.

This kind of iterative approach, of course, induces ambiguity with regard to project status. Nevertheless, this iterative approach, and the ambiguity it entails, may be necessary to cope with three biases commonly observed in the evaluation of creative ideas. First, people tend to underestimate the originality of highly novel new ideas. Second, people tend to reject original ideas due the risk and ambiguity inherent in novel approaches. Third, due to their lack of familiarity with the ideas, people are poor judges of the requirements and outcomes associated with pursuing new ideas. Although these errors pervade the evaluation of creative efforts (Mumford, Blair, Dailey, Leritz, & Osburn, in press), the findings obtained by Dailey and Mumford (in press) and Licuanan et al. (in press) indicate that evaluations that actively seek to identify the original attributes of an idea and examine a variety of consequences of idea implementation tend to minimize errors in idea evaluation.

In addition to these cognitive biases, the certain organizational characteristics may act to undermine idea evaluation. For example, because new projects and new ideas are uncertain, decisions about whether to pursue a project and what kind of revisions are called for in an idea will often evoke political disputes (Mumford, Eubanks, & Murphy, 2006). Clearly, if these political disputes are not managed effectively, both the project and the project planning will be affected. Along related lines, in attempts to reduce ambiguity, people may search for other sources of information, such as the status of project champions, the reputation of the people doing the work, and the organization's record of success in pursuing projects in related areas (Kasof, 1995). The implication of these observations, of course, is that people must sell projects and project plans.

Institutionalization

In addition to scanning and monitoring, theme selection, and evaluation, institutionalization appears to represent a noteworthy influence on innovation at the organizational level. By the term *institutionalization*, we refer to those organizational structures, practices, and policies that contribute to or support the development and execution of plans for innovative projects. One illustration of the importance of institutionalization may be found in the studies linking an open achievement-oriented culture to innovation (Nystrom, 1990; Tesluk, Farr, & Klein, 1997). Perhaps somewhat more compelling support for the impact of institutionalization on planning for innovation may be found in Hage (1999). In his review of organizational-level influences or innovation, he found that a firm's history of innovation was one of the best predictors of its subsequent innovation.

One way that innovation and planning for innovation become institutionalized is through the structure of the organization. Across a variety of studies, two key structural variables consistently emerge as critical influences on innovation: horizontal structuring and professionalization (Damanpour, 1991; Russell & Russell, 1992). Horizontal structures contribute to innovation by permitting the rapid movement of people across projects while allowing projects to draw from multiple forms of expertise in project planning and development. The effects of professionalization on innovation are somewhat more complex. Professionalization, of course, helps ensure requisite expertise is available to the organization. At the same time, it results in a culture that places a premium on autonomy and generative intellectual activities. For their part, autonomy and intellectual engagement have been found to contribute to both innovation and planning across a variety of settings (Mumford & Gustafson, 1988; Mumford et al., 2002a). Structure is merely one aspect of institutionalization. For example, the kind of controls applied by the organization with regard to project development represent a potentially powerful influence on innovation (Abbey & Dickson, 1983; Cardinal, 2001). Broadly speaking, application of controls that contribute to innovation meet three criteria: (1) They recognize and reward the value of innovation; (2) they provide projects with autonomy in resolving issues encountered; and (3) they provide mechanisms for bringing projects and problems encountered to the attention of senior management (e.g., proposal review boards). Application of control strategies that ensure requisite resources are available and can be adjusted based on project needs also appear to contribute to innovation (Chandy & Tellis, 2000; Nohari & Gulatti, 1996).

In addition to controls, a number of other institutional practices appear to influence the planning and development of innovative projects. For example, planning and innovation are resource-intensive activities. Thus organizational practices that buffer projects from undue time pressures and other distractions appear necessary for planning and project development, especially during initial exploratory and template planning efforts (Amabile, Hadley, & Kramer, 2002; Cardinal & Hatfield, 2000). Along somewhat different lines, practices that contribute to organizational learning and information sharing, ranging from encouragement for professional engagement to the development of requisite information technology systems, appear necessary when organizations are planning for innovation (Andriopoulos & Lowe, 2000).

GROUP-LEVEL INFLUENCES

Organizations define the context in which innovation occurs. In organizational settings, the generation of ideas, and the development and fielding of projects flowing from these ideas, typically occurs in groups (Taggar, 2001; West, 2002). As a result, the nature and structure of group interactions can be expected to have a marked impact on creativity and innovation. This observation, when considered in light of the model for innovation planning presented earlier, suggests that four group-level phenomena will represent noteworthy influences on the nature and effectiveness of innovation planning: (1) mission definition, (2) team planning processes, (3) relationship formation, and (4) climate development.

Mission Definition

Perhaps the most important influence on creative achievement at the group level is the nature of the mission presented to the group. In contrast to a vision, which reflects an image of an idealized future (Conger & Kanungo, 1998), a mission represents a more delimited image of the future focused on a specific product to be produced or a particular set of goals to be attained. For example, Hounshell and Smith (1988), in their qualitative analysis of DuPont's work on the development of synthetic fibers, found that this effort was directed by reference to a relatively straightforward but challenging technical objective – to develop synthetic fibers that mimicked the properties of wool. Similarly, Kidder (1981), in his study examining the development of a new minicomputer, found that the effort was guided by the desire to exploit the processing capabilities provided by a 32-bit chip. Hughes (1989), in his study of Edison's work, found that electrical lighting systems – not simply the development of the light bulb – guided the work of Edison's laboratory over a period of 10–15 years.

These studies illustrating the impact of mission definition on innovation suggest a new question: How does mission definition contribute to creative efforts? In fact, mission definition appears to serve at least five critical functions in the planning and execution of projects that require innovation:

1. Missions define the goals of creative activities, and goal definition is commonly considered integral to planning (Earley & Perry, 1987).
2. Missions provide direction to creative efforts without placing constraints on how people explore mission-relevant issues (Trevelyan, 2001).
3. Missions provide a basis for allocating resources and evaluating the relevance of individuals' creative efforts.
4. Missions delimit the scope, or range, of creative activity.
5. Missions provide a structure that permits multiple autonomous contributions by individuals to a team effort – autonomous contributions that appear critical to creativity and innovation (Mumford, Scott, Gaddis, & Strange, 2002b).

The directive and integrative roles of missions highlight the importance of defining the missions assigned to groups in such a way that mission framing will facilitate creativity and innovation. Broadly speaking, viable missions evidence three key characteristics: (1) relevance to the fundamentals, or trends, being pursued by the organization; (2) appropriate scope; and (3) appropriate configuration with respect to the project planning stage under consideration.

Perhaps the most obvious desirable characteristic of a mission is that it should be consistent with the trends, or fundamentals, being pursued by the organization. Definition of missions in terms of these trends, or fundamentals, places the creative efforts in a context, ascribes organizational meaning to the effort, and establishes the legitimacy of the effort. Thus mission definitions, when framed in terms of fundamentals, establish the meaningfulness of innovation plans while providing a vehicle for sense making as people cope with novel, ill-defined tasks and the crises that invariably arise in planning and execution (Drazin et al., 1999; Ford, 1996).

Our foregoing observations with regard to mission content point to a second key characteristic of viable mission statements – the scope of the mission. Viable mission statements should not only define what is expected of the group, but also specify relevant restrictions on the group's activities (Kidder, 1981). Indeed, if missions are too broadly defined, it limits their value as a directive and integrative mechanism. By the same token, if missions are too narrowly defined and too many restrictions are attached to them, the exploration required for innovation will suffer. Thus mission definition requires balancing breadth and specificity.

With regard to mission scope, it is important to bear in mind the stage of innovation planning under consideration. Clearly, in initial exploratory and template planning efforts, where exploration of project parameters is a critical concern, missions should be defined in relatively broad terms. Moreover, the mission given to a group should be framed so as to allow exploration of various issues or potentialities without undue restrictions. As innovation planning moves into plan development, forecasting, and plan execution stages, however, greater specificity in outcome expectations and the imposition of more contingencies, requirements, and restrictions will be required. Missions, as a result, should not be viewed as a fixed directive structure but rather as a malleable structure specified to provide the level of detail appropriate for a project at a given stage in its development.

Team Planning Processes

The mission applicable at a given stage in a project development cycle provides the framework around which plans will be formulated to guide creative work. The planning of creative efforts, in principle, can be expected to proceed using some combination of the planning processes identified by Mumford et al. (2002a). In reality, the locus of innovation planning in the mission group and the various demands made by creative efforts result in some unique influences on planning that must be taken into account.

To begin, when planning innovative efforts, mission teams must necessarily frame plans around two key considerations. First, innovative efforts require adequate resources (Ekvall & Ryhammer, 1999; Nohari & Gulatti, 1996). Second, innovative efforts require adequate time to come to fruition (Amabile et al., 2002). In planning time and resource allocation, key components of the effort must be specified. Because expertise with regard to these components is distributed, time and resource requirements must be negotiated cooperatively as opposed to in a competitive manner, because these requirements stress the need for trust and mission commitment in planning.

Project planning teams in allocating time and resources must also take into account another phenomenon: The available research indicates that people's estimates of time and resource requirements tend to be inaccurate and typically prove to be overly optimistic (Dailey & Mumford, in press; Josephs & Hahn, 1995), particularly under conditions of ambiguity (Licuanan et al., in press). These findings are noteworthy because they suggest that mission planning teams must, in allocating time and resources, ask "what if" questions and employ "devil's advocate" techniques (Schwenk & Cosier, 1980). More centrally, these biases suggest that in mission planning, leadership teams must allow for some slack in available resources while establishing structures that permit rapid reallocation of these resources as new project needs emerge.

These observations suggest a broader conclusion with regard to the planning of innovative efforts. Project planning is an ongoing activity that requires progressive refinement and opportunistic adjustment of plans as the project unfolds and new information becomes available. As a consequence, there is not one project plan, but rather a series of plans. The need for organic adjustment and adaptation of plans, however, implies that commitment to prior decisions and groupthink may undermine the flexibility needed in mission planning teams. Instead, innovation planning requires an open, skeptical approach and careful ongoing monitoring of progress markers.

Because project planning occurs in a team setting involving multiple forms of expertise and ongoing monitoring and adjustment, effective mission planning requires participation. In keeping with this observation, studies of innovation in research and development organizations by Arvey, Dewhirst, and Boling (1976) and Mossholder and Dewhurst (1980) indicate that participation contributes to innovation. What should be recognized here is that plan formation and plan adjustment will become exceedingly difficult if too many individuals become involved in the planning process (Curral, Forrester, Dawson, & West, 2001). Instead, what is required is exchange among key staff, who should represent different constituencies. As a result, it is not surprising that the team leader's meeting has become the hallmark of work on creative projects.

Teamwork in project planning, like teamwork in general (Day, Gronn, & Salas, 2004), requires commitment, monitoring of others, backup behavior, and the availability of shared mental models. Some support for this proposition may be found in Dunbar's (1995) study of microbiology laboratories, which found that use of near-analogies – that is, analogies characteristic of shared mental models – contributes to innovation. The apparent need for teamwork in innovation planning, however, suggests that innovation is more likely to occur when four conditions exist: (1) teams have a clear mission; (2) explicit attempts are made to construct a shared mental model with respect to the mission and project plans; (3) critical issues and emerging problems are articulated in meetings or day-to-day interactions to facilitate backup activities; and (4) well-established criteria are identified for monitoring both team performance and project outcomes.

Of course, professional knowledge and values, by virtue of the fact that they are shared among members of a discipline, provide a basis for effective teamwork in project planning. In fact, the foundation that professionalization provides for teamwork in project planning may in part account for the tendency of innovative efforts to occur in isolated pockets of like-minded professionals. Professionalization, however useful in early-cycle efforts, will ultimately prove more problematic in late-cycle efforts (e.g., planning forecasting, implementation), in which more diverse expertise is required. Hence, in late-cycle efforts, establishing a shared model of the project per se is likely to prove essential.

Relationship Formation

Our earlier observations about mission planning teams fails to take into account another group-level phenomenon that has a potentially powerful effect on innovation planning – namely, incorporating requisite relationships in project plans. Traditionally, innovative efforts have been held to occur within the boundaries of a particular organization. As the complexity of innovative efforts has increased, however, innovation has been found to require exchange and collaboration among multiple organizations working within a broader network of enterprise (Mitra, 2000). For example, Gemünden, Heydebreck, and Herden (1992), in a study of new-product development efforts, found that project success (both technological and market) was positively related to alliance formation.

Alliances, of course, allow firms to acquire capabilities needed for innovation. Not only do alliances provide new capabilities, but they also provide information about customers, suppliers, and competitors needed for effective planning and product development (Adams & Day, 1998; Nellore & Balachandra, 2001); requisite technical support (Hargadon & Sutton, 1997); and new intellectual perspectives contributing to creative thought and plan generation (Alam, 2003).

The multiple benefits of alliances across organizations, or across units within an organization, have three noteworthy implications for innovation planning. First, identification of requisite alliance partners should be viewed as a core element of planning. Second, people who have a wide range of network connections should be included in mission planning teams to facilitate the identification of requisite partners. Third, plans should expressly define the roles and expected contributions of partners at different stages of plan development and execution.

Not only does innovation planning require the identification, recruitment, and management of relationships with internal and external partners, but it also necessitates systematic structuring of the relationships among subteams (Gassman & van Zedwitz, 2003) and facilitation of the requisite collaborations among people with complementary forms of expertise (Abra, 1994). Thus careful arrangement and structuring of peer relationships are critical elements of innovation planning.

Of course, project leadership cannot force people to establish collaborative relationships. Nevertheless, planning teams can take a number of steps to facilitate the formation of the requisite collaborations. For example, team members might be allowed to request that certain individuals, who possess select skills and expertise, be actively recruited for a project. Leadership teams might attempt to manage the mix of skills available. Finally, rewards, compensation, and recognition might be structured to recognize both collaborative and individual contributions to a project. It is important to bear in mind that collaborations will inevitably change in form as projects move through different stages of development. Early-cycle collaborations tend to be informal and rather dynamic, with the exact form of these relationships depending on the particular individuals involved. As projects progress, collaborative efforts tend to become more formalized and structured.

Climate Development

These observations with regard to collaboration bring us to a final group-level phenomenon that should be considered in planning for innovation – the climate to be established in the mission team. Climate (i.e., perceptions of the local work environment) has a marked impact on innovation, with well-developed climate inventories producing correlations in the 0.40–0.50 range, with measures of creative achievement ranging from supervisory evaluations to patent rates to return on investment (Amabile, Conti, Coon, Lazenby, & Herron, 1996; Bain, Mann, & Pirola-Merlo, 2001; Ekvall & Ryhammer, 1999; West et al., 2003).

Climate inventories differ somewhat with respect to the norms and practices held to contribute to innovation. Nonetheless, dimensions such as peer support, organizational support, autonomy, participative safety, challenge, intellectual stimulation, resources, and impediments appear in most climate inventories. In a recent meta-analysis of climate studies, Hunter, Bedell, and Mumford (in press) sought to identify the level at which climate exerted its strongest effects and the particular climate dimensions that appeared best able to account for these effects. Based on 42 studies meeting the criteria established for inclusion in the meta-analysis, it was found that climate exerted its strongest effects at the group level as opposed to the individual and organizational levels. Moreover, perceptions of challenge, intellectual stimulation, and collaboration were found to exert stronger effects on innovation than perceptions of autonomy and resource availability, although autonomy and resource availability still exerted non-trivial effects.

These findings indicate that leadership teams should plan not only mission, process, and collaborations, but also conduct of the work. That is, these teams should establish a structure, focus, and normative expectations for interactions that will promote active intellectual exchange with regard to challenging projects. This kind of active intellectual exchange might be facilitated in a number of ways. For example, meetings or colloquium might be initiated to explore, in a joint fashion, critical challenges being encountered in the project. Project space might be laid out in a manner that encourages discussion. Leaders might role-model or reward the formation and presentation of generative questions about others' work. Although other intervention strategies of this sort might be proposed, planning projects and day-to-day project interactions in such a way as to facilitate the emergence of a climate promoting dynamic intellectual exchange with regard to more challenging aspects of projects may well prove to be a critical aspect of innovation planning, given the impact of climate on creativity and innovation.

INDIVIDUAL-LEVEL INFLUENCES

Although operational planning will typically occur in mission teams, the nature and success of these efforts will be influenced by the characteristics of team members. A variety of individual level attributes have been identified that influence creativity and innovation, including intelligence (Sternberg & O'Hara, 1999), divergent thinking (Merrifield, Guilford, Christensen, & Frick, 1962; Vincent, Decker, & Mumford, 2002), achievement motivation (Feist & Gorman, 1998), and creative self-efficacy (Tierney & Farmer, 2002). From the perspective of innovation planning, however, three individual-level phenomena are likely to be viewed as crucial elements of plan generation and execution: leadership, staff capabilities, and staff engagement.

Leadership

Leadership, at least traditionally, has not been viewed as a critical influence on creativity and innovation. According to this view, the job of managers was to stand back and let the real creative people do the work. The evidence accumulated over the last 30 years, however, indicates that leaders exert a noteworthy influence not only on innovation planning, but also on the generation of new ideas and new products and services (Mumford et al., 2002b; Tierney, Farmer, & Graen, 1999; West et al., 2003). The available evidence indicates that leaders exert these effects through multiple mechanisms, including mission definition (Mumford et al., 2002b), problem framing (Farris, 1972), idea evaluation and revision (Mumford, Connelly, & Gaddis, 2003), task structure (Barnowe, 1975), mentoring (Zuckerman, 1977), role modeling (Mouly & Sankaran, 1999), and project promotion (Howell & Boies, 2004).

The varied effects of leaders' actions on the nature and success of creative efforts indicate that innovation planning must ultimately take into account the capabilities of the people who will be asked to lead the project. Perhaps the most clear-cut conclusion that may be drawn in this regard is that when selecting and recruiting people to lead creative efforts, it is necessary to seek out people who possess the requisite technical expertise. This point is nicely illustrated in studies by Andrews and Farris (1967) and Barnowe (1975). In studies examining the performance of research and development teams, these authors found that the technical skill of the group leader was the single best predictor of cross-group differences in creativity and innovation. When one considers the role of leaders in defining problems, evaluating and revising ideas, structuring the work, and allocating resources, it is perhaps not surprising that leader technical expertise has a marked impact on innovation.

Leader expertise, however, represents a necessary but not sufficient condition for innovation. Because leaders must be able to address the many unexpected problems that emerge in the planning and execution of a project, leaders must possess creative thinking skills (Tierney et al., 1999). Moreover, leaders will be needed who can manage project crises and place these crises in the context of a broader mission. These requirements, in turn, indicate that the leaders of creative efforts will need system thinking and sense-making skills (Drazin et al., 1999). Finally, because leaders must promote projects and recruit project staff, both political and "salesmanship" skills will be required (Mumford et al., 2002b).

These competencies will be required, at least to some extent, of all leaders who take responsibility for a project. By the same token, the unique demands imposed by different stages in the process of plan development and execution will result in shifts in the relative importance of these leader characteristics. For example, expertise and creative thinking skills will be at a premium in exploratory and template planning efforts – a phase in which ambiguity surrounds the project and many of the issues encountered are of a distinctly technical nature. Later in the planning and project development cycle, when greater resources must be acquired and the stress associated with organizing and integrating multi-functional teams becomes evident (Keller, 2001), a greater emphasis will be placed on interpersonal and social skills. These shifts in requisite leadership skills as project plans unfold indicate that some attention should be given to the different kinds of leadership required at different points in the project development cycle. Moreover, given cross-stage differences in project needs and the central role played by leaders in shaping creative efforts, it would seem desirable if plans were put in place to facilitate these leadership transitions as projects move from one stage of development to another.

Even bearing in mind the potential for transitioning leaders as projects progress, the many demands placed on the leaders of creative efforts suggest that it may be impossible to find one person who can do the job. Thus Hauschildt and Kirchmann (2001), in a study of 133 innovations emerging from engineering and manufacturing firms, found that the technical and financial success of creative efforts increased when multiple leaders, filling multiple distinct roles, were involved in the project. This need for multiple leaders and shared leadership (Gronn, 2002) suggests that innovation planning should consider not only which roles must be filled and what competencies are required in these roles, but also how these leaders will coordinate their activities, which process will be applied in decision making, and what the history of collaboration among those being considered for leadership roles is.

Staff Capabilities

In addition to identifying requisite leadership, project plans must take into account staff capabilities (Stringer, 2000). It is possible to take a straightforward approach in planning for requisite staff capabilities: One simply identifies the key components of a project and then recruits people who have the expertise needed to execute these key components. Given the role of expertise in shaping performance in creative efforts (Ericsson & Charness, 1994; Weisberg, 1999), there is much to be said for this approach. The realities of project planning and execution, however, will typically make the planning of requisite staff capabilities a far more complex and difficult undertaking.

Innovative projects are inherently uncertain (Sharma, 1999). Moreover, as a project proceeds, new, often unanticipated issues will emerge. As a result, it is difficult to say with complete certainty exactly which forms of expertise will be needed to develop and execute project plans. This point suggests that, in staffing, an attempt should be made to ensure the availability of a portfolio of expertise. One way expertise portfolios might be formulated is by identifying the different forms of core expertise needed for critical path activities and then searching for (or developing through exploratory efforts and other project assignments) individuals who not only possess one form of core expertise, but also bring to the project one or two forms of other expertise that, although not critical, may prove useful as the project unfolds (Root-Bernstein, Bernstein, & Garnier, 1995).

In addition to technical expertise, most innovative efforts will require at least some staff who possess requisite creative thinking skills (Tierney et al., 1999). In this regard, it is important to bear in mind Taggar's (2001) findings indicating that team performance suffers in groups where virtually all members evidence substantial creativity – the old problem of "too many chiefs and too few Indians." This finding, in turn, suggests that in staff planning exercises creativity should not be sought in all staff but rather in those staff who will assume responsibility for significant generative activities. Moreover, given the stress and demands of creative work, along with the need for support (Amabile et al., 1996), substantial attention in staff planning should be given to the number and nature of the requisite support personnel. Indeed, it is not uncommon to underestimate support staff needs due to a tendency to focus on salient technical issues.

As was the case for leadership, staffing mix appears to depend on the stage of the project and the kind of project plans under consideration. In early exploratory and template planning efforts, staffing will involve only a few forms of expertise – typically, expertise relevant to exploration and analysis of the fundamentals being addressed. A marked shift in this staffing mix will occur as projects proceed to late-cycle activities, where a premium is placed on implementation. As projects move toward implementation, a broader mix of organizational expertise becomes necessary, leading to a preference for the use of multi-functional teams. Although the use of multi-functional teams clearly contributes to both the speed and the success of new-product development efforts (Cooper & Kleinschmidt, 2000; Thamhain, 2003), it is important to recognize that not all individuals working in a functional area will prove equally valuable as members of these teams. Multi-functional teams require staff who not only know their own field, but can also communicate with, and adapt to, people who come from different professional backgrounds. Thus, in staffing multi-functional teams, people must be sought who display characteristics that are likely to promote cross-disciplinary collaboration, such as organizational commitment, a service orientation, openness, and communication skills.

Staff Engagement

Regardless of their stage in the project development cycle, creative projects are demanding efforts that require a substantial investment of time and resources on the part of the people doing the work (Sternberg, O'Hara, & Lubart, 1997). As a result, creative people evidence substantial achievement motivation (Collins & Amabile, 1999; Mumford & Gustafson, 1988). Nevertheless, this achievement motivation is unlikely to be manifest in highly autonomous individuals, the individuals who pursue creative work (Feist, 1999), unless they find value in the work at hand. These observations led Mumford et al. (2002a) to argue that the success of creative efforts depends not on motivation per se but rather on engaging people in the project.

Accordingly, in project planning, some attention must be given to the strategies that will be used to bring about engagement. Engagement, of course, is influenced by a number of factors, ranging from creative self-efficacy (Tierney & Farmer, 2002) to opportunities for professional recognition (Chalupsky, 1953). Although many considerations influence engagement, West (2002) has argued that engagement among creative people is strongly influenced by challenge and the substantive significance of both the mission and the work being pursued as part of the mission. This observation, in turn, indicates that engagement will require identification and articulation of the challenges posed by the mission.

The identification and articulation of challenges is critical to innovation planning because it provides a basis for ensuring engagement through recruitment of project staff. One of the most clear-cut findings to emerge from studies of creativity is that creative people evidence an early and abiding interest in certain types of challenges (Heinzen, Mills, & Cameron, 1993). Performance on creative efforts improves when people are allowed to pursue those challenges they find intrinsically interesting (Collins & Amabile, 1999). By articulating the challenges involved in a mission and allowing people to choose the projects they are willing to "sign up" for, self-selection mechanisms will serve to maximize engagement. To capitalize on this self-selection phenomenon, project plans must include a communication effort that makes people aware of both the project and the professional challenges that make this project unique (Mumford, 2000).

Of course, as projects evolve over time, the nature of the challenges involved will also change. Early in the project development cycle, the challenges encountered will be predominately technical in nature, leading to a need to recruit staff with strong professional interests. As projects move toward implementation, however, the challenges will become more organizational and interpersonal in nature, leading to a need to recruit staff who find satisfaction in shaping ideas into viable products. One implication of these observations is that project plans must recognize the need for periodic restaffing of projects. Another implication of these observations is that some movement across projects should be expected, and perhaps encouraged. This movement, by transferring skills acquired on one project in one thematic area to other projects in other thematic areas, may serve as a stimulus for additional innovation (Mumford, 2000).

CONCLUSIONS

Before turning to the broader conclusions flowing from our observations with regard to organizational-, group-, and individual-level influences on innovation planning, certain limitations of the present efforts should be noted. In this chapter, we have examined innovation planning from a general cross-domain perspective. As a result, we have said little about potential domain-specific (Baer, 2003) or field-specific (Csikszentmihalyi, 1999) differences with regard to the requirements for innovation planning. This limitation is of some importance because cross-domain and cross-field differences in the nature of the projects being pursued may lead to shifts in planning requirements. At the same time, it seems likely that these shifts will be more a matter of emphasis (e.g., the criticality of certain stages or the difficulty of certain planning operations) than a reconfiguration of the basic operations called for in innovation planning.

Likewise, we have not discussed potential differences in the planning activities required for different types of creative efforts. It is possible, and perhaps likely, that processes involved in innovation planning will differ with the type of project under consideration – specifically, process versus product innovations (Damanpour, 1991). Prior studies have not found noteworthy differences with respect to the basic operations across process and product innovations (Mumford & Hunter, 2005), even though it is clear that the key considerations involved in innovation planning – for example, relevant restrictions – will vary across different types of creative efforts.

Finally, we have said little about potential environmental influences on innovation and innovation planning. This limitation is of some concern because prior studies (Wise, 1992) have demonstrated that innovation occurs in waves with the possibility and likely success of innovative efforts varying with respect to basic capability, technological infrastructure, and market readiness (Hughes, 1989). These environmental differences in the feasibility of and need for innovation – however important in shaping the kind of creative efforts initiated – typically do not exert a marked influence on the basic operations required for planning and execution of creative efforts.

Even bearing these limitations in mind, this chapter has some noteworthy implications for understanding how organizations can plan for innovation. Clearly, it has proven difficult to develop viable general models for the planning and execution of creative efforts (Kamoche & Cunha, 2001). The difficulty in developing general models of innovation planning, however, seems linked to two major issues.

First, given the nature of creative thought and the inherent uncertainty of creativity and innovation (Simon, 1993), it has proven difficult to identify the basic elements, or entities, around which plans should be formulated. The nature of creativity and innovation suggests that planning becomes possible if it focuses on multiple projects that are initiated around themes defined on the basis of emerging long-term trends and the fundamentals (i.e., basic operational issues) that the organization must address to be able to respond to and exploit these trends.

The second problem that has blocked the development of models of innovation planning arises from the tendency of scholars to focus on a single level of analysis. Thus some models stress organizational considerations (e.g., Sharma, 1999), whereas other models stress individual-level considerations (e.g., O'Connor, 1998). The conclusions flowing from the present effort, however, suggest that the development of viable planning models will require a multi-level approach that considers organizational-, group-, and individual-level phenomena. We argue that variables operating at each of these three levels operate in a synergistic fashion to shape the missions of project teams – the basis for innovation in organizational settings (West, 2002). More specifically, planning operations occurring at the organizational level define the types of projects and the missions to be pursued by project teams, with organizational planning both legitimizing projects and providing the institutional structures needed to initiate and support project work. The nature and success of teams in pursuing a mission, however, is contingent on three capabilities of team members – namely, leadership, staff capabilities, and staff engagement.

This multi-level framing implies that the planning and execution of creative efforts must take into account variables operating at the organizational, group, and individual levels. Our examination of the variables operating at these levels suggests that the planning of creative efforts can be described in terms of the general model presented in Fig. 2. Within this model, scanning and monitoring of the internal and external environment of the organization is held to give rise to: (1) the themes to be pursued, (2) the initial exploratory projects needed to provide absorptive capacity, and (3) a framework for identifying fundamentals, establishing evaluation criteria, and developing appropriate institutional structures. Definition of the fundamentals of interest allows missions to be established for project teams vis-à-vis the stage of project development. Mission definition, in turn, permits team mission planning, which must itself consider both the kind of partnerships needed and the climate required to facilitate creativity and innovation. Given that creative work is, ultimately,

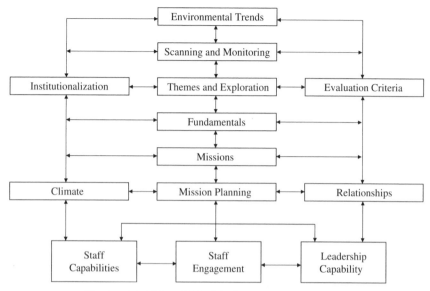

Fig. 2.   Multi-Level Model of Innovation Planning.

the work of people, mission planning must consider the capabilities of leaders, the capabilities of staff, and staff engagement in the mission being pursued at a given point in the project development cycle.

The general model for the planning and execution of creative efforts presented in Fig. 2 points to another conclusion. Innovation planning must consider not only the variables operating within a given level of analysis, but also the potential cross-level interactions. For example, the culture and institutional structures of the organization will influence the climate operating at the group level (Tesluk et al., 1997). Potential leaders must be selected, recruited, and developed with the goal of establishing the requisite partnering relationships in mind. Moreover, the mission being pursued at a given point in the project development cycle will condition the kind of evaluation criteria that can appropriately be applied in appraising project efforts.

These observations about the operation of potential cross-level interactions in the planning and execution of creative efforts are noteworthy in part because they suggest a number of potential directions for future research. For example, staff engagement influences not only mission planning, but also the use of internal information in theme identification and exploration. Unfortunately, relatively little is known about how staff ideas are brought to the attention of managers and how senior managers' scanning and monitoring activities influence reactions to staff proposals.

Another area for future research pertains to the application of relevant evaluation criteria. Traditionally, evaluative standards have been defined primarily with respect to products (e.g., Cooper, 2000; Lonergan et al., 2004). However, given the model of innovation planning presented in Fig. 2, there would seem to be value in extending current evaluation practices to consider various processes known to contribute to the success of creative efforts. For example, project evaluations might consider the availability of the requisite partnering and collaborative relationships, the effectiveness of interactions among members of the project leadership team, staff perceptions of the climate of the team, and overall levels of engagement.

Yet another potential direction for future cross-level research may be found in mission definition. Although it seems plausible to argue that projects, and project missions, must be framed in terms of fundamentals, we know little about the considerations that lead organizations to see certain fundamentals as critical or the process by which these fundamentals are defined. Research examining these issues will prove especially useful if it takes into account potential institutional influences that moderate the ability of the organization to identify the kind of fundamentals that should be pursued in project planning (Hage, 1999) and the way in which institutional structures shape mission definition and the problems encountered in mission planning (Dutton & Dukerich, 1991).

In addition to pointing out some noteworthy cross-level relationships that should be considered in future research, this model of innovation planning points to the need to extend current research on within-level influences. For example, the available literature has much to say about how leadership capabilities influence staff engagement (e.g., Mumford et al., 2002b). Far less attention has been given to the influence of staff capabilities and collaborative relationships on staff engagement. Along similar lines, although we know that viable partnerships and alliances contribute to innovation, the literature has little to say about how these relationships should be managed in mission planning and how these relationships operate to shape the climate of a project. Finally, we need to know far more about how institutional structures shape the definition and success of exploratory efforts and the application of the knowledge gained through exploration in mission planning (Andriopoulos & Lowe, 2000).

When one considers the research needs indicated by this model of innovation planning, it is clear that we lack a complete description of the within-level and cross-level relationships that influence the planning and execution of creative efforts. By providing an initial model of innovation planning that moves us beyond the traditional "weed" and "seed" approaches (Sharma, 1999), this chapter should serve as an impetus for further research and, more centrally, the development of sound guidelines that will make possible the sustained innovation that is essential if organizations are to thrive and prosper in the dynamic twenty-first-century economy.

ACKNOWLEDGMENTS

We thank Stephen Murphy and Dawn Eubanks for their contributions to the present effort. Correspondence should be addressed to Michael D. Mumford, Department of Psychology, The University of Oklahoma, Norman, Oklahoma, 73019 or mmumford@ou.edu

REFERENCES

Abbey, A., & Dickson, J. (1983). R&D work climate and innovation in semiconductors. *Academy of Management Journal, 25*, 362–368.
Abra, J. (1994). Collaboration in creative work: An initiative for investigation. *Creativity Research Journal, 8*, 205–218.
Acs, Z. J., & Audretsch, D. B. (1988). Innovation in large and small firms: An empirical analysis. *American Economic Review, 78*, 678–690.
Adams, J. E., & Day, G. S. (1998). Enhancing new product development performance: An organizational learning perspective. *Journal of Product Innovation Management, 15*, 403–422.
Alam, I. (2003). Commercial innovations from consulting engineering firms: An empirical exploration of a novel source of new product ideas. *Journal of Product Innovation Management, 20*, 300–313.
Allen, T. J., & Cohen, S. I. (1969). Information flow in research and development laboratories. *Administrative Science Quarterly, 14*, 12–19.
Amabile, T. M., & Conti, R. (1999). Changes in the work environment for creativity during downsizing. *Academy of Management Journal, 42*, 630–641.
Amabile, T. M., Conti, R., Coon, H., Lazenby, J., & Herron, M. (1996). Assessing the work environment for creativity. *Academy of Management Journal, 39*(5), 1154–1184.
Amabile, T. M., Hadley, C. N., & Kramer, S. J. (2002). Creativity under the gun. *Harvard Business Review, 80*, 52–61.
Anacona, D., & Caldwell, D. (1992). Demography and design: Predictors of new product team performance. *Organization Science, 3*, 321–341.

Andrews, F. M., & Farris, G. F. (1967). Supervisory practices and innovation in scientific teams. *Personnel Psychology, 20*, 497–515.

Andriopoulos, C. (2003). Six paradoxes in managing creativity: An embracing act. *Long Range Planning, 36*, 375–388.

Andriopoulos, C., & Lowe, A. (2000). Enhancing organizational creativity: The process of perpetual challenging. *Management Decision, 38*, 734–774.

Anzai, Y. (1984). Cognitive control of real-time event driven systems. *Cognitive Science, 8*, 221–254.

Arvey, R. D., Dewhirst, H. D., & Boling, J. C. (1976). Relationships between goal clarity, participation in goal setting, and personality characteristics on job satisfaction in a scientific organization. *Journal of Applied Psychology, 61*, 103–105.

Baer, J. (2003). Evaluative thinking, creativity, and task specificity: Separating wheat from chaff is not the same as finding needle in haystacks. In: M. A. Runco (Ed.), *Critical creative processes* (pp. 129–152). Cresskill, NJ: Hampton.

Bain, P. G., Mann, L., & Pirola-Merlo, A. (2001). The innovation imperative: The relationships between team climate, innovation, and performance in research and development teams. *Small Group Research, 32*(1), 55–73.

Barnowe, J. T. (1975). Leadership and performance outcomes in research organizations. *Organizational Behavior and Human Performance, 14*, 264–280.

Berger, C. R., & Jordan, J. M. (1992). Planning sources, planning difficulty and verbal fluency. *Communication Monographs, 59*, 130–149.

Blair, C. (2005). *Criteria used in appraising ideas.* Unpublished master's thesis, University of Oklahoma.

Bluedorn, A. C. (2002). *The human organization of time: Temporal realities and experience.* Stanford, CA: Stanford Business Books.

Bluedorn, A. C., Johnson, R. A., Cartwright, D. K., & Barringer, B. R. (1994). The interface and convergence of the strategic management and organizational environment domains. *Journal of Management, 20*, 201–263.

Bonnardel, N., & Marmeche, E. (2004). Evocation processes by novice and expert designers: Towards stimulating analogical thinking. *Creativity and Innovation Management, 13*, 176–186.

Brophy, D. R. (1998). Understanding, measuring, and enhancing individual creative problem-solving efforts. *Creativity Research Journal, 11*, 123–150.

Brown, S., & Eisenhardt, K. (1995). Product development: Past research, present findings, and future directions. *Academy of Management Review, 20*, 343–378.

Bullinger, H. J., Auernhammer, K., & Gomeringer, A. (2004). Managing innovation networks in the knowledge driven economy. *International Journal of Production Research, 42*, 3337–3353.

Cardinal, L. B. (2001). Technological innovation in the pharmaceutical industry: The use of organizational control on managing research and development. *Organization Science, 12*, 19–37.

Cardinal, L. B., & Hatfield, D. E. (2000). Internal knowledge generation: The research laboratory and innovative productivity in the pharmaceutical industry. *Journal of Engineering and Technology Management, 17*, 247–272.

Castrogiovanni, G. J. (1991). Environmental munificence: A theoretical assessment. *Academy of Management Review, 16*, 452–565.

Chalupsky, A. B. (1953). Incentive practices as viewed by scientists and managers of pharmaceutical laboratories. *Personnel Psychology, 6,* 385–401.

Chandy, R. K., & Tellis, G. J. (2000). The incumbent's curse? Incumbency, size and radical innovation. *Journal of Marketing, 64,* 1–17.

Chernow, R. (1998). *Titan: The life of John D. Rockefeller, Sr.* New York, NY: Vintage.

Cohen, W. M., & Levinthal, D. A. (1990). Absorptive capacity: A new perspective on learning and innovation. *Administrative Science Quarterly, 35,* 128–152.

Collins, M. A., & Amabile, T. M. (1999). Motivation and creativity. In: R. J. Sternberg (Ed.), *Handbook of creativity* (pp. 297–312). Cambridge, UK: Cambridge University Press.

Conger, J. A., & Kanungo, R. N. (1998). *Charismatic leadership in organizations.* Thousand Oaks, CA: Sage.

Cooper, R. G. (2000). Product innovation and technology strategy. *Research Technology Management, 43,* 38–41.

Cooper, R. G., & Kleinschmidt, E. J. (2000). New product performance: What distinguishes the star products. *Australian Journal of Management, 25*(1), 17–46.

Csikszentmihalyi, M. (1999). Implications of a systems perspective for the study of creativity. In: R. T. Sternberg (Ed.), *Handbook of creativity* (pp. 312–338). Cambridge, UK: Cambridge University Press.

Curral, L. A., Forrester, R. H., Dawson, J. F., & West, M. A. (2001). It's what you do and the way that you do it: Team task, team size, and innovation-related group processes. *European Journal of Work and Organizational Psychology, 10,* 187–204.

Dailey, L. R., & Mumford, M. D. (in press). Evaluative aspects of creative thought: Errors in appraising the implications of new ideas. *Creativity Research Journal.*

Damanpour, F. (1991). Organizational innovation: A meta-analysis of effects of determinants and moderators. *Academy of Management Journal, 34,* 555–590.

Danneels, E., & Kleinschmidt, E. J. (2001). Product innovativeness from the firm's perspective: Its dimensions and their relation with project selection and performance. *Journal of Product Innovation Management, 18,* 357–363.

Day, D. V., Gronn, P., & Salas, E. (2004). Leadership capacity in teams. *Leadership Quarterly, 15,* 857–880.

Dean, J. W., & Sharfman, M. P. (1996). Does decision process matter: A study of strategic decision making effectiveness. *Academy of Management Journal, 39,* 368–396.

Debruyne, M., Moenaert, R., Griffin, A., Hart, S., Hultink, E. J., & Robben, H. (2002). The impact of new product launch strategies on competitive reaction to industrial markets. *Journal of Product Innovation Management, 19,* 159–170.

Dess, G. G., & Pickens, J. C. (2000). Changing roles: Leadership in the 21st century. *Organizational Dynamics, 28,* 18–34.

Dougherty, D., & Hardy, B. F. (1996). Sustained innovation production in large mature organizations: Overcoming organization problems. *Academy of Management Journal, 39,* 826–851.

Dougherty, D., & Heller, T. (1994). The illegitimacy of successful product innovation in established firms. *Organization Science, 5,* 200–281.

Drazin, R., Glynn, M. A., & Kazanjian, R. K. (1999). Multilevel theorizing about creativity in organizations: A sense making perspective. *Academy of Management Review, 24,* 286–329.

Dunbar, K. (1995). How do scientists really reason: Scientific reasoning in real-world laboratories. In: R. J. Sternberg & J. E. Davidson (Eds), *The nature of insight* (pp. 365–396). Cambridge, MA: MIT Press.

Dutton, J. E., & Dukerich, J. M. (1991). Keeping an eye on the mirror: Image and identity in organizational adaptation. *Academy of Management Journal, 34*, 517–554.

Earley, P. C., & Perry, B. C. (1987). Work plan availability and performance: An assessment of task strategy priming on subsequent task completion. *Organizational Behavior and Human Decision Processes, 39*, 279–302.

Eisenhardt, K. M., & Tabrizi, B. N. (1995). Accelerating adaptive processes: Product innovation in the global computer industry. *Administrative Science Quarterly, 40*, 84–110.

Ekvall, G., & Ryhammer, L. (1999). The creative climate: Its determinants and effects at a Swedish university. *Creativity Research Journal, 12*, 303–310.

Ericsson, K. A., & Charness, W. (1994). Expert performance: Its structure and acquisition. *American Psychologist, 49*, 725–747.

Farris, G. F. (1972). The effect of individual role on performance in innovative groups. *R&D Management, 3*, 23–28.

Feist, G. J. (1999). The influence of personality on artistic and scientific creativity. In: R. J. Sternberg (Ed.), *Handbook of creativity* (pp. 273–296). Cambridge, UK: Cambridge University Press.

Feist, G. J., & Gorman, M. E. (1998). The psychology of science: Review and integration of a nascent discipline. *Review of General Psychology, 2*, 3–47.

Feldman, D. H. (1999). The development of creativity. In: R. J. Sternberg (Ed.), *Handbook of creativity* (pp. 169–188). Cambridge, UK: Cambridge University Press.

Finke, R. A., Ward, T. B., & Smith, S. M. (1992). *Creative cognition: Theory, research, and applications*. Cambridge, MA: MIT Press.

Florida, R. (2002). *The rise of the creative class*. New York, NY: Basic Books.

Ford, C. M. (1996). A theory of individual creative action in multiple social domains. *Academy of Management Review, 21*, 1112–1142.

Ford, C. M., & Gioia, D. A. (2000). Factors influencing creativity in the domain of managerial decision making. *Journal of Management, 26*, 705–732.

Gaddis, B. (2005). *Training articulation of key causes, key resources, and key goals. Content-based training as an alternative to improving planning performance*. Unpublished doctoral dissertation, University of Oklahoma.

Gailbraith, J. R. (1982). Designing the innovation organization. *Organizational Dynamics, 10*, 5–25.

Gassman, O., & van Zedwitz, M. (2003). Trends and determinants of managing virtual R&D teams. *R&D Management, 33*, 243–263.

Gemünden, H. G., Heydebreck, P., & Herden, R. (1992). Technological interweavement: A means of achieving innovation success. *R&D Management, 22*, 359–376.

Georgsdottir, A. S., & Getz, I. (2004). How flexibility facilitates innovation and ways to manage it in organizations. *Creativity and Innovation Management, 13*, 166–175.

Gronn, P. (2002). Distributed leadership as a unit of analysis. *Leadership Quarterly, 13*, 423–451.

Gruber, H. E., & Wallace, D. B. (1999). The case study method and evolving systems approach for understanding unique creative people at work. In: R. J. Sternberg (Ed.), *Handbook of creativity* (pp. 93–115). Cambridge, UK: Cambridge University Press.

Hage, J. T. (1999). Organizational innovation and organizational change. *Annual Review of Sociology, 25*, 597–622.

Halbesleben, J. R., Novicevic, M. M., Harvey, M. G., & Buckley, M. (2003). Awareness of temporal complexity in leadership of creativity and innovation: A competency-based model. *Leadership Quarterly, 14*, 433–455.

Hammond, K. J. (1990). Case-based planning: A framework for planning from experience. *Cognitive Science, 14,* 385–443.

Hargadon, A., & Sutton, R. I. (1997). Technology brokering and innovation in a product development firm. *Administrative Science Quarterly, 42,* 716–749.

Hauschildt, J., & Kirchmann, E. (2001). Teamwork for innovation – the "troika" of promoters. *R&D Management, 31,* 41–49.

Hayes-Roth, B., & Hayes-Roth, F. (1979). A cognitive model of planning. *Cognitive Science, 3,* 275–310.

Heinzen, J. E., Mills, C., & Cameron, P. (1993). Scientific innovation potential. *Creativity Research Journal, 6,* 261–270.

Henderson, R. (1994). Managing innovation in the information age. *Harvard Business Review, 1,* 100–105.

Hershey, D. A., Walsh, D. A., Read, S. J., & Chulef, A. S. (1990). The effects of expertise on financial problem-solving: Evidence for goal-directed problem-solving scripts. *Organizational Behavior and Human Decision Processes, 46,* 77–101.

Hitt, M. A., Hoskisson, R. E., Johnson, R. A., & Moesel, D. D. (1996). The market for corporate control and firm innovation. *Academy of Management Journal, 39,* 1084–1196.

Hounshell, D. A., & Smith, J. K. (1988). *Science and corporate strategy: Dupont R&D, 1902–1980.* New York, NY: Cambridge University Press.

Howell, J. M., & Boies, K. (2004). Champions of technological innovation: The influences of contextual knowledge, role orientation, idea generation, and idea promotion on champion emergence. *Leadership Quarterly, 15,* 130–149.

Huber, J. C. (1998). Invention and inventivity as a special kind of creativity with implications for general creativity. *Journal of Creative Behavior, 32,* 58–72.

Hughes, T. P. (1989). *American genesis: A history of the American genius for invention.* New York, NY: Penguin.

Hull, F. M. (2003). Simultaneous involvement in service product development: A strategic contingency approach. *International Journal of Innovation Management, 7,* 339–370.

Hunter, S. T., Bedell, K. E., & Mumford, M. D. (in press). Climate for creativity: A quantitative review. *Creativity Research Journal.*

Janssen, O., van de Vliert, E., & West, M. (2004). The bright and dark sides of individual and group innovation: A special issue introduction. *Journal of Organizational Behavior, 25,* 129–146.

Jelinek, M., & Schoonhoven, C. B. (1990). *The innovation marathon: Lessons learned from high technology firms.* Oxford, UK: Blackwell.

Johannsen, G., & Rouse, W. B. (1983). Studies of planning behavior of aircraft pilots in normal, abnormal, and emergency situations. *IEEE Transactions on System, Man and Cybernetics, 13,* 267–278.

Josephs, R. A., & Hahn, E. D. (1995). Bias and accuracy in estimates of task duration. *Organizational Behavior and Human Decision Processes, 61,* 202–213.

Kamoche, K., & Cunha, M. P. (2001). Minimal structures: From jazz improvisation to product innovation. *Organization Studies, 22,* 733–764.

Kanigel, R. (1997). *The one best way: Frederick Winslow Taylor and the enigma of efficiency.* New York, NY: Penguin.

Kasof, J. (1995). Explaining creativity: The attribution perspective. *Creativity Research Journal, 8,* 311–366.

Keegan, A., & Turner, J. R. (2002). The management of innovation in project-based firms. *Long Range Planning, 35*, 367–388.

Keller, R. T. (2001). Cross-functional project groups in research and new product development: Diversity, communications, job stress, and outcomes. *Academy of Management Journal, 44*, 547–559.

Kickul, J., & Gundry, L. K. (2001). Breaking through boundaries for organizational innovation: New managerial roles and practices in e-commerce firms. *Journal of Management, 27*, 347–361.

Kidder, T. (1981). *The soul of a new machine.* New York, NY: Avon.

Kitchell, S. (1995). Corporate culture, environmental adaptation, and innovation adoption: A quantitative/qualitative approach. *Journal of the Academy of Marketing Science, 23*, 195–205.

Koberg, C. S., Uhlenbruck, N., & Sarason, Y. (1996). Facilitators of organizational innovation: The role of life-cycle stage. *Journal of Business Venturing, 11*, 133–149.

Langley, P., Simon, H. A., Bradshaw, J. M., & Zytkow, J. M. (1987). *Scientific discovery: An account of the creative processes.* Cambridge, MA: MIT Press.

Li, H., & Atuahene-Gima, K. (2001). Product innovation strategy and the performance of technology ventures in China. *Academy of Management Journal, 44*(6), 1123–1134.

Licuanan, B., Dailey, L., & Mumford, M. D. (in press). Idea evaluation: Error in evaluating highly original ideas. *Journal of Creative Behavior.*

Lonergan, D. C., Scott, G. M., & Mumford, M. D. (2004). Evaluative aspects of creative thought: Effects of idea appraisal and revision standards. *Creativity Research Journal, 16*, 231–246.

Lubart, T. I. (2001). Models of the creative process: Past, present, and future. *Creativity Research Journal, 13*, 295–308.

Majumdar, S. K., & Venkataraman, S. (1993). New technology adoption in US telecommunications: The role of competitive pressures and firm-level inducements. *Research Policy, 22*, 521–536.

Makridakis, S. (1991). Forecasting in the 21st century. *International Journal of Forecasting, 7*, 123–126.

Marcy, R. T., & Mumford, M. D. (in press). Social innovation: Enhancing creative performance through causal analysis. *Creativity Research Journal.*

Merrifield, P. R., Guilford, J. P., Christensen, P. R., & Frick, J. W. (1962). The role of intellectual factors in problem solving. *Psychological Monographs, 76*, 1–21.

Mintzberg, H. (1991). Learning-1, planning-0-reply. *Strategic Management Journal, 12*, 463–466.

Mintzberg, H., Raisinghani, D., & Theoret, A. (1976). The structure of unstructured decision processes. *Administrative Science Quarterly, 21*, 246–275.

Mintzberg, H., & Waters, J. (1985). Of strategies, deliberate and emergent. *Strategic Management Journal, 6*, 257–272.

Mitra, J. (2000). Making corrections: Innovation and collective learning in small businesses. *Education and Training, 42*, 228–237.

Monge, P. R., Cozzens, M. D., & Contractor, N. S. (1992). Communication and motivational predictors of the dynamics of organizational innovation. *Organization Science, 3*, 250–274.

Mossholder, K. W., & Dewhurst, H. D. (1980). The appropriateness of management by objectives for development and research personnel. *Journal of Management, 6*, 145–156.

Mouly, V. S., & Sankaran, J. K. (1999). The "permanent" acting leader: Insights from a dying Indian R&D organization. *Leadership Quarterly, 10*, 637–652.

Mumford, M. D. (2000). Managing creative people: Strategies and tactics for innovation. *Human Resource Management Review, 10*, 1–29.

Mumford, M. D., Baughman, W. A., Supinski, E. P., & Maher, M. A. (1996). Process-based measures of creative problem-solving skills: II. Information encoding. *Creativity Research Journal, 9*, 77–88.

Mumford, M. D., Blair, C., Dailey, L. R., Leritz, L. E., & Osburn, H. K. (in press). Errors in creative thought? Cognitive biases in a computer processing activity. *Journal of Creative Behavior.*

Mumford, M. D., Connelly, M. S., & Gaddis, B. (2003). How creative leaders think: Experimental findings and cases. *Leadership Quarterly, 14*, 411–432.

Mumford, M. D., Eubanks, D. L., & Murphy, S. T. (2006). Creating the conditions for success: Best practices in leading for innovation. In: J. A. Conger & R. Riggio (Eds), *The practice of leadership* (pp. 129–149). San Francisco, CA: Jossey-Bass Publishers.

Mumford, M. D., & Gustafson, S. B. (1988). Creativity syndrome: Integration, application, and innovation. *Psychological Bulletin, 103*, 27–43.

Mumford, M. D., & Hunter, S. T. (2005). Innovation in organizations: A multi-level perspective on creativity. In: F. J. Yammarino & F. Dansereau (Eds), *Research in multi-level issues: Volume IV* (pp. 11–74). Oxford, UK: Elsevier.

Mumford, M. D., Mobley, M. I., Uhlman, C. E., Reiter-Palmon, R., & Doares, L. (1991). Process analytic models of creative capacities. *Creativity Research Journal, 4*, 91–122.

Mumford, M. D., Schultz, R. A., & Osburn, H. K. (2002a). Planning in organizations: Performance as a multi-level phenomenon. In: F. J. Yammario & F. Dansereau (Eds), *Research in multi-level issues: The many faces of multi-level issues* (Vol. 1, pp. 3–35). Oxford, UK: Elsevier.

Mumford, M. D., Schultz, R. A., & Van Dorn, J. R. (2001). Performance in planning: Processes, requirements, and errors. *Review of General Psychology, 5*, 213–240.

Mumford, M. D., Scott, G. M., Gaddis, B., & Strange, J. M. (2002b). Leading creative people: Orchestrating expertise and relationships. *Leadership Quarterly, 13*, 705–750.

Nellore, R., & Balachandra, R. (2001). Factors influencing success in integrated product development (IPD) projects. *IEEE Transactions on Engineering Management, 48*(2), 164–173.

Nohari, K., & Gulatti, S. (1996). Is slack good or bad for innovation. *Academy of Management Journal, 39*, 799–825.

Nutt, P. C. (1984). A strategic planning network for nonprofit organizations. *Strategic Management Journal, 5*, 57–75.

Nyström, H. (1979). *Creativity and innovation.* New York, NY: Wiley.

Nystrom, H. (1990). Organizational innovation. In: M. S. West & J. L. Farr (Eds), *Innovation and creativity at work: Psychological and organizational strategies* (pp. 143–162). New York, NY: Wiley.

O'Connor, G. C. (1998). Market learning and radical innovation: A cross case comparison of eight radical innovation projects. *Journal of Product Innovation Management, 15*, 151–166.

O'Hara, K. P., & Payne, S. J. (1998). The effects of operator implementation cost on planfulness of problem solving and learning. *Cognitive Psychology, 35*, 34–70.

Olson, E. M., Walker, O. C., Ruekert, R. W., & Bonner, J. M. (2001). Patterns of cooperation during new product development among marketing, operations, and R&D. *Journal of Product Development Management, 18*(4), 258–271.

Patalano, A. L., & Seifert, C. M. (1997). Opportunistic planning: Being reminded of pending goals. *Cognitive Psychology, 34*, 1–36.

Pelz, D. C. (1983). Quantitative case histories of urban innovation: Are there innovating stages? *IEEE Transactions on Engineering Management, 30*, 60–67.

Perry-Smith, J. E., & Shalley, C. E. (2003). The social side of creativity: A static and dynamic social network perspective. *Academy of Management Review, 28*(1), 89–106.

Quinn, J. B. (1985). Managing innovation: Controlled chaos. *Harvard Business Review, 3*, 73–84.

Robinson, R. B., & Pearce, J. A., II. (1988). Planned patterns of strategic behavior and their relationship to business-unit performance. *Strategic Management Journal, 9*, 43–60.

Rodan, S. (2002). Innovation and heterogeneous knowledge in managerial contact networks. *Journal of Knowledge Management, 6*, 152–163.

Root-Bernstein, R. S., Bernstein, M., & Garnier, H. (1995). Correlations between avocations, scientific style, work habits, and professional impact of scientists. *Creativity Research Journal, 8*, 115–137.

Russell, R. D., & Russell, C. J. (1992). An examination of the effects of organizational norms, organizational structure, and environmental uncertainty on entrepreneurial strategy. *Journal of Management, 18*, 639–656.

Schwenk, C. R., & Cosier, R. A. (1980). Effects of the expert, devil's advocate, and dialectical inquiry methods on prediction performance. *Organizational Behavior and Human Decision Processes, 26*, 409–424.

Scott, G. M., Lonergan, D. C., & Mumford, M. D. (2005). Contractual combination: Alternative knowledge structures, alternative heuristics. *Creativity Research Journal, 17*, 21–36.

Sharma, A. (1999). Central dilemmas of managing innovation in large firms. *California Management Review, 41*, 65–85.

Simon, H. (1993). Strategy and organizational evolution. *Strategic Management Journal, 14*, 131–142.

Simonton, D. K. (1999). Talent and its development: An emergenic and epigenetic model. *Psychological Review, 106*, 435–457.

Souitaris, V. (2001). External communication determinants of innovation in the context of a newly industrialized country: A comparison of objective and perceptual results from Greece. *Technovation, 21*, 25–34.

Sternberg, R. J. (2005). We want creativity! No, we don't! In: F. J. Yammarino & F. Dansereau (Eds), *Research in multi-level issues* (Vol. IV, pp. 93–104). Oxford, UK: Elsevier.

Sternberg, R. J., & O'Hara, L. A. (1999). Creativity and intelligence. In: R. J. Sternberg (Ed.), *Handbook of creativity* (pp. 297–312). Cambridge, UK: Cambridge University Press.

Sternberg, R. J., O'Hara, L. A., & Lubart, T. I. (1997). Creativity as investment. *California Management Review, 40*, 8–32.

Stringer, R. (2000). How to manage innovation. *California Management Review, 42*, 70–89.

Taggar, S. (2001). Group composition, creative synergy, and group performance. *Journal of Creative Behavior, 35*, 261–286.

Tesluk, P. E., Farr, J. L., & Klein, S. R. (1997). Influences of organizational culture and climate on individual creativity. *Journal of Creative Behavior, 31*, 27–41.

Thamhain, H. J. (2003). Managing innovative R&D teams. *R&D Management, 44*(3), 297–322.

Tierney, P., & Farmer, S. M. (2002). Creative self-efficacy: Its potential antecedents and relationship to creative performance. *Academy of Management Journal, 45*(8), 1137–1148.

Tierney, P., Farmer, S. M., & Graen, G. B. (1999). An examination of leadership and employee creativity: The relevance of traits and relationships. *Personnel Psychology, 52*, 591–620.

Topalian, A. (2000). The role of innovation leaders in developing long-term products. *International Journal of Innovation Management, 4*, 149–171.

Trevelyan, R. (2001). The paradox of autonomy: A case of academic research scientists. *Human Relations, 54*, 495–525.

Troy, L. C., Szymanski, D. M., & Rajan, V. P. (2001). Generating new product ideas: An initial investigation of the role of market information and organizational characteristics. *Journal of Academy of Marketing Science, 29*(1), 89–101.

Tushman, M. L., & O'Reilly, C. A. (1997). *Winning through innovation.* Cambridge, MA: Harvard Business School Press.

Van de Ven, A. H. (1986). Central problems in the management of innovation. *Management Science, 32*, 590–607.

Verhaeghe, A., & Kfir, R. (2002). Managing innovation in a knowledge intensive technology organization (KITO). *R&D Management, 32*, 409–417.

Vincent, P. H., Decker, B. P., & Mumford, M. D. (2002). Divergent thinking, intelligence, and expertise: A test of alternative models. *Creativity Research Journal, 14*, 163–178.

Ward, T. B., Patterson, M. J., & Sifonis, C. M. (2004). The role of specificity and abstraction in creative idea generation. *Creativity Research Journal, 16*, 1–9.

Weingart, L. R. (1992). Impact of group goals, task component complexity, effort, and planning on group performance. *Journal of Applied Psychology, 77*, 682–693.

Weisberg, R. W. (1999). Creativity and knowledge: A challenge to theories. In: R. J. Sternberg (Ed.), *Handbook of creativity* (pp. 226–259). Cambridge, UK: Cambridge University Press.

Weldon, E., Jehn, K. A., & Pradhan, P. (1991). Processes that mediate the relationship between a group goal and improved group performance. *Journal of Personality and Social Psychology, 61*, 555–569.

West, M. A. (2002). Sparkling fountains or stagnant ponds: An integrative model of creativity and innovation implementation in work groups. *Applied Psychology: An International Review, 51*, 355–387.

West, M. A., Borill, C. S., Dawson, J. F., Brodbeck, F., Shapiro, D. A., & Howard, B. (2003). Leadership clarity and team innovation. *Leadership Quarterly, 14*, 246–278.

Wilensky, R. W. (1983). *Planning and understanding: A computational approach to human reasoning.* Reading, MA: Addison-Wesley.

Wise, G. (1992). Inventions and corporations in the maturing electrical industry. In: R. J. Weber & D. N. Perkins (Eds), *Inventive minds: Creativity in technology* (pp. 291–310). New York, NY: Oxford University Press.

Woods, M. F., & Davies, G. B. (1973). Potential problem analysis: A systematic approach to problem prediction and contingency planning: An aid to the smooth exploitation of research. *R&D Management, 4*, 25–32.

Xiao, Y., Milgram, P., & Doyle, D. J. (1997). Capturing and modeling planning expertise in anesthesiology. Results of a field study. In: C. Zsambok & G. Klein (Eds), *Naturalistic decision making* (pp. 197–205). Hillsdale, NJ: Lawrence Erlbaum Associates.

Zuckerman, H. (1977). *Scientific elite: Nobel laureates in the United States.* New York, NY: Free Press.

TEMPLATES FOR INNOVATION

John E. Ettlie

ABSTRACT

In their chapter, Mumford, Bedell-Avers, and Hunter (this volume) confront the nontrivial issue of whether creativity and innovation can be planned, and proceed to support an affirmative answer with a well-organized treatment of the applied research literature relevant to this topic. They outline and reference an incremental approach to this planning process at multiple levels of analysis (organization, group, and individual), and present both a state-of-the-art review and a general, normative approach to this daunting challenge. In reviewing this chapter, this commentary addresses what is worthwhile and important in their presentation that students of this field should find noteworthy. Next, it takes up the issue of what is underdeveloped or missing that would fit nicely into Mumford et al.'s framework, or might provide food for thought to those wanting to go forward with research on the topic of planning for innovation. Finally, it presents conclusions about this topic and the field in general that were stimulated by Mumford et al.'s chapter, including the role of information technology and knowledge management for innovation planning.

Multi-Level Issues in Creativity and Innovation
Research in Multi-Level Issues, Volume 7, 155–167
Copyright © 2008 by Elsevier Ltd.
ISSN: 1475-9144/doi:10.1016/S1475-9144(07)00006-9

PLANNING FOR INNOVATION: NOTEWORTHY CONTRIBUTIONS

Mumford, Bedell-Avers, and Hunter (this volume) have done a credible review of the wide-ranging issues associated with this most important topic: Can innovation be planned and, if so, how? Perhaps the most important contribution they make is that they develop the point that if appropriate constraints (i.e., staged project planning) are applied to the creative process, they enhance innovative outcomes. Few, if any, formal treatments of the R&D management or new-product development process give this insight much attention, even though case reports such as Thomke's (2003) work on efforts to effectively constrain the design process at BMW, and other treatments (e.g., Ettlie & Stoll, 1990), illustrate how boundaries can set the creative mind free. Of course, there are limits, and what we have yet to see is the calculus of planning that will give us the optimal level of constraint by a plan that maximizes outcomes. Nevertheless, some constraints will clearly promote creativity and *learning*.

In a way, any plan is a constraint, and the optimal plan is probably one that allows for efficient learning as the innovation process unfolds. For example, one common challenge encountered in the innovation process is that as participants learn the nature of the new technology – which, by definition, can unfold only gradually or it would not be an innovation – the specifications of the technology project change. This also occurs when environmental conditions change, as pointed out by Mumford et al. This specification "creep" is maddening to those who supply new technology to customers and who want to exploit that technology for economic gain according to an aggressive time deadline. In fact, radical technology cannot be scheduled, which is one of the major lessons of any basic course on the subject.

For example, in our study of manufacturing software development and implementation, we found that satisfaction among key plant managers and technical personnel trying to modernize their factories was much higher when some significant part of the software development was delayed until after first launch of the new advanced manufacturing system (Ettlie & Gentner, 1989). As plant personnel learned what the new system could and could not do, and as the project unfolded over time, the specifications changed. This evolution is something all suppliers of new technology have to plan for because they cannot learn the particulars of every customer and still make money. Even if suppliers did understand customer needs and specifications perfectly (which rarely happens), it is the product's adopters who must ultimately understand their new system. These users must learn at their pace, which may be at variance with the planned milestones. Not surprisingly, many projects of this magnitude underestimate the cost and time of training, because such training often has to be done more than once and in a manner not anticipated at the project outset. Rarely is classroom training alone an effective way to support a new technology introduction.

Another illustration might help capture this essential and subtle point of the implications of gradual unfolding of innovation projects, which resist planning and thrive on learning. Many firms practice the art of technology and design reuse (Sivaloganathan, 2001; Busby, 1999; Zangwill, 1993), primarily in an effort to reduce cost and time to market. For example, Mercedes-Benz, in an effort to improve quality and reduce cost, has reorganized its product-development process around six cross-functional teams (e.g., powertrain, design, electronics). Instead of vehicle programs developing components separately, the goal is to share more parts across vehicle lines (Meiners, 2005). How does the company intend to avoid the obvious problem that this practice restricts creativity in finding the best component for the particular vehicle? The answer given is that program managers can now concentrate on those areas that are unique to their models, making project management more efficient and accountable. There is also an intergenerational effect: Engineers must identify more components to use from outgoing models. Again, the idea is that constraining the design process can set engineers free to be more creative in unique parts of total product characteristics. The benefits of planning include the synergistic effects that this example illustrates, and Mumford et al. develop this point thoroughly in their chapter. How to achieve integration is less clear (Rubenstein, 1989).

Given these examples, any reader would benefit by attending to the important feature of the authors' treatment of innovation planning: They allow for learning along the way. Mumford and colleagues say early on that people will not plan unless two conditions are met: (1) the task is difficult and (2) interdependence (complexity) is high. The most successful innovators are those companies that learn faster than their competitors, an ability that is derived from the dynamic capabilities model of the firm (Teece, Pisano, & Shuen, 1997).

We offer one final example of this critical point (the interaction of planning or anticipation and learning and execution) here. If the present discussion seems belabored and redundant, it is because we have found that this issue is not obvious and often is appreciated only by people who have actually experienced the unfolding nature of the innovation process over time. In our work (Ettlie & Reza, 1992) and the work of many others (e.g., Small & Yasin, 2000), it has been found that if an organization – usually a business firm – attempts to adopt a significant new operations process or information technology system and the workforce is organized in a union, at least one essential element of the implementation will be necessary for success: a union–management technology agreement.

Union–management technology agreements are typically signed before the new technology arrives on the scene for installation, although some or most of the planning may have gone forward before the official start date. They typically set the new conditions of work, because job descriptions of the workforce often change, new skills are required, and new standard operating procedures need to be followed, including maintenance and support of the new technology.

Unions want to protect their members and, of course, health, safety, and job security are important concerns for all. Management wants to continue to exercise the flexibility needed to capture the benefits of the technology as specified. As conditions and outcomes change, learning will occur that can improve the process. Union–management agreements, along with a host of other organizational innovations, have been shown to be associated with highly successful cases of innovative process and information technology projects.

Interestingly, the actual contract language in these agreements does not predict success. That is, if one compares successful and less successful projects of this type, the language of union–management agreement will not matter. Having the agreement matters, but the specifics are relatively unimportant. The simple reason for this phenomenon, and one that is missed by many, is that the successful companies learn the most. Having the agreement allows both parties to learn what is actually needed to be successful, including the proper specifications, and this learning will obsolete the details of any prior agreement signed before the real work was started. The limits of planning are reached quickly in these cases.

Mumford et al. discuss adoption of the portfolio approach to illustrate how planning can be framed and implemented. This exploration points to another critical issue across all settings: *resources.* To their observations that people underestimate innovation when it is first introduced as well as the length of time that project work takes, I would add that the official portfolio, which is often overloaded with longer-term projects that cannot be sustained, does not account for "off the books" work that research and engineering professionals often engage in to ensure that project deadlines are actually satisfied. An example can be found in the case of the Chevrolet Corvette project team that was tasked with beating Mercedes and Toyota to market with an active suspension model in 1990. This emergency project with the last-minute goal to be first to market with active suspension was carried out, essentially, by engineering staff who were officially assigned to other funded projects. This anecdote also leads to a methodological warning: To study planning for innovation, survey data probably will not be sufficient. Only in-depth comparative cases will get to this type of data.

Another essential point of the innovation process that is so often forgotten, but Mumford et al. are keen about, is the amount of *time* it takes to accomplish real innovation. ("Radical" is one way of describing these breakthroughs, but the terms "disruptive," "discontinuous," and "field-changing" have also been used in this context.) Whenever a company changes its platform, we look for a different process unfolding. This evolution offers an opportunity to study real innovation, in the context of a portfolio that must do other things as well. Thus, placing the right bets is part of the essential role of general managers. The strategic planning idea that some possible futures are derived from a vision and some emerge unexpectedly is very consistent with their observations.

Mumford et al. discuss environmental scanning, mentioning five examples as they do so: customer feedback, supplier feedback, market research, competitor monitoring, and technology monitoring. Perhaps without knowing it, they give us a blueprint (which can already be found in the literature) for focusing our planning effort. Although environmental uncertainty comes from many sources, managers can effectively attend to only a few of these possibilities. We have shown in our work (Ettlie, Bridges, & O'Keefe, 1984), along with other authors more recently (e.g., Bstieler, 2005), that paying attention to competitors, customers, and technology are the three key areas for planning innovation successfully. One must add government to this list of key factors when in a regulated environment. Unfortunately, because internal environments dominate the process, the voice of the customer tends to be trumped by benchmarking and internal process management (Ettlie & Johnson, 1994). Hence the best innovators often get their competitive information from their best customers to make sure that these two data points are properly weighted in the process.

Many other good points are attended to (though not explicitly cited) in Mumford et al.'s chapter:

- The strength of weak connections (Granovetter, 1973).
- The way that evaluation can kill potentially good ideas, although Mumford et al. miss the issue of timing – Too early kills ideas too soon (Hage, 1980).

- Structuring for innovation, although Mumford et al. miss the literature on corporate venturing (Miles & Covin, 2002).
- The importance of goals, although Mumford et al. miss the key point of the power of goal setting (Latham & Locke, 1991).
- "Make or buy" decisions at the heart of the planning process and capability assessment and development that help top managers guide important teams on innovation quests (Narayanan, Douglas, Guernsey, & Charnes, 2002).

Other emergent issues worthy of note are as follows:

- Alliance formation and the presence of multiple organizations involved in planning, which is a real challenge.
- The climate for innovating, although this is not clarified with respect to culture (Denison, 1996) and philosophy, such as in the case studies of Honda Corporation (the Honda effect).
- The idea that innovation occurs in waves. Although Mumford et al. cite Hounshell and Smith (1998), the authors do not discuss the waves of exploration and exploitation at DuPont, which seem to follow seven- to nine-year cycles.

In sum, Mumford et al.'s chapter is a broad, comprehensive, if not exhaustive, treatment of an important topic and a rewarding read for any serious student of the subject. For any student of planning, project management, and the innovation process generally, this chapter is highly recommended.

PLANNING FOR INNOVATION: NOTEWORTHY OMISSIONS

In many ways, Mumford et al.'s chapter begs to be augmented, and it is noteworthy that omissions come to mind easily when reading this treatment of the planning process for innovation – it is generally that well written. Five areas leap to mind:

- Although the chapter deals reasonably well with structure, with the exception of the literature on corporate venturing, it does not cover the strategy for innovating quite so adeptly.

- Leadership is an important issue, and championship is also introduced in the chapter. But what is the conceptual difference between the two?
- The chapter deals almost exclusively with incumbent firms, but new entrants are important to any innovation system.
- Teamwork is mentioned, but a classical view of "more is better" is the summary treatment. In reality, innovation often thrives on tension, especially between functions.
- The emerging role of information technology and knowledge management for innovation planning and execution as well as the numerous planning tools that have been successfully adopted (with the exception of stage-gate process, which is often modified) are conspicuous by their absence.

Strategy and Innovation

Strategy precedes structure in organizations, even if some part of that strategy emerges from learning (Amburgey & Dacin, 1994). Here, I allude specifically to business unit and R&D strategy, corporate strategy for innovation, and functional strategies that support these innovative plans. This is a broad and rich area, so only a few citations will be provided here. For an introduction to the subject of the corporate strategy issues associated with innovation planning, two books are worth consideration: Shilling's (2005) book and the Burgelman, Grove, and Meza (2004) text.

As far as empirical studies, many come to mind, but the research dealing with entrepreneurial orientation (Miller & Friesen, 1982) and the relationship between strategy and structure of innovating (Ettlie et al., 1984) are two seminal works. With regard to the planning context, the notion of disruptive technology (Christensen, 1997) and reflections on the research agenda for this topic are reviewed effectively in the recent special issue of the *Journal of Product Innovation Management* (Danneels, 2006). In the long haul, strategy will likely be more important to get right, with structure coming along – even if kicking and screaming – in the end, just as goal setting (Latham & Locke, 1991) and the relationship between R&D and marketing (e.g., Sherman, Berkowitz, & Souder, 2005) will trump most other issues in effective innovation planning. Ultimately, that is what Mumford et al.'s chapter needs: Some priorities need to be attached to all those issues that are reviewed so well in each section, but with no real indication of why, say, climate trumps structure. What comes first? What is second? Who is on third (with apologies to Bud Abbott)?

Leadership and Championship

The literature has revealed a resurgence in interest regarding the role of championship in the innovation process (e.g., Howell, Shea, & Higgins, 2005). The chapter by Mumford et al., however, never really comes to grips with the possible overlap between this concept and leadership, especially as it relates to innovation planning. The championship notion is becoming more expansive, with some authors seeking to include almost any role that might influence the initiation and implementation of innovation concepts. This is especially true for radical innovation, and we need more research on reconciliation of these two important research streams.

One hopeful "beginning of this end" is the series of articles published by Jane Dutton and her colleagues on *issue selling* and framing (Dutton, Ashford, O'Neill, Hayes, & Wierba, 1997; Dutton, Ashford, O'Neill, & Lawrence, 2001; Dutton, Ashford, Lawrence, & Miner-Rubino, 2002). If one considers issue selling to be an essential part of championship behaviors and organizational change processes, then this line of research shows great promise in elucidating how planning actually takes shape in organizations. What this series of studies demonstrates is that issue selling is an essential skill – including issue-selling moves of packaging, involvement, and timing – in changing organizations. Indeed, it may turn out to be one of the essential distinguishing features in leadership behaviors for all people engaged in innovation planning.

Another potentially important feature of the leadership skill set is orchestration of *personnel flows* in the innovation process. A strong correlation exists between initiation of radical innovation operations process adoption in manufacturing and service firms and the change of key general managers of a firm (Ettlie, 1980, 1985). As the plan goes forward for adoption of new process technology, movement of technical personnel into middle management, including project management, is paramount to ultimate implementation success.

Incumbent versus New Entrants

Entrepreneurship has become a cottage industry in academe, and it is wonderful to see it enjoy, at last, the attention that it deserves. However, most new firms are started by teams (Aldrich & Cliff, 2003), and the similarities and differences between planned and unplanned innovation start-ups are just beginning to be revealed in the literature.

Furthermore, there is a nasty conceptual debate smoldering in this "next big thing": Researchers in the entrepreneurship area are beginning to redefine and expand their field much as quality mavens expanded their field to answer all questions. I heard the following dialogue recently at a seminar: Practitioner: "What is entrepreneurship?" Professor's answer: "Innovation."

Teamwork

Would anyone deny the importance of teamwork for innovation planning and execution? Not me. However, I would suggest that what is needed here is an emphasis on the approach to teamwork that is unique for the innovating context (e.g., Katz, 2003). We know teams are important for innovation planning and implementation, and these groups are likely to be two different teams when truly radical change is at hand. But which particular team at which stage of the process plays the larger role, along with their unique unfolding, is important to emphasize.

For example, a real tension exists between R&D and marketing in the most critical first stage of the innovation process because of the very nature of these two functions in a firm and the cultures of the disciplines they represent (Ettlie, 2002). This tension needs to be managed to successfully capture the significant inputs of both important functions for, especially, early planning of innovation. We still do not know how these two cultures can clash like titans yet still produce innovation success for an organization. The idea that we work happily in teams with smiles on our faces, all joyfully embracing the bliss of teamwork and valuing the notion of being a team player, is woefully naive.

The original gatekeeper model so effectively documented by Allen, Tushman, and Lee (1979) and others clearly needs updating. Firms are effectively sourcing ideas much more broadly now in the technical ranks, including marketing, which puts real pressure on teamwork management (Ettlie & Elsenbach, 2005). This scenario is no longer a matter of a single gatekeeper managing the effective flow ideas in an R&D lab.

Munford et al. cite Barnowe's (1975) article is an important contribution on leadership and innovation. One of the essential findings in that work, however, is that there is considerable variance in how much leaders influence innovative outcomes. Granted, a small variance (15%) might actually be practically significant in the long run. By contrast, when technical teams are disadvantaged (e.g., many new junior hires), leaders exert much greater influence. Perhaps the shift in the gatekeeper model to broader sourcing of ideas internally for information processing shows how these teams have become less disadvantaged over the past two decades. It is not clear whether this is a broad trend or precisely what accounts for this shift.

We have also begun to believe that products and services have fundamental differences long ignored in the literature, which we intend to rectify. These variations include how ideas are effectively sourced and how the process is planned, which seem to be quite different in these two settings (Ettlie & Rosenthal, 2006).

Information Technology and Knowledge Management

The role of information technology in the innovation process has continued to increase in importance. At this point, it is probably not a stretch to say that every organization has two technical functions: (1) the technical core of knowledge associated with the prime responsibility for new products and services and (2) the information and knowledge technical core.

A number of recent studies, for example, have examined the importance of information technology in virtual engineering teams (Malhotra, Majchrzak, Carman, & Lott, 2001) and the attendant changes required in strategy and structure needed to make these new approaches to new-product development work. Clearly, the potential to improve the introduction of anything new can be enhanced by information and knowledge management. Nevertheless, questions remain about whether this will take place, given that – using one of Mumford et al.'s terms – there is no planning template as yet to guide this process.

This brings us to the final point, which focuses on the importance of *tools* in the innovation planning process and their contributions to knowledge management. To the credit of Mumford et al., they do discuss the stage-gate process, which has a well-known role in product development. This staging method is also modified in many settings (Ettlie & Elsenbach, 2007), which shows how planning will be augmented by learning, as discussed earlier. In addition to stage management tools, many other well-documented methods for improving the planning and execution process are available, including innovation roadmapping (Radnor & Probert, 2004), quality function deployment (QFD; Ettlie & Johnson, 1994), and many more.

REFERENCES

Aldrich, H. E., & Cliff, J. E. (2003). The pervasive effects of family on entrepreneurship: Toward a family embeddedness perspective. *Journal of Business Venturing, 18*, 573.

Allen, T. J., Tushman, M. L., & Lee, D. M. S. (1979). Technology transfer as a function of position in the spectrum from research through development to technical services. *Academy of Management Journal, 22*, 694–708.

Amburgey, T. L., & Dacin, T. (1994). As the left foot follows the right? The dynamics of strategic and structural change. *Academy of Management Journal, 37*, 1427–1452.

Barnowe, J. T. (1975). Leadership and performance outcomes in research organizations: The supervisor of scientists as a source of assistance. *Organizational Behavior and Human Performance, 14*, 264.

Bstieler, L. (2005). The moderating effect of environmental uncertainty on new product development and time efficiency. *Journal of Product Innovation Management, 22*, 266.

Burgelman, R. A., Grove, A. S., & Meza, P. E. (2004). *Strategic dynamics: Concepts and cases.* New York: McGraw-Hill/Irwin.

Busby, J. S. (1999). The problem with design reuse: An investigation into outcomes and antecedents. *Journal of Engineering Design, 10*, 277–296.

Christensen, C. M. (1997). *The innovator's dilemma.* Boston, MA: Harvard Business School Press.

Danneels, E. (2006). Dialogue on the effects of disruptive technology on firms and industries. *Journal of Product Innovation Management, 23*, 2–4.

Denison, D. R (1996). What is the difference between organizational culture and organizational climate? A native's point of view on a decade of paradigm wars. *Academy of Management Review, 21*(3), 619–656.

Dutton, J. E., Ashford, S. J., Lawrence, K. A., & Miner-Rubino, K. (2002). Red light, green light: Making sense of the organizational context for issue selling. *Organization Science, 13*(4), 355–372.

Dutton, J. E., Ashford, S. J., O'Neill, R. M., Hayes, E., & Wierba, E. E. (1997). Reading the wind: How middle managers assess the context for selling issues to top managers. *Strategic Management Journal, 18*(5), 407–425.

Dutton, J. E., Ashford, S. J., O'Neill, R. M., & Lawrence, K. A. (2001). Moves that matter: Issue selling and organizational change. *Academy of Management Journal, 44*(4), 716–737.

Ettlie, J. E. (1980). Manpower flows and the innovation process. *Management Science, 26*(11), 1086–1095.

Ettlie, J. E. (1985). The impact of inter organizational manpower flows on the innovation process. *Management Science, 31*(9), 1055–1071.

Ettlie, J. E. (2002). Research-based pedagogy for new product development: MBAs vs. engineers in different countries. *Journal of Product Innovation Management, 19*(1), 46–53.

Ettlie, J. E., Bridges, W., & O'Keefe, R. (1984). Organizational strategy and structural differences for radical versus incremental innovation. *Management Science, 30*(6), 682–695.

Ettlie, J. E., & Elsenbach, J. (2007). Modified stage-gate regimes in new product development. *Journal of Product Innovation Management, 24*(1), 20–33.

Ettlie, J. E., & Elsenbach, J. M. (2005). *Idea reservoirs and new product commercialization.* Working paper, College of Business, Rochester Institute of Technology, Rochester, NY.

Ettlie, J. E., & Gentner, C. E. (1989). Manufacturing software maintenance. *Manufacturing Review, 2*(2), 129–133.

Ettlie, J. E., & Johnson, M. D. (1994). Product development benchmarking versus customer focus in applications of quality function deployment. *Marketing Letters, 5*(2), 107–116.

Ettlie, J. E., & Reza, E. (1992). Organizational integration and process innovation. *Academy of Management Journal, 34*(4), 795–827.

Ettlie, J. E., & Rosenthal, S. R. (2006). *Exploratory study of service and manufacturing innovation.* Working paper, College of Business, Rochester Institute of Technology, Rochester, NY.

Ettlie, J. E., & Stoll, H. (1990). *Managing the design-manufacturing process.* New York: McGraw-Hill.

Granovetter, M. S. (1973). The strength of weak ties. *American Journal of Sociology, 78*(6), 1360–1380.

Hage, J. (1980). *Theories of organizations.* New York: Wiley.

Hounshell, D. A., & Smith, J. K. (1998). *Science and corporate strategy: DuPont R&D, 1902–1980.* New York: Cambridge University Press.

Howell, J. M., Shea, C. M., & Higgins, C. A. (2005). Champions of product innovations: Defining, developing and validating a measure of champion behavior. *Journal of Business Venturing, 20*(5), 641.

Katz, R. (2003). *Managing technological innovation: A collection of readings* (2nd ed.). New York: Oxford University Press.

Latham, G. P., & Locke, E. A (1991). Self-regulation through goal setting. *Organizational Behavior and Human Decision Processes, 50*(2), 212–247.

Malhotra, A., Majchrzak, A., Carman, R., & Lott, V. (2001). Radical innovation without collocation: A case study at Boeing-Rocketdyne. *MIS Quarterly, 25*(2), 229–249.

Meiners, J. (2005, September 12). M-B changes product development. *Automotive News, 81*, 18.

Miles, M. P., & Covin, J. G. (2002). Exploring the practice of corporate venturing: Some common forms and their organizational implications. *Entrepreneurship Theory and Practice, 26*(3), 21–40.

Miller, D., & Friesen, P. H. (1982). Innovation in conservative and entrepreneurial firms: Two models of strategic momentum: Summary. *Strategic Management Journal (pre-1986), Chichester, 3*(1), 1–24.

Mumford, M. D., Hunter, S. T., & Bedell-Avers, K. E. (Eds), (this volume). Planning for innovation: A multi-level perspective. *Research in multi-level issues: Multi-level issues in creativity and innovation* (Vol. 7). Oxford: Elsevier.

Narayanan, V. K., Douglas, F. L., Guernsey, B., & Charnes, J. (2002). How top management steers fast cycle teams to success. *Strategy and Leadership, 30*(3), 19–27.

Radnor, M., & Probert, D. R. (2004). Viewing the future. *Research Technology Management, 47*(2), 25–27.

Rubenstein, A. H. (1989). *Managing technology in the decentralized firm.* New York: Wiley.

Sherman, J. D., Berkowitz, D., & Souder, W. E. (2005). New product development performance and the interaction of cross-functional interaction and knowledge management. *Journal of Product Innovation Management, 22*(5), 399–411.

Shilling, M. (2005). *Strategic management of technological innovation.* New York: McGraw-Hill.

Sivaloganathan, S. T. M. S. (2001). Use of design interpretation for developing new generation products in small and medium enterprises. *International Journal of Manufacturing Technology and Management, 3*(4/5), 469–487.

Small, M. H., & Yasin, M. (2000). Human factors in the adoption and performance of advanced manufacturing technology in unionized firms. *Industrial Management & Data Systems, 100*(8), 389–401.

Teece, D. J., Pisano, G., & Shuen, A. (1997). Dynamic capabilities and strategic management. *Strategic Management Journal, 18*(7), 509–533.

Thomke, S. (2003). *Experimentation matters: Unlocking the potential of new technologies for innovation.* Boston, MA: Harvard Business School Press.

Zangwill, W. L. (1993). *Lightning strategies for innovation.* New York: Free Press.

INNOVATION AS A CONTESTED TERRAIN: PLANNED CREATIVITY AND INNOVATION VERSUS EMERGENT CREATIVITY AND INNOVATION

Christine Miller and Richard N. Osborn

ABSTRACT

This commentary challenges researchers to include grounded social processes generated by individual action and interaction as they study managerial efforts in an attempt to impose prescriptive innovation models on them. Specifically, innovation planning for the middle of the organization and the middle stages of the innovation process should consider a variety of social processes that emerge from the interaction of individuals in their grounded setting. Researchers in this area should place much more emphasis on interpretation and further explore how leaders might facilitate interaction to increase the changes of dynamic adaptive emergence. We also suggest a consideration of managerial mindsets to determine how executives attempt to influence those in the middle, and we call on researchers to explicitly recognize differences in types of innovations and technological discontinuities.

Multi-Level Issues in Creativity and Innovation
Research in Multi-Level Issues, Volume 7, 169–189
Copyright © 2008 by Elsevier Ltd.
All rights of reproduction in any form reserved
ISSN: 1475-9144/doi:10.1016/S1475-9144(07)00007-0

INTRODUCTION

Innovation in the form of modernization, improvement, advance, or the truly original is probably one of the most commonly researched topics across the subfields of management – from organization behavior's fascination with creativity, to organization theory's focus on organizational innovation, to strategy's emphasis on patents, to technology management's search for the next big idea. A simple search of the standard academic search engines yields thousands of entries. Why? In the United States, it is generally recognized that companies cannot compete on the basis of simple efficiency but rather must develop new products, services, processes, and ways of managing if they are to compete successfully in a global economy. Thus it is no real criticism to note Mumford, Bedell-Avers, & Hunter (this volume) have left out more than they have included. To the contrary, it is important to note the issues that they have discussed and the delicate balancing act that managers interested in promoting innovation must perform. In addition, it is important to acknowledge that a different way of examining parts of the planning process for innovation is feasible.

WHAT IS INCLUDED

In many respects, Mumford et al.'s chapter is an extraordinary, broad-based effort to partially integrate research conducted across diverse fields so as to develop a multi-level perspective on planning for innovation. Specifically, Mumford et al. argue for the criticality of planning for innovation, thereby identifying the forces that influence, and should influence, planning, innovation, and creativity at the organizational, group, and individual levels. The authors recognize that innovative and creative processes require an approach to planning that is different from that taken in routine organizational tasks. To this end, they propose a normative model for "effective planning" for innovation based on a multi-dimensional, "incremental approach involving a viable portfolio of projects." The incremental approach implies that plans must necessarily unfold slowly over time because of the uncertainty inherent in planning creative efforts. In these authors' model, planning is to occur simultaneously across a viable portfolio of projects in different stages of development in which the multiple projects are prioritized on, and organized around, an integrated set of themes.

Sophisticated Planning across Levels of Analysis

Mumford et al. reject the simple forecasting/budgeting outcome specification models so common in the applied literature on innovation planning
dating from the 1950s. They recognize and attempt to deal with the
complexity of both the planning and innovation processes. As their chapter
suggests, however, there is as much controversy as insight in the literature,
such that it yields a series of vague prescriptions suggestive of the early
process views of management. To wit, we find the following: Thus ongoing
active monitoring, especially during the initial phases of plan execution, will
be required along with additive tailoring of plans to meet the unique
challenges that arise during the initial phases of plan execution. While
evaluation can proceed using standard business models, it is important to
bear in mind a notable exception to the general rule of thumb. More
specifically, the difficulties encountered in initial plan execution should not
be overweighed in appraising project performance.

As with the earlier process management perspective, one cannot disagree
with their statements calling for active monitoring, additive tailoring of
plans, and taking care not to overweight the initial plan in appraising
performance. We are just not sure at what point active monitoring becomes
onerous oversight (Bonner, Ruekert, & Walker, 2002; McGrath, 2001;
Morris, 1996) or additive tailoring becomes retrospective revisionism. And
we wonder about the viability of initial plans to predict uncertain outcomes
in an uncertain world, for we know all too well the predilections of senior
executives to institute process and outcome controls that reach toward an
obsolete initial plan (Van de Ven, 1986). We agree with Mumford et al.:
Senior executives and managers who want innovation must perform a very
delicate balancing act. Rather than following a formula or a simple process,
it appears that the management of innovation may be as complex as the
innovation itself.

Teleological-Stage Models

Having established the distinct characteristics of innovative and creative
efforts that necessitate a different planning approach from routine activities,
Mumford et al. identify five stages of the planning process. Carefully
unbundling the key elements of each stage, these authors draw upon a rich
variety of extant studies to provide lists of antecedent conditions,
characteristics, and qualities. Furthermore, they show that a multi-level

perspective – incorporating organizational, group, and individual levels – is essential in drawing attention to the interdependencies that significantly influence creativity and innovation at all levels. The authors provide observations that demonstrate how actions that occur at each level should impact the overall effectiveness of plan construction and execution throughout the project development cycle. This effort should not be taken lightly. Few, if any, innovation studies recognize all three levels. Likewise, few theoretical perspectives cover all three levels.

The reviewed studies are summarized in a stage model of planning that features several subcomponents at each stage. The stages in the planning process can generally be matched to an implicit innovation development process. The planning model starts with scanning (e.g., acquisition of expertise) and ends in execution (e.g., implementation). There seems to be little question about the importance of planning and senior management direction in the scanning or plan execution phases, albeit for entirely different reasons. Without some sort of "plan" and top management support, it would be virtually impossible for the organization to acquire the personnel and resources necessary to mount an innovation effort. And, of course, it is inconceivable that implementation would proceed without clear expectations of both the desired outcome and the means to get there.

In some respects, Mumford et al.'s proposed model echoes the findings of Van de Ven and his colleagues in their more than a decade-long investigations of innovation (Van de Ven, Polley, Garud, & Venkataraman, 1999). Innovation in organizations is neither a chaotic, random series of accidents nor a planned program sequence of orchestrated events. And yet, as Van de Ven et al. (1999) show, without some chaos and some teleology emphasized by management, innovation will not occur. The question, then, is how to navigate the challenge of innovation with selectively planned chaotic anticipation of the unknown. How should directed action for innovation be undertaken?

STRATEGIES FOR NAVIGATION

Consider two alternative views – contrasting exemplars – of directed action taken from ethnographic accounts of European and Trukese navigators. The trope of metaphor or comparison, which is common in anthropological studies, is used here to illustrate how observationally based accounts of different approaches to directed action can open new ways of thinking about planning, innovation, creativity, and strategy.

Thomas Gladwin's (1964) comparison of the methods by which European and Trukese navigators navigate the open sea has been used to describe contrasting approaches to purposeful action (Berreman, 1966; Suchman, 1987). Gladwin notes that the European navigator starts out with a plan – "a course" that is charted according to certain universal principles. The voyage is conducted by relating all decisions back to that plan; all effort is directed to remaining "on course." Unexpected events require that the plan first be altered to respond to the changing conditions. In contrast, the Trukese navigator begins the voyage with an objective: getting to a particular island. He responds to events in an ad hoc manner as they emerge. Information gathered from the surroundings – wind, waves, tides and currents, stars, clouds, birds and sea creatures – is read moment by moment. Effort is directed at reaching the objective, whatever it takes.

Both navigators employ a system of techniques: The European navigator applies general principles to whatever case he encounters, whereas the Trukese navigator works from a system of cues that are interpreted as they emerge. If asked, the European navigator might be able to show and tell about the techniques he uses, whereas the Trukese might not be able to articulate his methods. Gladwin argues that the European system of navigation can be taught relatively easily, whereas the Trukese system must be learned through apprenticeship and experience. Both systems "work," and neither is superior to the other. What this example illustrates are *different styles of thought*, rather than better or worse methodologies. Each system is superior under certain circumstances and for specific purposes. And, of course, there are good and bad navigators among both Europeans and Trukese.

The Truk and Complexity

The importance of co-evolutionary dynamics for innovation (the Truk view of navigation) is echoed in some analyses by those following a complexity theory perspective (Brown & Eisenhardt, 1995; Browning, Beyer, & Shetler, 1995). For many who assume this viewpoint, there is a concern for the adaptation of an organization to an uncertain environment, where adaptation is judged in terms of a fitness landscape (possible adaptive outcomes with higher fitness being preferred to those with lower fitness). Strategies for development are similar to the later stages of the Mumford et al. planning approach, and there is an emphasis on altering the interdependencies among component parts of the organization (architecture).

Specifically, following Caldart and Ricart (2004), senior executives at the strategic apex are to develop a representation of the inter-firm fitness landscape, position the organization to climb a basin of attraction using preferred evolutionary strategies, and develop an architecture of the firm via manipulation of interdependencies. Consistent with Levinthal and his colleagues (Levinthal, 1997; Levinthal & Warglien, 1999), the choices regarding the representation of a fitness landscape, the positioning of a firm, and its architecture, in part, depend on the characteristics of the firm's environment, the breadth of the managerial leader's vision, and the history of the firm's evolutionary path (Tzeng, 2006). Choices are neither environmentally determined nor unrestrained.

While some complexity-based views share an emphasis on vision and environmental positioning with the Mumford et al. model (Browning et al., 1995), it is important to note key differences among these perspectives. In the planning view (European system of navigation), system coordination emanates from above and cascades down through the lower echelons to achieve the goal of innovation. In a complexity perspective, organizational adaptation arises from interaction among individuals within the system and is emphasized as an initiating innovation, while both positively internally reinforced and positively environmentally reinforced innovation attempts are expected to create an upward spiral of improvement yielding greater fitness.

To achieve both the initiating innovation and the necessary positive reinforcement, the complexity perspective emphasizes the management of networks and interdependencies rather than controls over process or outcomes. This perspective is supported by recent work – for example, a study of the social processes involved in innovation networks is provided by Obstfeld (2005). Rather than specific goals and detailed plans, a complexity perspective emphasizes evolutionary strategies rather than definitive plans, because the actual innovation and the specifics of the innovation in the market may be considered unpredictable. In the jargon of complexity theory, order is free at the edge of chaos. Unfortunately, the resulting free order may not be the one initially desired by senior management (Osborn, Hunt, & Jauch, 2002).

Upward Innovative Dynamics

It is important to stress four major points about a complexity perspective of innovation. The first point is the need to understand the power of emergent dynamics. Each entity operating within the organization, in adapting to its own context, itself interacts with and adjusts to others. In larger, more sophisticated organizations, some entities are themselves complex systems replete with ever-changing internal interactions among members and operating in a highly fluid context. These entities have been labeled adaptive agents (Maguire & McKelvey, 1998). As entities adjust to one another and to their specific context, a new self-organized order describing their collective adaptations may emerge. This emergent order is extremely powerful because it meets the collective needs of the component entities.

The second point concerns the apparent novelty of complexity. In some respects, complexity is revolutionary. For innovation, however, its underlying message reinforces the message conveyed by some researchers, such as Mumford et al. For decades, researchers studying innovation have noted the importance of the individual and group factors mentioned by Mumford et al., whether they be creativity, professionalism, leadership, group dynamics, or the like. The underlying message is that individuals, their interactions, the tasks that they are asked to complete, and the settings in which they operate matter a great deal when explaining and predicting innovation. The message from a complexity perspective is similar. The subtle difference is the emphasis that a complexity view places on interaction among the elements and management of this interaction (Caldart & Ricart, 2004). The bottom line: Innovation is likely to occur if management does not kill it.

The third point is that history matters. While new managers want to believe they start with a clean slate, the complexity perspective emphasizes the important role played by past adaptations as a basis for new co-evolutionary alterations. Jump-starting innovation in a rigid bureaucracy with a history of stability is a much greater challenge than doing so in an organization with a history of more flexibility (Tzeng, 2006). In many large organizations, as managers attempt to put their stamp on the firm, efforts at change often seem to take on a "flavor of the month" aura. Management by objectives is followed by process improvement, which is in turn followed by another new approach to technological innovation. How management has attempted change in the past – and not just the apparent success of these efforts – may well set the tone for how those asked for innovation see new attempts to foster innovation. Their interpretations are likely molded by past experience.

The fourth point takes some extended discussion. The innovation emerging upward from local adaptation may or may not fit the type, form, or character of change desired by management. Also, the process of emergence is far from the orderly planned perspective of many managers. The very attempts by managers to control the process of emergence could actually dampen the dynamics needed to encourage innovation (McGrath, 2001). At this stage of research, however, it is not clear precisely which managerial plans, processes, and controls inhibit emergent dynamics and which enhance their value to the organization. As suggested by Mumford et al., both failure to plan and rigid planning may inhibit innovation. What happens versus what should happen in the vast middle, however, remains a matter of hot debate.

It seems clear that Mumford et al. would like to be European navigators. At the beginning and end of the process, we, too, would look like European navigators. However, there is the vast middle to be traversed during this journey – the middle of the innovation process and the middle of the organization. What should happen after leaving port and before entering the final destination?

THE MESSY MIDDLE

Whether one adopts a European or Trukese perspective in examining the overall navigation strategy for innovation, organizations still confront the problem of the messy middle. The middle comprises both (1) the middle of the innovation process in the Mumford model and (2) middle management. Specifically, as a research idea moves from conceptual possibility (template planning) to project action (plan development) to the beginning of the development cycle with forecasting, its costs, risks, and uncertainty escalate. In these middle stages, middle management dominates, and middle management is where the pressure for innovation meets the reality of the necessity for immediate performance. Stated in March's (1991) terms, this is where exploration meets exploitation, and where both may not be sought simultaneously by the same individuals.

While the planning process can rightfully be represented as a series of sequential steps in a linear process from point A to point B (European view), in real time the vast middle is inherently nonlinear. Beyond the course set by senior executives in the first stage, project participants at all levels negotiate how, when, where, and what work will be performed by whom. As abstract conceptual possibilities are explored and transformed into concrete prototypes for testing and evaluation, there is often intense pressure for immediate performance. Managers no longer ask, "Can this be done?," but rather emphasize how the innovation can be accomplished efficiently. In this middle phase, uncertainty re-enters the innovation process as the abstract conceptual possibility explodes in a myriad of divergent directions and tasks. An entirely new level of complexity, both in the management and technical direction, is introduced. It is here that negotiating the inherent interdependencies at multiple levels becomes crucial.

Recognition of the interdependencies is fundamental to understanding innovation and creative processes from an organization-wide perspective. While it is clear that the top-down planning processes outlined in Mumford et al.'s chapter are exceedingly complex, the authors imply that a high level of coordinated planning across all of these levels is achievable. In reality, grounded studies of organizational initiatives to impose order on creative and innovative efforts suggest that few organizations have adapted to function at this level of sophistication and effectiveness.

Failure in the Middle

Recent research on the introduction of innovation cells within a Tier One automotive supplier (Miller, 2006) suggests that an alternative interpretive perspective – one that considers the ways in which participants define a situation, develop, and maintain shared understandings, and make sense of their own and others' beliefs (Daft & Weick, 1984; Dougherty & Corse, 1995; Smircich & Stubbart, 1985; Weick, 1979) – can highlight complications resulting from top-down planning processes. Rather than being a story of success, however, it is a tale of how expectations were set and confounded, teams lacking confidence were high-jacked by advocates with strong personalities, and lessons learned were abbreviated and ignored so that mistakes were repeated. Our tale concerns projects at the middle stage of development. It provides a concrete example of how a top-down planning process can become entangled with "empowerment" of a bottom-up planning model.

Similar to many large organizations organized along the bureaucratic model, the top-level management of this particular automotive supplier supported the development and implementation of a stage-gate process for innovation management similar to the stage-gate approach characterized in the Mumford et al. model. Beginning with idea generation at stage 0, ideas theoretically proceeded through the development process to stages 1, 2, and 3, at which point they were handed off for production. For a variety of reasons, including financial constraints and shifts in strategic direction, not all ideas were sanctioned by management to proceed along the development track. Many were "killed" or "book-shelved" in stages 1 or 2. As in many other firms, metrics were developed to track and monitor various aspects of the stage-gate process, such as percentage of sales of new products – specifically, those innovations developed within the previous 24 months. Given that management was keen on moving innovations along, it closely monitored the time between gate 1 and gate 2. As prior research would suggest and Mumford et al. note, this is a critical transition and one that is often successfully traversed with the use of innovation cells.

Senior management hired an expert who was known for his success with innovation cells – that is, empowered cross-functional teams consisting of a small number of individuals (five to six) who, for a limited period of time, were exclusively dedicated to focusing intensely on evaluating and moving forward specific innovative product concepts. For the supplier, the innovation cell initiative represented a process innovation within the product development division. While it was a departure of sorts from the formal stage-gate process, management hoped it would both show their commitment to innovation and help engineers move projects along.

Middle managers proceeded to plan for innovation cells based on their interpretation of a book authored by the new expert. Of course, the middle managers designing the new innovation cells called for adaptations reflecting the organization's history and current conditions – for example, adaptations based on the traditionally dominant role of functional engineering groups, the poor financial condition of the firm, and the firm's lack of experience with cross-functional innovation teams. As a consequence, they modified the book's rules for their own situation. Instead of five or six volunteers, a large number of engineers were assigned as participants, and these participants retained many of their other job responsibilities. Instead of maintaining co-location even in the face of conflict, subgroups were allowed to move their work back to their initial locations to work on "their part of the project." While assured the cell members would have "full control," a senior manager (what some would call a "project champion") maintained his active involvement to provide "coordination."

As the innovation cell concept was new to this particular organization, both the team and the leadership of the division were on a learning curve; they had embarked on exploration. An elaborate and well-attended briefing to describe and explain the innovation cell process and goals was held to launch the team. In the weeks following the team's send-off, it became increasingly clear that each member of the team represented his or her functional area and came with his or her own goals and style of thought shaped by the individual's prior professional training. Cell members maintained their functionally based rules, policies, and procedures, even though they were initially told to be creative, ignore the rules, and develop their own views. Consequently, they struggled to reach agreement on a shared understanding of their goal and a common plan for how to proceed. A facilitator had been assigned; however, this individual's understanding of his role was that he was to oversee logistics, but not process.

Although the team members were given a charter, confusion arose regarding the conflict between the explicit messages regarding the team's autonomy and the implicit "guidance" it received from the project champion. Over time, team members' confidence diminished. They looked for direction and reassurance that the "course" they were on was the "right" one. Such direction and reassurance had always been provided in the past. By the third week, many of the team members had stopped participating in the cell, instead taking their "part" of the project back to their own work area. The team was adrift, with neither a detailed plan nor the experience needed to engage in creative cross-functional collaborative work. A coup among some of the remaining team members resulted in settling on "something" – a planned course of action to deliver an acceptable "innovation." They provided some engineering improvements to the initial idea and called it a success.

At the end of the project, leadership applauded the effort. A "lessons learned debriefing" was conducted at the conclusion of the first innovation cell. Here, team members were given the opportunity to provide positive and negative feedback on their experiences. The manager who was the cell's champion "facilitated" the session. A number of significant insights and lessons surfaced during the team debriefing session. However, meaningful details relating to the experiences and social processes in which team members engaged were scrubbed from the final report by the sponsoring manager. In its final form, the report recommended that subsequent innovation cells would benefit from more intensive planning.

The final product of the "lessons learned debriefing" was served up in bullet points that were reported to other senior managers. These senior managers agreed the initial innovation cell was a success and authorized the second cell. Many of the same participants in the first cell were reassigned to participate in the second cell. The lessons learned from the first team, having been scrubbed and sanitized, did not seem meaningful or particularly relevant to the organizers of the new cell; consequently, they were ignored. Not surprisingly, the second cell's experience was a repeat of the first. Both projects for the first and second cell disappeared somewhere in stage 2 in the stage-gate innovation process.

This brief example illustrates some of the unanticipated consequences of the planning view system in which coordination emanates from above and cascades down through the lower echelons, whose residents are expected to achieve the goal of innovation. The story highlights the power of existing interpretive systems to influence actions and interactions even after individuals are explicitly told they have the freedom to create, the freedom to break the rules, the right to challenge norms and change paradigms, and the luxury of failure. What this example implies, and what Mumford et al. identify as an area for further research, are the ways in which institutional structures shape the definition and success of exploratory efforts and the application of the knowledge gained through exploration in mission planning.

Organizations are Both Bureaucratic and Interpretative Systems

Further research might take an interpretive approach – one in which organizations are conceptualized as interpretive systems that exercise social control of cognition. How is innovation defined and practiced at different echelons? What are the ways in which knowledge gained through exploratory efforts is applied at later stages of the innovation process? How is a shared understanding of success and failure negotiated? An interpretive approach may complement the conventional bureaucratic view in which an organization is perceived as a relatively static "network of roles and relationships which channel information, decisions, and authority" (Dougherty & Corse, 1995, p. 72). While normative prescriptions from a senior management perspective instruct workers on what "should" and "must" occur, an interpretive perspective brings to light what is: the implicit rules and unspoken values that direct and shape both individual and collective behavior. In complex organizations, research on both simultaneously is clearly needed.

History, Bureaucracy, and the Problem of Continuity

Many firms, much like our example auto supplier, find themselves in a classic double bind (Bateson, Don, Johnson, Haley, & Weakland, 1956, 1963) when undertaking a major innovation effort. Middle managers are caught in a paradox in which they must innovate, but at the same time are required to maintain bureaucratic efficiency. In theory, bureaucracy and innovation "do not mix" (Dougherty & Corse, 1995). Yet, the new must be developed in a setting historically designed for the old.

Ample evidence indicates that the history of the firm and its structure are important factors in analyzing innovation. For some, a history of success yields absorptive capacity (Cohen & Levinthal, 1990); for others, it yields intransigence (Tushman & Anderson, 1986). And, of course, there is the dismal prospect from population ecology of almost total bureaucratic intransigence (Hannan & Freeman, 1977, 1989). Recent work in strategy has even started to recognize the importance of historically emergent social processes because they may provide the organization with a sustained competitive advantage (Bapuji & Crossan, 2005; Nahapiet & Ghoshal, 1998). Specifically, there is a growing emphasis on developing knowledge and "social capital" as enduring characteristics of a successful firm (Matusik, 2002). Finally, dating back to the work of Burns and Stalker (1966), there is the prospect that fundamental overall structural change may be needed to transform an organization from placing an emphasis on efficiency to pursuing innovation. In sum, researchers have long recognized the mixed pressures from history and structure on the potential for innovation.

Several case studies suggest that larger firms might be able to pursue both efficiency and innovation with periodic chaos followed by temporary stability or with modular designs (Galunic & Eisenhardt, 2001). The use of modular designs is consistent with many successful models of innovation practice within large organizations where firms carve out space for short-lived disruptive (i.e., creative) efforts (Wördenweber & Weissflog, 2005). And yet, as Mumford et al. point out, there are very difficult individual and group issues involved with effectively planning for even short-term period adjustments. In addition to the factors they point out, we suggest future research might include investigations of the bureaucratic model as a worldview. That is, the problem with bureaucracy may lie less in formal structures and the historical drive for efficiency than in the bureaucratic mindset that is so prevalent in large firms.

The bureaucratic model may be seen as an institutionalized system of knowledge and beliefs (Berger & Luckmann, 1967) that evokes a particular set of shared understandings and cognitive maps. Such shared under-standings and cognitive maps are not as much determined by management as they co-evolve with history and experience. History is not automatically fixed, but rather interpreted. Clearly, some aspects of the bureaucratic cognitive map are not compatible with conditions that nurture and support innovation. However, a more detailed analysis may suggest areas of greater compatibility. We clearly need to know more about the evolution and development of the cognitive maps of those who are asked to actually be creative, drive innovation, and successfully move projects from one phase to the next. Can individuals rapidly switch from stability to adaptation? While individuals may have sufficient cognitive capability to make this switch, the Mumford et al. model also alerts us to the potential that group dynamics and processes may block adaptation. These group factors may be yielding "a collective cognitive map" that is much less pliable than the cognitive maps of their members.

We suggest that researchers should rethink the concept of planning in the messy middle. With ephemeral creative spaces, twentieth-century notions of planning "with an eye to efficiency" may need to be replaced by the concept of "situated action"[1] (Suchman, 1987), the product of social processes that are self-organizing, nonlinear, and messy. The notion of "situated action" recognizes the importance of emergent structuration from social processes in the success of innovative efforts.

The recommendation to cultivate situated action suggests that models precisely prescribing how planning should be conducted and how management should control innovation may be limited. They are limited because they assume a high level of managerial control not only over goals, structures, and resources, but also over social processes. These assumptions seem to reconfirm a bureaucratic worldview where planning is separated from doing and control. In this worldview, subordinates do; they do not plan and they do not evaluate. Thus planning for innovation may merely bring forth the very intransigence often attributed to history and structure. In contrast, the analysis of "situated action" calls for interpretations of history as well as active engagement in planning and evaluation by those doing the work. The emphasis is on evolving social processes. These would include, for example, social processes that involve network building (Obstfeld, 2005).

For instance, phenomena such as collaboration (or the lack thereof) are first and foremost products of social processes that result from the actions and interactions of individuals in response to conditions at each level. The outcomes of these social processes are at least as unpredictable and uncertain as the outcome of creative efforts themselves. Furthermore, these social processes are likely to be heavily influenced by interpretations of the history and structure of the organization, including an understanding that most organizations must pursue efficiency just for survival. If emergent social processes characterized as collaborative, trustful, knowledge seeking, and adaptable are viewed as a strategic asset that fosters innovation, senior managers will need to consider how these processes evolve. Consistent with Boal (2004), we suggest that as a part of the planning process researchers should consider how managers link past, present, and future to provide new interpretations of history and structure. Without reinterpretation, the bureaucratic mindset of a fixed history and structure of the firm may dominate and have a deleterious influence on the evolutionary social processes in the middle of the firm.

Perhaps the bureaucratic worldview of senior managers needs adjustment more than the middle needs plans, processes, and coordination. In the messy middle of the organization and the innovation process, we need research suggesting when the mental models of senior executives yield actions consistent with innovation. For instance, recent research suggests that leadership emphasizing patterning of attention and network development may be more appropriate in stimulating innovation than leadership emphasizing transformational visioning or instrumental rewards (Osborn & Marion, 2006). That is, leaders increase the chances of innovation when they do not tell subordinates what to do and how to do it, but rather suggest which issues are important to resolve. To the extent that planning identifies issues, it would be consistent with these results. To the extent that planning tells individuals what to do and how to do it, it could be dysfunctional for innovation. Furthermore, this research suggests that leader-developed networks were also important for greater innovation. Again, planning that helps individuals find connections may be beneficial, whereas planning that specifies connections may be dysfunctional.

It is important to note that this research was based on a conceptual foundation emphasizing emergence from interaction among individuals rather than the more typical emphasis on the traditional bureaucratic model found in many leadership studies. Based on the findings of other studies that are reported in the Mumford et al. chapter, the authors suggest that leadership teams should plan not only mission, process, and collaborations, but also *how the work will occur*. This approach implies that leadership teams are somehow better positioned and more qualified to plan creative and innovative projects than are the individuals and groups that are actually performing the work. Not only does this approach minimize the potential importance of numerous emergent social processes that must be addressed as part of collective collaborative effort, but it also assumes a higher level of managerial control over outcomes and processes than may be possible or desirable.

To the degree managers specify both outcomes and processes, managerial controls in the form of "plans" may restrict and/or conflict with the emergent order that project groups and teams on the ground need. We might think of this condition as "over-systemization." We obviously need research to suggest at what point "planning" and "leadership" devolve into over-systemization. Mumford et al.'s proposed model suggests, and we concur, that some planning and leadership are needed. Clearly, emergent social processes can yield an "order" not desired by management. For this reason, we echo Mumford et al.'s call for more research on when, how, and how much planning is needed. We also call for much more emphasis on social processes.

Although Mumford et al. acknowledge social processes, we believe their treatment, and that of many others taking a managerial perspective, places them in a nearly idealized setting. For example, the authors stress the need for trust and mission commitment in planning, but have not provided insight based on grounded study as to how real people arrive at this state. We are concerned about this omission because managers are advised to develop a portfolio of projects. This portfolio is likely to include both winners and losers – projects selected for further development and those eliminated, respectively. It would seem difficult to develop an aura of trust and mission commitment for those working on projects when it is quite obvious that the algorithm for individual survival and development is a race for short-term commercial success, and not an exploration (cf. March, 1991). Finally, we agree it is nice to develop trust and mission commitment. However, is it necessary, and is such a condition related to innovative success?

WHAT TYPE OF INNOVATION

Finally, we would be remiss not to point out the potential technological boundary conditions of Mumford et al.'s proposed model. All models have boundary conditions (Dubin, 1969). These boundary conditions stipulate areas where they are and are not applicable. Numerous works suggest that the type of technological innovation being pursued may make an important difference regarding how the innovation should be planned and managed (Abernathy & Clark, 1985; Henderson & Clark, 1990; Tushman and Anderson, 1986; Van de Ven et al., 1999). With the emphasis on planning and systemization, it seems clear that Mumford et al.'s model is applicable to what the technological researchers label as incremental innovation – for example, process improvements, the addition of new features to existing designs, or the "D" in "R&D."

Nevertheless, the question remains as to how the model needs to be adjusted to account for radical innovation, technological discontinuities, and technological alterations yielding architectural change. Each of these well-known types of technological innovations calls for fundamental adjustments. These adjustments go far beyond just the introduction of new products, changes in features, extensions into new markets, or improvements in production processes. A quick examination of each suggests some potential boundary conditions on the Mumford et al. model.

Henderson and Clark (1990) suggest that some technological changes call for readjustments well beyond the technical core of the organization. To be successfully implemented, some technological innovations require the organization to alter its managerial infrastructure, change its policies, and, perhaps, adjust its strategy. These reconfigurations would allow the firm to mesh their technological and administrative subsystems. DeSantis, Glass, and Ensing (2002) address this issue in their discussion of organizational designs for R&D. In the Mumford et al. model, managers would be expected to anticipate the administrative requirements from a proposed innovation and plan for a new administrative support subsystem. It is not clear from the model how such adjustments might be undertaken or which planning and processes would be needed to make such adjustments. Clearly, more research on managerial and administrative innovation that occurs to match technological change is warranted.

What we find most interesting is that managerial and administrative innovations often seem to be separated from technological innovations, marketing innovations, or financial innovations. If corporate success is influenced by all of these functional areas, and if each area needs innovation to thrive in a highly competitive environment, we can understand the call to build social capital, intellectual capital, and absorptive capacity (Cohen & Levinthal, 1990; Nahapiet & Ghoshal, 1998) via both exploration and exploitation (March, 1991). At the same time, we would ask Mumford and his colleagues to consider the ramifications of a successful technological innovation program across a wide variety of functional areas for the planners and senior management in their next article. We suggest that our emphasis on dynamic emergence, social processes, history, and organizational structure mentioned earlier may be even more important in the simultaneous implementation of administrative and managerial innovation to cope with technological, marketing, and financial innovation.

Some 20 years ago, Tushman and Anderson (1986) introduced the notion of technological discontinuities. That is, a technological change is seen as being able to invalidate the knowledge and experience base used to successfully manage an older technology. The classic example was transistors replacing tubes. In our mind, there is a question of whether the Mumford et al. model is applicable to innovations involving technological discontinuities. For that matter, we also question whether extensions of existing corporate knowledge and intellectual capital are applicable when technological discontinuities are a dominant feature of a new regime. While few technological innovations are so radical that they invalidate *all* prior knowledge of the old technology, many innovations call for unlearning as well as learning. Managers may need to extinguish part of the old as they build the new. Precisely how managers identify what needs to be discarded and how they discard elements of the old without eliminating what needs to be kept are clearly beyond the capabilities of the proposed model. It is clear to us, however, that future work on the Mumford et al. model should consider the larger-scale integration questions posed by multi-function integration and the elements of technological discontinuities.

CONTESTED TERRAIN

There is little question that the Mumford et al. chapter makes a significant contribution to the emerging stream of literature on creativity and innovation. However, we are concerned that the tone seems overly positive in assuming that prescriptive models are generally uncontested in organizational settings. When the fundamental influences of grounded social processes generated by individual action and interaction are not taken into account, managerial efforts to impose prescriptive models could create a condition of over-systemization. In the messy middle, a little planning may go a long way. We can easily envision managers over-specifying outcomes, processes, and ways to do the work (Bonner et al., 2002). To question the applicability of the model in the messy middle, we charted two quite different approaches to navigation and briefly presented some recent findings of failed innovation. While we, like Mumford et al., provide more questions than answers, it is quite clear that we are calling for much more research emphasis on interpretation by those doing the work, facilitating interaction to increase the changes of dynamic adaptive emergence, and alteration in managerial mindsets to alter how managers attempt to influence those in the middle.

We recognize the value of the contributions made by the authors in establishing how and why planning can contribute to innovative and creative efforts. We also recognize the difficulty of providing an integrative model that would cover individual, group, and organization levels for all stages of the innovation process. Nevertheless, we wonder about the applicability of the model to radical innovations calling for architectural changes and innovations involving technological discontinuities.

We suggest that innovation planning for the middle of the organization and the middle stages of the innovation process should consider a variety of social processes – emergent from the interaction of individuals in their grounded setting. A consideration of these social processes might fundamentally alter how management plans and which questions researchers ask in the future.

NOTE

1. Suchman argues that "planned, purposeful actions are inevitably *situated actions*. By situated actions I mean simply actions taken in the context of particular, concrete circumstances" (1987, p. viii).

REFERENCES

Abernathy, W., & Clark, K. (1985). Innovation: Mapping the winds of creative destruction. *Research Policy, 14*(1), 3–22.

Bapuji, H., & Crossan, M. (2005). Co-evolution of social capital and knowledge: An extension of the Nahapiet and Ghoshal framework. Paper presented at the Academy of Management, Honolulu, HI.

Bateson, G., Don, D., Johnson, M. D., Haley, J., & Weakland, J. H. (1956). Toward a theory of schizophrenia. *Behavioral Science, 1*, 251–264.

Bateson, G., Don, D., Johnson, M. D., Haley, J., & Weakland, J. H. (1963). A note on the double bind-1962. *Family Process, 2*, 154–161.

Berger, P., & Luckmann, T. (1967). *The social construction of reality*. New York, NY: Anchor Books.

Berreman, G. D. (1966). Anemic and emetic analyses in social anthropology. *American Anthropologist, 68*(2), 346–354.

Boal, K. B. (2004). Strategic leadership, organizational learning, and network ties. *Strategic leadership on both sides of the Atlantic: Symposium on strategic leadership*. Lausanne, Switzerland: International Institute for Management Development.

Bonner, J. M., Ruekert, R. W., & Walker, J. O. C. (2002). Upper management control of new product development projects and project performance. *Journal of Product Innovation Management, 19*(3), 233–245.

Brown, S., & Eisenhardt, K. (1995). Product development: Past research, present findings, and future directions. *Academy of Management Review*, *20*, 343–378.

Browning, L., Beyer, J. M., & Shetler, J. C. (1995). Building cooperation in a competitive industry: Sematech and the semiconductor industry. *Academy of Management Journal*, *38*(1), 113–151.

Burns, T., & Stalker, G. M. (1966). *The management of innovation*. London: Tavistock.

Caldart, A. A., & Ricart, J. E. (2004). Corporate strategy revisited: A view from complexity theory. *European Management Review*, *1*, 96–103.

Cohen, W. M., & Levinthal, D. A. (1990). Absorptive capacity: A new perspective on learning and innovation. *Administrative Science Quarterly*, *35*(1), 128–152.

Daft, R. L., & Weick, K. E. (1984). Toward a model of organizations as interpretive systems. *Academy of Management Review*, *9*, 284–295.

DeSantis, G., Glass, J. T., & Ensing, I. M. (2002). Organizational designs for R&D. *Academy of Management Executive*, *16*, 55–66.

Dougherty, D., & Corse, S. (1995). When it comes to product innovation, what is so bad about bureaucracy? *Journal of High Technology Management Research*, *6*, 55–76.

Dubin, R. (1969). *Theory building*. New York, NY: Free Press.

Galunic, D. C., & Eisenhardt, K. M. (2001). Architectural innovation and modular corporate forms. *Academy of Management Journal*, *44*(6), 1229–1249.

Gladwin, T. (1964). Culture and logical process. In: W. H. Goodenough (Ed.), *Explorations in cultural anthropology: Essays in honor of George Peter Murdock* (pp. 167–178). New York, NY: McGraw-Hill.

Hannan, M. T., & Freeman, J. (1977). The population ecology of organizations. *American Journal of Sociology*, *82*, 929–964.

Hannan, M. T., & Freeman, J. (1989). *Organization ecology*. Cambridge, MA: Harvard University Press.

Henderson, R., & Clark, K. (1990). Architectural innovation: The reconfiguration of existing product technologies and the failure of established firms. *Administrative Science Quarterly*, *35*(1), 9–30.

Levinthal, D. A. (1997). Adaptation on rugged landscapes. *Management Science*, *43*(7), 934–950.

Levinthal, D. A., & Warglien, M. (1999). Landscape design: Designing for local action in complex worlds. *Organization Science*, *10*(3), 342–357.

Maguire, S., & McKelvey, B. (1998). Complexity and management: Moving from fad to firm foundations. *Emergence*, *1*, 5–49.

March, J. G. (1991). Exploration and exploitation in organizational learning. *Organization Science*, *2*(1), 71–87.

Matusik, S. F. (2002). An empirical investigation of firm public and private knowledge. *Strategic Management Journal*, *23*(5), 457.

McGrath, R. G. (2001). Exploratory learning, innovative capacity, and managerial oversight. *Academy of Management Review*, *44*(1), 118–131.

Miller, C. (2006). *The impact of formalization on innovation: An ethnographic study of process formalization*. Unpublished Ph.D. dissertation. Wayne State University, Detroit, MI.

Morris, J. A. (1996). The dimensions, antecedents, and consequences of emotional labor. *Academy of Management Review*, *21*(4), 986.

Mumford, M., Bedell-Avers, K., & Hunter, S. (this volume). Planning for Innovation: A multi-level perspective. In: M. Mumford, S. Hunter & K. Bedell-Avers (Eds), *Multi-level issues in creativity and innovation* (Vol. 7). Oxford: Elsevier.

Nahapiet, J., & Ghoshal, S. (1998). Social capital, intellectual capital, and the organizational advantage. *Academy of Management Review*, *23*(2), 242–266.

Obstfeld, D. (2005). Social networks, the tertius lungens orientation, and involvement in innovation. *Administrative Science Quarterly*, *50*(1), 100–131.

Osborn, R., & Marion, R. (2006). *Complexity leadership, transformational leadership and the performance of international innovation seeking alliances.* Detroit, MI: Wayne State University Department of Business.

Osborn, R. N., Hunt, J. G., & Jauch, L. R. (2002). Toward a contextual theory of leadership. *Leadership Quarterly*, *13*, 797–837.

Smircich, L., & Stubbart, C. (1985). Strategic management in an enacted world. *Academy of Management Review*, *10*, 724–737.

Suchman, L. A. (1987). *Plans and situated actions.* New York, NY: Cambridge University Press.

Tushman, M., & Anderson, P. (1986). Technological discontinuities and organizational environments. *Administrative Science Quarterly*, *31*, 439–465.

Tzeng, C. H. (2006). Lenovo computer in Beijing Zhongguancun: From entrepreneurial startup to large innovative firm. Paper presented at the Academy of Management, Atlanta, GA.

Van de Ven, A. H. (1986). Central problems in the management of innovation. *Management Science*, *32*(5), 590–607.

Van de Ven, A. H., Polley, D., Garud, R., & Venkataraman, S. (1999). *The innovation journey.* New York, NY: Oxford University Press.

Weick, K. E. (1979). *The social psychology of organizing* (2nd ed.). Reading, MA: Addison-Wesley.

Wördenweber, B., & Weissflog, U. (2005). *Innovation cell: Agile teams to master disruptive innovation.* Berlin: Springer.

CONSTRAINTS ON INNOVATION: PLANNING AS A CONTEXT FOR CREATIVITY

Michael D. Mumford, Samuel T. Hunter and Katrina E. Bedell-Avers

ABSTRACT

Plans and planning have a long and checkered history. In their commentaries, Ettlie (this volume) and Miller and Osborn (this volume) take rather different views on the need for planning in innovative projects. In this commentary, we take the position that innovation requires constraints. These constraints induce certain risk factors that warrant attention, such as oversystemization. By the same token, they produce conditions, including social conditions that make sustained innovation possible. Based on these observations, some potential directions for future research are discussed.

INTRODUCTION

Creativity and innovation – that is, the translation of new ideas into visible products and processes – are critical to organizational performance in the twenty-first-century economy (Florida, 2002; Janssen, van de Vliert, &

Multi-Level Issues in Creativity and Innovation
Research in Multi-Level Issues, Volume 7, 191–200
Copyright © 2008 by Elsevier Ltd.
ISSN: 1475-9144/doi:10.1016/S1475-9144(07)00008-2

West, 2004). The fundamental importance of creativity to organizational performance, in turn, suggests that organizations must plan for creativity. Unfortunately, the weed or seed models that have been traditionally used as a basis for planning for creativity are ultimately inadequate. This observation led Mumford, Bedell-Avers, and Hunter (this volume) to propose a new framework that might be used to facilitate organizational planning for creativity. More specifically, we proposed a multi-level framework that took into account organizational-, group-, and individual-level influences within a dynamic system where creative projects unfold over time as organizations create and explore the implications of new ideas.

Both Ettlie (this volume) and Miller and Osborn (this volume), in their commentaries, conclude that the multi-level model of creative planning proposed by Mumford et al. is plausible. Nonetheless, both also raise certain questions about the model we have proposed. Accordingly, we will, in the present commentary, attempt to answer the questions broached by Ettlie as well as Miller and Osborn. Before turning to these questions, however, we will briefly return to certain key assumptions underlying this model as anticipated by Ettlie.

CONSTRAINTS

Ettlie (this volume) begins his commentary by articulating three key assumptions underlying the model of innovation planning proposed by Mumford et al. (this volume) – specifically, assumptions involving learning, time, and constraints. It is, of course, difficult to conceive of any model of organizational planning for innovation that does not involve learning. New ideas, however valuable, must be developed if they are to prove useful to an organization. And, by virtue of their novelty, the organization must learn about both the implications of these ideas and their consequences for organizational operations. This learning process unfolds over time, with planning requiring decision making about the value of continued exploration (March, 1991).

Few scholars would dispute the necessity of assumptions made about learning and time in any viable model of organizational innovation. More controversial is the assumption implicit in our model about the importance of constraints. Ettlie (this volume) correctly argues that implicit in any plan are a set of constraints. At least taken at face value, the imposition of such constraints would seem to inhibit creativity and innovation. In fact, our naive conceptions of the creative person see a person who transcends the manifold constraints imposed by the day-to-day world in which others live.

The literature on creative thought, however, paints a rather different picture of the need for, and relevance of, constraints to the production of viable new ideas. Expertise, or knowledge, ultimately represents a set of constraints as the creator works within a body of extant knowledge. What should be recognized here is that virtually all studies indicate that expertise is critical to the production of viable new ideas (Ericsson & Charness, 1994; Weisberg, 1999). Moreover, Finke, Ward, and Smith (1992), in their experimental studies of creative thought, have shown that the imposition of constraints during idea generation is a critical influence – specifically, a positive critical influence – on the generation of viable new ideas.

There is, in fact, no reason to expect that the imposition of constraints would prove any less important to innovation in organizational settings. Rather, we would expect that the imposition of these constraints would prove ever more important. In organizations, ideas often fail to be developed into viable new products and services because organizational capital is not effectively brought to bear on their development. Organizational capital, however, is necessarily a constraint on idea generation. Moreover, the organization's operating environment, customers, suppliers, competitors, and technology all represent constraints on the development of new ideas and innovative new products. Essentially, then, we would argue that innovation in organizations is inherently a constrained activity.

Not only is organizational innovation an inherently constrained activity, but also the plans organizations formulate for innovation can also be viewed as a set of self-imposed constraints. The fundamental importance of these constraints is perhaps best illustrated by the need for the organization to consider fundamentals in its planning process for innovation (Hughes, 1989). Ultimately, the decision to pursue one set of fundamentals implies that other fundamentals will not be pursued by the organization. This rather straightforward observation has an important implication, one noted by both Ettlie (this volume) and Miller and Osborn (this volume): Planning for innovation will ultimately depend on the decisions made by leaders as they place constraints on the innovation process (Mumford, Scott, Gaddis, & Strange, 2002).

In our view, the key to understanding planning for innovation is, in fact, the selection of appropriate constraints to be imposed on the generation and development of new ideas. What should be recognized in this regard is that planning for innovation is something more than simply formulating a set of constraints. Planning for innovation in part depends on the nature of the constraints imposed and the timing of constraint imposition. Thus, immediate practical benefits, such as financial evaluation criteria, should not be applied in initial exploratory efforts. By the same token, an adequate research base indicating precisely which constraints should be imposed at which point in the idea development process is woefully lacking. This lack of information on relevant constraints and the optimal timing of their implementation represents what is perhaps one of the potentially important directions for future research on organizational innovation.

OVERSYSTEMIZATION

These observations about the constraints imposed by planning for innovation bring us to the commentary of Miller and Osborn (this volume). These authors bring to the fore a problem likely to be broached in any discussion of planning for innovation – that is, the possibility that planning might lead to oversystemization. Oversystemization, in turn, may represent a significant block to the production of new ideas and thus the fielding of viable new products and services.

Although we would not dispute that oversystemization is a risk, it may not be a necessary outcome of planning for innovation. Oversystemization can inhibit creativity and innovation when the standards applied in appraising ideas are inappropriate (Mumford, Blair, Dailey, Leritz, & Osborn, 2006). What should be recognized in this regard, however, is that not all standards applied in evaluating ideas inherently inhibit creativity and innovation (Mumford, Connelly, & Gaddis, 2003). For example, Kitchell (1995) found that if the criteria applied in the evaluation process stress growth and adaptability, rather than short-term financial return, innovation will be enhanced. In fact, one might argue that planning for innovation will often prove useful in enhancing innovation precisely because such planning exercises serve to disseminate appropriate evaluation standards throughout the organization.

Of course, in Miller and Osborn's (this volume) commentary, the risks attached to oversystemization are not simply a matter of the standards applied in appraising ideas. In their view, the development of a systematic process for innovation planning will often "shut out people and their ideas" based on their position. In fact, Ettlie (this volume) makes a similar comment in his discussion of the importance of "off-the-books" work in creative ventures. At one level, shutting out people, and their ideas, may seem to inhibit innovation. Nevertheless, one must remember that innovation in organizations is inherently a slow process in which requisite expertise is acquired over time. One implication of this observation is that, ultimately, it may be necessary to shut out some people, and some ideas, as organizations invest their resources in exploring certain avenues as opposed to others. It is, in fact, this exploration that provides the background needed for subsequent "off-the-books" work and results in the production of ideas that are likely to prove of value to the organization.

Clearly, we do not believe oversystemization to be as great a risk as Miller and Osborn (this volume) suggest. In fact, we would argue that if the initial stages of the idea generation and development process are managed as suggested in the model we proposed, the likelihood of oversystemization is rather small. Most initial template planning and plan development efforts can be, and should be, expected to fail. It is these failures, and the learning they engender, that build the capabilities needed for sustained innovation.

Although we do not perceive oversystemization as significant a risk to innovation in the model proposed by Mumford et al. (this volume), we believe this comment leads to a broader question: Oversystemization with respect to what? Innovation suffers in an organization because (1) fundamentals and themes are not adequately explored (Hughes, 1989), (2) adequate sustained resources are not provided (Dougherty & Hardy, 1996), and (3) organizational operations are not realized to take the implications of the innovation into account (Tushman & O'Reilly, 1997). Under these conditions, oversystemization of the innovation process may be the only answer.

COMPLEXITY

Underlying Miller and Osborn's (this volume) views concerning over-systemization is a broader theoretical model based on organizational complexity theory. Within this model, interactions occurring among networks of individuals give rise to new ideas. The ideas that "bubble up" from these complex patterns of interchange are assumed, if viable, to develop a kind of "gravitational pull" such that the organization intuitively realigns itself to pursue these ideas. This complexity theory model is, of course, similar to Eisenhardt and Tabrizi's (1995) seed model. We would question its value as a basis for innovation on several grounds.

First, complex systems are overdetermined. By the term "overdetermined," we mean that interactions and inter-reactions shape individuals' appraisal and evaluation of ideas. In a complex, overdetermined system, people will generate ideas. More often than not, these ideas will represent incremental extensions of current operations. Although these naturally emerging incremental extensions of current operations may prove useful in enhancing efficiency, it is open to question whether they will, in fact, produce anything truly new – in other words, radical, major innovations.

Second, radical major innovations, regardless of whether they are process or product innovations, are almost by definition alien to a complex organizational system. On the one hand, the alien nature of major, radical innovations arises from the fact that they lie outside the system. On the other hand, the alien nature of these ideas arises from the lack of expertise that members of the organizational system have in working with them. Under these conditions, complex systems will tend to reject new ideas unless expertise is progressively built up over time. This learning, which admittedly may occur in a complex fashion, is critical to planning for innovation.

Third, the idea that new ideas "bubble up" overlooks a critical set of constraints. As Ettlie (this volume) points out, development of innovative new ideas requires a substantial amount of time and a substantial invest-ment of organizational resources. The time and cost involved in nurturing innovations, especially radical innovations, require that informed decisions be made as to whether an idea is worth pursing. Moreover, the organization must develop the expertise, and systems, needed to pursue this idea. Given these constraints, it is difficult to see how ideas can simply "bubble up."

These points about complexity can be made more concrete by considering two major innovations: IBM's development of its first personal computer and DuPont's development of synthetic fibers. Although IBM did successfully develop a personal computer, this development occurred outside the normative organization, which was viewed as a significant impediment to efforts along these lines due to its prior investments in the mainframe computer market. DuPont's development of synthetic fibers was ultimately based on the recognition that the gunpowder business was waning and that organic chemistry was a promising new avenue for exploiting extant corporate expertise in chemistry. DuPont's profits from World War I were thus expended to find an extended research and development effort that became a basis for building a new business.

SOCIAL SYSTEMS

Although we do not see the "bubble-up" model proposed by Miller and Osborn (this volume) as having much value in planning for innovation, it did lead these authors to ask questions about social systems and their role in the process of planning for innovation. A similar question is broached by Ettlie (this volume) in his discussion of leadership, entrepreneurship, and teamwork. Of course, social interactions do influence the process of planning for innovation. At the same time, we would caution all those interested in innovation not to underestimate the complexity of these influences.

Studies of innovation are often informed primarily by impressions. But do these "naive" impressions, in fact, hold over time? An illustration of this point may be found in the work of Miller and Osborn (this volume), who argue that middle managers by virtue of the production pressure placed on them will constitute a noteworthy blockage to the acceptance of creative ideas "bubbling up" from the people actually doing the work. As plausible as this idea might seem at first glance, it is open to question whether this is, in fact, the case.

Mumford, Marks, Connelly, Zaccaro, and Reiter-Palmon (2000) developed a set of measures examining leaders' creative thinking skills (e.g., problem construction, conceptual combination). When these measures were administered to 1,818 junior, mid-level, and senior army officers, it was found that creative thinking skills peaked in the mid-career period, with more-senior officers demonstrating stronger idea-evaluation skills. Given the relatively strong creative thinking skills evidenced by this particular sample of middle managers, it seems to us open to question whether middle managers are truly adverse to creative ideas.

We bring up the results of this study not just to dispute the arguments being made by Miller and Osborn (this volume), but also to illustrate a critical point. We often do not know enough to make strong statements about social system influences on innovation. To reiterate this point, consider two conclusions often drawn about social influences on organizational innovation. First, it is often assumed that diversity facilitates innovation. Perhaps this is true in idea evaluation, but the problems posed by a lack of shared structures may limit diversity's value in initial idea generation (Mumford, Feldman, Hein, & Nago, 2001). Second, we tend to assume that supportive leaders will facilitate innovation. In truth, the bulk of the available findings indicate that leaders who define and articulate challenging technical missions are the individuals who are most likely to stimulate innovation (Mumford et al., 2002).

In our view, these observations point to a need for further research on exactly how social interactional variables shape the process of planning for innovation. In fact, Ettlie (this volume) lays out at least three key areas that warrant further attention. First, within the model of planning under consideration, leaders will play a key role (Mumford et al., 2002). Thus, there is a need for research examining the mental models applied by leaders in planning for innovation as well as studies examining the criteria applied in evaluating creative work at different stages of development. Second, creative work is held to occur in teams, with these teams changing in composition as ideas are progressively refined. What we do not know, however, is how these teams should structure themselves and how changes in team composition should be managed. Third, in framing innovative projects, both "push" (new technological capabilities) and "pull" (customer demand) factors are operating. What is unclear is how these push and pull forces are evaluated and integrated as organizations plan innovations.

Research along these lines will likely prove most valuable if it takes into account other considerations. First, as noted by Ettlie (this volume), innovation, and planning for innovation, is inherently controversial. Innovation planning occurs under conditions of uncertainty and ambiguity. This uncertainty and ambiguity indicates that conflict, debate, and politics will surround innovation planning. What we do not know much about is how innovative organizations act to manage this political debate and which strategies they apply in resolving this debate.

Second, innovation ultimately requires sharing information. People and organizations, however, are inherently limited information processes. These constraints inevitably result in restrictions on individuals' forecasting abilities – a limitation that may undermine the entire innovation planning process. These observations not only suggest a need for information sharing and planning tools, but also point to a need for studies examining the social process variables – for example, idea selling and entrepreneurship – that serve to offset the limitations that constrain individuals' information processing and forecasting.

Innovation planning is an inherently social process. It not only builds absorptive capability, but also sends a message to the organization about which ideas are valued and why they are valued. Thus, in research examining social influences on innovation planning, it may not be sufficient simply to examine social influences on planning. We may also need to examine the social influences of the planning process on organizational innovation.

CONCLUSIONS

As implied by our foregoing observations, planning for innovation is an inherently complex phenomenon – a phenomenon that is shaped by the organization just as it shapes the organization and its future. Mumford et al. (this volume) presented a normative model describing how effective planning for innovation might occur in organizational settings. The viability of this model, development of which is unique in its own right, is most aptly illustrated in the depth of the questions broached by these commentaries. Indeed, these commentaries point to some noteworthy, and potentially significant, directions for future research.

These commentaries, moreover, remind us of a basic point: Creativity and innovation do not operate in a free and open fashion. Rather, creativity and innovation are constrained phenomena – constrained by the questions we ask and the lessons we learn as we work through these questions over time. Ultimately, the importance of innovation planning may derive as much from the questions formulated and the issues explored through this process as from the particular ideas developed into viable new products and services.

REFERENCES

Dougherty, D., & Hardy, B. F. (1996). Sustained innovation production in large mature organizations: Overcoming organization problems. *Academy of Management Journal, 39*, 826–851.

Eisenhardt, K. M., & Tabrizi, B. N. (1995). Accelerating adaptive processes: Product innovation in the global computer industry. *Administrative Science Quarterly, 40*, 84–110.

Ericsson, K. A., & Charness, W. (1994). Expert performance: Its structure and acquisition. *American Psychologist, 49*, 725–747.

Ettlie, J. E. (this volume). Templates for innovation. In: M. D. Mumford, S. T. Hunter & K. E. Bedell-Avers (Eds), *Research in multi-level issues vol. 7: Multi-level issues in creativity and innovation.* Oxford, UK: Elsevier.

Finke, R. A., Ward, T. B., & Smith, S. M. (1992). *Creative cognition: Theory, research, and applications.* Cambridge, MA: MIT Press.

Florida, R. (2002). *The rise of the creative class.* New York: Basic Books.

Hughes, T. P. (1989). *American genesis: A history of the American genius for invention.* New York: Penguin.

Janssen, O., van de Vliert, E., & West, M. (2004). The bright and dark sides of individual and group innovation: A special issue introduction. *Journal of Organizational Behavior, 25*, 129–146.

Kitchell, S. (1995). Corporate culture, environmental adaptation, and innovation adoption: A quantitative/qualitative approach. *Journal of the Academy of Marketing Science, 23*, 195–205.

March, J. G. (1991). Exploration and exploitation in organizational learning. *Organization Science, 2*, 71–87.

Miller, C., & Osborn, R. N. (this volume). Innovation as contested terrain: Planned creativity and innovation versus emergent creativity and innovation. In: M. D. Mumford,

S. T. Hunter & K. E. Bedell-Avers (Eds), *Research in multi-level issues vol. 7: Multi-level issues in creativity and innovation.* Oxford, UK: Elsevier.

Mumford, M. D., Bedell-Avers, K. E., & Hunter, S. T. (Eds). (this volume). Planning for innovation: A multi-level perspective. *Research in multi-level issues vol. 7: Multi-level issues in creativity and innovation.* Oxford, UK: Elsevier.

Mumford, M. D., Blair, C., Dailey, L. R., Leritz, L. E., & Osborn, H. K. (2006). Errors in creative thought? Cognitive biases in a computer processing activity. *Journal of Creative Behavior, 40,* 75–109.

Mumford, M. D., Connelly, M. S., & Gaddis, B. (2003). How creative leaders think: Experimental findings and cases. *Leadership Quarterly, 14,* 411–432.

Mumford, M. D., Feldman, J. M., Hein, M. B., & Nago, D. J. (2001). Tradeoffs between ideas and structure: Individual versus group performance in creative problem-solving. *Journal of Creative Behavior, 35,* 1–23.

Mumford, M. D., Marks, M. A., Connelly, M. S., Zaccaro, S. T., & Reiter-Palmon, R. (2000). Development of leadership skills: Experiences and timing. *Leadership Quarterly, 11,* 87–114.

Mumford, M. D., Scott, G. M., Gaddis, B., & Strange, J. M. (2002). Leading creative people: Orchestrating expertise and relationships. *Leadership Quarterly, 13,* 705–750.

Tushman, M. L., & O'Reilly, C. A. (1997). *Winning through innovation.* Cambridge, MA: Harvard Business School Press.

Weisberg, R. W. (1999). Creativity and knowledge: A challenge to theories. In: R. J. Sternberg (Ed.), *Handbook of creativity* (pp. 226–259). Cambridge, UK: Cambridge University Press.

PART III:
CREATIVITY AND COGNITIVE PROCESSES

CREATIVITY AND COGNITIVE PROCESSES: MULTI-LEVEL LINKAGES BETWEEN INDIVIDUAL AND TEAM COGNITION

Roni Reiter-Palmon, Anne E. Herman and
Francis J. Yammarino

ABSTRACT

This chapter provides an in-depth understanding of the cognitive processes that facilitate creativity from a multi-level perspective. Because cognitive processes are viewed as residing within the individual and as an individual-level phenomenon, it is not surprising that a plethora of research has focused on various cognitive processes involved in creative production at the individual level and the factors that may facilitate or hinder the successful application of these processes. Of course, individuals do not exist in a vacuum, and many organizations are utilizing teams and groups to facilitate creative problem solving. We therefore extend our knowledge from the individual to the team level and group level, providing more than 50 propositions for testing and discussing their implications for future research.

Multi-Level Issues in Creativity and Innovation
Research in Multi-Level Issues, Volume 7, 203–267
Copyright © 2008 by Elsevier Ltd.
All rights of reproduction in any form reserved
ISSN: 1475-9144/doi:10.1016/S1475-9144(07)00009-4

INTRODUCTION

Innovation has been claimed to be a critical force in organizational performance and survival (Dess & Picken, 2000; Ford & Gioia, 1995; Mumford & Hunter, 2005; Shalley, Zhou, & Oldham, 2004). Changes in technology, globalization, and increased competition have all created an environment in which creativity and innovation are needed to cope with the situational and economic pressures and frequent changes (Mumford, Scott, Gaddis, & Strange, 2002c; Shalley et al., 2004; West, Hirst, Richter, & Shipton, 2004; Woodman, Sawyer, & Griffin, 1993). More recently, it has been suggested that the rise and fall of economic development of cities is based on the "creative class" – those individuals who engage in creative work (Florida, 2002). Not surprisingly, then, organizational researchers have become increasingly interested in understanding the antecedents of creativity in organizations.

One important factor affecting creative problem solving is that of creative thought processes. Much of the work on creative thought processes has focused on understanding these processes at the individual level (Mumford, Mobley, Uhlman, Reiter-Palmon, & Doares, 1991; Ward, Smith, & Finke, 1999). Only limited information is available on how these cognitive processes operate at the team level or group level. Therefore, this chapter seeks to provide an understanding of both the individual and the team or group cognitive processes involved in creative problem solving. It opens with a discussion of models of cognitive processes involved in creative problem solving developed at the individual level. This exploration is followed by a comprehensive review of each core process and the research conducted at the individual level on the various factors that influence the effective application of that process. When available, research extending the application of the process at the team and group levels is also reviewed; if no such research has been conducted to date, hypotheses about the effect and nature of the aggregation of the individual cognitive efforts are offered.

Because of the limited research available at the team or group level, and the extensiveness of the research at the individual level, the propositions offered in this chapter focus on the team and group.

FACTORS INFLUENCING CREATIVITY

Rhodes (1987) has suggested that four factors or categories of variables have an influence on creativity. His "four P's of creativity" scheme provides a useful tool for organizing the research on creativity:

- Person – characteristics of the individual that make him or her creative
- Product – an outcome approach to creativity, focusing on an idea, solution, or product
- Press – environmental and contextual factors that influence creative performance
- Process – cognitive process and thinking techniques that lead to more creativity

Early work on creativity tended to concentrate on the person and individual difference variables that led to creativity. Creativity was identified as a phenomenon residing within an individual; consequently, the study of creativity focused on the characteristics that make that individual unique, different, and creative (Mumford, 2003). The result was a study of eminent individuals and an understanding of creativity from the perspective of traits that distinguish creative individuals from those who are not creative (Barron & Harrington, 1981; Feist, 1999). Individual difference characteristics that were studied included intelligence; personality variables such as openness to experience, independence, and thinking styles; and motivational variables such as achievement motivation and intrinsic motivation (Amabile, 1983; Barron & Harrington, 1981; Shalley et al., 2004). Another important variable studied at the individual level was that of cognitive processes involved in creative production, whose exploration started with the work of Guilford (1950).

Of course, creativity does not exist in a vacuum. Contextual variables exert a strong influence on creative production. Research on contextual factors that facilitate or inhibit creativity has also typically evaluated creativity from the individual's perspective, however. Issues of organizational culture, leadership, organizational structure, and rewards have all been studied in this context (Amabile & Gryskiewicz, 1989; Arad, Hanson, & Schnieder, 1997; Shalley et al., 2004).

Finally, the product approach to creativity permeates all of these research streams. Most of the research on creativity today identifies creativity in terms of the outcome. Creativity is defined as a product (i.e., idea, solution) that is both novel or original, and useful or appropriate (Amabile, 1996; Mumford & Gustafson, 1988; Woodman et al., 1993).

Although all of these factors are important in the study and understanding of creativity and innovation, this chapter focuses on one aspect – that is, it provides an in-depth understanding of the cognitive processes that facilitate creativity from a multi-level perspective. Because cognitive processes are viewed as residing within the individual and as an individual-level phenomenon, not surprisingly, a plethora of research has focused on cognitive processes involved in creative production at the individual level and the various factors that may facilitate or hinder the successful application of these processes (Brophy, 1998a; Mumford, Baughman, & Sager, 2003; Mumford et al., 1991; Ward et al., 1999).

Groups and teams have emerged as a strong force in how organizations respond to and cope with the need for change (Devine, Clayton, Phillips, Dunford, & Melner, 1999; West et al., 2004). It has been suggested that creativity and innovation, because of the complexity of the problems currently facing organizations, is not a solitary activity today. Rather, the need to have diverse skills and knowledge requires the use of teams (Dunbar, 1997; Paulus & Nijstad, 2003). However, research on the cognitive processes of creative problem solving at the group level is more limited. While quite a bit of research has investigated brainstorming (Brophy, 1998b; Paulus & Paulus, 1997; Rickards, 1999), other cognitive processes relating to team creative performance have not been as heavily researched. Further, even when the term "team cognition" is used in team research, it typically connotes team member schemas about team interactions and other team members – a social cognitive phenomenon (Rentsch & Woehr, 2004; Salas & Fiore, 2004). Finally, models of team cognition typically focus on individual cognition, paying only limited attention to the effect of the group on these individual cognitive processes (Brophy, 1998b; Santanen, 2006; Smith, Gerkens, Shah, & Vargas-Hernandez, 2006).

Therefore, the purpose of this paper is to provide a comprehensive review of the cognitive process involved in creative problem solving. The paper will open with a discussion of models of cognitive processes involved in creative problem solving developed at the individual level, then followed by a comprehensive review of each core process and the research conducted at the individual level on factors that influence the effective application of that process. When available, team and group research extending the application of the process at the team level and group level will also be reviewed, and if not, hypotheses about the effect and nature of the aggregation of the individual cognitive efforts will be offered. Finally, in each section focusing on team- or group-level processes, a number of propositions for extending the research beyond our current understanding will be developed. Because the individual-level literature on creativity and cognitive processes is fairly well established, we see no need to re-state propositions that have been eloquently and generally stated, and in many cases tested, previously. As such, we focus on new or newer group-level or team-level propositions as well as multi-level propositions regarding creativity and cognitive processes that heretofore have not been explicitly advanced nor fully tested in prior work.

Table 1. Summary of Propositions.

Process Title	Proposition
Problem identification and construction	1–9
Information search and encoding	10–19
Idea and solution generation	20–34
Idea evaluation and selection	35–40
Implementation planning and monitoring	42–50
Conclusions	51–54

At this point it is important to note that this chapter does not address all the possible influences on the creative problem solving process in individuals and teams. There are multiple other factors that affect the application of these processes at the individual level such as affect (James, Brodersen, & Eisenberg, 2004; Lubart & Getz, 1997), personality variables (Barron & Harrington, 1981; Feist, 1999), and motivation (Amabile, 1996). Further these variables may have different effects depending on the process (Kaufmann & Vosburg, 2002). In addition, similar and additional factors that may influence the application at the team level include team composition (West et al., 2004), social processes (Drach-Zahavy & Somech, 2001), leadership (Howell & Boies, 2004; Shalley & Gilson, 2004), and team and organizational culture (Mathisen & Einarsen, 2004). These factors are important but are beyond the scope of this chapter.

Moreover, while there is a distinction in the literature between the notions of "groups" and "teams," these differences are not always clear to all researchers or without controversy (Paulus, Nakui & Putman, 2006). As such, for our purposes in this article, we tend to use the terms "groups" and "teams" interchangeably, as our focus is on the next higher level of analysis above the "individual" rather than on the distinction between groups and teams per se.

To facilitate the reading of this paper, Table 1 provides a summary of the various propositions advanced in the text, organized by the specific processes discussed. The table is provided as both a starting point and a summary for the information presented in further detail below.

COGNITIVE MODELS OF CREATIVE PROBLEM SOLVING

Creative problem-solving models are based on the same cognitive processes that are used for solving more routine problems that do not call for creativity. Not all problems require creative solutions, and not all applications of the cognitive processes result in a creative outcome (Brophy, 1998a). It is only when the need for a creative solution exists and successful application of the cognitive process follows that creativity is observed. Creative problem solving is more likely to occur when the problem is ill defined and novel (Dillion, 1982; Mumford et al., 1991). When the problem presented to the problem solver is novel, he or she cannot rely on tried-and-true solutions or approaches; rather, the problem calls for non-routine application of cognitive processes. Ill-defined problems are characterized by multiple possible goals, multiple possible approaches to solving the problem, and multiple possible and acceptable solutions (Dillion, 1982; Mumford et al., 1991; Schraw, Dunkle, & Benedixen, 1995).

Multiple models of cognitive processes relevant to creative problem solving exist (e.g., Finke, Ward, & Smith, 1992; Merrifield, Guilford, Christensen, & Frick, 1962; Mumford et al., 1991; Osborn, 1953; Silverman, 1985; Sternberg, 1988). Several core processes can be identified that cut across these models, including problem construction or problem identification, information search and gathering, idea generation, idea evaluation and selection, and implementation planning and monitoring. The first three processes are typically viewed as part of the idea-generation phase, whereas the last two are considered part of the implementation phase (Basadur, 1997; Ford, 1996; Mumford, 2001; West, 2002a).

A few points regarding these processes should be noted. First, most models suggest that people may cycle back to earlier processes, either routinely or as a result of difficulties encountered at a later process, so that the progression from one process to the next may not be linear. Second, the quality of the later processes may depend on the effort and quality of earlier processes, suggesting that all processes are critical for creative problem solving.

PROBLEM IDENTIFICATION AND CONSTRUCTION

Individual Level

Problem construction is defined as the process of identifying that a problem exists and defining the goals and parameters of the problem-solving effort (Basadur, Ellspermann, & Evans, 1994; Mumford, Reiter-Palmon, & Redmond, 1994; Pitz, Sachs, & Heerboth, 1980). The same ill-defined problems that give rise to creative problem solving also place a premium on problem construction. Well-defined problems, by definition, are those problems where the goals and parameters are defined, and the appropriate solution is known, if not to the problem solver then to someone else – for example, a teacher (Dillion, 1982; Getzels, 1979). Ill-defined problems, in contrast, do not have known goals or solutions, and they may have multiple goals and solutions (Dillion, 1982; Schraw et al., 1995). As a result, the first step in the creative problem-solving effort is problem identification, definition, and construction (Basadur, Runco, & Vega, 2000; Finke et al., 1992; Lubart, 2001; Mumford et al., 1991). Because this structuring is the first step in creative problem solving, it provides the context for the application of later processes and, therefore, is viewed as having a marked impact on creative problem solving as a whole as well as on later processes (Adelman, Gualtieri, & Stanford, 1995; Mumford et al., 1994; Rostan, 1997; Scott, Leritz, & Mumford, 2004).

Research on problem identification and problem construction at the individual level reveals that this process is critical for effective creative problem solving. In one of the first studies on problem construction, Getzels and Csikszentmihalyi (1975, 1976) observed art students as they prepared to paint a still-life painting. This preparation, which included the number of objects and uniqueness of objects investigated before a final setup was selected and the amount of time used for exploration prior to actually painting, was identified as problem identification. The paintings of the art students who engaged in more problem construction activities were judged to be more creative by expert judges. Further, a longitudinal follow-up of the same students found that students who engaged in more problem construction activities also were more successful artists seven years later. Other studies have found that problem construction is related to solution quality and originality in solving real-life problems, and that problem construction ability explains creativity above and beyond intelligence and divergent thinking (Okuda, Runco, & Berger, 1991; Reiter-Palmon, Mumford, & Threlfall, 1998; Runco & Okuda, 1988; Smilansky, 1984).

Mumford et al. (1994) presented a model that attempted to explain how problem construction exerts its influence on creative problem solving and to identify the variables that may influence this process. Their model is based on the notion of problem representations (Gick & Holyoak, 1983; Holyoak, 1984). Problem representations are categories or schemas constructed to represent previous problem-solving efforts and include four elements: (1) the goals of the problem-solving effort; (2) key information necessary to solve the problem; (3) key procedures needed to solve the problem; and (4) the constraints placed on the solution.

Mumford et al. (1994) suggested that the first step involves attention. Specific cues would indicate that further attention to the situation and the problem is necessary. They may include personally relevant cues, surprising or incongruent cues, and cues that signal a discrepancy from the desired state. Some of these cues will be associated with one or more problem representations from previous experiences. When the problem is ill defined or novel, there are no direct matches between all the features from an available problem representation and the new situation. As a result, problem representations may be activated based on partial similarity to the cues. In addition, multiple problem representations will be activated. To complete the problem construction process, either one of the activated problem representations must be selected as the one used to define the current problem or a new problem representation must be created from some or all of the activated problem representations.

This model underscores the importance of attentional resources to the problem construction process. Problem construction can occur more automatically when the problem solver frames the problem in ways that fit with past experiences and existing problem representations (Bagozzi & Dholakia, 2005; Holyoak, 1984; Johnson, Daniels, & Huff, 2001; Mumford et al., 1994). Research supports the notion that when problem construction is more deliberate, and more time is spent, more creative solutions result. Deliberate problem construction has been manipulated by requesting participants to think about some or all of the different elements of the problem representation prior to solving the problem or by training the problem construction process, thereby calling attention to the need for problem construction (Baer, 1988; Basadur, Graen, & Green, 1982; Redmond, Mumford, & Teach, 1993; Reiter-Palmon, Mumford, O'Connor Boes, & Runco, 1997; Scott et al., 2004).

Because problem construction is based on past experience and familiarity with similar problems, and attention to cues signaling a problem, it is expected that expertise will play a role in problem construction. Studies comparing experts and novices suggest that experts spend more time constructing ill-defined problems, whereas novices spend more time attempting to solve ill-defined problems (Kay, 1991; Rostan, 1994; Voss, Wolfe, Lawrence, & Engle, 1991). However, because experts have a well-organized set of problem representations that are linked to specific trigger cues, they may be more likely to rely on tried-and-true solutions, represented by a single problem representation, and possibly more automatic application of the problem construction process; this factor may explain the curvilinear relationship observed between expertise and creativity (Basadur, 1994; Hoover & Feldhusen, 1994; Mumford & Gustafson, 1988).

Finally, attention to one or more elements of the problem representation may influence the problem construction process. Mumford, Baughman, Threlfall, Supinski, and Costanza (1996b) investigated the importance of the four elements of the problem representation in relation to the development of creative solutions. In this study, participants first read a problem, and then were presented with 16 different ways in which it could be redefined. Participants were asked to read through these 16 alternative problem definitions and select the four best definitions. The 16 statements reflected one of the four main elements of a problem representation, goals, key information, key procedures, or restrictions. Within each content area, statements reflected either high or low quality and/or originality. Participants read six different problems and selected problem restatements for each one. In addition, participants were asked to solve two different problems, and their solutions were then scored for quality and originality. The results suggest that a focus on high-quality elements – especially restrictions – may result in more creative solutions.

As this discussion makes clear, at the individual level, problem construction is an important process that has a strong influence on later processes and the outcome of creative problem solving. Problem construction is triggered by environmental cues, which in turn trigger problem representations, which are themselves based on past experiences. Rote application of problem representations typically results in less creative solutions, whereas a more deliberate and effortful application of the process results in more creative solutions. Further, attention to high-quality elements of the representations (specifically restrictions) will lead to more creative solutions.

Team Level

A construct similar to problem representation exists in the team literature. In recent years, the concept of shared mental models has been used to explain team performance (Cannon-Bowers, Salas, & Converse, 1993; Klimoski & Mohammed, 1994). Shared mental models are a representation of knowledge shared by team members regarding the task, team interaction, and teammates (Cannon-Bowers et al., 1993; Mathieu, Goodwin, Heffner, Salas, & Cannon-Bowers, 2000; Smith-Jentsch, Mathieu, & Kraiger, 2005). Cannon-Bowers et al. (1993) suggest that four distinct types of mental models exist:

- The first type of mental model includes knowledge about the technology and equipment used, such as operating procedures and system limitations.
- The second type of mental model includes knowledge about the task or job, such as procedures, likely contingencies, constraints, and strategies.
- The third type of mental model includes knowledge about team interactions, such as roles and responsibilities, information sources, and interaction patterns.
- The fourth type of mental model includes knowledge about team members, such as teammate skills and attitudes.

Of these four types of mental models, the task knowledge version is the most similar to the problem representations discussed at the individual level. It includes some of the dimensions represented in the problem representation, such as procedures, strategies, and constraints. Cannon-Bowers et al. (1993) hypothesized that when tasks are unpredictable, it is more important that team members have a shared mental model of task knowledge; they also suggested that shared mental models will improve the effectiveness of team performance. Unpredictable tasks share similar features with ill-defined problems – namely, these tasks also may not have known solutions or even correct solutions.

Previous empirical work using shared mental models has typically found positive relationships between the degree of agreement or sharedness of these models and various measures of team effectiveness and team processes (e.g., Marks, Zaccaro, & Mathieu, 2000; Mathieu et al., 2000; Smith-Jentsch et al., 2005). Most empirical studies, however, have not differentiated between the different types of mental models possible, or focused on team interaction and team members' mental models. Furthermore, measures of team performance typically include efficiency, safety, task completion, or effectiveness – but not measures of creativity.

Pearce and Ensley (2004) have used the shared mental model approach to measure shared vision in product and process innovation teams (PPITs). Their study collected information about shared vision, teamwork, and perceptions of innovation, as well as customer and managerial ratings of innovation, from 71 PPITs during two time periods. These researchers found that shared vision predicted perception of innovation by both team members and external sources (customers and management). Similarly, Gilson and Shalley (2004) found that when team members had shared goals, they engaged in creative processes more frequently.

Research on mental models suggests that agreement among group members should facilitate group processes and interactions, and improve effectiveness and efficiency. However, agreement on the task mental model may be the result of automatic selection of the problem representation at the individual level followed by similar selection at the group level. While this practice increases efficiency – less time is spent discussing how the problem should be framed – at the individual level automatic application of a problem representation leads to lowered creativity. This outcome is more likely when team members have homogeneous backgrounds and experiences and, therefore, have similar problem representations. In addition, when tasks are simple and routine, similar problem representations will emerge from this shared experience. Of course, these types of tasks do not typically call for creative solutions.

Proposition 1. Shared mental models in teams will lead to more creative solutions, especially for complex or unpredictable tasks.

Proposition 2. Shared mental models in teams resulting from automatic application of a single problem representation will result in less creative solutions.

Proposition 3. Homogeneous groups are more likely to have similar problem representations, and to apply those problem representations automatically, resulting in less creative solutions.

Heterogeneous teams, such as project teams, cross-functional teams, and interdisciplinary teams, face a unique situation relating to problem construction. The tasks typically facing these types of teams tend to be more complex, are often novel, and frequently call for creative solutions (Lovelace, Shapiro, & Wiengart, 2001). In addition, team members have different experiences and backgrounds (e.g., education, industry, department), which would lead individual team members to construct the problem in different ways. Because the problem construction process is typically automatic, team members might potentially have very different conceptualizations of the goals, procedures, information, and restrictions that must be attended to when solving the problem, but will not discuss this information. However, just as at the individual level, where the diversity of information and the combination of problem representations to construct a new problem representation results in more creative solutions, the diversity of cross-functional or interdisciplinary teams may be expected to lead to more creative solutions. This outcome becomes more likely if team members can develop a problem representation that encompasses elements from the multiple problem representations possessed by the various team members. Additionally, integrating the diverse representations would be more time-consuming and require greater effort than using a single problem representation, and would require paying attention to this integration process. Research on team diversity has suggested that functional diversity – in terms of educational background, knowledge, or skills – is related to creativity and innovation (Dougherty, 1992; Dunbar, 1997; Paulus, 2000; West, 2003; West, Sacramento, & Fay, 2006). Nevertheless, the integration of the team members' different points of view and elements of the disparate problem representations will require time and attention, which will be achieved only if team members engage actively in problem construction as a team (De Dreu & West, 2001; Tjosvold, 1998; Watson, Kumar, & Michaleson, 1993).

An emerging concept in team research that is relevant here is that of cognitive consensus (Mohammed & Dumville, 2001). Cognitive consensus refers to agreement among group members regarding how key issues are defined. The concern here is not so much about consensus in reaching an agreement about a final decision or solution (although that is certainly part of cognitive consensus), but rather about how group members reach cognitive consensus or agreement on the interpretation of issues (Bettenhausen, 1991; Mohammed & Dumville, 2001). Although only minimal research has been conducted on cognitive consensus to date, some studies have found that – similar to shared mental models – cognitive consensus results in more efficient group decisions because group members tend to attend to, interpret, and communicate about issues in a similar manner (Mohammed & Ringseis, 2001). In other studies, cognitive diversity or consensus early in the team process was not found to be related to team success, although cognitive consensus at the end was important for team success (Fiol, 1994; Kilduff, Angelmar, & Mehra, 2000).

Some initial evidence on how teams reach cognitive consensus is provided in a study by Mohammed and Ringseis (2001), in which student groups engaged in a multiple-issue decision-making exercise. Among the antecedents of team consensus was a requirement for reaching a consensus decision and group members' behaviors. Specifically, when group members made an effort to understand the reasons for other members' preferences and accepted other points of view as legitimate, more cognitive consensus resulted. Additional support for the importance of understanding other team members' frames of reference comes from a study by Mitchell (1986), who found that performance in management groups improved when an intervention was introduced that facilitated understanding of the diverse members' frames of reference.

Proposition 4. Disagreements within a group about the right solution to a problem may represent disagreements about how to construct and define the problem that were never discussed and never resolved.

Proposition 5. Teams that are able to resolve disagreements about problem representations will generate more creative solutions.

Proposition 6. Knowledge, understanding, and acceptance of the problem representations of other group members will facilitate development of a shared problem representation.

Proposition 7. Heterogeneous groups will generate more complex problem representations, resulting in more creative solutions, if team members actively engage in problem construction in the team and incorporate elements from multiple team members' representations.

Some factors that operate in group environments are likely to restrict the complexity of the final problem representation, even in a heterogeneous group. Because of the need to reach agreement about what the problem representation should include and the need to take into account multiple problem representations, with multiple and possibly conflicting goals and restrictions, the process will be even more time-consuming in a team environment. Under conditions of time pressure, groups will tend to create a less complex problem representation that may not incorporate all possible elements of the various problem representations. Alternatively, if groups are encouraged to explore differences and to take into account different points of view, and if they spend time doing so, more complex problem representations may be derived. This outcome is more likely when diverse groups are assembled on purpose, such as in interdisciplinary teams, where members are often selected to represent different points of view or backgrounds.

Proposition 8. Groups under time pressure will be less likely to develop complex and representative problem representations.

Proposition 9. Groups whose members are encouraged to spend time understanding one another's perspectives are more likely to construct the problem in a more complex fashion and to incorporate elements from multiple individual problem representations.

INFORMATION SEARCH AND ENCODING

Individual Level

Problem construction provides the map for developing a solution to the problem, which includes the identification of necessary information. Information necessary to solve the problem can come from internal sources (e.g., knowledge already available to the problem solver) or external sources (e.g., books, articles, other people, the Web). Very rarely will individuals have all the information necessary for developing a solution available to them, however. Even if all the information is available in memory, individuals must still determine which information is relevant to the problem-solving effort and which is not. Studies have found that the goals provided influence the information search strategies used (Gilliland & Landis, 1992). The more complex and ill-defined the problem, the larger and more diverse the set of information that must be gathered and that might potentially be useful in developing a solution to the problem (Reiter-Palmon & Illies, 2004). It is, therefore, not surprising that studies on information searches have found that time and effort in this stage are related to creative problem solving. That is, individuals who spend more time and effort searching for information subsequently generate more creative solutions (Illies & Reiter-Palmon, 2004; Mumford, Baughman, Supinski, & Maher, 1996a).

One key issue influencing the results of an information search is the type of information gathered and the particular information attended to. One avenue of research targets the search for confirming information, or the confirmation bias phenomenon. Much of the research in this area has focused on gathering supportive information once a decision has been made. However, based on studies on confirmation bias, it is clear that people are more likely to attend to information that supports their position and to ignore disconfirming information (Jonas, Schultz-Hardt, Frey, & Thelen, 2001; Pinkley, Griffith, & Northcraft, 1995). Although these studies tend to address issues related to the information search after a decision is made, it is likely that similar influences will prevail even before a final decision has been made. In other words, the problem representations will guide the information search; information that fits with the problem construction will be attended to and processed, whereas information that is disconfirming may be ignored.

Searching for and encoding only confirming information will likely result in less creative solutions. Research on creative problem solving and information search has suggested that individuals who are able to use diverse and inconsistent information develop more creative solutions (Baughman & Mumford, 1995; Dunbar, 1995; Reiter-Palmon et al., 1997; Rodan, 2002). In addition, evidence of confirmation bias in information search is available in a study by Illies and Reiter-Palmon (2004). These researchers found that when individuals solve a problem that engages their values, those individuals tend to spend less time on information search activities and attend less to each piece of information, compared with other problems; their solutions to the value-laden problem are also less creative.

Although this finding suggests that having a wide variety of information will always be beneficial to creative problem solving, casting such a wide net may result in information overload and confusion, and is more time-consuming than specific information search. Therefore, it is important to have just the right kind of diverse information. This idea is supported by research suggesting that knowing when the diverse and inconsistent information is relevant to the problem-solving task at hand is critical. Indeed, research has shown that the ability to attend to relevant information and to discount irrelevant information is related to creative performance (Davidson, 1995; Mumford et al., 1996a).

These studies do not indicate precisely how individuals make the determination that specific information is relevant, particularly when information is inconsistent or diverse, and hence potentially irrelevant. Further, these studies underscore the importance of the management of the diverse and large amount of information gathered. Research on expertise may provide some clues about how individuals determine the relevance of information and how they go about managing this information. Experts are able to identify, organize, and understand information that is needed to solve problems more efficiently than novices do (Bedard & Chi, 1992; Chi, Glaser, & Rees, 1982; Ericsson & Lehman, 1996; Glaser & Chi, 1988). Experts have more domain-relevant knowledge than novices, and their knowledge is better organized and interconnected, allowing for the retrieval of more information that is well organized and more relevant to the problem at hand (Charness, 1991; Ericsson & Kintsch, 1995). Experts are also more likely to search information more systematically, coherently, and efficiently; to ignore task-irrelevant information; and to search for more high-level information (Charness, Reingold, Pomplun, & Stampe, 2001; Ericsson, 1999; Hershey, Walsh, Read, & Chulef, 1990; Salterio, 1996).

These findings suggest that experts, owing to the organization of their knowledge, are more likely to search for information in a way that facilitates creativity. In reality, some research suggests that expertise may sometimes be a disadvantage for creative problem solving. Because existing knowledge is typically used to evaluate the need to search for additional information and to judge the relevance of new information (Barrick & Spilker, 2003), experts may achieve information search efficiency by not attending to important information and dismissing apparently irrelevant information. This proposition is supported by findings that suggest domain knowledge may be constraining under some conditions, possibly contributing to the "inverted U" relationship observed between creativity and expertise (Bonnardel & Marmeche, 2004; Plucker & Beghetto, 2004; Lubart & Guignard, 2004; Wiley, 1998).

Although expertise can guide the direction of information search and determination of relevance, less is known about how people decide when to stop looking for information. Stopping rules are heuristics that allow the problem solver to decide when to stop searching for additional information (Browne & Pitts, 2004). Limited research has been conducted in this area of decision making as yet, with the majority of the research on stopping rules having focused on information search in support of choosing a specific solution from a list of possible options (Couger, 1996).

In contrast, stopping rules for design problems, which include the early stages of problem solving and decision making, and for idea generation have received less attention. In their study, Browne and Pitts (2004) asked information system analysts to identify system requirements for the development of a new online grocery store. Analysts performed the task individually, and these sessions were recorded. A verbal protocol analysis was used to determine stopping rules. The results suggested that use of specific stopping rules was related to the quantity and quality of the information gathered, but experience was not. Overall, using the difference threshold stopping rule – that is, a decision maker assesses the incremental value of the most recent piece of information, and once that value falls below a prespecified threshold, the decision maker stops looking for more information – resulted in higher quantity and quality of information search.

Team Level

Information search and encoding are also important at the team level. Free flow of information between team members has been found to be related to solution quality, increased flexibility, and innovation in problem-solving teams (Atuahene-Gima, 2003; Brown & Eisenhardt, 1995; Drach-Zahavy & Somech, 2001). Further, some have speculated that one advantage of diverse teams – especially those that are functionally diverse – is the wide knowledgebase that members bring (i.e., the differences in their perspectives and their access to different knowledge sources) (Bantel & Jackson, 1989; Cummings, 2004; Perry-Smith & Shalley, 2003; West et al., 2004). Individual team members can serve as knowledge banks for the group regarding their particular topic of expertise, and they may have access to different sources of information, increasing the amount of knowledge possessed by the group has a whole. However, just as information overload is a concern at the individual level, so, too, this consideration arises at the team level. Indeed, it may be even more critical for groups, as the team may have access to more information. Research on communication and its effect on creativity at the team level has shown mixed results, however.

Several studies suggest that communication and socialization of team members result in those members becoming more engaged in team creative problem solving and more innovation (Drach-Zahavy & Somech, 2001; Gilson & Shalley, 2004). In contrast, a study by Kratzer, Leenders, and van Englen (2004) found that the frequency of communication between team members was inversely related to creative performance, suggesting that more communication and information sharing is not always beneficial. These contradictory results suggest that merely evaluating frequency of communication may not be enough. Rather, the nature and quality of the communication need to be investigated. Thus issues that need to be addressed at the team level include how teams share and effectively manage the information available to all of their members.

Proposition 10. More information sharing within a team is not always beneficial for creative problem solving. Information sharing within a team will facilitate creative problem solving when the information shared is appropriate and relevant to the problem.

When working in a team, other group members can serve to provide information that is needed to solve the problem. This type of sharing is particularly important when only some team members have access to knowledge or specific information that might prove useful in solving the problem.

Research on information sharing in groups has focused on this issue – namely, how information that is not shared initially by all group members is pooled. Numerous studies have investigated this phenomenon using the hidden profile paradigm. In these studies, group members read information about possible solution alternatives and are told that that they may have information that other members do not have. Some information is shared by all group members, but information that is necessary to support the best decision choice is generally not shared. This line of research has consistently found that group members are more likely to discuss the information that group members share (all group members know) and are less likely to discuss information that is not shared (known by one or only a few group members). This is the case even when the unshared information supports a better solution to the problem than the shared information (e.g., Devine, 1999; Hollingshead, 1996; Stasser & Titus, 1985, 1987; Wittenbaum, 1998).

Additional research on information sharing using the hidden profile paradigm has sought to elucidate the circumstances under which group members are more likely to discuss unshared information. These studies suggest that the number of individuals who have knowledge or information is important. Shared information is discussed more frequently than partially shared information (information shared by some but not all group members), which is in turn discussed more frequently than unshared information (information available to only one group member).

Further supporting this finding is a study on the effect of functional diversity on team performance in business unit management teams (Bunderson & Sutcliffe, 2002). This investigation found that having a degree of overlap in experiences and functions between team members facilitates information sharing and performance. Bunderson and Sutcliffe argue that this overlap in information provides a common ground that facilitates information sharing by allowing for easier communication among peers.

In contrast, some research suggests that disagreement about the solution is likely to facilitate information sharing among group members (Galinsky & Kray, 2004; Hollingshead, 1996; Schittekatte & van Hiel, 1996). It is possible that some degree of overlap in experience and background is necessary to assure that group members are able to effectively communicate with one another (and not past one another). Too little overlap will result in ineffective communication and lack of understanding, however, whereas too much overlap will result in similarity of thinking and a tendency to ignore potential solutions or problems.

Proposition 11. Functional diversity of team members will have a curvilinear relationship with information sharing.

Other studies on information sharing have found that the task provided to the group influences the degree to which information is shared. When groups are asked to select the best option, they are less likely to discuss unshared information compared to when groups are asked to discuss the information prior to making a decision (Stewart & Stasser, 1995) and when they are asked to discuss all alternatives (Parks & Cowlin, 1995). These findings underscore the importance of discussion as part of the information sharing process. Given that different group members possess different information, the most likely way to share this information would be through discussion. If discussion is discouraged or viewed as unnecessary, less information will be shared. Factors that might suggest discussion is not necessary or that might serve to discourage it include time pressure and a climate that discourages exploration and discussion.

Proposition 12. Teams that emphasize discussion and exploration will engage in more information sharing.

Proposition 13. Time pressure will result in less information sharing among team members.

Group members who are designated as experts tend to discuss more information – including unshared information – especially when the group is aware of their expert status (Franz & Larson, 2002; Stasser & Stewart, 1995). It has been suggested that one reason for this finding is that experts may feel more confident in speaking up in the group setting, and when group members know that someone is an expert they are more likely to seek his or her input. Shared information tends to be viewed as more valuable, important, and relevant (Wittenbaum, Holligshead, & Botero, 2004), indicating that it might be more difficult to communicate unshared information. This finding supports the notion that experts may be more likely to share information as a result of the confidence in their expertise, because experts typically have access to unshared information, which is more difficult to communicate. It is possible that one reason members of cross-functional teams are able to communicate diverse information is because all members are believed to have their own area of expertise and, therefore, are more likely to communicate unshared information.

Proposition 14. Experts in a team are more likely to communicate unshared information to team members.

Proposition 15. Communication of unshared information in a team will be higher in cross-functional teams where multiple members are considered experts.

The studies investigating information sharing and the conditions under which group members are likely to share information that is not shared by all provide us with an understanding of when and how group members decide to share information. However, these studies have typically used a paradigm where there is one correct answer, which is not a relevant characteristic for ill-defined problems that call for creative solutions. Under those conditions, even if group members decide to share information and know that they hold unique information, it is less clear precisely which information is relevant to the problem at hand and will facilitate problem solving, and which information is irrelevant. Distinguishing between the two forms of information can be particularly problematic when information seems irrelevant or inconsistent. As discussed in the individual-level section, a determination of which information is relevant for problem solving is a critical aspect of the information search, and the quality of the information used may ultimately affect the creativity of the solution. At the team level, several additional issues arise with regard to this process.

The first issue in determining the relevance of information relates to confirmation bias. Confirmation bias at the individual level is a well-documented phenomenon (Ditto & Lopez, 1992; Klayman & Ha, 1987; Nickerson, 1998). Although fewer studies have been conducted with groups, confirmation bias also appears to exist at this level. In a series of studies looking at confirmation bias in groups, Schultz-Hardt, Frey, Luthgens, and Moscovici (2000) found that confirmation bias occurred in homogeneous groups or when a small minority existed. Group homogeneity was defined based on the preferred answer or solution to the problem. When groups had similar-size majority and minority subgroups (e.g., in a five-person group, a three-two division of members), confirmation bias was not significant, although cell means revealed a preference for confirming information. This confirmation bias occurred as a result of stronger commitment of group members to the group decision as well as higher confidence in the decision in homogenous groups.

Schultz-Hardt et al. (2000) hypothesized that confirmation bias in groups represents a reliance on social consensus to determine the optimal point for stopping the information search and finalizing a solution to the problem. It is likely that in cross-functional teams, where members excel in different areas of expertise, the resulting group would be more heterogeneous, leading to less confirmation bias.

In addition to minority influence on confirmation bias, task routine has an effect on whether confirmation bias occurs. Betsch, Haberstroh, Glockner, Haar, and Fiedler (2001) found that when task routine and instructions were manipulated, less confirmation bias occurred. Specifically, in routine tasks participants searched for confirming information; in contrast, for non-routine tasks or tasks framed as novel, the confirmation bias disappeared. As a consequence, indicating that the problem-solving effort is non-routine and requires creative thought is likely to facilitate more through and less biased information search in a group.

Proposition 16. Cross-functional teams and other heterogeneous teams will engage in more information search and less confirmation bias compared to homogeneous teams.

Proposition 17. When the purpose of the problem-solving effort in a team is to reach a creative solution, or when the task is nonroutine, the group will engage in more information search and less confirmation bias compared to routine tasks.

The confirmation bias literature addresses one aspect of how individuals and teams determine whether information is relevant. One difficulty in determining information relevance in a team situation, however, is that some information may seem irrelevant to some members while it may seem relevant to others because of the information available to them. For example, one group member may decide that a specific piece of information is not relevant to the problem at hand, not encode it, and not share it with the team. Other team members might potentially find that specific information useful or relevant, but do not have access to it. This failure to share information may be particularly problematic if the neglected information might potentially affect how other information is perceived and interpreted. Similarity in team members' problem construction processes would facilitate agreement on which information is considered important by all group members. Of course, even agreement on the problem construction may not result in full agreement on the relevance of information, and it will not alter the outcome when one team member's lack of knowledge affects which information is deemed relevant or shared. One possible solution is to encourage team members to communicate about what additional information will be supportive or relevant.

Proposition 18. Shared problem representation resulting from the problem construction phase will increase agreement among team members on what information is relevant to problem solving.

Proposition 19. Agreement among team members about what types of information are viewed as relevant will increase information sharing.

IDEA AND SOLUTION GENERATION

Individual Level

Idea generation is the process of coming up with alternative solutions to a problem. Ill-defined situations – those that foster creativity – are characterized by having multiple plausible solutions (Mumford et al., 1991). It is therefore not surprising that of all of the steps in the creative problem-solving process, idea generation is the one most typically associated with creativity. In fact, a common misconception about creativity is that it is equivalent to the process of idea generation.

The majority of studies on idea generation at the individual level have focused on divergent thinking, or the generation of multiple ideas related to undefined/indefinite and typically unrealistic scenarios. The concept of divergent thinking, which was first suggested by Guilford (1950, 1967), has had a major influence on the field of creativity. In fact, for many years it was synonymous with creativity. When originally suggested, the idea-generation process provided a stark contrast to previous measures and conceptualizations focusing on convergent thought (Mumford, 2001). This process was seen as important because without the generation of the idea, an idea will not be available for later steps such as idea evaluation and selection. Studies examining the relationship between divergent thinking indices and creativity have yielded mixed results. Some studies have found no relationship or only a weak relationship between divergent thinking and creative performance (Hocevar, 1980), whereas other studies have found stronger relationships in a variety of settings and populations (Mumford, Marks, Connelly, Zaccaro, & Johnson, 1998; Plucker, 1999; Runco, 1991).

A typical test of divergent thinking is one where the individual is asked to generate as many ideas as possible given a presented stimulus. For example, the "Uses" test (Guilford, 1967) asks individuals to generate as many ideas as they can for uses for a brick or a newspaper. The most common methodology used for scoring divergent thinking tests has focused on the quantity of ideas generated – that is, ideational fluency, which refers to the number of unique solutions generated to a problem. The focus on the quantity of solutions or ideas was popularized by brainstorming research (e.g., Kramer, Fleming, & Mannis, 2001; Mullen, Johnson, & Salas, 1991).

Although the quantity of ideas may be of importance in certain circumstances, a more practical assessment of solutions is found through gauging the quality or originality of the solution. Originality, which can be conceptualized as the frequency of occurrence, has been used more frequently as a scoring procedure for divergent thinking tests than quality defined as the appropriateness or feasibility of the idea. Although some research has found a relationship between quantity and measures of quality and originality, this is not always the case, suggesting that the relationship between quantity and quality and originality is a complex one (Mouchiroud & Lubart, 2001; Runco & Marz, 1992). In addition, other scoring procedures exist, such as scoring for flexibility (i.e., how many different groups of ideas the individual identifies) or complexity of the ideas generated (Runco, 1999; Mumford et al., 1998).

Because idea generation has been viewed as a critical process in creativity, attention has been focused on what contributes to successful idea generation and how to facilitate it. Some divergence has emerged in the field regarding how idea generation can be facilitated. Some researchers have stated that this process is facilitated through the arranging, amalgamation, and ordering of previously established categories (Mumford, Mobley et al., 1991). Other researchers have focused on the process of decomposition, or the presentation of goals to the problem solver, as a method for facilitating idea generation (e.g., Adelman et al., 1995; Butler & Scherer, 1997; Pitz et al., 1980; Shalley, 1991; Yates, 1990). Still other approaches have evaluated the effect of instructions or examples on idea generation (e.g., Runco, Illies, & Eisenman, 2005a; Runco, Illies, & Reiter-Palmon, 2005b; Runco & Okuda, 1991; Shalley, 1995; Smith, Ward, & Schumacher, 1993). Furthermore, analogies have been used successfully to facilitate solution or idea generation (Holyoak, 1984; Reeves & Weisberg, 1994). Finally, some researchers have focused on the notion of "insight" as key to coming up with creative solutions to problems (Hogarth, 1980; Schilling, 2005).

Mumford and his colleagues have investigated extensively the concept of category combination as a way of developing new ideas (Baughman & Mumford, 1995; Mobley, Doares, & Mumford, 1992; Mumford, Baughman, Maher, Costanza, & Supinski, 1997). The primary theme of this research is the identification of how categories of information and knowledge are combined and organized to create new and creative ideas. Early work by Mobley et al. (1992) found that when participants were asked to combine divergent categories, the resulting new category were more original conversely, higher quality was obtained when similar categories were presented. Mumford, Supinski, Baughman, Costanza, and Threlfall (1997) found that this category combination ability was related to performance on a different creative problem-solving task. Those individuals who were able to combine categories in new and meaningful ways were also able to develop more creative advertising campaigns at a later point in the study.

Other studies have focused on how people combine and reorganize categories to create new categories. Mumford et al. (1997) have investigated the factors that affect category combination in terms of the strategy used. In their study, categories were designed to be either similar or related to each other or to be divergent. In addition, instructions to the participants led them to focus on identifying features in each category that were similar or, alternatively, asked the participants to identify features and think about what they represent. Results of this study indicated that when similar categories were used, the first strategy (identifying similar features across categories) resulted in more original and higher-quality ideas; when diverse categories were used, however, the second strategy was more effective. Along similar lines, Baughman and Mumford (1995) found that identifying shared atypical features and non-common typical features resulted in more original ideas.

Scott, Lonergan, and Mumford (2005) have studied the category combination process using a more realistic problem. Prior studies used stimulus material that did not present a real-life situation. In addition to replicating the results of previous studies with their new test, Scott et al. (2005) sought to compare the outcomes of using two different approaches for category combination. In this study, participants were asked to develop a new educational curriculum and a new teaching method. Participants read through background materials about a hypothetical school, and they were provided with information about possible methods that could be used in generating the new teaching methods.

The manipulations involved varying the content and structure of the different methods presented to participants. One manipulation in this study intended to alter the strategy individuals used in category combination. By changing the prompts and questions individuals viewed as part of the materials, the researchers caused participants to use either an analogical or a case-based approach. In addition, the number of example problems, the similarity of the example programs to each other, and the similarity to current instructional methods were manipulated. The results suggested that when a larger number of programs was presented, the analogical approach resulted in more creative ideas. With fewer programs, the case-based approach resulted in more creative solutions. In addition, the effectiveness of the application of the approach (either case-based or analogical) was significantly related to creative performance.

Taken together, these studies suggest that category combination plays an important role in generating creative ideas. Specifically, the ability to use the appropriate strategy facilitates the category combination process. The research by Mumford and his colleagues suggests several factors might potentially influence the effect of strategy selection, including category similarity, amount of information presented, and typicality of category features.

Another strategy used to facilitate idea generation is that of decomposition – that is, the act of breaking down the problem into individual parts. Studies looking at goal presentation have found that when goals are presented one at a time, participants generate more solutions; by comparison, presenting multiple goals or no goals results in fewer solutions generated (Butler & Scherer, 1997; Pitz et al., 1980). Butler and Scherer (1997) also found that participants who received two conflicting goals at the same time generated higher-quality solutions compared to participants who received one goal at a time and participants who did not receive any goals. These results suggest that the effect of decomposition on idea generation depends on how decomposition is presented (one goal at a time or multiple goals) and the criterion used to evaluate the ideas generated (fluency or quality).

Similar to presenting specific goals embedded in the problem, other studies have focused on using more general goals to enhance solution generation (Gilliland & Landis, 1992; Shalley, 1991, 1995). Gilliland and Landis (1992) found that participants given more difficult goals generated more solutions than those given easy goals. Shalley (1995) found that simply telling people to do their best to be creative led participants to generate more creative solutions, compared to giving them no goal at all.

In a different study, Shalley (1991) manipulated productivity and creativity goals as well as personal discretion. Productivity and creativity goals were manipulated in one of three ways: (a) difficult goals were provided by instructing participants to attain a specific high number of memos or a high percentage of creative work respectively, (b) were told to do their best, or (c) were provided with no goal. Personal discretion was manipulated by telling participants that they had complete freedom on how to work on the task (high discretion) or that the tasks needed to be performed in a specific order (low discretion).

The results of this study suggest a complex relationship between goals and creativity. Participants assigned either do-your-best or difficult creativity goals were significantly more creative than participants given no creativity goals. The least creative responses were found when participants were assigned either a difficult or do-your-best productivity goal but no creativity goal. Also, creative responses were lower when participants were assigned no creativity goal and completed the tasks in a specified order. Productivity goals did result in participants generating a greater number of solutions, and creativity goals did result in more creative solutions. This study suggests that assigning a specific type of goal (creativity or productivity) would lead to an improvement in that specific measure, and possibly lower performance on the other measure, unless both productivity and creativity goals are specified.

Taken collectively, these studies suggest that decomposition of the problem affects creativity primarily through its effect on goal selection and attention to goals. When only one goal is presented, participants attend to that goal to the exclusion of other goals. By contrast, the presentation of multiple goals forces individuals to take into account the competing demands of the different goals, resulting in fewer but more creative ideas.

Shalley (1991, 1995) altered the goals provided to participants by manipulating the instructions provided (or not provided). Other research, while not directly manipulating goals, has focused on the effect of instructions on the idea-generation process. Runco and Okuda (1991) realized that the type of instructions has a differential effect on the different aspects of solution creativity evidenced. Specifically, participants were given multiple divergent thinking tests on different days (over a five-day span) with differential instructions in the following order:

1. Generate as many ideas as you can.
2. Be original with your ideas.
3. Generate as many different ideas as you can and be flexible.

When participants were given explicit flexibility instructions, they generated more different ideas than when they were provided with either the more generic or originality instructions. Interestingly, participants' originality scores decreased when they were given the flexibility instructions. This is a particularly important finding because it is assumed that the flexibility of ideas is strongly related to the originality of ideas. Additionally, results indicated that transfer between idea-generation tasks did not occur.

In addition to the influence of the type of instructions provided, the level of specificity of instructions provided to problem solvers will influence the creativity of solutions. In their study, Ward, Patterson, and Sifonis (2004) provided either very specific instructions on how to solve the problem or very ambiguous instructions on how to solve the problem; they found that the more ambiguous instructions resulted in more novel solutions relative to the more specific instructions. Similarly, Runco et al. (2005b) investigated not only the level of explicitness of instructions, but also the type of instructions used. Participants were presented with one of two types of instructions that differed in their level of precision and ambiguity (low, moderate, or high). Instructions were either conceptual (e.g., be original when generating ideas) or procedural (e.g., think of ideas that no one else will). Providing procedural instructions relative to conceptual instructions had the most striking influence on idea generation in terms of fluency, flexibility, and originality. When evaluating the ideas for originality, the level of explicitness of instructions mattered, with more ambiguous and less precise instructions resulting in more original idea production.

Runco et al. (2005a) went beyond simply the role of instructions and looked at how task qualities – specifically, realistic versus unrealistic tasks – influenced the ideas generated. Participants were randomly divided into groups and asked to generate creative solutions to both an unrealistic problem and a realistic problem. They were provided with brief descriptions of how ideas are evaluated (originality, appropriateness, and creativity). The study participants were then randomly assigned to one of four instruction conditions: (1) generate as many ideas as you can, (2) generate only original ideas, (3) generate only appropriate ideas, and (4) generate only creative ideas. The instructions influenced how the groups performed on the creative idea-generation tasks. Specifically, the realistic task resulted in more appropriate ideas, whereas the unrealistic task resulted in more original and flexible ideas. Runco et al. (2005a) also found that the type of task modified the effect of the instruction on the production of ideas, such that the magnitude of the instruction effects depended on the type of task.

These studies imply that several facets of instructions, as well as the conditions in which they are given, influence idea generation. The level of explicitness can either constrain the ideation (if the instructions are highly explicit) or allow for individualistic interpretation (if the instructions are less explicit and more ambiguous). Although only one study explicitly considered the difference between using conceptual or procedural instructions, the results do suggest that procedural directions (i.e., how-to directives) contain additional information suggesting how to identify the desired aspects of the ideas.

Another technique that has been used to enhance creative idea generation is analogical transfer – that is, the use of remote stimuli to stimulate new ideas (Reeves & Weisberg, 1994). Dahl and Moreau (2002) found that when developing new products, more extensive use of analogical transfer, use of a "near" analogy (i.e., an analogy drawn from a close domain), and use of external priming agents (i.e., benchmarks) all resulted in more original products and features. Hender, Dean, Rodgers, and Nunamaker (2002) provided additional support for the usefulness of analogies in enhancing creative idea generation. In their study, use of analogies resulted in the production of fewer but more creative ideas than did idea generation without analogies.

One caveat to consider, however, is that the applicability of analogical transfer to idea generation depends on the individual's ability to see the relationship between the analogy and the current problem. Likewise, providing examples to people when they are generating ideas influences creative idea generation (e.g., Marsh & Landau, 1996; Smith et al., 1993; Ward, Smith, & Vaid, 1997). In particular, providing examples or asking people to think of previous examples of similar problems has been shown to result in conformity, or less originality, of the ideas that are subsequently generated (Marsh & Landau, 1996; Smith et al., 1993).

Expertise provides the individual with many examples that may be used in the development of new ideas, and it has been shown to influence idea generation (Mumford et al., 1998; Vincent, Decker, & Mumford, 2002). When Mumford et al. (1998) used a multiple-attribute approach to assess the expertise of participants, they found that experts generated more ideas that were also higher in both quality and originality than participants who had less expertise. Unlike previous work on examples, expertise provides the problem solver with a number of different examples in context, along with the knowledge of when and how to use these examples as a starting point. For these reasons, it may not constrain idea generation.

Team Level

Past investigations into group influences on creative problem solving have concentrated on the idea-generation process for quite some time (e.g., Taylor, Berry, & Block, 1958). Historical efforts have often focused on techniques to improve idea generation, and more specifically efforts toward group idea generation. Additionally, some of the original work done on group processes and idea generation investigated the effects of groups on individual creativity (e.g., Andre, Schumer, & Whitaker, 1979). This chapter, however, focuses on team and group creativity as the product.

Another focus of the research efforts into group idea generation is brainstorming. An extremely large number of studies have been done on group brainstorming, which is a specific technique for the facilitation of idea generation in groups. Brainstorming is the act of generating ideas while attempting to suspend evaluative thought (Lamm & Trommsdorff, 1973). Most of this research has addressed the quantity of solutions or ideas, and not the quality of ideas (e.g., Kramer et al., 2001; Mullen et al., 1991). Because the results of the idea-generation process can be evaluated in many different ways (e.g., originality, appropriateness, flexibility), the focus on quantity provides an incomplete understanding of the effect of brainstorming on group creativity.

A review of the brainstorming literature suggests that in most cases, individuals working alone or nominal groups (when individual output is pooled) outperform groups in terms of the number of ideas generated (e.g., Andre et al., 1979; Asmus & James, 2005; Diehl & Stroebe, 1987; Dunnette, Campbell, & Jaastad, 1963; Larey & Paulus, 1999; Leggett Dugosh & Paulus, 2005; McGlynn, McGurk, Effland, Johll, & Harding, 2004; Mullen et al., 1991). By contrast, research on the effects of brainstorming on quality or originality of ideas is more limited and not as conclusive (Barki & Pinsonneault, 2001; Diehl & Stroebe, 1987; Grawitch, Munz, Elliott, & Mathis, 2003; Mullen et al., 1991; Sutton & Hargadon, 1996).

Research has attempted to address the reasons for the unexpected lack of superiority by groups compared to individuals. One concern with using teams for any task is that a pattern of non-participation often emerges. This tendency may reflect members' reluctance to share ideas with others or their evaluation apprehension (e.g., social anxiety). Some group members, in an attempt to be polite, may wait and take turns to express ideas. This may result in a twofold loss of ideas: The person waiting may lose track of the idea, and the failure to share the idea means that it will not spark any other ideas from other team members. Regardless of the reason for non-participation, it remains a popular criticism of group work.

Another factor that may contribute to non-participation is the size of the group. Examining the effect group size on idea generation is not a new idea, and most efforts have found that smaller groups generate more ideas than larger groups (e.g., Bouchard & Hare, 1970; Renzulli, Owen, & Callahan, 1974). In fact, Hackman (1992) advised that group size should be limited to the minimum number of people needed to complete the job at hand. Although no prescriptions are available for the proper size of groups needed for creative output, we have begun to understand differences between smaller and larger groups. Curral, Forrester, Dawson, and West (2001), for example, investigated the influence of group size on processes necessary for creativity and innovation. In their study, team size was a significant predictor of processes that support innovation such as participation, information sharing, and understanding the importance of innovation; in particular, size was inversely related to the success of processes that support innovation.

Others have tried to find methods that will counteract the productivity loss due to the size of brainstorming groups (e.g., using facilitators, training, modeling, or cognitive exercises). A popular option has come from the advent of technology to facilitate idea generation, also known as electronic brainstorming (e.g., Dennis & Valacich, 1999; Gallupe et al., 1992; Pinsonneault, Barki, Gallupe, & Hoppen, 1999; Shepherd, Briggs, Reinig, Yen, & Nunamaker, 1996). Gallupe et al. (1992) found that electronic brainstorming techniques, as compared with face-to-face interaction, resulted in less productivity loss in larger groups (e.g., 12 members relative to six; six members relative to two or four members).

Proposition 20. Groups brainstorming will result in fewer ideas generated by groups relative to individuals, but better or similar quality and originality of ideas.

Proposition 21. A curvilinear relationship exists between group size and idea generation.

Proposition 22. Large groups will inhibit idea generation through lowered participation of group members.

One way that technology may counteract productivity loss is by preventing or minimizing production blocking (Diehl & Stroebe, 1987; Stroebe & Diehl, 1994). The production of ideas may decline when group members are able to present their ideas only one at a time, which may result in a reduced amount of time for each person to share (Paulus, Larey, & Dzindolet, 2004). The reduction in time allowed to think about the ideas that have been exchanged may also influence productivity. Paulus and Yang (2000) found that groups that focused more attention on the ideas exchanged by group members and spent more time reflecting on group members' ideas following idea exchange performed better than groups that did not focus on the sharing aspect of group work or groups that completed the task as part of a nominal group. Similarly, research suggests that encouraging group members to write down ideas so they will not forget them shows that this technique allows groups to perform better (Dennis & Williams, 2003).

Proposition 23. Using techniques (such as writing ideas, electronic brainstorming) that allow team members to continue to develop new ideas while still interacting with others will facilitate idea generation in groups.

Proposition 24. Groups that spend more time sharing and reflecting on ideas will generate more ideas and more creative ideas than groups that do not.

Group membership has been investigated as an antecedent of group idea generation. Researchers have integrated the social influence of group members themselves on the production of ideas in a group context (Milliken, Bartel, & Kurtzberg, 2003). It has been suggested that shifting membership will facilitate idea generation by exposing the group to new ideas generated by those individuals who are new to the team (Levine, Choi, & Moreland, 2003).

Choi and Thompson (2005) investigated the influence of group membership change on group creativity. Two types of groups were compared with respect to their fluency and flexibility of ideas generated. One type of group had an open membership, where the members of the group changed by rotating a small group of participants during the series of group tasks. The other groups had closed membership, where the members in the group remained the same for the entire series of tasks. The groups that experienced membership change generated more ideas, as well as more different ideas in terms of category representation, than the closed membership groups. Furthermore, the newly added members of the groups were responsible for positive performance by improving the production of the tenured members of the group, in terms of both the quantity and the flexibility of the ideas provided.

Proposition 25. Membership change in teams will be positively related to creative performance relative to groups where membership stays stagnant.

Proposition 26. Membership change in teams will be positively related to creative performance only if new members are willing to share ideas.

Adding or including new members is merely one way in which group membership may influence creative problem solving. Team diversity has been conceptualized in multiple ways, including personality variables, demographic variables, cognitive style, knowledge, expertise, and functional roles (Milliken et al., 2003). Because this chapter focuses on cognitive processes, it reviews only those variables that have a more direct effect on cognitive process, such as knowledge, expertise, and cognitive style.

Chirumbolo, Mannetti, Pierro, Areni, and Kruglanski (2005) investigated how a group's need for closure (measured as an aggregate of the individuals' levels of need for closure) related to idea generation. High-need-for-closure groups generated more ideas relative to low-need-for-closure groups, but the degree of elaboration and the creativity of those ideas were lower in the former groups. This relationship most likely reflects the fact that the need for closure restricts hypothesis generation and the production of conventional ideas. Taking a different approach, Basadur and Head (2001) investigated the effect of group cognitive style homogeneity or heterogeneity on group creative problem solving. Heterogeneous groups outperformed homogeneous groups, providing additional support to the positive relationship between diversity and creativity.

Another aspect relevant to group membership is the extent of domain knowledge that group members bring to the idea-generation task. Expertise at the group level incorporates not only individual experience, but also knowledge that is collective and shared. The extent to which shared knowledge structures are activated is an aspect that must be considered at the group level, but it is not relevant at the individual level of idea generation. Furthermore, in a group context there may be a better chance for a member to have familiarity with the problem, as at least one person may have had a similar prior experience. This expertise can enhance productivity both in terms of coming up with new ideas and in terms of avoiding costly mistakes (Paulus et al., 2004).

The differences in the expertise of group members may result in a need to share more information so as to develop a group understanding of individual members' relevant knowledge. This additional integration of relevant information for idea generation may provide opportunities for further exchange, which may then result in added input from the non-expert members of the group. The valuable information from the expert members, combined with the fresh perspectives of the group members, may help to resist the temptation to apply what has been done in the past to the current idea-generation task.

Because group idea generation occurs in a social context, aspects of group behavior are important to understand when considering this process. De Dreu (2002) concluded that the processes during team meetings determined innovation success; successful teams dealt with contradictory results, had some diversity in team makeup, and engaged in effective collaborative reasoning. The notion that group interaction has a strong influence on creativity and idea generation is far from radical (e.g., Andre et al., 1979), but the importance of the social influence on the cognitive processes necessary to facilitate idea generation is quite strong.

Proposition 27. Diverse teams in terms of cognitive style and expertise will generate more creative ideas than homogeneous teams.

Proposition 28. Team diversity will facilitate idea generation if team members discuss different ideas and share their different perspectives.

Proposition 29. Team diversity will allow team members to integrate and utilize contradictory information and results, and therefore will facilitate idea generation.

Just as instructions given to individuals who are asked to generate creative ideas have been shown to have strong influences on their performance, a focus on strategies or instructions given to groups who are responding to creativity tasks has been shown to affect creative performance. Specifically, Santanen, Briggs, and DeVreede (2004) examined the differential effects of either free or directed brainstorming strategies. Free brainstorming occurred without any facilitation, but the directed efforts had three different patterns of facilitation. The quartet method involved four different prompts on one topic, followed by four different prompts on another topic; these prompts occurred every 8 min. The duet method entailed two prompts on one topic, which continued every 4 min. The solo method relied on one prompt per topic presented every 2 min.

Overall brainstorming efforts with directed facilitation resulted in more solutions generated with higher creativity ratings, higher average creativity ratings, and a greater concentration of creative solutions. When comparing the facilitation methods, both the solo and quartet methods resulted in significantly more creative solutions than the duet method. Although the solo and quartet methods both resulted in higher creativity, there were differences in the solutions generated. The solo method resulted in solutions that focused more specifically on the criterion provided in the prompts. As such, this facilitation method may be better when the problem-solving effort demands a focus on solutions with a more specific target. Furthermore, the solo method may be more appropriate when the solution does not need to satisfy a wide contingent of others. The quartet method, however, resulted in more broad solutions with a wider focus. This method may be better employed when the problem calls for a wider contingent of people to be satisfied. These results mirror the results obtained by Butler and Scherer (1997) with individuals.

Other studies have focused on the rules or instructions used for brainstorming and their effect on idea generation. Paulus and Brown

(2003) found that providing additional guidelines for brainstorming increased the fluency of idea-generation groups. Similarly, the use of facilitators who stress brainstorming rules also increased idea generation (Oxley, Dzindolet, & Paulus, 1996).

Proposition 30. Structuring the idea generation task by presenting probes or providing rules will facilitate idea generation in groups.

Proposition 31. Groups that focus on one goal at time will generate more ideas.

Proposition 32. Groups that focus on multiple and competing ideas will generate more creative ideas.

The usefulness of examples has mixed support (e.g., Smith, 2002). Leggett Dugosh and Paulus (2005) also investigated facilitation processes that occurred during idea-generation tasks. Groups were presented with either a large or small number of either unique or common ideas. Groups that were exposed to a larger number of common ideas resulted in higher fluency. Furthermore, researchers found that the groups' ability to recall the ideas that were provided to them was related to enhanced idea generation.

Similarly, Connolly, Routhieaux, and Schneider (1993) compared the introduction of rare and common ideas to groups. Although they expected exposure to rare ideas to stimulate further ideas in groups, their research did not support this hypothesis. This unexpected non-finding may be explained by referring to work done by Mumford and colleagues (1997). When individuals were presented with either unique or common categories of ideas, the ultimate outcome (i.e., ideas that were original or of high quality) depended on the strategy used to generate ideas. It is possible that when presented with unique or rare ideas, instructions on how to leverage those diverse examples to generate new ideas (e.g., try to identify features of the example and think about what that information represents) may be necessary to realize the expected benefits from this approach to idea generation.

Proposition 33. Providing common examples for idea generation will facilitate idea generation fluency in teams.

Proposition 34. Providing teams with instructions on how to utilize examples to generate new ideas will result in higher-quality and more original ideas.

IDEA EVALUATION AND SELECTION

Individual Level

Once the individual problem solver has generated ideas, the next step involves evaluating the ideas generated and selecting the best one. This effort is considered part of the implementation phase of creative problem solving (Basadur, 1997; Mumford, 2001), but has not received as much attention as earlier phases in the creative problem-solving process. The idea evaluation process includes the evaluation of an idea or set of ideas against a standard and the determination of whether any of the ideas from the previous idea-generation process can be implemented, should be rejected, or may be revised (Mumford, Lonergan, & Scott, 2002a).

While idea evaluation has not received as much attention as idea generation, it is no less critical for creative problem solving. In organizational settings, many ideas are generated, but only a few reach the implementation phase (Sharma, 1999). Furthermore, the quality and originality of the final idea selected for implementation will depend on the quality of the evaluation and selection process. When presented with multiple options, individuals do not always select the best one, so understanding the factors that facilitate the evaluation and choice of a creative solution is important. One possible reason that the idea evaluation process has not received as much attention as other processes in the past is because it seems to require more convergent thought relative to the previously discussed processes, which tend to involve more divergent thought (Basadur, 1995). The idea evaluation process also relies on the external evaluation of creative work by other individuals. Evaluation by external sources has an important effect on creativity (Amabile, 1996; Shalley, 1995; Shalley & Perry-Smith, 2001) but is not considered a cognitive process; for this reason, it is not reviewed here.

The first question that arises is whether people are able to evaluate ideas accurately. Runco and his colleagues, in a series of studies on idea evaluation using diverse populations including children, teachers, undergraduate students, and managers, found that individuals are, indeed, able to accurately evaluate ideas for originality and novelty (Basadur et al., 2000; Runco & Basadur, 1993; Runco & Chand, 1995; Runco & Smith, 1992; Runco & Vega, 1990). Furthermore, Runco and Smith (1992) found that evaluative accuracy is not correlated with a measure of critical thinking (convergent thinking). Likewise, several other studies have found that evaluative thinking is correlated with divergent thinking scores of fluency and flexibility, suggesting that although idea evaluation may seem to be a convergent thought process, it is more likely a divergent process (Runco, 1991; Runco & Chand, 1995). These findings also suggest that being able to identify an original idea is related to being able to generate original ideas.

The next issue is how individuals determine that they should stop generating ideas and move on to this next phase of evaluation and selection. This issue has not received attention on the individual side, but it has been investigated at the team level and so will be addressed in the next section.

Another issue that needs to be addressed is how people go about evaluating ideas. A model of idea evaluation suggested by Mumford, Schultz, and Osburn (2002b) begins with forecasting. According to this model, the first step in idea evaluation requires the prediction of the outcomes or consequences of idea implementation. These consequences are specific to the idea evaluated and the context in which it is implemented. In addition, the idea is compared to a set of goals and standards to determine whether the idea satisfies all, some, or none of the goals identified.

The Mumford et al. (2002a) model suggests that goals and standards will have a pronounced effect on the evaluation and selection process. It is therefore important to understand how goals and standards are developed. Ill-defined problems, by definition, have multiple goals, and some of these goals may conflict with one another, such that the attainment of one reduces the likelihood of the attainment of another. The problem construction process may provide some of the guidelines for goals and standards, as goals may be included as part of the problem representation.

Another factor that may influence the type of standards used for evaluation is the domain of interest. Feist (1991) has suggested that evaluation will depend on the domain such that evaluation of art is more intuitive whereas evaluation of science is more analytical. In a similar vein, Yuan and Zhou (2002) have suggested that evaluation of art focuses more on originality whereas evaluation of solutions to organizational problems focuses more on appropriateness or practicality. In a study designed to assess these domain differences, Sullivan and Ford (2005) found that the type of problem presented to participants (strategic choice vs. advertising) resulted in different evaluations of choices. The strategic choice evaluations produced two specific factors of novelty and value, whereas a combined factor emerged for the advertising campaign. These findings indicate that the standards for evaluation do, indeed, differ from one type of problem to the next.

In another empirical investigation on the effects of standards on creative problem solving, Lonergan, Scott, and Mumford (2004) specifically manipulated the standards used. These researchers asked 148 undergraduate students to assume the role of a marketing manager and evaluate three proposals for a new product campaign. After reading through the product description and the proposals, the participants were asked to provide an evaluation of each idea using an idea appraisal form. The idea appraisal form was designed to allow the manipulation of standards by focusing the participants on either innovative or operating efficiency standards. In addition, the originality of the plans presented to participants varied and included one low-originality, one average-originality, and one high-originality plan. Finally, two types of plans were provided. Half of the participants reviewed television ad campaigns (considered a more ill-defined task), and the other half reviewed magazine ad proposals (considered a more well-defined task). In addition to the evaluation, participants were asked to provide ideas for revisions and formulate plans for implementation. The implementation plans were then rated based on their quality and originality and served as the dependent variables.

The results indicated that innovative standards resulted in more creative implementation plans for the ill-defined TV ads. In contrast, more creative plans for the magazine ads were generated when operative efficiency standards were provided. Focusing on innovative standards was beneficial for less innovative ideas (the low-originality plans), but operating efficiency standards were more beneficial when the ideas were more innovative.

The results from this study underscore the importance of the type of standards applied in the idea evaluation process for final idea selection and on the next process of implementation planning. The study by Lonergan et al. (2004) manipulated standards through the appraisal form given to participants. In other studies, standards and goals may be manipulated through the instructions provided. Research on goal setting and instructions to be creative has found that these factors can influence the outcome of the creative problem-solving effort, in a way that is consistent with the goal or instruction (Runco et al., 2005b; Runco & Okuda, 1991; Shalley, 1991, 1995).

A final issue relating to standards and their effect on evaluation is the possibility of shifting standards. This relationship may be particularly relevant for ill-defined problems, as the goals and standards may change as the individual engages in the actual creative problem-solving effort (Necka, 2003). As a result of new information, new combinations, and the like, the standards applied to the evaluation of the solution set may potentially change. It is possible, therefore, that the timing of evaluation may result in different effects due to the shift in goals and standards.

In the only study to evaluate the effect of timing of the evaluation on creativity, Lubart (2001) asked participants to compose a short story or create a still-life drawing. Participants were instructed to evaluate their work either early in the creative process or later. Lubart found that students who evaluated their work early in the writing process wrote more creative stories than those who evaluated their work later. No differences were found for the drawing task.

Team Level

It has been suggested that teams may provide the most benefit to the creative problem-solving process in the later stages of the creative process – namely, during idea evaluation and selection and implementation (Milliken et al., 2003; Mumford, Feldman, Hein, & Nagao, 2001a; Nijstad, Rietzschel, & Stroebe, 2006; West, 2002b). Research in this area has yielded somewhat mixed results. Nijstad et al. (2006) found that while groups generated fewer ideas and fewer ideas of high quality than did nominal groups, the ideas selected for final consideration were of equivalent quality, suggesting that groups may not be better than individuals at this task. The study by Mumford, Schultz, and Van Doorn (2001b) found that under certain conditions, groups were better at evaluating and selecting a solution than were individuals. This study provides some clues as to when groups will be more effective than individuals in evaluating and selecting ideas.

Mumford et al. (2001a) asked participants to solve one of two problems: one that was social in nature or one that was cognitive in nature. Participants were assigned to one of three training conditions: (1) consistent training (match between training and problem-solving exercise); (2) inconsistent training (no match between training and problem-solving exercise); or (3) no training. In addition, half of the participants were asked to respond to a priming questionnaire prior to the problem-solving exercise, whereas the other half did not complete any survey before solving the problem. Creativity was evaluated in two ways – fluency (i.e., the number of solutions generated by the individual or the group) and a rating of the creativity of the solution selected as the best.

In this study, the researchers found that very different factors influenced individual versus group creativity. Individuals benefited from priming and generated more alternatives compared to the no-priming condition. This distinction, in turn, was related to the selection of a more creative solution. For groups, while priming led to the development of more alternatives, it did not necessarily lead to the selection of a more creative solution. Instead, groups benefited from having all individuals be exposed to the same training when no priming condition was available. Moreover, this group (matched training, no priming) outperformed all individuals as well as all other groups in the study.

Mumford et al. (2001a) suggest that groups perform better when fewer alternatives are available, such that time and coordination requirements are minimized. Because fewer resources are expended on the review of multiple alternatives, groups are able to fully elaborate and expand on the better, more optimal choices for the solution to be implemented. In addition, having a shared understanding or a shared mental model facilitates production and selection of creative solutions in groups. These results further underscore the importance of having an appropriate and shared understanding of the problem (i.e., a problem representation). In this context, a shared understanding of the problem representation created a shared understanding of how to evaluate the solutions generated or standards, which in turn allowed the selection of the most creative solution.

Proposition 35. Groups will outperform individuals in solution evaluation and selection.

Proposition 36. Groups that agree on the problem representation to use for constructing the problem and have an appropriate representation will evaluate and select a more creative solution.

Proposition 37. While fluency in the idea generation phase may be beneficial to individuals, it may be detrimental to, or have no effect on group creative problem solving.

Proposition 38. Group agreement and identification of the appropriate standards for evaluation will facilitate creative problem solving in groups.

Limited data exist on the issue of idea evaluation and selection both at the individual and group levels, so much more research in this area is clearly needed. Extrapolating from the model developed by Mumford et al. (2002a) on idea evaluation suggests that just as standards are critical for individual evaluation, so they are also important for group evaluation and selection. The study by Mumford et al. (2001a) suggests that agreement on these standards through a shared mental model may lead to more effective evaluation and better idea selection by groups. At the same time, some degree of disagreement – particularly on the relative importance of various goals or standards – may potentially lead to the selection of a more innovative solution, one that takes into account multiple standards. As previous research suggests, the degree of disagreement matters. Either too much disagreement or not enough common ground may lead to difficulty in communication and shared understanding.

Proposition 39. A curvilinear relationship will exist between agreement on standards and solution creativity in teams.

Proposition 40. Cross-functional and other heterogeneous groups will be more likely than homogeneous groups to disagree on which standards should apply to the idea evaluation and selection process.

Proposition 41. Multiple competing standards in teams will result in the selection of more creative solutions than a single standard or complementary standards.

IMPLEMENTATION PLANNING AND MONITORING

Individual Level

After an idea has been selected, it needs to be implemented. Much of the work on implementation of creativity and innovation has focused on the actual implementation process itself. As a result, the literature tends to consider factors that influence the initial implementation (e.g., persuasion, coordination, or support for the innovation) as well as factors that influence long-term acceptance and use of the innovation (Clegg, Unsworth, Epitropaki, & Parker, 2002; Klein, Conn, & Sorra, 2001; Klein & Sorra, 1996; West, 2002a, 2002b, 2003). Not surprisingly, much of the theoretical and empirical work on innovation implementation has focused on teams and organizations, and not individuals. While theoretical approaches to planning have indicated that planning is important to creativity, research in the creativity arena targeting individual-level cognitive factors that influence implementation has been lacking (Naglieri & Kaufman, 2001). As stated earlier, this chapter concentrates on the cognitive processes related to creativity and innovation. While implementation is, indeed, a more social phenomenon, both the planning involved in developing an implementation plan and the monitoring of the results of implementation are cognitive in nature.

Early work on planning focused on the sequencing of actions to attain a goal and monitoring of the plan's success (Covington, 1987; Hayes-Roth &

Hayes-Roth, 1979). Later work has emphasized not only the development of an action plan, but also the mental simulation of the action sequences, anticipation of those actions' consequences, and identification of goals, constraints, and development of a solution to the problem as part of plan development (Mumford et al., 2001b, 2002b; Scholnick & Friedman, 1987).

Some of these aspects of planning are similar to the problem construction processes discussed earlier (e.g., identification of goals and constraints) and, therefore, will not be discussed here. Other aspects of planning have not been considered yet and will be covered in this section. Mumford and his colleagues (Mumford et al., 2001b, 2002b) have identified several key planning activities and processes. Among the important aspects of planning for the purpose of developing an implementation plan for a creative solution are generating a basic plan for implementation, identifying the consequences of the implementation action, identifying important milestones that would indicate success or failure, developing backup plans to address problems, monitoring the implementation and the attainment of the milestones, and revising the implementation plan (Mumford et al., 2001b, 2002b).

The problem representation developed in the problem construction phase will provide the goals necessary for the implementation plan. In addition to the problem representation, information gathered in the information encoding processes, coupled with the solution selected for implementation, will inform the individual about possible constraints in the implementation, identify needed resources, and point to possible difficulties in implementation. Berger and Dibattista (1992) found that the amount of information accessed in the information search phase influenced how elaborate the plans were. Likewise, the diversity of the information obtained influenced how elaborate plans were and how many contingency plans were developed.

While earlier processes contribute to plan development, several important key issues emerge specifically in the implementation planning and monitoring process. One important concern has to do with identifying the consequences of actions as developed in the implementation plan. Identifying these consequences allows the problem solver not only to anticipate positive outcomes, but also to evaluate possible negative outcomes, identify actions that would minimize the effects of the negative outcomes, and develop contingency plans. It is not surprising that forecasting has been found to be important for the development of plans and to planning ability (Berger, Guilford, & Christensen, 1957; Isenberg, 1986; Serfaty, MacMillan, Entin, & Entin, 1997).

The importance of forecasting calls attention to another important aspect of implementation plans: Successful plans allow for flexibility and possible change if the implementation does not proceed as originally planned. Berger et al. (1957) found that adaptability and flexibility were important factors in planning activities. Several empirical studies have found that individuals typically engage in plan revision as part of the planning process (Jaarsvled & van Leeuwen, 2005; Keane, 1996; Woods & Davies, 1973).

The need for revision may emerge as a result of identification of a gap between the desired state and actual state as it relates to plan execution. Specifically, planning identifies milestones that would indicate progress toward the goals and determines the need for plan adjustment based on this progress. In a study of physicians and planning of treatment, Kuipers, Moskowitz, and Kassinger (1988) found that effective plans were iterative based on specific treatment outcomes and patient status. Similarly, Xiao, Milgram, and Doyle (1997), in a study of anesthesiologists, found that after initial plan development, plans were revised based on key milestones indicating progress (or lack thereof). The need for revisions also indicates that planning includes the development of backup plans. The study by Xiao et al. suggested that better planners also developed backup plans, and Eisenhardt (1989) suggests that more effective decision makers develop and consider more alternative plans.

Finally, the need for the revision of a plan becomes particularly apparent when one considers the nature of the environment in which the implementation occurs and the type of problems for which the solution was developed. Creative solutions developed to address organizational problems represent solutions to ill-defined and complex problems, typically have multiple goals, influence multiple constituents, represent a departure from normal operations, and occur in an environment that is constantly changing. These factors suggest another important issue in the development and execution of effective plans – namely, opportunistic planning.

Opportunistic planning refers to fact that individual problem solvers will identify potential opportunities for goal satisfaction, even if the initial plan does not account for those opportunities (Gollwitzer & Schaal, 1998; Seifert & Patalano, 2001). In this way, individuals may adapt plans based on changes that occur in the environment, thereby taking advantage of those changes. Opportunistic planning requires that problem solvers scan their environment for cues that suggest an opportunity. In a series of studies on opportunistic planning, Patalano and Seifert (1997) and Seifert, Patalano, and Hammond (1997) found that developing a plan allowed individuals to recognize relevant cues, even when they were not part of the original plan. Similarly, studies on implementation intentions, which link specific goals with environmental or situational cues, found that implementation intentions are related to identification of relevant cues, opportunistic planning, and goal attainment (Gollwitzer, 1999; Sheeran & Orbell, 1999; Webb & Sheeran, 2004). Studies on managerial planning have found similar results, where managers were more aware and considered information more opportunistically in light of a developed plan (Eisenhardt, 1989; Oswald, Mossholder, & Harris, 1997; Thomas & McDaniel, 1990).

Team Level

Innovation, which may be defined as the implementation of a creative idea, has received a great deal of attention at the team level. According to West (2002a), innovation includes the implementation of an idea. Implementation of innovation requires coordination of different departments in the organization (i.e., product development, production, marketing, finance), so it is not surprising that much of the research on innovation and implementation has emerged from team-focused literature (West et al., 2004).

According to West (2002b), understanding innovation – that is, the implementation of ideas – is more critical for organizational success than understanding creativity. Furthermore, West argues, implementation is more complex and difficult than generating ideas. However, much of the research on team innovation implementation has concentrated on issues of coordination, persuasion, organizational climate that supports innovation, and other social phenomena, rather than the role of the team in implementation planning and monitoring (Gilson, Mathieu, Shalley, & Ruddy, 2005; Klein & Knight, 2005; Scott & Bruce, 1994; Shalley et al., 2004; West et al., 2004).

One reason that innovation implementation is viewed as so important at the team level is because of the need to coordinate different parties and address their concerns. Although these considerations have distinct implications for interactions and social processes, they also have important implications from a cognitive perspective. As discussed in the section on individual-level effects, the primary issues in implementation planning are developing a plan, anticipating problems with implementation, developing ways to address those potential problems, developing backup plans, and identifying and monitoring milestones that indicate progress. Monitoring is particularly important because planners typically cannot anticipate every possible obstacle. As a consequence, in implementation, the team must be attentive to cues that would indicate the plan's success or possible obstacles, and should be prepared to revise the original plan (Leudar & Costal, 1996). Developing an implementation plan is particularly important at the team level because it provides individual members of the team with a shared understanding of the process and their specific roles and responsibilities in that process (Janicik & Bartel, 2003; Mumford et al., 2001a; Weingart, 1992). For that reason, planning at the team level is more time-consuming and requires more effort.

Because this process is so effortful, teams do not always engage in planning. Hackman, Brousseau, and Weiss (1976) found that teams engaged in planning only when instructed to do so. Others have found that planning does not occur even for novel or difficult tasks, even though it might be expected that planning would be most beneficial in these circumstances (Weingart, 1992). Still others have found that those teams that engage in planning when tasks are complex and difficult goals are set perform better (Marta, Leritz, & Mumford, 2005; Weingart, 1992).

Weingart (1992) hypothesized that when goals are easy and the task is simple, planning is not as important. In contrast, complex tasks and difficult goals might benefit more substantially from planning, even though there is a competition for cognitive resources between planning and execution. In addition, studies have suggested that more interdependency between subgoals or subtasks might require more planning and coordination from team members (Marks & Panzer, 2004; Weldon, Jehn, & Pradhan, 1991).

Other studies have focused on the effects of external demands on planning. West (2002a) suggests that external demands are an important issue that facilitates innovation and innovation planning. External demands can be viewed in this context as contributing to task complexity. In a series of studies, West and his colleagues found that innovation implementation and implementation planning were direct responses to external demands such as workload, consumer demands, interpersonal conflicts, and procedural difficulties (Bunce & West, 1995; West et al., 2004).

Proposition 42. Teams will be more likely to plan and coordinate activities when instructed to do so.

Proposition 43. Teams will be more likely to plan and coordinate activities when the task is complex or goals are difficult.

Proposition 44. Teams will be more likely to plan and coordinate activities when tasks are interdependent.

Implementation planning in teams will occur for more complex tasks. Implementing creative solutions, by definition, is difficult. Because the initial task facing the team is ill defined, agreement about the best solution or idea both within and outside the team is not guaranteed. Even if team members reach agreement about the best solution through the cognitive processes outlined previously, to implement the idea, typically more than just the team needs to accept the solution. External demands, organizational policies and procedures, resources, and the like all play important roles in the acceptance of an innovation and its successful implementation (Klein et al., 2001; Klein & Knight, 2005; West et al., 2004).

Part of the implementation planning challenge facing the team is how to address these possible constraints. The first step the team needs to take is to anticipate and forecast the possible constraints and difficulties in implementation. Because members of cross-functional or multi-disciplinary teams will have different perspectives and will belong to different networks within and outside the organization, these teams will have access to more information about possible objections and constraints on implementation. In a qualitative study in which they conducted interviews with members of multi-disciplinary product development teams, Vissers and Dankbaar (2002) found that one advantage of multi-disciplinary teams is the team members' knowledge of the various constraints, which enables them to forecast the difficulties that might be faced by the multiple constituents involved in the implementation process. However, team members will need to share this information with the rest of the team before a plan for implementation that addresses all of these concerns can be devised. Teams that engage in discussions about planning, including discussions of the possible constraints, have been found to have more effective performance (Lewis, 2004; Tschan, 1995; Zaccaro, Gualtieri, & Minionis, 1995).

Proposition 45. Heterogeneous teams will be able to anticipate more possible obstacles to plan implementation and develop better plans to address those obstacles.

Proposition 46. Heterogeneous teams that spend more time discussing possible constraints in plan development will develop more effective implementation plans.

Further, planning allows heterogeneous teams to maximize the effectiveness of their diversity of experience and expertise. Using discussion and planning, team members become aware of more aspects of how the plan should be carried out, what roles different members will fulfill, and which potential difficulties each person may need to address. Indeed, Stout, Cannon-Bowers,

Salas, and Milanovich (1999) have found that planning offers a way to develop shared mental models that facilitate team performance. In turn, these shared mental models can facilitate the effectiveness of implementation planning in general, and the modification and revision of plans in particular.

Plans may change and shift as a result of changes to the external environment, as a result of unanticipated difficulties in implementation, or because new opportunities for attaining certain goals emerge. This propensity for change requires the team to be able to adapt and change the plan, revise the plan, or use backup plans as necessary for successful implementation. Shared mental models will allow team members to respond more quickly to changes in plans and to refine plans. Accordingly, Mumford et al. (2001a) found that shared mental models in groups facilitate the elaboration and refinement of plans.

Other work has suggested that more diverse teams are better able to respond to change and engage in opportunistic planning. Marta et al. (2005) found that diverse groups engaged in more planning and more effective planning when change was introduced, whereas homogeneous groups were more successful when no such change occurred. Stout et al. (1999) found that teams that engage in more planning were able to anticipate other team members' needs for information and provide that information more efficiently. In addition, this awareness of informational requirements and other concerns relating to the implementation plan allows team members to be alert and attend to cues that suggest opportunistic planning.

Proposition 47. Planning activities allow team members to exchange and discuss information relevant to plan development.

Proposition 48. Planning will facilitate the development of shared mental models in heterogeneous teams.

Proposition 49. Shared mental models in teams will facilitate effective responses to plan revision and refinement.

Proposition 50. Heterogeneous groups will adapt better to plan changes and will be able to engage in more opportunistic planning.

CONCLUSIONS

It is also important to look at the entire creative problem-solving process as a whole. One critical issue is when and how individuals cycle through the various processes. Although the discussion in this chapter might seem to suggest that this process follows a linear progression from problem construction, to information search, to idea generation, to idea evaluation and selection, and finally to implementation planning and monitoring, this is probably not the case. While individuals or teams may sometimes progress from one process to the other in a linear fashion, it is quite likely that for most the progression will not be so neatly prescribed. In some cases, processes may be applied so automatically that it may seem as if they did not occur at all. In other cases, individuals and teams may return to earlier processes.

Return to earlier processes may occur as a result of difficulties in applying a later process, an event suggesting that a previous process resulted in an ineffective outcome (Mumford et al., 1991). For example, an individual who cannot solve the problem may realize that his or her problem construction and resulting problem representation were incomplete and, therefore, may return to that process. By contrast, difficulties in developing an implementation plan may suggest that the solution selected in the previous process was not the optimal solution. An individual may also return to previous processes as a result of new information or insight that emerged as the result of a later process.

Finally, these processes are not as neatly separated as discussed here. Although much of the information search occurs early in the processes to support the development of alternative solutions, individuals may also search for information later in the process to provide support for the selection or elimination of a specific alternative or to identify potential obstacles for the implementation plan. Ford and Sullivan (2004) proposed that novel contributions made during the problem construction, information search, and alternative generation phases might contribute to solution quality and originality, but that novel contributions made later in the cycle will be more disruptive and perhaps even reduce the likelihood of creative solutions. In the only study to empirically test the timing effect, Lubart (2001) found that evaluation early in the writing process had a different effect on the creativity of a short story than evaluation later in the writing process.

Whereas at least a little empirical research has focused on the effect of timing of the process, even less is known about this effect in the team context. Two specific issues need to be addressed at the team level that are unique to team creative problem solving.

The first issue relates to the fact that different team members may move through these cognitive processes at different rates. Thus, while some team members are moving toward alternative generation, others may still be formulating the problem. The effect of having different team members progressing at different rates is not clear. Some team members or the team as a whole might potentially be pushed to move faster through the process. The opposite might also occur, with some team members being slowed down. Accordingly, this may be a source of tension in team creative problem solving. It is also unclear how the fact that different team members progress through the process at different rates might affect the outcome of the creative problem solving.

The second issue relates to when and how the team as a whole cycles back through earlier processes. Just as different team members may progress through the process at different rates, so different team members may vary in terms of their need to revisit earlier processes and the processes to which they choose to return. Again, it is not clear what happens in the team environment – that is, whether the team as a whole revisits earlier processes, or only some members do. In addition, the conditions that signal the need to return to earlier processes might have to be particularly strong, as teams may show greater resistance than individuals to revisiting issues that are deemed as settled. Because teams need to invest additional time coordinating their problem-solving efforts relative to individuals, a return to an earlier process would be particularly time-consuming in a team setting. Ford and Sullivan (2004) alluded to this issue when they claimed that novel contributions would be disruptive later in the creative problem-solving cycle.

Proposition 51. The specific effect of different rates of progression of team members on the team creative problem-solving process and its outcomes is subject to speculation and needs to be investigated.

Proposition 52. Teams will be more resistant to returning to earlier processes (or parts of earlier processes) than individuals.

Finally, two common threads appear in our discussion of all processes. First is the finding that all processes require time and effort. For almost all processes, studies suggest that spending more time on the process will result in a higher-quality outcome for the specific process and affect the creative problem-solving process as a whole (Illies & Reiter-Palmon, 2004; Johns & Morse, 1997; Reiter-Palmon et al., 1997). In the team environment, not only are the creative problem-solving processes time-consuming, but more time also needs to be invested in the coordination, discussion, sharing, and integration of different points of view. Studies on creative problem solving and decision making in the group environment suggest that effective communication is key to successful outcomes (Hinsz, Tindale, & Vollrath, 1997; Gibson, 2001). As a result, creative problem solving in teams is even more time-consuming and effortful than the corresponding process is for the individual.

The second common thread is the tension between convergent and divergent thinking. Early work by Guilford (1950) has focused our attention on divergent processes and their effect on creative problem solving. More recent theory and research, however, suggest that both are important for successful creative problem solving (Basadur, 1995; Brophy, 2001). While individuals may have a preference for one type of cognitive style (Brophy, 1998a) and, therefore, excel in some processes and not necessarily others, teams may utilize the strength of each individual. Teams that consist of individuals who favor both convergent thinking and divergent thinking, and that have a balance of these two styles, may be more likely to execute all of the different processes equally well. Indeed, Basadur and Gelade (2005) found that teams that had a balance between the preference for divergent thought and for convergent thought were more successful.

Proposition 53. Creative problem solving in teams will be more time-consuming than creative problem solving conducted by individuals.

Proposition 54. Teams consisting of individuals with a preference for divergent and convergent thought will be more successful across all aspects of the creative problem-solving process.

In conclusion, this chapter has provided an in-depth review of the cognitive processes that influence creative problem solving at the individual level, and from a multi-level perspective it has sought to understand what happens when these cognitive processes are "aggregated" in team and group situations.

Much of the work on group creativity has focused on only one process – that of idea generation – and then typically on only one criterion – that of fluency (Paulus et al., 2006). This stream of research has concluded, quite consistently, that individuals and nominal groups outperform groups, and that individuals and nominal groups generate more ideas than groups do (Mullen et al., 1991; Paulus & Brown, 2003).

If that is the case, why do we continue to see the extensive use of groups and teams in businesses and organizations? One possibility is that for various reasons we would like to believe that groups are better than individuals; as the old adage concludes, "Two heads are better than one."

We are predisposed to believe, even in the face of reality, that groups perform better than individuals (Hackman, 1998; Naquin & Tynan, 2003). Another possibility is that we have not fully investigated how groups operate, particularly from a cognitive perspective. To date, group research has tended to focus on one cognitive process and one outcome. If we investigate other criteria (such as quality and originality) or other cognitive processes, we might find evidence supporting the superiority of groups and teams. This idea is echoed in the title of West's (2002b) article, "Ideas are ten a penny: It's team implementation, not idea generation, that counts." This chapter has speculated about how teams might influence other cognitive processes in the creative problem-solving effort (beyond idea generation), suggesting possible avenues for investigation of the specific aspects of creative problem solving and the specific conditions under which teams might be more effective than individuals.

REFERENCES

Adelman, L., Gualtieri, J., & Stanford, S. (1995). Examining the effect of causal focus on the option generation process: An experiment using protocol analysis. *Organizational Behavior and Human Decision Processes, 61,* 54–66.

Amabile, T. M. (1983). The social psychology of creativity: A componential conceptualization. *Journal of Personality and Social Psychology, 45,* 357–376.

Amabile, T. M. (1996). *Creativity in context: Update to the social psychology of creativity.* Boulder, CO: Westview Press.

Amabile, T. M., & Gryskiewicz, N. D. (1989). The creative environment scales: Work environment inventory. *Creativity Research Journal, 2,* 231–253.

Andre, T., Schumer, H., & Whitaker, P. (1979). Group discussion and individual creativity. *Journal of General Psychology, 100,* 111–123.

Arad, S., Hanson, M. A., & Schnieder, R. J. (1997). A framework for the study of the relationship between organizational characteristics and organizational innovation. *Organizational Dynamics, 24,* 20–35.

Asmus, C. L., & James, K. (2005). Nominal group technique, social loafing, and group creative project quality. *Creativity Research Journal, 17,* 349–354.

Atuahene-Gima, K. (2003). The effects of centrifugal forces on product development speed and quality: How does problem solving matter? *Academy of Management Journal, 46,* 359–373.

Baer, J. M. (1988). Long-term effects of creativity training with middle school students. *Journal of Early Adolescence, 8,* 183–193.

Bagozzi, R. P., & Dholakia, U. M. (2005). Three roles of past experience in goal setting and goal striving. In: T. Betsch & S. Haberstroh (Eds), *The routines of decision making* (pp. 21–38). Mahwah, NJ: Lawrence Erlbaum Associates.

Bantel, K. A., & Jackson, S. E. (1989). Top management and innovations in banking: Does the demography of the top team make a difference? *Strategic Management, 10*, 107–124.

Barki, H., & Pinsonneault, A. (2001). Small group brainstorming and idea quality: Is electronic brainstorming the most effective approach? *Small Group Research, 32*, 158–205.

Barrick, J. A., & Spilker, B. C. (2003). The relations between knowledge, search strategy, and performance in unaided and aided information search. *Organizational Behavior and Human Decision Processes, 90*, 1–18.

Barron, F., & Harrington, D. M. (1981). Creativity, intelligence, and personality. *Annual Review of Psychology, 32*, 439–476.

Basadur, M. S. (1994). Managing the creative process in organizations. In: M. A. Runco (Ed.), *Problem finding, problem solving, and creativity* (pp. 237–268). Norwood, NJ: Ablex.

Basadur, M. S. (1995). Optimal ideation-evaluation ratios. *Creativity Research Journal, 8*, 63–75.

Basadur, M. S. (1997). Organizational development interventions for enhancing creativity in the workplace. *Journal of Creative Behavior, 31*, 59–72.

Basadur, M. S., Ellspermann, S. J., & Evans, G. W. (1994). A new methodology for formulating ill-structured problems. *OMEGA: The International Journal of Management Science, 22*, 627–645.

Basadur, M. S., & Gelade, G. (2005). Using the creative problem solving profile (CPSP) for diagnosing and solving real-world problems. *Emergence, 5*, 22–47.

Basadur, M. S., Graen, G. B., & Green, S. G. (1982). Training in creative problem solving: Effects on ideation and problem finding in an applied research organization. *Organizational Behavior and Human Performance, 30*, 41–70.

Basadur, M. S., & Head, M. (2001). Team performance and satisfaction: A link to cognitive style within a process framework. *Journal of Creative Behavior, 35*, 227–248.

Basadur, M. S., Runco, M. A., & Vega, L. A. (2000). Understanding how creative thinking skills, attitudes, and behaviors work together: A causal process model. *Journal of Creative Behavior, 34*, 77–100.

Baughman, W. A., & Mumford, M. D. (1995). Process-analytic models of creative capacities: Operations influencing the combination-and-reorganization process. *Creativity Research Journal, 8*, 37–62.

Bedard, J., & Chi, M. T. H. (1992). Expertise. *Current Directions in Psychological Science, 1*, 135–139.

Berger, C. R., & Dibattista, P. (1992). Information seeking and plan elaboration: What do you need to know to know what to do? *Communication Monographs, 59*, 368–387.

Berger, R. M., Guilford, J. P., & Christensen, P. R. (1957). A factor-analytic study of planning abilities. *Psychological Monographs, 71*, 31.

Betsch, T., Haberstroh, S., Glockner, A., Haar, T., & Fiedler, K. (2001). The effects of routing strength on adaptation and information search in recurrent decision making. *Organizational Behavior and Human Decision Processes, 84*, 23–53.

Bettenhausen, K. L. (1991). Five years of group research: What we have learned and what needs to be addressed. *Journal of Management, 17*, 345–381.

Bonnardel, N., & Marmeche, E. (2004). Evocation processes by novice and expert designers: Towards stimulating analogical thinking. *Creativity and Innovation Management, 13*, 176–186.

Bouchard, T. J., & Hare, M. (1970). Size, performance, and potential in brainstorming groups. *Journal of Applied Psychology, 54*, 51–55.

Brophy, D. R. (1998a). Understanding, measuring, and enhancing individual creative problem-solving efforts. *Creativity Research Journal, 11,* 123–150.

Brophy, D. R. (1998b). Understanding, measuring, and enhancing collective creative problem-solving efforts. *Creativity Research Journal, 11,* 199–229.

Brophy, D. R. (2001). Comparing the attributes, activities, and performance of divergent, convergent, and combination thinkers. *Creativity Research Journal, 13,* 439–455.

Brown, S. L., & Eisenhardt, K. M. (1995). Product development: Past research, present findings, and future directions. *Academy of Management Review, 20,* 343–378.

Browne, G. J., & Pitts, M. G. (2004). Stopping rule use during information search in design problems. *Organizational Behavior and Human Decision Processes, 95,* 208–224.

Bunce, D., & West, M. A. (1995). Self perceptions and perceptions of group climate as predictors of individual innovation at work. *Applied Psychology: An International Review, 44,* 199–215.

Bunderson, J. S., & Sutcliffe, K. M. (2002). Comparing alternative conceptualizations of functional diversity in management teams: Process and performance effects. *Academy of Management Journal, 45,* 875–893.

Butler, A. B., & Scherer, L. L. (1997). The effects of elicitation aids, knowledge, and problem content on option quantity and quality. *Organizational Behavior and Human Decision Processes, 72,* 184–202.

Cannon-Bowers, J. A., Salas, E., & Converse, S. (1993). Shared mental models in expert team decision making. In: N. J. Castellan, Jr (Ed.), *Individual and group decision making: Current issues* (pp. 221–246). Hillsdale, NJ: Lawrence Erlbaum Associates.

Charness, N. (1991). Expertise in chess: The balance between knowledge and search. In: K. A. Ericsson & J. Smith (Eds), *Toward a general theory of expertise* (pp. 39–63). New York, NY: Cambridge University Press.

Charness, N., Reingold, E. M., Pomplun, M., & Stampe, D. M. (2001). The perceptual aspect of skilled performance in chess: Evidence from eye movements. *Memory and Cognition, 29,* 1146–1153.

Chi, M. T. H., Glaser, R., & Rees, E. (1982). Expertise in problem solving. In: R. J. Sternberg (Ed.), *Advances in the psychology of human intelligence* (Vol. 1, pp. 1–75). Hillsdale, NJ: Lawrence Erlbaum Associates.

Chirumbolo, A., Mannetti, L., Pierro, A., Areni, A., & Kruglanski, A. (2005). Motivated closed-mindedness and creativity in small groups. *Small Group Research, 36,* 59–82.

Choi, H., & Thompson, L. (2005). Old wine in a new bottle: Impact of membership change on group creativity. *Organizational Behavior and Human Decision Processes, 98,* 121–132.

Clegg, C., Unsworth, K., Epitropaki, O., & Parker, G. (2002). Implicating trust in the innovation process. *Journal of Occupational and Organizational Psychology, 75,* 409–422.

Connolly, T., Routhieaux, R. L., & Schneider, S. K. (1993). On the effectiveness of group brainstorming: Test of one underlying cognitive mechanism. *Small Group Research, 24,* 490–503.

Couger, J. D. (1996). *Creativity and innovation in information system organizations.* Danvers, MA: Boyd and Fraser.

Covington, M. V. (1987). Instructions in problem solving and planning. In: S. L. Friedman, F. K. Scholnick & R. R. Cocking (Eds), *The role of planning in cognitive development* (pp. 469–514). Cambridge, MA: Cambridge University Press.

Cummings, J. N. (2004). Work groups, structural diversity, and knowledge sharing in a global organization. *Management Science, 50,* 352–364.

Curral, L. A., Forrester, R. H., Dawson, J. F., & West, M. A. (2001). It's what you do and the way that you do it: Team task, team size, and innovation-related group processes. *European Journal of Work and Organizational Psychology, 10,* 187–204.

Dahl, D. W., & Moreau, P. (2002). The influence and value of analogical thinking during new product ideation. *Journal of Marketing Research, 39,* 47–60.

Davidson, J. E. (1995). The suddenness of insight. In: R. J. Sternberg & J. E. Davidson (Eds), *The nature of insight* (pp. 125–155). Cambridge, MA: MIT Press.

De Dreu, C. K. W. (2002). Team innovation and team effectiveness: The importance of minority dissent and reflexivity. *European Journal of Work and Organizational Psychology, 11,* 285–298.

De Dreu, C. K. W., & West, M. A. (2001). Minority dissent and team innovation: The importance of participation in decision-making. *Journal of Applied Psychology, 86,* 1191–1201.

Dennis, A. R., & Valacich, J. S. (1999). Research note: Electronic brainstorming: Illusions and patterns of productivity. *Information Systems Research, 10,* 375–377.

Dennis, A. R., & Williams, M. L. (2003). Electronic brainstorming: Theory, research, and future directions. In: P. B. Paulus & B. A. Nijstad (Eds), *Group creativity: Innovation through collaboration* (pp. 160–178). New York, NY: Oxford University Press.

Dess, G. G., & Picken, J. C. (2000). Changing roles: Leadership in the 21st century. *Organizational Dynamics, 28,* 18–34.

Devine, D. J. (1999). Effects of cognitive ability, task knowledge, information sharing, and conflict on group decision-making effectiveness. *Small Group Research, 30,* 608–634.

Devine, D. J., Clayton, L. D., Phillips, J. L., Dunford, B. B., & Melner, S. B. (1999). Teams in organizations: Prevalence, characteristics, and effectiveness. *Small Group Research, 30,* 678–711.

Diehl, M., & Stroebe, W. (1987). Productivity loss in brainstorming groups: Toward the solution of a riddle. *Journal of Personality and Social Psychology, 53,* 497–509.

Dillion, J. T. (1982). Problem finding and solving. *Journal of Creative Behavior, 16,* 97–111.

Ditto, P. H., & Lopez, D. F. (1992). Motivated skepticism: Use of differential decision criteria for preferred and nonpreferred conclusions. *Journal of Personality and Social Psychology, 63,* 568–584.

Dougherty, D. (1992). Interpretive barriers to successful product innovation in large firms. *Organization Science, 3,* 179–202.

Drach-Zahavy, A., & Somech, A. (2001). Understanding team innovation: The role of team processes and structures. *Group Dynamics: Theory, Research, and Practice, 5,* 111–123.

Dunbar, K. (1995). How do scientists really reason: Scientific reasoning in real-world laboratories. In: R. J. Sternberg & J. E. Davidson (Eds), *The nature of insight* (pp. 365–396). Cambridge, MA: MIT Press.

Dunbar, K. (1997). How scientists think: On-line creativity and conceptual change in science. In: T. B. Ward, S. M. Smith & J. Vaid (Eds), *Creative thought: An investigation of conceptual structures and processes* (pp. 461–493). Washington, DC: American Psychological Association.

Dunnette, M. D., Campbell, J., & Jaastad, K. (1963). The effects of group participation on brainstorming effectiveness for two industrial samples. *Journal of Applied Psychology, 47,* 30–37.

Eisenhardt, K. M. (1989). Making fast strategic decisions in high-velocity environments. *Academy of Management Journal, 32,* 543–576.

Ericsson, K. A. (1999). Creative expertise as superior reproducible performance: Innovative and flexible aspects of expert performance. *Psychological Inquiry, 10*, 329–361.

Ericsson, K. A., & Kintsch, W. (1995). Long-term working memory. *Psychological Review, 102*, 211–245.

Ericsson, K. A., & Lehman, A. C. (1996). Expert and exceptional performance: Evidence of maximal adaptation to task constraints. *Annual Review of Psychology, 47*, 273–305.

Feist, G. J. (1991). Synthetic and analytic thought: Similarities and differences among art and science students. *Creativity Research Journal, 4*, 145–155.

Feist, G. J. (1999). The influence of personality on artistic and scientific creativity. In: R. J. Sternberg (Ed.), *Handbook of creativity* (pp. 273–296). New York, NY: Cambridge University Press.

Finke, R. A., Ward, T. B., & Smith, S. M. (1992). *Creative cognition: Theory, research, and applications.* Cambridge, MA: MIT Press.

Fiol, C. M. (1994). Consensus, diversity, and learning in organizations. *Organization Science, 5*, 403–420.

Florida, R. L. (2002). *The rise of the creative class: And how it's transforming work, leisure, community and everyday life.* New York, NY: Basic Books.

Ford, C. M. (1996). A theory of individual creative action in multiple social domains. *Academy of Management Review, 21*, 1112–1142.

Ford, C. M., & Gioia, D. A. (1995). *Creative action in organizations: Ivory tower visions and real world voices.* Thousand Oaks, CA: Sage.

Ford, C., & Sullivan, D. M. (2004). A time for everything: How the timing of novel contributions influences project team outcomes. *Journal of Organizational Behavior, 25*, 279–292.

Franz, T. M., & Larson, J. R. (2002). The impact of experts on information sharing during group discussion. *Small Group Research, 33*, 383–411.

Galinsky, A. D., & Kray, L. J. (2004). From thinking about what might have been to sharing what we know: The effects of counterfactual mind-sets on information sharing in groups. *Journal of Experimental Social Psychology, 40*, 606–618.

Gallupe, R. B., Dennis, A. R., Cooper, W. H., Valacich, J. S., Bastianutti, L. M., & Nunamaker, J. F., Jr. (1992). Electronic brainstorming and group size. *Academy of Management Journal, 35*, 350–370.

Getzels, J. W. (1979). Problem finding: A theoretical note. *Cognitive Science, 3*, 167–171.

Getzels, J. W., & Csikszentmihalyi, M. (1975). From problem solving to problem finding. In: I. A. Taylor & J. W. Getzels (Eds), *Perspectives in creativity* (pp. 90–116). Chicago, IL: Aldine.

Getzels, J. W., & Csikszentmihalyi, M. (1976). *The creative vision: A longitudinal study of problem finding in art.* New York, NY: Wiley.

Gibson, C. B. (2001). From knowledge accumulation to accommodation: Cycles of collective cognition in work groups. *Journal of Organizational Behavior, 22*, 121–134.

Gick, M. L., & Holyoak, K. J. (1983). Schema induction and analogical transfer. *Cognitive Psychology, 15*, 1–38.

Gilliland, S. W., & Landis, R. S. (1992). Quality and quantity goals in a complex decision task: Strategies and outcomes. *Journal of Applied Psychology, 77*, 672–681.

Gilson, L. L., Mathieu, J. E., Shalley, C. E., & Ruddy, T. M. (2005). Creativity and standardization: Complementary or conflicting drivers of team effectiveness. *Academy of Management Journal, 48*, 521–531.

Gilson, L. L., & Shalley, C. E. (2004). A little creativity goes a long way: An examination of teams' engagement in creative processes. *Journal of Management, 30,* 453–470.

Glaser, R., & Chi, M. T. H. (1988). Overview. In: M. T. H. Chi, R. Glaser & M. J. Farr (Eds), *The nature of expertise* (pp. xv–xxiii). Hillsdale, NJ: Lawrence Erlbaum Associates.

Gollwitzer, P. M. (1999). Implementation intentions: Strong effects of simple plans. *American Psychologist, 54,* 493–503.

Gollwitzer, P. M., & Schaal, B. (1998). Metacognition in action: The importance of implementation intentions. *Personality and Social Psychology Review, 2,* 124–136.

Grawitch, M. J., Munz, D. C., Elliott, E. K., & Mathis, A. (2003). Promoting creativity in temporary problem solving groups: The effects of positive mood and autonomy in problem definition on idea-generating performance. *Group Dynamics, 7,* 200–213.

Guilford, J. P. (1950). Creativity. *American Psychologist, 5,* 444–454.

Guilford, J. P. (1967). *The nature of human intelligence.* New York, NY: McGraw-Hill.

Hackman, J. R. (1992). Group influences on individuals in organizations. In: M. D. Dunnette & L. M. Hough (Eds), *Handbook of industrial organizational psychology* (pp. 199–267). Palo Alto, CA: Consulting Psychologists Press.

Hackman, J. R. (1998). Why teams don't work. In: R. S. Tindale, L. Heath, J. Edwards, E. J. Posavac & F. B. Bryant (Eds), *Theory and research on small groups* (pp. 245–267). New York, NY: Plenum Press.

Hackman, J. R., Brousseau, K. R., & Weiss, J. A. (1976). The interaction of task design and group performance strategies in determining group effectiveness. *Organizational Behavior and Human Performance, 16,* 350–365.

Hayes-Roth, B., & Hayes-Roth, F. (1979). A cognitive model of planning. *Cognitive Science, 3,* 275–310.

Hender, J. M., Dean, D. L., Rodgers, T. L., & Nunamaker, J. F., Jr. (2002). An examination of the impact of stimuli type and GSS structure on creativity: Brainstorming techniques in a GSS environment. *Journal of Management Information Systems, 18,* 59–85.

Hershey, D. A., Walsh, D. A., Read, S. J., & Chulef, A. S. (1990). The effects of expertise on financial problem solving: Evidence for goal-directed, problem-solving scripts. *Organizational Behavior and Human Decision Processes, 46,* 77–101.

Hinsz, V. B., Tindale, T. R., & Vollrath, D. A. (1997). The emerging conceptualization of groups as information processors. *Psychological Bulletin, 121,* 43–64.

Hocevar, D. (1980). Intelligence, divergent thinking, and creativity. *Intelligence, 4,* 25–40.

Hogarth, R. M. (1980). *Judgment and choice: The psychology of judgment.* New York, NY: Wiley-Interscience Publication.

Hollingshead, A. B. (1996). The rank-order effect in group decision making. *Organizational Behavior and Human Decision Processes, 68,* 181–193.

Holyoak, K. J. (1984). Mental models in problem solving. In: J. R. Anderson & K. M. Kosslyn (Eds), *Tutorials in learning and memory* (pp. 193–218). New York, NY: Freeman.

Hoover, S. M., & Feldhusen, J. F. (1994). Scientific problem solving and problem finding: A theoretical model. In: M. A. Runco (Ed.), *Problem finding, problem solving, and creativity* (pp. 201–219). Westport, CT: Ablex.

Howell, J. M., & Boies, K. (2004). Champions of technological innovation: The influence of contextual knowledge, role orientation, idea generation, and idea promotion on champion emergence. *Leadership Quarterly, 15,* 123–143.

Illies, J. J., & Reiter-Palmon, R. (2004). The effects of type and level of personal involvement on information search and problem solving. *Journal of Applied Social Psychology, 34*, 1709–1729.

Isenberg, D. J. (1986). Thinking and managing: A verbal protocol analysis of managerial problem solving. *Academy of Management Journal, 29*, 775–788.

Jaarsvled, S., & van Leeuwen, C. (2005). Sketches from the design process: Creative cognition inferred from intermediate products. *Cognitive Science, 29*, 79–101.

James, K., Brodersen, M., & Eisenberg, J. (2004). Workplace affect and workplace creativity: A review and preliminary model. *Human Performance, 17*, 169–194.

Janicik, G. A., & Bartel, C. A. (2003). Talking about time: Effects of temporal planning and time awareness norms on groups' coordination and performance. *Group Dynamics: Theory, Research, and Practice, 7*, 122–134.

Johns, G. A., & Morse, L. W. (1997). Research note: Divergent thinking as a function of time and prompting to "be creative" in undergraduates. *Journal of Creative Behavior, 31*, 156–165.

Johnson, P., Daniels, K., & Huff, A. (2001). Sense making, leadership, and mental models. In: S. J. Zaccaro & R. J. Klimoski (Eds), *The nature of organizational leadership: Understanding the performance imperatives confronting today's leaders* (pp. 79–103). San Francisco, CA: Jossey-Bass.

Jonas, E., Schultz-Hardt, S., Frey, D., & Thelen, N. (2001). Confirmation bias in sequential information search after preliminary decisions: An expansion of dissonance theoretical research on selective exposure to information. *Journal of Personality and Social Psychology, 80*, 557–571.

Kaufmann, G., & Vosburg, S. K. (2002). The effects of mood on early and late idea production. *Creativity Research Journal, 14*, 317–330.

Kay, S. (1991). The figural problem solving and problem finding of professional and semiprofessional artists and nonartists. *Creativity Research Journal, 13*, 185–195.

Keane, M. T. (1996). On adaptation in analogy: Tests of pragmatic importance and adaptability in analogical problem solving. *Quarterly Journal of Experimental Psychology A: Human Experimental Psychology, 49*, 1062–1085.

Kilduff, M., Angelmar, R., & Mehra, A. (2000). Top management-team diversity and firm performance: Examining the role of cognitions. *Organization Science, 11*, 21–34.

Klayman, J., & Ha, Y. W. (1987). Confirmation, disconfirmation, and information in hypothesis testing. *Psychological Review, 94*, 211–228.

Klein, C. G., & Knight, A. P. (2005). Innovation implementation. *Current Directions in Psychological Science, 14*, 243–246.

Klein, K. J., Conn, A. B., & Sorra, J. S. (2001). Is everyone in agreement? An exploration of within-group agreement in employee perceptions of the work environment. *Journal of Applied Psychology, 86*, 3–16.

Klein, K. J., & Sorra, J. S. (1996). The challenge of innovation implementation. *Academy of Management Review, 21*, 1055–1080.

Klimoski, R., & Mohammed, S. (1994). Team mental model: Construct or metaphor? *Journal of Management, 20*, 403–437.

Kramer, T. J., Fleming, G. P., & Mannis, S. M. (2001). Improving face-to-face brainstorming through modeling and facilitation. *Small Group Research, 32*, 533–557.

Kratzer, J., Leenders, R. T. A. J., & van Englen, J. M. L. (2004). Stimulating the potential: Creative performance and communication innovation teams. *Creativity and Innovation Management, 13*, 63–71.

Kuipers, B., Moskowitz, A. J., & Kassinger, J. P. (1988). Critical decisions under uncertainty: Representations and structure. *Cognitive Science, 12*, 177–210.

Lamm, H., & Trommsdorff, G. (1973). Group-induced extremization: Review of evidence and a minority-change explanation. *Psychological Reports, 33*, 471–484.

Larey, T., & Paulus, P. B. (1999). Group preference and convergent tendencies in small groups: A content analysis of group brainstorming performance. *Creativity Research Journal, 12*, 175–184.

Leggett Dugosh, K., & Paulus, P. B. (2005). Cognitive and social comparison processes in brainstorming. *Journal of Experimental Social Psychology, 41*, 313–320.

Leudar, I., & Costal, A. (1996). Situating action IV: Planning as situated action. *Ecological Psychology, 8*, 153–170.

Levine, J. M., Choi, H. S., & Moreland, R. L. (2003). Newcomer innovation in work teams. In: P. B. Paulus & B. A. Nijstad (Eds), *Group creativity: Innovation through collaboration* (pp. 202–224). New York, NY: Oxford University Press.

Lewis, K. (2004). Knowledge and performance in knowledge-worker teams: A longitudinal study of transactive memory systems. *Management Science, 50*, 1519–1533.

Lonergan, D. C., Scott, G. M., & Mumford, M. D. (2004). Evaluative appraisal of creative thought: Effects of appraisal and revision standards. *Creativity Research Journal, 16*, 231–246.

Lovelace, K., Shapiro, D. L., & Wiengart, L. R. (2001). Maximizing cross-functional new product teams' innovativeness and constraint adherence: A conflict communications perspective. *Academy of Management Journal, 44*, 779–793.

Lubart, T., & Guignard, J. H. (2004). The generality-specificity of creativity: A multivariate approach. In: R. J. Sternberg, E. L. Grigorenko & J. L. Singer (Eds), *Creativity: From potential to realization* (pp. 43–56). Washington, DC: American Psychological Association.

Lubart, T. I. (2001). Models of the creative process: Past, present, and future. *Creativity Research Journal, 13*, 295–308.

Lubart, T. I., & Getz, I. (1997). Emotion, metaphor, and the creative process. *Creativity Research Journal, 10*, 285–301.

Marks, M. A., & Panzer, F. J. (2004). The influence of team monitoring on team processes and performance. *Human Performance, 17*, 25–41.

Marks, M. A., Zaccaro, S. J., & Mathieu, J. E. (2000). Performance implications of leader briefings and team-interaction training for team adaptation to novel environments. *Journal of Applied Psychology, 85*, 971–986.

Marsh, R. L., & Landau, J. D. (1996). How examples may (and may not) constrain creativity. *Memory and Cognition, 24*, 669–680.

Marta, S., Leritz, L. E., & Mumford, M. D. (2005). Leadership skills and group performance: Situational demands, behavioral requirements, and planning. *Leadership Quarterly, 16*, 97–120.

Mathieu, J. E., Goodwin, G. F., Heffner, T. S., Salas, E., & Cannon-Bowers, J. A. (2000). The influence of shared mental models on team processes and performance. *Journal of Applied Psychology, 85*, 273–283.

Mathisen, G. E., & Einarsen, S. (2004). A review of instruments assessing creative and innovative environments within organizations. *Creativity Research Journal, 16*, 119–140.

McGlynn, R. P., McGurk, D., Effland, V. S., Johll, N. L., & Harding, D. J. (2004). Brainstorming and task performance in groups constrained by evidence. *Organizational Behavior and Human Decision Processes, 93*, 75–87.

Merrifield, P. R., Guilford, J. P., Christensen, P. R., & Frick, J. W. (1962). The role of intellectual factors in problem solving. *Psychological Monographs, 76,* 1–21.

Milliken, F. J., Bartel, C. A., & Kurtzberg, T. R. (2003). Diversity and creativity in work groups: A dynamic perspective on the affective and cognitive processes that link diversity and performance. In: P. B. Paulus & B. A. Nijstad (Eds), *Group creativity: Innovation through collaboration* (pp. 32–62). New York, NY: Oxford University Press.

Mitchell, R. (1986). Team building by disclosure of internal frames of reference. *Journal of Applied Behavioral Science, 22,* 15–28.

Mobley, M. I., Doares, L. M., & Mumford, M. D. (1992). Process analytic models of creative capacities: Evidence for the combination and reorganization process. *Creativity Research Journal, 5,* 125–155.

Mohammed, S., & Dumville, B. C. (2001). Team mental models in a team knowledge framework: Expanding theory and measurement across disciplinary boundaries. *Journal of Organizational Behavior, 22,* 89–106.

Mohammed, S., & Ringseis, E. (2001). Cognitive diversity and consensus in group decision making: The role of inputs, processes, and outcomes. *Organizational Behavior and Human Decision Processes, 85,* 310–336.

Mouchiroud, C., & Lubart, T. I. (2001). Social creativity: A cross-sectional study of 6- to 11-year old children. *International Journal of Behavioral Development, 26,* 60–69.

Mullen, B., Johnson, C., & Salas, E. (1991). Productivity loss in brainstorming groups: A meta-analytic integration. *Basic and Applied Psychology, 12,* 3–24.

Mumford, M. D. (2001). Something old, something new: Revisiting Guilford's conception of creative problem solving. *Creativity Research Journal, 13,* 267–276.

Mumford, M. D. (2003). Where have we been, where are we going? Taking stock in creativity research. *Creativity Research Journal, 15,* 107–120.

Mumford, M. D., Baughman, W. A., Maher, M. A., Costanza, D. P., & Supinski, E. P. (1997). Process-based measures of creative problem-solving skills: IV. Category combination. *Creativity Research Journal, 10,* 59–71.

Mumford, M. D., Baughman, W. A., & Sager, C. E. (2003). Picking the right material: Cognitive processing skills and their role in creative thought. In: M. A. Runco (Ed.), *Critical creative processes* (pp. 19–68). Cresskill, NJ: Hampton Press.

Mumford, M. D., Baughman, W. A., Supinski, E. P., & Maher, M. A. (1996a). Process-based measures of creative problem-solving skills: II. Information encoding. *Creativity Research Journal, 9,* 77–88.

Mumford, M. D., Baughman, W. A., Threlfall, K. V., Supinski, E. P., & Costanza, D. P. (1996b). Process-based measures of creative problem-solving skills: I. Problem construction. *Creativity Research Journal, 9,* 63–76.

Mumford, M. D., Feldman, J. M., Hein, M. B., & Nagao, D. J. (2001a). Tradeoffs between ideas and structure: Individuals versus group performance in creative problem solving. *Journal of Creative Behavior, 35,* 1–23.

Mumford, M. D., & Gustafson, S. B. (1988). Creativity syndrome: Integration, application, and innovation. *Psychological Bulletin, 103,* 27–43.

Mumford, M. D., & Hunter, S. T. (2005). Innovation in organizations: A multi-level perspective on creativity. *Multi-level Issues in Strategy and Methods, 4,* 11–73.

Mumford, M. D., Lonergan, D. C., & Scott, G. (2002a). Evaluating creative ideas: Processes, standards, and context. *Inquiry: Critical Thinking Across the Disciplines, 22,* 21–30.

Mumford, M. D., Marks, M. A., Connelly, M. S., Zaccaro, S. J., & Johnson, J. F. (1998). Domain-based scoring of divergent-thinking tests: Validation evidence in an occupational sample. *Creativity Research Journal, 11*, 151–163.

Mumford, M. D., Mobley, M. I., Uhlman, C. E., Reiter-Palmon, R., & Doares, L. M. (1991). Process analytic models of creative capacities. *Creativity Research Journal, 4*, 91–122.

Mumford, M. D., Reiter-Palmon, R., & Redmond, M. R. (1994). Problem construction and cognition: Applying problem representations in ill-defined domains. In: M. Runco (Ed.), *Problem finding, problem solving, and creativity* (pp. 3–39). Norwood, NJ: Ablex.

Mumford, M. D., Schultz, R. A., & Osburn, H. K. (2002b). Planning in organizations: Performance as a multi-level phenomenon. In: F. J. Yammarino & F. Dansereau (Eds), *The many faces of multi-level issues* (pp. 3–65). Cambridge, MA: Elsevier Science.

Mumford, M. D., Schultz, R. A., & Van Doorn, J. R. (2001b). Performance in planning: Processes, requirements, and errors. *Review of General Psychology, 5*, 213–240.

Mumford, M. D., Scott, G. M., Gaddis, B., & Strange, J. M. (2002c). Leading creative people: Orchestrating expertise and relationships. *Leadership Quarterly, 13*, 705–750.

Mumford, M. D., Supinski, E. P., Baughman, W. A., Costanza, D. P., & Threlfall, K. V. (1997). Process-based measures of creative problem-solving skills: V. Overall prediction. *Creativity Research Journal, 10*, 73–86.

Naglieri, J. A., & Kaufman, J. C. (2001). Understanding intelligence, giftedness and creativity using PASS theory. *Roeper Review, 23*, 151–156.

Naquin, C. E., & Tynan, R. O. (2003). The team halo effect: Why teams are not blamed for their failures. *Journal of Applied Psychology, 88*, 332–340.

Necka, E. (2003). Creative interaction: A conceptual schema for the process of producing ideas and judging the outcomes. In: M. A. Runco (Ed.), *Critical creative processes* (pp. 115–117). Cresskill, NJ: Hampton Press.

Nickerson, R. S. (1998). Confirmation bias: A ubiquitous phenomenon in many guises. *Review of General Psychology, 2*, 175–220.

Nijstad, B. A., Rietzschel, E. F., & Stroebe, W. (2006). Four principles of group creativity. In: L. Thompson & H. S. Choi (Eds), *Creativity and innovation in organizations teams* (pp. 161–179). Mahwah, NJ: Lawrence Erlbaum Associates.

Okuda, S. M., Runco, M. A., & Berger, D. E. (1991). Creativity and the finding and solving of real-world problems. *Journal of Psychoeducational Assessment, 9*, 45–53.

Osborn, A. F. (1953). *Applied imagination: Principles and procedures for creative problem-solving.* New York, NY: Charles Scribner & Sons.

Oswald, S. L., Mossholder, K. W., & Harris, S. G. (1997). Relations between strategic involvement and managers' perceptions of environment and competitive strengths: The effect of vision salience. *Group and Organization Management, 22*, 343–365.

Oxley, N. L., Dzindolet, M. T., & Paulus, P. B. (1996). The effects of facilitators on the performance of brainstorming groups. *Journal of Social Behavior and Personality, 11*, 633–646.

Parks, C. D., & Cowlin, R. (1995). Group discussion as affected by number of alternatives and by a time limit. *Organizational Behavior and Human Decision Processes, 62*, 267–275.

Patalano, A. L., & Seifert, C. M. (1997). Opportunistic planning: Being reminded of pending goals. *Cognitive Psychology, 34*, 1–36.

Paulus, P. B. (2000). Groups, teams, and creativity: The creative potential of idea-generating groups. *Applied Psychology: An International Review, 49*, 237–262.

Paulus, P. B., & Brown, V. R. (2003). Enhancing ideation creativity in groups: Lessons from research on brainstorming. In: P. B. Paulus & B. A. Nijstad (Eds), *Group creativity: Innovation through collaboration* (pp. 110–136). New York, NY: Oxford University Press.

Paulus, P. B., Larey, T. S., & Dzindolet, M. T. (2004). Creativity in groups and teams. In: M. E. Turner (Ed.), *Groups at work: Theory and research* (pp. 319–338). Mahwah, NJ: Lawrence Erlbaum Associates.

Paulus, P. B., Nakui, T., & Putman, V. L. (2006). Group brainstorming and teamwork: Some rules for the road to innovation. In: L. Thompson & H. S. Choi (Eds), *Creativity and innovation in organizational teams* (pp. 69–86). Mahwah, NJ: Lawrence Erlbaum Associates.

Paulus, P. B., & Nijstad, L. E. (2003). Group creativity: An introduction. In: P. B. Paulus & B. A. Nijstad (Eds), *Group creativity: Innovation through collaboration* (pp. 110–136). New York, NY: Oxford University Press.

Paulus, P. B., & Paulus, L. E. (1997). Implications of research on group brainstorming for gifted education. *Roeper Review, 19*, 225–229.

Paulus, P. B., & Yang, H. C. (2000). Idea generation in groups: A basis for creativity in organizations. *Organizational Behavior and Human Decision Processes, 82*, 76–87.

Pearce, C. L., & Ensley, M. D. (2004). A reciprocal and longitudinal investigation of the innovation process: The central role of shared vision in product and process innovation teams (PPITs). *Journal of Organizational Behavior, 25*, 259–278.

Perry-Smith, J. E., & Shalley, C. E. (2003). The social side of creativity: A static and dynamic social network perspective. *Academy of Management Review, 28*, 89–106.

Pinkley, R. L., Griffith, T. L., & Northcraft, G. B. (1995). "Fixed pie" a la mode: Information availability, information processing, and the negotiation of suboptimal agreements. *Organizational Behavior and Human Decision Processes, 62*, 101–112.

Pinsonneault, A., Barki, H., Gallupe, R. B., & Hoppen, N. (1999). Research note: The illusion of electronic brainstorming productivity: Theoretical and empirical issues. *Information Systems Research, 10*, 378–380.

Pitz, G. F., Sachs, N. J., & Heerboth, J. (1980). Procedures for eliciting choices in the analysis of individual decisions. *Organizational Behavior and Human Decision Processes, 26*, 396–408.

Plucker, J. A. (1999). Reanalyses of student responses to creativity checklists: Evidence of content generality. *Journal of Creative Behavior, 33*, 126–137.

Plucker, R. A., & Beghetto, J. A. (2004). Why isn't creativity more important to educational psychologists? Potentials, pitfalls, and future directions in creativity research. *Education Psychologist, 39*, 83–96.

Redmond, M. R., Mumford, M. D., & Teach, R. (1993). Putting creativity to work: Effects of leader behavior on subordinate creativity. *Organizational Behavior and Human Decision Processes, 55*, 120–151.

Reeves, L., & Weisberg, R. W. (1994). The role of content and abstract information in analogical transfer. *Psychological Bulletin, 115*, 381–400.

Reiter-Palmon, R., & Illies, J. J. (2004). Leadership and creativity: Understanding leadership from a creative problem-solving perspective. *Leadership Quarterly, 15*, 55–77.

Reiter-Palmon, R., Mumford, M. D., O'Connor Boes, J., & Runco, M. A. (1997). Problem construction and creativity: The role of ability, cue consistency, and active processing. *Creativity Research Journal, 10*, 9–23.

Reiter-Palmon, R., Mumford, M. D., & Threlfall, K. V. (1998). Solving everyday problems creatively: The role of problem construction and personality type. *Creativity Research Journal, 11,* 187–197.

Rentsch, J. R., & Woehr, D. J. (2004). Quantifying congruence in cognition: Social relations modeling and team member schema similarity. In: E. Salas & S. M. Fiore (Eds), *Team cognition: Understanding the factors that drive process and performance* (pp. 11–31). Washington, DC: American Psychological Association.

Renzulli, J. S., Owen, S. V., & Callahan, C. M. (1974). Fluency, flexibility, and originality as a function of group size. *Journal of Creative Behavior, 8,* 107–113.

Rhodes, M. (1987). An analysis of creativity. In: S. G. Isaksen (Ed.), *Frontiers of creativity research: Beyond the basics* (pp. 216–222). Buffalo, NY: Bearly.

Rickards, T. (1999). Brainstorming. In: M. A. Runco & S. R. Pritzker (Eds), *Encyclopedia of creativity* (Vol. 1, pp. 219–228). San Diego, CA: Academic Press.

Rodan, S. (2002). Innovation and heterogeneous knowledge in managerial contact networks. *Journal of Knowledge Management, 6,* 152–163.

Rostan, S. M. (1994). Problem finding, problem solving, and cognitive controls: An empirical investigation of critically acclaimed productivity. *Creativity Research Journal, 7,* 97–110.

Rostan, S. M. (1997). A study of young artists: The development of artistic talent and creativity. *Creativity Research Journal, 10,* 175–192.

Runco, M. A. (1991). The evaluative, valuative, and divergent thinking abilities of children. *Journal of Creative Behavior, 25,* 311–319.

Runco, M. A. (1999). Divergent thinking. In: M. A. Runco & S. R. Pritzker (Eds), *Encyclopedia of creativity* (Vol. 1, pp. 219–228). San Diego, CA: Academic Press.

Runco, M. A., & Basadur, M. S. (1993). Assessing ideational and evaluative skills and creative styles and attitudes. *Creativity and Innovation Management, 2,* 166–173.

Runco, M. A., & Chand, I. (1995). Cognition and creativity. *Educational Psychology Review, 7,* 243–268.

Runco, M. A., Illies, J. J., & Eisenman, R. (2005a). Creativity, originality, and appropriateness: What do explicit instructions tell us about their relationships? *Journal of Creative Behavior, 39,* 137–148.

Runco, M. A., Illies, J. J., & Reiter-Palmon, R. (2005b). Explicit instructions to be creative and original: A comparison of strategies and criteria as targets with three types of divergent thinking tests. *Korean Journal of Thinking and Problem Solving, 15,* 5–15.

Runco, M. A., & Marz, W. (1992). Scoring divergent thinking tests using total ideational output and a creativity index. *Educational and Psychological Measurement, 52,* 213–221.

Runco, M. A., & Okuda, S. M. (1988). Problem-discovery, divergent thinking, and the creative process. *Journal of Youth and Adolescence, 17,* 211–220.

Runco, M. A., & Okuda, S. M. (1991). The instructional enhancement of the flexibility and originality scores of divergent thinking tests. *Applied Cognitive Psychology, 5,* 435–441.

Runco, M. A., & Smith, W. R. (1992). Interpersonal and intrapersonal evaluations of creative ideas. *Personality and Individual Differences, 13,* 295–302.

Runco, M. A., & Vega, L. (1990). Evaluating the creativity of children's ideas. *Journal of Social Behavior and Personality, 5,* 439–452.

Salas, E., & Fiore, S. M. (2004). *Team cognition: Understanding the factors that drive processes and performance.* Washington, DC: American Psychological Association.

Salterio, S. (1996). Decision support and information search in a complex environment: Evidence from archival data in auditing. *Human Factors, 38,* 495–505.

Santanen, E. L. (2006). Opening the black box of creativity: Causal effects in creative solution generation. In: L. Thompson & H. S. Choi (Eds), *Creativity and innovation in organizational teams* (pp. 69–86). Mahwah, NJ: Lawrence Erlbaum Associates.

Santanen, E. L., Briggs, R. O., & DeVreede, G. J. (2004). Causal relationship in creative problem solving: Comparing facilitation interventions for ideation. *Journal of Management Information Systems, 20*, 167–197.

Schilling, M. A. (2005). A "small-world" network model of cognitive insight. *Creativity Research Journal, 17*, 131–154.

Schittekatte, M., & van Hiel, A. (1996). Effects of partially shared information and awareness of unshared information on information sampling. *Small Group Research, 27*, 431–450.

Scholnick, E. K., & Friedman, S. L. (1987). The planning construct in the psychological literature. In: S. L. Friedman, E. K. Scholnick & R. R. Cocking (Eds), *Blueprints for thinking: The role of planning in cognitive development* (pp. 3–38). New York, NY: Cambridge University Press.

Schraw, G., Dunkle, M. E., & Benedixen, L. D. (1995). Cognitive processes in well-defined and ill-defined problem solving. *Applied Cognitive Psychology, 9*, 523–538.

Schultz-Hardt, S., Frey, D., Luthgens, C., & Moscovici, S. (2000). Biased information search in group decision making. *Journal of Personality and Social Psychology, 78*, 655–669.

Scott, G. M., Leritz, L. E., & Mumford, M. D. (2004). The effectiveness of creativity training: A quantitative review. *Creativity Research Journal, 16*, 361–388.

Scott, G. M., Lonergan, D. C., & Mumford, M. D. (2005). Conceptual combination: Alternative knowledge structures, alternative heuristics. *Creativity Research Journal, 17*, 79–98.

Scott, S. G., & Bruce, R. A. (1994). Determinants of innovative behavior: A path model of individual innovation in the workplace. *Academy of Management Journal, 37*, 580–607.

Seifert, C. M., & Patalano, A. L. (2001). Opportunism in memory: Preparing for chance encounters. *Current Directions in Psychological Science, 10*, 198–201.

Seifert, C. M., Patalano, A. L., & Hammond, K. J. (1997). Experience and expertise: The role of memory in planning for opportunities. In: P. J. Feltovich, K. M. Ford & R. R. Hoffman (Eds), *Expertise in context: Human and machine* (pp. 101–123). Menlo Park, CA: American Association for Artificial Intelligence.

Serfaty, D., MacMillan, J., Entin, E. E., & Entin, E. B. (1997). The decision-making expertise of battle commanders. In: C. E. Zsambok & G. Klein (Eds), *Naturalistic decision making* (pp. 233–246). Hillsdale, NJ: Lawrence Erlbaum Associates.

Shalley, C. E. (1991). Effects of productivity goals, creativity goals, and personal discretion on individual creativity. *Journal of Applied Psychology, 76*, 179–185.

Shalley, C. E. (1995). Effects of coaction, expected evaluation, and goal setting on creativity and productivity. *Academy of Management Journal, 38*, 483–503.

Shalley, C. E., & Gilson, L. L. (2004). What leadership needs to know: A review of social and contextual factors that can foster or hinder creativity. *Leadership Quarterly, 15*, 33–53.

Shalley, C. E., & Perry-Smith, J. E. (2001). Effects of social-psychological factors on creative performance: The role of informational and controlling expected evaluation and modeling experience. *Organizational Behavior and Human Decision Processes, 84*, 1–22.

Shalley, C. E., Zhou, J., & Oldham, G. R. (2004). The effects of personal and contextual characteristics on creativity: Where should we go from here? *Journal of Management, 30*, 933–958.

Sharma, A. (1999). Central dilemmas of managing innovation in large firms. *California Management Review, 41*, 65–85.

Sheeran, P., & Orbell, S. (1999). Augmenting the theory of planned behavior: Roles for anticipated regret and descriptive norms. *Journal of Applied Social Psychology, 29*, 2107–2142.

Shepherd, M. M., Briggs, R. O., Reinig, B. A., Yen, J., & Nunamaker, J. F., Jr. (1996). Invoking social comparison to improve electronic brainstorming: Beyond anonymity. *Journal of Management Information Systems, 12*, 155–170.

Silverman, B. G. (1985). The use of analogs in the innovation process: A software engineering protocol analysis. *IEEE Transactions on Systems, Man, and Cybernetics, 15*, 30–44.

Smilansky, J. (1984). Problem solving and the quality of invention: An empirical investigation. *Journal of Educational Psychology, 76*, 377–386.

Smith, S. M. (2002). The constraining effects of initial ideas. In: P. B. Paulus & B. A. Nijstad (Eds), *Group creativity: Innovation through collaboration* (pp. 15–31). New York, NY: Oxford University Press.

Smith, S. M., Gerkens, D. R., Shah, J. J., & Vargas-Hernandez, N. (2006). Empirical studies of creative cognition in idea generation. In: L. Thompson & H. S. Choi (Eds), *Creativity and innovation in organizational teams* (pp. 3–20). Mahwah, NJ: Lawrence Erlbaum Associates.

Smith, S. M., Ward, T. B., & Schumacher, J. S. (1993). Constraining effects of examples in creative generation tasks. *Memory and Cognition, 21*, 837–845.

Smith-Jentsch, K. A., Mathieu, J. E., & Kraiger, K. (2005). Investigating linear and interactive effects of shared mental models on safety and efficiency in a field setting. *Journal of Applied Psychology, 90*, 523–535.

Stasser, G., & Stewart, G. (1995). Expert role assignment and information sampling during collective recall and decision making. *Journal of Personality and Social Psychology, 69*, 619–628.

Stasser, G., & Titus, W. (1985). Pooling unshared information in group decision making: Biased information sampling during discussion. *Journal of Personality and Social Psychology, 48*, 1467–1478.

Stasser, G., & Titus, W. (1987). Effects of information load and percentage of shared information on the dissemination of unshared information during group discussion. *Journal of Personality and Social Psychology, 53*, 81–93.

Sternberg, R. J. (1988). A three-facet model of creativity. In: R. J. Sternberg (Ed.), *The nature of creativity: Contemporary psychological perspectives* (pp. 125–147). New York, NY: Cambridge University Press.

Stewart, D. D., & Stasser, G. (1995). Expert role assignment and information sampling during collective recall and decision making. *Journal of Personality and Social Psychology, 69*, 619–628.

Stout, R. J., Cannon-Bowers, J. A., Salas, E., & Milanovich, D. M. (1999). Planning shared mental models, and coordinated performance: An empirical link is established. *Human Factors, 41*, 61–71.

Stroebe, W., & Diehl, M. (1994). Why are groups less effective than their members? On productivity loss in idea generating groups. In: W. Stroebe & M. Hewstone (Eds), *European review of social psychology* (Vol. 5, pp. 271–303). Chichester, UK: Wiley.

Sullivan, D. M., & Ford, C. M. (2005). The relationship between novelty and value in the assessment of organizational creativity. *Korean Journal of Thinking and Problem Solving, 15*, 117–131.

Sutton, R. I., & Hargadon, A. (1996). Brainstorming groups in context: Effectiveness in a product design firm. *Administrative Science Quarterly, 41*, 685–718.

Taylor, D. W., Berry, P. C., & Block, C. H. (1958). Does group participation when using brainstorming facilitate or inhibit creative thinking. *Administrative Science Quarterly, 3*, 23–47.

Thomas, J. B., & McDaniel, R. R. (1990). Interpreting strategic issues: Effects of strategy and the information-processing structure of top management teams. *Academy of Management Journal, 33*, 286–306.

Tjosvold, D. (1998). Cooperative and competitive goal approach to conflict: Accomplishments and challenges. *Applied Psychology: An International Review, 47*, 285–342.

Tschan, F. (1995). Communication enhances small group performance if it conforms to task requirements: The concept of ideal communication cycles. *Basic and Applied Social Psychology, 17*, 371–393.

Vincent, A. S., Decker, B. P., & Mumford, M. D. (2002). Divergent thinking, intelligence, and expertise: A test of alternative models. *Creativity Research Journal, 14*, 163–178.

Vissers, G., & Dankbaar, B. (2002). Creativity in multidisciplinary new product development teams. *Creativity and Innovation Management, 11*, 31–42.

Voss, J. F., Wolfe, C. R., Lawrence, J. A., & Engle, R. A. (1991). From representation to decision: An analysis of problem solving in international relations. In: R. J. Sternberg & P. S. Frensch (Eds), *Complex problem solving: Principles and mechanisms* (pp. 119–158). Hillsdale, NJ: Lawrence Erlbaum Associates.

Ward, T. B., Patterson, M. J., & Sifonis, C. M. (2004). The role of specificity and abstraction in creative idea generation. *Creativity Research Journal, 16*, 1–9.

Ward, T. B., Smith, S. M., & Finke, R. A. (1999). Creative cognition. In: R. J. Sternberg (Ed.), *Handbook of creativity* (pp. 189–212). New York, NY: Cambridge University Press.

Ward, T. B., Smith, S. M., & Vaid, J. (1997). Conceptual structures and processes in creative thought. In: T. B. Ward, S. M. Vaid & J. Vaid (Eds), *Creative thought: An investigation of conceptual structures and processes* (pp. 1–27). Washington, DC: American Psychological Association.

Watson, W. E., Kumar, K., & Michaleson, L. K. (1993). Cultural diversity's impact on interaction process and performance: Comparing homogenous and diverse task groups. *Academy of Management Journal, 36*, 590–602.

Webb, T. L., & Sheeran, P. (2004). Identifying good opportunities to act: Implementation intentions and cue discrimination. *European Journal of Social Psychology, 34*, 407–419.

Weingart, L. R. (1992). Impact of group goals, task component complexity, effort, and planning on group performance. *Journal of Applied Psychology, 77*, 682–693.

Weldon, E., Jehn, K. A., & Pradhan, P. (1991). Processes that mediate the relationship between a group goal and improved group performance. *Journal of Personality and Social Psychology, 61*, 555–569.

West, M. A. (2002a). Sparkling fountains or stagnant ponds: An integrative model of creativity and innovation implementation in work groups. *Applied Psychology: An International Review, 51*, 355–387.

West, M. A. (2002b). Ideas are ten a penny: It's team implementation, not idea generation, that counts. *Applied Psychology: An International Review, 51*, 411–424.

West, M. A. (2003). Innovation implementation in work teams. In: P. B. Paulus & B. A. Nijstad (Eds), *Innovation through collaboration* (pp. 245–276). New York, NY: Oxford University Press.

West, M. A., Hirst, G., Richter, A., & Shipton, H. (2004). Twelve steps to heaven: Successfully managing change through developing innovative teams. *European Journal of Work and Organizational Psychology, 13,* 269–299.

West, M. A., Sacramento, C. A., & Fay, D. (2006). Creativity and innovation implementation in work groups: The paradoxical role of demands. In: L. Thompson & H. S. Choi (Eds), *Creativity and innovation in organizational teams* (pp. 137–159). Mahwah, NJ: Lawrence Erlbaum Associates.

Wiley, J. (1998). Expertise as a mental set: The effects of domain knowledge in creative problem solving. *Memory and Cognition, 26,* 716–730.

Wittenbaum, G. M. (1998). Information sampling in decision-making groups: The impact of members' task-relevant status. *Small Group Research, 29,* 57–84.

Wittenbaum, G. M., Holligshead, A. B., & Botero, I. C. (2004). From cooperative to motivated information sharing in groups: Moving beyond the hidden profile paradigm. *Communication Monographs, 71,* 286–310.

Woodman, R. W., Sawyer, J. E., & Griffin, R. W. (1993). Toward a theory of organizational creativity. *Academy of Management Review, 18,* 293–321.

Woods, M. F., & Davies, G. B. (1973). Potential problem analysis: A systematic approach to problem prediction and contingency planning: An aid to the smooth exploitation of research. *R&D Management, 4,* 25–32.

Xiao, Y., Milgram, P., & Doyle, J. D. (1997). Capturing and modeling planning expertise in anesthesiology: Results of a field study. In: C. E. Zsambok & G. Klein (Eds), *Naturalistic decision making* (pp. 197–205). Hillsdale, NJ: Lawrence Erlbaum Associates.

Yates, F. (1990). *Judgment and decision making.* Englewood Cliffs, NJ: Prentice Hall.

Yuan, R., & Zhou, J. (2002). Expected evaluations and creativity: New answers to an old question. Presented at the Annual Conference of the Academy of Management, Denver, CO.

Zaccaro, S. J., Gualtieri, J., & Minionis, D. (1995). Task cohesion as a facilitator of team decision making under temporal urgency. *Military Psychology, 7,* 77–95.

TEAM CREATIVITY: MORE THAN THE SUM OF ITS PARTS?

Claudia A. Sacramento, Jeremy F. Dawson and
Michael A. West

ABSTRACT

Reiter-Palmon, Herman, and Yammarino (this volume) put forward a series of useful propositions about the nature of team creativity, its connection with individual creativity and cognitive processes, and its antecedents. This commentary highlights some issues raised by these propositions, and explores the emergence of team creativity in greater depth. In particular, it discusses existing principles of multi-level theory and measurement, and considers how they might be applied to team creativity. We conclude that there is no single unified way to treat the concept of team creativity, but just as the antecedents of creativity may change in different situations, so may the way in which the construct is defined.

INTRODUCTION

Creativity is the root of innovation, and the failure to innovate is often associated with market losses and eventual company extinction. It is therefore understandable that researchers have started to study creativity in

Multi-Level Issues in Creativity and Innovation
Research in Multi-Level Issues, Volume 7, 269–287
Copyright © 2008 by Elsevier Ltd.
ISSN: 1475-9144/doi:10.1016/S1475-9144(07)00010-0

work settings (see Paulus & Nijstad, 2003). Work-related creativity research draws mostly on a social-personality paradigm, driven in great part by the model put forward by Amabile (1988). This trend has been chiefly focused on the interactions between individual characteristics and social context features as predictors of creativity (see e.g., George & Zhou, 2001; Madjar & Oldham, 2002). The creative cognition approach, by contrast, focuses on the cognitive processes and structures that underlie creative thinking, aiming to improve the understanding of creativity by applying concepts and methods of cognitive science (Finke, Ward, & Smith, 1992). Cognitive research on creativity is quite diverse, tapping into cognitive processes such as memory, attention, and knowledge (Runco, 2003), and is considerably more extensive than the social interaction literature.

In their chapter, Reiter-Palmon, Herman, and Yammarino (this volume) link these two bodies of literature and apply the configural approach of individual creative cognition to the study of work teams charged with creative endeavors. Although cognitive processes have been taken into account in models of workplace creativity (Agrell & Gustafson, 1996; Woodman, Sawyer, & Griffin, 1993), they have not been fully incorporated in the empirical research. Only a few studies have so far investigated cognitive and social-personality variables at the same time. Whereas the cognitive approach has minimized the importance of personal or contextual variables, the interactionist approach has not contributed to the under-standing of the mental representations and processes underlying creativity (Sternberg & Lubart, 1999). By taking a multidisciplinary perspective and linking these two areas together, Reiter-Palmon et al. establish a path that enables work-related creativity research to benefit from the vast extant research on creative cognition. As such, their contribution stimulates organizational creativity research and promotes an integrative under-standing of creativity.

What we consider to have been missed – not only in this chapter, but also in general team creativity research – is a critical reflection about the nature of the construct. Theory building should start with the designation and definition of the theoretical phenomenon and the endogenous construct of interest (Kozlowski & Klein, 2000), but team creativity theory has developed without careful consideration of the nature and characteristics of this creativity. Is creativity an exclusive product of the single minds of individuals, whereas only implementation of those ideas can be attributed to teams? Or does it make sense to consider team creativity as having its own properties? Five individuals working on their own in an open task will never achieve the same output as when they work together in a team (the output could be better or worse, but is very unlikely to be the same), so team creativity appears to hold face validity as a concept. And if we assume the collective nature of creativity, how does it originate? When conducting multi-level research, what implications does the concept of team creativity have for the operationalization and measurement of variables? Should researchers use a single measure of team creativity, or should they instead obtain individual measures of team members' creativity? If the latter, how should these measures be combined to form a single indicator?

Although we do not intend to provide definitive answers to these questions, it is our aim here to raise awareness of the importance of having a precise idea about the nature of the phenomenon when developing theory on team creativity. In line with this reasoning, our commentary is organized in two main parts. The first part introduces our overall perception of Reiter-Palmon et al.'s chapter. We highlight some aspects that we considered to be less consensual or in need of further clarification. In the second part, which constitutes the bulk of this commentary, we reflect about the nature of team creativity and its implications for multi-level research practices.

CRITIQUE

Reiter-Palmon et al. adopted a consensual five-stage model of cognitive problem solving as the underlying framework against which they systematized several decades of cognition research. The authors summarized the variables considered to be influential at each of the stages involved in creative problem solving: problem identification and construction; information search and encoding; idea and solution generation; idea evaluation and selection; and implementation, planning, and monitoring.

Based on the review compiled for each stage, the authors draw a parallel between the individual-level and team-level constructs they consider to be similar. For example, when discussing the first stage (problem construction), Reiter-Palmon et al. suggest that team mental models about the team task are analogous to individual problem representations. Having established the parallels between individual cognition and team research, the authors develop 54 propositions about the factors influencing team creativity. By the end of their chapter, the reader can picture a model for each of the five stages accounting for the respective influencing variables.

Overall, this chapter constitutes a valuable effort in linking together two streams of research. The review is insightful and comprehensive, drawing on different literatures such as those dealing with expertise, hidden profiles, team mental models, and team diversity. The analogies established between individual- and team-level constructs are, on the whole, theoretically sound and thought provoking.

This chapter draws attention to an area that as yet has been the subject of little research – namely, team cognitive processes and creativity. Despite the burgeoning research on creativity, the study of the associated creative processes has been restricted to the individual level and mostly to the laboratory. Furthermore, Reiter-Palmon et al. do not adopt the usual distinction between groups and teams to differentiate between experimental and field research, but instead use the concepts interchangeably, assuming that their propositions should be generalizable and valid for both settings. This makes the chapter appealing and relevant for experimental and field researchers, as well as for practitioners.

Summarizing all of the research on cognition that might be of relevance for team creativity and linking it to team research is a difficult endeavor, and although we agree with many of the propositions elaborated by the authors, we have a number of concerns. These concerns are organized into theoretical, research-related, and practical implications and are discussed next.

Theoretical Contribution

It is not easy to take stock of all the factors influencing the cognitive processes involved at each stage of the creative production. Reiter-Palmon et al. do an excellent job of systematizing the review that informs their propositions, but some omissions are worth noting.

For instance, time pressure is assumed to have an impact on problem identification and construction and on information search and encoding. However, the authors do not theorize about the effect of time pressure on any of the other stages discussed. Some empirical studies suggest time pressure has a pervasive effect throughout the process. For instance, time pressure impairs idea and solution generation in individuals (Rokeach, 1950), and it is reasonable to expect that groups under time pressure will also be less fluent in terms of ideas generated. Time restrictions will reduce information exchange, impairing the probability of new ideas being put forward, and force the group to move on to the next stage, limiting the number of new contributions.

We recognize the difficulty in acknowledging the impact that all variables have at each stage, and a trade-off between breadth and depth is always necessary. A future contribution might complement Reiter-Palmon et al.'s chapter by systematically addressing the impact of a limited number of variables throughout the five stages, focusing also on research methodology. This limited set of variables should consist of the most pervasive factors identified here: Team diversity, task characteristics, and time pressure emerge as potential candidates. This would offer a parsimonious and hopefully elegant model.

Another aspect that is not totally clear to us is the criterion for selection of the variables deemed to influence each stage of the creative process. Reiter-Palmon et al. inform us that their purpose is to provide an understanding of both individual and team cognitive processes involved in creative problem solving and that they will, therefore, devote their energy to elucidating variables that might affect the application of cognitive processes. These authors recognize that they do not address all the possible influences on creative problem-solving processes and all variables that affect creative processes at the individual and team levels, such as affect, personality, motivation, team composition, social processes, leadership, and team and organizational culture. However, the authors include in their propositions the effect of team size, which in terms of category does not appear to us to differ that much from, for example, team composition. Moreover, the authors discuss the effect of time pressure on team idea generation without explaining how the impact of this variable actually occurs via alteration of cognitive processes. We suspect that there is a logical rationale for the selection of variables, but we did not find it clearly stated.

Research Implications

A first concern that is applicable to all multi-level research is the level of the constructs involved. The parallelism established between individual cognition and team-analogous constructs shifts all of Reiter-Palmon et al.'s propositions to the team level. But where no parallelism was available, the authors theorized on the aggregation of individual-level constructs – that is, consensus models, to use Chan's (1998) typology. These aggregations, however, raise questions about theoretical and empirical justification, and researchers need to bear that in mind when empirically addressing these propositions. These authors are among the most prominent multi-level researchers, and we are certain their proposals obey such assumptions. Nevertheless, further elucidation about these cases would have been informative – not least in explaining why the authors believe team members would display the necessary agreement about these individual-level constructs to justify their aggregation.

In particular, although Reiter-Palmon et al. argue that teams are likely to be more creative if they reach cognitive consensus, it is not clear how team creativity could be measured if cognitive consensus is not reached, as this implies there would be insufficient agreement to justify aggregation. This leads to a methodological impasse where it is impossible to measure low team creativity.

Another issue of concern is the testing of the proposals that relate to specific outcomes of each stage. For instance, whereas Proposition 1 ("Shared mental models will lead to more creative solutions, especially for complex or unpredictable tasks.") does not seem to instigate many problems in terms of measurement, Proposition 4 ("Disagreements within a group about the right solution to a problem may represent disagreements about how to construct and define the problem that were never discussed before.") is extremely difficult to test. In the laboratory it is possible to evaluate how certain variables influence a specific stage of the creative process (see e.g., Redmond, Mumford, & Teach, 1993), but this relationship is much harder to disentangle in field settings. The researcher can assume a developmental approach and assess each stage sequentially. Logistically, this approach is not viable given all the constraints of field research. Furthermore, teams do not follow a linear development across the stages of creativity but rather use a more iterative approach, so the design would not capture the entire performance level within each stage.

Alternatively, the researcher might assess the output relative to each stage a posteriori, via self-ratings or an expert informant. However, the evaluation of the outcomes relative to each stage – problem construction, information sharing, fluency and quality of ideas, or selection of the best ideas – would be very much influenced by the final project output, which is not a pure measure of creativity but an overall indicator of innovation.

We do not question the value of the propositions forwarded by Reiter-Palmon et al., but some further guidance about the best way to empirically validate them would be useful.

Practical Implications

Embedded in this chapter are a valuable and broad set of recommendations that have the potential to be useful to practitioners who want to maximize the creativity of the teams with which they are associated. However, these implicit recommendations are sometimes confusing, as some of the propositions seem to be contradictory. For example, Proposition 11 ("Functional diversity of team members will have a curvilinear relationship with information sharing."), Proposition 24 ("Groups that spend more time sharing and reflecting on ideas will generate more ideas and more creative ideas than groups that do not."), and Proposition 27 ("Diverse teams in terms of cognitive style and expertise will generate more creative ideas than homogeneous teams.") all make sense on their own. However, Propositions 11 and 24 taken together would suggest a curvilinear relationship between diversity of expertise and creativity, whereas Proposition 27 does not.

A key point noted by Reiter-Palmon et al. is that teams work in circles and not linearly (i.e., moving in an orderly fashion from one stage to the next). The emergence of a problem during the implementation stage might redirect the team to idea evaluation and selection, if the team aims to identify the best option omitted before; or it might send the team to problem construction, if the team wants to develop a completely new idea; or it might even cause the team to begin an information search, if the best option is to gather information that will enable team members to overcome the new problem representation. As it is, this transition across stages might represent a critical factor for team creativity. However, as Reiter-Palmon et al. note in Proposition 52, teams are generally more resistant to returning to earlier processes (or parts of earlier processes) than individuals.

Given the difficulty associated with promoting the conditions that facilitate the creative process at each stage, researchers should aim to identify the factors that help teams to effectively transition between stages. One such potential factor is team reflexivity. Reflexivity is the extent to which teams reflect on their objectives, strategies, processes, and environments; make plans based on perceived needs to change these aspects of their tasks and social environments; and then implement these plans (West, 1996, 2000). Teams that are highly reflexive are more likely to perceive the need to transition between stages at appropriate times and thus to be more effective throughout the creative process than teams that are less reflexive.

DOING MULTI-LEVEL RESEARCH ON CREATIVITY: FIRST THINK ABOUT *TEAM CREATIVITY*

Multi-level research on creativity remains underdeveloped. This gap in our knowledge base can easily be understood – and excused – by considering the youth of the field. Nevertheless, if researchers continue to fail to adopt a multi-level framework, the understanding of work-related creativity may be undermined. Mumford and Hunter (2004) suggest that most of the contradictory findings on innovation can be accounted for by taking a multi-level perspective and assuming that different requirements for innovation exist at different levels, with the contradictions being a consequence of the interactions between cross-level variables. A particularly compelling example provided by Reiter-Palmon et al. is the obvious contradiction between studies showing a negative impact of extrinsic rewards on creativity (Oldham, 2003) and studies suggesting that goals, output processes, and extrinsic rewards are positively related to organizational innovation (Abbey & Dickson, 1983).

Despite the pleadings for multi-level research, most of the studies conducted to date have focused on a single level of analysis, most commonly the individual level (e.g., Zhou & George, 2001). Some exceptions that have begun to expand the field should be applauded, such as Hirst, van Knippenberg, and Zhou's (2006) study on the relationship between team learning behavior, team supports for learning, goal orientation, and employee creativity; Taggar's (2002) study on the relationship between team creativity-relevant processes and individual and team creativity; and Drazin, Glynn, and Kazanjian's (1999) theoretical proposal on how creativity unfolds across levels in long-duration organizational projects.

Scholars engaged in multi-level research on team (rather than individual) creativity are on a somewhat difficult footing, and will face increased difficulties concerning theoretical, measurement, and analysis issues. Hitherto the work-related creativity literature has been dominated by individual-level studies. Even when the research setting involves teams, the outcome under analyses is usually individual creativity (e.g., Amabile, Barsade, Mueller, & Staw, 2005). These studies do not entail major measurement decisions, as the level of data collection is obviously the individual. Team innovation research, by contrast, is not centered on the generation of ideas but rather on their implementation, and the outcome to be assessed is usually associated to the final product developed by the team, which informs the methodological design (West, 2002; West & Anderson, 1996). When the outcome of interest is not individual creativity but rather team creativity, the researcher faces more difficult choices about the level of data collection. For instance, is it preferable to collect measures for each single team member, or is it more appropriate to gather one score for the whole team?

By aiming to study *team creativity*, the researcher is assuming that creativity – at least in that specific situation – is a collective construct.

The emergence of collective constructs takes place via social interactions between the lower-level systems. In organizational settings, many collective constructs have their roots in the cognition, affect, behavior, and characteristics of individuals that emerge via social interaction and are manifested at different levels (Morgeson & Hofmann, 1999).

Emergence processes vary along a continuum ranging from composition to compilation (Kozlowski & Klein, 2000). For the sake of simplicity, and given the introductory character of our contribution, we will focus solely on the two extreme forms of emergence as a means to stimulate reflection on the emergence of team creativity. It is not possible to determine the exact position of the nature of the collective construct across the continuum, as this will likely vary across different domains, so we considered that anchoring our discussion on the two extreme types would best fit our aim of encouraging research into this topic. It is important to note, however, that when analyzing the nature of the construct, the researcher should keep in mind the whole continuum and not merely the extreme forms.

Composition is based on assumptions of some level of isomorphism, and describes phenomena that are to some extent the same as they emerge across levels. The collective construct (designated shared unit properties) results from the convergence of similar lower-level properties. Shared unit properties originate at the individual level and converge among group members as a function of attraction, selection, attrition, socialization, or social interaction (Kozlowski & Klein, 2000).

Compilation, by comparison, is based on assumptions of discontinuity. It refers to situations in which lower-level characteristics, behaviors, and perceptions do not coalesce, but instead the higher-level phenomenon (designated as configural unit properties) is a more complex combination of the individual-level contributions. The phenomenon comprises a common domain but is distinctively different across levels. Configural unit properties capture the array of different individual contributions to the whole. They also originate at the individual level, but unlike shared properties, are not assumed to converge among members of a unit (Kozlowski & Klein, 2000).

The question about the nature of team creativity is a pertinent one here. Does team creativity emerge as a result of the convergence of the essentially identical contributions of individual members, as would be suggested by a direct consensus model (Chan, 1998), so that team creativity is a mere sum or average of individual creativity? Or does team creativity result from the array or pattern of individual team members' creativity – the complex combination of one team member's contribution on one issue, another team member's contribution on a second issue, and the lack of contribution from a third member?

If we think of a string quartet in which each player performs his or her own part of the same music and contributes equally to the overall creative performance of the quartet, we can assume the overall level of creativity follows a compositional emergence. The same conclusion applies if we consider the tendency for less-creative individuals to start expressing themselves more freely and being more creative once given a role model for doing so (Jaussi & Dionne, 2003). It is likely that in teams that are initially dominated by the creative output of one or two individuals, less-creative members may eventually increase their creative output via role modeling to match the level provided by the more creative members. In this case, team creativity is a shared construct that emerges from the convergence of individual members' creativity.

Conversely, if we think of a soccer team, a creative midfielder is often responsible for the level of creative soccer played by the team. The team can adopt a more or less creative style of play as a consequence of the input of one member. It is still a unit construct that we are looking at – the overall level of team creativity – but a configural one rather than a shared one. That is, different members make different contributions and these contributions are not assumed to converge across individuals.

Theoretical proposals relating to team creativity have reflected the two underlying emergence forms. In their cognitive model of group creativity, Smith, Gerkens, Shah, and Vargas-Hernandez (2005) proposed that group creativity could be seen as an analogue of the individual cognitive system. Individual cognitive components have specific roles and functions that contribute to creative and noncreative thinking, and the individuals in a group play the roles of these cognitive components in such a way that the group works as if it had an overall mind. This isomorphism of the construct across levels (even though Smith et al. state the isomorphism is not complete) sets the model closer to a compositional emergence form. By contrast, Woodman et al's. (1993) interactionist theory of creative behavior emphasizes the different nature of individual and team creativity when describing two completely different sets of variables influencing the two outputs. This last proposition is thus closer to a configural ideal type.

As Kozlowski and Klein suggest, the type of emergence is influenced by the nature of the social–psychological interactions and can vary for a given phenomenon across situations, such as task types. Team creativity might, therefore, be compositional in some domains and compilational in others. The research question can also determine which processes are examined.

(This leads to a situation not dissimilar to Heidinger's uncertainty principle: The role of the investigator and the processes being examined are inextricably linked, meaning that "true" answers can never be completely achieved.) For instance, if the researcher hypothesizes the normative effect of groups and the convergence of creative contributions across team members toward a group norm over time, the underlying model would be closer to a compositional one.

Despite this uncertainty (or perhaps because of it), it is essential that researchers have a clear idea about the nature of the emergence of team creativity in the specific situation they wish to investigate. It is of critical importance to be clear about the type of unit-level construct because this information should drive the form of measurement and strategy for analysis. The multi-level literature has provided a valuable set of recommendations, so researchers can adequately address the phenomena they are studying. This knowledge, however, can be beneficial only if the researcher is conscious about the level and nature of the constructs involved. Individual-level constructs should be measured with individual-level data. The measurement of unit-level constructs can be performed either with individual-level data that are afterward combined or with unit-level data (e.g., an expert source provides one single rating for the whole unit) (Kozlowski & Klein, 2000).

There is no universal agreement about this last point, however. Indeed, some researchers argue that unit-level constructs should be accessed using unit-level data, as this avoids the ambiguity inherent in aggregated data (Rousseau, 1985). Others argue that by using a global measure, the researcher lacks the data needed to test whether members are, indeed, homogeneous on the variables under consideration, so researchers should use unit-level data only when there is absolute certainty about the level of the construct (Klein, Dansereau, & Hall, 1994).

According to this line of reasoning, if the researcher is just interested in studying individual creativity, the level of measurement is logically the individual. Self-ratings, peer ratings, or leader/supervisor/expert informant ratings of the level of creativity demonstrated by each individual would be adequate forms of collection. Examples of this situation are abundant in the literature (e.g., George & Zhou, 2002).

If the researcher is interested in team creativity, two options remain open. The first option is to obtain a rating for the team as a whole. This might be a subjective rating of an expert informant (e.g., Tierney & Farmer, 2002) or other objective measures such as number of patents (e.g., Oldham & Cummings, 1996). The second option is to collect individual ratings (either self-ratings or external ratings) that are to be combined in some form later. The manner in which these individual ratings are combined depends to a large extent on the form of the ratings and the level of isomorphism with the team-level construct (Bliese, 2000). Chan (1998) provides a useful typology of composition models ("composition" in this terminology has a broader meaning, including what Kozlowski and Klein (2000) described as compilation models), which includes both consensus models (those most closely aligned to the earlier description of composition models) and compilation models. Chan described five types of composition models, any three of which might be used for measuring team creativity under certain circumstances.

The first is the additive model that specifies that individual constructs combine additively to form the higher-level construct. For example, under the Smith et al. (2005) model, the level of team creativity might be viewed as simply the total sum of all individual members' levels of creativity, in which case, measuring individual members' creativity and aggregating the results would be all that is necessary to capture the level of team creativity.

Alternatively, if team creativity were to be considered a team-level construct without an individual-level analogue (as suggested by Woodman et al., 1993), then it could still be captured from individual data in two ways. Chan's referent-shift consensus model attempts to measure group-level properties by asking individuals about the group as a whole – for example, questions such as "To what extent does your team try out new ideas and approaches to problems?" As with all consensus models, it is necessary to demonstrate agreement of team members' views before data can be aggregated to the team level to form the team construct.

The third of Chan's models that could be useful is the dispersion model. This compilation model effectively measures the diversity of a lower-level construct to obtain a higher-level construct that is not isomorphic. For example, it may be that team creativity is a function of differing viewpoints or skills or abilities within a team. Therefore, the individual constructs could be measured and the amount of diversity among them calculated to form the measure of team creativity.

Recalling our earlier point, to further inform this decision, the researcher must have a precise idea about the nature of team creativity under the situation investigated. Does it obey a composition or a compilation emergence model? Is it a shared or a configural unit property? According to Kozlowski and Klein (2000), shared unit properties emerge from shared perceptions, affect, and responses, and have their roots at the psychological level. Hence, the data to access these constructs should match the level of origin – that is, the individual level. Collecting data at the individual level has the additional advantage that the researcher can test whether the construct does, in fact, result from a compositional emergence. If the researcher assumes the compositional nature of creativity (via either an additive or a consensus model), collecting individual-level data is not only appropriate but also a requirement to prove this assertion. One factor that will influence the type of emergence is the nature of the creative task. If the team has to perform an additive task (team performance is the sum of team members' performances; Steiner, 1972), the model of emergence is very likely to be a compositional one. The most appropriate form of measuring in this circumstance is the average of the individual-level ratings.

Configural properties result from individuals' characteristics, cognitions, or behaviors, but in this case they do not coalesce. Kozlowski and Klein (2000) recommend a variety of data-combination techniques, such as minimum and maximum scores, indices of variation, profile similarity, and multidimensional scaling. The choice of a technique is highly dependent on the type of creativity task that the team is facing. Taking Steiner's terminology as an example, if the task at stake is a disjunctive one (team performance is determined by the performance of the best team member), the adequate representation is the maximum score of the most creative team member. If the task is conjunctive (team performance equals the worst performance of any team member), the researcher should take the minimum score obtained by a team member. If the task falls somewhere between an additive task and a disjunctive task, then the researcher should calculate a weighted average (Pirola-Merlo & Mann, 2004). How this calculation should be performed is not clear and probably varies across different situations, depending chiefly on the type of task. Systematic efforts at measuring configural creativity are necessary to shed light on this problem.

Two empirical studies have started a movement to address the nature of the emergence of team creativity by looking at the relationship between individual and team creativity. The results found by each study support a different model, providing confirmation of the contingent nature of the emergence.

Taggar (2002) examined 94 student groups performing 13 open-ended tasks over 13 weeks. The author hypothesized that "group creativity is an interactive function of aggregated individual creativity and the specific behaviors within a team that measure team creativity-relevant processes" (p. 320). This assertion implies a synergistic perspective of creativity more easily associated with a compilation model. In this study, individual-relevant (e.g., preparation, participation) and team-relevant creative processes (e.g., effective communication, involving others), and individual creativity, were peer rated at the end of week 13. Team creativity was the average of the 13 weekly assessments provided by an expert judge (team members received weekly feedback reports of these ratings). Taggar verified that the aggregation of the individual ratings predicted group creativity as rated by the external judge. Furthermore, he found that creativity-relevant processes accounted for variation in team creativity beyond the variance explained by the aggregation of individual creativity. The results suggest not only that team creativity is the addition of individual-level creativity but also that team-relevant creative processes that emerge as part of the group interaction are important.

Pirola-Merlo and Mann (2004) challenged these conclusions, arguing that it was possible to account for the findings reported by Taggar without accepting that team creativity is more than the aggregated creativity of group members. These authors claimed that in a typical interdependent project team, creativity emerges from the combination of individual creativity as the result of a fuzzy compositional form of emergence. This form is distinct from the compositional emergence presented by Kozlowski and Klein (2000); in fuzzy compositional models, the aggregate variable contains influences that are not captured by the lower-level construct (Bliese, 2000). Contrary to Taggar's (2002) findings, Pirola-Merlo and Mann (2004) claimed that team creativity is simply the aggregation of the creativity of individual members. They predicted that group processes would not account for significant variance in team creativity, after individual creativity had been accounted for.

To test these assumptions, the authors analyzed the relationship between individual and team creativity in a sample of 54 R&D teams over nine months. As part of their study, they measured individual, team, and project creativity. Individual creativity was computed as the average of three items: self-report and leader ratings of creativity plus leader ratings of performance, rated monthly. Team creativity was assessed by asking members to rate the overall innovativeness of the work on the project completed in the last month. "Time-general" creativity was measured by asking all team members at the start of the project to what extent they agreed with the item "This team has developed innovative solutions to problems" presented in the initial questionnaire. Project creativity was assessed by asking team members to indicate the number of new products, processes, or patents produced by the group and to rate the outcomes in terms of novelty, usefulness, creativity, and innovativeness.

As a result of this study, Pirola-Merlo and Mann (2004) concluded that team creativity could be explained by aggregation processes across both people and time: Team creativity at a particular point in time could be explained by either the average or a weighted average of team member creativity, and the creativity of the project could be explained by either the maximum or the average of team creativity across time points. The differing conclusions reached by these researchers and Taggar highlight how important it is to consider the nature of emergence when deciding upon the way the construct is measured.

Earlier, researchers may have been distracted from the problems associated with defining team creativity, with Kozlowski and Klein (2000) stating that "At first glance, the construct of unit creativity appears straightforward .... But a further, multilevel perspective indicates much work to be done in defining, explicating, and operationalizing the nature and emergence of unit-level creativity" (p. 41). However, creativity scholars have dismissed this point in their theoretical frameworks, assuming by default a configural or compositional structure without explaining their assumptions.

For instance, Gilson and Shalley (2004) measured engagement in team creative processes by using the leader to determine the overall rating for the team. As described earlier, this technique is more suitable when the construct follows a configural model of emergence. However, the definition of the team creative processes – "Members working together in such a manner that they link ideas from multiple sources, delve into unknown areas to find better or unique approaches to a problem, or seek out novel ways of performing a task" (p. 454) – is more suggestive of a shared property (and implies a compositional emergence). As such, data should have been collected at the individual level. It is possible that the level of measurement is adequate, but the authors fail to clarify the nature of the construct or to describe how it informed the level of data collection.

As an example of the assumption by default of compositional emergence, one can cite the research on brainstorming, in which the performance of the team is usually obtained by averaging the individual contributions. This methodology assumes – without adequate theoretical justification – that team creativity is simply the aggregation of individual creative efforts. This assumption (which is both untested and unverified) is the basis for a long and extensive tradition of research in social psychology. We do not claim that this procedure is incorrect. Rather, we suggest that for the good development of team creativity theory, scholars should describe the theory underlying the emergence of the construct and explain how that theory informed the measurement and analysis.

In summary, it is not possible to generalize at this point about the nature of the emergence of team creativity. In certain domains, creativity is a shared construct; in other domains, it is a configural construct; and in still other domains, it will lie somewhere along the continuum described by Kozlowski and Klein (2000). Furthermore, there is no single best way of measuring team creativity, either when it is assumed to be a shared property or when it is assumed to be a configural property. The general rule that applies to configural and shared properties is that they should be assessed at the level of origin, and the model of data aggregation, combination, and representation should be informed by the theoretical definition of the construct and the nature of its emergence (Kozlowski & Klein, 2000).

Knowledge about the particular situation will allow the researcher to develop assumptions about the nature of the emergence of the construct under the specific situation. Systematic reflection across studies on the level of emergence of team creativity would facilitate our understanding of team creativity and inform best practice to measure both shared and configural types.

CONCLUSION

The linkage between individual cognitive processes and team processes makes an essential contribution to the development of team creativity research, and the chapter by Reiter-Palmon et al. constitutes an excellent initial step in establishing this relationship. We would extend the contribution made by these authors by discussing the nature of the collective construct of team creativity and its implications in terms of measurement. For the good development of team creativity research, it is vital that scholars cautiously reflect about the emergence of the phenomenon in the context they are studying, and this reflection should, in turn, inform their choices in terms of measurement and analysis. Systematic research on the nature of collective creativity across a range of different domains will contribute to better understanding of when team creativity should be operationalized as the average of individual contributions, and when this average is not the ideal form of representation. In the latter case, research can also illuminate which forms of aggregation are more appropriate and in which situations.

REFERENCES

Abbey, A., & Dickson, J. W. (1983). R&D work climate and innovation in semiconductors. *Academy of Management Journal, 26*(2), 362–368.

Agrell, A., & Gustafson, R. (1996). Innovation and creativity in work groups. In: M. A. West (Ed.), *Handbook of work group psychology* (pp. 317–343). Chichester, UK: Wiley.

Amabile, T. M. (1988). A model of creativity and innovation in organizations. In: B. M. Staw & L. L. Cummings (Eds), *Research in organizational behavior* (Vol. 10, pp. 123–167). Greenwich, CT: JAI Press.

Amabile, T. M., Barsade, S., Mueller, J. S., & Staw, B. M. (2005). Affect and creativity at work: A daily longitudinal test. *Administrative Science Quarterly, 50*, 367–403.

Bliese, P. D. (2000). Within group agreement, non-independence, and reliability: Implications for data aggregation and analysis. In: K. J. Klein & S. W. J. Kozlowski (Eds), *Multilevel theory, research, and methods in organizations* (pp. 349–381). San Francisco, CA: Jossey-Bass.

Chan, D. (1998). Functional relations among constructs in the same content domain at different levels of analysis: A typology of composition models. *Journal of Applied Psychology, 83*, 234–246.

Drazin, R., Glynn, M. A., & Kazanjian, R. K. (1999). Multilevel theorizing about creativity in organizations: A sensemaking perspective. *The Academy of Management Review, 24*(2), 286.

Finke, R. A., Ward, T. B., & Smith, S. M. (1992). *Creative cognition: Theory, research, and applications.* Cambridge, MA: MIT Press.

George, J. M., & Zhou, J. (2001). When openness to experience and conscientiousness are related to creative behavior: An interactional approach. *Journal of Applied Psychology, 86*(3), 513–524.

George, J. M., & Zhou, J. (2002). Understanding when bad moods foster creativity and good ones don't: The role of context and clarity of feelings. *Journal of Applied Psychology, 87*(4), 687–697.

Gilson, L. L., & Shalley, C. E. (2004). A little creativity goes a long way: An examination of team's engagement in the creative process. *Journal of Management, 30*(4), 453–470.

Hirst, G., van Knippenberg, A., & Zhou, J. (2006). A multi-level perspective on employee creativity: Goal orientation, team supports for learning, and individual creativity. Submitted for publication.

Jaussi, K. S., & Dionne, S. D. (2003). Leading for creativity: The role of unconventional leader behavior. *Leadership Quarterly, 14*(4–5), 475–498.

Klein, K. J., Dansereau, F., & Hall, R. J. (1994). Levels issues in theory development, data-collection, and analysis. *Academy of Management Review, 19*(2), 195–229.

Kozlowski, S. W. J., & Klein, K. J. (2000). A multilevel approach to theory and research in organizations: Contextual, temporal, and emergent processes. In: K. J. Klein & S. W. J. Kozlowski (Eds), *Multilevel theory, research, and methods in organizations: Foundations, extensions, and new directions* (pp. 3–90). San Francisco, CA: Jossey-Bass.

Madjar, N., & Oldham, G. R. (2002). Preliminary tasks and creative performance on a subsequent task: Effects of time on preliminary tasks and amount of information about the subsequent task. *Creativity Research Journal, 14*(2), 239–251.

Morgeson, F. P., & Hofmann, D. A. (1999). The structure and function of collective constructs: Implications for multilevel research and theory development. *The Academy of Management Review, 24*(2), 249–265.

Mumford, M. D., & Hunter, S. T. (2004). Innovation in organizations: A multilevel perspective on creativity. In: F. Dansereau & F. J. Yammarino (Eds), *Research in multi-level issues* (Vol. 4, pp. 11–73). Oxford, UK: Elsevier.

Oldham, G. R. (2003). Stimulating and supporting creativity in organizations. In: S. Jackson, M. Hitt & A. DeNisi (Eds), *Managing knowledge for sustained competitive advantage* (pp. 243–273). San Francisco, CA: Jossey-Bass.

Oldham, G. R., & Cummings, A. (1996). Employee creativity: Personal and contextual factors at work. *Academy of Management Journal, 39*(3), 607.

Paulus, P., & Nijstad, B. A. (2003). *Group creativity: Innovation through collaboration.* Oxford, UK: Oxford University Press.

Pirola-Merlo, A., & Mann, L. (2004). The relationship between individual creativity and team creativity: Aggregating across people and time. *Journal of Organizational Behavior, 25*(2), 235–257.

Redmond, M. R., Mumford, M. D., & Teach, R. (1993). Putting creativity to work: Effects of leader-behavior on subordinate creativity. *Organizational Behavior and Human Decision Processes, 55*(1), 120–151.

Reiter-Palmon, R., Herman, A., & Yammarino, F. (this volume). Creativity and cognitive processes: Multi-level linkages between individual and team cognition. In: M. Mumford, S. Hunter & K. E. Bedell-Avers (Eds), *Multi-level issues in creativity and innovation* (Vol. 7). Oxford: Elsevier.

Rokeach, M. (1950). The effect of perception of time upon the rigidity and concreteness of thinking. *Journal of Experimental Psychology, 40*, 206–216.

Rousseau, D. M. (1985). Issues of level in organizational research. In: B. M. Staw & L. L. Cummings (Eds), *Research in organizational behavior* (Vol. 17, pp. 1–37). Greenwich, CT: JAI Press.

Runco, M. A. (2003). *Critical creative processes.* Cresshill, NJ: Hampton Press.

Smith, S. M., Gerkens, D. R., Shah, J., & Vargas-Hernandez, N. (2005). Empirical studies of creative cognition in idea generation. In: L. Thompson & H. Choi (Eds), *Creativity and innovation in organizational teams* (pp. 3–20). Mahwah, NJ: Lawrence Erlbaum Associates.

Steiner, I. D. (1972). *Group process and productivity.* New York: Academic Press.

Sternberg, R. J., & Lubart, T. (1999). The concept of creativity: Prospects and paradigms. In: R. J. Sternberg (Ed.), *Handbook of creativity* (pp. 3–15). Cambridge, UK: Cambridge University Press.

Taggar, S. (2002). Individual creativity and group ability to utilize individual creative resources: A multilevel model. *Academy of Management Journal, 45*(2), 315–330.

Tierney, P., & Farmer, S. M. (2002). Creative self-efficacy: Its potential antecedents and relationship to creative performance. *Academy of Management Journal, 45*(6), 1137.

West, M. A. (1996). Reflexivity and work group effectiveness: A conceptual integration. In: M. A. West (Ed.), *Handbook of work group psychology* (pp. 555–579). Chichester, UK: Wiley.

West, M. A. (2000). Reflexivity, revolution, and innovation in work teams. In: M. M. Beyerlein, D. A. Johnson & S. T. Beyerlein (Eds), *Product development teams: Advances in interdisciplinary studies of work teams* (pp. 1–29). Stanford, CT: JAI Press.

West, M. A. (2002). Sparkling fountains or stagnant ponds: An integrative model of creativity and innovation implementation in work groups. *Applied Psychology – An International Review, 51*(3), 355–387.

West, M. A., & Anderson, N. R. (1996). Innovation in top management teams. *Journal of Applied Psychology, 81*(6), 680–693.

Woodman, R. W., Sawyer, J. E., & Griffin, R. W. (1993). Toward a theory of organizational creativity. *The Academy of Management Review, 18*(2), 293.

Zhou, J., & George, J. M. (2001). When job dissatisfaction leads to creativity: Encouraging the expression of voice. *Academy of Management Journal, 44*(4), 682.

TEAM COGNITION: THE IMPORTANCE OF TEAM PROCESS AND COMPOSITION FOR THE CREATIVE PROBLEM-SOLVING PROCESS

Christina E. Shalley

ABSTRACT

This commentary suggests areas that could be further developed in Reiter-Palmon, Herman, and Yammarino's call for a multi-level analysis of the underlying cognitive structures of both teams and individuals. The chapter by Reiter-Palmon, Herman, and Yammarino effectively demonstrates the importance of cognition in the understanding of individual and team creativity. However, the importance of other issues – in particular, team process and composition – also needs to be more fully considered when moving from the individual level to the team level. This commentary addresses the conceptual challenge of attempting to take a purely cognitive approach for teams, and presents some further arguments for considering how team process and composition influence team cognition and ultimately team creative problem solving. It also discusses the value of using some type of team intervention to enhance team creative

Multi-Level Issues in Creativity and Innovation
Research in Multi-Level Issues, Volume 7, 289–304
Copyright © 2008 by Elsevier Ltd.
ISSN: 1475-9144/doi:10.1016/S1475-9144(07)00011-2

problem-solving processes. Finally, it argues for the importance of considering the dynamic nature of some teams and examining how changes in team membership can affect team cognition.

INTRODUCTION

Reiter-Palmon, Herman, and Yammarino (this volume) do an excellent job of summarizing the extant literature on individual cognition. Their chapter provides a comprehensive review and update of the literature on individual cognition. Quite a bit of research has been conducted in this area, and these authors present the results of this research in a clear, organized fashion while also pointing out directions that additional research might explore. Along the way, this part of the chapter focuses strongly on the antecedents of team creativity and cognitive processes (i.e., individual creative cognition).

In addition, Reiter-Palmon et al. correctly point out that only very limited research has targeted the cognitive processes of creative problem solving at the group level, with the exception of the brainstorming literature. In their own chapter, they explore a number of cognitive-related issues that are raised by their extensive survey of the literature. Likewise, they highlight a number of issues that warrant further examination when moving from individual cognition to the team level. They provide a very good case for exploring the multi-level linkages between individual and team cognition, and they present many sound testable propositions for examining team cognition in particular.

Their well-stated introductory objective is "to provide an understanding of both the individual and team or group cognitive processes involved in creative problem solving." Reiter-Palmon et al. are very clear in their introduction to this piece that they are limiting their multi-level discussion to cognition. They state that the purpose of their chapter is to "provide a comprehensive review of the cognitive process involved in creative problem solving." They briefly acknowledge other variables that could be considered, such as team process and composition, but state that these are beyond the scope of their chapter. Although I understand these authors' rationale for constraining their discussion of individual and team cognition to a manageable level for their chapter's purposes, the question remains: Can you truly discuss team cognition without bringing in the issues of team composition and process?

Given that team cognition involves the cognition of a collection of individuals, who these individuals are and what they potentially bring to the table can make a huge difference in the analysis of team cognition. Therefore, when moving from the individual level to the team level, issues become more complex, as team composition and team members' interactions can affect the team's cognition. When discussing team cognition, inputs such as differences in personality, cognitive processing, functional experience, and knowledge and skills are potentially very important. For example, if teams are composed of some members who have similar cognitive styles, this shared style may facilitate the effective functioning of their team. Also, teams that include members who rate highly on certain personality factors, such as openness to experience, may be more willing to listen to different ideas and consider the worthiness of various viewpoints.

In addition, how the team interacts can influence team cognition at multiple points in time. For example, the process the team employs can affect whether ideas are freely shared and discussed, which ultimately affects the team's cognition. Therefore, although Reiter-Palmon and colleagues state that these matters are beyond the scope of their chapter, they appear to be very intimately linked to team cognition. That is, team cognition includes team member schemas about team interactions and other team members, and is a social cognitive phenomenon. For example, if the team is composed of two or more members who have a history of effectively working together, this past experience could smooth the initial team interaction because these members could rely on their common team schema of how to integrate their ideas effectively.

This commentary highlights some important factors having to do with team process and composition that should also be considered when examining team cognition, and it points out a number of propositions where Reiter-Palmon and colleagues are already touching on team composition (i.e., diversity) and particular facets of team process (e.g., Propositions 3–6). It briefly discusses some training and interventions that might be used to facilitate team creative problem solving. In addition, it argues that the dynamic nature of teams needs to be considered because changes in team membership can influence team cognition. Further consideration of these issues could lead to the refinement and extension of some of Reiter-Palmon et al.'s original propositions and the addition of potentially other testable propositions. Ultimately, this could lead to a more complete understanding of multi-level cognition.

THE IMPORTANCE OF TEAM COMPOSITION AND PROCESS

Researchers of teams have generally followed the well-accepted input–process–outcome (IPO) framework (e.g., Cohen & Bailey, 1997; Tannenbaum, Beard, & Salas, 1992). Inputs can include the task the team is working on, the composition of the group (including individual cognition), and the organizational context. As for process, the effectiveness of many work teams depends on whether members with different backgrounds help one another to fulfill their tasks. Essentially, it is usually the team members themselves who need to be able to effectively harness and use the different knowledge, skills, and abilities (KSAs) that different team members possess. As such, teams need to develop effective integration or group process skills to function. Also, for members to meaningfully contribute to the team, they need self-direction, self-motivation and self-monitoring, effective communication techniques, and productive management of conflict. Therefore, at the team level, team creative processes mediate the relationship between individual creativity and team creativity (Taggar, 2002; Woodman, Sawyer, & Griffin, 1993).

Research indicates that factors that influence the coordination of team members' activities are particularly critical for performance in general (e.g., Hackman, 1987; McIntyre & Salas, 1995). It has been proposed that team members require appropriate team integration skills that are distinct from technical skills relevant to team performance (Stevens & Campion, 1994). Stevens and Campion (1994) grouped these team integration skills into two categories. The first category concerns self-management KSAs such as goal setting, performance management, and task coordination. The second category deals with interpersonal KSAs, such as communication skills, conflict-resolution skills, and collaborative problem-solving skills. The more the team members possess these skills, the more effectively they would presumably function as a team.

When individuals work in teams, they are potentially exposed to a broad range of skills, perspectives, and information that can be used to generate more ideas and form better options for how work is performed. Creativity, in part, comes from bringing together knowledge from disparate places. Access to diverse information, ideas, and alternatives stimulates creativity and groundbreaking advancements (Amabile, Conti, Coon, Lazenby, & Herron, 1996; Perry-Smith, 2006; Perry-Smith & Shalley, 2003). When teams have some level of internal variety and some degree of external reach to others outside the team, they should be able to be more successful in creative problem solving. As Kanter (1988) argues, "Contact with those who see the world differently is a logical prerequisite to seeing it differently ourselves" (p. 175). Weak ties, where individual team members have access to disconnected others with non-redundant information (i.e., external social capital), should also increase a team's ability to explore and reach diverse information that might then help the team solve problems creatively (Perry-Smith, 2006; Perry-Smith & Shalley, 2003). External social capital increases the heterogeneity of available information, can encourage deeper deliberations and discussions about reasons for variety, and may result in more debate and the surfacing of new alternatives (Beckman, 2006).

As such, team creativity relies on tapping into the diverse knowledge base of its members and then combining and applying this knowledge. In organizations, the availability of diverse knowledge is shaped and constrained by the realities of deadlines, resources, collaborators, and workloads. Diversity of knowledge in teams is deep-level (rather than surface-level) diversity or cognitive diversity. Indeed, the value of working in teams is that it exposes individuals to a broader set of perspectives and cross-fertilization of ideas, potentially resulting in more creative outcomes (Perry-Smith & Shalley, 2003). Given that team members may have different cognitive strategies and career experiences, this leads to a variation in knowledge and problem-solving approaches that can help teams identify and use multiple knowledge components. Individuals develop their own knowledge and network ties with other knowledgeable persons, both of which could help the team retrieve and apply knowledge components that may prove useful for a given task.

Of course, team members must have the ability and motivation to share and develop their ideas, as well as to integrate different components of a task. That is, team members have a choice as to whether to engage in creative processes (Drazin, Glynn, & Kazanjian, 1999). For teams to be creative, members need to generate a number of ideas, share these ideas, critically process the ideas generated, select those ideas that are most promising, and work together to transform creative ideas into workable methods, products, and services. During this process, members will inevitably challenge assumptions and approaches, which in turn may stimulate more creative thought (as long as the team shares common goal or interests). Furthermore, the use of "devil's advocates" or the encouragement of minority dissent in teams seems to prevent premature movement to consensus, promotes cognitive complexity, and facilitates better decision making (DeDreu & West, 2001). Finally, the absorptive capacity of a team (i.e., the ability to recognize the value of new information, assimilate it, and apply it) will be higher when team members participate in decision making, because participation stimulates the exchange and integration of information (DeDreu & West, 2001).

TEAM COMPOSITION AND PROCESS IN RELATION TO CREATIVE PROBLEM SOLVING

At all levels of analysis, the interactions between individuals and their context shape and constrain what they do. Individuals generate the initial ideas. If they are organized into collective entities (e.g., teams, networks), these individuals are nested in and influenced by their own psychological context and the team context. Therefore, team composition and process affects all of the core cognitive processes relevant to creative problem solving. According to the chapter by Reiter-Palmon et al., the core cognitive processes are twofold:

• The idea-generation phase, which includes three stages: problem construction or identification, information search and gathering, and idea generation
• The implementation phase, which includes two stages: idea evaluation and selection, and implementation planning and monitoring

For each of the two phases, I will discuss some issues to consider with regard to team process and composition, and highlight where Reiter-Palmon et al.'s propositions could benefit from further consideration and development of these issues.

Idea-Generation Phase

In presenting their team-level propositions for problem construction, Reiter-Palmon et al. argue that homogeneity of teams may hinder the team creative problem-solving process. Specifically, Proposition 3 states that homogeneous groups would be more likely to apply similar problem representations automatically, which would be expected to lead to less creative problem solutions. It would be beneficial for these authors to take a more fine-grained approach in discussing diversity. That is, which aspects of diversity are important for team creative problem solving? Is it only diversity that is present on a deep-level versus surface-level characteristics? Alternatively, is it beneficial for the team to be diverse on deep-level issues but similar on surface-level characteristics? For example, diversity on some factors (e.g., cognitive style) may be more important for creative problem solving, whereas homogeneity on other compositional factors (e.g., conscientiousness) might enhance the team's engagement in the process of creative problem solving.

Reiter-Palmon et al.'s discussion highlights the importance of attention and the use of attentional resources for problem construction. These authors state that specific cues can indicate that further attention to the situation and problem is necessary. They also argue that attention to high-quality elements of the problem representations should result in more creative solutions. Given that problem solvers frame the problem in ways that fit with their past experiences and existing problem representations, the composition of the team seems to be a critical factor for problem construction. That is, based on their past experiences and skill levels, team members may vary in their use of attentional resources, which in turn would affect the team's cognition.

As Reiter-Palmon et al. note, it is important to have a shared mental model of task knowledge that should improve the effectiveness of team performance. For example, Gilson and Shalley (2004) found that when team members had shared goals, they engaged more frequently in creative processes. This finding suggests that it is essential to identify the stage at which shared mental models are most important for groups. When does having shared mental models or goals enhance creative problem solving versus constrain it? For teams, it makes sense that there is a strong need for shared mental models, particularly in diverse teams. In addition to facilitating problem construction, such a shared model should be helpful during the idea-generation process and the evaluation of solutions.

As Reiter-Palmon and colleagues argue, the value of team diversity is the integration of different points of view and elements of the problem representation. They state that all members of the team need to actively engage in problem construction. Therefore, the team process comes into play. As such, Reiter-Palmon et al.'s Propositions 4 and 5 deal with team disagreements and whether they are effectively resolved, while Propositions 6 and 9 concern the understanding of and acceptance of others' problem representations.

As the authors point out, the concept of cognitive consensus (Mohammed & Dumville, 2001) could be very important. According to them, cognitive consensus results in group members attending to, interpreting, and communicating about issues in a similar manner. If group members make an effort to understand the reasons for other preferences and accept other points of view as legitimate, higher cognitive consensus results (Mohammed & Ringseis, 2001). Therefore, key to Reiter-Palmon and colleagues' arguments with problem construction is the teams' under-standing of diverse members' frame of references. This requires listening, engaging, and understanding where each team member is coming from (e.g., functional background, prior experiences).

Next, they discuss the important role of searching for and encoding information. They discuss research that found that it is critical for individuals to be motivated to exert the time and effort needed to be more creative at this stage. Presumably, this motivation would be very important or more important for teams, because one would expect that it would be needed to encourage team members to spend more time sharing their own unique knowledge and experiences. Having variance in knowledge and expertise should also result in the greater use of diverse and inconsistent information, which should help to develop creative solutions. Therefore, teams with a high level of expertise would not be desirable, nor would a team composed entirely of novices. The added value of using teams over individuals derives from the range of experience that can be called on to search and evaluate information.

Proposition 10 states that information sharing will facilitate creative problem solving only when the information shared is appropriate and relevant to the problem. It is unclear, however, precisely how the team members will know what information is appropriate and relevant to share at this stage of the problem-solving process. This may explain why Bunderson and Sutcliffe (2002) found that when team members have some degree of overlap in experiences and functions, information sharing and performance are facilitated. Perhaps this overlap in knowledge facilitates team discussion of whether certain information is relevant. If there is no overlap, then team members may not consider information that they are not sure is pertinent to the problem representation at hand. Therefore, it may be critical for team members to know the functional background and experiences of other team members.

As stated in Proposition 11, functional diversity may have a curvilinear relationship with information sharing, but the key could lie in the awareness of the team composition and the knowledge assets that exist with each team member. Team compositional issues are touched on in Propositions 14, 15, and 16. Finally, Proposition 12 deals with team process issues – namely, the hypothesis that teams that emphasize discussion and exploration will engage in more information sharing.

According to Proposition 20, "Group brainstorming will result in fewer ideas generated by groups relative to individuals, but better or similar quality and originality of ideas." The first part of this proposition makes sense, but the authors do not really present arguments or research to support the idea that groups – relative to individuals – will produce better or similar quality and originality of ideas. The actual outcome might depend a great deal on whether the team members had good group process to capture the potential diversity of knowledge in the team. Also, the diversity of the group could moderate this effect.

In the section on the idea-generation stage, Reiter-Palmon and colleagues begin to bring in more of a focus on team compositional factors and review some relevant literature (see Propositions 25–27). They also state that team process is important as well (see Propositions 28 and 29).

Implementation Phase

In Reiter-Palmon et al.'s discussion of the evaluation of ideas, it is not clear if the evaluating team is the same as the idea-generation team. Some of the research cited involves individuals evaluating others' ideas rather than their own ideas. This may represent a different process than when the team was involved in generating the ideas. As Runco and Chand (1995) note, a judge evaluating the work of another person will have a different perspective than the idea generator. Also, it may be worthwhile to evaluate the cognitive process of the decision makers. How can an idea be presented in such a way that it will be evaluated more favorably by others? Interestingly, research has found that being able to identify an original idea is related to being able to generate original ideas. Thus, the implication for managers is that if the managers are not creative, even when creative ideas are generated by individual employees or work teams, the ideas may stagnate because they will not be evaluated favorably.

I agree with Reiter-Palmon and colleagues' suggestion that you need to have a shared problem representation along with some disagreement on evaluation standards for creative problem solving. Indeed, some disagreement about the relative importance of various goals and standards should ultimately lead to more creative solutions. Therefore, their Proposition 40, which deals with team composition, states that more diverse teams are expected to disagree more on standards for evaluation.

Reiter-Palmon et al.'s discussion of the need to have a number of contingency plans and the need to identify the consequences of actions is very important, as both of these topics are under-researched areas for both individuals and teams. For teams, if planning is done ahead of time, roles can be assigned (e.g., identifying who should be a devil's advocate in idea evaluation). Also, one or more members of the team may be assigned to monitor team progress and plan accordingly. Ideally, the authors might expand their discussion of cross-functional or multidisciplinary teams' use of different perspectives and networks to gain access to possible objections and constraints on implementation, along with ways to incorporate this information more fully into these teams' plans. As these authors point out, a critical issue is that to gain the benefit of team diversity, information needs to be shared. How do you get teams to communicate in a common language so that all members understand what each member is saying? Proposition 45 deals with team composition, and Proposition 46 deals with how team process can affect the implementation of plans.

Reiter-Palmon and colleagues cite research that suggests that more diverse teams are better able to respond to change and engage in opportunistic planning. This enhanced ability to adapt to change may arise because these teams recognize their diversity and realize the need to plan accordingly. There may be a false assumption going on within more homogeneous groups: Because team members see themselves as similar, they assume they understand one another and do not spend the time evaluating and planning. This may be particularly true for groups that are homogenous on surface-level characteristics but do not realize that there is variance on deep-level characteristics. Reiter-Palmon et al.'s Proposition 47 is about process, and Propositions 48, 50, and 54 are about team composition.

THE POTENTIAL USE OF INTERVENTIONS AND TRAINING

Managers can take a variety of steps to help teams function more effectively. Specifically, a body of work focuses on team building and other interventions (e.g., Tannenbaum et al., 1992; Woodman & Sherwood, 1980). Team-building efforts generally try to improve team performance by improving communication, reducing conflict, and increasing commitment and cohesion among team members (Bettenhausen, 1991). Team coaching is an intervention that inhibits process losses and fosters process gain by helping members coordinate their efforts and make task-appropriate use of their collective resources in accomplishing the team's work.

Research has also explored ways to train teams (e.g., Dyer, 1984; Swezey & Salas, 1992). Moreover, the training literature has begun to focus on training meta-cognitive skills (e.g., Kraiger, Ford, & Salas, 1993; Marks, Zaccaro, & Mathieu, 2000). If teams are provided with the cognitive capability to diagnose, interpret, and respond to shifting task demands, they ultimately should be more effective. Research has indicated that the induction of shared mental models through training leads to enhanced team performance (Cannon-Bowers, Salas, & Converse, 1993; Stout, Cannon-Bowers, & Salas, 1996; Zaccaro, Gualtieri, & Minionis, 1995). When teams are encouraged to discuss how they view the problem, what evaluation standards they employ, and so forth, the process should help them understand where each of the members is coming from and why each may react in a certain way to new information, and ultimately help the team to be more successful and creative. Teams may need training to reach this level of understanding, and possibly the use of a team facilitator at times. Therefore, it might make sense for a manager to provide some type of intervention to help a team be better able to accomplish this goal.

Reiter-Palmon et al.'s chapter could be extended by the inclusion of some discussion of how to enable groups to more effectively solve creative problems. Although these authors touch on this issue in a few places throughout the chapter (e.g., Propositions 33 and 34), further treatment of the issue would be useful.

DYNAMIC NATURE OF MANY ORGANIZATIONAL TEAMS

A final issue to consider and potentially develop further with regard to team cognition is the dynamic nature of many organizational teams, such as project teams that change often in response to their environment (Gersick, 1988). In most teams, changes in membership are inevitable as time passes. Any changes in team membership result in changes in the team's knowledge base and interactions among members. This evolution, in turn, may affect the team's cognition, social relations, and performance.

Changes in team membership may potentially be a positive development in terms of the team's creative problem solving. There is a real value in having new members join teams because they may potentially bring a fresh perspective that could spark new ideas. However, the new members also need to learn how to function effectively in the team, so that their ideas are attended to by the rest of the team, before the team can reap the benefits of having new members.

Each team works in its own unique way, and changes in team membership may potentially disrupt the established work process. It has been argued that when team members hold similar team-related knowledge, they are better able to anticipate the information team members need, their actions and reactions, and their ability to respond effectively (Salas, Dickinson, Converse, & Tannenbaum, 1992). Teams that have worked together for a while have a shared understanding of how work should be managed and coordinated. They also have a shared language, culture, and narratives about the organization. A shared language suggests a common perspective and trustworthiness (Tsai & Ghosal, 1998). A shared organizational culture provides a common frame of reference, a shared vision and set of goals, and a conceptual filter that helps generate expectations about work (Nahpiet & Ghosal, 1998). Common work experiences affect the development of shared beliefs and cultures as well as performance (Beckman, 2006; Chattopadhay, Glick, Miller, & George, 1999). Also, there is cohesion from having worked together in the past (Eisenhardt & Schoonhoven, 1990; Taylor & Greve, 2006). Teams with sufficient experience to have established communication can more easily utilize member diversity. Finally, common understandings facilitate execution and implementation of ideas (Williams & O'Reilly, 1998).

Reiter-Palmon and colleagues discuss membership changes in the team with regard to idea generation and ways that new members bring new ideas to the team (i.e., Propositions 25 and 26). In their conclusion, they state that each of the stages discussed is not necessarily a separate process and that individuals and teams can cycle back and forth between the different stages. Also, they discuss how tension may arise between team members if some members are slower or quicker at cycling through the process or if some members want to revisit stages and others are resistant to doing so. These issues are important for team development. Furthermore, when one considers the potentially dynamic nature of the team, this adds another level of complexity to these issues. For instance, if the team is midway in the process and a new member joins the team, the new member may want to revisit the initial problem-solving stages. Also, the new member may need to be informed of the team's cognition at each stage of the process so that he or she understands where the team is at this point and which standards team members chose to use.

When changes in team personnel occur, the new members may not share a common language or coding scheme for information, which could prove detrimental for their communication and team cognition. Furthermore, over time, communication tends to become more centralized around one or two team members (Kratzer, Leenders, & van Engelen, 2004). This could potentially be a problem for the team if one of the more central members is rotated off of the team.

Clearly, then, it is critical to think about how to manage changes in team personnel so that the team can still operate smoothly. For example, how do you build common team cognition with personnel changes? How can teams effectively pass on shared mental models and scripts to new members so as not to disrupt the creative problem-solving process while also reaping the benefits of having new perspectives? Furthermore, team members are often selected for certain teams and rotated through other work teams. Presumably they are selected on the basis of the particular skills they bring to the table or their ability to work well with the existing team members. Therefore, selection mechanisms potentially may reduce the existence of potential team conflicts and process losses. There needs to be a strong focus on the value of planning and monitoring, especially when team membership is changing and evolving.

CONCLUSION

Reiter-Palmon et al's multi-level analysis of the underlying cognitive structure of both teams and individuals makes a valuable contribution to the literature. Their review of the extant research on individual and team cognition is extremely useful. The primary issue for the present commentary is whether one can truly examine team cognition without a full considera-tion of the members of the team (i.e., team composition) and their team interactions (i.e., team process). Therefore, the bulk of the discussion here has focused on the importance of team process and composition for team cognition, and ultimately team creative performance. I have presented arguments for Reiter-Palmon and colleagues to consider that they might potentially refine and extend their existing propositions. I have also discussed how managers might facilitate more effective team processes, such as trying to invoke shared mental models and encouraging the sharing of information and the evaluative standards used by each team member. Finally, I have suggested the importance of considering the dynamic nature of some teams and the issues that may arise when team members leave the team or join a new team, in an effort to further the development of the concept of team cognition.

REFERENCES

Amabile, T. M., Conti, R., Coon, H., Lazenby, J., & Herron, M. (1996). Assessing the work environment for creativity. *Academy of Management Journal, 39*, 1154–1184.

Beckman, C. (2006). The influence of founding team company affiliations on firm behavior. *Academy of Management Journal, 49*, 741–758.

Bettenhausen, K. L. (1991). Five years of group research: What we have learned and what needs to be addressed. *Journal of Management, 17*, 345–381.

Bunderson, J. S., & Sutcliffe, K. M. (2002). Comparing alternative conceptualizations of functional diversity in management teams: Process and performance effects. *Academy of Management Journal, 45*, 875–893.

Cannon-Bowers, J. A., Salas, E., & Converse, S. (1993). Shared mental models in expert team decision-making. In: N. J. Castellan, Jr. (Ed.), *Individual and group decision making: Current issue* (pp. 221–246). Hillsdale, NJ: Lawrence Erlbaum Associates.

Chattopadhay, P., Glick, W., Miller, C., & George, H. (1999). Determinants of executive beliefs: Comparing functional conditioning and social influence. *Strategic Management Journal, 20*, 763–789.

Cohen, S. G., & Bailey, D. E. (1997). What makes teams work: Group effectiveness research from the shop floor to the executive suite. *Journal of Management, 23*, 239–290.

DeDreu, C. K. W., & West, M. A. (2001). Minority dissent and team innovation: The importance of participation in decision making. *Journal of Applied Psychology, 86*, 1191–1201.

Drazin, R., Glynn, M. A., & Kazanjian, R. K. (1999). Multilevel theorizing about creativity in organizations: A sense-making perspective. *Academy of Management Review, 24*, 286–329.

Dyer, J. L. (1984). Team research and team training: A state-of-the-art review. In: F. A. Muckler (Ed.), *Human factors review* (pp. 285–323). Santa Monica, CA: Human Factors Society.

Eisenhardt, K. M., & Schoonhoven, C. B. (1990). Organizational growth: Linking founding teams' strategy, environment and growth among US semi-conductor ventures. *Administrative Science Quarterly, 28*, 274–291.

Gersick, C. J. (1988). Time and transition in work teams: Toward a new model of group development. *Academy of Management Journal, 31*, 9–41.

Gilson, L. L., & Shalley, C. E. (2004). A little creativity goes a long way: An examination of teams' engagement in creative processes. *Journal of Management, 30*, 453–470.

Hackman, J. R. (1987). The design of work teams. In: J. Lorsch (Ed.), *Handbook of organizational behavior* (pp. 315–342). Englewood Cliffs, NJ: Prentice-Hall.

Kanter, R. M. (1988). When a thousand flowers bloom: Structural, collective, and social conditions for innovation. *Research in Organizational Behavior, 10*, 169–211.

Kraiger, K., Ford, J. K., & Salas, E. (1993). Application of cognitive, skill-based, and affective theories of learning outcomes to new methods of training evaluation. *Journal of Applied Psychology, 78*, 311–328.

Kratzer, J., Leenders, A. J., & van Engelen, M. L. (2004). Stimulating the potential: Creative performance and communication in innovation teams. *Creativity and Innovation Management, 13*, 63–71.

Marks, M. A., Zaccaro, S. J., & Mathieu, J. E. (2000). Performance implications of leader briefings and team-interaction training for team adaptation to novel environments. *Journal of Applied Psychology, 85,* 971–986.

McIntyre, R. M., & Salas, E. (1995). Measuring and managing for team performance: Lessons from complex environments. In: R. A. Guzzo & E. Salas (Eds), *Team effectiveness and decision-making in organizations* (pp. 9–45). San Francisco, CA: Jossey-Bass.

Mohammed, S., & Dumville, B. C. (2001). Team mental models in a team knowledge framework: Expanding theory and measurement across disciplinary boundaries. *Journal of Organizational Behavior, 22,* 89–106.

Mohammed, S., & Ringseis, E. (2001). Cognitive diversity and consensus in group decision making: The role of inputs, processes and outcomes. *Organizational Behavior and Human Decision Processes, 83,* 310–336.

Nahpiet, J., & Ghosal, S. (1998). Social capital, intellectual capital, and the organizational advantage. *Academy of Management Review, 23,* 242–266.

Perry-Smith, J. E. (2006). Social yet creative: The role of social relationships in facilitating individual creativity. *Academy of Management Journal, 49,* 85–102.

Perry-Smith, J. E., & Shalley, C. E. (2003). The social side of creativity: A static and dynamic social network perspective. *Academy of Management Review, 28,* 89–106.

Reiter-Palmon, R., Herman, A., & Yammarino, F. (this volume). Creativity and cognitive processes: Multi-level linkages between individual and team cognition. In: M. Mumford, S. Hunter & K. Bedell-Avers (Eds), *Multi-level issues in creativity and innovation* (Vol. 7).Oxford: Elsevier.

Runco, M. A., & Chand, I. (1995). Cognition and creativity. *Educational Psychology Review, 7,* 243–267.

Salas, E., Dickinson, T. L., Converse, S. A., & Tannenbaum, S. I. (1992). Toward an understanding of team performance and training. In: R. W. Swezey & E. Salas (Eds), *Teams: Their training and performance* (Vol. xvi, pp. 3–29). Westport, CT: Ablex.

Stevens, M. J., & Campion, M. A. (1994). The knowledge, skill, and ability requirement for teamwork: Implications for human resource management. *Journal of Management, 20,* 503–530.

Stout, R. J., Cannon-Bowers, J. A., & Salas, E. (1996). The role of shared mental models in developing team situation awareness: Implications for training. *Training Research Journal, 2,* 85–116.

Swezey, R. W., & Salas, E. (1992). *Teams: Their training and performance.* Westport, CT: Ablex.

Taggar, S. (2002). Individual creativity and group ability to utilize individual creative resources: A multilevel model. *Academy of Management Journal, 45,* 315–330.

Tannenbaum, S. I., Beard, R. L., & Salas, E. (1992). Team building and its influence on team effectiveness: An examination of conceptual and empirical developments. In: K. Kelley (Ed.), *Issues, theory, and research in industrial/organizational psychology* (Vol. xviii, p. 477). Oxford, UK: North-Holland.

Taylor, A., & Greve, H. R. (2006). Superman or the fantastic four? Knowledge combination and experience in innovative teams. *Academy of Management Journal, 49,* 723–740.

Tsai, W., & Ghosal, S. (1998). Social capital and value creation: The role of intrafirm networks. *Academy of Management Journal, 41,* 464–476.

Williams, K. Y., & O'Reilly, C. A. I. (1998). Demography and diversity in organizations. *Research in Organizational Behavior, 20*, 77–140.

Woodman, R. W., Sawyer, J. E., & Griffin, R. W. (1993). Toward a theory of organizational creativity. *Academy of Management Review, 18*, 293–321.

Woodman, R. W., & Sherwood, J. J. (1980). The role of team development in organizational effectiveness: A critical review. *Psychological Bulletin, 88*, 166–186.

Zaccaro, S. J., Gualtieri, J., & Minionis, D. (1995). Task cohesion as a facilitator of team decision making under temporal urgency. *Military Psychology, 7*, 77–95.

BEYOND COGNITIVE PROCESSES: ANTECEDENTS AND INFLUENCES ON TEAM COGNITION

Roni Reiter-Palmon, Anne E. Herman and Francis J. Yammarino

ABSTRACT

In this reply, we offer responses to two commentaries on our work on individual and team cognition and team creative problem-solving processes. We first acknowledge the contributions and depth of expansions to our work by Sacramento, Dawson, and West and by Shalley. We next clarify our views on some issues they raise. Finally, we offer additional multi-level extensions on these processes by incorporating ideas on leadership and organizational context.

INTRODUCTION

We thank Sacramento, Dawson, and West (this volume) as well as Shalley (this volume) for the insightful comments and a critique of our chapter on individual and team cognition. We are encouraged by the positive review of our current approach linking individual and team cognition research and extrapolating from these areas to team creativity. Both commentaries also

Multi-Level Issues in Creativity and Innovation
Research in Multi-Level Issues, Volume 7, 305–313
ISSN: 1475-9144/doi:10.1016/S1475-9144(07)00012-4

emphasize that, while our chapter provides a useful start to the conversation on the relationship between individual and team cognition, more work, both theoretical and empirical, remains to be done. We agree. Our chapter provides an initial attempt to bridge the divide between individual and team cognition and offers a preliminary discussion of multi-level issues in this domain. Nevertheless, additional conceptual and empirical work will need to provide more depth as well as more breadth in this research arena. Toward this end, we first address some of the comments and concerns raised by the two commentaries, and then explore additional issues that may affect individual and team cognition that have not been addressed previously.

RESPONSE TO SACRAMENTO ET AL.

The commentary by Sacramento et al. raises several concerns about our work. First, these authors point out the lack of in-depth discussion on certain aspects or factors that influence the application of cognitive processes in a team environment. They suggest that a follow-up article, in which a limited number of constructs are reviewed in detail, might provide a useful framework for further understanding the relationship between individual and team cognition and their association with team creativity. We agree that in our chapter we made a choice favoring breadth over depth of coverage, and we welcome a more focused review of a select set of variables in future work.

Another concern raised by Sacramento et al. is that "a critical reflection on the nature of the construct" of team creativity is lacking. These authors devote the bulk of their commentary to addressing this issue. This criticism, as they note, is not unique to our work, but rather plagues many of the theoretical and empirical studies in the field of team creativity. Sacramento et al. present this issue, implicitly and explicitly, as one of a definition of team creativity that has important implications for the operationalization of the construct, its measurement, and, as a result, study design.

Sacramento et al. suggest that the emergence of team creativity can range from simple aggregation or composition models to more discontinuous, compilation models (Chan, 1998; Klein & Kozlowski, 2000). Each model has implications for the research design, process, and measurement of the construct of interest. We agree with Sacramento et al. that the issue of definitional clarity and measurement of multi-level constructs is critical. This caveat holds for all multi-level research, of course. Sacramento et al. have nevertheless done a good job of applying these issues to the individual and team cognition approach presented, as well as providing examples of how the different models might be applied and tested.

What is less clear from the discussion by Sacramento et al. is whether these authors believe that the definition of team creativity can shift and change based on the situation, or whether the definition is stable and only the operationalization of team creativity, its manifestation, or measurement changes. They state, "In certain domains creativity is a shared construct, whereas in others it is configural..." The concern we have is that if the basic definition of team creativity changes from situation to situation, the construct becomes not only more difficult to measure but potentially not particularly useful. In our view, shifting definitions are generally problematic, whereas changes in measures, manifestations, and operationalizations present fewer challenges.

Implicit in their discussion is the process by which team cognition emerges from individual cognition. Sacramento et al. note that this is a familiar theme in multi-level research. A similar question can be asked regarding any construct that is evaluated from a multi-level perspective: How do we get from here – that is, the individual-level construct – to there – that is, the group-level construct? Identifying the process by which team cognition emerges or how individual cognitions converge is critical. This issue of emergence or convergence is only now starting to draw the attention of multi-level researchers. An example of such work is a chapter in this series by McComb (2007), which focuses on how individual mental models become team shared mental models. Similarly, Kozlowski and Ilgen (2006), in their recent review of team research, suggest that team emergent processes are critical for team effectiveness and may come about in a variety of ways, which, to date, remain relatively unexplored.

RESPONSE TO SHALLEY

The issue of how individual cognition becomes team cognition and the process by which this evolution takes place constitute the focus of Shalley's commentary. Specifically, Shalley asserts that to better understand team cognition and its relationship to creativity, researchers must attend to team processes and team composition – two aspects that were covered only minimally in our chapter. Shalley argues that team social interactions and team composition are instrumental in explaining how individual cognition emerges or converges into team cognition.

Shalley's commentary focuses attention on factors that affect either the application of individual cognitive processes or the integration of these individual processes into team cognition. The various processes at the team level are influenced by individuals' abilities and their motivations to engage in cognitive processes as well as by the processes' coordination, integration, sharing of information, and discussion. The former factors point to team composition variables, while the latter emphasize the importance of team process variables. The comments by Shalley further delineate how these variables may affect the propositions presented in our chapter.

The final section in Shalley's commentary provides a discussion of the practical implications of the propositions presented in our chapter. While work on team cognition does have implications for interventions such as training and development, we are concerned that it is premature to discuss such interventions. The empirical findings are fairly robust as they relate to individual cognition. However, understanding of team cognition and, as was pointed out in the two commentaries, the processes by which team cognition emerge, are less clear. Providing recommendations for interventions and other applications should come after well-replicated tests and empirical results regarding these propositions have been established. Developing training and other applications prior to rigorous testing of these propositions is premature, in our view, and may lead to inappropriate recommendations for practice.

ADDITIONAL ISSUES

Both commentaries provided a more in-depth review of several issues that were not addressed in our chapter. The discussion of those concerns has caused us to think about some additional issues that were not addressed either in our chapter or in the two commentaries – specifically, the role of leadership in these processes and the fact that teams are embedded in a larger organizational context.

Leadership

One area that has important effects on team creativity in general and on the application of creative problem-solving processes in particular is that of leadership, a multi-level phenomenon (see Yammarino, Dionne, Chun, & Dansereau, 2005). Researchers have found that leaders can exert a significant influence on creativity and innovation (Howell & Avolio, 1993; West et al., 2003). Leaders can affect creativity in individuals and teams in many ways, including through goal setting (Shalley, 1991), feedback (Shalley, 1995), providing role models for creativity (Zhou & Shalley, 2003), influences on the team culture (Jung, Chow, & Wu, 2003), management of the social processes within the team such as team conflict (Tjosvold, Hui, & Yu, 2003), and direct support for creativity by providing resources (Egan, 2005). All of these factors may have a direct effect on the application of the cognitive processes at both the individual and team levels of analysis.

Previous efforts have documented the effect that leaders can have on individual creativity – specifically, cognitive processes affecting creative problem solving (cf. Mumford, Scott, Gaddis, & Strange, 2002; Reiter-Palmon & Illies, 2004). Here, we will briefly address some aspects of leadership that can influence the application and emergence of these processes in a team. For example, a leader may facilitate the development of a shared mental model by providing a shared vision or encouraging discussions that would lead to the development of a shared mental model, thereby moving team members from individual cognition to team cognition. Other aspects of leadership may also facilitate the development of shared mental models, such as developing an open team culture that would allow for the discussion of disagreements. Similarly, leaders who encourage discussion and open communication will have a direct effect on knowledge and information sharing and may reduce confirmation bias in teams.

Leaders can also play an important role in idea generation. One way to reduce production loss in groups is by the use of trained facilitators (Straus, 2002). Leaders can provide the same structure and guidance as trained facilitators, such as setting goals and providing structure, developing norms and culture, smoothing conflict, and encouraging participation. Leaders can also provide support for the group in the idea evaluation and selection phases by providing guidance regarding goal importance and standards for evaluation, thereby facilitating team convergence. Leaders can facilitate implementation planning by role modeling (planning themselves), requesting planning from the team (instructions), and encouraging the integration of multiple points of view in the plan (through culture and trust). Finally, leaders can affect the entire team creative problem-solving effort.

Our Proposition 51 suggests that the effect of team members progressing at different rates within these processes needs to be investigated. It is possible that one effect the team leader may have is to minimize any negative effects related to this differential progression, by providing guidance and structure for the rate of progression, thereby ensuring that all team members are "on the same page." Alternatively, leaders may minimize the difficulties associated with different rates of progression by providing an environment in which differences are accepted and questions are welcomed.

In addition, although the previous discussion focused on the effect of a single leader on a group, current research is investigating the effect of shared leadership in teams (Bligh, Pearce, & Kohles, 2006). Shared leadership may be particularly important in cross-functional teams, as such teams are more likely to lack a natural hierarchical structure for knowledge work, suggesting that teams that engage in creative problem-solving routinely may be more likely to develop shared leadership (Pearce & Manz, 2005). The same factors that give rise to effective shared leadership (openness and trust, discussion of disagreements, sharing of information) also facilitate the emergence of team cognition.

Context

One implication of the previous discussion is the importance of team culture and team norms to the application of the individual and team cognitive processes. While leaders have a strong influence on the culture within the team, other forces play a role in the development of team culture. Both the organizational culture and the broader national culture also influence the development of team culture, for example. Organizational culture has been found to play an important role in organizational innovation (Amabile, Conti, Coon, Lazenby, & Herron, 1996). This culture will influence the importance the team places on creativity and innovation and, therefore, the willingness and motivation of individual members to engage in creative processes. In addition, it will affect group processes such as coordination, information sharing, trust, and openness, all of which may have an effect on the emergence of group cognition.

Similarly, leaders and organizations in which teams are embedded can influence the availability of resources. The resources that are provided to the leader in terms of personnel, and therefore workload and financial resources, will determine what is available to the leader to allocate to the team. While leaders have some control and can negotiate for resources, broader factors such as organizational policies and goals as well as economic conditions will also play roles in determining the availability of resources.

Social networks are also important determinants of creativity (Csikszentmihalyi, 1988), though these networks can take many forms.

Perry-Smith and Shalley (2003) discuss the effect of strong or weak ties to these networks on creativity. Ties outside the team and the organization, and even outside the workplace, may also provide sources of information and support for creativity.

In addition, we suspect that the type of team (e.g., cross-functional teams, one-time project teams, or a standing committee) and the task facing the team exert strong influences on both individual cognition and the emergence of team cognition. For example, cross-functional teams, by their nature, include more diverse members than other types of teams. Service on cross-functional teams or project teams may be merely one aspect of the job required from the members, such that team members have multiple and competing job demands, and possibly multiple supervisors. Further, teams of this nature may be more limited in terms of the time they spend in the team context, limiting members' social interaction. This limited social interaction can then give rise to less communication, more misunderstandings, and more disagreements, all of which hurt the team creative cognitive process.

Finally, another point that is relevant to our discussion of context is that our chapter provides a limited multi-level view of cognition and creativity. Our work focuses on only two levels of analysis: the individual and the team. Lacking from our discussion are the effects and processes at the department level (or other aggregation of teams into larger units), the organizational level, and the multi-organizational level.

CONCLUSION

Our chapter was designed to focus on the relationship between individual cognitive processes and team cognitive processes as both relate to creative team performance. The two commentaries provide insightful extensions to this effort by pointing out (1) that these individual and team cognitive processes do not occur in a vacuum and (2) that other variables can exert a strong influence on the application of individual and team processes and on the emergence of team cognition. In this reply we have highlighted additional factors, such as leadership and context, that may likewise influence team cognitive processes and, therefore, team creativity. We believe that this effort is only a first step in an important research stream on multi-level approaches to team cognition and team creativity.

REFERENCES

Amabile, T. M., Conti, R., Coon, H., Lazenby, J., & Herron, M. (1996). Assessing the work environment for creativity. *Academy of Management, 39*, 1154–1185.

Bligh, M. C., Pearce, C. L., & Kohles, J. C. (2006). The importance of self- and shared leadership in team based knowledge work. *Journal of Managerial Psychology, 21*, 296–318.

Chan, D. (1998). Functional relations among constructs in the same content domain at different levels of analysis: A typology of composition models. *Journal of Applied Psychology, 83*, 234–246.

Csikszentmihalyi, M. (1988). Society, culture, and person: A systems view of creativity. In: R. J. Sternberg (Ed.), *The nature of creativity: Contemporary psychological perspectives* (pp. 229–325). New York, NY: Cambridge University Press.

Egan, T. M. (2005). Creativity in the context of team diversity: Team leader perspectives. *Advances in Developing Human Resources, 7*, 207–225.

Howell, J. M., & Avolio, B. J. (1993). Transformational leadership, transactional leadership, locus of control, and support for innovation: Key predictors of consolidated-business-unit performance. *Journal of Applied Psychology, 78*, 891–902.

Jung, D. I., Chow, C., & Wu, A. (2003). The role of transformational leadership in enhancing organizational innovation: Hypotheses and some preliminary findings. *Leadership Quarterly, 14*, 525–545.

Klein, K. J., & Kozlowski, S. W. J. (2000). From micro to meso: Critical steps in conceptualized and conducting multi-level research. *Organizational Research Methods, 3*, 211–237.

Kozlowski, S. W. J., & Ilgen, D. R. (2006). Enhancing the effectiveness of work groups and teams. *Psychological Science in the Public Interest, 7*, 77–124.

McComb, S. A. (2007). Mental model convergence: The shift from being an individual to being a team member. In: F. Dansereau & F. J. Yammarino (Eds), *Multi-level issues in organizations and time* (Vol. 6, pp. 95–147). Oxford: Elsevier Science Ltd.

Mumford, M. D., Scott, G. M., Gaddis, B., & Strange, J. M. (2002). Leading creative people: Orchestrating expertise and relationships. *Leadership Quarterly, 13*, 705–751.

Pearce, C. L., & Manz, C. C. (2005). The new silver bullets of leadership: The importance of self-and shared leadership in knowledge work. *Organizational Dynamics, 34*, 130–141.

Perry-Smith, J. E., & Shalley, C. E. (2003). The social side of creativity: A static and dynamic social network and dynamic social network perspective. *Academy of Management Review, 28*, 89–106.

Reiter-Palmon, R., & Illies, J. J. (2004). Leadership and creativity: Understanding leadership from a creative problem-solving perspective. *Leadership Quarterly, 15*, 55–78.

Sacramento, C., Dawson, J., & West, W. (this volume). Team creativity: More than the sum of its parts. In: M. D. Mumford, S. T. Hunter & K. E. Bedell-Avers (Eds), *Multi-level issues in creativity and innovation*. Research in multi-level issues (Vol. 7). Oxford, UK: Elsevier.

Shalley, C. E. (1991). Effects of productivity goals, creativity goals, and personal discretion on individual creativity. *Journal of Applied Psychology, 76*, 179–185.

Shalley, C. E. (1995). Effects of coaction, expected evaluation, and goal setting on creativity and productivity. *Academy of Management Journal, 38*, 483–504.

Shalley C. E. (this volume). Team cognition: The importance of team process and composition for the creative problem-solving process. In: M. D. Mumford, S. T. Hunter & K. E. Bedell-Avers (Eds), *Multi-level issues in creativity and innovation*. Research in multi-level issues (Vol. 7). Oxford, UK: Elsevier.

Straus, D. (2002). *How to make collaboration work: Powerful ways to build consensus, solve problems, make decisions.* San Francisco, CA: Berrett-Koehler.

Tjosvold, D., Hui, C., & Yu, Z. (2003). Conflict management and task reflexivity for team in-role and extra-role performance in China. *International Journal of Conflict Management, 14,* 141–163.

West, M. A., Borril, C. S., Dawson, J. F., Brodbeck, F., Shapiro, D. A., & Haward, B. (2003). Leadership clarity and team innovation in health care. *Leadership Quarterly, 14,* 393–410.

Yammarino, F. J., Dionne, S. D., Chun, J. U., & Dansereau, F. (2005). Leadership and levels of analysis: A state-of-the-science review. *Leadership Quarterly, 16*(6), 879–919.

Zhou, J., & Shalley, C. E. (2003). Research on employee creativity: A critical review and directions for future research. In: J. J. Martoccio & R. Gerald (Eds), *Research in personnel and human resources management* (pp. 165–217). London, UK: Elsevier Science.

PART IV:
SUBSYSTEM CONFIGURATION

SUBSYSTEM CONFIGURATION: A MODEL OF STRATEGY, CONTEXT, AND HUMAN RESOURCES MANAGEMENT ALIGNMENT

Simon Taggar, Lorne Sulsky and Heather MacDonald

ABSTRACT

This chapter presents a contextual model of human resources management (HRM). The hallmarks of this model are that (1) the most advantageous HRM practices vary conditionally upon strategic considerations; (2) each organization has multiple substrategies within it, and each substrategy is aligned with a unique bundle of HRM practices; (3) within each organization, three substrategies are associated with three subsystems; and (4) in terms of contributing to sustainable competitive advantage, the innovation subsystem is the most valuable regardless of the organization in question.

INTRODUCTION

Context – that is, the circumstance or setting surrounding organizational events – has been studied in numerous ways. For instance, strategists, being

Multi-Level Issues in Creativity and Innovation
Research in Multi-Level Issues, Volume 7, 317–376
Copyright © 2008 by Elsevier Ltd.
ISSN: 1475-9144/doi:10.1016/S1475-9144(07)00013-6

Fig. 1. SHRM Approach to Context.

concerned with the organizational level of analysis, have primarily focused on the environment (e.g., economic, technological, political, legal, social/ cultural, and competitive activities; Czinkota & Kotabe, 2001) surrounding the organization. For them, strategy is often a reflection of context. The strategic human resources management (SHRM) approach also considers context through strategy. This approach, which is illustrated in Fig. 1, suggests that "for a company to be successful, human resources (HR) must align the company's people strategies and management processes with its business strategies" (Gubman, 1995, p. 15) regardless of whether business strategies are planned or emergent.

By contrast, HRM, industrial-organizational psychology (I-O), and organizational behavior (OB) scholars typically think of context as having a moderating or direct effect on dependent or criterion variables. These criteria are generally individual-level variables. Fig. 2 illustrates the HRM/ I-O/OB orientation.

Both views of context depicted in Figs. 1 and 2 have merit as well as scientific and practical utility, yet neither sufficiently captures the role of context in organizations for researchers who want to link strategy to employee attitudes and behavior. A more comprehensive definition of context needs to incorporate elements from both perspectives. Hence, this chapter introduces and describes an integrated model of strategy alignment (IMSA); this model is illustrated in Fig. 3.

In brief, the IMSA consists of multiple subsystems existing within a larger organizational system and espouses a fit between the external environment, grand strategy, substrategies, and HR bundles. Whereas most previous research has focused on aligning HR with business strategy, we argue that a firm's overall strategy (grand strategy) can be decomposed into several substrategies, each of which should be aligned with separate HR practices.

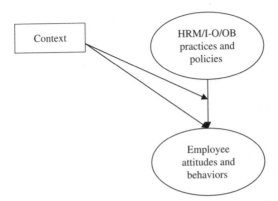

Fig. 2.   Human Resources Management, Industrial-Organizational Psychology, and
Organizational Behavior Approach to Context.

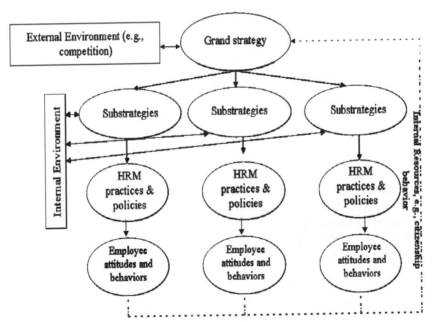

Fig. 3.   Integrated Model of Strategy Alignment.

The IMSA includes two levels of analysis at which we will consider context – the level of grand strategy and the level of substrategy. Thus the IMSA provides a multi-level framework. The impetus for developing this model was the realization that the majority of theories in the HRM, I-O, and OB fields are developed with little thought given to context, or assuming a stable context, at both the system and subsystem levels (cf. Ilinitch, D'Aveni, & Lewin, 1996). This assumption is a limitation in several ways:

• Scholars and practitioners who disregard context may take a "best practices" approach that fails to recognize that policies and practices may be more or less appropriate in differing organizational settings.
• Policies and practices may be linked to unsuitable criteria when establishing validity or utility.
• The value of bundles of policies and practices to the achievement of organizational goals may be underestimated or overestimated.
• Firm efficiency and effectiveness will suffer when policies and practices do not align with firm strategy to achieve firm goals.

Rather than a "best practices" approach, the IMSA provides a contingency framework for understanding the effects of strategic context on both groups and individual employees. It provides a "line of sight" showing how employee contributions may have a measurable effect on their organizations' ability to meet more proximal substrategy goals. In many organizations, the HRM function continues to face a battle in justifying its contribution to organizations (Becker & Huselid, 1998; Pfau & Cundiff, 2002). Modeling of a link between HRM practices and strategy is important to winning this battle and represents one of the most pressing issues for HRM professionals and researchers alike.

It is useful to consider strategy as a key contextual factor when deciding upon appropriate HRM practices. Strategy has the potential to help scholars and practitioners understand the context for events at multiple levels of an organization. For instance, strategy formulation and implementation facilitates organization–external environmental alignment (Hitt & Ireland, 1985). Strategy is also the basis of organization design (structure); organization design, in turn, defines the managerial decision orientation (Camillus, 1986). In addition, strategy is used to assess the activities of a firm's employees. For instance, strategic diagnosis involves identifying a link between strategy and employees' behaviors, attitudes, and values. Behavioral diagnosis and motivational diagnosis are used to determine whether employees are performing in ways that enhance competitive strategy. Research has also attempted to identify management belief systems that are consistent with different strategy types. Studies have generally confirmed that a higher level of organizational performance results when an organization's decision-making characteristics (e.g., willingness to take risks, openness of decision making) and strategy are aligned (e.g., Govindarajan, 1988, 1989).

Much SHRM literature has advocated an alignment between HRM and strategy (e.g., Gubman, 1995). The benefits of alignment within organizations are a major theme in several literatures. For instance, Barney (1986) argued that an organization's culture defines how an organization conducts its business. To support a competitive advantage, that culture must not be common to other organizations and must promote a capability to perform functional activities in a manner that increases the value-added of the firm. Problems related to misalignment of HR practices with strategy are apparent in the classic article entitled "On the Folly of Rewarding for A while Hoping for B," which deals with the concept of misaligned reward systems that discourage the very behavior they wish to promote (Kerr, 1995). Nadler and Trushman state that "the degree to which the strategy, work, people, structure, and culture are smoothly aligned will determine the organization's ability to complete and succeed" (1997, p. 34). We will touch upon all five of Nadler and Trushman's key areas that organizations should seek to monitor for alignment or fit to ensure organizational success in our model of context within organizations.

This chapter begins with a detailed description of the IMSA. After outlining the model, we consider the relationship between our model and organizational culture, to illustrate how the IMSA accommodates additional variables of potential interest. Next, we examine some complicating factors arising from our formulation. Finally, we examine the implications of our model for one particular example HRM activity – namely, performance management.

Before describing the IMSA, however, we must define three concepts important to understanding the model and its development: strategy, substrategy, and subsystem.

Defining Strategy and Substrategy

Strategy has been conceptualized in a number of different ways within organizations, including business strategy, corporate strategy, and grand strategy. *Business strategy* concerns the actions and the approaches crafted by management to produce successful performance in one specific line of business. *Corporate strategy* concerns how a diversified company intends to establish business positions in different industries.

Central to our thesis is the idea that most firms develop *grand strategies* that reflect the "firm's primary action plans for accomplishing long-run sales and profitability objectives"; "firms should and do formulate grand strategies that dominate corporate activities for a period of time ... corporate and business level strategies influence a firm's performance" (Hitt & Ireland, 1985, p. 794). Grand strategies may take a number of forms, and several typologies have been offered in the literature (e.g., Treacy & Wiersema, 1995). Porter (1980) describes a commonly cited typology. He notes that competitive advantage tends to come from two sources: (1) whether a firm's products are differentiated in any way (e.g., most innovative or of the highest quality), or (2) whether the firm is the lowest-cost producer in an industry.

Strategy formulation involves monitoring and analyzing the external environmental factors influencing the organization (Ansoff, 1965; Butler, Ferris, & Napier, 1991; Gunnigle & Moore, 1994; Walker, 2001). Strategic choices are shaped by the need to align organizational resources (e.g., human capital) with environmental opportunities and threats (Powell, 1992).

Strategy implementation seeks to align resources with strategy so that management's vision for the company becomes reality. It represents the game plan for moving the company into an attractive business position and for building a sustainable competitive advantage.

Grand strategy can be conceptualized as being composed of a variety of substantial activities that must be completed as part of strategy implementation. *Substrategies* are important in that they describe activities that employees and managers of an organization undertake to enact the strategic plan, thereby achieving the organization's grand strategy. As illustrated in Fig. 3, substrategies correspond to discernable HRM strategies made up of discrete practices and policies that complement one another. If grand strategy is a declaration of a firm's intent and goals, then substrategies represent a declaration of the intent and goals of different subsystems within the organization. The achievement of an organization's strategic goals should follow from the fulfillment of its substrategies.

Defining Subsystems

Organizations can be viewed as being composed of interacting subsystems. *Subsystems* are often defined as groupings of organizational activities, functions, and processes that are classified solely based on their purpose in organizational effectiveness (Katz & Kahn, 1978). More specifically, a subsystem may be defined as the "set of distinct but interrelated activities, functions, and processes that are directed at attracting, developing, and maintaining (or disposing of) a firm's human resources" (Lado & Wilson, 1994, p. 107).

INTEGRATED MODEL OF STRATEGY ALIGNMENT

The development of the IMSA was inspired by a number of research streams. We believed that it would be fruitful to integrate this diverse body of literature with the goal of developing a model for HRM – a model that is subject to scientific scrutiny and potentially useful for HRM practitioners who are charged with developing and implementing HRM systems.

First, in developing the IMSA, it is important to acknowledge the influence of theory and research in the area of SHRM. Over the last decade, this field has been actively exploring the role that management practices can play in the realization of an organization's grand strategy (Pfeffer, 1994). A study conducted by Brockbank, Ulrich, and James (1997), for example, found that in both 1992 and 1997, firm performance was higher when HRM departments focused more on the strategic aspects of HRM and relatively less on operational agendas.

Much SHRM research is based on the contention that due to increasing competitive pressures, firms seek a competitive advantage – "a relatively enduring form of competitive superiority based on some distinctive and enviable competence or capability which rivals have become frustrated trying to copy" (Boxall, 1999, p. 267). The resource-based view of the firm (Barney, 1986), which has been the backdrop for much of the work in SHRM, explains competitive advantage, and its dynamics, with respect to organizational resources. According to this theory, competitive advantage is derived from resources such as human capital (an aggregate of employees' knowledge, skills, experience, and commitment to the organization), physical capital, and organizational capital. Human capital is considered particularly difficult for competitors to imitate. Accordingly, it is a potentially important source of sustainable competitive advantage.

The resource-based view promotes a "fit" between the organization's human capital and capabilities and the external factors of market and competition (which are reflected in the organization's strategy). In addition, Barney (1991) notes that the environmental context in which an asset is applied will determine whether that asset is actually a resource. According to the contingent resource-based view, "the value of a resource cannot be determined in a vacuum, but depends on the context in which it is used" (Katila & Shane, 2005, p. 825).

The resource-based view postulates that HRM can provide the foundation for sustained competitive advantage if it contributes *rare* or *exceptional* value to the firm's strategic position (Boxall, 1999; Barney, 1991; Peteraf, 1993; Wright, McMahan, & McWilliams, 1994). Becker and Huselid note "with as much emphasis on the effective *implementation* of corporate strategies as their *content*, organizational policies and infrastructure are increasingly considered a potential source of sustainable competitive advantage" (Becker & Huselid, 1998, p. 57).

Because a critical firm resource is human capital, one source of competitive advantage may come from aligning the management of human capital with the grand strategy of the organization (Becker & Huselid, 1998):

> An internally consistent and coherent HRM system that is focused on solving operational problems and implementing the firm's competitive strategy is the basis for the acquisition, motivation, and development of the underlying intellectual assets that can be a source of sustained competitive advantage. (Becker & Huselid, 1998, p. 55)

In sum, the IMSA makes the assumption that aligning HRM practices with organizational strategy is the best way to leverage human capital to achieve organizational objectives. However, this assumption alone offers nothing of significant incremental value. Our intent was to develop a model that takes this basic assumption and extends it in a number of ways.

The IMSA is based on five guiding principles. These principles were derived from research in the areas of organizational strategy, organizational culture, organizational theory, and management theory. Next, we identify these guiding principles, review the pertinent research inspiring each principle, and describe the model in greater detail.

Principle 1: HRM Should be Linked to Organizational Substrategies

Miles and Snow (1984) have argued that HRM practices should be consistent with strategic choices. However, theory and research exist suggesting the benefits of aligning HRM practices with substrategies – in particular, substrategies that work together to achieve an organization's grand strategy. Inspection of Fig. 3 reveals that the IMSA links the organization's grand strategy with specific organizational substrategies.

In early work, Barnard (1938) argued that an organization's purpose and objectives should be broken into fragments ordered in time and assignment for cooperation. Implicit in this model, as well as in some other models (e.g., Huselid, 1995; Truss & Gratton, 1994), is the idea that overall organizational goals can be differentiated at hierarchical levels, with outcomes at one level contributing (along with other outcomes) to outcomes at a higher level. Ansoff (1965) suggested that strategic objectives were best implemented through a series of goals cascading down through the organization. Plans of specific action may serve as linking pins between organizational levels on the way to goal achievement (e.g., Likert, 1961). Implementing strategy through cascading goals remains a popular concept (e.g., Drucker, 1954; Sy & D'Annunzio, 2005; Walker, 2001).

Lawrence and Lorsch (1967) have argued that organizations must break complex tasks into simpler activities and develop subsystems to specialize in these activities. Similarly, Mintzberg (1973) has suggested that organizations consist of subsystems or subunits. For instance, the technostructure is responsible for strategic planning, operations research, systems analysis and design, and the operating core, which itself consists of assemblers, machine operators, and shippers.

A central premise of the IMSA is that organizations consist of subsystems that complete activities important to achieving a super-ordinate goal. Lawrence and Lorsch (1967) define an organization as a system of interrelated behaviors of people who are performing a task that has been differentiated into several distinct subsystems. Each subsystem performs a part of the task. These authors argue that without differentiation and specialization, an organization's activities would become unmanageable. The goal of differentiation is inherent in subsystem development and causes each subsystem to behave differently and develop particular attributes. For instance, groups that are organized to perform simpler, more certain tasks (e.g., production groups) usually have a more formal structure than groups that focus on more uncertain tasks (e.g., research and development). Although differentiation may simplify task execution, it complicates task coordination. The activities of each subsystem must be integrated to achieve the outputs and goals of the organization as a whole.

If each subsystem has its own activities and goals, it follows that to achieve the organization's grand strategy, the goals associated with particular subsystems must be achieved (cf. Miles & Snow, 1986; Tichy, 1983). Similarly, substrategies, which represent the intentions and goals of different subsystems, must be realized to achieve the grand strategy. This, in turn, requires that appropriate HRM practices must be aligned with substrategies to produce positive employee attitudes and optimal behavior – both of which are required to realize the organization's substrategies and, ultimately, the grand strategy (cf. Bart, Bontis, & Taggar, 2001; Pfau & Cundiff, 2002). As Fig. 3 shows, multiple substrategies are expected to reside within an organization, and each is aligned with a set of unique HRM practices and policies.

Principle 2: HRM Should not Adopt a "Best Practices" Mentality

Our second guiding principle is a direct result of our first principle, which suggested that HRM should be aligned with substrategies. Specifically, we assume that different "best" HRM practices exist for each distinct employee group. Each employee segment is aligned with a specific bundle of HRM practices. The specific bundle in question is aligned to the extent that it helps the specific employee segment achieve its own unique substrategy. As a consequence, no single universal HRM system can be applied throughout the entire organization.

Building on the resource-based view (Barney, 1986), contingency theorists (e.g., Delery & Doty, 1996) propose that HRM strategies within a firm should reinforce the firm's choice of core competencies that create its competitive advantage. Specifically, this contingency approach advocates different HRM practices for different business strategies. Not surprisingly, academic debates arisen over the question of a universalistic (best practices) approach versus the contingency approach to HRM practices (Delery & Doty, 1996; Gibb, 2001; Pfeffer, 1994, 1998).

The prevalent "best practices" approach (see Bowen, Galang, & Pillai, 2002; Delaney, Lewin, & Ichniowski, 1989; Huselid, 1993, 1995; Osterman, 1994) takes the position that certain HRM practices are appropriate for all firms regardless of strategy. It advocates that effective HRM is achieved through implementing the best practice (Boam & Sparrow, 1992) and suggests that ineffective HRM is a consequence of failing to do so (Gibb, 2001; Pfeffer, 1998). According to institutional theory (Meyer & Rowan, 1977), many organizational practices are adopted because a few legitimate organizations serve as models for others to imitate by way of perceived best practices.

The best practices view has been challenged, with some empirical evidence supporting the contingency approach instead. When Youndt, Snell, Dean, and Lepak (1996) compared contingency theory with the universal approach in a manufacturing setting, they found that the relationship between organizational strategy and HRM practices was best explained by the contingency approach. More recently, Datta, Guthrie, and Wright (2005) reported that HRM systems' impact on productivity is influenced by industry, capital intensity, growth, and differentiation. Nevertheless, most studies have failed to find support for the efficacy of "fit" between HRM and strategy, perhaps because of a failure to recognize the most appropriate dependent variables (Wright & Sherman, 1999).

Principle 3: Employees do not Equally Contribute to the Grand Strategy

In our formulation of the IMSA, employees will be members of one of four employee groups or segments. Each segment is aligned with one of the substrategies depicted in Fig. 3. Fig. 4 illustrates the existence of four distinct employee segments: (a) inner core, (b) outer core, (c) inner peripheral, and (d) outer peripheral.

Each of these segments represents a somewhat discrete context or subsystem uniquely defined in terms of the role played in realizing the organization's grand strategy. Because some segments are more "central" or important for realizing the organization's grand strategy, we refer to Fig. 4

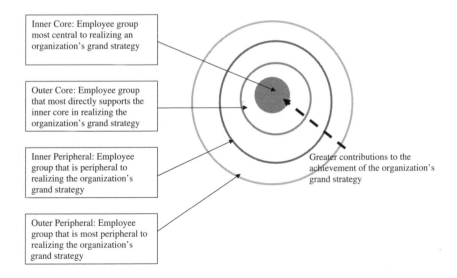

Fig. 4. Employee Centrality Sphere of Organizational Subsystems.

as the employee centrality sphere (ECS). The segments that make up the ECS are not necessarily formal structures within organizations (e.g., functional departments); instead, they describe the internal activities of employees who are linked by a shared super-ordinate goal. The idea behind the ECS came from, and is consistent with, the work of Boxall (1999) and Purcell (1996). The existence of distinct employee segments is important because not all employees constitute equivalent sources of rare value. This resource-based view of the organization (Barney, 1991) leads us to distinguish between core and peripheral resources (i.e., between resources that contribute rare or exceptional value and those that do not). Specifically, it suggests that a firm's human capital complement may be of two types: that which contributes rare or exceptional value and that which does not. Those employees who contribute rare or exceptional value in a firm may be referred to as the core segment of the ECS. This segment contributes most directly to formulating and implementing the organization's grand strategy.

Employees of the organization who do not contribute rare or exceptional value may be referred to as the peripheral segment of the ECS. Members of the peripheral segment generally play a small, if any, direct role in formulating the overall strategic intent (tangible organizational goals) or determining the overall strategic plan and its implementation. Nonetheless, peripheral members are vital in actually carrying out some of the activities in strategic implementation.

The core workforce can be said to make the most "value-added" contribution to the organization because it performs at a strategic level and contributes substantially to designing and achieving the firm's goals through strategy formulation and implementation (Purcell, 1996). That is, core members are responsible for the systematic determination of organizational goals and the plans to achieve those goals. Core employees are critical to value creation and have "product, service, or organizational knowledge that can never be bought but has to be created" (Purcell, 1996, p. 19). They are responsible for understanding the environment external to the organization and identifying the internal resources available to best meet external threats and opportunities. Some of the core's knowledge is unique to the particular organization (e.g., a function of the company's history). Boxall provides further elaboration:

> The Inner Core are the managers, technical specialists, and strategically located who are responsible for valuable innovations or for successful imitation ... Arguably, an open, egalitarian management process is best suited to these "key value generators" so that

criticism can be used creatively to generate new ways of operating, to foster the kind of "contention" that stimulates variety and adaptability ...

... the Outer Core consists of those employees ... with whom stable employment relations must be built if the firm is to meet its commitments to customers without process disruptions. Furthermore, these are the employees on whom the firm will depend for continuous improvement within a given strategic paradigm. (1999, p. 268)

The inner core consists of those employees who are responsible for the innovations, or "value generators" (Boxall, 1999, p. 267). These members are responsible for establishing market leadership. "Loss of key members of the Inner Core undermines the firm's capacity to adapt to a changing environment and to lead adaptive change" (p. 268).

Outer core employees are also relatively high "value generators" but are more focused on the operations of the firm in its attempt to gain or maintain a competitive advantage. These individuals have the industry skills and are the employees "with whom stable employment relations must be built if the firm is to meet its commitments to customers without process disruptions" (Boxall, 1999, p. 268). The outer core depends on the flexibility of the inner core (Atkinson, 1984). During periods of stable growth, outer core employees are relied upon for their dependable service and incremental learning.

The two core groups are expected to be found in any industry and almost all organizations. For example, in the inner core, one organization may employ individuals who produce new and innovative products, while another organization may have its inner core employees focus on excelling through innovative branding. Innovation is common to the inner core of both firms; however, innovation is manifested in different ways in the two organizations. In one firm, innovation may be directed toward marketing and branding of products; in the other firm, it may be applied to the development of new products. In both cases, sustained competitive advantage is thought to be associated with recruiting creative and intelligent individuals for the inner core and establishing highly positive working relations with a well-qualified outer core.

Purcell (1996) differentiated core from periphery employees on the basis of the ease of their replacement and the employees' value contributions to the grand strategy. Peripheral employees are replaceable and do not add great value to the grand strategy. They conduct the day-to-day operational aspects of the firm (Purcell, 1996). These employees may include secretaries and other administrators, assembly-line workers, and other non-exempt workers. We do not mean to imply that the activities of peripheral workers are not important to an organization's success: As mentioned previously, strategic goals cannot be achieved unless the organization includes a peripheral group of employees. Nonetheless, from a strategy formulation and implementation standpoint, we contend that these individuals do not generally add rare or exceptional value to achieving overall strategic goals.

By way of example, assume we have a fast-food restaurant whose grand strategy centers on low cost and growth. An individual working at a counter can have a major impact on customer satisfaction and, therefore, might be considered important to a given franchise. From the standpoint of realizing the grand strategy, however, this counter worker is not nearly as important as the vice president in charge of franchising. If an aggregation of counter workers provides poor customer service, we would contend that the problem is systemic. Accordingly, one would have to identity members of the inner core who are responsible for this problem, such as the vice president of HRM.

There may be two models for organizing peripheral work. The first is to keep it in house. This approach may be appropriate when outsourcing is not feasible, such as when the work being performed is unique to the firm yet has low relative value. Alternatively, when the work is not unique or strategically relevant to the firm and can be performed by another organization for lower cost (due to economies of scale for example), outsourcing makes economic sense. There are numerous companies whose competitive strategy is to sell "periphery" services at a cost that is lower than a company would otherwise incur. For example, contracting out payroll to a bank that specializes in the distribution of money and keeps pace with legislative changes in payroll contributions is usually less expensive for an organization than handling payroll activities on an in-house basis. Hence, peripheral employees need not be direct employees of the firm; they may simply work for the firm, but not necessarily derive compensation from it. For instance, Hewlett-Packard outsources personnel administration activities when "it proves cost-effective and provides a higher-quality service" (Laabs, 1993, p. 41).

Thus the work done by the inner peripheral segment may often be relatively low value-added yet unique to the organization, while the outer peripheral often completes work that is relatively low value and not unique to the organization. On some occasions, however, the outer peripheral contributors do add significant value to the organization. These contributors may be on either a temporary (e.g., consultant) or open-ended contract (e.g., investment firm) with the organization. Services that are often outsourced include the manufacturing of parts, trucking, catering, data processing, and accounting.

Based on our discussion of the first three guiding principles, we offer the following research propositions:

Proposition 1. Organizations distinguish between employee groups based on their contributions to the firm. These groups have separate substrategies – that is, missions, goals, objectives, and action plans for achievement that explicitly recognize each group's place within the organization and environmental forces outside the organization.

Proposition 2. The inner core segment, as a function of the quality and quantity of decisions and activities within the segment, makes the greatest contribution to achieving an organization's grand strategy.

*Principle 4: HRM Should Uniquely Align with Specific
Employee Segments*

Although a majority of published studies have shown a significant relationship between HRM and firm performance, these relationships are neither universal nor consistent (Becker & Gerhart, 1996). These mixed results may arise because models of SHRM employ firm performance as the dependent variable. Within the strategy field, the focus of attention has been almost entirely on financial measures of firm performance (Rowe, Morrow, & Finch, 1995). Whereas contingency theorizing to date suggests alignment between a firm's HRM practices and organizational strategy, the IMSA suggests aligning HRM practices with substrategies.

Substrategies may mediate between HRM bundles and grand strategy. As a consequence, a more appropriate examination of the impact of HRM practices may be to determine whether appropriate HRM bundles (discussed later in this chapter) affect substrategy goals. Consideration of the purpose of each ECS segment is important for performance measurement because it is not the simple possession of an attribute (e.g., creativity) but rather the utilization of that attribute toward some end (e.g., innovation) that reflects on performance. A specific utilization implies a purpose or goal toward which the resource can be used either efficiently or poorly.

HRM practices should be tailored to employees such that these practices support the employees in achieving their job mandates. This recommendation suggests that a higher-fidelity alignment between HRM and goals for different employee groups is necessary than is presently considered under the contingency perspective. A higher-fidelity HRM alignment allows better integration with other organizational practices, such as financial practices that routinely assign budgets to employee groups based on the goals and value of each employee group. A misalignment of HRM systems and the goals of different employee groups would represent inefficiencies in the pursuit of substrategy goals. Because one immediate purpose of strategy is often the achievement of higher-than-normal returns on assets and resources (e.g., to do better than the competition), it is hardly surprising that attention is focused on employee contributions to achieving those returns by strategists, accountants, and financial managers within an organization, both at the individual level and in terms of categories of work and workers.

The thrust of our argument is that researchers should pay closer attention to the ECS segments when measuring HRM practices. Creating a measure by averaging the use of HRM practices across an organization (e.g., jobs in the particular organization are designed for teamwork) seems to assume that all employee groups are equivalent. Clearly, this may not be the case. Tsui, Pearce, Porter, and Tripoli (1997) provide strong evidence that organizations use different HRM systems for employees in different jobs. This finding suggests that a particular HRM system may be required to fit a particular job or grouping of jobs. For instance, Snell (1992) provides evidence that the knowledge of cause–effect relations and the presence of crystallized standards of desirable performance in jobs influence the HRM control systems selected by organizations for those jobs. These job characteristics appear to vary both within and between organizations. Focusing on HRM systems within the context of ECS segments, therefore, may provide greater insight into how organizations can gain a competitive advantage through human capital.

We are not the first to consider the level of analysis at which HRM practices and policies are measured. Huselid (1995), for instance, measured HRM practices for exempt and non-exempt employees separately. Arthur (1994), Delery and Doty (1996), Ichniowski, Shaw, and Prennushi (1997), and MacDuffie (1995) measured HRM practices for a particular group of employees performing the same or similar jobs within a firm. Similarly, Tsui et al. (1997) measured HRM practices at the job level both within and across organizations. Doty and Delery (1997) proposed a framework of SHRM where it is more important that some employees – namely, the core workforce – be managed by a high-performance work system. However, most previous studies have sought to link HRM practices with firm-, business-, or plant-level outcomes (Rogers & Wright, 1998). With regard to specific HRM practices, the strongest link between HRM and performance has been found at the plant or site level (MacDuffie, 1995; Arthur, 1994; Delery & Doty, 1996).

Based on the guiding principles discussed thus far, we offer the following research proposition:

Proposition 3. The ECS represents a parsimonious typology of employee contributions to the grand strategy. Each segment of the ECS has a substrategy, and an associated unique organizational context, that requires a unique bundle of HRM practices.

Principle 5: There are Universal Organizational Substrategies, with Unique HRM Bundles for Each Substrategy

Another feature of the IMSA is based on the strategic frameworks developed by Porter (1980) and Schuler and Jackson (1987). Porter (1980) introduced two grand strategies, low cost and differentiation, and suggested they defined two ends of the strategy continuum. Porter's model is probably the most commonly referenced strategy typology. The low-cost leader in any market gains competitive advantage from being able to produce at the lowest cost. Labor is recruited and trained to deliver the lowest possible costs of production. Costs are shaved off every element of the value chain. Products tend to be "no frills" versions. Low cost does not always lead to low price, however: Producers could price their products at competitive parity, exploiting the benefits of a larger margin than competitors.

Differentiated goods and services satisfy the needs of customers through a sustainable competitive advantage. As a consequence, companies can desensitize customers to prices and focus on value that generates a comparatively higher price and a better margin. The benefits of differentiation require producers to segment markets so as to target their goods and services at specific segments, generating a higher-than-average price. The differentiating organization will incur additional costs in creating such a competitive advantage, and these costs must in turn be offset by the increase in revenue generated by sales. Of course, there is always the chance that any differentiation strategy could be copied by competitors. Therefore, companies always have an incentive to innovate and continuously improve on the product or service.

Research has demonstrated that managers practicing a differentiation strategy and those employing a cost leadership strategy tend to possess different attributes. For example, managers pursuing strategies of differentiation have greater risk-taking propensities, have greater tolerances for ambiguity, and have a more internal locus of control relative to their counterparts who are pursuing strategies of cost leadership (Miller & Toulouse, 1986).

Building on Porter's (1980) work, Schuler and Jackson (1987) took a behavioral perspective. They assumed that firms develop HRM practices as a means for managing the behaviors of employees and that different strategies impose differing behavioral imperatives. They defined an effective HRM system as one that (1) accurately identifies the behaviors needed to implement the firm's strategy, (2) provides opportunities for employees to engage in the behaviors needed, (3) ensures employees have the competencies required, and (4) motivates employees to behave as needed. Schuler and Jackson then focused on three strategic activities: innovation, quality improvement, and cost reduction.

Increasing innovation has been identified as a common grand strategy (Schuler & Jackson, 1987). Innovation, with its reliance on creativity and originality, is not easily imitated and, therefore, can provide an organization with a sustained competitive advantage (cf. Wright et al., 1994). Twomey and Harris (2000) suggested that the more an organization uses innovation as a strategy, and the more the firm's HRM practices align with this strategy, the better its performance will be.

Innovation Substrategy

Innovation is not simply a mandate passed down to employees by management; rather, employees must be provided with an environment in which they can be creative and take risks without fear of reprisal. Thus, to successfully implement an innovation strategy, it is essential that the organization align its HRM practices accordingly (Gupta & Singhal, 1993). For a comprehensive review of climate dimensions conducive to creativity, the reader is referred to Mumford and Hunter (2005).

Building on the contingency approach to SHRM, certain HRM practices will be more effective than others for increasing innovation – specifically, HRM practices that allow for flexibility, knowledge, and empowerment, and that provide employees with the tools and freedom they need to be innovative. Broad perspectives and experience sets, plus information-sharing and participatory mechanisms, all enhance the prospects for spontaneity, innovation, and alternative strategy generation (Wright & Snell, 1999).

Table 1 provides an example of an appropriate HRM bundle for innovation. In contrast to these HRM practices, cost-cutting measures are

Table 1. Example HRM Bundles of Complementary Practices for Business Strategies.

Practice	HRM Bundle for Cost Reduction	HRM Bundle for Innovation	HRM Bundle for Quality
General orientation and HRM planning	• Cost-based approach • Lean production • Transactional relationships • High levels of reliable role behavior while being minimally staffed • Relatively moderate amounts of employee initiative, innovation, and spontaneity • Workers who can be relatively easily replaced • Consolidation • Reengineering • Downsizing • Use of temporary workers, part-time workers, and overtime • Outsourcing • Tight controls • Overhead minimization • Economies of scale • Centralized decision making to control costs • Minimal succession planning	• Employees are viewed as an asset (e.g., firms consider the aggregate present value of the employee's net future contributions, with salary often acting as a proxy for expected contribution) • Attracting creative employees for long-term relationships • Focus on enabling individuals to concentrate their attention on products and product breakthroughs • Succession planning and retention is important. • Comfortably staffed – not too lean	• Attracting cooperative employees for long-term relationships • Some succession planning • Retention programs are important • Comfortably staffed – not too lean
Job design	• Mechanistic in structure (i.e., narrow span of control, many levels of authority) • Routine jobs • Relatively low worker discretion (e.g., direct supervision/	• Organic in structure (e.g., wide span of control, few levels of authority, high knowledge-based authority) • Negotiated job roles • Broadly defined jobs/autonomy/ empowerment	• Organic in structure (e.g., moderate span of control, moderate levels of authority, high knowledge-based authority) • Broadly defined jobs/autonomy/ empowerment

Table 1. (*Continued*)

Practice	HRM Bundle for Cost Reduction	HRM Bundle for Innovation	HRM Bundle for Quality
	standardization of work processes/standardization of outputs)	• Flexible job design • Problem-solving teams • Employee interaction and participation encouraged	• Employee suggestion programs • Flexible job design • Problem-solving teams • Self-directed work groups
Recruiting	• Tap into a large local labor supply • Walk-ins • Write-ins • Employee referrals to save costs • Local advertising (e.g., newspapers) • Private employment agencies • Educational institutes (e.g., trades schools) • Internet • Word of mouth • Government employment centers	• Often tap into a national or international labor market • Professional recruiting/professional search firms • Employee referrals to get professional skills (e.g., employees recommend their friends from a professional organization) • Targeted advertising in professional journals (e.g., law journals) • Educational institutes (e.g., executive MBA programs).	• Often from a national or international labor market • Employee referrals • Targeted advertising in professional journals (e.g., law journals) • Educational institutes (e.g., executive MBA programs) • Professional search firms
Selection	• Internal promotions • Large selection pools • Seniority-based systems • Interview(s) with immediate supervisor • Reference checks • Multiple-cutoff decision-making model (i.e., successful job performance requires a set of minimum attributes)	• Significant investment in assessment (e.g., assessment centers) • Broad competencies (e.g., creativity, initiative/integrity/leadership skills) • Senior management team composition is considered (e.g., diversity of perspectives) • Compensatory decision-making model (i.e., the presence of some attributes or experiences in	• Significant amounts of assessment • Broad competencies (e.g., project management initiative/integrity/leadership/teamwork • Compensatory decision-making model (i.e., the presence of some attributes or experiences can compensate for a lack of others)

Training	• Relatively minimal amounts • Efficiency topics	candidates can compensate for a lack of others) • Generally the strongest HRM systems • Broad competencies (e.g., creativity, initiative/integrity/leadership/teamwork • Continuous development – principles of a "learning organization." • International work assignments • Extensive orientation programs • Networking with other industry leaders	• Broad competencies (e.g., creativity, initiative/integrity/leadership/teamwork • Continuous development – principles of a "learning organization" • Understanding of all functional aspects of the organization
Performance appraisal	• Explicit job design • Short-term focus • Promotes individual behavior	• Long-term focus • Promotes interpersonal behavior • Performance standards – process (e.g., consensus building and ethics) and outcomes • Focus on empowerment, diversity sensitivity, teams, extra-role behavior, and other broader competencies	• Intermediate to long-term focus • Promotes cooperative behavior. • Focused on tangible improvements in efficiency or costs • Focus on empowerment, diversity sensitivity, teams, extra-role behavior, and other broader competencies
Compensation	• Lower end of market rates • Green-fields/off-shore/outsourcing/contingent and part-time workers • Pay-for-performance • Rewards for meeting goals • Piece rate • Commissions • Gain sharing	• Competitive or above-market base salaries • Profit sharing and/or merit bonus	• Team-based pay • Profit sharing and/or merit bonus

not likely to increase innovation; in fact, they may actually suppress innovation if employees lack the resources needed to create new products. Similarly, a focus on quality may not be conducive to innovation because a zero-error policy may discourage employees from taking the risks required for innovation. Mumford and Hunter (2005) note that financial controls may likewise hinder the development of innovative products, perhaps by creating an excessive burden of proof on ideas, fostering management processes that inhibit communication and collaboration, and restricting the exploration of ideas. For an organization to increase innovation among its inner core workers, it must encourage creative behavior with a long-term focus, interdependent behavior, risk taking, and flexibility (cf. Schuler & Jackson, 1987).

Quality Improvement Substrategy
Another competitive strategy outlined by Schuler and Jackson (1987) is based on product and/or service quality. Quality strategies involve a commitment to both quality processes and quality output within the organization. Although quality has been identified as a precursor to innovation (Bolwijn & Kumpe, 1996), empirical evidence suggests that quality is effective on its own as a key strategy for organizational success in increasingly competitive environments (Briggs & Keogh, 1999).

According to Schuler and Jackson (1987), quality strategies should take a long-term or an intermediate-term focus and should encourage cooperative behavior and commitment to organizational goals. Key HRM practices that align with a quality improvement strategy include feedback systems, teamwork, autonomy, and flexible job classifications. Practices that increase organizational commitment are also likely to affect quality positively. Table 1 shows an example of an appropriate HRM bundle of practices associated with the quality improvement substrategy.

Cost-Reduction Substrategy
In a recent Labor Force 2000 survey, one-third of the companies surveyed listed the need to cut costs or improve their profitability as the strategic issue of greatest concern to them (Mirvis, 1997). Although organizations may choose cost reduction as a short-term measure to combat temporary dips in the economy, this approach is increasingly being employed as a grand strategy in positioning an organization as the lowest-cost producer, and hence the most competitive organization (Schuler & Jackson, 1987).

According to Schuler and Jackson, the main characteristics of a cost-reduction strategy include "tight controls, overhead minimization, and pursuit of economies of scale" (Schuler & Jackson, 1987, p. 210). These characteristics work together either to increase the level of output per employee or to reduce the costs associated with the output of each employee. Table 1 provides an example of an appropriate HRM bundle of practices associated with the cost-reduction substrategy.

Organizational Examples
Nike has a grand strategy of innovation. This company continually introduces new products that make its own and its competitors' products seem obsolete, and it utilizes marketing innovation and branding to provide differentiation. Even though Nike is concerned with innovation as a grand strategy, it also includes subsystems that have their own strategic intentions. For example, the inner core has to be innovative in branding and product development. The outer core must ensure that products are delivered in sufficient quantities, and at sufficient levels of quality, to numerous markets around the world. For instance, merchandise planning analysts develop, execute, and report on detailed demand, inventory, purchase, and/or delivery plans for products. The inner periphery includes warehouse operatives who process orders for shipment. Nike also supports a low-cost outer peripheral employee group that focuses on manufacturing via contractors in the developing world, taking advantage of local labor laws and working at low cost.

Reebok's core segment also focuses on innovation – for example, in marketing of brand products. Its peripheral segment is characterized by low-cost manufacturing in facilities located in developing countries. Like Nike, Reebok has gained a competitive advantage by concentrating on designing and marketing high-tech fashionable sports and fitness footwear while avoid investing in fixed assets. Both companies achieve this goal by contracting out production to suppliers in countries with low-cost labor (e.g., Taiwan and South Korea).

McDonald's core segment consists of a head office that is very concerned with quality in terms of standardization, quality products, consistent value propositions, and innovation (such as the company's new health-conscious menu). The outer core includes employees who have the job title "Business Consultants" and help owner/operators and field service managers protect the McDonald's brand by ensuring that their restaurants meet McDonald's food quality and restaurant safety standards. The inner peripheral comprises the labor force made up of young, easily replaced staff members with low compensation rates; these employees perform jobs that are designed so that they consist of simple tasks and require little training or succession planning. In the outer peripheral, organizations such as Danone, Heinz, McCain, Minute Maid, Mother Parker's, and Nestle supply food that needs very little preparation before serving. For instance, rather than restaurants buying potatoes to make their own French fries, Nestle is contracted to make fries for the restaurants according to McDonald's formula.

Whirlpool's grand strategy involves cost reduction. Even though the company as a whole has adopted a low-cost grand strategy, it still has an inner core that is charged with formulating and implementing strategy, such as how to deal with poor stock performance. The inner core initiated a 3-year global restructuring in 2003, and made acquisitions in Mexico and Poland. The outer core is concerned with maintaining world-class logistics. It also demands a 5% total cost/productivity improvement per year and 10 times improvements in speed and quality. The periphery includes assembly plant positions.

Similarly, Target's ability to offer low-cost products at its store is part of its grand strategy. This strategy is dependent on the core's ability to improve distribution, pursue aggressive buying with long-term vendors, and providing constant training on team-oriented approaches to customer service.

Now that we have discussed our five guiding principles, we suggest some additional research propositions:

Proposition 4. The implementation of the substrategy of the inner core requires innovation from segment employees.

Proposition 5. The inner core segment is most likely to achieve its substrategy goals when it is supported by an innovation-oriented HRM bundle (see Table 1).

Proposition 6. The outer core segment, by maintaining and ensuring the quality of the organization's daily operations, products, and/or services, makes the second greatest contribution to achieving the grand strategy.

Proposition 7. The implementation of the substrategy of the outer core requires a quality orientation from segment employees – that is, a focus on maintaining the quality of the organization's products and/or services (e.g., designing and maintaining quality control systems).

Proposition 8. The outer core segment is most likely to achieve its substrategy goals when it is supported by a quality-oriented HRM bundle.

Proposition 9. The inner peripheral segment, through the execution of routine job tasks, makes a relatively small contribution to grand strategy.

Proposition 10. The implementation of the substrategy of the inner peripheral segment requires that the quality of the product and/or service is obtained at the lowest possible cost.

Proposition 11. The inner peripheral segment is most likely to achieve its substrategy goals when it has a low-cost HRM bundle.

Proposition 12. The outer peripheral may be outsourced and may contribute rare or exceptional value in some instances.

Model Summary

In summary, the model proposed in Fig. 3 makes the following key assumptions:

- Organizational grand strategy is realized through the achievement of distinct organizational substrategies.
- Each organizational substrategy is associated with a specific employee segment, because the segments do not equally contribute rare or exceptional value.
- The substrategies take the form of innovation, quality, and low-cost substrategies.
- Each substrategy is associated with a unique bundle of HRM practices and policies.

Overall, the intent of the IMSA is to advance the understanding of how to conduct HRM by aligning HRM bundles to one of three distinct substrategies, with the choice of HRM bundle being conditional upon the employee segment in question.

One might argue that this model is incomplete, insofar as it does not incorporate a myriad of variables linked to organizational strategy (e.g., adaptability). These variables may also influence how HRM is conceptualized and operationalized within organizations. We now examine one of these variables – organizational culture – to illustrate how the IMSA may incorporate additional contextual factors when considering HRM.

THE IMSA: UNDERSTANDING THE RELATIONSHIP BETWEEN STRATEGY AND CULTURE

Organizational culture can be defined as a system of shared values and beliefs that produce norms and patterns of behavior and that establish an organizational way of life (Chatman & Jehn, 1994; Koberg & Chusmir, 1987; Rousseau, 1990). Although numerous dimensions and attributes of organizational culture have been proposed in the last couple of decades, we have chosen to examine the competing values framework (Cameron & Quinn, 1999).

The competing values framework has been found to have a high degree of congruence with well-known and well-accepted categorical schemes that organize individuals' cognitive processing of information as well as their values and assumptions (e.g., Jung, 1923; McKenney & Keen, 1974; Mason & Mitroff, 1973; Mitroff & Kilmann, 1978). Furthermore, there is a good fit between this framework and the substrategies proposed in the IMSA. According to Cameron and Quinn's framework (1999), four major clusters of values define organizational cultures:

- Clan (e.g., values cohesion, participation, and teamwork)
- Adhocracy (e.g., values creativity and innovation)
- Hierarchy (e.g., values efficiency and reliability)
- Market (e.g., values productivity and competitiveness)

These values, like grand strategy, have generally been studied at the organizational level.

Cameron and Quinn (1999) suggest that any one of these sets of values may reflect an organization's culture (i.e., its grand culture), although each subunit within an organization may have its own subculture and hence its own set of values. That is, an organization may be fragmented into groups that think about the world in very different ways or hold different beliefs about what their organization should be (Morgan, 1997). For example, a hierarchical culture might exist at the organizational level, yet one or more subgroups have an adhocracy culture. Such patterns of values, fragmented or integrated, and supported by various operating norms and rituals, can have a decisive influence on the organization's overall success (Morgan, 1997). This relationship is consistent with the IMSA, in which we define one grand strategy as well as a series of substrategies for different employee segments.

Interestingly, a number of management scholars suggest that a HR manager should invoke practices that reinforce the organization's grand culture (e.g., Cabrera & Bonache, 1999; Jehn & Bezrukova, 2004; Morgan, 1993; Ulrich, 1995). For instance, the HR manager might concentrate on improving efficiencies in a hierarchical culture, whereas employee development and work processes emphasizing teamwork might be pursued in a clan culture. This idea of aligning HRM practices with cultural considerations is similar to the notion of aligning HRM practices with grand strategy. One key difference, however, is our postulation that different HRM practices are needed for different employee segments, based on the substrategy associated with the segment in question. From a contingency approach, HRM systems should be situationally specific; different environments require different organizational systems for optimal effectiveness (Morgan, 1993).

The preceding (albeit brief) discussion of culture leads us to pose a fundamental two-part question: What is the relationship between culture and strategy, and what implications does the IMSA have for this relationship? According to Morgan (1993), culture is a driver of organizational strategy. Therefore, the organization's culture may be an antecedent to the strategic choices made. It is also possible that culture and strategy are reciprocally related (Burke & Litwin, 1992). That is, culture may influence strategy, and strategy may influence culture. Regardless of the causal relations between culture and strategy, it is clear that a link exists between the two. As Ashkanasy and Jackson note, "HRM outcomes and processes are inextricably linked with culture" (2001, p. 406). For instance, organizational socialization practices (e.g., new-employee orientation) are crucial for transmitting and perpetuating culture.

Assuming an organization has a grand strategy such as innovation, should all employees within the organization have an aligned culture (i.e., an adhocracy)? That is, should every employee group value change, entrepreneurialism, excitement, and dynamism? Should every employee group show an acceptance of experimentation, risk, challenge, and creativity?

The IMSA offers an answer to these questions. It suggests an alternative to aligning culture with grand strategy – specifically, aligning culture with substrategies. This relationship implies that culture would not be homogeneous throughout an organization, but rather varied between different employee groups. Homans (1950) argues that employees within groups that interact with one another socially, share activities, and share sentiments will experience social cohesion, a prototype of culture. Geertz (1964) suggests that a communal ideology is a precursor to culture. Thus subcultures may emerge in subsystems consisting of employees who are working on activities of similar value to an organization and with a common super-ordinate goal.

In the past, the idea of a unitary, monolithic organizational culture has been challenged by numerous scholars (e.g., Hofstede, 1998; Jordon, 1994; Schneider, 1975). While grand culture appears useful in differentiating one organization from another in inter-organizational studies, it has limitations when trying to explain people's intra-OB (Schneider, 1975). Organizations have been shown to contain distinct subcultures (Brown, 1995; Hofstede, 1998; Martin, 1992; Ott, 1989; Trice & Beyer, 1993), which form around organizational groups on the basis of a range of factors such as location, functional focus, and professional background (Bloor & Dawson, 1994). Indeed, Schneider (1975) has suggested that the focus on a grand culture limits the potential of the culture construct.

The notion of subcultures does not violate the notion of grand culture, just as the notion of substrategies does not violate the notion of grand strategy. Indeed, viewed conceptually, subculture is a subset of grand culture and as such is similarly constituted and functionally equivalent; the difference is merely one of scale (Lok, Westwood, & Crawford, 2005). Subcultures, like cultures, consist of distinctive values, beliefs, and norms about patterns of segment members' behaviors (Chatman & Jehn, 1994). Within one subculture, a high degree of consistency would be expected between employees in their shared belief structures, values, and norms. These elements and their gestalt make any subculture distinctive, both with respect to other subcultures and with respect to the grand culture. Subcultures, then, can also resemble grand cultures – making it feasible to talk about clan, adhocracy, hierarchy, and market subcultures.

The notion of subcultures is supported by Martin's (1992) differentiation view of culture, which sees organizations as complex, dynamic, and characterized not by unity and harmony but rather by diversity and even inconsistency. The relationship between subculture and grand culture is suggested by the IMSA, with subcultures, in a sense, being embedded in grand cultures. Nevertheless, to be conceptually differentiated and viable, a subculture must contain elements that are distinct from the grand culture, including a particular value set that aligns with substrategies. Thus subcultures can be defined as distinct clusters of understandings, behaviors, and cultural forms that identify segments of people in the ECS. They differ noticeably from the grand organizational culture in which they are embedded, by either intensifying its understandings and practices or deviating from them (Trice & Morand, 1991). This last point is important, because it makes clear the point that subcultures may be either in alignment with the grand strategy and culture, or antithetical to it (cf. Brown, 1995).

It has been argued that subculture takes precedence over grand culture and gains commitment from, or exerts control over, individual employees (Bloor & Dawson, 1994). Subcultures provide a more immediate and engaged work context for people, one in which particular values and attitudes are formed and routinely reinforced. They provide a common basis for identification and are more focused and coherent than organizational cultures. For example, employees tend to identify more closely with their work area than with the organization as a whole (Prestholdt, Lane, & Mathews, 1987).

Based on the IMSA, it can be inferred that, in general, an organization contains at least three subcultures with different sets of values adopted from the competing values framework. The inner core would be an adhocracy (e.g., values creativity and innovation), the outer core would be a hierarchy (e.g., values efficiency and reliability), and the inner periphery would be a market culture (e.g., values productivity and competitiveness). Furthermore, any segment may also have a clan culture (e.g., values cohesion and teamwork). Outer periphery members are members of some other organization.

There is empirical support for the idea that numerous subcultures exist within the same organization. For example, Hofstede (1998) studied organizational culture in a large Danish insurance company (3,400 employees). Employee questionnaire responses were subjected to a hierarchical cluster analysis, which produced a dendrogram. This dendrogram revealed the presence of three distinct subcultures within the company: (1) a professional subculture consisting of highly educated employees in management roles, (2) an administrative subculture, and (3) a customer interface subculture consisting of personnel in sales offices. Hofstede noted that "sales persons and appraisers appear together, although they belonged to quite different parts of the organization" and that "the customer interface subculture represents a 'counter-culture' to the professional culture, which includes higher management" (p. 8). Consistent with the IMSA, Hofstede's study found that the three subcultures had distinct sets of values that were unique from other subcultures within the organization. Also consistent with the IMSA, it suggested that organizations may have three subcultures within them that correspond with adhocracy, hierarchy, and market values.

The notion that a number of subcultures coexist within an organization (and that each subculture has a unique set of values) corresponds to the theoretical work by Jones (1983). Jones distinguished three ideal-typical organizational cultures: production culture, bureaucratic culture, and professional culture. The production culture arises when work is routine and standardized; the bureaucratic culture arises when tasks include non-routine elements; and the professional culture arises when the task is very non-routine and difficult, and the work is completed by skilled specialized personnel. These three cultures appear to correspond well to the inner core (professional subculture), outer core (bureaucratic subculture), and inner peripheral (production subculture) employee segments.

In summary, the IMSA can accommodate the ideas that organizations are likely to contain a number of subcultures and that these subcultures map onto the ECS segments. Evidence does, indeed, suggest that organizations contain subcultures (Brown, 1995; Martin, 1992; Trice & Morand, 1991). Perhaps one reason researchers have been unable to resolve the question of whether culture and organizational performance are linked (Ashkanasy & Jackson, 2001) is because, according to the IMSA, the strongest relations are likely to be those between subculture and outputs of ECS segments.

THE IMSA: SOME COMPLICATING FACTORS

Although we believe that the IMSA goes one step beyond the traditional SHRM by narrowing the focus down to the level of substrategies, some complicating factors must be addressed if the model hopes to be useful to both HRM science and practice. In this section, we explore three of these complicating factors.

Undoubtedly, some additional complicating factors are not addressed here, such as the existence of collective bargaining, which may limit organizational autonomy in developing specific HRM bundles. Although admittedly selective, this discussion may stimulate the reader to consider how the IMSA may incorporate some of these additional factors.

Organizational Configuration

One immediate question arising from the IMSA is "How do these segments interact with one another as organizations strive to achieve the grand strategy?" The type of organization (e.g., manufacturing facility, government, not-for-profit agency) and other contextual variables such as organizational structure and culture will all likely influence how jobs are configured across the segments, and the extent to which certain positions contribute to achieving the substrategies of more than one segment. To help edify our conceptual framework, we provide some examples.

Example 1: Government Organization
Consider Fig. 5, which illustrates the ECS segments for a hypothetical government organization (e.g., a city). Inspection of the figure reveals that each segment is represented by a circle, with each circle overlapping with at least one other circle. For example, while the head of a city department may be in the inner core, a department head, who is primarily in the outer core, may sometimes be asked to provide input or feedback relating to strategy formulation and implementation requiring innovation and may interact directly with the inner core (e.g., being invited to sit on a committee with the chief operating officer). This department head may best be depicted as residing in the overlap between the inner and outer core of the organization in Fig. 5. Likewise, a member of the inner core (e.g., the director of parks and recreation) may interact with members of the outer core (e.g., the head of a department within parks and recreation) to provide guidance relating to quality of government services.

Notice also that the outer peripheral intersects with all of the other segments. Some employees may, of course, reside within the outer peripheral and not contribute much to the organization in terms of either quality or innovation (e.g., cleaning staff who are subcontracted to clean offices do not

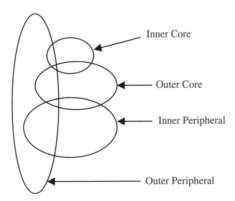

Fig. 5. Government Configuration.

substantially and directly contribute to quality and innovation, although they make an indirect contribution in that clean offices may lead to increased rates of job satisfaction). At the same time, other outer peripheral members might be quite important from the standpoint of quality, innovation, or both. For example, an HR consultant who is hired to improve efficiencies and eliminate redundancies may contribute to quality and provide innovative solutions to help the city achieve its goals – a grand strategy such as providing the best possible services to the citizenry while keeping costs as low as possible. This consultant may best be depicted as situated in the overlap between the outer peripheral, outer core, and inner core.

Of course, this scheme seemingly challenges our earlier assertion that peripheral employees add the least amount of value to a firm. Admittedly, some organizations will derive considerable value from the outer periphery. The important caveat here is that when peripheral contributors become important from the standpoint of value generation, they are not full-time employees; rather, they are under temporary contracts.

Example 2: University
Fig. 6 presents an example of an organization that many of our readers will be quite familiar with: a university. This figure is meant to illustrate another feature of our model: Each position within an organization may be spatially located to indicate its relative emphasis in terms of strategic

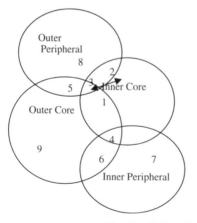

1.	University president
2.	University dean
3.	Professor
4.	Executive secretary/office manager
5.	Contract teaching
6.	Secretary to professor
7.	Cleaning staff
8.	Security system maintenance
9.	IT technician

Fig. 6. University Configuration.

objectives. Thus we can see the university president and dean are both members of the inner core, yet the dean is spatially located farther from the center of the inner core circle. By positioning the dean toward the periphery of the inner core circle, we recognize that a dean is required to interact with the outer core, and to work with outer core members to help ensure quality.

Another implication of this spatial configuration is also best explained by way of example. Consider two positions associated with the outer core (e.g., "3" and "4") that both overlap with the same neighbor segment (i.e., the inner core). Our assumption is that the position closer to the center of the neighbor will be relatively more concerned with the strategic emphasis of the neighbor segment. For this example, the professor position is assumed to be more concerned with innovation compared to the executive secretary position. Their relative positions from the center of their own circles, however, also indicate their relative concern for their own strategic emphasis (in this case, quality).

Overall, inspection of the university example suggests that several areas of overlap exist among the different segments. This implies that relative to the government example, a more complex series of interactions occurs between members of the various segments as they potentially contribute to innovation, quality, or both.

Example 3: Insurance Company

Our third example (Fig. 7) demonstrates that the outer peripheral segment may, in fact, be quite important from the standpoint of innovation. In some insurance companies, for example, investment decisions are outsourced to investment firms that make important decisions concerning the company's

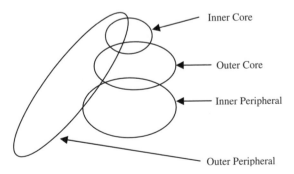

Fig. 7. Insurance Company Configuration.

financial assets. Insurance companies generally earn the lion's share of their income from investments (as opposed to insurance premiums).

Example 4: Law Firm

Our fourth example (see Fig. 8) is a law firm, and our intent here is to illustrate that the lawyers who belong to the outer core are quite heavily involved in innovation. After all, these employees ultimately produce the services – and they must be creative in building their personal client bases. A managing partner who is in the inner core is also concerned with innovation, albeit innovation of a different sort. Issues surrounding growth of the firm, diversification, and other concerns fall within the province of the managing partners. The strategic decisions made by managing partners may occur irregularly in established firms; yet, when they do occur, they affect the very nature of the firm.

This example demonstrates that members within one segment may be heavily involved in the strategic emphasis of a neighbor segment. Here, the lawyers, and not just the managing partners, play a central role in innovation for the law firm. This example also illustrates the distinction between quantity and quality of strategic acts. For instance, lawyers may

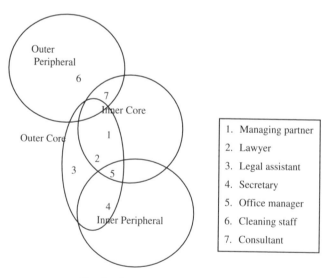

Fig. 8. Law Firm Configuration.

contribute to the firm's innovation substrategy through their daily actions and can, therefore, be considered to produce a high quantity of innovations, yet the importance or quality of the managing partners' decisions is what places them squarely in the inner core.

Example 5: Conglomerate
Our fifth example (Fig. 9) concerns a conglomerate and illustrates another common configuration. Given the existence of multiple business units with varying degrees of independence, we see the inclusion of multiple inner cores for each segment. For example, there are three inner cores (one each for the business units and one for the corporation) in this simplified and partial exhibition of the Pepsi Co. conglomerate.

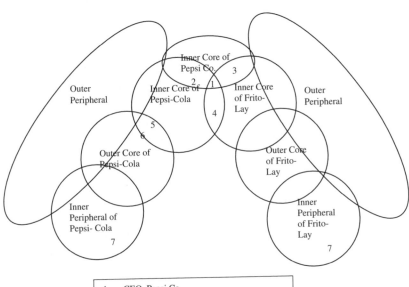

1.	CEO, Pepsi Co.
2.	COO, Pepsi-Cola
3.	COO, Frito-Lay
4.	Vice president of supply chain management
5.	Vice president of HRM, Pepsi-Cola
6.	Director of HRM, bottling plant
7.	Production-line workers

Fig. 9. Conglomerate Configuration.

Summary of Examples

Taken together, these five selective and restrictive examples serve to capture the inherent diversity in how segments may be related to one another, how jobs are potentially located within particular segments, and how jobs may be involved, to varying degrees, in the strategic imperatives of more than one segment.

So far, we have chosen to focus on alternative types of organizational configurations. Nevertheless, it is clear that the IMSA could be broadened to encompass contextual complexities arising from variations in both organizational culture and organizational structure. For example, we might assume that the degree of overlap between adjoining segments is partially a function of structural and cultural considerations. For instance, an organic structure might lead to greater overlap between segments. A culture high in power distance might lead to a scenario in which the outer core is given little latitude in the area of innovation, yet the inner core is quite heavily involved in ensuring high levels of both innovation and quality.

Placing Job Positions into Employee Segments

The reader may assume that certain job positions will predictably fall into specific segments. For example, CEOs (where relevant), presidents, and vice presidents are likely the exclusive members of the inner core, with various levels of management falling into either the outer core or perhaps the inner peripheral segment. Hourly employees would be classified as belonging to the periphery.

Unfortunately, the placement of particular employees into specific segments is not so easy to predict. For instance, some managers might be members of the inner core and some hourly employees could conceivably be members of the outer core. In fact, differences between organizations in the same industry in the placement of employee groups in the ECS may be a key source of competitive advantage. For example, at Second Cup coffee retail locations, baristas are viewed as trained professionals who cultivate their passion for coffee knowledge through an exclusive Coffee College and extensive in-café training programs. That is, they appear to be treated like core employees, a factor that differentiates Second Cup from its competition.

Similarly, in multiple-division organizations, each division will have its own inner core. The corporation will also have an inner core consisting of the board of directors. The corporation's inner core decides whether top-level employees will be given the autonomy to make strategic decisions that will, in effect, make division managers become members of the corporation's inner core. Hence, a business unit's inner core members may also be inner core members of the corporation.

The reason why we cannot assume group membership from job descriptions or job titles is a by-product of the fact that organizational structure is rarely simple or predictable. Moreover, organizations sometimes transform themselves through organizational development. As a consequence, employees may switch from one group to another following some organizational change (e.g., job redesign, changes in reporting relationships). For instance, a job-enrichment initiative (Hackman & Oldham, 1980) may give some employees decision-making autonomy, essentially elevating them from one ECS group to another (e.g., from the inner peripheral segment to the outer core). Flatter organizational structures tend to push decision-making powers downward in the organization because a given number of decisions are apportioned among fewer levels. Such a structure results in an organization that tends to have a smaller peripheral and larger core. Generally, there is a North American trend toward flatter organizations and, therefore, toward a smaller peripheral segment.

As Cascio (1995) described it, the world of work is in a state of flux and change, with many structural and process-related changes taking place as a result. Many organizations are becoming more organic in structure partly due to increasing global competition (Courtright, Fairhurst, & Rogers, 1989). We are witnessing a blurring of the distinction between hourly employees and management. Employees are increasingly being empowered to make decisions and solve problems through a team-based approach (Hedge & Borman, 1995). The proliferation of total quality management (TQM; Waite, Newman, & Krzystofiak, 1994) and its offspring is yet a further illustration of how employees are becoming empowered to help organizations improve, making it difficult to predict where employees (based on their work activities) should be placed within the ECS framework.

In sum, it is not simply a matter of reading an individual's job description and instituting ECS segment membership as a result. Although some organizations have highly formalized job structures and hierarchies (e.g., fast-food restaurants) that make it possible to infer ECS segment membership from job descriptions, this is not the case for all organizations. We view the ECS segments as fluid entities, with individuals moving from segment to segment as organizations reconceptualize and reconfigure in their quest to remain competitive.

Overlap among Employee Segments

So far, we have not considered the overlap between segments in the ECS model. Referring to Fig. 6, we will first focus on position 6, which represents the job of a secretary to a professor. This individual is in the inner peripheral segment, yet can make contributions to the outer core. For instance, a secretary may contribute to quality by ensuring that all pages making up an exam are present when he or she receives exams back from printing. Nevertheless, the secretary's contribution to quality is fundamentally different from that of a professor, who may contribute to the quality of an exam by ensuring that its content is valid. The HRM bundle for the secretary must match the nature of his or her job, and likewise for the professor.

Now consider a secretary who is asked to develop Web pages for the purposes of assisting a professor in data collection. The task requires a high degree of data manipulation and synthesis. A key question is how many of these high-level tasks the secretary performs and whether these tasks are part of the secretary's designated job responsibility or are extra-role duties. If the secretary engages in a number of important activities that make meaningful contributions to quality, we may question the wisdom of an HRM bundle designed exclusively around low-cost considerations.

One way of determining the appropriate HRM bundle for the secretary is to conduct a detailed and thorough job analysis. For example, functional job analysis (FJA; Fine, 1989) can be used to determine which specific tasks contribute to quality and the extent to which the employee has discretion in completing those tasks. FJA can also be used to identify low base-rate tasks and to determine how central these tasks are to the grand strategy of the organization. For instance, it can help clarify the types of contributions to innovation that a lawyer in Fig. 8 may make compared to the contributions made by the managing partner (e.g., negotiating mergers and acquisitions). If the FJA indicates that the job involves enough activities to warrant the position being considered as part of the next highest ECS segment, we would suggest an HRM bundle appropriate for that higher segment. A hybrid HRM bundle is not advocated because of the need to avoid a lack of horizontal alignment or congruence between HR practices and policies forming a bundle. Horizontal alignment occurs when various elements of the HRM system reinforce one another and send consistent signals regarding valued behaviors.

Complicating Factors: Summary

This section reviewed three complicating factors that should be considered if the IMSA is to have scientific or practical benefits with respect to SHRM. First, we must acknowledge that a variety of organizational configurations exist, and this proliferation has immediate implications for how the various employee segments are likely to interact. Second, it may be difficult to predict membership in a specific employee segment based on a specific job description. Rather, a variety of factors will influence the placement of a given job within the ECS framework. Third, a given job position may contribute to more than one segment, although it will be primarily linked to one of the four ECS segments.

THE IMSA AND A SPECIFIC HRM SYSTEM: PERFORMANCE MANAGEMENT

In this section, we consider the implication of the IMSA for a specific HRM function. For illustration purposes, this section focuses on the performance management system. Here the primary focus will be vertical fit of HRM practices with specific ECS segments, although we will consider linkages among various systems (i.e., horizontal fit) where appropriate.

Performance Management

Historically, research examining performance management can be divided into studies concerned with performance appraisal (where the unit of analysis typically is the individual) and studies examining various aspects of the feedback and development process. A commonality characterizing this research is an implicit assumption that some "best practices" approach exists. Thus these studies include the use of optimal measurement techniques, the use of best training approaches for performance raters, and the use of research-proven techniques for delivering feedback and motivating employees through the feedback and development process.

For example, previous research has attempted to identify the "best" rating format (e.g., Borman et al., 2001; Tziner & Kopelman, 2002), rater training program (e.g., Noonan & Sulsky, 2001; Woehr & Huffcut, 1994), and approach to feedback delivery (e.g., Jelley & Goffin, 2001; Zhou, 1998). This avenue of research has proven quite fruitful, leading to the introduction of technologies and procedures that unquestionably assist organizations in the management of individual employee performance. Nonetheless, missing from this research is a consideration of strategic context and its ability to moderate the success of any performance management tool or practice. To illustrate this void, this section considers the case of rater training research.

For many years, the "best practices" approach to rater training research involved instructing raters in how to avoid "rating errors" such as halo and leniency errors; this approach is generally referred to as rater-error training (cf. Landy & Farr, 1980; Woehr & Huffcut, 1994). However, with the realization that these errors suffer from both conceptual and methodological limitations, it became clear that eliminating them may not lead to rating improvements and, in fact, could yield deleterious psychometric consequences for performance ratings (Bernardin & Pence, 1980; Murphy & Balzer, 1989). For example, rendering uniformly high ratings across employees may or may not constitute a leniency error. If true performance is high across employees, the ratings are warranted and, therefore, are accurate. In sum, high levels of leniency may or may not constitute a rating error, so it might be erroneous to consider ratings invalid if operationally defined leniency is deemed to be high.

With the increased attention given to cognitive models of the rating process (e.g., DeNisi, Caffery, & Meglino, 1984), combined with the increased use of accuracy scores to operationalize rating quality (instead of traditional rater-error measures such as halo) (Sulsky & Balzer, 1988), new "best" training programs emerged, such as frame-of-reference (FOR) training (Bernardin, Buckley, Tyler, & Wiese, 2000). Unlike rater-error training, which is primarily concerned with a rater's motivation to rate employees inaccurately, FOR training focuses on rater ability. In FOR training, the goal is to calibrate all raters such that they agree upon the appropriate rating for a particular level of performance on a specific performance dimension.

If we simply examine the research in a disinterested manner, it is clear that FOR training is superior to rater-error training from the standpoint of the psychometric quality of the resultant performance ratings (see the meta-analysis by Woehr & Huffcut, 1994). At the same time, it is clear that this research has not considered the strategic context that might potentially complicate the meaning of the "best" training approach.

Consider, for example, inner core employees who are required to be innovative. From the standpoint of the inner core, managers want to stimulate creativity; the last thing they want to do is to appear punitive, which could stifle intrinsic motivation. For at least some of these managers, accurate performance ratings are not necessarily a desired endpoint (see also Murphy & Cleveland, 1995). In fact, they may perceive rating inflation as a desirable strategy for motivating and enhancing employee creativity. Performance rating is motivated behavior, and just because raters have the ability to rate accurately does not necessarily mean they will be motivated to do so (Banks & Murphy, 1985), with or without FOR training.

Now consider the outer core, and managers charged with evaluating inner peripheral employees. Outer core managers are concerned with the quality of the daily operations of the organization. They would want performance evaluations to be accurate inasmuch as accurate evaluations help identify employees who adhere to routines and procedures, leading to optimal decisions regarding merit and potential promotion. Viewed through this lens, FOR training makes a great deal of sense: All raters should operate on "a level playing field," ensuring that each employee is evaluated using a common metric and with a consensual understanding of the meaning of performance.

Does this mean that FOR training is doomed to fail (or at least be less effective) if a cohort of managers operates from a "rating-as-motivational-tool" agenda? Perhaps the better question isn't whether the training is necessary, but whether it is sufficient in a well-functioning performance management system. It is difficult to argue that calibrating raters is a bad idea. Conversely, maybe more calibration is needed in certain instances. Although FOR training may be sufficient for calibrating raters who are charged with evaluating lower-level employees doing routine work (i.e., peripheral segment of the ECS), a more enhanced training protocol that addresses the issue of rater motivation may be required when raters operate (at least somewhat) from a motivational agenda. Training raters on how to effectively motivate employees through the feedback and development process is a good starting point. Incorporating some of the elements from rater-error training might also be fruitful if it brings to light the motivational underpinnings for inflated rating behavior.

Here, we have attempted to illustrate how HRM strategy may influence the choice of optimal training programs – conditional upon the particular imperatives of employees from different segments of the ECS. This line of reasoning can be extended to any specific parameter of the performance management system, from the rating format selected to the specific approaches employed during feedback and development. Next, we consider how differences in the perception of HRM strategy add yet another layer of complexity when attempting to conceptualize an optimal personnel practice such as performance management.

Strategy and the ECS: Potential Conflicts and Complexities

Matters would be relatively straightforward if a specific set of optimal HRM practices existed for each ECS segment. In reality, an ECS segment may be characterized by a lack of consensus within the firm as to which HRM practices support a particular segment-specific HRM strategy. That is, how a HRM strategy is operationalized may be in the "eye of the beholder," and a uniform and consensual operationalization of HRM strategy may be too simplistic.

Consider, for example, a university that decides to adopt a grand strategy of innovation improvement. Its idea is to improve public/government and private sector perceptions concerning the university's innovation capabilities, thereby maximizing secured funding as well as donations and grants. At the level of senior members of the inner core (e.g., university president, select vice presidents), adoption of this grand strategy may lead them to emphasize measurable outcomes that are easily quantifiable, such as mean publication rate per faculty member or aggregate dollars obtained from research grants. Here, the emphasis is placed on quantity, and the goal of maximizing benchmarks of success makes sense from the standpoint of bolstering outsiders' perceptions of the institution as innovative.

By way of comparison, consider the deans, who are also part of the inner core. For them, success for the individual researcher may have a more complex meaning. Although numbers of publications may be relevant, the quality of the research and the visibility/prestige of the publication outlet are also relevant success parameters for many faculty members.

Sulsky and Keown (1998) argue that we have expended considerable research energy in trying to determine how to measure performance, but devoted relatively little research attention to the meaning of performance. Following through on our example, does performance mean the same thing for different members of the inner core? We suggest in some instances (as illustrated in this example) a consensual perception does not exist. What implications, if any, does its absence have for how we design a performance management system?

At the most basic level, a performance management system must begin with some agreed-upon notion concerning what is meant by various levels of performance. This shared definition, in turn, should help inform particular components of the system, such as how rewards are allocated, what the criteria for promotion are, and which performance goals should be set, to name a few. If a senior member of the inner core defines performance in such a way that it leads to a reward system based on numbers of publications with no regard given to the issue of quality, how will this relationship be perceived by other members of the inner core who do not share the same conceptualization? Moreover, if promotions to a higher rank are largely based on quantity, what effect might this policy have on the affective commitment and morale of faculty who sacrifice quantity to maximize research quality?

This example demonstrates that a given HRM strategy does not necessarily imply that all constituent groups, or all members within an ECS segment, share similar goals with respect to that strategy. Moreover, it may not be possible to satisfy the goals of one ECS segment, or one group within a segment, without adversely affecting the goals of another segment or group (Schein, 1980). A basic question concerns how we identify the specific goals emanating from a particular HRM strategy. According to Cameron and Whetten (1981), it may be difficult to nail down these goals for employee groups, as goals may change over time. Nonetheless, without a clear explication of the goals for ECS segments, it will be difficult to identify how to best conduct performance management within an organization.

Balzer and Sulsky (1990) suggest that it is important to differentiate between goals and objectives when considering performance management system characteristics. Specifically, objectives are deemed to be more specific than goals, and an individual goal can lead to numerous objectives for the performance management system. For instance, consider an inner peripheral employee group with a cost-reduction strategy that decides to develop a performance management system that is consistent with this HRM strategy. In this case, the overall goal would be to maximize performance and productivity while minimizing costs. In reality, a number of specific system characteristics become potentially appealing in this context:

- Rewards based on achieving certain preordained performance levels, as opposed to simply rewarding the top performers (i.e., absolute vs. relative reward system)
- Development of rating criteria that specifically address cost factors either directly or indirectly
- Use of inexpensive technologies for collecting and tracking ongoing performance (e.g., rating forms instead of computer-based performance tracking)

The obvious challenge is to address the likelihood that with potentially different goals across various ECS segments, and possibly within segments, different objectives may come to light. Although we cannot detail all of the possible objectives for a given goal within a segment, Table 2 does provide some examples of how this scenario might play out.

Table 2 presents a series of questions that are addressed when developing a performance management system. For example, critical questions include exactly what should be measured (e.g., traits vs. behaviors) and who should do the measuring (i.e., who will render the performance evaluations). Furthermore, we consider each of the employee groups in the ECS, and describe some likely objectives that each group has for a given question. These objectives, of course, will stem directly from the strategic goals of a given ECS segment.

To further illustrate the meaning behind Table 2, consider the "What to measure?" question. For the inner core group, the strategic imperative of innovation will likely lead to a concentration on rather broad competencies such as creativity and problem-solving ability. Thus the appraisal system would likely be non-analytic, requiring the evaluator(s) to use human judgment and identify performance levels for broad competency areas based on observed performance (Feldman, 1992). For the inner peripheral group, by contrast, the focus for evaluation is more likely to be on behaviors that are readily observed and "countable" – such things as safety violations or production errors. Thus, for these employees, the appraisal system would be an analytic one, implying that little or no human judgment is necessary to render evaluations (Bernardin, 1992). In sum, simply counting the occurrence of particular behaviors is an analytic task that does not require the types of judgmental inferences involved when deciding whether an employee is highly creative.

Inspection of Table 2 also reveals that some segments have overlapping objectives for the performance management system. For example, concerning "how to measure" (see Table 2), both inner core and outer core members might be best served by a trait-based approach to ratings, while the other groups would be optimally evaluated using behaviorally based approaches to evaluation (e.g., Behavioral Observation Scales; Latham & Wexley, 1977).

Previous research examining rating formats has not considered the strategic context and the implications for rating format choice. This research has generally concluded that behaviorally based formats are superior to trait-based approaches from the standpoint of psychometric integrity (cf. Bernardin & Beatty, 1984), although some of the comparative research is flawed insofar as poor criteria (Murphy & Balzer, 1989) are used as the basis for comparing alternative formats. In addition, behaviorally based

Table 2. How Performance Appraisal may Differ for ECS Segments.

Goals	Employee Groups in the ECS			
	Inner core: innovation	Outer core: quality	Inner peripheral: low cost	Outer peripheral: low cost
What to measure?	o High-bandwidth constructs (e.g., creativity, integrity, and teamwork) o Specific cognitive abilities o Processes and outcomes	o Moderate-bandwidth constructs (e.g., organization and dependability) o General cognitive abilities o Processes and outcomes	o Specific behaviors and outcomes, such as those related to efficiency, waste, error, and health and safety	o Objective outcome criteria (e.g., productivity) from outsourcing organization
Who does the measuring?	o Multiple raters, such as board of directors, fellow team members, peers, shareholders, key customers, and self	o 360-degree rating, such as by supervisor, peer, customers, subordinates, and self	o Manager/supervisor o Management by objectives	o Outsourcing organization
When is performance measured?	o Continuous feedback, development, and coaching	o Regularly scheduled formal appraisals (e.g., annually or biannually)	o Annual formal appraisals o Feedback upon poor performance	o Outsourcing organization
How?	o Trait-based scales o Goal setting o Targets met	o Trait- and behavioral-based scales o Goal setting o Targets met	o Behavioral-based scales o Objectives met	o Objectives met

Table 2. (Continued)

Goals	Employee Groups in the ECS			
	Inner core: innovation	Outer core: quality	Inner peripheral: low cost	Outer peripheral: low cost

Why?	○ Feedback and development
	○ To motivate
	○ Pay/bonuses
	○ Accountability (e.g., integrity)
	○ Retention
		○ Feedback and development
		○ To motivate
		○ Pay/bonuses
		○ Accountability (e.g., quality-related goals)
		○ Retention
			○ Accountability (e.g., identify potential problems around waste or customer service)
			○ Gain knowledge/evaluate
			  • Evaluate selection and promotion decisions/ T&D programs
			  • Errors in job analysis, descriptions, and so on
			  • Errors in job design
			  • Avoid discrimination
			  • Get to know what is happening
				○ Compare suppliers

approaches are preferable from a legal standpoint (Arvey & Murphy, 1998). In sum, although the general consensus is that behaviorally based assessment is superior to trait-based assessment, strategic context is not factored into the evaluative equation.

One implication arising from this situation is the need for evaluative research targeted at specific segments of the ECS. Later in this chapter, we offer some specific research propositions related to this issue. If legal concerns mitigate the use of trait-based evaluation, it might be necessary to supplement trait-based scales with information stipulating the behavioral requirements associated with alternative rating levels. That is, raters would be provided with the specific behavioral expectations associated with alternative levels of performance on subjective dimensions such as "creativity." Beyond meeting legal imperatives, this makes sense insofar as raters have a frame of reference in which to ground their evaluations, which should in turn enhance both reliability and rating accuracy.

As mentioned earlier, Table 2 also reveals variability concerning "what to measure." Interestingly, HRM practitioners are generally taught that performance assessment should follow a detailed and comprehensive job analysis. This is also considered to be a key element for the legal defensibility of appraisal systems (Murphy & Cleveland, 1995). However, previous performance appraisal research has not examined how strategic imperatives might help inform the specific type of job analysis conducted when developing appraisal systems. Instead, the type of rating format is often used as the point of departure for informing the specific type of analysis to be conducted. For example, behaviorally anchored rating scales (Smith & Kendall, 1963) require a critical-incidents approach to job analysis, whereas trait-based rating scales require job analyses focusing on the identification of knowledge, skills, abilities, and other characteristics (KSAOs).

Ideally, the specific strategic goals for particular ECS segments should help inform the type of job analysis initiatives undertaken when developing technologies for evaluating work performance. The inner core, by focusing on broad competencies, suggests the need for job analysis technologies that are less focused on employee behaviors and more focused on identifying critical KSAOs necessary to be effective on the job. The focus is on both process (e.g., was the behavior ethical?) and outcome. Alternatively, for inner peripheral employees, job analysis will likely be used to identify critical work outcomes that are countable. These outcomes (e.g., units produced, amounts of waste) then become the focus of evaluation. When process is measured for inner peripheral employees, critical-incidents job analysis techniques are appropriate. In contrast, for inner core employees, the process measures will be concerned with broader traits such as integrity, problem solving, team building, and leadership.

In the next section, we explore one important implication arising from our position that there will not necessarily be an optimal bundle of HRM practices/policies that implements a grand strategy. Rather, as just illustrated with the performance management example, HRM systems should vary as a function of ECS segment. Specifically, we turn our attention now to the following proposition: Because each segment may have specific goals, we need to examine whether, and to what extent, a HRM system is effective in the context of the particular segment in question. This brings us to a familiar concept: validity.

Meeting Objectives: An Issue of Validity

Within the research community, the concept of validity has evolved over the past 20 years. Whereas in the past we considered alternative types of validity (e.g., content vs. construct validity), we now conceptualize validity in terms of an inference (Landy, 1986; Society for Industrial and Organizational Psychology, 1987). For example, when we talk about test validity, we are really considering the validity of the inferences drawn from the test scores. It is the inferences that are valid or invalid, not the test itself.

In the same way, we might consider the validity of a set of performance evaluations from the standpoint of the inferences we draw from those evaluations. But what inferences will we likely want to draw from a set of performance evaluations, and might these inferences vary as a function of ECS segment?

Another way of thinking about this issue is to consider the objectives held by particular constituents within a particular segment, such as the inner core. Assuming an innovation HRM strategy, we might surmise that employees within this segment would require a performance management system that helps support innovation. Following this perspective, objectives would include ensuring that top employees are rewarded and that feedback concentrates on ways of improving creativity. This might take the form of multi-source (360-degree) feedback, it might involve setting up regularly scheduled performance feedback meetings, or perhaps a management-by-objectives program will be developed. Thus, from the perspective of the inner core, a "valid" system allows one to infer (1) that employees' true performance levels are based on available performance data and (2) that the effects of performance feedback on subsequent performance are positive. In sum, validity boils down to a question of whether, and to what extent, specific objectives emanating from substrategy-related goals are met successfully.

If employees of another segment (e.g., the outer core) are considered, a new set of objectives and requirements for validity may become evident. Thus, for a group of employees who must meet quality standards, outer core members who serve as performance evaluators may want a system that is easy to use and does not require a substantial time investment. Any activity (including performance management) deemed to distract these employees from the goal of ensuring quality may be seen in a negative light. If a performance management system considered "valid" by the inner core is perceived as a hindrance to other activities considered more important for ensuring quality, then outer core members might not infer that the system meets their own segment objectives. Thus the performance management system is not "valid" in this sense.

Returning to the earlier example from the academic context where the university adopts an innovation improvement grand strategy, the university's performance appraisal system may be considered invalid by senior administration (e.g., president) if it rewards quality of output and ignores quantity. Deans who are members of the inner core might perceive the reward system to be valid, however – at least insofar as the system meets the objective of rewarding professors based on the quality of their scholarly output.

Clearly, validity is in the eye of the beholder, and conflicts will arise to the extent that organizational members conceptualize validity differentially. The IMSA can be understood from the lens of validity because fundamentally, strategic context is the driver of validity judgments. At least two factors will influence a particular validity judgment: (1) the job position and its placement within the ECS, and (2) the extent to which the position interacts with and may be influenced by adjoining segments. For example, a dean who is part of the inner core understands the necessity for quantity of output, yet also is sympathetic to the outer core's emphasis on quality research. Because the dean position resides in the area of overlap between the inner and outer cores (as illustrated in Fig. 6), the dean's understanding of validity will likely be influenced by both ECS segments.

Performance Management System: Summary and Implications

Our central thesis is that it is not possible to identify a best approach to performance management or its components (e.g., training raters) insofar as substrategy will influence how the performance management (or any HR) system should be designed and implemented. In addition, we suggest that within different ECS segments, specific objectives might arise for the system that are, at least somewhat, unique to that segment. To the extent that this differentiation in objectives occurs, the same performance management system might be perceived as "valid" by members of one ECS segment and "invalid" by others. Moreover, members of the same segment could conceivably arrive at somewhat different validity conceptualizations. The ultimate judgment concerning validity should be the degree to which the performance management system supports substrategy implementation.

These arguments have direct implications for the development of HRM bundles. To give this some context, let us reexamine the issue of performance management. First, there is the potential for conflict among different constituent groups concerning how the performance management system should be designed and administered. Bargaining among the different ECS segments to arrive at a single management system that is mutually agreeable may provide a solution to this dilemma (cf. Katz & Kahn, 1978). More likely, however, is the emergence of a system that largely serves the needs of one constituent group (i.e., ECS segment). For example, a system perceived as overly cumbersome and time-consuming by managers charged with evaluation might lead to managerial shortcuts in how the system is utilized (e.g., not keeping performance diaries as stipulated by the system and instead relying on overall impressions when evaluating employees). In the university example, professors unhappy with an emphasis on performance quantity might devote more time to activities (e.g., consulting) that do not directly benefit the organization as a way of compensating for their failure to accrue significant merit pay or bonuses. This behavior could adversely affect other activities of benefit to the organization, such as professors' service-related activities.

What these two examples share in common is the unfortunate outgrowth of conflict: Employees may not ultimately contribute to meeting the strategic goals of the organization. This implies that the development of any performance management system might need to be approached from a change-process model, whereby representatives from various interested subgroups or organizational segments are involved in system development.

An alternative approach might be to design different performance management systems, each of which best fits a particular ECS segment. For instance, if the organization chooses to pursue a quality strategy (outer core jobs), it would make sense to provide feedback and development to employees in the outer core, with minimal or no feedback provided to employees performing more routine activities in the inner peripheral. Such a system might be especially relevant when inner peripheral jobs are designed

to leave little worker autonomy in an effort to make them "fool-proof."
This approach, however, is possible only if employees at this level are not (or
are only minimally) involved in helping the organization achieve its strategic
direction.

Assume for a moment that we were successful in tailoring the
performance management system to each individual segment: Members of
the outer core receive structured feedback with goal setting, while inner
peripheral members are simply appraised with little or no provision for
formal feedback and development. Although this system might seem to be a
tenable solution to the inherent reality of alternative segments with distinct
substrategies, complications arise when we acknowledge that a given
position may reside in the area of overlap between segments (e.g., the dean's
position, number 6 in Fig. 6). In such a case, the organization must decide
what the appropriate HRM bundle would be.

In this chapter, we used a specific HRM system, performance management, to exemplify the implications of the IMSA for all possible HRM
systems (e.g., employee selection, training). Specifically, we attempted to
show how the IMSA links grand strategy to segment-specific substrategies,
and how these substrategies in turn link to HRM bundles. Although we will
not attempt to provide an exhaustive set of propositions, we will illustrate
the implication of this model by providing example research propositions
for the performance management system used for inner core employees.
Specifically, our thesis is that no one optimal performance management
system is suitable for all ECS segments. Alignment of any HRM system
should be to the ECS segment to which it is applied. The resource-based
view of the organization suggests that benefits would accrue from such an
alignment. Accordingly, we put forth the following propositions:

Proposition 13. Performance management systems for inner core positions that include appraisal and development around innovation will lead to
achievement of substrategies and contribute to achieving the grand strategy.

Proposition 14. Maximal organizational performance is realized when
innovation is given the greatest emphasis and weighting in the overall
appraisal and development process for inner core employees.

Proposition 15. Inner core employees who spend relatively more of their
time concentrating on innovation-related activities will contribute more to
achieving the substrategy and, therefore, contribute more to the grand
strategy.

CONCLUSIONS

There is a need for a theory of context within organizations to better understand the environments within which people work. In helping to bridge this gap, this chapter presented a parsimonious model of subsystem configuration in which strategy is the focal concept. An important objective of the IMSA is to promote classification of work environments. Our classification system provides a means for defining sets of homogeneous work contexts and cultures in an effort to significantly increase levels of explained variance of key variables both within and across organizations. Also, the determination and explanation of work environments within firms enhances the development of normative theory (i.e., when and where certain HR practices should be used in firms).

The IMSA takes a configurational approach to understanding organizations. For our purposes, we view "configuration" to be synonymous with both "gestalt" and "archetype." Configurations are a means of achieving parsimony while presenting rich and complex descriptions of organizations (Mintzberg, 1973, 1978). Configuration research allows for the aggregation and organization of a large body of theory and empirical research into a meaningful set, thereby allowing propositions to be developed. It also provides a means for further developing the study of workplace behavior to help ascertain and explain why some organizations are more effective and efficient than others.

In the past, HR strategy has typically been conceptualized as the "pattern of decisions regarding the policies and practices associated with the HR system," and the prevailing assumption has been that HR strategy both contributes to and emerges from grand strategy (Bamberger & Fiegenbaum, 1996, p. 931). The IMSA suggests that rather than aligning HRM with grand strategy, aligning HRM with organizational substrategies is the best way for an organization to achieve its grand strategy.

In elaborating on the IMSA, we have suggested that different subsystems contain activities of varying value to the firm. It is well accepted that employees should be treated as unique individuals, yet fairly. The notion that all employee groups should not be treated the same is also not new to HRM. Different substrategies may require different work environments – leading to the need for different HRM practices for different substrategies.

Consider, for example, compensation systems. Because labor costs are often closely linked to budgets, and budgets flow directly from judgments of the contributions that an employee group makes to achieving organizational goals, most compensation systems (e.g., point factor system) take into account the perceived value (i.e., contribution to helping the organization implement its strategy) of an employee group. Even with seniority-based compensation systems, members of senior management are generally paid more than line supervisors because the former are thought to be more valuable to achievement of the strategic goals of the organization. That is, seniority-based compensation systems usually apply within employee groups rather than between employee groups. Between employee groups, in general, valued employees (e.g., corporate executives) are paid more than employees who are lower in the hierarchy and who contribute less to achieving the firm's strategic goals (e.g., line workers).

Value is often defined in the broader compensation system by the organizational goals that are to be reached. That employee groups often are, and should be, treated differently based on their contributions to achieving organizational goals is a basic premise of the IMSA.

Crotts, Dickson, and Ford (2005) noted that the formulation of strategy and mission is generally accomplished with less difficulty than their implementation. Moreover, in the strategic planning process it is often financial performance that gets measured and managed, "while the other equally important parts of the mission get lost in noble words" (Crotts et al., 2005, p. 54). If the most critical task facing HRM functions today is to align the company's "people strategies" and management processes with its grand strategy (cf. Gubman, 1995), HRM practitioners need to satisfy the following criteria:

- Understand the grand strategy and the value the company offers to its customers.
- Understand the core and peripheral employee segments and their substrategies.
- Correctly assign jobs to employee segments.
- Create HRM bundles that cue employees to act in support of the defined substrategies (e.g., which elements of performance are measured and reinforced).

Such HRM practices will help ensure that managers are consistent in what they say, do, and reward, and that employees receive consistent signals about what is expected from them.

In this chapter, we considered extant conceptualizations of context in the strategy, HRM, I-O, and OB literatures by forging linkages between HRM and strategy. Ideally, our exploration here will stimulate further thinking about context as it pertains to HRM and strategy implementation. We call upon researchers to carefully consider the meaning of "best" or "validity."

If nothing else, the IMSA suggests that achieving grand strategic objectives requires an acknowledgment that there may be no one best approach to HRM.

In closing, this chapter builds on the work of previous scholars (e.g., Mumford & Hunter, 2005) who have linked innovation and creativity to grand strategy. In particular, it elaborates on the role played by innovation. Innovation is central to the success of any firm, regardless of its grand strategy. This view is consistent with that held by Pfeffer (1994, 1998), who argues (1) that organizational success depends less on advantages associated with economies of scale, technology, patents, and access to capital and more on innovation, and (2) that this source of competitive advantage is largely derived from the firm's HR. Accordingly, Pfeffer and others advocate investment in high-performance and high-involvement HRM systems that are designed to enhance employee skills, commitment, and productivity (Datta et al., 2005). Of course, these investments may be more beneficial in some contexts than in others (i.e., inner core segment). Nevertheless, the innovation subsystem – although necessary for reaching firm goals – is not sufficient. The quality and low-cost subsystems must also reach their substrategy goals before successful organizational performance will be realized.

REFERENCES

Ansoff, H. I. (1965). *Corporate strategy: An analytical approach to business policy for growth and expansion.* New York. NY: McGraw-Hill.

Arthur, J. B. (1994). Effects of human resource systems on manufacturing performance and turnover. *Academy of Management Journal, 37,* 670–687.

Arvey, R. D., & Murphy, K. R. (1998). Performance evaluation in work settings. *Annual Review of Psychology, 49,* 141–168.

Ashkanasy, N. M., & Jackson, C. R. A. (2001). Organizational culture and climate. In: N. Anderson, D. S. Ones, H. K. Sinangil & C. Viswesvaran (Eds), *Handbook of industrial work, and organizational psychology* (pp. 398–415). London: Sage.

Atkinson, J. (1984). Manpower strategies for flexible organizations. *Personnel Management, 15,* 28–31.

Balzer, W. K., & Sulsky, L. M. (1990). Performance appraisal effectiveness. In: K. R. Murphy & F. E. Saal (Eds), *Psychology in organizations: Integrating science and practice* (pp. 133–156). Hillsdale, NJ: Erlbaum.

Bamberger, P., & Fiegenbaum, A. (1996). The role of strategic reference points in explaining the nature and consequences of human resources strategy. *Academy of Management Review, 21,* 926–958.

Banks, C. G., & Murphy, K. R. (1985). Toward or narrowing the research–practice gap in performance appraisal. *Personnel Psychology, 38,* 335–345.

Barnard, C. I. (1938). *The functions of the executive*. Cambridge, MA: Harvard University Press.

Barney, J. (1986). Organizational culture. *Academy of Management Review, 11*, 656–665.

Barney, J. (1991). Firm resources and sustained competitive advantage. *Journal of Management, 17*, 99–120.

Bart, C., Bontis, N., & Taggar, S. (2001). A model of the impact of mission statements on firm performance. *Management Decision, 39*, 19–36.

Becker, B., & Gerhart, B. (1996). The impact of human resource management on organizational performance: Progress and prospects. *Academy of Management Journal, 39*, 779–801.

Becker, B. E., & Huselid, M. A. (1998). High performance work systems and firm performance: A synthesis of research and managerial implications. *Research in Personnel and Human Resources Management, 16*, 53–101.

Bernardin, H., & Beatty, R. (1984). *Performance appraisal: Assessing human behavior at work.* Boston, MA: Kent.

Bernardin, H. J. (1992). An analytic framework for customer-based performance content development and appraisal. *Human Resource Management Review, 2*, 81–102.

Bernardin, H. J., Buckley, M. R., Tyler, C. L., & Wiese, D. S. (2000). A reconsideration of strategies in rater training. *Research in Personnel and Human Resources Management, 18*, 221–274.

Bernardin, H. J., & Pence, E. C. (1980). Effects of rater error training: Creating new response sets and decreasing accuracy. *Journal of Applied Psychology, 65*, 60–66.

Bloor, G., & Dawson, P. (1994). Understanding professional culture in organizational context. *Organizational Studies, 15*, 275–295.

Boam, R., & Sparrow, S. (1992). *Designing and achieving competency*. London: McGraw-Hill.

Bolwijn, P. T., & Kumpe, T. (1996). About facts, fiction and forces in human resources management. *Human Systems Management, 15*, 161–172.

Borman, W. C., Buck, D. E., Hanson, M. A., Motowidlo, S. J., Stark, S., & Drasgow, F. (2001). An examination of the comparative reliability, validity, and accuracy of performance ratings made using computerized adaptive rating scales. *Journal of Applied Psychology, 86*, 965–973.

Bowen, D. E., Galang, C., & Pillai, R. (2002). The role of human resource management: An exploratory study of cross-country variance. *Human Resource Management, 41*, 103–122.

Boxall, P. (1999). Achieving competitive advantage through human resource strategy: Towards a theory of industry dynamics. *Human Resource Management Review, 8*, 265–288.

Briggs, S., & Keogh, W. (1999 July). Integrating human resource strategy and strategic planning to achieve business excellence. *Total Quality Management, 10*, 447.

Brockbank, W., Ulrich, D., & James, C. (1997). *Trends in human resource competencies.* Third Conference on Human Resource Competencies. University of Michigan School of Business, Ann Arbor, MI.

Brown, A. (1995). *Organizational culture*. London: Pitman.

Burke, W. W., & Litwin, G. H. (1992). A causal model of organizational performance and change. *Journal of Management, 18*, 523–545.

Butler, J. E., Ferris, G. R., & Napier, N. K. (1991). *Strategy and human resource management.* Cincinnati, OH: South-Western.

Cabrera, E. F., & Bonache, J. (1999). An expert HR system for aligning organizational culture and strategy. *Human Resource Planning, 22*, 51–60.

Cameron, K. S., & Quinn, R. E. (1999). *Diagnosing and changing organizational culture: Based on the competing values framework.* New York, NY: Addison-Wesley.

Cameron, K. S., & Whetten, D. A. (1981). Perceptions of organizational effectiveness over organizational life cycles. *Administrative Science Quarterly, 26*(4), 525–544.

Camillus, J. C. (1986). *Strategic planning and management control.* Lexington, MA: Lexington Books.

Cascio, W. F. (1995). Whither industrial and organizational psychology in a changing world of work? *American Psychologist, 50,* 928–939.

Chatman, J. A., & Jehn, K. A. (1994). Assessing the relationship between industry characteristics and organizational culture: How different can you be? *Academy of Management Journal, 37,* 522–553.

Courtright, J. A., Fairhurst, G. T., & Rogers, L. E. (1989). Interaction patterns in organic and mechanistic systems. *Academy of Management Journal, 32,* 773–802.

Crotts, J. C., Dickson, D. R., & Ford, R. C. (2005). Aligning organizational processes with mission: The case of service excellence. *Academy of Management Executive, 19,* 54–68.

Czinkota, M. R., & Kotabe, M. (2001). *Marketing management* (2nd ed.). Cincinnati, OH: South-Western.

Datta, D. K., Guthrie, J. P., & Wright, P. M. (2005). Human resource management and labor productivity: Does industry matter? *Academy of Management Journal, 48,* 135–145.

Delaney, J. T., Lewin, D., & Ichniowski, C. (1989). *Human resource policies and practices in American firms.* Washington, DC: US Government Printing Office.

Delery, J. E., & Doty, D. H. (1996). Modes of theorizing in strategic human resource management: Tests of universalistic, contingency and configurational performance predictions. *Academy of Management Journal, 39,* 802–835.

DeNisi, A. S., Caffery, T., & Meglino, B. (1984). A cognitive view of the performance appraisal process: A model and research propositions. *Organizational Behavior and Human Performance, 33,* 360–396.

Doty, D. H., & Delery, J. E. (1997). The importance of holism, interdependence, and equifinality assumptions in high performance work systems: Toward theories of the high performance work force. Presented at the National Meetings of the Academy of Management, Boston, MA.

Drucker, P. F. (1954). *The practice of management.* New York, NY: Harper and Row.

Feldman, J. M. (1992). The case for non-analytic performance appraisal. *Human Resource Management Review, 2,* 9–35.

Fine, S. A. (1989). *Functional job analysis scales: A desk aid.* Milwaukee, WI: Author.

Geertz, C. (1964). Ideology as a cultural system. In: D. E. Apter (Ed.), *Ideology and discontent* (pp. 47–76). London: Free Press of Glencoe.

Gibb, S. (2001). The state of human resource management: Evidence from employees' views of HRM systems and staff. *Employee Relations, 23,* 318–336.

Govindarajan, V. (1988). A contingency approach to strategy implementation at the business unit level: Integrating administrative mechanisms with strategy. *Academy of Management Journal, 31,* 828–853.

Govindarajan, V. (1989). Implementing competitive strategies at the business unit level: Implications of matching managers with strategies. *Strategic Management Journal, 10,* 251–269.

Gubman, E. L. (1995). Aligning people strategies with customer value. *Compensation and Benefits Review, 27,* 15–22.

Gunnigle, P., & Moore, S. (1994). Linking business strategy and human resource management. *Personnel Review, 23,* 63–84.

Gupta, A., & Singhal, A. (1993). Managing human resources for innovation and creativity. *Research Technology Management, 36*, 41–48.

Hackman, R. J., & Oldham, G. R. (1980). *Work redesign.* Redding, MA: Addison-Wesley.

Hedge, J. W., & Borman, W. C. (1995). Changing conceptions and practices in performance appraisal. In: A. Howard (Ed.), *The changing nature of work* (pp. 451–482). San Francisco, CA: Jossey-Bass.

Hitt, M. A., & Ireland, R. D. (1985). Strategy, context factors, and performance. *Human Relations, 38*, 793–812.

Hofstede, G. (1998). Identifying organizational subcultures: An empirical approach. *Journal of Management Studies, 35*, 1–12.

Homans, G. C. (1950). *The human group.* New York, NY: Harcourt, Brace.

Huselid, M. A. (1993). Estimates of the impact of human resource management practices on turnover and productivity. Paper presented at the annual meeting of the Academy of Management, Atlanta, GA.

Huselid, M. A. (1995). The impact of human resource management practices on turnover, productivity and corporate financial performance. *Academy of Management Journal, 38*, 635–672.

Ichniowski, C., Shaw, K., & Prennushi, G. (1997). The effects of human resource management practices on productivity. *American Economic Review, 87*, 291–313.

Ilinitch, A. Y., D'Aveni, R., & Lewin, A. Y. (1996). New organizational forms and strategies for managing in hypercompetitive environments. *Organization Science, 7*, 211–220.

Jehn, K. A., & Bezrukova, K. (2004). A field study of group diversity, workgroup context, and performance. *Journal of Organizational Behavior, 25*, 703–729.

Jelley, R. B., & Goffin, R. D. (2001). Can performance-feedback accuracy be improved? Effects of rater priming and rating-scale format on rating accuracy. *Journal of Applied Psychology, 86*, 134–144.

Jones, G. R. (1983). Transition costs, property rights, and organizational culture: An exchange perspective. *Administrative Science Quarterly, 28*, 454–467.

Jordon, A. T. (1994). Organizational culture: The anthropological approach. In: A. T. Jordon (Ed.), *Practicing anthropology in corporate America: Consulting on organizational culture* (pp. 3–16). Arlington, VA: American Anthropological Association.

Jung, C. G. (1923). *Psychological types.* London: Routledge & Kegan Paul.

Katila, R., & Shane, S. (2005). When does lack of resources make new firms innovative? *Academy of Management Journal, 48*, 814–829.

Katz, D., & Kahn, R. L. (1978). *The social psychology of organizations.* New York, NY: Wiley.

Kerr, S. (1995). On the folly of rewarding A, while hoping for B. *Academy of Management Executive, 9*, 7–14.

Koberg, C. S., & Chusmir, L. H. (1987). Organizational culture relationships with creativity and other job-related variables. *Journal of Business Research, 15*, 397–409.

Laabs, J. J. (1993). Hewlett-Packard's core values drive HR strategy. *Personnel Journal, 72*, 38–46.

Lado, A. A., & Wilson, M. (1994). Human resource systems and sustained competitive advantage: A competency-based perspective. *Academy of Management Review, 19*, 699–727.

Landy, F. J. (1986). Stamp collecting versus science. *American Psychologist, 41*, 1183–1192.

Landy, F. J., & Farr, J. L. (1980). Performance rating. *Psychological Bulletin, 87*, 72–107.

Latham, G. P., & Wexley, K. N. (1977). Behavioral observation scales. *Personnel Psychology, 30*, 255–268.

Lawrence, P., & Lorsch, J. (1967). Differentiation and integration in complex organizations. *Administrative Science Quarterly, 12,* 1–30.

Likert, R. (1961). *New patterns of management.* New York, NY: McGraw-Hill.

Lok, P., Westwood, R., & Crawford, J. (2005). Perceptions of organizational subculture and their significance for organizational commitment. *Applied Psychology: An International Review, 54,* 490–514.

MacDuffie, J. P. (1995). Human resource bundles and manufacturing performance: Organizational logic and flexible production systems in the world auto industry. *Industrial and Labor Relations Review, 48,* 194–221.

Martin, J. (1992). *Cultures in organizations: Three perspectives.* New York, NY: Oxford University Press.

Mason, R. O., & Mitroff, I. (1973). A program of research in management. *Management Science, 19,* 475–487.

McKenney, J. L., & Keen, P. G. W. (1974). How managers' minds work. *Harvard Business Review, 51,* 79–90.

Meyer, J. W., & Rowan, B. (1977). Institutional organizations: Formal structures as myths and ceremony. *American Journal of Sociology, 83,* 340–363.

Miller, D., & Toulouse, J. M. (1986). Chief executive personality and corporate strategy and structure in small firms. *Management Science, 32,* 1389–1409.

Miles, R. E., & Snow, C. (1986). Organizations: New concepts for new forms. *California Management Review, 28,* 62–73.

Miles, R. H., & Snow, C. C. (1984). Fit, failure and the hall of fame. *California Management Review, 24,* 10–28.

Mintzberg, H. (1973). Strategy-making in three modes. *California Management Review, 16,* 44–53.

Mintzberg, H. (1978). Patterns in strategy formation. *Management Science, 24,* 934–948.

Mirvis, P. H. (1997). "Soul work" in organizations. *Organization Science, 8,* 193–206.

Mitroff, I. I., & Kilmann, R. (1978). *Methodological approaches to social science.* San Francisco, CA: Jossey-Bass.

Morgan, G. (1997). *Images of organizations.* Thousand Oaks, CA: Sage.

Morgan, M. J. (1993). How corporate culture drives strategy. *Long Range Planning, 26,* 110–118.

Mumford, M. D., & Hunter, S. T. (2005). Innovation in organizations: A multi-level perspective on creativity. In: F. Dansereau & F. Yammarino (Eds), *Multi-level issues in strategy and methods* (Vol. 4, pp. 11–73). Oxford, UK/Holland: Elsevier.

Murphy, K. R., & Balzer, W. K. (1989). Rater errors and rating accuracy. *Journal of Applied Psychology, 74,* 619–624.

Murphy, K. R., & Cleveland, J. N. (1995). *Understanding performance appraisal.* Thousand Oaks, CA: Sage.

Nadler, D. A., & Trushman, M. L. (1997). *Competing by design.* New York, NY: Oxford University Press.

Noonan, L., & Sulsky, L. M. (2001). Examination of frame of reference and behavioral observation training on alternative training effectiveness criteria in a Canadian military sample. *Human Performance, 14,* 3–26.

Osterman, P. (1994). How common is workplace transformation and who adopts it? *Industrial and Labor Relations Review, 47,* 173–188.

Ott, J. (1989). *The organizational culture perspective.* San Francisco, CA: Brooks/Cole.

Peteraf, M. (1993). The cornerstones of competitive advantage: A resource-based view. *Strategic Management Journal, 14*, 179–191.

Pfau, B. N., & Cundiff, B. B. (2002). Seven steps before strategy. *Workforce, 81*, 40–45.

Pfeffer, J. (1994). *Competitive advantage through people*. Boston, MA: Harvard Business School Press.

Pfeffer, J. (1998). *The human equation*. Boston, MA: Harvard Business School Press.

Porter, M. E. (1980). *Competitive strategy: Techniques for analyzing industries and competitors*. New York, NY: Free Press.

Powell, T. (1992). Organizational alignment as competitive advantage. *Strategic Management Journal, 13*, 119–135.

Prestholdt, P., Lane, I., & Mathews, R. (1987). Nurse turnover as reasoned action: Development of a process model. *Journal of Applied Psychology, 72*, 221–227.

Purcell, J. (1996). Contingent workers and human resource strategy: Rediscovering the core–periphery dimension. *Journal of Professional HRM, 5*, 16–23.

Rogers, E. W., & Wright, P. M. (1998). Measuring organizational performance in strategic human resource management: Problems, prospects, and performance information markets. *Human Resource Management Review, 8*, 311–331.

Rousseau, D. M. (1990). Assessing organizational culture: The case for multiple methods. In: B. Schneider (Ed.), *Organizational climate and culture* (pp. 153–192). San Francisco, CA: Jossey-Bass.

Rowe, W. G., Morrow, J. L. J., & Finch, J. F. (1995). Accounting, market, and subjective measures of firm performance: Three sides of the same coin? Unpublished manuscript, University of Waterloo, London, Canada.

Schein, E. (1980). *Organizational psychology* (3rd ed.). Englewood Cliffs, NJ: Prentice-Hall.

Schneider, B. (1975). Organizational climates: An essay. *Personnel Psychology, 28*, 447–479.

Schuler, R. S., & Jackson, S. E. (1987). Linking competitive strategy with human resource management practices. *Academy of Management Executive, 1*, 207–219.

Smith, P. C., & Kendall, L. M. (1963). Retranslation of expectations: An approach to the construction of unambiguous anchors for rating scales. *Journal of Applied Psychology, 47*, 149–155.

Society for Industrial and Organizational Psychology, Inc. (1987). *Principles for the validation and use of personnel selection procedures* (3rd ed.). College Park, MD: Author.

Snell, S. (1992). Control theory in strategic human resource management: The mediating effect of administrative information. *Academy of Management Journal, 35*, 292–327.

Sulsky, L. M., & Balzer, W. K. (1988). Meaning and measurement of performance rating accuracy: Some methodological and theoretical concerns. *Journal of Applied Psychology, 73*, 497–506.

Sulsky, L. M., & Keown, J. L. (1998). Performance appraisal in the changing world of work: Implications for the meaning and measurement of work performance. *Canadian Psychology, 39*, 52–59.

Sy, T., & D'Annunzio, L. S. (2005). Challenges and strategies of matrix organizations: Top-level and mid-level managers' perspectives. *Human Resource Planning, 28*, 39–49.

Tichy, N. (1983). *Managing strategic change*. New York, NY: Wiley.

Treacy, M., & Wiersema, F. (1995). *The discipline of market leaders: Choose your customers, narrow your focus, dominate your market*. New York, NY: Addison-Wesley.

Trice, H., & Morand, D. (1991). Organisational subculture and countercultures. In: G. Miller (Ed.), *Studies in organizational sociology* (pp. 45–69). Greenwich, CT: JAI Press.

Trice, H. M., & Beyer, J. M. (1993). *The cultures of work organizations.* New Jersey, NJ: Prentice-Hall.

Truss, C., & Gratton, L. (1994, September). Strategic human resource management: A conceptual approach. *International Journal of Human Resource Management, 5,* 663–686.

Tsui, A. S., Pearce, J. L., Porter, L. W., & Tripoli, A. M. (1997). Alternative approaches to the employee–organization relationship: Does investment in employees pay off? *Academy of Management Journal, 40,* 1089–1122.

Twomey, D. F., & Harris, D. L. (2000). From strategy to corporate outcomes: Aligning human resource management systems with entrepreneurial intent. *International Journal of Commerce and Management, 10,* 43–55.

Tziner, A., & Kopelman, R. E. (2002). Is there a preferred performance rating format? A non-psychometric perspective. *Applied Psychology: An International Review, 51,* 479–503.

Ulrich, D. (1995). *Human resource champions.* Boston, MA: Harvard Business School Press.

Waite, M. L., Newman, J. M., & Krzystofiak, F. J. (1994). Association among performance appraisal, compensation, and total quality programs. *Psychological Reports, 75,* 524–526.

Walker, J. W. (2001). Perspectives. *Human Resource Planning, 24,* 12–14.

Woehr, D. J., & Huffcutt, A. I. (1994). Rater training for performance appraisal: A quantitative review. *Journal of Occupational and Organizational Psychology, 67,* 189–205.

Wright, P., McMahan, G., & McWilliams, A. (1994). Human resources and sustained competitive advantage: a resource-based perspective. *International Journal of Human Resource Management, 5,* 301–326.

Wright, P. M., & Sherman, W. S. (1999). The failure to find fit in strategic human resource management: Theoretical and empirical considerations. In: P. Wright, L. Dyer, J. Boudreau & G. Milkovich (Eds), *Research in personnel and human resource management* (pp. 53–74). Greenwich, CT: JAI Press, Supplement A.

Wright, P. M., & Snell, S. A. (1999). Toward a unifying framework for exploring fit and flexibility in strategic human resource management. *Academy of Management Review, 23,* 756–772.

Youndt, M. A., Snell, S. A., Dean, J. W., & Lepak, D. P. (1996). Human resource management, manufacturing strategy, and firm performance. *Academy of Management Journal, 39,* 836–866.

Zhou, J. (1998). Feedback valence, feedback style, task autonomy, and achievement orientation: Interactive effects on creative performance. *Journal of Applied Psychology, 83,* 261–276.

LINKING INNOVATION AND CREATIVITY WITH HUMAN RESOURCES STRATEGIES AND PRACTICES: A MATTER OF FIT OR FLEXIBILITY?

James L. Farr and Veronique Tran

ABSTRACT

Innovation is an important component of the overall strategy for contemporary organizations. In parallel, strategic human resources management scholars have argued that human resources management practices should help to motivate behaviors and attitudes among organizational employees that will contribute to the successful implementation of the overall strategy. Taggar, Sulsky, and MacDonald suggest that the employee sector they label as the inner core is most critical to the attainment of an innovative substrategy goal, and specific human resources bundles should be designed to encourage creative and innovative behaviors among inner core employees. This commentary argues that innovation, as an inherent part of the overall strategy, should be an important goal for all employee sectors, although the nature of their needed innovative behavior may differ. Thus, the Taggar et al. model should be integrated with the multi-level model of organizational

Multi-Level Issues in Creativity and Innovation
Research in Multi-Level Issues, Volume 7, 377–392
Copyright © 2008 by Elsevier Ltd.
ISSN: 1475-9144/doi:10.1016/S1475-9144(07)00014-8

innovation and creativity developed by Bains and Tran (2006) to account better for the requirements of innovation in complex organizations.

INTRODUCTION

In their chapter in this volume Taggar, Sulsky, and Macdonald (this volume) present a multi-level model that addresses the linkages between organizational strategy, human resources (HR) practices, and employee behavior and attitudes. Their model is consistent with the general arguments stated by advocates of strategic human resources management (SHRM; e.g., Tichy, Fombrun, & Devanna, 1982; Miles & Snow, 1984; Snell, Youndt, & Wright, 1996). That is, Taggar and colleagues assert that aligning organizational HR practices with organizational strategy is the most effective way to ensure that the organization's human capital is directed toward the achievement of organizational objectives. However, their model makes additional assumptions that lead to a more nuanced approach to linking strategy and HR practices. Thus, we can view the integrated model of strategy alignment (IMSA) proposed by Taggar et al. as a response to the call for more theory to help provide content for the "black box" connecting SHRM and measures of organizational effectiveness (cf. Dyer & Shafer, 1999; Becker & Gerhart, 1996). Taken together, these additional assumptions describe two important contingencies regarding the alignment of HR practices and organizational strategy.

First, an organization's overall or "grand strategy" consists of (generally) "universal" substrategies of innovation, quality, and cost/efficiency (cf. Schuler & Jackson, 1987; Porter, 1980). These three substrategies exist to some (varying) degree in most organizations, and they are usually in (at least) partial conflict with each other. That is, an organization cannot typically emphasize and achieve all three substrategies to an equally high degree but rather must choose among them. Taggar et al. note that differing integrated bundles or complementary groupings of HR practices enable the achievement of each substrategy.

Second, every organization includes clusters of employees who are differentially linked to the development, attainment, and modification of the grand strategy (and substrategies) and to the development, attainment, and modification of HR practices and policies that support the substrategies and grand strategy. In addition, the HR practices and policies appropriate for achieving attainment of the substrategies may differ for the various employee clusters.

Thus, Taggar et al. argue that an organization must align its HR practices for each of four employee clusters, which they label as the inner core, the outer core, the inner peripheral, and the outer peripheral. We do not describe these clusters in detail here, but refer the reader to Taggar et al.'s chapter. For our purposes, it is sufficient to note that the inner core cluster is most central to achievement of the organization's grand strategy, and the outer peripheral cluster is least central to this endeavor. Furthermore, the relative importance of the three substrategies varies by employee cluster, which allows for partial resolution of the usual conflict among the substrategies. Taggar et al. suggest that the innovation substrategy is primary for the inner core, the quality substrategy is primary for the outer core, and the cost reduction substrategy is primary for both peripheral employee segments. Therefore, the bundle of HR practices most appropriate for each employee cluster varies in accordance with its primary substrategy. This point is discussed in more detail later in this commentary.

The approach that Taggar et al. have developed in the IMSA is partly a response to several criticisms that have been made of earlier SHRM theory and research. For example, Chadwick and Cappelli (1999) argue that the use of generic strategy typologies – such as that described by Porter (1980) – to provide an overall categorical label for the strategy followed by an organization (e.g., "cost leadership" or "cost focus" in Porter's typology) often leads to overly simplistic and even inaccurate characterizations of organizational strategy. The substrategies offered by Taggar et al. (i.e., innovation, quality improvement, and cost reduction) are similar to Porter's (1980) strategic types. Nevertheless, in the Taggar et al. model, an organization's grand strategy includes all three substrategies in some mixture. Thus, many forms of organizational grand strategy exist, and it would be a straightforward extension of Taggar et al.'s model to apply the IMSA to organizational subunit levels, such as strategic business units or functional divisions, thereby bringing the mixed strategy notion to these lower organizational levels.

In their depiction of the IMSA (shown in Fig. 3 in the Taggar et al. chapter), these authors do not indicate direct interactions or integration among the substrategies or the HR practices and policies that follow from them. Instead, they include only indirect influences on these entities through iterative changes in the grand strategy arising from feedback concerning the employee attitudes and behaviors occurring in response to the HR bundles.

Thus, we must infer that such interactions among the substrategies are consistent with Taggar et al.'s reasoning.

Another criticism of some approaches to SHRM theory and research is that concepts and measures are directed toward HR practices and policies that are treated as applying in a similar fashion to all employees of the organization (Chadwick & Cappelli, 1999; Ichniowski, Shaw, & Prennushi, 1997; Jackson, Schuler, & Rivero, 1989). Taggar and colleagues also avoid this concern. Following the findings of several studies (e.g., Rumelt, 1991; Lepak & Snell, 2002; MacDuffie, 1995) that show that HR practices differ across groupings of employees and that the links between HR practices and various outcome measures are stronger when examined within industrial or employee sectors rather than at aggregated levels, Taggar et al. argue that HR alignment should occur within the four employee segments that they describe (inner core, outer core, inner peripheral, outer peripheral).

One important conclusion that Taggar et al. reach is that the innovation substrategy and the associated innovation-focused HR subsystem are of primary importance to the level of sustainable competitive advantage that any organization can maintain. However, they note that success in achieving the innovation substrategy goals is not sufficient, because true organizational effectiveness can be realized only when the quality and cost substrategy goals are also met. The remainder of the present commentary focuses on issues associated with the innovation substrategy, given its centrality to Taggar et al.'s model and our own research interests.

THE INTEGRATED MODEL OF STRATEGY ALIGNMENT AND ORGANIZATIONAL INNOVATION

Taggar et al. present innovation either as being a general concept (i.e., the innovation substrategy) or as being focused on product development with an emphasis on marketing or branding aspects. In the former case, innovation appears like a "single entity" or a homogenous whole, and the generality of the term prevents us from outlining more precisely what can be expected from various actors in the organization. In the latter case, the concept is narrower than most definitions of organizational innovation imply. Thus, we would suggest adopting West and Farr's (1990) definition of innovation: "the intentional introduction and application within a role, group, or organization of ideas, processes, products, or procedures, new to the relevant unit of adoption, designed to significantly benefit the individual, the group, the organization, or wider society" (p. 9). This definition provides a broader scope for innovation and also suggests that innovation has the potential to occur at every level and in any part of the organization.

The overall innovation process can be parsed into four subprocesses: problem identification, idea generation, idea evaluation, and implementation of innovation. Farr, Sin, and Tesluk (2003) suggest that creativity is concerned with problem identification and idea generation, whereas innovation is concerned with idea evaluation and implementation of the innovation. Consistent with Farr et al. (2003) and other authors (e.g., Amabile, 1983; Kanter, 1988; Patterson, 2002; Staw, 1990), Bains and Tran (2006) propose a multi-level model of innovation in organizations (see Fig. 1). Their model is based on two underlying concepts: (1) these four subprocesses, which one can find at all levels of analysis and (2) Kanter's (1988) four-stage model, which includes coalition building, selling, transfer, and diffusion. Although the Bains–Tran model might appear to suggest that the innovation process is linear, these authors note that the process of innovation is nonlinear (cf. Anderson, De Dreu, & Nijstad, 2004), chaotic, iterative (cf. Drazin, Glynn, & Kazanjian, 1999), cyclical, and dynamically

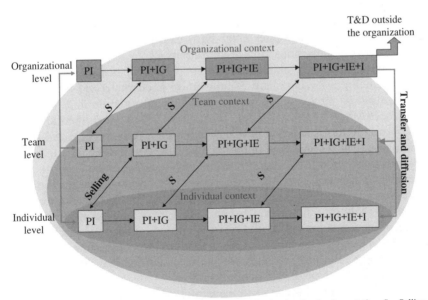

PI = Problem Identification; IG = Idea Generation; IE = Idea Evaluation; I = Implementation; S = Selling

Fig. 1. A Multi-Level Model of Creativity and Innovation.

evolving over time. That is, each innovation initiative goes in spirals of influencing, selling, sharing, dissenting, or converging within and across levels. The cycle of problem identification, idea generation, idea evaluation, and implementation repeats itself as necessary, within and across each level of analysis (i.e., individual, team, and organization).

The Inner Core and Innovation

In their second proposition (P2), Taggar et al. posit that the inner core employee segment makes the greatest contribution to achieving an organization's grand strategy. They further suggest that innovation is the single substrategy through which the grand strategy can be achieved. Thus, the inner core segment is responsible for generating and implementing innovation (P4). This section examines how innovation unfolds within the inner core through the lens of the Bains–Tran (2006) model.

For simplification purposes, we start from the individual level, which would apply to any individual belonging to the inner core. Because individuals are the conduits of idea generation, decision making, coalition building, implementation, and other mechanisms, processes, and tasks relevant to innovation, individuals will begin and complete the process of innovation, even though they may be organized into collective entities (teams, networks, divisions, and organizations).

The initial step in the innovation process is *problem identification* (PI; the first cell in Fig. 1). This phase of innovation is characterized by problem presentation or discovery, as well as gathering information and obtaining resources (Amabile, 1983; Kanter, 1988; Staw, 1990). Once the individual has been able to identify the problem, he or she enters the *idea generation* (IG) phase, which consists of initiating a new process that departs from the organization's routine (Kanter, 1988) and of generating possibilities through available pathways and the exploration of relevant features in the environment (Amabile, 1983). Even while generating ideas and working toward a solution, however, the individual may choose to revisit the problem identification phase and revise his or her conceptualization of the problem. Thus, the second cell at the individual level of the model depicted in Fig. 1 (i.e., PI + IG) represents the first step in the iterative process contributing to the prospective innovation.

Next, the individual proceeds to the *idea evaluation* (IE) phase. This phase consists of response validation, during which the response possibility chosen on a particular trial is considered. It is during this stage that the individual determines whether the product or response will be appropriate, useful, correct, or valuable (Amabile, 1983). A second iteration (the third cell in Fig. 1; PI + IG + IE) takes place during which the individual, while evaluating ideas to approach a solution to the problem, may reconsider some aspects of the problem and generate additional or different ideas that better fit the possible solution.

During the *implementation* (I) phase, the individual carries out a plan based on the decision processes that occurred during response validation (Amabile, 1983). At this point, effort is required to apply the solution to the current problem (Farr et al., 2003). During this stage, a third iteration occurs, which is the cumulative effect of PI + IG + IE + I. This iteration could indicate that an individual is ready to implement an innovation resulting from the three previous stages, or that, while ready to implement the innovation, the individual is reviewing all options to ensure that no stone has remained unturned. The individual may choose to return to an alternative stage (PI, IG, IE, I) sequentially or haphazardly depending on some combination of his or her cognitive style and working style.

At any stage, individuals may feel limited in their capacity to advance the innovation cycle, and they may decide to proceed with selling and coalition building (Kanter, 1988) to diffuse their ideas to higher levels (i.e., group or organization). Selling is a crucial part of the innovation process, as it acts to enable or diffuse an innovation. The extent of selling required may depend on the magnitude of the innovation considered. For example, it may be easier to convince team members to work on the improvement of a procedure; by contrast, it may require more time, resources, and commitment to work on the launch of a new product line. (The issue of incremental versus radical innovations is discussed in more detail later in this commentary.) Once the idea is sold to others – whether to a team or to the organization as a whole – the various stages of the innovation process are reiterated. This sequence is similar to the one described at the individual level, but the involvement of groups with a larger number of individuals ensures that complexity becomes increasingly greater as the level increases.

In their fifth proposition (P5), Taggar et al. posit that the inner core segment is most likely to achieve its substrategy goals when it is supported by an innovation HRM bundle. This is where grand strategy, HRM, and innovation come together. As Taggar et al. point out, top management may be a selected subgroup in the inner core, but the inner core also includes different levels of employees. Let us focus a moment on the inner core as top management team (TMT). In Bains and Tran's (2006) model, the organizational level can be represented by the CEO and his or her direct reports, which collectively form the TMT. Thus, the innovation process may be carried through by an individual or several individuals forming a team, similar to what we have described earlier in this commentary, except that the CEO and the TMT hold an overview of the organization. The problems they identify, the ideas they generate and evaluate, and their implementation decisions are made with a bird's-eye view of the organization and are similarly applicable to the entire organization. The actual implementation of those decisions, however, may be delegated to lower levels.

The organizational level can also be embedded in structures, networks, climate and culture, and organizations can provide support (or not) for innovation through these elements. A climate characterized by procedures, systems, and norms that encourage risk-taking behaviors, experimenting, cooperation, and tolerance for ambiguity and unpredictability (see Tesluk, Farr, & Klein, 1997) will increase the likelihood that all phases of the innovation process will be realized. Top managers can also influence creativity by endorsing and enacting assumptions, beliefs, and values that define an organizational culture supportive of innovation (Tesluk et al., 1997). Kanter (1988) recommends a culture encouraging diversity, flexibility, quick action, cross-fertilization, collective pride, and ultimately integration. Individuals and teams are more likely to implement ideas if they receive support from leaders and management (Axtell et al., 2000), their mistakes are tolerated (Zhou & Woodman, 2003), and they have more opportunities to participate in decision making (Axtell et al., 2000; West, 2002).

Organizational support becomes most important in the evaluation and implementation phases, as well as in the phase of diffusion and transfer of innovation outside the organization or back to the individual or group level for further iterations of the innovation process. Organizational-level factors essentially provide the structures and mechanisms by which innovation is enabled (or not). As components of an HRM bundle for innovation, Taggar et al. mention organic structure, knowledge-based authority, autonomy, empowerment, flexible job design, problem-solving teams, and encouragement of employee interaction and participation. These features are all included in the kind of organizational support described previously.

When examining creativity and innovation at the individual, group, organizational, and environmental levels, Mumford and Hunter (2005) point out the challenge of contradicting forces pulling processes in different directions. More specifically, it appears that the requirements for creativity and innovation observed at one level of analysis are not necessarily consistent with those observed at other levels of analysis. Mumford and

Hunter suggest how difficult it could be to form a truly comprehensive theory of creativity and innovation in organizations without understanding the nature and form of these interactions. For example, they note that creativity and innovation at the workgroup level depend on active, open, and collaborative exchanges and cooperation among group members, but that such cooperative exchanges are often not part of the typical behavior patterns of autonomous, competitive people who are focused on individual achievement.

In addition, Mumford and Hunter (2005) describe many of the contextual and social factors influencing collaboration among workgroup members, including leadership, justice perceptions, resource allocation norms, and social interaction norms. These factors suggest that effective performance management systems must be able to encourage both individual creative behaviors and group-based collaboration and knowledge-sharing behaviors that are required for the implementation of organizational innovation. Both Oldham (2003) and Lawler (2003), for example, note how various types of individual-, group-, and organization-based reward systems influence creativity, knowledge sharing, and individual behavior. Lawler (2003) further distinguishes reward systems that are focused on top management from those designed for lower levels of the organization.

It is also reasonable to suggest that individuals are not simply influenced by the groups in which they have formal membership, but can simultaneously occupy multiple roles within an organization (Drazin et al., 1999), thus creating multiple overlapping or non-overlapping networks through multiple memberships. During the process of selling, members of the inner core will necessarily reach out to other parts of the organizations and to other employee segments. The existence of that type of "networking" suggests that we should examine how creativity and innovation may emerge in these other segments.

Innovation in Other Employee Segments

In their sixth and seventh propositions (P6 and P7), Taggar et al. posit that the outer core is the second greatest contributor to achieving the grand strategy by maintaining and ensuring quality (or products, services, operations, and so on), and that employees of the outer core should be quality oriented. While focusing on this effort, managers and employees of this segment might potentially engage in various process-reengineering initiatives or continuous improvement programs, each of which requires the innovation sequence outlined by Bains and Tran (2006). We view quality-focused programs such as process reengineering and continuous improvement as being consistent with West and Farr's (1990) definition of innovation. In addition, while working on maintaining quality, members of the outer core may discover larger problems that need to be communicated to the inner core. Thus, effective communication between members of the two employee groups is vital.

The inner core might be the primary segment that focuses on major (or radical) innovation projects, but its primacy in this area should not and does not preclude the possibility that creativity and innovation might unfold in the other employee segments. For example, although Taggar et al. suggest the inner and outer periphery employee segments tend to focus on the cost reduction substrategy, the achievement of such strategic goals is likely to require novel approaches. Global competition creates economic pressures that necessitate cost reduction as an organizational goal. The proverb "Necessity is the mother of invention" notes the important role of creativity and innovation in implementing new cost reduction programs. The next section expands our thinking regarding the need for creativity and innovation in all employee segments with a more detailed consideration of the distinction between radical and incremental innovation.

INCREMENTAL VERSUS RADICAL INNOVATION

Given the framework of Bains and Tran (2006), creativity and innovation have the potential to occur at every level and in any part of the organization. The challenge comes from the processes that allow (or do not allow) for an idea to migrate to other parts of the organization, so that it gains greater legitimacy and wider support and ultimately becomes an innovation that is effectively implemented. We would argue that the encouragement of creative and innovative behaviors for all employee clusters is important for the effective accomplishment of the innovative substrategy of an organization. But, consistent with Taggar et al., we agree that the various employee clusters are differentially linked to the innovation process. We believe, however, that the importance of the employee clusters for achieving innovation goals is contingent on several attributes of the specific innovation process being considered.

Organizational innovations can be categorized in many ways. For purposes of illustrating our point, we will simply contrast radical innovations with incremental innovations. According to Subramaniam and

Youndt (2005), incremental innovations refine and improve existing products, services, and technologies, whereas radical innovations are major transformations that often result in making the current products, services, and technologies obsolete. Abernathy and Clark (1985) further note that incremental innovations apply the organization's existing knowledgebase, whereas radical innovations considerably reduce or even destroy the value of that knowledge.

While we might expect inner core employees to be especially critical for radical innovations (and perhaps outer core employees as well), the roles of the outer core and peripheral clusters may be more important for incremental innovations. Ideas for completely new products and services or the applications of cutting-edge technologies within an organization are likely to arise from the problem identification and idea generation processes of those employees charged with strategic thinking and environmental monitoring (i.e., the inner core). Inner core employees also exert control over organizational resources that can initiate implementation of large-scale change or radical innovation. Thus, the arguments of Taggar et al. that the inner core employee cluster is most important for achieving the innovation substrategy seem most applicable to radical innovation.

Conversely, creative ideas about how to improve existing products, services, and procedures often arise from those employees who are closest to the production of products, provision of services, and administration of operating procedures (i.e., the outer core and peripheral employees). Such incremental innovations may not require extensive resources or high-level approval to be implemented, so the outer core and peripheral clusters may be frequently critical in all phases of the incremental innovative process. For example, Axtell et al. (2000) describe research investigating factors that led shop-floor employees to suggest work process improvements and to implement effectively selected workplace changes.

Our point that the employee clusters described by Taggar et al. may be differentially important for various types of organizational innovations also implies that the organization's HR bundles of practices and policies should recognize that creative and innovative work behaviors and attitudes are desired in all employee clusters. Taggar et al. argue that the inner core cluster should have an HR bundle that emphasizes the innovation substrategy achievement, the outer core's HR bundle should emphasize achievement of the quality substrategy, and the inner peripheral's HR bundle should emphasize attainment of the low-cost substrategy. We agree that the HR bundles for the several employee clusters should differ, but suggest that organizations should consider both the types of innovations (radical, incremental, or both) needed to meet their substrategies (and grand strategy) and the general stages of the innovation process when designing the HR bundles.

Rank, Pace, and Frese (2004) note that the predictors of the creativity and innovation implementation stages of the overall innovation process differ in terms of the level or amount of the predictor variable that has been shown to encourage or facilitate effective employee behaviors for each stage. These authors discuss predictive differences in various individual, team, and organizational factors that can be linked to the presence of HR practices and policies. For example, they indicate that lower levels of external demands (e.g., low time pressure) are more conducive to idea generation, whereas strong external demands (e.g., high-performance goals) facilitate innovation implementation. Similarly, high levels of individualism may facilitate creativity, whereas moderate levels are associated with effective implementation of innovations. These findings are not inconsistent with Taggar et al.'s general point that HR and performance management systems require differentiation across employee segments, but add to the complexity of the issue by suggesting that organizational innovation is not a single entity, but rather is composed of multiple processes that themselves require differentiated HR and performance management approaches.

CONCLUSIONS

Taggar et al. argue that organizations should differentiate their HR practices for four employee sectors and that the HR bundle for the inner core sector should focus on enhancing innovation. Based on our line of arguments developed in this commentary, we propose to merge Taggar et al.'s IMSA with Bains and Tran's model (see Fig. 2). This merged model would address the need for greater flexibility in the organizational structures and for a flow of communication between the four segments to enhance the innovation process. We have argued that innovation can emerge in any of the four segments, even though the inner core has innovation (and probably more radical innovation than incremental innovation) as its primary performance objective. The three other segments contribute to the grand strategy by either developing incremental innovations or making contributions to the radical innovations initiated by the inner core.

We further suggest integrating the model shown in Fig. 2 with Wright and Snell's (1998) framework of fit and flexibility in SHRM, in which the authors propose three points of flexibility: "(1) developing HR systems that

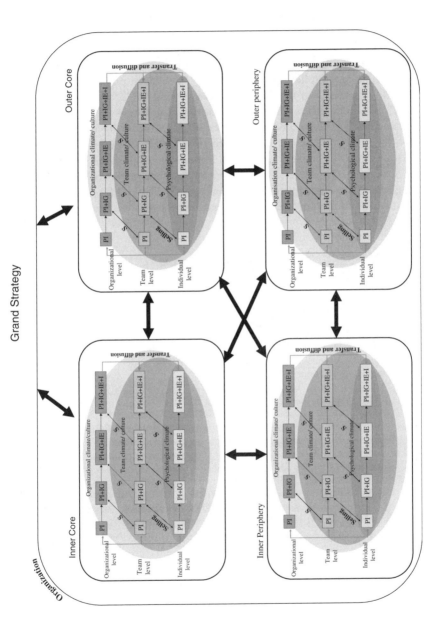

Fig. 2. An Integration of Taggar et al.'s IMSA and Bains and Tran's Multi-Level Model of Creativity and Innovation.

can be adapted quickly, (2) developing a human capital pool with a broad array of skills, and (3) promoting behavioral flexibility among employees" (p. 761). When the organizational strategy emphasizes innovation, the organization's intellectual and human capital is especially important. The many changes implied by innovation further emphasize the need for flexibility in terms of employee knowledge and skills. Amabile (1983) has noted the importance of domain-relevant knowledge for creativity and innovation. The dynamics of *which* knowledge and skills are relevant in an organization characterized by innovation further support the need for flexibility in HR practices to support knowledge acquisition and application to novel settings. Behavioral flexibility may be achieved only with the support of top organizational management to build and maintain an organizational climate and culture that fosters creativity and innovation.

REFERENCES

Abernathy, W. J., & Clark, K. (1985). Mapping the winds of creative destruction. *Research Policy, 14*, 3–22.

Amabile, T. M. (1983). The social psychology of creativity: A componential conceptualization. *Journal of Personality and Social Psychology, 45*, 357–376.

Anderson, N. R., De Dreu, C. K. W., & Nijstad, B. A. (2004). The routinization of innovation research: A constructively critical review of the state-of-the-science. *Journal of Organizational Behavior, 25*, 147–173.

Axtell, C. M., Holman, D. J., Unsworth, K. L., Wall, T. D., Waterson, P. E., & Harrington, E. (2000). Shopfloor innovation: Facilitating the suggestion and implementation of ideas. *Journal of Occupational and Organizational Psychology, 73*, 265–285.

Bains, P., & Tran, V. (2006, May 5–6). *Creativity and innovation: Taking it to the next level.* Paper presented at the 21st SIOP Annual Conference, Dallas, TX.

Becker, B., & Gerhart, B. (1996). The impact of human resource management on organizational performance: Progress and prospects. *Academy of Management Journal, 39*, 779–801.

Chadwick, C., & Cappelli, P. (1999). Alternatives to generic strategy typologies in strategic human resource management. In: P. Wright, L. Dyer, J. Boudreau & G. Milkovich (Eds), *Research in personnel and human resources management, supplement 4* (pp. 1–29). Stamford, CT: JAI Press.

Drazin, R., Glynn, M. A., & Kazanjian, R. K. (1999). Multilevel theorizing about creativity in organizations: A sensemaking perspective. *Academy of Management Review, 24*, 286–307.

Dyer, L., & Shafer, R. A. (1999). Creating organizational agility: Implications for strategic human resources management. In: P. Wright, L. Dyer, J. Boudreau & G. Milkovich (Eds), *Research in personnel and human resources management, supplement 4* (pp. 145–174). Stamford, CT: JAI Press.

Farr, J. L., Sin, H.-P., & Tesluk, P. E. (2003). Knowledge management processes and work group innovation. In: L. V. Shavinina (Ed.), *International handbook on innovation* (pp. 574–586). Amsterdam: Elsevier Science.

Ichniowski, C., Shaw, K., & Prennushi, G. (1997). The effects of human resource management practices on productivity: A study of steel finishing lines. *American Economic Review, 87*, 291–313.

Jackson, S. E., Schuler, R. S., & Rivero, J. C. (1989). Organizational characteristics as predictors of personnel practices. *Personnel Psychology, 42*, 727–786.

Kanter, R. M. (1988). When a thousand flowers bloom: Structural, collective, and social conditions for innovation in organizations. *Research in Organizational Behavior, 10*, 169–211.

Lawler, E. E. (2003). Reward systems in knowledge-based organizations. In: S. E. Jackson, M. A. Hitt & A. S. DeNisi (Eds), *Managing knowledge for sustained competitive advantage: Designing strategies for effective human resource management* (pp. 274–302). San Francisco: Jossey-Bass.

Lepak, D. P., & Snell, S. A. (2002). Knowledge management and the HR architecture. In: S. E. Jackson, M. A. Hitt & A. S. DeNisi (Eds), *Managing knowledge for sustained competitive advantage: Designing strategies for effective human resource management* (pp. 127–154). San Francisco: Jossey-Bass.

MacDuffie, J. (1995). Human resource bundles and manufacturing performance: Organizational logic and flexible production systems in the world auto industry. *Industrial and Labor Relations Review, 48*, 197–221.

Miles, R. H., & Snow, C. C. (1984). Fit, failure, and the hall of fame. *Academy of Management Review, 26*, 10–28.

Mumford, M. D., & Hunter, S. T. (2005). Innovation in organizations: A multi-level perspective on creativity. In: F. Dansereau & F. Yammarino (Eds), *Multi-level issues in strategy and methods* (Vol. 4, pp. 11–74). Oxford, UK: Elsevier.

Oldham, G. R. (2003). Stimulating and supporting creativity in organizations. In: S. E. Jackson, M. A. Hitt & A. S. DeNisi (Eds), *Managing knowledge for sustained competitive advantage: Designing strategies for effective human resource management* (pp. 274–302). San Francisco: Jossey-Bass.

Patterson, F. (2002). Great minds don't think alike? Person-level predictors of innovation at work. In: C. L. Cooper & I. T. Robertson (Eds), *International review of industrial and organizational psychology* (Vol. 17, pp. 115–144). Chichester, UK: Wiley.

Porter, M. E. (1980). *Competitive strategy: Techniques for analyzing industries and competitors.* New York: Free Press.

Rank, J., Pace, V. L., & Frese, M. (2004). Three avenues for future research on creativity, innovation, and initiative. *Applied Psychology: An International Review, 53*, 518–528.

Rumelt, R. P. (1991). How much does industry matter? *Strategic Management Journal, 12*, 167–186.

Schuler, R. S., & Jackson, S. (1987). Linking competitive strategies with human resource management practices. *Academy of Management Executive, 1*, 207–219.

Snell, S. A., Youndt, M. A., & Wright, P. M. (1996). Establishing a framework for research in strategic human resource management: Merging resource theory and organizational learning. In: G. R. Ferris (Ed.), *Research in personnel and human resources management* (Vol. 14, pp. 61–90). Greenwich, CT: JAI Press.

Staw, B. M. (1990). An evolutionary approach to creativity and innovation. In: M. A. West & J. L. Farr (Eds), *Innovation and creativity at work* (pp. 287–308). Chichester, UK: Wiley.

Subramaniam, M., & Youndt, M. A. (2005). The influence of intellectual capital on the types of innovative capabilities. *Academy of Management Journal, 3*, 450–463.

Taggar, S., Sulsky, L., & MacDonald, H. (this volume). Sub-system configuration: A model of strategy, context, and human resource management alignment. In: M. D. Mumford, S. T. Hunter & K. E. Bedell-Avers (Eds), *Research in multi-level issues* (Vol. VII). Oxford, UK: Elsevier.

Tesluk, P. E., Farr, J. L., & Klein, S. A. (1997). Influences of organizational culture and climate on individual creativity. *Journal of Creative Behavior, 31*, 27–41.

Tichy, N. M., Fombrun, C. J., & Devanna, M. A. (1982). Strategic human resource management. *Sloan Management Review, 23*(2), 47–60.

West, M. A. (2002). Sparkling fountains or stagnant ponds: An integrative model of creativity and innovation implementation in work groups. *Applied Psychology: An International Review, 51*, 355–424.

West, M. A., & Farr, J. L. (1990). Innovation at work. In: M. A. West & J. L. Farr (Eds), *Innovation and creativity at work* (pp. 3–13). Chichester, UK: Wiley.

Wright, P. M., & Snell, S. A. (1998). Toward a unifying framework for exploring fit and flexibility in strategic human resource management. *Academy of Management Review, 23*, 756–772.

Zhou, J., & Woodman, R. W. (2003). Managers' recognition of employees' creative ideas: A socio-cognitive model. In: L. V. Shavinina (Ed.), *The international handbook on innovation* (pp. 631–640). Amsterdam: Elsevier Science.

MULTI-LEVEL STRATEGIC HRM: FACILITATING COMPETITIVE ADVANTAGE THROUGH SOCIAL NETWORKS AND SUPPLY CHAINS

Anthony R. Wheeler, Jonathon R. B. Halbesleben and M. Ronald Buckley

ABSTRACT

Taggar, Sulsky, and MacDonald have presented an integrated model that links organizational strategy, the environment, and human resources management. This commentary analyzes their model, identifying a number of missed opportunities that are not adequately integrated into the model. Moreover, we propose two directions for expanding their model, including a consideration of social network theory and the global supply chain. By expanding Taggar et al.'s model to consider social networks and the supply chain, we believe that it will better capture the complexity of contemporary organizations while supporting the fecund ideas that Taggar et al. have proposed.

Multi-Level Issues in Creativity and Innovation
Research in Multi-Level Issues, Volume 7, 393–409
Copyright © 2008 by Elsevier Ltd.
All rights of reproduction in any form reserved
ISSN: 1475-9144/doi:10.1016/S1475-9144(07)00015-X

INTRODUCTION

Organizations are always on the lookout for ways to add value and increase their competitive advantage in the increasingly flat competitive marketplace. The last decade of research on strategic human resources management (SHRM) has unequivocally established the strong linkage between an organization's HRM effectiveness and its financial performance, primarily through increased employee productivity and retention (e.g., Datta, Guthrie, & Wright, 2005; Huselid, 1995). Moreover, Barney's (1991) resource-based view (RBV) of the organization has served as much of the theoretical reasoning behind the link between SHRM and organization performance (Wright, Dunford, & Snell, 2001). RBV posits that organizations primarily gain competitive advantage through "resources which are rare, valuable, inimitable, and nonsubstitutable" (Wright et al., 2001, p. 703). While RBV provides a sound theoretical base to support the voluminous empirical SHRM research, SHRM researchers have grappled with the practical implications of this theory (Barney, Wright, & Ketchen, 2001; Wright et al., 2001).

Among the main critiques of RBV applied to SHRM, SHRM proponents have questioned how organizations can truly develop and implement unique HRM systems that are not quickly imitated, absorbed, and adopted by competitor organizations (Lepak & Snell, 1999). Thus, many SHRM researchers have directed considerable attention to the issue of SHRM "configuration" or "architecture" (e.g., Lepak & Snell, 2002; Wright & Snell, 1998), which must support the organization's overall strategy. The level of analysis further compounds the analysis of the HRM configuration–strategy link. For example, Wright, Gardner, and Moynihan (2003) concluded that most SHRM research focuses on the organizational level, leaving the business-unit level underrepresented in SHRM research. Huselid (1995), in his seminal article, reasons that the SHRM–performance/turnover relationship logically extends from the organization level to the business-unit level to the individual level, so long as the SHRM systems support the organization strategy. It is this complex issue – the reciprocal nature of multi-level system configuration and corporate strategy – that Taggar, Sulsky, and MacDonald skillfully address in their chapter.

Taggar, Sulsky, and MacDonald (this volume) develop an integrated model of strategy alignment (IMSA) that addresses how organizations can develop and implement HRM systems that primarily add or create value for an organization at the unit or department level. Their model proposes that HRM system configuration necessarily depends on the organization's overall strategy, which consists of multiple unique substrategies. Taking full advantage of the organization's human capital becomes a function of configuring HRM systems around the substrategies that guide (or should guide) the work being accomplished in that unit. Taggar et al. then demonstrate how a particular HRM function – namely, performance appraisal – can be flexible enough to adapt to any substrategy of a unit in any organization. That is, the issue of SHRM configuration, in essence, is a strategy development issue, as a wide array of flexible HRM functions exist to simultaneously meet broad organization-level and narrow unit-level needs.

Building upon the strengths and opportunities presented by Taggar et al.'s chapter this commentary proposes that the issue of multi-level SHRM configuration is enhanced through examination of social network theory (Burt, 1982; Granovetter, 1973; Nadel, 1957) and the idea of the global supply chain (Bowersox, Daugherty, Droge, Rogers, & Wardlow, 1989). For anyone who has read Friedman's (2005) *The World Is Flat*, the issue of connectivity within organizations and between organizations necessarily influences how organizations can sustain competitive advantages by creating unique SHRM systems. Thus, this commentary seeks to suggest how social networks rooted within SHRM systems can provide that competitive advantage at multiple levels across, within, and between organizations.

In this commentary, we first examine Taggar et al.'s IMSA applied to SHRM. We then present social network theory (Burt, 1982; Granovetter, 1973; Nadel, 1957) as a plausible alternative to the IMSA. Next, we discuss implications for multi-level socially networked SHRM in the context of global supply chain management. Finally, we present future research suggestions based on our fusion of Taggar et al.'s model with our suggested modifications.

OPPORTUNITIES SEIZED AND OPPORTUNITIES MISSED

Taggar et al.'s rationale for the IMSA is logically linear; therefore, we do not summarize their main points here as much as we discuss their implications and the opportunities for clarification of the IMSA. We highlight four outstanding issues that need to be addressed by the IMSA:

- The IMSA, for the most part, resembles top-down or even matrix management, especially in its focus on independent subunit strategies and on the notion that only "core" employees add value to an organization.

• The IMSA emphasizes vertical fit between an organization's grand strategy, substrategies, and HRM practices to the detriment of horizontal fit among the HRM functions.
• The IMSA fails to address the legal ramifications – particularly equal employment opportunity and fair labor employment practices laws – of differentially bundling HRM practices within the same organization.
• While Taggar et al. explicitly shun "best practices" recommendations, they overlook several HRM practices that are, by definition, malleable.

Although we view these four issues as being interdependent, their root causes all relate to the lack of a coherent theoretical grounding.

Fig. 3 in Taggar et al.'s chapter illustrates the IMSA. The implications of this model are clear: While the environment or context influences the organization, it does so in a manner that influences the grand strategy of the organization. Any contextual forces buffeting the organization are then filtered through that grand strategy into lower substrategies. The internal environment of the organization, which is later defined as the organizational culture of the organization, links to neither the external environment nor the grand strategy. The unique HRM bundles then flow directly from each substrategy. The desired employee attitudes and behaviors – which we think should be attitudes related to turnover intentions and behaviors related to performance, but which Taggar et al. term "internal resources" such as organizational citizenship behaviors – then link back to the organization's grand strategy. No links exist between substrategies or the HRM bundles of the substrategies. Moreover, Taggar et al. do not specify whether the desired attitudes and behaviors that flow from each substrategy through the HRM bundles are related. In short, the IMSA emulates a traditional top-down, hierarchical model of organizational operation.

Our reading of the current SHRM literature places us at odds with such a traditional model. We find it easy to interpret Barney's (1991) RBV as a de facto call for independent HRM bundles, as Barney et al. (2001) summarize organizational resources and capabilities as "bundles of tangible assets, including ... organizational processes and routines" (p. 625). Wright et al. (2001), however, eschew the idea of HRM independence. Instead, they posit that organizations gain competitive advantages through SHRM practices only if resources and capabilities are interrelated. Moreover, consistent with Fiol, O'Conner, and Aguinis (2001), these authors note that in rapidly changing markets, SHRM practices are limited or hindered in developing sustained competitive advantages: SHRM systems simply cannot easily keep up with environmentally-induced changes in corporate strategy. That is, changes in the corporate strategy necessarily force organizations to adapt their HRM systems to those changes. Clearly, the more chaotic the environment in which an organization operates, the more slowly a top-down strategy with independent substrategies would respond to change (Webb & Pettigrew, 1999).

Our second issue relating to the IMSA centers on the lack of integration between HRM functions or bundles. Delery and Doty (1996) defined two types of SHRM integration: horizontal fit, which refers to "the internal consistency of the organization's HR policies and practices," and vertical fit, which refers to "the congruence of the HR system with other organizational characteristics, such as firm strategy" (p. 804). For SHRM to effectively yield increased performance at any level and decreased turnover, organizations must achieve both types of fit (Delery, 1998; Wright & McMahan, 1992). The IMSA appears to focus primarily on vertical fit. Assuming that each HRM bundle is strategically and operationally independent from other HRM bundles, any SHRM model must account for how each HRM function, even with a bundle, is integrated (Delery, 1998).

The SHRM literature regarding internal and external fit is clear on the issue of integration, yet this same literature presents many difficulties in achieving this integration. Wright and Snell (1998) postulate that "vertical fit is viewed as directing human resources toward the primary initiatives of the organization, whereas achievement of horizontal fit is viewed as instrumental for efficiently allocating those resources" (p. 756). MacDuffie (1995) found strong evidence that horizontally consistent HRM bundles increased productivity. Huselid (1995), by contrast, found that *both* horizontal and vertical fit increased organization financial performance. That is, Huselid found no evidence that either type of fit provided increased performance as compared with the other.

The need to balance these types of fit presents organizations with a number of difficult obstacles to overcome. An organization must first identify the skills and behaviors of employees that are dictated by the organization strategy, which then leads to the development and implementation of HRM practices that support those identified skills and behaviors (Wright & Snell, 1998). However, while the fairly straightforward link between strategy, horizontally and vertically integrated HRM systems, and performance in a stable environment makes sense, these relationships are more difficult to elucidate in unstable environments (Wright & Snell, 1998). Delery (1998) also notes that measuring HRM effectiveness across multiple levels of an organization is often difficult, yet is ultimately necessary for organizations that seek to maximize human capital even in unstable and changing environments. Thus, an organization must have enough technical expertise to measure HRM effectiveness accurately as well as enough flexibility in its HRM configuration across levels of the organization to adapt to any environment.

Wright and Snell (1998) give the most persuasive recommendations for balancing horizontal and vertical fit. They suggest utilizing HRM practices that grant lower-level managers the greatest flexibility in implementing them. Nevertheless, however they are implemented, these functions must be uniformly applied across jobs. That is, an organization can construct malleable HRM systems at the macro-level that give front-line managers enough flexibility to tailor them to specific jobs within subunits of the organization. We suggest and will later address some HRM practices that can help organizations achieve this delicate balance.

Our third concern relating to the IMSA focuses on the legal ramifications of independent HRM bundling across the same organization. If organizations implement truly unique HRM bundles across departments based on subunit strategy, those organizations could promote and even encourage employee behavior, at the managerial level, that violates fair pay and antidiscrimination laws. Suppose a manager in a subunit needs to hire a marketing employee, and that manager views marketing as a valuable function in achieving the unit's strategy. Would we recommend that this manager develop a completely unique and independent selection system for this position, even though the skills and aptitudes required for a marketing position would be fairly constant across an organization regardless of the unit or strategy? Likewise, we could imagine similar scenarios related to promotion and pay administration.

Clearly, providing too much discretion at lower levels of an organization might potentially lead to unforeseen adverse employment issues. These adverse employment issues would carry high costs for organizations when they would have to be addressed. Indeed, entire areas of organizational research are dedicated to understanding how perceived differences in selection, promotion, and pay policies may lead to destructive organizational attitudes and behaviors or inhibit positive behaviors (Ambrose & Cropanzano, 2003; Greenberg, 1993; Organ & Konovsky, 1989; Scandura, 1999).

All industrialized nations possess some form of employment discrimination and fair labor laws. These policies range from fairly liberal to conservative with the intention of protecting employees from unfair HRM-related practices (Aycan & Kanungo, 2001). Gender, race, religious, and disability biases have been demonstrated to creep into recruitment, selection, and promotion practices in organizations around the world

(Aycan et al., 2000; Cleveland, Murphy, & Williams, 1989; Katz, Hass, & Bailey, 1988).

For example, according to the US Department of Labor's Bureau of Labor and Statistics' (BLS) most recent summary of wages in the United States, US women on average earn four fifths of the wages paid to men holding the same job (BLS, 2004). Women also bump up against a *glass ceiling* that artificially limits promotion opportunities for females. While these wage and promotion differences have been attributed to the belief that women tend to take more breaks in their careers, purportedly to raise children, recent empirical research has discredited this myth (Lyness & Judiesch, 2001). An alternative hypothesis suggests that women and men differ in negotiation intensity, and managers, whether intentional or not, allow these pay and promotion differences to persist (Barron, 2003).

Our point here is that non-coordinated HRM policies allow human bias to adversely affect groups of employees. The more discretion, less direction, and less oversight a manager receives from the organization, the larger the opportunities for these biases to appear. In this regard, utilizing independent HRM bundles may lead to more costs than benefits; moreover, justifying biased bundles based on different substrategies may pose legal limitations.

Finally, we address the issue of flexible HRM best practices. We find a certain tautology to Taggar et al.'s avoidance of "best practices" recommendations. While we understand their underlying logic with respect to organizational variables (no two organizations share the exact strategies, operate in the exact same environment, and face the exact same competition), we do not share their avoidance of "best practices." Don't some organizations choose "best practices" HRM configurations that are entirely consistent with their firm strategies? Of course, organizational culture will dictate the adoption of certain HRM practices. Nevertheless, to completely shun "best practices" HRM configurations, even at the subunit level, ignores quite a bit of multi-level empirical evidence to the contrary. At the macro-level, Huselid (1995) identified 13 HRM practices and examined their influence on 968 organizations' financial performance. While he did not control for organizational culture, his large sample and robust statistical findings across organizations provide strong evidence that some HRM practices are, indeed, better than others, regardless of organizational culture or firm strategy.

Taggar et al. use the performance management function as an example of how organizations can implement HRM practices in accordance with the IMSA. As a counterpoint, we would mention the reliability and validity issues and the adverse behavioral consequences (Graves, 1982) of using the performance management practice of paired comparison. If we fail to recommend some form of a "best practice" for any given HRM function within a HRM bundle, do we run the risk of implying that *any* HRM practice will best serve an organization, even if that HRM practice is unreliable and invalid? An organization's strategy and culture might, in fact, support a HRM practice such as paired comparison that inevitably leads to adverse consequences for that organization. Echoing this point, Delery and Doty (1996) note that "conducting more valid performance appraisals or using more valid selection devices should always be better than using less valid measure" (p. 806). We would suggest that recognition and emulation of "best practices" – and not outright imitation – may be a simple way to increase the performance of an organization.

Decades of research at the micro-level on HRM practices strongly suggest that certain HRM practices are, in fact, more reliable and valid than others and promote individual performance and retention (Jackson & Schuler, 1995). Barrick and Mount's (1991) influential meta-analysis of the "Big Five" personality traits reported that conscientiousness predicts more variability in job performance across job titles, organizations, and industries than any of the remaining Big Five traits. Rynes, Brown, and Colbert (2002) conclude that intelligence is the single best predictor of performance across the board. Judge, Higgins, and Cable (2000) found that, depending on the type of interview used, interviews predict less performance variability than other selection tests but predict person–organization fit very well. The IMSA suggests that each unit of an organization pursue differential HRM bundling that is consistent with that unit's strategy. Would a multiple-hurdle selection system consisting of an IQ test, a conscientious test, and a behaviorally based interview fail to predict employee post-hire performance in any unit of any organization? If so, that unit would represent a massive series of human behavior anomalies.

The missing link in Taggar et al.'s supposition that each organizational unit must necessarily pursue unique HRM bundling is that HRM systems must be built around the job within the organization. Moreover, because most – if not all – organizations pursue performance-based missions, HRM bundles within an organization must support performance. In fact, several HRM "best practices" exist that allow organizations ample flexibility to adjust to subunit strategies. Job or work analysis is always contingent on the context of the organization, but it must be conducted so as to achieve horizontal integration among HRM practices. Management by objectives (MBO) performance management plans, as Taggar et al. note, distill organizational-level goals down to individual employees. MBO plans are individually negotiated, not universally applied. Broadband compensation plans allow organizations to pursue hybrid pay policies to meet external hiring and retention demands while maintaining employee motivation. These "best practices" can be bundled across units within organizations; moreover, they are easily horizontally integrated.

The SHRM configuration literature also clarifies this issue of "best practices" regardless of how someone conceptualizes the term "best practice." Similar to Taggar et al.'s IMSA, Lepak and Snell (2002) grappled with the issue of HRM configuration and organizational characteristics by examining four types of employment contracts (knowledge based, job based, contract, and alliance/partnership). They predicted that, based on the type of employment contract utilized, organizations should implement different HRM configurations to promote performance and retention. Lepak and Snell (2002) found that knowledge-based employment, which is characterized by core employees who "contribute to a firm's strategic objective" (p. 520), required commitment-based HRM configurations, which Arthur (1994) described as "systems [that] shape desired employee behaviors and attitudes by forging psychological links between organizational and employee goals" (p. 671). Commitment-based HRM systems likely include rigorous training and development, job designs that promote empowerment, commitment to employment security, aptitude-focused recruitment and selection, developmental performance appraisal systems, knowledge-based pay systems (e.g., skill-based pay versus job-based pay), and long-term incentives such as stock options (Lepak & Snell, 2002).

As organizations move to adopt job-based, contractual, or alliance/partnership-based employment contracts, their HRM configurations move toward productivity-based, compliance-based, or collaborative-based versions, respectively. The value of the relationship between the organization and the employee, which is based on the value that an individual employee adds to the organization, should dictate the level of HRM investment in an individual employee. For highly valued employees, an organization will invest in HRM to help maximize their performance while also working to retain those employees. Taggar et al.'s IMSA makes similar arguments; however, the IMSA does not address "nonvalued" employees in as much detail as it does valued employees. This neglect of nonvalued employees leaves us with the impression that the IMSA would decrease performance and increase turnover of these individuals. While poorer performance and retention of nonvalued employees would not cost an organization as much as it would if the same pattern held among valued employees, this neglect would certainly hurt an organization's bottom line in terms of turnover-associated costs (see Cascio, 1991).

We cannot overemphasize the need for close relationships between SHRM architecture, HRM bundling, performance, and turnover. The value of any conceptual model that is theoretically grounded is its ability to address *what*, *when*, *how*, and *why* (Bacharach, 1989). Our reading of Taggar et al.'s and interpretation of the IMSA lead us to conclude that this model clearly addresses the *what* and *when* issues, but does not fully address the *how* and *why* issues. We believe that Taggar et al. could improve the IMSA by adding social network theory (Burt, 1982; Granovetter, 1973; Nadel, 1957) to better integrate the HRM-bundling concept between substrategies.

SOCIAL NETWORK THEORY: AN ALTERNATIVE

Wasserman and Faust (1994) described the basic components of a social network: the actor, the relational tie, the number and level of others tied to the actor (e.g., dyad, triad, subgroup, group, department, division, organization), the relation among those parties, and the total network. Social networks describe the connectivity of actors within any given network. Some actors and connections within a network become so central or valued to other actors in the network that they are recognized as resources (termed *social capital*) to others in the network (Borgatti & Foster, 2003). In a strong network, each actor adds unique value to the entire network; thus, weak ties and actors are either eliminated from the network or provided intra-network resources to succeed (Burt, 1992). We believe that the addition of social network theory will strengthen Taggar et al.'s IMSA, as both social networks and SHRM focus on adding value at multiple levels in an organization.

In reading Taggar et al.'s chapter, we noted several opportunities where social network theory would strengthen the rationale behind the IMSA. First, social network theory will address the lack of horizontal and vertical fit in the IMSA. As the grand strategy of the organization permeates all levels of the organization, certain employees will most likely drive the distilling of this strategy (e.g., CEO, heads of divisions). While Taggar et al.'s Principle 3 states that employees do not equally contribute to the grand strategy, we wonder if these authors would agree that the more the employees who do contribute to the grand strategy, the better that organization's performance will become. In social network-speak, spanning the structural holes within the network makes the network strong and better performing. HRM scholars have begun to apply social network principles to various HRM systems, and have found encouraging empirical support for the application of social networks in HRM (Collins & Clark, 2003; Evans &

Davis, 2005; Williamson & Cable, 2003). Later in this commentary, we outline how the IMSA can become socially networked HRM.

The IMSA and SHRM literature inherently assume that HRM will be part of the organization's strategy; thus, a senior HRM executive will likely be responsible for converting the grand strategy into HRM terminology. As we have suggested, several HRM practices exist that are broadly defined and flexible (e.g., MBO). These broad HRM practices will serve as the guiding principle for organizations to gain value through SHRM practices; moreover, having broadly stated HRM practices at the organization level, which will be uniformly applied across divisions and departments of the organization, should satisfy legal requirements. The senior HRM executive then becomes, in social network terminology, an actor at the top level. To the extent that this senior HRM executive engages other employees at every level of the organization, preferably communicating the purposes and practices of HRM in the organization, he or she creates strong HRM-related ties, which will add value to the organization.

Not only should this senior HRM executive create strong ties among other senior executives, but he or she should also foster strong dyadic ties with the employees at the head of each substrategy in the IMSA. Ideally, each subunit should employ a top-level HRM employee. These subunit HRM heads will then have triadic ties across subunits with one another. In this way, the HRM subunit leaders will strengthen ties among subunits and share resources. Finally, these HRM subunit heads will create strong ties with the managers and employees within each subunit. It is in these subunit ties that innovative applications of grand-level HRM strategies will be implemented to customize the final HRM bundles within each subunit. A stronger HRM social network should develop if the HRM employees at each level strengthen ties both vertically and horizontally within the network. A social network model of these relationships appears in Fig. 1.

Finally, a socially networked SHRM system will facilitate increased responsiveness to environmental demands. Taggar et al.'s IMSA specifies that environmental factors influence only macro-level strategic formulation. Modern organizations, however, typically experience these environmental forces at every level of the organization, including the micro-level selection of specific HRM practices (Chow, 2004). Taggar et al. also properly note the role of an organization's culture in the process of developing its grand strategy, substrategies, and HRM practices. The organizational culture must support and reinforce these components, which necessarily means that this culture must also support and reinforce any social networks with the organization. Stronger social HRM networks are more "plugged in," both

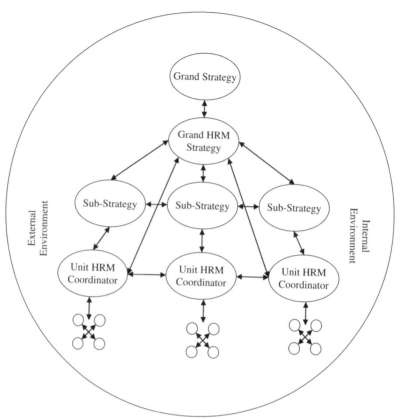

Fig. 1. Socially Networked SHRM Version of IMSA Focusing on Performance.

internally and externally, so that individual, unit, and organization performance are maximized. In fact, when we examined the different industry configurations presented by Taggar et al., we thought that these configurations looked like social network models.

MULTIPLE LEVELS OF HRM WITHIN GLOBAL SUPPLY CHAINS

The parsimony of social network theory is that it provides a meaningful logic describing how resources are shared across multiple levels of organizations and between organizations to add value (Oh, Labianca, & Chung, 2006). We previously addressed intra-organization social networks; we now turn to inter-firm social networks. While Taggar et al. did not address between-firm issues related to the IMSA, organizations increasingly operate in an environment of global supply chains in an effort to efficiently deliver their products to the intended markets. Hult, Ketchen, & Slater (2004) describe a supply chain as "a network of actors that transforms raw materials in distributed products" (p. 241). Consistent with Taggar et al.'s focus on core employees, global supply chain operations consist of numerous organizations that are integrated strategically, operationally, and technologically (Hult et al., 2004), working in a coordinated effort, from research, development, and manufacturing to distributing and marketing, to bring sometimes a single product to consumers.

As organizations seek to increase productivity and efficiency within their global supply chains through continuous improvement practices (Hult, Ketchen, & Nichols, 2002), supply chain scholars and HRM scholars have posited that one area of improved efficiency within a supply chain might improve HRM effectiveness (Richey & Wheeler, 2004). However, with the exception of examining discrete HRM functions such as selection (Richey, Tokman, & Wheeler, in press) and training (Gowen & Tallon, 2003), no research exists examining wholesale SHRM effectiveness within organizations in a single supply chain as a means of increasing performance and employee retention. Taggar et al.'s IMSA, with its emphasis on vertical fit, coupled with a more expansive view provided by social network theory, might provide a feasible model of understanding SHRM within the global supply chain context. If organizations with a single supply chain share SHRM resources throughout the supply chain, it seems logical that the entire supply chain should become higher performing.

FUTURE RESEARCH AND CONCLUSIONS

The process of investigating SHRM and multi-level social networks presents numerous opportunities and obstacles. Little research currently exists that examines multi-level HRM, with Whitener (2001) being a notable exception. Compounding the paucity of multi-level HRM analysis is the dearth of SHRM research that utilizes social network theory. This is a great example of where "a negative times a negative does not equal a positive." While the theory appears promising, the methodological and analytical difficulties surrounding both multi-level research and social network research (Contractor, Wasserman, & Faust, 2006) are daunting. Nevertheless, Taggar et al.'s IMSA, with some modifications, might help to better elucidate some of these issues.

An industry that highlights the benefits of integrating social networks and supply chain thinking with the IMSA is health care. The US health-care industry poses some challenges for the IMSA, particularly because it requires unusual combinations of substrategies (e.g., innovation is required to address complex and unique cases, but it must incorporate principles of quality such as zero error tolerance) and a challenging employee centrality sphere where it is difficult to separate core and peripheral employees (e.g., the cleaning staff of a hospital would rarely be considered peripheral, as they are absolutely critical to maintaining hygiene and, therefore, to the health of patients). Adding complexity is the unique nature of staffing, where a key driver in the grand strategy (physicians) may actually be a part of the external environment and outside the reach of HRM policies and practices. Finally, supply chain issues are critical, as the efficiency and quality goals of payers (e.g., insurance companies, government) are increasingly driving the manner in which care is provided.

As a result, to support the grand strategy of health care, a fully networked approach to HRM that takes into account integration of the supply chain is absolutely essential. The creation of independent substrategies and different HRM practices and policies has been particularly problematic for health care in the past because it reinforces the silos that have developed between occupational groups and that have led to lower-quality or more expensive health care (cf. Khatri, Baveja, Boren, & Mammo, 2006). As yet, research has not examined these relationships in the health-care industry, so this industry may serve as a valuable subject for testing the IMSA and some of our suggested modifications.

In summary, while we acknowledge the fine contributions that Taggar et al. have made in modeling the important linkages between organizational strategy, the environment, and human resources management, further consideration of their model suggests a myriad of opportunities for expansion. By expanding the model and integrating social networks and the supply chain, we believe the model will be able to better capture the complexity of contemporary organizations while supporting the novel and insightful ideas that Taggar et al. have proposed.

REFERENCES

Ambrose, M. L., & Cropanzano, R. (2003). A longitudinal analysis of organizational fairness: An examination of reactions to tenure and promotion decisions. *Journal of Applied Psychology, 88*, 266–275.

Arthur, J. B. (1994). Effects of human resource systems on manufacturing performance and turnover. *Academy of Management Journal, 37*, 670–687.

Aycan, Z., & Kanungo, R. M. (2001). Cross-cultural industrial and organizational psychology: A critical appraisal of the field and future direction. In: N. Anderson, D. S. Ones, H. K. Sinangil & C. Viswesvaran (Eds), *Handbook of industrial, work and organizational psychology* (Vol. 1, pp. 385–408). Thousand Oaks, CA: Sage.

Aycan, Z., Kanungo, R. M., Mendonca, M., Yu, K., Deller, J., Stahl, J., & Kurshid, A. (2000). The impact of culture on human resource management practices: A ten-country comparison. *Applied Psychology: An International Review, 49*, 192–220.

Bacharach, S. B. (1989). Organizational theories: Some criteria for evaluation. *Academy of Management Review, 14*, 496–515.

Barney, J. B. (1991). Firm resources and sustained competitive advantage. *Journal of Management, 17*, 99–120.

Barney, J. B., Wright, M., & Ketchen, D. J., Jr. (2001). The resource-based view of the firm: Ten years after. *Journal of Management, 27*, 625–641.

Barrick, M. R., & Mount, M. K. (1991). The big-five personality dimensions and job performance: A meta-analysis. *Personnel Psychology, 44*, 1–26.

Barron, L. A. (2003). Ask and you shall receive: Gender differences in negotiators' beliefs about requests for higher salary. *Human Relations, 56*, 635–662.

Borgatti, S. P., & Foster, P. C. (2003). The network paradigm in organizational research: A review and typology. *Journal of Management, 29*, 991–1013.

Bowersox, D. J., Daugherty, P. J., Droge, C. L., Rogers, D. S., & Wardlow, D. L. (1989). *Leading edge logistics: Competitive positioning for the 1990s.* Oak Brook, IL: Council of Logistics Management.

Bureau of Labor and Statistics. (2004). Median usual weekly earnings of full-time wage and salary workers by detailed occupation and sex. www.bls.gov

Burt, R. S. (1982). *Toward a structural theory of action.* New York: Academic Press.

Burt, R. S. (1992). *Structural holes: The social structure of competition.* Cambridge, MA: Harvard University Press.

Cascio, W. F. (1991). *Costing human resources.* Boston: PWS-Kent.

Chow, F. H. (2004). The impact of institutional context on human resource management in three Chinese societies. *Employee Relations, 26*, 626–642.

Cleveland, J. N., Murphy, K. R., & Williams, R. E. (1989). Multiple uses of performance appraisal: Prevalence and correlates. *Journal of Applied Psychology, 74*, 130–135.

Collins, C. J., & Clark, K. D. (2003). Strategic human resource practices, top management team social networks, and firm performance: The role of human resource practices in creating organizational competitive advantage. *Academy of Management Journal, 46*, 740–751.

Contractor, N. S., Wasserman, S., & Faust, K. (2006). Testing multitheoretical, multilevel hypotheses about organizational networks: An analytic framework and empirical example. *Academy of Management Review, 31*, 681–703.

Datta, D. K., Guthrie, J. P., & Wright, P. M. (2005). Human resource management and labor productivity: Does industry matter? *Academy of Management Journal, 48*, 135–145.

Delery, J. E. (1998). Issues of fit in strategic human resource management: Implications for research. *Human Resource Management Review, 8*, 289–309.

Delery, J. E., & Doty, D. H. (1996). Modes of theorizing in strategic human resource management: Tests of universalistic, contingency, and configurational performance predictions. *Academy of Management Journal, 39*, 802–835.

Evans, W. E., & Davis, W. D. (2005). High-performance work systems and organizational performance: The mediating role of internal social structure. *Journal of Management, 31*, 758–775.

Fiol, C. M., O'Conner, E. J., & Aguinis, H. (2001). All for one and one for all? The development and transfer of power across organization levels. *Academy of Management Review, 26*, 224–242.

Friedman, T. L. (2005). *The world is flat: A brief history of the twenty-first century*. New York: Farrar, Straus, and Giroux.

Gowen, C. R., III., & Tallon, W. J. (2003). Enhancing supply chain practices through human resource management. *Journal of Management Development, 22*, 32–44.

Granovetter, M. (1973). The strength of weak ties. *American Journal of Sociology, 78*, 1360–1380.

Graves, J. P. (1982). Let's put the appraisal back in performance appraisal: II. *Personnel Journal, 61*, 918–923.

Greenberg, J. (1993). Stealing in the name of justice: Informational and interpersonal moderators of theft reactions to underpayment inequity. *Organizational Behavior and Human Decision Processes, 54*, 81–104.

Hult, G. T. M., Ketchen, D. J., Jr., & Nichols, E. L., Jr. (2002). An examination of cultural competitiveness and order fulfillment cycle time within supply chains. *Academy of Management Journal, 45*, 577–586.

Hult, G. T. M., Ketchen, D. J., Jr., & Slater, S. F. (2004). Information processing, knowledge development, and strategic supply chain performance. *Academy of Management Journal, 47*, 241–253.

Huselid, M. A. (1995). The impact of human resource management practices on turnover, productivity, and corporate financial performance. *Academy of Management Journal, 38*, 635–672.

Jackson, S. E., & Schuler, R. S. (1995). Understanding human resource management in the context of organizations and their environments. *Annual Review of Psychology, 46*, 237–264.

Judge, T. A., Higgins, C. A., & Cable, D. M. (2000). The employment interview: A review of recent research and recommendations for future research. *Human Resource Management Review, 10*, 383–406.

Katz, I., Hass, R. G., & Bailey, J. (1988). Attitudinal ambivalence and behaviors toward people with disabilities. In: H. E. Yuker (Ed.), *Attitudes toward persons with disabilities* (pp. 47–57). New York: Springer.

Khatri, N., Baveja, A., Boren, S. A., & Mammo, A. (2006). Medical errors and quality of care: From control to commitment. *California Management Review, 48*(3), 113–141.

Lepak, D. P., & Snell, S. A. (1999). The human resource architecture: Toward a theory of human capital allocation and development. *Academy of Management Review, 24*, 31–48.

Lepak, D. P., & Snell, S. A. (2002). Examining human resource architecture: The relationships among human capital, employment, and human resource configurations. *Journal of Management, 28*, 517–543.

Lyness, K. S., & Judiesch, M. K. (2001). Are female managers quitters? The relationships of gender, promotion, and family leaves of absence to voluntary turnover. *Journal of Applied Psychology, 86*, 1167–1178.

MacDuffie, J. (1995). Human resource bundles and manufacturing performance: Organizational logic and flexible production systems in the world auto industry. *Industrial and Labor Relations Review, 48*, 197–221.

Nadel, S. F. (1957). *The theory of social structure.* Glencoe, IL: Free Press.

Oh, H., Labianca, G., & Chung, M. H. (2006). A multilevel model of group social capital. *Academy of Management Review, 31*, 569–582.

Organ, D. W., & Konovsky, M. (1989). Cognitive versus affective determinants of organizational citizenship behavior. *Journal of Applied Psychology, 74*, 157–164.

Richey, R. G., Tokman, M., & Wheeler, A. R. (in press). A supply chain manager selection methodology empirical test and suggested application. *Journal of Business Logistics.*

Richey, R. G., & Wheeler, A. R. (2004). A three hurdle model of supply chain manager selection. *Journal of Marketing Channels, 11*, 89–104.

Rynes, S. L., Brown, K. G., & Colbert, A. E. (2002). Seven common misconceptions about human resource practices: Research findings versus practitioner beliefs. *Academy of Management Executive, 16*, 92–103.

Scandura, T. A. (1999). Rethinking leader-member exchange: An organizational justice perspective. *Leadership Quarterly, 10*, 25–40.

Taggar, S., Sulsky, L., & MacDonald, H. (this volume). Sub-system configuration: A model of strategy, context, and human resource management alignment. In: M. D. Mumford, S. T. Hunter & K. E. Bedell-Avers (Eds), *Research in multi-level issues* (Vol. VII). Oxford, UK: Elsevier.

Wasserman, S., & Faust, K. (1994). *Social network analysis: Methods and applications.* New York: Cambridge University Press.

Webb, D., & Pettigrew, A. (1999). The temporal development of strategy: Patterns in the UK insurance industry. *Organization Science, 10*, 601–621.

Whitener, E. M. (2001). Do "high commitment" human resource practices affect employee commitment? A cross-level analysis using hierarchical linear modeling. *Journal of Management, 27*, 515–536.

Williamson, I. O., & Cable, D. M. (2003). Organizational hiring patterns, interfirm network ties, and interorganizational imitation. *Academy of Management Journal, 46*, 349–358.

Wright, P. M., Dunford, B. B., & Snell, S. A. (2001). Human resources and the resource based view of the firm. *Journal of Management, 27*, 701–721.

Wright, P. M., Gardner, T. M., & Moynihan, L. M. (2003). The impact of HR practices on the performance of business units. *Human Resource Management Journal, 13*, 21–36.

Wright, P. M., & McMahan, G. C. (1992). Theoretical perspectives for strategic human resource management. *Journal of Management, 18*, 295–320.

Wright, P. M., & Snell, S. A. (1998). Toward a unifying framework for exploring fit and flexibility in strategic human resource management. *Academy of Management Review, 23*, 756–772.

A MODEL OF STRATEGY, CONTEXT, AND HUMAN RESOURCE MANAGEMENT ALIGNMENT

Simon Taggar, Heather MacDonald and Lorne Sulsky

ABSTRACT

This response addresses the central issues raised by the commentaries on our earlier chapter. The intent here is to clarify issues that may have been insufficiently explicated in our original treaties. These include the distinction between core and other employee groups, the importance of horizontal fit among the human resources management (HRM) practices, and the importance of job analysis principles when considering innovative activities throughout firms.

INTRODUCTION

We thank the authors of the commentaries related to our earlier chapter for their insights on the model we presented. For purposes of organization, the present response begins with the commentary provided by Wheeler, Halbesleben, and Buckley (this volume) and addresses the four primary

Multi-Level Issues in Creativity and Innovation
Research in Multi-Level Issues, Volume 7, 411–420
Copyright © 2008 by Elsevier Ltd.
All rights of reproduction in any form reserved
ISSN: 1475-9144/doi:10.1016/S1475-9144(07)00016-1

concerns that form the basis of their commentary. Next we turn our attention to the interesting insights offered by Farr and Tran (this volume), highlighting the opportunities they introduce for furthering the theoretical and practical import of our model.

Before turning our attention to the commentaries, however, we must emphasize that our earlier chapter was largely based on systems theory (Bertalanffy, 1950) and, as such, has its roots in coherent theoretical grounding. Wheeler at al. (this volume) note a lack of theoretical grounding as problematic for our model. Perhaps some of the commentaries' questions actually stem from a lack of understanding or appreciation of our theoretical orientation. In case we were not clear enough in our previous chapter concerning this point, we would like to briefly review the conceptual foundation that underlies our model.

SYSTEMS THEORY

Becker and Huselid (2006) state that the "HR system – firm performance link is not as direct as suggested by the prior SHRM [strategic human resources management] literature" (p. 901). That is, intermediate outcomes exist that must be explored (Becker & Gerhart, 1996). Kozlowski and Klein (2000) take a systems theory perspective to understanding multi-level issues in organizations. Accordingly, we adopt a systems theory perspective for examining potential intermediate mechanisms and business processes involved in business strategy implementation.

The overarching theme of systems theory is the formalization and rationalization of work processes and rewards to achieve organizational goals (Waring, 1992). The key assumption underlying this theory is that work processes can be formalized and rationalized to optimize productivity. This is in contrast to normative approaches where "satisfaction of employees' needs by organizations, teams, and their leaders not only causes employees' personal satisfaction, trust, and loyalty, but also unleashes powerful drives in them to achieve the collective's goals and to freely, creatively, and continuously improve the processes necessary to achieve these goals" (Abrahamson, 1997, p. 496).

A system (e.g., a business unit) is composed of regularly interacting or interrelating groups of activities (subsystems) that, when taken together, form a new whole (Kauffman, 1980). In most cases, this whole has properties that cannot be found in its constituent elements. From a human resources

(HR) perspective, we proposed three constituent parts of a business unit based on the three distinct HR strategies, or HR management (HRM) systems, put forth by Schuler and Jackson (1987). In the integrated model of strategy alignment (IMSA), subsystems were not organizational units (see Figs. 4 to 9 in our chapter). Rather, employees contribute to the grand strategy through the achievement of the goals associated with subsystems (i.e., innovation, low cost, or quality goals).

RESPONSE TO WHEELER ET AL.'S COMMENTARY

Issue 1

Having briefly reviewed the origins of our model, we now address the major themes arising from the critical analysis provided by Wheeler et al. (this volume). The first issue these authors raise suggests that we adopted a top-down perspective whereby value added is related to where employees reside within the organization (i.e., core versus peripheral).

In terms of strategy formulation and implementation, we did, indeed, adopt a top-down model. Wheeler et al., however, are incorrect when they suggest our analysis indicates that *only* "core" employees add value to an organization. Rather, the word "especially" is a more accurate portrayal of our viewpoint. That is, we maintain that inner-core employees, by virtue of their position and influence, are *especially* able to create and maintain the most value. This statement does not logically imply that other employees, including those in the outer core or even in the periphery, cannot or should not add value. In fact, organizational success depends on the goal associated with each substrategy being achieved effectively and efficiently.

In addition to being based on systems theory, the IMSA is consistent with the traditional management approach, which starts with top management's identification of strategic goals based on an analysis of the external business environment (i.e., situational analysis). In this sense, the model is supported by research showing that most business goals and objectives are developed at top management levels (Bartlett & Ghoshal, 1993; Chandler, 1962), as depicted in Fig. 3 in our original chapter (Taggar, Sulsky, & MacDonald, this volume). Consistent with our model and grounded in the theory of upper echelons (Hambrick & Mason, 1984), research on the top management teams (TMTs) suggests that firm performance is the result of the collective characteristics and actions of a central group of managers.

Fig. 3 illustrates how grand strategies help align substrategies or subsystem goals. That is, although the external business environment influences the organization at multiple points, top management generally develops the overall *strategic direction* of the organization by taking into account both the external environment and the internal employee behavior. Although Fig. 3 does not address organizational culture, we note in the chapter that the degree to which the strategy, work, people, structure, and culture are smoothly aligned will determine the organization's ability to compete and succeed. We go on to explain that each subsystem develops a supporting culture that can, in turn, be influenced by the external environment. For instance, perceptions of external wage inequity will affect employee attitude and behavior. As shown in Fig. 3, both attitudes and behaviors (of which intentions to quit, absenteeism, exiting, citizenship, and commitment are just a few of many possible examples) influence the organization's ability to achieve its grand strategy.

Deciding on goals at the highest level and then cascading those goals throughout an organization is considered efficient (Sy & D'Annunzio, 2005; Galbraith, 2000). However, it does not logically follow that management ignores bottom-up information or that such information is unimportant. As Farr and Tran (this volume) note in their commentary, such information is critical both in making the correct strategic decisions and in implementing a chosen strategy. Nonetheless, we maintain that goals associated with subsystems are still tied to the organization's vision and that top management decides which goals are the most important.

Issue 2

The second issue raised by Wheeler et al. (this volume) concerns our ostensible overemphasis of vertical fit without due regard to the importance of horizontal fit. In fact, horizontal fit is a central feature of the IMSA, although this point might not have been immediately obvious. To understand our position, it is instructive to briefly review how we perceive the link between HR and substrategies.

Consider the case of innovation. Innovation is a goal of one organizational subsystem. Achievement of the goal of innovation is facilitated by the HR polices, practices, and culture in the innovation subsystem. That is, the work context should encourage innovation, and employees should be selected in part because they possess attributes related to creativity. According to Schuler and Jackson (1987), this outcome can be achieved through adoption of policies and practices that make up an innovation HR strategy.

The IMSA makes salient contextual heterogeneity in substrategies, subsystems, and HR bundles. Based on systems theory, it notes the need for HR bundles to vertically align with substrategies (e.g., innovation) rather than with the grand strategy. Also, the model makes salient the need to align HR practices horizontally within a bundle to achieve the goal espoused by the substrategy.

As Becker and Huselid (2006) note, "first, internal fit should have no value in the absence of external fit," and "second, if the HR architecture, and by definition this means the elements within that architecture, is focused on executing the strategic business process, the architecture will necessarily have internal fit" (p. 909). Fig. 3 and its accompanying text illustrate the point that vertical alignment requires goals and substrategies to be congruent with each other. Consistent with Becker and Huselid's view, careful assessment of the IMSA should also lead the reader to conclude that HR practices elicit appropriate behaviors necessary to achieve substrategy goals (i.e., horizontal alignment).

Of course, the focus on fit makes the IMSA vulnerable to two concerns common to all fit-based models. Specifically, we make normative statements about what organizations *should* do rather than descriptive statements about what they *actually* do (cf. Zajac, Kraatz, & Bresser, 2000). In addition, as the commentators correctly note, fit-based approaches create a tension between the benefits of fit and its constraints on flexibility (cf. Becker & Huselid, 2006).

Issues 3 and 4

Wheeler et al. (this volume) raise important issues concerning legal defensibility and best practices. Rather than adopting a strict contextual or situational framework, we endorse an integrationist perspective. This perspective acknowledges best practices while addressing the need to tailor HR practices and policies commensurate with the needs of the subsystem in a legally defensible manner. The application of a best practice should take into account strategic considerations as a contextual influence (as the example on performance appraisal validity in our previous chapter demonstrates).

Consider, for example, jobs that involve innovation. One could argue that innovation is a competency required for any job. Of course, we do not advocate an allocation of all jobs that involve innovation to the inner core.

Part of a job analysis should involve the determination of how critical innovation is for the job under scrutiny. In job analysis terms, (1) if a large amount of the total time on a job is spent being innovative, (2) if innovation contributes to differentiating successful employees from the less successful ones, and (3) if innovation is very important to successful job performance, then the job should be considered part of the inner core. Even when innovation is an appropriate job descriptor for two jobs, operationalizing innovation in terms of its importance, frequency of use, and contribution to variance in performance or level required is important to understanding how two jobs differ in terms of innovation.

Now suppose that job analysis determines that innovation is not critical for a job, but the organization believes that competitive advantage may be achieved by stressing and promoting innovation within a particular job. Such a job may currently reside in the outer core or even in the periphery. The organization could redesign this job such that innovation becomes a critical component, effectively moving it into the inner core.

Determining which job is, or should be, placed under which HR bundle will force HR/OB/I-O psychology practitioners and researchers to think strategically. For instance, in our chapter we described how Second Cup is unique in that retail baristas are treated like core employees. In this case, these employees have the potential to improve customer service through innovation. By contrast, Porter (1996) described strategic activity systems in airline, retail furniture, and financial service industries, noting how "limited" customer service is as a dimension of effective strategy in two of the three companies he studied.

RESPONSE TO FARR AND TRAN'S COMMENTARY

We appreciated the analysis conducted by Farr and Tran (this volume) because it allows us the opportunity to elaborate on the issue of criticality of innovation within a job. West and Farr (1990) define innovation as the "the intentional introduction and application within a role, group, or organiza-tion of ideas, processes, products, or procedures, new to the relevant unit of adoption, designed to significantly benefit the individual, the group, the organization, or wider society" (p. 9). Consistent with this definition, Bains and Tran (2006) note that creativity and innovation have the potential to occur at every level and in any part of the organization.

Porter (1996) distinguished between managerial decisions that create competitive advantage and those that simply improve operational excellence.

In a similar way, IMSA seeks to distinguish between innovation that creates competitive advantage and innovation that improves operational excellence. Although we agree that creativity and innovation have the potential to occur and add some value at every level of a firm, the types of creativity and innovation that may arise in different jobs within an organization should be assessed in pragmatic terms through a job analysis.

In considering job analyses, it becomes clear that innovation is a central part of some jobs, is not so important for other jobs, and is potentially detrimental for still other jobs (e.g., nuclear operator). Thus, HR practitioners must ensure that an environment conducive to innovation [e.g., one that emphasizes risk taking (Jackson & Schuler, 1995); one that rewards outcomes rather than procedures (Miles & Snow, 1994)] exists for those jobs that would substantially benefit from such a context. Few successful organizations provide all organizational members with an innovation HR bundle (e.g., attracting creative employees, enabling individuals to concentrate their attention on products and product breakthroughs, allowing slack but "not-too-lean" staffing levels).

When conducting job analyses, a critical decision is the level of detail or specificity selected to analyze jobs (Ash, 1988). This issue is often referred to as the bandwidth–fidelity problem. On the one hand, jobs may be assessed at a broad but shallow range (high bandwidth). If job analysis is conducted at a high bandwidth, jobs that are essentially different will start to look the same (Harvey, 1991). On the other hand, jobs can be described in great depth and in highly specific terms (high fidelity). If fidelity is too high in job analysis, jobs that are essentially the same will begin to look different (Harvey, 1991). In addition, a high-fidelity job analysis results in the proliferation of the number of knowledge, skills, and abilities (KSAs, i.e., activities that appear to be required to do that job). Thus, when fidelity is too high, both a CEO's job and a janitor's job could arguably require innovation. When a high-fidelity assessment of jobs suggests that all jobs in a firm require innovation, a somewhat higher-bandwidth assessment of jobs may help differentiate when creativity is critical for the job and when it is not.

One consequence of a job analysis conducted at a too-high fidelity level may be that the HR manager institutes training programs, or other interventions, to enable a janitor to develop innovation when this course of action will not result in the best return on investment (ROI) for the firm as a whole. The ROI for a training program on innovation for inner-core members, for example, will be greater than the ROI if the same training course is developed for peripheral segment members. If HR/OB/I-O psychology practitioners and researchers are to understand organizational context, they must include ROI and utility analysis in their deliberations because firm resources are finite and optimal resource allocation is important to achieving a competitive advantage. Of course, this argument does not logically lead to the conclusion that any employee group should be "neglected" to the extent that employees in that group experience declining performance and increased turnover.

The IMSA recognizes that "some jobs are strategic (or more valuable) and others are not" (Becker & Huselid, 2006, p. 917). An offshoot of the notion of strategic and nonstrategic jobs is the sometimes uncomfortable, but practical, recognition that the "level of investment directed to the employees in those job categories would be significantly different" (Becker & Huselid, 2006, p. 918). Careful reading of the "Employee Centrality Sphere of Organizational Subsystems" section of our chapter (Taggar et al., this volume) will show that we do not claim that "only *core* employees add value to an organization," as suggested by Wheeler et al. (this volume). In fact, this idea runs counter to the economic assessment undercurrent flowing through the chapter. Specifically, organizations would likely not recruit, select, develop, and retain employees who do not add value. At the same time, the IMSA claims that core employees add more value than other employees.

Thus, the IMSA suggests an incongruity with Farr and Tran's statement that encouragement of creative and innovative behaviors for all employee clusters is important for the effective accomplishment of the innovative substrategy of an organization if in practical terms this means that all employees should receive an innovation HR bundle. The financial costs of developing an innovation HR bundle for peripheral employees could put an organization at a competitive disadvantage compared to other organizations that apply a low-cost HR bundle to the same group of employees. Moreover, selecting creative people for jobs that do not require a substantial amount of creativity may lead to dissatisfaction, absenteeism, and turnover due to poor person-job fit.

CONCLUSION

In a recent review of the SHRM literature, Becker and Huselid (2006) note that the link between an organization's HRM effectiveness and its financial performance is not unequivocal. There is still much work to be done to elucidate this relationship. For instance, these authors write that one "common concern expressed in the empirical literature is the caveat that the positive cross-sectional HR–firm performance relationship is, in part, influenced by mutual causation or simultaneity bias" (p. 913). They suggest that part of the solution to this problem is to make theory more elaborate. The IMSA responds to the call by Becker and Huselid (2006) for researchers to "extend SHRM theory in a way that formally integrates the mechanism through which HR architecture actually influences firm performance" (p. 900). Our approach takes the perspective espoused by systems theory, and our resulting model suggests that competitive advantage is a function of (1) how well a firm aligns its HR policies and practices with its substrategies and (2) which jobs are placed under these substrategies. Accordingly, we provide a parsimonious and pragmatic operationalization of strategy implementation.

Priem and Butler (2001) note the need for delineation of "the specific mechanism purported to generate competitive advantage" and "actionable prescripts" (p. 31). Porter (1996) notes that strategic positioning "means performing different activities from rivals or performing similar activities in different ways" (p. 62). Our IMSA suggests that competitive advantage may be gained through redesigning jobs so they are placed in different subsystems – for example, treating selected shop-floor workers as inner-core employees by giving them an adhocracy culture and innovative HR bundle. Accordingly, substrategies represent intermediate outcomes between HR practices and firm performance. To test our model, substrategies must be strategically validated to demonstrate their importance to effective strategy implementation, which itself will require in-depth, context-specific analyses of firms.

REFERENCES

Abrahamson, E. (1997). The emergence and prevalence of employee management rhetorics: The effects of long waves, labor unions, and turnover, 1875 to 1992. *Academy of Management Journal, 40*, 491–532.

Ash, R. A. (1988). Job analysis in the world of work. In: S. Gael (Ed.), *Job analysis handbook for business, industry, and government* (Vol. 1, pp. 3–13). New York: Wiley.

Bains, P., & Tran, V. (2006, May 5–6). *Creativity and innovation: Taking it to the next level.* Paper presented at the 21st SIOP Annual Conference, Dallas, TX.

Bartlett, C. A., & Ghoshal, S. (1993). Beyond the M-form: Toward a managerial theory of the firm. *Strategic Management Journal, 14*, 23–46.

Becker, B. E., & Gerhart, B. (1996). Human resources and organizational performance: Progress and prospects. *Academy of Management Journal, 39*, 779–801.

Becker, B. E., & Huselid, M. A. (2006). Strategic human resources management: Where do we go from here? *Journal of Management, 32*, 898–925.

Bertalanffy, L. von. (1950). An outline of general systems theory. *Philosophy of science, 1,* 134–165.

Chandler, A. D. (1962). *Strategy and structure.* Cambridge, MA: MIT Press.

Farr, J.L., & Tran, V. (this volume). Linking innovation and creativity with human resource strategies and practices: A matter of fit or flexibility? In: M. Mumford, S. T. Hunter & K. E. Bedell-Avers (Eds), *Research in multi-level issues: Multi-level issues in creativity and innovation* (Vol. 7). Oxford, UK: Elsevier.

Galbraith, J. R. (2000). *Designing the global corporation.* San Francisco, CA: Jossey Bass.

Hambrick, D. C., & Mason, P. A. (1984). Upper echelons: The organization as a reflection of its top managers. *Academy of Management Review, 9,* 193–207.

Harvey, R. (1991). Job analysis. In: M. Dunnette & L. M. Hough (Eds), *Handbook of industrial and organizational psychology* (Vol. 2, pp. 71–163). Palo Alto, CA: Consulting Psychologists.

Jackson, S. E., & Schuler, R. S. (1995). Understanding human resource management in the context of organizations and their environments. *Annual Review of Psychology, 46,* 237–264.

Kauffman, D. L. (1980). *Systems 1: An introduction to systems thinking.* Minneapolis, MN: Future Systems.

Kozlowski, S. W. J., & Klein, K. J. (2000). A multilevel approach to theory and research in organizations: Contextual, temporal, and emergent processes. In: K. J. Klein & S. W. J. Kozlowski (Eds), *Multilevel theory, research, and methods in organizations: Foundations, extensions, and new directions* (pp. 3–90). San Francisco, CA: Jossey-Bass.

Miles, R. E., & Snow, C. C. (1994). *Fit, failure and the hall of fame.* New York: Free Press.

Porter, M. (1996). What is strategy? *Harvard Business Review, 74,* 61–78.

Priem, R. L., & Butler, J. E. (2001). Is the resource-based theory a useful perspective for strategic management research? *Academy of Management Review, 26,* 22–40.

Schuler, R. S., & Jackson, S. E. (1987). Linking competitive strategies with human resources practices. *Academy of Management Executive, 1,* 207–220.

Sy, T., & D'Annunzio, L. S. (2005). Challenges and strategies of matrix organizations: Top-level and mid-level managers' perspectives. *Human Resource Planning, 28,* 39–49.

Taggar, S., Sulsky, L., & MacDonald, H. (this volume). Sub-system configuration: A model of strategy, context, and human resource management alignment. In: M. D. Mumford, S. T. Hunter & K. E. Bedell (Eds), *Research in multi-level issues: Multi-level issues in creativity and innovation* (Vol. 7). Oxford, UK: Elsevier.

Waring, S. P. (1992). Peter Drucker, MBO, and the corporatist critique of scientific management. In: D. Nelson (Ed.), *A mental revolution: Scientific management since Taylor* (pp. 205–236). Columbus, OH: Ohio State University Press.

West, M. A., & Farr, J. L. (1990). *Innovation and creativity at work: Psychological and organizational strategies.* Oxford, England: Wiley.

Wheeler, A. R., Halbesleben, J. R. B., & Buckley, M. R. (this volume). Multi-level strategic HRM: Facilitating competitive advantage through social networks and supply chains. In: M. Mumford, S. T. Hunter & K. E. Bedell-Avers (Eds), *Research in multi-level issues: Multi-level issues in creativity and innovation* (Vol. 7). Oxford, UK: Elsevier.

Zajac, E. J., Kraatz, M. S., & Bresser, R. K. F. (2000). Modeling the dynamics of strategic fit: A normative approach to strategic change. *Strategic Management Journal, 21,* 429–453.

PART V:
NEW VENTURE EMERGENCE

A MULTI-LEVEL PROCESS VIEW OF NEW VENTURE EMERGENCE

Cameron M. Ford and Diane M. Sullivan

ABSTRACT

Entrepreneurship research has grown in both quality and quantity over the past decade, as many theoretical innovations and important empirical research findings have been introduced to the field. However, theoretical approaches to understanding entrepreneurship remain fragmented, and empirical findings are unstable across different contexts. This chapter describes features of a multi-level process view of new venture emergence that adds coherence to the entrepreneurship theory jungle and brings order to idiosyncratic empirical results, by explaining how ideas become organized into new ventures. The centerpiece of this effort is enactment theory, a general process approach specifically developed to explain organizing processes. Enactment theory – and Campbellian evolutionary theorizing more generally – has a long history of use within and across multiple levels of analysis. Consequently, the description here illustrates how organizing unfolds across multiple levels of analysis and multiple phases of development. After describing the theorizing assumptions and multi-level process view of new venture organizing, the chapter explores implications of applying this perspective by suggesting new research directions and interpretations of prior work. The aim is to advocate process theorizing as a more productive approach to understanding new venture emergence.

Multi-Level Issues in Creativity and Innovation
Research in Multi-Level Issues, Volume 7, 423–470
Copyright © 2008 by Elsevier Ltd.
All rights of reproduction in any form reserved
ISSN: 1475-9144/doi:10.1016/S1475-9144(07)00017-3

INTRODUCTION

This chapter pulls together several different strands of organizational inquiry to weave a story about how novel ideas grow into organizations. This story describes a process that begins with an insight by an individual, and seeks to explain how that insight evolves, gains momentum, attracts enthusiasts, and culminates in a network of economic relationships that define a new business venture. This tale spans multiple levels of analyses and developmental phases, and relies on an eclectic set of theoretical characters drawn from research traditions in psychology, organizational behavior (OB), organizational theory, strategy, economics, and, of course, entrepreneurship. Unfortunately, this is not a short story. Consequently, we are grateful for the opportunity to present our musings on new venture emergence processes in a venue that encourages wide-ranging proposals and interdisciplinary discourse.

We are motivated to investigate new venture emergence processes for four reasons. First, the question "Where do new ventures come from?" was recently singled out in a review of research published in the *Academy of Management Journal* as a key, underdeveloped research issue to be addressed by future entrepreneurship studies (Ireland, Reutzel, & Webb, 2005). Although the quantity and quality of research on entrepreneurship have increased dramatically in the past decade, our understanding of how visions become ventures remains limited (Alvarez, 2005).

Second, entrepreneurship research has not emphasized multi-level theory capable of capturing the interplay among founders, founding management teams, new ventures, and their value networks. The most prominent approaches to studying entrepreneurship follow either an economics tradition that emphasizes environmental determinants of venture creation and performance (Hayek, 1945; Shane, 2000; Yates, 2000) or a psychological tradition that emphasizes founder traits or characteristics associated with venture creation and performance (Shaver & Scott, 1991; Shook, Priem, & McGee, 2003). Neither an environment-centric nor a person-centric approach has produced a comprehensive understanding of entrepreneurial processes (Shane, 2003). Approaches that consider how entrepreneurial processes emerge at the nexus of persons and environments (cf. Shane, 2003) are needed to enrich our understanding of how new ventures emerge and succeed (Ireland et al., 2005). The need to address entrepreneurship at this nexus suggests that multi-level theorizing is necessary to improve future research.

Third, process theories of entrepreneurship are rare in the literature, despite an acknowledged need to investigate how the entrepreneurial process unfolds (Shane, 2006). This lack of process theorizing implies that important dynamic processes are underrepresented in both environment-centric and person-centric approaches to entrepreneurship. Both of these approaches suffer from problems associated with variance approaches to understanding organizational phenomena (cf. Mackenzie, 2004). For instance, we lack descriptions of how conceptions of opportunities evolve, how entrepreneurs learn, how stakeholder networks form and grow, and how consumer preferences shift during the new venture organizing process. Empirical research findings in entrepreneurship tend to be unstable from one context to another (Shane, 2006), owing in part perhaps to the wide application of variance approaches to entrepreneurship research.

Many of the factors complicating the interpretation of entrepreneurship studies might be understood more clearly and more generally if considered from a process perspective. For example, contrasting assumptions regarding whether opportunities exist in an objective sense or whether they are created through entrepreneurial action (Alvarez, 2005) might be reconciled by employing dynamic approaches such as enactment theory or Giddens' structuration theory (Ford, 1996). Giddens (1984), for example, describes how individual action and social structures relate to each other and how routine actions reproduce these structures. Thus, while different domains offer established ways of doing things, these structures can be changed by individuals who ignore them, replace them, or enact them differently than other persons do. [See Gioia and Pitre (1990) for a discussion of how dynamic theorizing allows researchers to "transition" between objectivist and subjectivist perspectives; see Ford (1996) for a discussion of how structuration theory can be applied to understanding evolution processes associated with creative action.]

Fourth, new venture emergence could be considered a "pure" form of organizing (i.e., making something from nothing), capable of enriching our general ability to create and employ theories describing important processes that lead to organizing (cf. Heath & Sitkin, 2001). Indeed, understanding the process of organization creation may help further our understanding of organization revisions that occur on an ongoing basis. Thus, while this chapter raises and addresses issues of particular interest in entrepreneurship research, we also hope to appeal to more general interests within the management field.

In sum, new venture emergence is an important practical problem about which we know relatively little. This chapter uses multiple levels of analysis to explore this topic because the process of shifting the locus of causation from a founder to a management team to a venture is inherent in the evolution of an idea to a firm. It investigates emergence as a process because this concept explains *how* new ventures form (rather than *under what circumstances* or in *what form*, for example, organizations form). Finally, it is hoped that the ideas presented here will spur additional research and inspire new insights that can be employed in other domains of OB research where organizing processes are a key concern.

We begin by describing several guiding assumptions and the general theoretical context within which we hope to position our contribution. This section is organized by following the description of process models offered by Mackenzie (2004), which requires us to identify the levels of analyses and phases of processes we consider, as well as the actors, considerations, resources involved, and outcomes associated with various processes. Thus the opening section provides a general explanation of our perspective on new venture emergence, with particular attention being paid to explicating the key assumptions incorporated in our logic and addressing the requirements of process and multi-level theorizing.

The latter sections in the chapter illustrate potential research issues that arise from this multi-level process view of new venture emergence. The second section describes the opportunity discovery process that occurs at the individual, founder level of analysis. The third section depicts subsequent opportunity evaluation processes that occur once a founder engages others to join in the formulation of the venture. Thus this section generalizes the general framework to the team level of analysis. Once a team has formulated a clear statement of its venture (often in the form of a business plan) and has accumulated sufficient resources, we generalize our description again to the venture level, whereby the firm begins economic activity (e.g., contracting, hiring, selling) and enters into the opportunity exploitation phase of the emergence process.

The boundaries of our description are drawn at the point where the venture becomes an ongoing business enterprise. That is, we do not attempt to describe or predict competitive success or firm survival. These questions have been studied extensively in the economics and entrepreneurship literature, and have been recently reviewed by Shane (2003). Finally, we conclude by suggesting contributions that a multi-level process view of new venture emergence offers to entrepreneurship research, education, and practice.

UNDERSTANDING NEW VENTURE EMERGENCE AT THE NEXUS OF FOUNDERS AND OPPORTUNITIES

Levels and Phases of New Venture Emergence

In describing our multi-level process view of new venture emergence, we incorporate several important recent contributions that we believe provide a robust foundation for developing proposals that span levels of analyses and phases of development (Rousseau, 2004). In doing so, we heed the advice offered by Alvarez (2005) to be explicit about key assumptions underlying our proposals.

For example, we have adopted Hackman's (2003) notion of bracketing as a means of clearly delineating our focal levels of analysis. Bracketing requires theorists to examine influences on a focal phenomenon that are located one level of analysis above and one level below the focal phenomenon. This important contribution to multi-level theorizing provides clear guidance to those developing new theory, and is a hallmark of rigorous multi-level research (Rousseau, 2004). Hackman asserts that in theoretical and empirical analyses of focal phenomena, constructs likely exist at both higher and lower levels that explain constructs at the focal level. Although much multi-level research tends to examine phenomena at a level below the focal phenomenon (Rousseau, 2004), Hackman believes that studying both lower- and higher-level phenomenon can help uncover relationships that fully address all of the "parts" and all of the "wholes." Hackman summarizes the usefulness of bracketing for studying multi-level phenomena by stating:

> Bracketing can (1) enrich understanding of one's focal phenomena, (2) help one discover non-obvious forces that drive those phenomena, (3) surface unanticipated interactions that shape an outcome of special interest, and (4) inform the choice of constructs in the development of actionable theory. (Hackman, 2003, p. 907)

Examining phenomena one level up refers to considering phenomena that exert influence downward on the focal phenomena (e.g., institutional processes that affect a founding team's ideation processes). Examining phenomena one level down refers to considering parts that make up the whole of the focal phenomena (e.g., studying how a founder's biases affect the judgments of a founding team) (Rousseau, 2004). The discipline enforced on a theorist by the process of bracketing promotes rigorous multi-level theorizing by requiring: (1) that constructs at each level be clearly specified in terms of their characteristics and appropriate levels of generalization and (2) that linkages among constructs between each pair of adjacent levels be identified (Mackenzie, 2004; Rousseau, 1985). As Hackman's work suggests, failure to consider both higher- and lower-level influences places a theorist at risk of under-specifying the functional relationships that influence constructs at various levels of analysis.

The perspective described in this chapter explains new venture emergence processes at three levels of analysis: the founder, the founding team, and the venture. For each of these levels, we bracket them by describing influences emerging from the level's "parts" and from uncertainty imposed on each focal level by its environment.

For instance, in bracketing the *founder* as a level of analysis, we look one level lower – at cognitive and motivational attributes (e.g., aspirations, knowledge, decision considerations) – and one level higher – at uncertainty in the (new venture) environment. The processes we describe whereby founders consider novel business proposals correspond to the *opportunity discovery phase* of the new venture emergence process.

When examining *founding teams*, we bracket our descriptions by looking one level lower at attributes of the founder/champion and one level higher, again including uncertainty in the new venture environment. This allows us to describe the *opportunity evaluation phase* of the new venture emergence process.

Finally, we define the *venture* as a "nexus of contracts" in a manner that follows Coase (1937) and transaction-cost theory (Williamson, 1975, 1985, 1991) as the focal level of analysis during the *opportunity exploitation phase* of the new venture emergence process (see also Alvarez & Barney, 2005). The venture is defined by the assignment of decision rights that determine resource allocation choices within a firm (Alvarez & Barney, 2005). The lower adjacent level bracketing the venture is the founding team; the upper level is again described by environmental uncertainty.

Thus the first assumption guiding our theorizing efforts is as follows:

Assumption 1. Multi-level bracketing is necessary to avoid theoretical under-specification of the new venture emergence process.

A second important contribution that informs our theorizing is the one offered by Heath and Sitkin's (2001) forceful critique of the character of OB research. Their essay describes three prevalent styles of theory in OB.

First, they describe "Big-B" research, defined as OB work that emphasizes interesting *behavior* that may be relevant to organizations. A problem with Big-B research is that it does not satisfy what Heath and

Sitkin describe as the Core Competence Test, which asks, "Is this a topic on which OB researchers have unique insights that are not likely to be shared by researchers in related social science disciplines like psychology, sociology, political science, or economics?" Heath and Sitkin (2001, p. 50). Heath and Sitkin's point is that the behaviors under research in Big-B work may not tell us much about organizations, and OB researchers are in a relatively poor position to offer unique theoretical insights.

Next, Heath and Sitkin describe "Contextualized-B" research, which "emphasizes behavior *in an organizational context*" Heath and Sitkin (2001, p. 51). This style of theorizing "may solve some problems with Big-B definitions because they specify that behavior must occur within an organizational context ... [but it] also creates ... two problems: *re-labeling and peripheral topics*" (p. 52). The re-labeling problem deals with borrowing theoretical constructs from other disciplines and simply generalizing them to organizational settings (e.g., investigating whether self-esteem beliefs affect employee performance). Peripheral topics are those that "are not central to understanding how organizations accomplish their task of organizing" (p. 53). To identify peripheral topics Heath and Sitkin propose the Organizational Centrality Test, which asks, "How much would we understand about organizations if we understood everything there was to know about____?" (p. 53). Thus, while Contextualized-B theorizing addresses interesting behavior in organizational settings; its emphasis on modest, incremental contributions to the understanding of relatively unimportant issues limits its overall impact.

Finally, Heath and Sitkin propose a third way of defining OB that they believe addresses problems associated with Big-B and Contextualized-B research: "Big-O" research. Under the Big-O definition of OB, topics should be "*more central in research* when they capture something that is *more central to the task of organizing*" (p. 54). Heath and Sitkin draw on the work of Weick (1979) in using the verb form of "organizational," because they believe that OB research would be more appropriate if it focused on how "people solve the dynamic problems of aligning goals and coordinating action" (p. 54). This type of theorizing should help organizational researchers gain an understanding of general insights about organizing. Heath and Sitkin propose two other benefits of Big-O theorizing that are germane to our current theorizing efforts: (1) "topics are more likely to be cross-level" and (2) "such topics are less likely to lend themselves to simple studies that simply correlate a laundry-list of behavioral variables" (p. 56).

As we describe in a moment, we follow Heath and Sitkin's advice as closely as we believe possible by using enactment theory (Weick, Sutcliffe, & Obstfeld,

2005) to bracket new venture emergence processes at different levels of analysis and through different phases of development. Consequently, our proposals enthusiastically embrace the call for Big-O theorizing put forth by Heath and Sitkin. This leads us to articulate a second assumption that guides our theorizing:

Assumption 2. New venture emergence is inherently a form of enactment that simultaneously involves making sense of relatively stable, "objective" social structures (e.g., markets, industries, institutions) and enacting novel variations that may ultimately alter those structures (see Ford, 1996). In adopting this assumption, we reject the distinction between objective opportunities and subjective creation as a false dichotomy that acts as a barrier to theoretical advances in the entrepreneurship discipline.

A third consideration we incorporate in our theorizing that is closely aligned with our goal of describing new venture *organizing* is to adopt a process, rather than a variance, approach to theorizing. Specifically, we follow the descriptions of Mackenzie (2004) and Van de Ven and Engleman (2004) regarding research that examines processes involved with organizing. Van de Ven and Engleman, for example, assert that studying event-driven processes of organizations is of paramount concern, as it helps to develop an understanding of how change occurs within an organization, how the orientation of time occurs within these changes, and how changes more generally occur within the organizational sciences (Van de Ven & Engleman, 2004). Mackenzie further develops this perspective by noting that "organizations are processual in nature … and [they] resemble collectives of processes in the process of becoming" Mackenzie (2004, p. 351).

We utilize the premises developed by Mackenzie (2004) that are important to developing an organizational process framework when we build our general description of new venture emergence. We then generalize this description across levels of analysis and developmental phases as an initial exploration of the utility of our approach. Thus we adopt a third premise:

Assumption 3. Process theorizing is required to adequately describe new venture emergence processes. Process theorizing is less sensitive to variations in context that produce unstable empirical findings in studies that employ a variance approach (Shane, 2006); as a consequence, it offers a more promising scheme for future entrepreneurship theorizing.

To summarize, the guidance offered by these important theory-building premises leads us to identify three important levels of analysis that are associated with the key events (cf. Mackenzie, 2004) or phases of the new venture emergence process:

- Founders' efforts are associated with the opportunity discovery phase.
- Founding management teams are associated with the opportunity evaluation phase.
- Venture efforts are the focal level for describing the opportunity exploitation phase.

Both the within- and between-phase events in our process view correspond to the different processes described in enactment theory – environmental change, enactment, selection, and retention. We will soon describe processes associated with strategic momentum that energize these processes and create "escape velocity" events that propel a new venture proposal from one level and phase to the next.

With our meta-theoretical premises in place, we now offer a definition of entrepreneurship consistent with these assumptions. Fortunately, considerable debate among entrepreneurship scholars has resulted in significant advances with respect to defining the domain of entrepreneurship research. Our discussion to this point resonates most closely with the defining elements of entrepreneurship that Shane (2003) offered in his extensive review of the field:

> Entrepreneurship is an activity that involves the discovery, evaluation, and exploitation of opportunities to introduce new goods and services, ways of organizing, markets, processes, and raw materials through organizing efforts that previously had not existed. (Shane, 2003, p. 4)

We adopt this definition for two reasons: (1) It describes entrepreneurship in terms of "activity" and "organizing efforts" that introduce ventures that "previously had not existed," and (2) the phases it identifies – discovery, evaluation, and exploitation – are compatible with the variation, selection, and retention phases specified in enactment and ESR theory. (To simplify our presentation, we use the abbreviation ESR for enactment–selection–retention theory rather than the synonymous, but more traditional, VSR abbreviation used to describe variation–selection–retention models.) Consequently, we adopt Shane's definition of entrepreneurship to guide our description of the new venture emergence process across different phases. Adopting the three theoretical premises mentioned earlier enables us to represent the richness inherent in the new venture emergence process by considering idiosyncratic contextual and historical circumstances within a general process framework. The proposals that follow should help academics and practitioners alike to understand the recurring challenges inherent in organizing new ventures to exploit novel business proposals.

Sequencing of Events and Phases in New Venture Emergence

The previous section addressed meta-theoretical assumptions and adopted and addressed Mackenzie's (2004) first requirement of articulating a process theory: identifying the key events in the process (environmental change–enactment/discovery–selection/evaluation–retention/exploitation). Mackenzie's second requirement is that we specify a time-dependent sequence of events capable of explaining "how change unfolds" (Van de Ven & Engleman, 2004; p. 345) within the context of new venture creation. We rely on Campbell's (1960) widely employed variation and selective-retention model of creativity and social change, and Weick et al. (2005) updated description of enactment theory in particular, as a meta-theoretical framework for explaining the sequence of phases leading to new venture emergence, as well as the processes that occur within and between each phase. We have used this perspective previously to explain the evolution of creative endeavors in general terms (Ford, 1996; Ford, 2005; Ford & Sullivan, 2005). In particular, we have found Campbellian theorizing to be especially impressive with respect to its broad application across research traditions and levels of analysis. Before continuing with our utilization of enactment theory, we offer a brief overview of the sequence of processes suggested by this approach and the approach from which enactment theory originated – namely, Campbell's (1960) variation and selective-retention theory.

The tenets of evolutionary theories have primarily been developed within the biological and ecological sciences but have been broadly applied in the behavioral and social sciences. Campbell's sophisticated descriptions of variation and selective-retention processes have been especially influential because he was the first to use Darwinian theory to explain creativity and social change (Campbell, 1960, 1965). Campbell describes the nature and tension inherent in evolution processes as follows:

> For an evolutionary process to take place there needs to be variations (as by mutation, trial, etc.), stable aspects of the environment differentially selecting among such variations, and a retention-propagation system rigidly holding on to the selected variations. The variation and the retention aspects are inherently at odds. Every new mutation represents a failure of reproduction of a prior selected form. Too high a mutation rate jeopardizes the preservation of already achieved adaptations. There arise in evolutionary systems, therefore, mechanisms for curbing the variation rate. The more

elaborate the achieved adaptation, the more likely are mutations to be deleterious, and therefore the stronger the inhibitions on mutation. For this reason we may expect to find great strength in the preservation and propagation systems, which lead to the perpetuation of once-adaptive traits long after environmental shifts have removed their adaptedness. (Campbell, 1965; pp. 306–307)

Building from this work, the ESR model proposes that a population can evolve as it is presented with variations to the previously retained status quo. Selection processes screen newly presented variants for their fitness relative to the demands imposed by the environment. Those variants that survive this selection process are retained as elaborations of the population. One of the creativity literature's most prolific contributors, Dean Keith Simonton, has strenuously argued for the superiority of ESR theory based on its comprehensiveness and versatility: "Because the variation–selection model can encompass such a diversity of processes, at some profound level creativity must be Darwinian. In both cultural and biological evolution, it may constitute the most important explanation for creative innovations" (Simonton, 1999; p. 322).

Thus, to simplify our task of identifying and sequencing processes that can be clearly specified at multiple levels of analysis, we adopt enactment theory (Weick et al., 2005) as an ESR process description that is uniquely capable of capturing the richness of processes characteristic of the entrepreneur–opportunity nexus at multiple levels of analysis. Enactment theory was originally proposed by Weick (1979) as an extension of Campbellian variation and selective-retention theory applied specifically to organizing processes. It is especially well suited to the focus in this chapter because of the extensive prior use of ESR theory to explain the evolution of creative endeavors (e.g., Campbell, 1960; Ford, 1996; Simonton, 1999). These previous process descriptions can be readily generalized to new venture emergence processes because entrepreneurship is inherently a creative act (Shane, 2003). More importantly, the fact that ESR theory has been used in so many ways, across so many levels of analysis, suggests that the key processes described in enactment theory (Weick, 1979; Weick et al., 2005) – that is, enactment, selection, retention, and environmental change – and the relationships among these processes can be effectively generalized to multiple levels of analysis. Weick et al. (2005) make this point explicitly:

The beauty of making ESR the microfoundation of organizing and sensemaking is that it makes it easier to work with other meso- and macro-level formulations that are grounded in Campbell's work. (e.g., Aldrich, 1999; Baum & Singh, 1994; Ocasio, 2001) (p. 414)

Adopting enactment theory enables us to satisfy the first and second criteria for rigorous multi-level theorizing (Mackenzie, 2004) by clearly specifying the processes we believe generalize across levels of analysis and explaining the sequences that constitute these processes. It also allows us to address the admonitions of Heath and Sitkin (2001) to develop organizational theories that identify *processes* that explain *organizing*.

Fig. 1 summarizes the multiple levels of analysis and multiple process phases that the rest of this chapter will describe. It illustrates how we bracket our three focal levels of analysis during three different phases of new venture emergence, and it shows how strategic momentum can reach a level of escape velocity (Jansen, 2004) that propels venture proposals to higher levels of organizing.

Fig. 2 illustrates how enactment can be used to identify and sequence the events that occur within each developmental phase. This figure, which is based on the recent work of Weick et al. (2005), shows how entrepreneurial enactment serves as the nexus that joins considerations at a higher level of analysis (i.e., environmental uncertainty) with influences derived from lower-level selective retention processes (e.g., decision considerations, knowledge, resources, relationships).

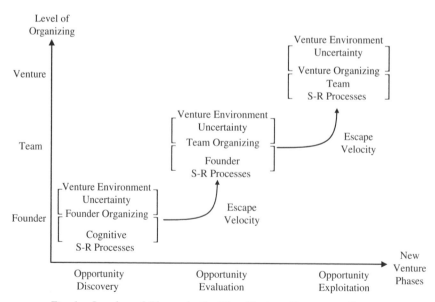

Fig. 1.   Levels and Phases in the New Venture Emergence Process.

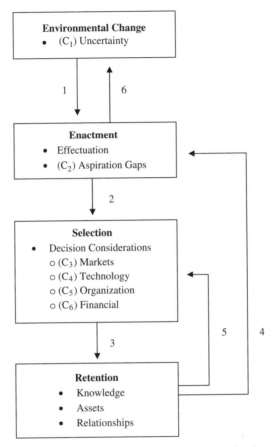

Fig. 2. Enactment Theory as a Model of the Entrepreneurship–Opportunity Nexus.

So far, we have addressed Mackenzie's requirements of specifying events and event sequences that make up our processes (environmental change–enactment–selection–retention cycles within each phase; opportunity discovery, evaluation, and exploitation as stages of a higher-order enactment process). We now examine the five distinct components necessary to fully describe a process framework:

- The people who perform a process
- Considerations that describe related decision criteria for determining outcomes when consideration values are applied [Mackenzie offers the familiar Vroom and Yetton (1973) leadership strategy process framework

as an example that employs several considerations to help managers select a leadership style]
- Relationships among the considerations
- Links to other processes
- Enabling task resources

Components of New Venture Emergence Processes

Satisfying the second criteria of rigorous multi-level theorizing – offering well-specified linkages among constructs that link adjacent levels – is especially challenging. We draw from several important recent contributions to the OB, entrepreneurship, and strategy research literatures to inform our speculations regarding cross-level linkages. Our efforts here are speculative, in that we have not yet established functional relationships indicating how lower- and higher-level constructs provide necessary and sufficient conditions that explain focal-level constructs (cf. Mackenzie, 2004). Instead, we rely at this point in our intellectual journey on identifying constructs that (1) have a history of generalization to multiple levels of analysis and (2) have been employed in recent theoretical advances that we believe are closely aligned with the tenets of enactment theory.

The enactment-based story illustrated in Fig. 2 begins, somewhat arbitrarily, with a description of *uncertainty* in the task environment one level above our focal level of analysis. A key attribute identified in both enactment theory and economics is uncertainty, typically resulting from environmental change. McMullen and Shepherd (2006) reviewed perspectives from economics to help advance a "theory of the entrepreneur" and identified uncertainty as the key attribute of the venture environment that initiates venture creation processes. Obviously, uncertainty has been an important construct at all levels of organizational and economic analysis. Here uncertainty is considered to be synonymous with Weick's (1979) description of ambiguity as the key attribute of the environment addressed by enactment. The influence of uncertainty on an actor's enactment processes is designated by arrow 1 in Fig. 2.

We continue our story by adopting Sarasvathy's important work on *effectuation* theory to describe the decision processes whereby entrepreneurs create variations when they "take a set of [previously retained] means as given, and focus on selecting between possible effects that can be created with that set of means" (Sarasvathy, 2001; p. 245). The idea that individual-, team-, or organization-level variation processes are simultaneously facilitated and constrained by previously retained routines also has a robust history in the field (e.g., Hargadon & Sutton, 1997; March, 1991). We follow decades of decision-making and strategy research by proposing *aspiration–achievement gaps* as key to motivating search and action at the individual, team, and venture levels (March & Simon, 1958; McMullen & Shepherd, 2006). The point where the value of novel proposals is assessed occurs when enactments are put through the selection process, as depicted by arrow 2 in Fig. 2.

Our description of *decision considerations* in the selection process draws from works by Astebro and Elhedhli (2006), Delmar and Shane (2004), Hughes and Chapin (1996), and Ford (2005) to describe how market, product/service (technology), organization, and financial considerations serve as screens that determine the plausibility and likely value of a novel business proposal. Those attributes of a proposal that survive the selection process are retained as tentative knowledge subject to further testing, as illustrated by arrow 3 in Fig. 2.

As proposals generate traction, they may also attract resources and relationships that can be used to further enact the venture proposal. *Retained knowledge, resources, and relationships* may be employed to modify a venture proposal, aspiration levels, and decision considerations through the feedback arrows 4 and 5 depicted in Fig. 2. These feedback processes describe how learning occurs during the new venture emergence process.

The outcomes associated with these processes vary by level of analysis, but generally feature benchmarks that define the growing plausibility of a new venture proposal. The extent to which a proposal satisfies new venture decision considerations will contribute to the degree of strategic momentum the proposition holds for future proposition development (Jansen, 2004). Proposals that fare well in these assessments (i.e., those that meet both aspiration and plausibility requirements) gain traction that can increase a proposal's momentum to a point when an "escape velocity" threshold is reached that motivates organizing processes that create the next higher level of analysis. For example, when a founder gets excited enough about a specific proposal, he or she might form a management team capable of launching the venture. This process of action taking is illustrated by arrow 6 in Fig. 2.

The remainder of this section offers additional details about each component of our process view as required by Mackenzie's (2004) process theory guidelines. We have not yet fully satisfied the criteria put forth by Mackenzie regarding the specification of functional relationships necessary to propose a process theory, which explains why we do not present our work as a model or theory at this point. Instead, we offer descriptions of our developing understanding of new venture emergence. These descriptions will form the narrative that will guide our subsequent stories depicting the opportunity discovery, evaluation, and exploitation phases of the new venture emergence process. Following prescriptions from Mackenzie (2004), we specify the: (1) people who perform a process, (2) considerations that describe related decision criteria for determining outcomes when consideration values are applied, (3) relationships among the considerations, (4) links to other processes, and (5) enabling task resources.

People who Perform the Processes
Individual founders are the focal level of the analysis during the opportunity discovery phase of the new venture emergence process. Proposals that develop sufficient momentum to reach escape velocity from this phase may instigate organizing of a founding team that undertakes the opportunity evaluation phase. Proposals that develop sufficient traction within a founding team may reach escape velocity that triggers venture formation. New ventures, defined as a nexus of contracts (Alvarez & Barney, 2005), are the focal level of analysis during the opportunity exploitation phase of the new venture emergence process.

Individuals are always the source of novel ideas in ESR theorizing (Ford, 1996, 2005). Interactions with others representing dimensions of the environment, or others in one's team or venture, however, may facilitate or constrain an individual's propensity to create novel proposals (Perry-Smith & Shalley, 2003).

Considerations That Describe Related Decision Criteria
Enactment theory serves as a useful general guide for identifying the sequence of considerations that determine, at least in part, the plausibility of a specific new venture proposal. The following considerations have been selected based in part on their extensive utilization at multiple levels of analysis in prior research, and in part on their correspondence to the phases of the enactment process.

(C_1) Environmental uncertainty. The first consideration relates to the downward influence of uncertainty in the task environment on founder, team, or venture enactment processes. In our perspective, we portray enactment at all focal levels of analysis as being affected by environmental uncertainty. Uncertainty has both a facilitating effect and a constraining effect on entrepreneurial enactment.

On the plus side, uncertainty suggests that the environment is changing and that the implications of these changes are unclear to many. Some theories of entrepreneurship suggest that such changes create objective opportunities, and that individuals with superior knowledge regarding those changes can benefit from possessing information asymmetries capable of generating economic rents (Ford, 2005).

On the negative side, recent work by McMullen and Shepherd (2006) describes uncertainty as a sense of doubt that blocks or delays action. This description of uncertainty suggests that it is subjective and likely to be affected by individual differences.

Weick et al. (2005) highlight ambivalence with respect to uncertainty in their description of sense making by noting that exchanges between actors and their environments can remain beneficial if retained content is both believed and doubted. Ambivalence allows actors to simultaneously benefit from past learning and adapt to changing circumstances in the environment. This tension is highly representative of the entrepreneurial enactment process, in that it captures both the excitement associated with recognizing a potential path for venture creation and the fear associated with undertaking that journey.

(C₂) Aspiration–performance gaps. Environmental uncertainty confronts sense makers with discontinuities whereby understanding of the environment becomes disorganized (Weick et al., 2005). Individuals' efforts to create order in their understandings may lead them to generate novel insights when previously retained knowledge is applied anew. We propose that individuals typically employ effectuation processes to create initial proposals that might serve as a solution to an observed problem.

To the extent that novel insights resolve uncertainties and address problematic aspects of the environment, individuals may envision action alternatives superior to their current circumstances. McMullen and Shepherd (2006) described this process as involving two stages: one in which the value of a novel insight is assessed with respect to third-party aspirations ("This would be a good opportunity for someone"), which may evolve into the second phase, in which it is identified as a first-person opportunity ("This would be a good opportunity for me"). The likelihood that a third-person opportunity will become recognized as a first-person opportunity is based in part on an individual's current circumstances in relation to the expected value presented by the opportunity. An individual with fewer opportunities would be expected to view a higher proportion of insights as representing first-person opportunities than would a person who is currently successful or has other lucrative employment options.

Thus we propose that individuals, teams, and ventures whose current circumstances are well below their individual or collective aspirations will be motivated to search for and create solutions to environmental uncertainties. To the extent that solutions arise that show promise toward fulfilling aspiration–achievement gaps (i.e., become first-person opportunities), momentum for the proposal will build and further effort will be expended to evaluate and exploit the opportunity.

As mentioned previously, research by Astebro and Elhedhli (2006), Delmar and Shane (2004), Hughes and Chapin (1996), and Ford (2005) suggest that new venture proposals face a limited set of relatively well-known valuation considerations. These considerations reflect four distinct organizing challenges that are often addressed by members of different professions and orientations (Ford, 2005). Collectively, consideration of market, technology (product/service), organizational, and financial plausibility (considerations C_3, C_4, C_5, and C_6 in our process description, respectively) is necessary to assess the overall plausibility of a new venture proposal.

(C₃) Market plausibility. Market plausibility consideration addresses issues such as existing market/customer size, sustainability, and customer switching costs. It also addresses whether the concept fulfills a genuine customer need, is priced appropriately, compares favorably to competition and substitutes, can be distributed through appropriate channels, and so forth.

(C₄) Technology plausibility. Technology – defined for our purposes as the knowledge required to deliver a product or service – can be effectively evaluated by addressing a few key considerations. For example, solution efficacy, reliability, and user learning curves need to be considered. Knowledge intensity, technology maturity, intellectual property characteristics, development costs, and potential obsolescence are other important factors with respect to the viability of a particular proposal.

(C₅) Organizational plausibility. Once a market need and a technology for addressing that need have been articulated, the ability to build an organization capable of delivering that solution to those in need of it must be considered. Assessments of the founder's and founding team's know-how, development of a viable business/revenue model, requirements for

specialized human resources, access to suppliers and distribution channels, and requirements to manufacture, store, and ship inventory are all key considerations related to the plausibility of the proposed venture. Collectively, these considerations are often referred to as the venture's business model.

(C₆) Financial plausibility. Selecting a venture proposal based on its characteristics as a creator of wealth and as an investment opportunity presents perhaps the most institutionally robust set of considerations in our presentation. Standard financial analyses can be developed to show the potential return that a founder, founding team member, employee, or investor might expect from implementing a particular new venture proposal. The most common methods of assessing financial plausibility involve estimating payback periods, net present values, growth potential, liquidation values, and other financial measures. These assessments can then be compared to the corresponding measures for other investment opportunities to determine the relative desirability, in terms of both magnitude of return and probability of return, of a particular new venture proposal.

Relationships Among the Considerations

Our description of the relationships between interdependent considerations is based largely on those depicted by enactment theory (Fig. 2) as well as our own experiences working with individuals and teams developing business proposals. We propose that environmental uncertainty fuels sense-making efforts by individuals who find current circumstances to be, in some fashion, problematic. Insights regarding proposed solutions to environmental uncertainties, which are typically produced through effectuation processes whereby one uses current knowledge and resources to create novel proposals, may invoke aspiration–achievement gaps held by a potential entrepreneur (i.e., the individual envisions a better circumstance for himself or herself). The resulting initial venture proposal then faces the selective-retention processes at the next lower level of analysis (e.g., founder/ cognitive level), which address both distinct organizing challenges and requirements common to all new ventures. (Retained cognitive structures are the lower level of analysis when we describe the founder, founders are the lower level when we describe founding teams, and teams are the lower level when we describe ventures.)

We tentatively propose that market considerations are evaluated first because they correspond most closely to the environmental uncertainty that cued entrepreneur effectuation and aspirations. In lay terms, this consideration is sometimes described as the "pain" in the market. This idea leads us to propose that technology (broadly defined as knowledge used to create a product or service) becomes meaningful in the context of this pain as a potential "painkiller" and, therefore, follows market considerations in the selection process.

Once a problem (pain) and solution (painkiller) have been assessed as a plausible pairing, the next consideration relates to one's ability to deliver the solution to those who need it. Organizing people, resources, alliances, and so forth is meaningful as a means to an end, defined in this case by market–technology considerations. Thus we argue that organizational considerations follow market and technology considerations in the evolution of a plausible new venture proposal.

Finally, we suggest that financial considerations logically follow organizational considerations because it is impossible to make projections regarding revenues and expenses without identifying the supply and demand considerations related to a market–technology pairing or appreciating the expenses likely to be incurred by the accumulation and deployment of organizational resources. If a new venture proposal is favorably selected based on market, technology, and organizational considerations, then traditional financial analyses and investment scenarios can be developed to test the economic value of the proposition.

Two additional consequences result from these enactment and selection processes. The first is the updating of previously retained knowledge, resources, and relationships as a result of the partial selection of a prior version of a new venture proposal (arrow 3 in Fig. 2). The second involves the modification of the process considerations in the selection and enactment phases of subsequent ESR trials (arrows 4 and 5 in Fig. 2). Thus entrepreneurs' effectuation processes, aspirations, and understanding of market, technology, organizational, and financial considerations may change as a result of their ongoing sense-making processes. This understanding is one of the more important and unique features of our process perspective: It explains how entrepreneurs learn as a result of the new venture enactment process.

Although we propose these consequences as a logical, and perhaps normatively useful, sequence of events, our enactment theory approach suggests that assessments of these considerations are likely to be uneven, biased, and revisited, depending on who is engaged in the selection process. In fact, many of these considerations may be overlooked, especially at lower levels of analysis, where individual bias and ignorance are likely to have their greatest impact. Thus, following Mackenzie, we argue that describing organizing process considerations reveals relatively invariant issues that emerging ventures must address, while remaining open to considering wide variations in context associated with the way in which these processes unfold in specific settings.

These selection considerations also work in an applied sense, and they reflect stable, institutionalized preferences held in different business domains. Astebro and Elhedhli (2006), for example, used data derived from years of invention assessments from a Canadian institute to determine how successfully their 35-item assessment procedure predicted venture commercialization. Their results showed that assessment accuracy could be as high as 92% utilizing a simplified 21-item inventory of market, technology, organizational, and financial considerations. This impressive showing suggests that current market, technology, organizational, and financial norms and methods are, in fact, important considerations with respect to new venture viability. It also suggests that the general success factors contributing to new venture success are not particularly numerous or difficult to consider. This is not to say that marshalling the knowledge, resources, and relationships necessary to articulate a credible venture organizing story is easy, however. Rather, it suggests that the considerations to be addressed during the enactment process are relatively well known.

Links to Other Processes
Links or transitions between processes are another necessary component of process theorizing. They specify how progress occurs from one consideration to the next, and from one level of organizing to higher levels of organizing. We explain transitions among ESR processes within each phase of the new venture emergence process – opportunity discovery, evaluation, and exploitation – as well as transitions between these phases by adopting Jansen's work on strategic momentum. Jansen summarizes the logic of her important contribution as follows:

> The proposed theory suggests that once created, change-based momentum becomes a dynamic element of organizational change that fluctuates in response to different change-related factors, including characteristics of social information conveyed during the change, changing commitments, and fluctuations in attentiveness. These relationships are expected to be cyclical, such that, for example, momentum enables progress, and progress fuels subsequent momentum ... Individuals use cues from the social environment to construct and interpret events (Salancik & Pfeffer, 1978). Because change-based momentum involves pursuing an unfamiliar trajectory, these social cues are likely to be especially salient as change participants attempt to make sense of the change. (Jansen, 2004; p. 279)

Jansen goes on to argue, as we have, that both urgency (aspiration–achievement gaps) and feasibility influence the attention and effort a novel proposal engenders. Finally, Jansen introduces the term "escape velocity" to describe "the critical threshold where recognizable traction (i.e., progress) along the new trajectory allows for an escape from the stasis-based path" Jansen (2004, p. 279). We like the visualization that Jansen's work offers to our description of new venture emergence – where ideas become more attention-grabbing, plausible, and "real" as they are considered, revised, and reconsidered, until they accelerate to a point where an individual's, team's, or venture's proposal reaches escape velocity and launches into the next higher level of analysis. As Jansen notes, this description of momentum often leads to non-incremental transitions akin to those described by punctuated equilibrium models of ecological and strategic change (cf. Gersick, 1988; Ford & Sullivan, 2004).

Enabling Task Resources
Resources that enable the processes described so far are an additional requirement of process theorizing (Mackenzie, 2004). We define resources in terms of knowledge, tangible resources, and relationships that have been retained through the course of previous enactment processes. In this sense, we follow a robust perspective from the strategy and entrepreneurship literatures, which suggests that entrepreneurs can be thought of in terms of the resource-based view of the firm (RBV) (Penrose, 1959; Wernerfelt, 1984; Barney, 1991). More specifically, their special alertness to opportunities, their abilities to acquire homogeneous resources, their ability to use homogeneous resources and assemble them into heterogeneous outcomes, and their specific prior knowledge and experience are resources that can be unique, inimitable, valuable, and non-substitutable (Alvarez & Busenitz, 2001). The basic argument of the RBV is that firms are bundles of resources and that the ability to accumulate rare, non-substitutable, valuable and inimitable resources can be the source of a competitive advantage (Penrose, 1959; Barney, 1991).

Knowledge has been deemed especially important as a strategic resource – in particular, privately held knowledge that serves as a basic source of advantage in competition (Conner & Prahalad, 1996). According to the knowledge-based view of the firm (KBV), knowledge is a major resource necessary for achieving favorable organizational outcomes, especially during early firm development.

Some work within entrepreneurship suggests that entrepreneurs, as a result of their prior experiences, hold specific sets of knowledge (Fiet, 1996;

Hills, Shrader, & Lumpkin, 1999; Ronstadt, 1988; Shane, 2000, 2003; Shook et al., 2003). Entrepreneurs' knowledge sets at any given period are inadequate due to the inherent limitations of their experiences (Shane, 2000, 2003). Furthermore, individuals are boundedly rational (Simon, 1947; Thompson, 1967), which also contributes to the shortcomings that exist in their knowledge sets. Work in economics describes this as "the knowledge problem" (Yates, 2000). According to the knowledge problem, there will always be information unknown to an individual that is relevant to his or her decision (Yates, 2000). Therefore, the relationship between entrepreneurs' knowledge and venture development is constrained by the limited knowledge that entrepreneurs' possess at any given point. Dew, Velamuri, and Venkataraman (2004) refer to this knowledge held by individuals as idiosyncratic knowledge and specialized knowledge.

One way in which knowledge and resource limitations can be addressed is through relationships with others, especially those whose access to knowledge and resources complements the developmental needs of a particular new venture proposal. In other words, social network and alliance relationships can serve as a source of knowledge relevant to venture development. Collinson and Gregson (2003) argue that start-up firms are constrained far more by knowledge limitations than by financial limitations, and that network relationships may act as the source of critical knowledge and expertise. Grant (1996) suggests that individuals are essentially specialists, in that they are only knowledgeable to the extent of their prior experience. Organizing requires the coordinated efforts of individual specialists who possess many different types of knowledge, so the creation of the firm requires conditions under which multiple individuals can integrate their specialist knowledge. Consequently, we include relationships, in addition to knowledge and tangible resources, as important retained resources that can be drawn on to facilitate the enactment process.

Outcomes of New Venture Emergence Processes

Up to this point, we have attempted to follow Mackenzie's requirements for process theorizing (Mackenzie, 2004). He describes four requirements:

- To describe the events that make up the process. In our case, we use enactment theory to categorize events as related to environmental change and uncertainty, enactment, section, or retention.

• To identify a time-dependent sequence of these events. We begin by considering environmental uncertainty, followed by enactment, selection, and retention, respectively, acknowledging that enactment is a recursive process that repeats itself until sufficient momentum is reach to jump to a new phase of venture emergence.
• To describe the people, considerations (steps), relationships among considerations, links to other processes, and resources included in a process. We attempted to address this requirement in the previous section.
• To describe the outcomes of our process view, at each phase and level of analysis, as well as at the end of the entire new venture emergence process (see Fig. 1).

We propose that the outcomes associated with each phase of the new venture emergence process take the form of increasingly sophisticated conversation pieces that serve to instigate further sense making and environmental change. Early-stage outcomes emerging from an individual founder may take the form of a useful analogy, story, or prototype. Teams are typically required to put together a credible business plan and professional presentation. Ventures often point to "alpha" customers or well-known alliance partners to help others visualize the value network within which the venture operates. These conversation pieces help others visualize key characteristics of the venture proposal and facilitate further sense making and collective organizing.

Weick et al. offer an image of sense making as an *activity that talks organizations into existence*:

> [Sense making] ... is about continued redrafting of an emerging story so that it becomes more comprehensive, incorporates more of the observed data, and is more resilient in the face of criticism. As the search for meanings continues, people may describe their activities as the pursuit of accuracy to get it right. However, that description is important because it sustains motivation ... The important message is that if plausible stories keep things moving, they are salutary. Action-taking generates new data and creates opportunities for dialogue, bargaining, negotiation, and persuasion that enriches the sense of what is going on (Sutcliffe, 2000). Actions enable people to assess causal beliefs that subsequently lead to new actions undertaken to test the newly asserted relationships. Over time, as supporting evidence mounts, significant changes in beliefs and actions evolve. (Weick et al., 2005, pp. 415–416)

This description of sense making resonates with both the narratives offered by seasoned entrepreneurs and our own observations working with individuals, teams, and fledgling ventures engaged in the new venture formation process.

To this point, this chapter has presented a way of thinking about entrepreneurship that promises to lead to more comprehensive and rich descriptions of how novel ideas develop into business ventures. Although our consideration of these complex dynamics remains at an early stage of development, we have attempted to follow the guidance offered by those who have described the requirements for rigorous multi-level and process theorizing. Specifically, we have suggested constructs that have been utilized effectively in previous theories describing different levels of analysis, and articulated linkages among constructs at different levels that affect founder-, team-, and venture-level enactment. The following sections illustrate the utility of adopting a multi-level process view of new venture emergence by proposing research questions suggested by this approach at the founder, founding team, and venture levels of analysis.

THE FOUNDER–OPPORTUNITY NEXUS: NEW VENTURE OPPORTUNITY DISCOVERY

Our description of enactment processes, whereby founders create and refine their new venture proposals, is bounded temporally by two events: It begins when an individual first notices an anomaly or change in the environment; it ends when a founder communicates a proposal to another person *with the intent of instigating an economic transaction* (e.g., pitching with the purpose of attaining partners, procuring professional services, making sales, creating formal alliances). The moment that individuals (whom we will refer to as founders to simplify our narrative) pitch their idea (cf. Elsbach & Kramer, 2003) to others with the intent of "organizing" economic activity – specifically, convincing others to join the venture – represents a developmental discontinuity. That is, the founder's proposal has gained enough momentum to attain escape velocity and instigate a second phase and higher level of organizing at the team level. Thus, as described previously, the founder is bracketed by higher-level environmental uncertainty and lower-level founder attributes such as aspiration–achievement gaps, knowledge, and relationships. The numbers associated with each section heading have been calibrated with the numbered arrows in Fig. 2 to help guide the reader through the bracketed enactment cycles that occur during each phase of the new venture emergence process.

Environmental Uncertainty and Enactment at the
Founder–Opportunity Nexus

Interesting research questions characteristic of understanding how higher-level environmental uncertainty affects founder enactment could examine how uncertainty influences founder motivation and ideation. For example, uncertainty may provoke negative emotions such as fear or frustration, which might in turn motivate search and creative problem solving. Insights from these processes are likely to be derived from effectuation processes that develop solutions by drawing upon previously retained knowledge, resources, and relationships (see arrow 5 in Fig. 2). Formulating an initial proposal that addresses a problematic source of uncertainty may raise founder aspirations or accentuate the gap between realized and desired achievement, thereby stimulating further motivation, search, and ideation. Subsequently, decision considerations reflecting the selection phase of the enactment process can be utilized as founders engage in thought trials or experiments that construct and evaluate hypothetical new venture scenarios.

Weick (1989) suggested that individuals subject abstract proposals to selection processes reflecting what is known about the concrete world and retain those ideas that survive this scrutiny. In the context of our current discussion, we propose that entrepreneurs act much like researchers by searching for knowledge retained in their schemas and drawn from their social network relationships that can inform their ideation processes. Once founders form an initial hypothesis about how a new venture can address a market problem with a technological solution, he or she can subject that proposal to already-familiar aspects of technology, market, management, and finance screens. Promising experiments can enhance subsequent motivation, thereby intensifying the search and increasing the rigor of subsequent selection screenings. The founder's creating processes can continue indefinitely as hypotheses are discarded, modified, or retained and schemas and networks are engaged and elaborated.

Of course, individual differences with respect to founders' aspiration levels; current achievements; effectuation prowess; awareness and understanding of market, technology, organization, and financial considerations; and knowledge, resources, and relationship assets are all likely to affect founder opportunity discovery. Thus, even though enactment processes may offer a useful description of how founders discover opportunities, they do not suggest that different individuals will recognize the same uncertainties, discover the same solutions, or experience the same motivation to exploit their opportunity.

Shane (2000) provides vivid evidence of these individual variations from a case study of eight entrepreneurs who were presented with a new technology. The study sought to determine whether each person would identify the same opportunities and express the same motivation to exploit those opportunities so identified. The results indicated that none of the entrepreneurs identified the same opportunity, and that not everyone exploited the opportunities recognized. Shane explains his findings based on differences among individuals' prior knowledge and experience, especially with respect to: (1) specific markets' characteristics, (2) ways to organize so as to serve specific markets, and (3) specific knowledge about customer problems.

Ardichvili, Cardoza, and Ray (2003) also argue that opportunity discovery is affected by individual differences (in terms of personality, creativity, and other characteristics), relationship networks, and prior knowledge. Specifically, they suggest that these differences create "entrepreneurial alertness" – a passive state where problematic uncertainties are noticed – that then leads entrepreneurs to discover and evaluate opportunities in an ongoing fashion whereby proposals are revised, reassessed, and so forth as momentum to continue builds or ebbs.

Social psychological processes related to the credibility of information sources through which founders acquire knowledge about environmental changes and uncertainties are also important to consider. Founders are likely to learn from family, friends, acquaintances, colleagues, and other social ties, as well as from news sources, purveyors of popular culture, and so forth. Broad exposure to diverse sources of information and discerning tastes regarding the relative weight given to information from sources of varying credibility are likely to enrich the effectuation and selection processes. This concept is consistent with proposals offered by Simonton (1999), which argue that an individual's creative potential is best nurtured by having many diverse sources of influence rather than just a single influence, and by maintaining robust relationship networks across one's life span. It is interesting to note that Simonton's proposals were also motivated by utilizing the ESR process theory we have adopted for our descriptions.

Selection Processes in Founder Thought Experiments

Interesting research questions related to selection considerations could address founders' differences with respect to understanding and prioritizing different value requirements that bolster the plausibility and momentum of new venture proposals. As discussed previously, novel venture proposals must address "real" selection factors in the environment. These factors are relatively well known and have been institutionalized in a myriad of entrepreneurship education programs, business planning guides, software products, government and private sector financing options, and technology commercialization agencies. The selection considerations we have identified, reflecting the practices, norms, and values of different task domains, include markets, technology, organization, and financing (Ford, 2005). These four domains and their respective selection considerations are even reflected in the table of contents of *Entrepreneur* magazine – it organizes stories under these primary headings – and in the standard format for business plans that articulate a venture proposal's attributes. The extent to which a founder's understanding of these selection considerations is closely aligned with how these considerations function in the environment will determine how effectively a founder assesses the value of novel venture proposals.

The most obvious issues to consider with regard to the effectiveness with which a founder will assess the value of novel venture proposals are founder bias and ignorance. Not surprisingly, individual differences among founders significantly affect the extent to which appropriate selection considerations are utilized, understood, or given appropriate weight.

Shaver and Scott (1991) propose that because entrepreneurs are required to make decisions under conditions of uncertainty, they will use decision-making heuristics to help them to proceed through the cognitive processes involved in entrepreneurship. These heuristics inevitably lead to biases of representativeness, anchoring and adjustment, and availability that influence the decision-making process. Shaver and Scott suggest that the use of these biases will affect which opportunities are recognized, how they are uncovered, and how they are developed.

Keh, Foo, and Lim (2002) also investigated the decision-making heuristic biases that influence the opportunity discovery and evaluation process of entrepreneurs. Specifically, they found that the relationship between illusion of control and opportunity evaluation was fully mediated by risk perceptions, indicating that entrepreneurs believe that they can control the situation, but not market forces. These biases, in addition to disciplinary specialization that limits broader understanding of different selection considerations, suggest that organizing a new venture on one's own is likely to be very difficult and fraught with surprises and mistakes. One could imagine exceptions to this rule, however – for example, a "serial entrepreneur" who has broad experience in all aspects of a new venture, or a scenario in which organizing considerations are relatively few (e.g., working as an independent contractor) or have been predetermined (e.g., purchasing a franchise).

Retention Processes and Managerial Capacity

Research questions related to founders' retention processes tend to focus on differences in founders' knowledge, resources, and relationships that provide access to additional knowledge and resources. Recent innovation and entrepreneurship research has depicted creative business outcomes, or innovations, as being the result of associations between previously retained forms of knowledge and technology (Hargadon & Sutton, 1997; Shane, 2000). This notion was captured by Thomas Edison, who noted that "To invent, you need a good imagination and a pile of junk" (quoted in Hargadon & Sutton, 2000; p. 160).

In the context of entrepreneurship, the initial generation of creative associations can motivate entrepreneurial exploration by producing information asymmetries – knowledge known to some but not to others – capable of creating economic value. Information asymmetries such as these are the foundation of the Austrian perspective on entrepreneurship (Hayek, 1945; described by Shane, 2000). This perspective argues that opportunities exist when all people do not possess the same information at the same time (a disequilibrium condition). According to the Austrian perspective, entrepreneurs may obtain resources below their equilibrium market price because others do not recognize the value of recombining those resources in a creative way. Because each potential entrepreneur's knowledge, resources, and relationships are unique, creative associations made by one entrepreneur are unlikely to be discovered by others.

Updating the Proposition and Assessing Momentum

Research questions related to the relationship between retention processes and further enactment trials might focus on learning, effectuation, and changing aspirations. Sarasvathy (2001) compares effectuation with the process of making dinner by examining the contents of one's pantry and determining what can be made with the ingredients on hand. We believe that it is important to investigate how founders' knowledge stocks change as a result of experience, and how the availability of new ingredients affects the recipes founders concoct.

Each enactment cycle, simulation, or thought experiment may result in the rejection of a proposition, either in the form of considering an opportunity to be plausible, albeit not for oneself (i.e., a third-person opportunity), or by identifying a selection consideration "showstopper" that makes the proposition seem implausible at the current time.

Alternatively, propositions may be partially selected. In this case, certain proposal attributes may survive selection considerations (e.g., "The technology works"), while others are deemed unworkable or underdeveloped (e.g., "I think I should target a different market"). This iterative "revise and resubmit" process may lead to proposals becoming more plausible as a result of continued effectuation processes that add missing ingredients to a venture recipe. To the extent that a founder perceives increased plausibility, and perhaps urgency related to increasingly vivid aspirations, we expect momentum to increase. When potential entrepreneurs believe they possess a creative idea not known to others, they may envision ways in which their proprietary, creative knowledge could lead to success. Their aspirations are especially likely to increase when the potential entrepreneur imagines a venture's profits to be both large and sustainable (Shane, 2001). The resulting momentum is likely to provoke increased attention, search, and ideation related to articulating the opportunity.

Enriching Founder Selection Considerations

A second learning process depicted by enactment theory suggests that founders' understandings of selection considerations should change as a result of the enactment process. For example, Ronstadt (1988) proposes the "corridor principle," which says that once an individual starts down a path of assessing an opportunity, other related venture proposals will become apparent. For instance, an individual who is seeking ways to address increasing fuel costs with solar energy (photovoltaic) panels may also discover characteristics of the solution that make it ideal for providing temporary electricity to disaster victims. Thus considerations that are not important in the context of assessing one venture proposal may prove to be powerful considerations that justify alternative proposals.

As a founder becomes increasingly immersed in modifying and assessing a proposal, lessons related to assessing key considerations should gradually enhance the quality and scope of that individual's selection processes. In other words, diligent founders are likely to learn what they don't know about assessing venture plausibility. Learning how to more accurately and comprehensively assess important environmental considerations is a key goal of entrepreneurship education, and an important advantage held by experienced entrepreneurs. In fact, we suggest that learning one's limitations is an important outcome of the enactment process that serves as an important motivator for seeking help from others and forming founding teams.

Opportunity Discovery, Escape Velocity, the "Pitch," and the Creating Coalition

A specific episode of founder creating processes can conclude in one of two ways, as founder investigations reduce uncertainty related to outcomes, both good and bad, that might result from a new venture proposal. First, a founder's new venture proposal may become more focused, elaborate, and comprehensive as it is infused with previously retained knowledge and knowledge obtained through social network relationships. This evolution may result in a proposal's momentum reaching escape velocity, such that the founder is motivated to "pitch" the proposal in an effort to build economic relationships that form a "creating coalition" or team necessary to launch the new venture. Alternatively, a founder's proposal may be confronted with too many gloomy assessments to support continued motivation, attention, and ideation.

The fact that a founder has developed sufficient confidence in the plausibility of a venture proposal to pitch the idea to potential partners suggests that certain outcome milestones have been achieved. In particular, we expect founders to continue working on their proposals until they are able to clearly articulate those proposals to others. The confidence this outcome brings to the founder may create sufficient momentum for the proposal to achieve escape velocity. Once escape velocity is achieved, founders may seek additional knowledge, resources, and relationships by presenting a vivid depiction of a proposal using narrative tools such as an analogy, story, model, or scenario that allows others to visualize how participating in the venture would address their aspirations.

We expect proposal momentum to be closely linked to the quality of the narrative strategies employed to articulate the variants of a proposal throughout the new venture emergence process. We also expect entrepreneurial pitches to be governed by the same social-psychological processes described by Elsbach and Kramer (2003) in the context of Hollywood pitch meetings. Thus we would expect a founder's success with respect to attracting others to join or support a venture to be affected by cues that govern person categorization and relationship categorization in the context of new venture creation.

For instance, "serial entrepreneurs" may be viewed similarly to the "showrunners" (pitchers who have a track record of successfully creating and executing new show ideas) identified by Elsbach and Kramer. Being classified in this fashion would likely add credibility to a founder's proposal and make its realization seem more plausible to those who are hearing the pitch. Elsbach and Kramer also note that pitcher–catcher relationships are more likely to flourish when the catcher views the relationship as a creative collaboration. When those listening to a founder's pitch view the founder as less competent than themselves, the outcome of the pitch is likely to be unfavorable and higher levels of organizing will be thwarted. Our multi-level process view emphasizes communication and sense-making processes like these, which create collective understandings and action from the visions of an individual.

THE TEAM–OPPORTUNITY NEXUS: NEW VENTURE OPPORTUNITY DISCOVERY

Few new venture opportunities are plausible enough to attract a team dedicated to evaluating and exploiting the proposal. Nevertheless, we propose that a novel proposal refined to a point where it is vivid and plausible enough to engage the aspirations of others is a prerequisite to venture team formation. The opportunity evaluation phase at the team level of analysis describes how novel proposals attract new participants and how new participants contribute to revising and improving the plausibility of the proposal. In this sense, our work follows previous research that describes how creative proposals and social networks co-evolve over time in a spiraling manner that leads proposals and relationships to become increasingly more organized (Perry-Smith & Shalley, 2003).

This phase of new venture emergence is temporally bound by two types of events. The first phase begins when an individual or several individuals make a commitment to work as partners who share decision rights and possibly share equity in a proposed venture. This phase concludes when the team creates contracts that establish economic commitments (e.g., lease agreements, manufacturing contracts, employment contracts, sales agreements). Once these commitments begin, the venture as an economic agent defined by a nexus of contracts is formed and the opportunity exploitation phase begins.

Environmental Uncertainty and Enactment at the Team–Opportunity Nexus

Research questions suggested by the nexus of environmental uncertainty and venture team enactment could focus on how a team's mix of aspirations, knowledge, resources, and relationships facilitate or hinder venture articulation and plausibility. This would entail examining how teams enact environmental uncertainty as a means of linking higher-level influences to team-level enactment. Given our attempt to incorporate multi-level bracketing into our theorizing, however, we are particularly interested in how (lower-level) founder characteristics affect the mix of participants attracted to a venture proposal (e.g., what kinds of partners would a star scientist be likely to attract?) and how founder attributes influence the effectuation and selection processes at the team level (e.g., do founders with prior venture organizing experience exert disproportional influence that hinders team-level effectuation?).

As described earlier, the complexities associated with articulating a plausible new venture proposal are likely to necessitate a search among the new and weak network relationships for those capable of spurring new creative associations and raising support for an entrepreneur's plans (Perry-Smith & Shalley, 2003). The additional knowledge acquired as a result of these interactions may affect the direction in which a venture proposal evolves, perhaps in unexpected ways. As the spiraling process that links the refinement of a novel business concept to the development of a social network supporting the entrepreneur evolves (cf. Perry-Smith & Shalley, 2003), important contributors with especially strong ties to the entrepreneur may join an entrepreneur's management team. This process serves to gather the diverse expertise necessary to fully articulate an entrepreneur's initial musings, and it helps establish a "creating coalition" capable of providing the technical, marketing, financial, and administrative expertise necessary to evaluate and enhance a venture proposal's plausibility. The character of a team's effectuation processes and collective aspirations influence this stage of the opportunity evaluation phase of the new venture emergence process.

Selection Processes in Founder–Team Sense-Making Conversations

Research questions directed toward understanding bracketed team-level selection processes could investigate how the diversity and quantity of team members' experience mitigate founders' bias and ignorance. The primary motivation for a founder to include others in a new venture proposition is to add knowledge, resources, and relationships to the emerging venture. The extent to which those assets are utilized (e.g., can a dominating founder limit the value of team member resources) or provide complementary contributions is interesting to consider. Given the faith that team members must show when committing to join a founder in a new venture, consensus-seeking dynamics might potentially emerge, especially with respect to validating proposals offered by the founder.

Teams are also likely to vary with respect to how aware they are of their founders' and their collective biases. For example, Simon, Houghton, and Aquino (2000) studied founder cognitive biases and found that founders tend to systematically underestimate the risks associated with their venture proposals. These researchers suggest that entrepreneurs can develop more realistic evaluations by incorporating other diverse perspectives into their opportunity discovery and evaluation processes. For example, adding team members with non-redundant knowledge and more extensive access to knowledge through network relationships should be expected to produce more rigorous assessments of new venture plausibility. This suggests a relationship between founding team selection and environmental uncertainty, whereby the match between team knowledge of selection factors and "real" environmental selection factors is an important factor for success.

Retention Processes and Managerial Capacity

Important research questions related to this part of the founding team enactment process might focus on how team members' knowledge and network relationships enrich effectuation processes and enhance the plausibility of a new venture proposal. Team members' knowledge, assets, and relationships supplement the limitations of the founder. This notion is analogous to Kogut and Zander's (1992) description of combinative capability, which they define as a dynamic ability of actors to synthesize current and acquired knowledge. As such, they include the existing knowledge of the founder as well as propose that knowledge can be obtained from others. In short, combinative capabilities comprise the ability to combine and effectively utilize both existing and new knowledge. In their work, Kogut and Zander propose that combinative capabilities are helpful in discovering and articulating opportunities.

Given the critical nature of attaining resources from others, it is not surprising that "solo entrepreneurs" who rely primarily on their own knowledge for discovering, evaluating, and exploiting novel venture ideas have limited success (Shane, 2000). By contrast, "network entrepreneurs" tend to create and exploit more opportunities because of their access to non-redundant knowledge and their exposure to the serendipitous associations that characterize many business initiatives (Aldrich & Kenworthy, 1999).

Updating the Proposition and Assessing Momentum

As we described at the individual level of analysis, effectuation processes are facilitated by available resources. We expect new ventures that utilize founding teams to have much more varied and higher-quality ingredients with which to improve their new venture recipes (to use Sarasvathy's cooking analogy). Shane (2003) reviews prior research that supports this notion. Specifically, he finds that ventures founded by individuals are less successful and more prone to mortality than ventures founded by teams.

Perry-Smith and Shalley's (2003) description of the interrelated spiraling processes that link concept formulation and network relationships offers a useful initial theoretical development suggesting that creative ideas and social networks evolve in tandem. We would expect that as the plausibility of the venture increases in this manner, associated increases in momentum would be moderated by the degree to which individual team members link the venture's success with their own personal aspirations. Specifically, momentum should increase more effectively when team decision rights and equity stakes are clearly defined from the onset of the venture team's formation. Unclear agreements may lead to ill will and conflict that detracts from a proposal's momentum.

Enriching Team Selection Considerations

Research questions related to this stage of team-level opportunity evaluation processes might emphasize the degree to which a team develops a collective understanding of important market, technology, organization, and financial issues, or whether team members remain specialized and rely on loosely coupled assessments. Obviously, conflict would be more likely to emerge when team members maintain narrow disciplinary perspectives by failing to learn from one another or failing to form team network relationships. Teams that are characterized by non-defensive, collaborative, interdisciplinary conversations, occasionally including outsiders, are especially likely to learn from one another and to improve their collective understanding of important environmental selection processes.

Another cross-level research question to consider is the degree of influence that a founder has on facilitating or restricting this learning process. Dogmatic or overconfident founders may hinder a team's ability to question assumptions about the environment or revisit prior assessments of important considerations.

Opportunity Evaluation, Escape Velocity, Resource Acquisition, and the Business Plan

As was the case at the founder level of analysis, the plausibility and vividness of a new venture proposal will determine the extent to which a founding team's confidence and excitement grow to the point where escape velocity leads to venture formation. Although the quality of analogies, stories, prototypes, and other narrative devices remains an important sense-making influence at this level, we argue that formal business plans represent the penultimate articulation of a new venture proposal. Just as "pitch meetings" are standard sense-making occasions in Hollywood (Elsbach & Kramer, 2003), business plan presentations are common practice during the venture evaluation phase. These presentations may be directed toward financial supporters (e.g., angel or venture capital investors), alliance partners (e.g., manufacturers, suppliers, distribution channels), lead customers, or even potential employees. We propose that a business plan is an especially critical sense-making conversation piece for two reasons. First, it forces founding teams to articulate their proposals in a comprehensive and compelling fashion, thereby allowing them to address the ultimate collective sense-making challenge: "How do we know what we think until we see what we say?" (Weick, 1979). Second, a business plan enables economic commitments to accumulate by presenting a consistent and complete description of a venture proposal.

We also think it is interesting to consider the role of simulations and prototypes as narrative tools that allow those who are unfamiliar with a venture proposition to comprehend the value of the proposal quickly and from their own perspective. We have helped entrepreneurs develop interactive Web sites, models, animated shorts, and non-functional "promo-types" to help them communicate the value of their proposals.

What is interesting about these kinds of sense-making devices is that they rely heavily on non-verbal cues that allow individuals who figuratively or literally speak a different language than the founding team to assess the proposal. We suspect that founding teams that create visualizations of their proposals in addition to authoring a formal business plan have considerable success, increasing momentum to the point of escape velocity that launches the venture as an economic agent participating in a value network of related interests (Christensen, 1997). These interests include customers, suppliers, competitors, service providers, and others who affect the market, technology, organization, and financial factors engaged by the venture.

THE VENTURE–OPPORTUNITY NEXUS: NEW VENTURE OPPORTUNITY EXPLOITATION

We employ two temporal boundary conditions to define the emergence of a venture and the beginning of the opportunity exploitation phase. The first is the establishment of economic contracts with interests outside the founding team. Although economic relationships often possess many of the same attributes as social network relationships, they often provide tangible resources and are regulated by contractual terms and authority. We believe this distinction is important to defining organizing as it pertains to new venture emergence. Thus a venture is born at the point when it begins exchanging economic value with other agents in its environment. We demarcate the end of this phase, somewhat arbitrarily, as the time when the venture's growth in revenues, assets, and personnel expenses (employee and service providers) are all positive for one quarter. Our logic is that this event – or an analogous event – would signal that a firm has become an ongoing, growing venture that has moved beyond the emergence stage (Hansen & Bird, 1997; Hansen, 1995; Reynolds & Miller, 1992; Katz & Gartner, 1988). We do not seek to describe what happens after the organization has reached this developmental milestone. Our story ends at the conclusion of the new venture emergence process.

Environmental Uncertainty and Enactment at the
Venture–Opportunity Nexus

Once a venture begins contracting with others, it accepts commitments that "lock in" certain facets of the venture proposal. At this point, the focus of

CAMERON M. FORD AND DIANE M. SULLIVAN

the search and ideation processes may shift away from deciding what to do and toward improving the means by which value is delivered. The shift from planning to doing, however, is likely to bring many lessons for the founding team and other venture participants. We suspect that effectuation processes are likely to remain relevant to venture emergence in this phase, but will be applied more often to improvising solutions to unanticipated problems.

We also believe it is important to examine the manner in which the founding team and venture aspirations shift as the venture opens. Greve (2003) examined the proposed influence of "performance minus aspiration level" gaps on search, research and development (R&D), and innovation in the shipbuilding industry. In his study, he found that performance minus aspiration level gaps had a substantial impact on search and innovation (performance below aspirations had a mild positive relationship to innovation; performance above aspirations had a strong negative relationship to innovation). Greve concluded that performance–aspiration gaps are an important "trigger" for search and creative action at the venture level. This suggests that initial disappointments in the opportunity exploitation phase are likely to be met by attempts to innovate and redeploy resources to better advantage.

Greve strongly advocates examining decision processes (e.g., aspiration levels, search, risk tolerance) related to innovation launch decisions as a means of better understanding differences between firms' propensity to innovate. He argues that performance–aspiration gaps represent a dynamic relationship between an individual's or firm's current situation and envisioned options (suggesting that this variable might be used at multiple levels of analysis).

Selection Processes in Venture–Value Network
Sense-Making Conversations

Research questions about selection processes at the venture level might focus on the relative importance and preferred sequence of addressing different considerations. One study along these lines was recently published by Delmar and Shane (2004). Their findings suggest a specific sequence of selection concerns that new ventures should undertake to promote further organizing processes and avoid venture team disbanding. Specifically, Delmar and Shane examined whether legitimating activities such as writing a business plan prevented the venture team from disbanding and promoted subsequent organizing of market, technology, organization, and financial aspects of the business. They discovered that ventures fared best when they addressed legitimating first. Consistent with the story we have been telling, their study suggests that helping others develop a collective understanding of the venture and building momentum with respect to the value of the venture are necessary prerequisites for processes related to acquiring and organizing tangible resources.

Retention Processes and Managerial Capacity

Research questions that address the character and quantity of the knowledge, resources, and relationships possessed by a venture and its founding team are salient to this phase of the venture emergence process. As described previously, RBV has become perhaps the dominant perspective for understanding competitive advantage and firm-level performance. In particular, previously retained knowledge expands the resources available to effectuation processes, leading to novel venture proposals. Evidence that previously retained knowledge enables innovation at the firm level is consistent with our prior descriptions.

For example, Hargadon and Sutton (1997) and Hargadon (2003) have presented extensive evidence examining new product and technology breakthroughs at the firm level of analysis. They argue that new proposals result from technology brokering, whereby information is taken from different industries and modified (i.e., fit) to industries in which this information is not currently being used to develop new solutions.

Hargadon's (2003) work, in particular, describes how specialized knowledge and interdisciplinary bridges combine to expand the array of retained resources available during an effectuation ideation process. Hargadon offers compelling evidence that novel breakthroughs are built from novel combinations of previously retained solutions, often drawn from diverse task domains or industries. His model is couched in a network and organizational memory perspective, whereby previously retained knowledge from diverse prior experiences is used to suggest analogies to new problems from different environments. Hargadon's important work highlights the importance of retained knowledge, tangible resources, and relationships (i.e., bridges) that link the effectuation and learning processes.

Updating the Proposition and Assessing Momentum

During this phase, the venture interacts with the "real" environment and, therefore, has an opportunity to learn from experience. An initial venture proposal is likely to include both components that work according to plan and other components that fail to meet expectations. Thus, the partial selection processes described previously are likely to require ventures to remain flexible, perhaps by taking a conservative approach to growth and financial commitments (Christensen, 1997). Ventures whose primary features fare well may find it relatively easy to keep their aspirations and momentum high while they modify secondary characteristics of their proposals. Conversely, firms that have difficulty with central aspects of their value proposition (e.g., margins are too low to fund the venture) will likely lose momentum and fail.

Interesting research questions related to this phase could address the extent to which emerging ventures adjust to environmental contingencies. Newly emerging ventures lack many of the forces of inertia described in prior research (Jansen, 2004). At the same time, they lack resources that might buffer them from exogenous shocks. Understanding the relative advantages offered by different types of resources when ventures need to improvise would shed light on this issue. For example, does a stockpile of strong network relationships help a venture quickly reconfigure its resources? Examining cross-level influences between the founding team and the emerging venture may reveal that team resources play a critical role in the improvisational capacity and staying power of a venture.

Enriching Venture Selection Considerations

Previous discussions of this process at lower levels of analysis and prior phases of organization have emphasized the sense-making processes that enable founders, founding teams, and others to "talk an organization into existence." The venture exploitation phase emphasizes action and business performance, rather than sense-making, outcomes as measures of progress and success. Research questions suggested by this phase might examine ways in which founding team members help or hinder the alignment of selection considerations with the experiences of the venture.

We suggest that early success may lead founding team members to overestimate the rigor and efficacy of their collective perspective on selection considerations, thereby making the team reach their understandings of the environment more slowly in the face of subsequent negative information. Alternatively, doubt (McMullen & Shepherd, 2006) may play an important role in venture and founding team learning. Specifically, ambivalence with respect to selection considerations may enhance founding team learning and vigilance, and improve the venture's responsiveness to unexpected events and environmental changes.

Opportunity Exploitation, Proposition Validation, and Capability Development

As opportunity exploitation processes continue, we expect firms to demonstrate the efficacy of their proposals by garnering outside investment, attaining sales, and growing their assets. Initial success is also likely to lead to further enrichment of knowledge, resources, and relationships, thereby increasing the momentum that led to the venture's launch. Research questions suggested by considering this final step in our journey might include investigations into how ventures effectively leverage endorsements from established, trusted associates as a means of enhancing their legitimacy. Emerging ventures require others to take leaps of faith with respect to trust, reliability, professionalism, and the like. They often rely on endorsements from well-known clients, suppliers or distributors, or associations with universities, investment firms, and other respected agencies to bolster their claims of legitimacy (Stuart, 2000; Stuart, Hoang, & Hybels, 1999; Ingram & Baum, 1997). This strategy of "legitimacy by association" is a common feature during new venture pitches, when names of prominent partners or promising leads are dropped in conversation as a cue to signal legitimacy.

Another interesting issue related to legitimacy has to do with the relationship between novelty and value assessments. Strategic management theory emphasizes differentiation (novelty) as the primary means by which firms create and sustain competitive advantage. Alternatively, institutional theory (DiMaggio & Powell, 1983) emphasizes conformity to accepted industry practice as the basis of firm survival. Deephouse (1996) conducted a competitive test of the relative explanatory power of these two theories and found that the relationship between novelty and strategic value is curvilinear: As strategic management theory predicts, firms must be somewhat novel to succeed, but as institutional theory predicts, too much novelty can be fatal.

We wonder if novelty is best applied to certain selection considerations while common practice is applied to others. For example, is novelty primarily important with respect to product or service offerings, but unimportant (or perhaps negatively associated with value) in financial arrangements? Knowing the most fruitful areas in which to leverage deviance and the best occasions for blending in with the crowd could enhance emerging ventures' odds of survival.

IMPLICATIONS OF A MULTI-LEVEL PROCESS VIEW OF NEW VENTURE EMERGENCE

We thank those of you who have stayed with us to the end of our journey. We warned that we did not have a short story to tell. Our purpose in presenting this tale has been twofold: to outline assumptions and possible foundations for a multi-level process approach to understanding and investigating new venture emergence, and to illustrate how one might think about explaining and studying new venture emergence with this approach. At the core of our effort has been enactment theory. Given our interest in enactment processes, we viewed the opportunity to author this far-reaching chapter as a self-learning opportunity to ask the ultimate sense-making question: "How do we know what we think until we see what we say?" Now that we have seen what we have said, here are a few key points that we think we thought.

First, it is critically important at this stage of development in entrepreneurship research to adopt event-driven or process theorizing. Entrepreneurship research has improved significantly in recent years and now offers many provocative empirical findings and theoretical arguments. These advances can be understood more coherently and can offer practical guidance more directly if reframed within a process perspective. This perspective examines the arduous journey between a founder's initial insight and the launch of a new venture. This journey can be described as an evolving communication, sense-making, and negotiation process among an entrepreneur/founder, members of a founding team, and critical stakeholders whose support is necessary to the venture's emergence and survival. In the beginning, the proposal is typically broad and relatively abstract. Over time, however, contributions from others and continued sense making help the proposal become more plausible as diverse stakeholder inputs and interests are considered and incorporated into the venture. At the end of this journey stands a venture proposal that is endorsed by those who shepherded the idea along. This new venture emergence process can cause great ideas to become corrupted or diluted by stakeholders or weighed down by convention, but the journey can also lead to novel associations that amplify the plausibility, value, and fitness of the venture.

Second, enactment theory is uniquely capable of describing the organizing of new ventures across multiple levels of analysis and phases of opportunity development. Enactment theory (and the robust evolutionary arguments from which it grew) provides a conceptual storyline that can be, and has been, generalized to multiple levels of analysis. It offers especially forceful arguments regarding the character of the entrepreneur–opportunity nexus by considering actor and contextual influences simultaneously. We especially like the notion that enactment-driven sense-making processes result in people talking organizations into existence. This insight may direct researchers' attention toward practical organizing problems that are well known to entrepreneurs, such as fashioning the pitch, naming the venture, fashioning tradeshow materials, writing the plan, building the prototype, and so forth. Researchers know little about how communication and social psychological processes influence the venture emergence process. We hope these issues draw more attention as we investigate processes through which visions are realized.

Third, we are excited about the potential of strategic momentum theory (Jansen, 2004) to sharpen our understanding of both the transitions among enactment processes and the discontinuous organizing leaps that literally create the next higher level of analysis. The intuitively appealing metaphor of ideas spinning faster and faster, and motivation growing as visions come into focus, is also consistent with important prior empirical studies on strategic change. It is also a versatile theoretical device. This metaphor can be employed just as effectively to describe why few founder insights survive more than a few minutes of scrutiny. It can also be used to explain why founders often fail to generate sufficient enthusiasm to create founding teams. Because momentum is a dynamic concept, it highlights the importance of small consistent wins, occasional endorsements, and communication of the achievement of important venture emergence milestones.

Fourth, because new venture emergence is ultimately an individual and collective sense-making process in the face of considerable uncertainty, communication processes within and among actors at different levels of analysis should be central to future entrepreneurship theorizing. We are especially interested in two promising avenues for research on entrepreneurial communication.

The first is to conduct research that generalizes and enriches Elsbach and Kramer's (2003) pioneering research on the pitching process. This process is rich in creativity, learning, communicating, and negotiating processes, with significant resources and strategic momentum at stake. We believe that research on pitching is a perfect example of Big-O theorizing, as this process is clearly central to organizing.

The second direction for future communication is to explore ways in which visualizations of venture attributes affect venture organizing. We argue that tangible, visible manifestations of a venture proposal such as analogies, success stories, models, Web sites, and prototypes are powerful narrative devices that can significantly influence assessments of venture plausibility. We suspect that early development of these types of proposal development milestones will improve venture momentum and increase the probability of venture launch.

Finally, writing this chapter has led us to wonder about the extent to which venture emergence processes are becoming institutionalized as a result of entrepreneurship education and research. Most major universities have entrepreneurship initiatives that support a handful of common classes (e.g., new venture finance, new venture marketing, business plan writing). The content of these courses is likely becoming more uniform as universities copy best practices from leading institutions and as textbooks become increasingly standardized as the field of entrepreneurship matures. Business plan competitions that utilize business planning templates or software are also held at many schools. Networking events with the express purpose of linking nascent entrepreneurship to experts and service providers are increasingly common.

It concerns us that entrepreneurship processes are being taught and supported in such a uniform way when we lack a strong research foundation for advocating such strong methodologies. One of our underlying goals in tackling this assignment has been to describe a multi-level process perspective that resonates with the tactical methods that characterize most entrepreneurship education and advising, while simultaneously providing a useful foundation for scholarly theory and research. This lofty aim would help align the rhetoric of entrepreneurship practitioners and scholars, and bring the rigor associated with evidence-based management training to the entrepreneurship field.

REFERENCES

Aldrich, H. (1999). *Organizations evolving.* London: Sage.

Aldrich, H. E., & Kenworthy, A. (1999). The accidental entrepreneur: Campbellian antinomies and organizational foundings. In: J. A. Baum & B. McKelvey (Eds), *Variations in organizational science: In honor of Donald T. Campbell* (pp. 19–33). Newbury Park, CA: Sage.

Alvarez, S. A. (2005). *Two alternative theories of entrepreneurship. Max Planck Knowledge Series.* Bristol, CT: NOW.

Alvarez, S., & Barney, J. (2005). How do entrepreneurs organize firms under conditions of uncertainty? *Journal of Management, 31*(5), 776–793.

Alvarez, S., & Busenitz, L. (2001). The entrepreneurship of resource-based theory. *Journal of Management, 27,* 755–775.

Ardichvili, A., Cardoza, R., & Ray, S. (2003). A theory of entrepreneurial opportunity identification and development. *Journal of Business Venturing, 18*(1), 105–123.

Astebro, T., & Elhedhli, S. (2006). The effectiveness of simple decision heuristics: Forecasting commercial success for early-stage ventures. *Management Science, 52*(3), 395–409.

Barney, J. B. (1991). Firm resources and sustained competitive advantage. *Journal of Management, 17,* 99–120.

Baum, J., & Singh, J. (1994). Organizational hierarchies and evolutionary processes: Some reflections on a theory of organizational evolution. In: J. A. C. Baum & J. V. Singh (Eds), *Evolutionary dynamics of organizations* (pp. 3–22). New York, NY: Oxford University Press.

Campbell, D. T. (1960). Blind variation and selective retention in creative thought as in other knowledge processes. *Psychological Review, 95,* 380–400.

Campbell, D. T. (1965). Variation and selective retention in socio-cultural evolution. In: H. R. Barringer, G. I. Blanksten & R. W. Mack (Eds), *Social change in developing areas: A reinterpretation of evolutionary theory* (pp. 19–48). Cambridge, MA: Schenkman.

Christensen, C. M. (1997). *The innovator's dilemma.* Cambridge, MA: Harvard Business School Press.

Coase, R. (1937). The nature of the firm. *Economica, 4*(16), 386–405.

Collinson, S., & Gregson, G. (2003). Knowledge networks for new technology-based firms: An international comparison of local entrepreneurship promotion. *R&D Management, 33*(2), 189–208.

Conner, K. R., & Prahalad, C. K. (1996). A resource-based theory of the firm: Knowledge versus opportunism. *Organization Science, 7*(5), 477–501.

Deephouse, D. (1996). Does isomorphism legitimate? *Academy of Management Journal, 39*(4), 1024–1039.

Delmar, F., & Shane, S. (2004). Legitimating first: Organizing activities and the survival of new ventures. *Journal of Business Venturing, 19,* 385–410.

Dew, N., Velamuri, S. R., & Venkataraman, S. (2004). Dispersed knowledge and an entrepreneurial theory of the firm. *Journal of Business Venturing, 19,* 659–679.

DiMaggio, P. J., & Powell, W. W. (1983). The iron cage revisited: Institutional isomorphism and collective rationality in organizational fields. *American Sociological Review, 48*(2), 147–160.

Elsbach, K. D., & Kramer, R. M. (2003). Assessing creativity in Hollywood pitch meetings: Evidence for a dual-process model of creativity judgments. *Academy of Management Journal, 46*(3), 283–301.

Fiet, J. O. (1996). The informational basis of entrepreneurial discovery. *Small Business Economics, 8,* 419–430.

Ford, C. (2005). Creative associations and entrepreneurial opportunities. In: L. Thompson & H. S. Choi (Eds), *Creativity and innovation in organizations* (pp. 216–227). Marwah, NJ: Lawrence Erlbaum.

Ford, C., & Sullivan, D. M. (2004). A time for everything: How the timing of novel contributions influences project team outcomes. *Journal of Organizational Behavior, 25*(2), 279–292.

Ford, C. M. (1996). A theory of individual creative action in multiple social domains. *Academy of Management Review, 21*(4), 1112–1142.

Ford, C. M., & Sullivan, D. M. (2005). Creating and organizing processes in the business domain. In: J. Kaufman & J. Baer (Eds), *Creativity across domains: Faces of the muse* (pp. 347–418). NJ: Lawrence Erlbaum.

Gersick, C. J. G. (1988). Time and transition in work teams: Toward a new model of group development. *Academy of Management Journal, 31*(1), 9–41.

Giddens, A. (1984). *The constitution of society.* Berkeley, CA: University of California Press.

Gioia, D. A., & Pitre, E. (1990). Multiparadigm perspectives on theory building. *Academy of Management Review, 15*(4), 584–602.

Grant, R. M. (1996). Toward a knowledge-based theory of the firm. *Strategic Management Journal, 17,* 109–122.

Greve, H. R. (2003). A behavioral theory of R&D expenditures and innovations: Evidence from shipbuilding. *Academy of Management Journal, 46*(5), 685–702.

Hackman, J. R. (2003). Learning more by crossing levels: Evidence from airplanes, hospitals, and orchestras. *Journal of Organizational Behavior, 24*(8), 905–922.

Hansen, E. L. (1995). Entrepreneurial network and new organization growth. *Entrepreneurship, Theory, and Practice, 19*(4), 7–20.

Hansen, E. L., & Bird, B. J. (1997). The stages model of high-tech venture founding: Tried but true? *Entrepreneurship, Theory, and Practice, 22*(2), 111–122.

Hargadon, A. B. (2003). *How breakthroughs happen.* Boston, MA: Harvard Business School Press.

Hargadon, A. B., & Sutton, R. I. (1997). Technology brokering and innovation in a product development firm. *Administrative Science Quarterly, 42,* 716–749.

Hargadon, A. B., & Sutton, R. I. (2000). Building an innovation factory. *Harvard Business Review, 78*(3), 157–166.

Hayek, F. (1945). The use of knowledge in society. *American Economic Review, 35*(4), 519–530.

Heath, C., & Sitkin, S. B. (2001). Big-B versus Big-O: What is organizational about organizational behavior? *Journal of Organizational Behavior, 22,* 43–58.

Hills, G. E., Shrader, R. C., & Lumpkin, G. T. (1999). Opportunity recognition as a creative process. In: P. D. Reynolds, W. D. Bygrave, S. Maingart, C. Mason, G. D. Meyer, H. Sapienza & K. G. Shaver (Eds), *Frontiers of entrepreneurship research* (pp. 216–227). Wellesley, MA: Babson College.

Hughes, G. D., & Chapin, D. C. (1996). Turning new product development into a continuous learning process. *Journal of Product Innovation Management, 13,* 89–104.

Ingram, P., & Baum, J. A. C. (1997). Opportunity and constraint: Organizations' learning from the operating and competitive experience of industries. *Strategic Management Journal, 18,* 75–98.

Ireland, R. D., Reutzel, C. R., & Webb, J. W. (2005). Entrepreneurship research in AMJ: What has been published, and what might the future hold? *Academy of Management Journal, 48*(4), 556–564.

Jansen, K. J. (2004). From persistence to pursuit: A longitudinal examination of momentum during the early stages of strategic change. *Organization Science, 15*(3), 276–294.

Katz, J., & Gartner, W. B. (1988). Properties of emerging organizations. *Academy of Management Review, 13*(3), 429–441.

Keh, H. T., Foo, M. D., & Lim, B. C. (2002). Opportunity evaluation under risky conditions: The cognitive processes of entrepreneurs. *Entrepreneurship Theory and Practice, 27*(2), 125–148.

Kogut, B., & Zander, U. (1992). Knowledge of the firm, combinative capabilities, and the replication of technology. *Organization Science, 3*(3), 383–397.

Mackenzie, K. D. (2004). The process approach to multi-level organizational behavior. In: F. Dansereau & F. J. Yammarino (Eds), *Multi-level issues in organizational behavior and processes* (Vol. 3, pp. 347–418). Oxford: Elsevier.

March, J. G. (1991). Exploration and exploitation in organizational learning. *Organization Science, 2*(1), 71–87.

March, J. G., & Simon, H. A. (1958). *Organizations.* New York, NY: Wiley.

McMullen, J. S., & Shepherd, D. A. (2006). Entrepreneurial action and the role of uncertainty in the theory of the entrepreneur. *Academy of Management Review, 31*(1), 132–152.

Ocasio, W. (2001). How do organizations think? In: T. K. Lant & Z. Shapira (Eds), *Organizational cognition: Computation and interpretation* (pp. 39–60). Mahwah, NJ: Erlbaum.

Penrose, E. (1959). *The theory of the growth of the firm.* New York, NY: Wiley.

Perry-Smith, J. E., & Shalley, C. E. (2003). The social side of creativity: A static and dynamic social network perspective. *Academy of Management Review, 28*(1), 89–106.

Reynolds, P., & Miller, B. (1992). New firm gestation: Conception, birth, and implications for research. *Journal of Business Venturing, 7*(5), 405–417.

Ronstadt, R. (1988). The corridor principle. *Journal of Business Venturing, 3*(1), 31–40.

Rousseau, D. M. (1985). Issues of level in organizational research: Multi-level and cross-level perspectives. *Research in Organizational Behavior, 7,* 1–37.

Rousseau, D. M. (2004). Now let's make multi-level research on trust doable. In: F. J. Yammarino & F. Dansereau (Eds), *Multi-level issues in organizational behavior and processes* (pp. 159–166). Oxford, UK: Elsevier.

Salancik, G. R., & Pfeffer, J. (1978). A social information processing approach to job attitudes and task design. *Administrative Science Quarterly, 23,* 224–253.

Sarasvathy, S. D. (2001). Causation and effectuation: Toward a theoretical shift from economic inevitability to entrepreneurial contingency. *Academy of Management Review, 26*(2), 243–263.

Shane, S. (2000). Prior knowledge and the discovery of entrepreneurial opportunities. *Organization Science, 11*(4), 448–469.

Shane, S. (2001). Technology opportunities and new firm creation. *Management Science, 47*(9), 1173–1181.

Shane, S. (2003). *A general theory of entrepreneurship.* Cheltenham, UK: Edward Elgar.

Shane, S. (2006). Introduction to the focused issue on entrepreneurship. *Management Science, 52*(2), 155–159.

Shaver, K. G., & Scott, L. R. (1991). Person, process, choice: The psychology of new venture creation. *Entrepreneurship Theory and Practice, 16*(2), 23–45.

Shook, C. L., Priem, R. L., & McGee, J. E. (2003). Venture creation and the enterprising individual: A review and synthesis. *Journal of Management, 29*(3), 379–399.

Simon, H. A. (1947). *Administrative behavior.* New York, NY: Macmillan.

Simon, M., Houghton, S. M., & Aquino, J. (2000). Cognitive biases, risk perception, and venture formation: How individuals decide to start companies. *Journal of Business Venturing, 15,* 113–134.

Simonton, D. K. (1999). Creativity as blind variation and selective retention: Is the creative process Darwinian? *Psychological Inquiry, 10*(4), 309–328.

Stuart, T. E. (2000). Interorganizational alliances and the performance of firms: A study of growth and innovation. *Strategic Management Journal, 21*(8), 265–284.

Stuart, T. E., Hoang, H., & Hybels, R. (1999). Interorganizational endorsements and the performance of entrepreneurial ventures. *Administrative Science Quarterly, 44,* 315–349.

Sutcliffe, K. M. (2000). Organizational environments and organizational information processing. In: F. M. Jablin & L. L. Putnam (Eds), *The new handbook of organizational communication* (pp. 197–230). Thousand Oaks, CA: Sage.

Thompson, J. D. (1967). *Organizations in action.* New York, NY: McGraw-Hill.

Van de Ven, A., & Engleman, R. (2004). Event- and outcome-driven explanations of entrepreneurship. *Journal of Business Venturing, 19*, 343–358.

Vroom, V. H., & Yetton, P. W. (1973). *Leadership and decision-making*. Pittsburgh, PA: University of Pittsburgh Press.

Weick, K. (1979). *The social psychology of organizing* (2nd ed.). New York, NY: McGraw-Hill.

Weick, K. E. (1989). Theory construction as disciplines imagination. *Academy of Management Review, 14*, 516–531.

Weick, K. E., Sutcliffe, K. M., & Obstfeld, D. (2005). Organizing and the process of sensemaking. *Organization Science, 16*(4), 409–421.

Wernerfelt, B. (1984). A resource-based view of the firm. *Strategic Management Journal, 5*, 171–180.

Williamson, O. E. (1975). *Markets and hierarchies: Analysis and antitrust implications*. New York, NY: Free Press.

Williamson, O. E. (1985). *The economic institutions of capitalism*. New York, NY: Free Press.

Williamson, O. E. (1991). Comparative economic organization: The analysis of discrete structural alternatives. *Administrative Science Quarterly, 36*, 269–296.

Yates, A. J. (2000). The knowledge problem, entrepreneurial discovery and Austrian market process theory. *Journal of Economic Theory, 91*(1), 59–85.

A MULTI-LEVEL PROCESS VIEW OF NEW-VENTURE EMERGENCE: IMPRESSIVE FIRST STEP TOWARD A MODEL

Claudia C. Cogliser and Jeffrey E. Stambaugh

ABSTRACT

Ford and Sullivan's piece makes a unique contribution to entrepreneurship studies, with the greatest being their multi-level, "bottom-up" theorizing about the process. These authors' focus is limited to one level during each temporal phase. To be consistent with enactment theory, this process should address the recursive nature between the micro (individual) and macro (team and venture) levels throughout the entrepreneurship process. Specifically, the individual level is relevant throughout the process. This commentary offers three mechanisms to link the micro and macro levels: situational, action formation, and transformation. The current work is not intended to diminish Ford and Sullivan's work; indeed, multi-level theorizing is messy and theirs is an ambitious first step.

Today, the entrepreneurial phenomenon is occurring at higher rates than ever before (Gartner & Shane, 1995; Thornton, 1999), with 4% of all US adults attempting a start-up venture at any given time (Reynolds & White,

Multi-Level Issues in Creativity and Innovation
Research in Multi-Level Issues, Volume 7, 471–477
Copyright © 2008 by Elsevier Ltd.
All rights of reproduction in any form reserved
ISSN: 1475-9144/doi:10.1016/S1475-9144(07)00018-5

1997). Accordingly, academe has responded with a concurrent growth in this field, as evidenced by an increase in research centers, professional organizations, and journals specific to its study (Katz, 1991). Not surprisingly, the number of research articles published across the last several decades, both in specialty entrepreneurship journals and more mainstream management outlets, has increased sharply (Busenitz et al., 2003; Davidsson, Low, & Wright, 2001; Ireland, Reutzel, & Webb, 2005a).

Despite the burgeoning interest in the phenomenon (as highlighted by Ford and Sullivan, this volume), the field is still a relatively young one when compared with its counterparts in management (Hitt & Ireland, 2000). Accordingly, it continues to struggle with low paradigmatic development (Ireland, Webb, & Coombs, 2005b) "marked by frequent and deep debates over legitimate methods, problems, and standards of solution" (Kuhn, 1996, p. 47–48). Part of the methodological debate is demonstrated by Low and MacMillan's (1988) groundbreaking call for scholars to study entrepreneurship at multiple (and complementary) levels of analysis. However, very few studies have actually done so in the ensuing decades; instead, research has tended to have a narrower focus, using either the firm or the individual as the unit of analysis (Chandler & Lyon, 2001; Davidsson & Wiklund, 2001; Ireland et al., 2005a).

We thus compliment Ford and Sullivan for several achievements in their chapter. First, in heeding calls to specify levels clearly (e.g., Chandler & Lyon, 2001; Low & MacMillan, 1988), Ford and Sullivan explore new-venture emergence at what they label as the level of the founder, the founding team, and the venture. This work is also notable for its focus on *teams*, identified as particularly fruitful for (but missing from) entrepreneurship research (Davidsson & Wiklund, 2001). Furthermore, their chapter applies a multi-level and process focus to what have been defined recently as the key levels of analysis for entrepreneurship (Busenitz et al., 2003) – namely, individuals, teams, and modes of organizing (or the venture) studied *in concert*.

As an aside, as yet another indication of low paradigmatic development, we note that there is not yet agreement within entrepreneurship on the typology of the levels. Low and MacMillan (1988) would have used the levels of the "individual," "group," and "organization" to tell this story, whereas Davidsson and Wiklund (2001) would have employed "individual," "team," and "firm."

Finally, Ford and Sullivan work toward a clear description of how they define entrepreneurship in their essay. They further provide the boundaries around their self-labeled "story" – that is, their process description stops at the point where the new venture becomes an ongoing business enterprise.

Ford and Sullivan's "story" is truly a complex one, as they introduce eclectic themes throughout their chapter. As our own backgrounds are in organizational behavior (Cogliser) and strategy (Stambaugh), we appreciated the opportunity to explore themes in greater detail throughout their chapter that we had studied previously only in an ancillary fashion. That being said, we also appreciated when sections of the chapter outlined simplify the connection between levels of analysis and the phases of entrepreneurial activity that form the basis of Ford and Sullivan's essay within the context of their various themes. In particular, it was helpful to see the authors' clear specification of which level of analysis was operative for each of the three phases of entrepreneurial activity (founder's efforts relevant for the opportunity discovery phase; founding team's efforts relevant for the opportunity evaluation phase; and venture efforts relevant for the opportunity exploitation phase).

However, this specification also pointed out a disconnect for us, in that each level of analysis is limited to a temporal phase in the entrepreneurship process. The use of Weick's (Weick, 1979; Weick, Sutcliffe, & Obstfeld, 2005) enactment model further convinced us that this constrained conceptualization limited a true multi-level perspective of entrepreneurship. We provide an example from our current work that demonstrates our rationale for disagreeing with this piece of the story.

Weick and colleagues' concept of enactment (Weick, 1979; Weick et al., 2005) involves perceptions and behaviors of individual actors within the context of a social system. As Weick and colleagues point out, a sense-making perspective is useful for organizational studies precisely because it provides a description of one means by which agency (individual actors) alters institutions and environments (enactment) (Weick et al., 2005, p. 419). The sense-making process also highlights how no organizing function (such as entrepreneurial discovery, evaluation, and exploitation, as described in Ford and Sullivan's chapter) "can properly be understood apart from its wider social and cultural context" (Scott, 1995, p. 151).

The process is recursive, in that three types of mechanisms link micro (individual) and macro (team and venture) levels of analysis (Stinchcombe, 1991). That is, "macro states at one point in time influence the behavior of individual actors [the founder, those on the founding team, and the broader number of individuals involved in the venture], and how these actions generate new macro states [the collectives of the team and the venture and associated outcomes] at a later time" (Hedström & Swedberg, 1998).

A *situational mechanism* involves the exposure of an actor to a social context that affects him or her in a certain way, linking a macro event to the person's beliefs, attitudes, and opportunities (Hedström & Swedberg, 1998). We believe this linkage occurs not only for the founder (individual level for Ford and Sullivan) at the opportunity discovery phase throughout the opportunity evaluation and exploitation stages, but also for *all* actors involved in the entrepreneurial process. Ford and Sullivan delineate the behavior of the individual (and the founder only) at only the opportunity discovery phase, and explore larger collectives (the team and the venture) at subsequent phases.

A second type of mechanism – an action-formation mechanism – is involved when a set of desires, beliefs, and action opportunities results in specific actions (Hedström & Swedberg, 1998). This shifts back to the individual's response to the social context that affected him or her with the situational mechanism described earlier. Ford and Sullivan describe facets of their story that encompass action-formation mechanisms as they point out how the various behaviors of the founders, members of the founding team, and the larger stakeholders involved with the venture respond to environmental factors. However, we believe the levels of analysis shown in Fig. 1 of Ford and Sullivan (this volume) are artificially imposed (such that individual, team, and firm/venture relationships occur at each stage of the entrepreneurship process).

A third mechanism described by Hedström & Swedberg (1998) – the transformation mechanism – shows how individual behaviors are transformed into a collective outcome. Multi-level theorizing is messy, of course, and it is difficult to *not* anthropomorphize macro entities in terms of their "behavior." Instead, macro-level entities (such as a founding team or a firm that is engaged in a new venture) or events (such as a new-venture formation) are linked by the combination of mechanisms described earlier such that behavior involves individual actors oriented toward the behavior of others.

In terms of enactment, Weick et al. (2005) describe how individuals "organize to make sense of equivocal inputs [environmental uncertainties] and enact this sense back into the world to make the world more orderly" (p. 410). This sense-making process occurs along the various phases of the entrepreneurship process involving multiple actors: the founder, members of the founding team, and a larger set of actors/stakeholders – both internal to the venture and perhaps external as well – who make up the venture.

We offer this example from some of our recent thinking to illustrate this point. We have theorized about the exploitation phase, where Ford and

Sullivan's story focuses on the venture level. We agree with their rationale, but suggest that the founder's (and the team's, to the extent that we homogenize the individuals) aspiration and plausibility requirements are still important as we examine which directions the venture takes in the face of continuing uncertainty (Fiegenbaum & Thomas, 2004; Kahneman & Tversky, 1979). Thus, the individual level may remain operative during the exploitation phase. Indeed, this observation suggests just how ambitious the effort to develop a multi-level process model for entrepreneurship truly is (as is the case, frankly, for multi-level theorizing in any organizational domain).

We end our commentary with a lingering question: Do processes at one level (the founder, the founding team, or the venture) affect outcomes at another level? Throughout their story, Ford and Sullivan demonstrate that the entrepreneurial process occurs at multiple levels. We agree with this conclusion, as organizations are hierarchically nested systems and it would be difficult to find single-level relationships that are unaffected by other levels in the entrepreneurship process. We would like to have seen explicit statements about theoretical relationships of the entrepreneurship process couched in multi-level terms (and the abstract teased us into thinking this is what we would find in Ford and Sullivan's chapter). Highlighting one of Klein and Kozlowski's (2000) principles for good multi-level theory, "conceptualization of emergent phenomena at higher levels should specify, theoretically, the nature and form of these bottom-up emergent processes" (p. 18).

In defense of Ford and Sullivan, these authors state at the outset in their introduction that their story is still speculative. However, we suggest that relationships can be specified and believe that the various themes throughout their chapter provide the theoretical "oomph" to move toward a clearly identified multi-level theoretical perspective on the entrepreneurial process. A quick review of the guiding principles for developing multi-level theory in Klein and Kozlowski's (2000) book as well as other explicit efforts that present frameworks for multi-level theorizing (Dansereau, Alutto, & Yammarino, 1984; House, Rousseau, & Thomas-Hunt, 1995; Klein, Dansereau, & Hall, 1994; Roberts, Hulin, & Rousseau, 1978; Rousseau, 1985) lend support to our point of view regarding Ford and Sullivan's work (while also recognizing how hard it is to do that – we leave with a "better them than us" statement with tongue-in-cheek).

This commentary is not intended to disparage the impressive contributions made by Ford and Sullivan's chapter. Their work addresses a significant gap in entrepreneurship research: multi-level theorizing about the process. Not only have scholars identified a need for more multi-level research, but also Ford and Sullivan have actually moved to fill that gap via a process model. That it is a "bottom-up" model makes their work all the more rare (Klein & Kozlowski, 2000). Actually, Ford and Sullivan are careful to acknowledge that their efforts do not yet constitute a model, but we believe that clearly the beginnings are there. We simply suggest that as they mature their story, they reflect the recursive links between the micro and macro levels. We wish them well, for as has been noted about multi-level models, "as with all maturation, however, the process has not proceeded without pain" (Klein & Koslowski, 2000, p. 4).

REFERENCES

Busenitz, L. W., West, G. P., Shepherd, D., Nelson, T., Chandler, G. N., & Zacharakis, A. (2003). Entrepreneurship research in emergence: Past trends and future directions. *Journal of Management, 29*(3), 285–308.

Chandler, G. N., & Lyon, D. W. (2001). Issues of research design and construct measurement in entrepreneurship research: The past decade. *Entrepreneurship Theory and Practice, 25*(4), 101–113.

Dansereau, F., Alutto, J. A., & Yammarino, F. J. (1984). *Theory testing in organizational behavior: The varient approach.* Englewood Cliffs, NJ: Prentice Hall.

Davidsson, P., Low, M. B., & Wright, M. (2001). Editor's Introduction: Low and MacMillan ten years on: Achievements and future directions for entrepreneurship research. *Entrepreneurship Theory and Practice, 26*(4), 5–15.

Davidsson, P., & Wiklund, J. (2001). Levels of analysis in entrepreneurship research: Current research practice and suggestions for the future. *Entrepreneurship Theory and Practice, 26*(4), 81–99.

Fiegenbaum, A., & Thomas, H. (2004). Strategic risk and competitive advantage: An integrative perspective. *European Management Review, 1*(1), 84–95.

Ford, C.M., & Sullivan, D.M. (this volume). A multi-level process view of new venture emergence. In: M. D. Mumford, S. T. Hunter & K. E. Bedell-Avers (Eds), *Research in multi-level issues vol. 7: Multi-level issues in creativity and innovation.* Oxford, UK: Elsevier.

Gartner, W. B., & Shane, S. A. (1995). Measuring entrepreneurship over time. *Journal of Business Venturing, 10*, 283–301.

Hedström, P., & Swedberg, R. (1998). Social mechanisms: An introductory essay. In: P. Hedström & R. Swedberg (Eds), *Social mechanisms: An analytical approach to social theory* (pp. 1–30). Cambridge, UK: Cambridge University Press.

Hitt, M. A., & Ireland, R. D. (2000). The intersection of entrepreneurship and strategic management research. In: D. L. Sexton & H. Landstrom (Eds), *The Blackwell handbook of entrepreneurship* (pp. 45–72). Oxford, UK: Blackwell.

House, R. J., Rousseau, D. M., & Thomas-Hunt, M. (1995). The meso paradigm: A framework for the integration of micro and macro organizational behavior. In: L. L. Cummings & B. M. Staw (Eds), *Research in Organizational Behavior* (pp. 71–114). Greenwich, CT: JAI Press.

Ireland, R. D., Reutzel, C. R., & Webb, J. W. (2005a). From the editors: Entrepreneurship research in AMJ: What has been published, and what might the future hold? *Academy of Management Journal, 48*(4), 556–564.

Ireland, R. D., Webb, J. W., & Coombs, J. E. (2005b). Theory and methodology in entrepreneurship research. In: D. J. Ketchen & D. D. Bergh (Eds), *Research methodology in strategy and management* (Vol. 2, pp. 1–32). Oxford, UK: Elsevier.

Kahneman, D., & Tversky, A. (1979). Prospect theory: An analysis of decision under risk. *Econometrica, 47*(2), 263–292.

Katz, J. A. (1991). The institution and infrastructure of entrepreneurship. *Entrepreneurship Theory and Practice, 15*(3), 85–102.

Klein, K. J., Dansereau, F., & Hall, R. J. (1994). Levels issues in theory development, data collection and analysis. *Academy of Management Review, 19*, 195–229.

Klein, K. J., & Kozlowski, S. W. J. (2000). *Multilevel theory, research, and methods in organizations.* San Francisco: Jossey-Bass.

Kuhn, T. S. (1996). *The structure of scientific revolutions* (3rd ed.). Chicago: University of Chicago Press.

Low, M. B., & MacMillan, I. C. (1988). Entrepreneurship: Past research and future challenges. *Journal of Management, 14*(2), 139–161.

Reynolds, P. D., & White, S. (1997). *The entrepreneurial process: Economic growth, men, women, and minorities.* Westport, CT: Quorum.

Roberts, K. H., Hulin, C., & Rousseau, D. M. (1978). *Developing an interdisciplinary science of organizations.* San Francisco: Jossey Bass.

Rousseau, D. M. (1985). Issues of level in organizational research: Multi-level and cross-level perspectives. In: L. L. Cummings & B. M. Staw (Eds), *Research in Organizational Behavior* (pp. 1–37). Greenwich, CT: JAI Press.

Scott, R. W. (1995). *Institutions and organizations.* Thousand Oaks, CA: Sage.

Stinchcombe, A. L. (1991). The conditions of fruitfulness of theorizing about mechanisms in social science. *Philosophy of the Social Sciences, 21*(3), 367–388.

Thornton, P. H. (1999). The sociology of entrepreneurship. *Annual Review of Sociology, 25*, 19–46.

Weick, K. E. (1979). *The social psychology of organizing* (2nd ed.). New York: McGraw Hill.

Weick, K. E., Sutcliffe, K. M., & Obstfeld, D. (2005). Organizing and the process of sensemaking. *Organization Science, 16*(4), 409–451.

DO LEVELS AND PHASES ALWAYS HAPPEN TOGETHER? QUESTIONS FOR CONSIDERING THE CASE OF NEW-VENTURE EMERGENCE

Kimberly S. Jaussi

ABSTRACT

In response to Ford and Sullivan's chapter, this commentary poses a number of questions intended to help future research efforts ascertain whether levels of analysis and phases of new-venture emergence happen concurrently. Strongly in agreement with Ford and Sullivan's call for a process approach toward the study of entrepreneurial ventures, the commentary focuses on the potential processes associated with different levels of analysis that might possibly underlie the enactment and effectuation processes depicted in their model. Through the examination of these underlying processes, questions for future research are raised to help address the question, "Do levels and phases of new-venture emergence always happen together?"

Multi-Level Issues in Creativity and Innovation
Research in Multi-Level Issues, Volume 7, 479–491
Copyright © 2008 by Elsevier Ltd.
ISSN: 1475-9144/doi:10.1016/S1475-9144(07)00019-7

INTRODUCTION

In their chapter "A Multi-Level Process View of New-Venture Emergence," Cameron Ford and Diane Sullivan bring forward something that the entrepreneurship literature has alluded to but not executed – that a multi-level framework would be useful for new theoretical insights and understandings of the entrepreneur and entrepreneurial action. In alignment with recent work by McMullen and Shepherd (2006), they call for and utilize a process approach to gain new perspectives on the emergence process of new ventures. Using a sense-making/enactment framework, Ford and Sullivan (this volume) put forth a multi-level model of the entrepreneurial process, whereby cross-level influences drive the enactment and effectuation process as the entrepreneurial venture itself moves from level to level of analysis.

In the abstract and first pages of their chapter, Ford and Sullivan (this volume) note that a process-based approach is necessary to understand how ideas become organized into new ventures, how visions become ventures, how the insight evolves, how the insight gains momentum, how the insight attracts enthusiasts, how the insight culminates in a network of economic relationships, how conceptions of opportunities evolve, how entrepreneurs learn, how stakeholder networks form and grow, and how the opportunity discovery process occurs at the individual level. In efforts to address these questions and to further understand new-venture emergence, the model put forth in their chapter describes an iterative process of enactment and effectuation.

As Ford and Sullivan note, underlying the enactment and effectuation processes are other processes that might also help answer these questions. This commentary focuses on many of those possibilities as it presents thoughts regarding further development of this model. In keeping with Ford and Sullivan's work, I would reiterate their statement of the value of and necessity for a process approach as well as the need to consider levels of analysis in any discussion of entrepreneurship. Through consideration of the underlying processes, the present commentary raises questions regarding whether movement to a new level of analysis occurs by default at each of the three phases of new-venture emergence. Depending on which processes do or do not occur, the venture may or may not be accurately represented at the corresponding level of analysis depicted in Ford and Sullivan's theorizing and Fig. 1 (which illustrates their model). In hopes of stimulating further work to determine the appropriate level of analysis at each phase, this commentary offers a wide range of questions applicable to future research that are raised by Ford and Sullivan's model.

As Ford and Sullivan mention, a number of processes could potentially drive the enactment and effectuation processes. Considering these underlying processes when examining the levels of analysis may yield different conclusions than considering the phases of emergence. To further this view and to consider the processes associated with each level of analysis in conjunction with the new-venture phase, this commentary closely considers two specific aspects of new-venture emergence. First, it addresses the venture at different levels and the processes that will help determine the level of analysis of the venture and its vision at different points in time. Second, it discusses the processes associated with movement both within each phase and between the various phases, particularly those processes and assumptions underlying escape velocity at different levels as well as the nature of the momentum at different stages. The commentary concludes with a general discussion of some other possible areas for future research regarding new-venture emergence and levels of analysis.

NEW-VENTURE VISION, UNDERLYING PROCESSES, AND LEVELS OF ANALYSIS

The first and overarching question relates to the definition of the emerging entrepreneurial venture at the three phases (opportunity discovery, opportunity evaluation, and opportunity exploitation) and the three levels of analysis (founder, team, and venture) as well as the processes that create the definition at those different levels of analysis. As I thought about how to reconcile Ford and Sullivan's model with the work done by Chan (1998), I first considered whether we mistakenly assume that the venture itself is the same construct across the different phases. Is the assumption of the model that the venture itself in concept and vision remains the same, but expands in numbers and robustness from the individual level to the team level to the venture level? Or does the venture's concept and vision become something qualitatively different at each level of analysis? Given the iterative processes outlined in Ford and Sullivan's model, either outcome seems plausible. In efforts to consider this issue further, this commentary first examines the vision of the new venture and investigates what the model suggests about its level of analysis at each phase. It then considers the processes outlined in the model and suggests future research questions that will help us better understand how those processes manage variance both between phases and within phases to determine the appropriate level of analysis for the venture.

Under Ford and Sullivan's model, the new-venture vision at Phase 1 would be that of the founder. Thus, it would be an individual-level construct. In the second phase, according to the model, at the team level, it would be the team's vision for the new venture. In the third phase, it would be the organizational vision. But how would these three visions be qualitatively similar or different? Ford and Sullivan clearly describe their process as iterative within each level, implying that sense-making and S-R processes might result in new meanings at each phase. Future research might explore what the S-R processes are, specifically, for reducing or creating variance *between* the levels and phases. In addition, it would be interesting to consider how the S-R processes might manage variance *within* a later stage. For example, when the venture is at the third (exploitation) phase, does one shared meaning about the vision exist among the employees, the organizing team, and the founder? Ideally, the answer would be yes – but, given the variety of agendas and backgrounds involved as well as the complexity of the processes at each level, how often might that concordance really occur? And if it does occur, *how* does it occur?

My fundamental question about whether the movement of levels of analysis corresponds to the phases stems from this line of thought. If the venture organization is *changing* due to the S-R processes and sense making of each stage, which processes drive the generation of the *understanding* of the organization at each level?

If we follow Ford and Sullivan's model, at each phase, the organization moves to a new level and abandons the previous level. For example, in the second phase, the organization is no longer an individual-level construct but instead becomes a team-level construct. Similarly, in the third phase, the organization is an organizational-level construct, and no longer a team-level construct. Ford and Sullivan's model describes the S-R processes of the lower level as driving the new, higher level of analysis, but which processes *within* the second phase, for example, are driving the coalescing of the team to create shared cognitions? At different levels of analysis, and at different phases of venture development, different processes occur. Whether the processes of each stage truly reflect a shift in the level of analysis in the definition of the entity remains to be determined by future research.

We must be careful not to assume that processes are automatically occurring at different levels of analysis, which would cause us to fall prey to the trap that diversity literature calls the "black box" (Lawrence, 1997; Dionne, Randel, Jaussi, & Chun, 2004). Jansen (2004) notes, "Organizational momentum is generated and maintained by shared perceptions and interaction. As momentum builds, there should be evidence of coalescing perceptions of momentum in the intraclass correlation coefficients over time" (p. 290). Her point is well taken, in that there should be evidence of shared (coalescing) perceptions over time to truly have organizational momentum. Similarly, for an entrepreneurial venture, we need to have evidence of this shared perception if we are to declare a level of analysis at Phases 2 and 3 for venture-related constructs that are built on the cognitions of members. Furthermore, we need to ensure that our process explanations address the processes by which those shared perceptions are generated, spread, and maintained at whatever level of analysis we assert.

A closer consideration of level-specific processes from other areas of research may help shed light on whether a concurrent relationship exists between levels of analysis shifts and phases of new-venture emergence. For example, future research might consider the "lens" for enacting the uncertainty (arrows 1 and 6 in Fig. 2 in Ford and Sullivan's chapter) and the processes associated with those lenses at each level. Ford and Sullivan describe knowledge as something that will influence enactment and effectuation; thus, it could be considered the "lens" in their model. In considering which processes might be related to the acquisition of that knowledge, one might ask, "What role might identity processes play in how uncertainty will be enacted?" That question, then, can be considered at each level of analysis with respect to individual-level identity, team-level identity, and organization-level identity, each of which is associated with its own unique processes.

Lines of inquiry might address how, at the individual level, processes related to the founder's functional background identity play a role in the founder's interpretation of the uncertainty in the environment, thereby shaping the opportunity discovery phase. Other identity-related processes linked to self-enhancement motives, such as prototyping or contrasting, may also play roles in the founder's perception and cognition of how the organization fits a market opportunity and might be considered by researchers. Similarly, future research might investigate how social identity processes influence the strategic group to which the founder considers the venture to belong, thereby shaping his or her development and articulation of the venture's fit with the market and the definition of the venture itself.

Another avenue for future research to address the levels issue with respect to the definition of the venture is to consider Ford and Sullivan's description of how and when the founder engages others and the venture moves to the team level of analysis at the second phase of emergence. However, the simple engagement of others does not make a team level. Further work would be useful if it addressed questions such as "What are the processes by which a founder puts together a team?" While Ford and Sullivan draw upon Elsbach and Kramer's (2003) "pitch" and "catch" process, many processes might potentially underlie how the founder selects a target audience. For example, what roles do processes related to similarity attraction, gender, or self-categorization play?

In fact, Ford and Sullivan (this volume) do touch upon this type of consideration when they state: Thus, we would expect a founder's success with respect to attracting others to join or support a venture to be affected by cues that govern person categorization and relationship categorization in the context of new venture creation. However, while Ford and Sullivan briefly mention this issue with respect to success in the formation, alluding to the reasons individuals would want to join the team, I wonder about it prior to that – namely, in the selection of *to whom* the founder targets a pitch. From a push/pull perspective, I wonder about the processes underlying the founder's choice regarding to whom the idea should be *pushed toward*, and as well as other processes that build on Ford and Sullivan's thoughts about who is likely *to pull the idea forward*. In terms of those pull processes, I suspect others warrant investigation, in addition to the person categorization and relationship categorization. For example, future studies might investigate whether attributional processes associated with "romancing the founder" occur within the team and lead to the pull, and whether those "romance" feelings come from drama used in the founder's "pitch." Furthermore, are those romance feelings shared, thereby making it a cross-level relationship, whereby a team pulls an individual founder and his or her idea?

While future research may be able to uncover other processes at work that explain why a founder is able to garner the support of a group of individuals who pull the venture to another phase, those processes will describe how the venture moves forward – which still leaves unanswered the question of whether a new level of analysis occurs simultaneously. To determine the appropriate level of analysis for the second phase, future research might consider the strength of the team's identity, examining how processes associated with that identity might influence whether the team can leverage its collective knowledge in its enactment and effectuation of the environment. If no team identity or processes create a collective team identity, then perhaps the team level of analysis is not appropriate at this stage.

As Ford and Sullivan (this volume) state, our multi-level processes view emphasizes communication and sense-making processes like these that create collective understandings and action from the visions of an individual. Future work should expand on the communication processes and sense-making processes at the group level that will create a collective understanding. Questions might be asked that address whether founding teams differ from cross-functional problem-solving teams in traditional organizations in terms of their processes for aligning the perspectives of individuals on the team. In the case of founding teams, members may have very different motives for being involved with the venture (e.g., investment, cause), with no overarching organizational culture or structure being available to provide the shared context and background that teams from traditional organizations might have. Thus, in founding teams, which processes will align the participants' various motives and opinions? Building on the "romance" possibility discussed earlier, might a group that is "romancing" a founder create shared meaning and team-level cognitions about things other than the value of the organization?

With careful investigation regarding the degree to which these processes are active, future research should be able to expand upon Ford and Sullivan's framework to identify which levels of analysis are occurring with respect to the venture itself. Once the levels of analysis are clear, we may then be able to determine whether those levels of analysis move concurrently with the phases of new-venture emergence.

MOVEMENT BETWEEN PHASES AND LEVELS

It is impossible to consider the entrepreneurial venture and the processes that might drive its vision and definition at each level of analysis without addressing the implications of the processes driving the movement, or momentum, *between* the levels of analysis. Ford and Sullivan assert that escape velocity is the process by which the entrepreneurial venture moves from the individual level to the team level and finally to the organizational level. This section suggests questions for future research regarding this application of escape velocity and levels of analysis, grounded in a discussion of types of momentum.

Momentum, Escape Velocity, and Processes That Create It at Different Levels of Analysis

Ford and Sullivan have used Jansen's (2004) work in a clever way by linking escape velocity to entrepreneurial venture emergence. I agree that escape velocity is a valuable construct to be considered as the mechanism by which an entrepreneurial venture may emerge. Yet I question the implications of asserting that it occurs between *each* phase of the venture emergence process. As Jansen (2004) describes it, escape velocity is the "recognizable traction (progress) that allows for an escape from the stasis-based path" (p. 279). Implicit in the application of that construct to the creation of an entrepreneurial venture is the assumption that change momentum (and not stasis momentum) is occurring between every phase of the process. Also implicit in the assumption that escape velocity occurs at the end of every phase is the notion that a stasis-based path occurs *within* each phase (because, according to Jansen's definition, escape velocity is escaping a stasis-based path).

As currently utilized, the framing of escape velocity implies that the venture is completely transformed at each phase. Depending on the answer to the question posed earlier about whether the venture is the same or different at each level and phase, we can consider whether escape velocity occurs. If the organization is moving through phases and levels but is qualitatively similar at each level and phase, then Jansen's theorizing suggests that stasis momentum occurs between phases because the venture follows the same trajectory. Conversely, if the vision and overall essence of the venture itself change dramatically between the phases (thereby changing the trajectory), then change-based momentum occurs and escape velocity may be the process by which it is facilitated. However, Jansen's definition of escape velocity suggests that for the venture to reach escape velocity, there must be stasis-based momentum *within* each phase and level, with true transformation occurring *between* each phase and level of analysis. Thus, a rich research agenda focusing on whether this stasis movement within, and change movement between, phases and levels occurs awaits researchers.

In fact, much of Jansen's (2004) work holds great potential for further integration into the examination of levels of analysis in the entrepreneurial venture process. During their efforts to answer the "within and between" question posed earlier, scholars might also uncover whether the venture-launching process is different for ventures with stasis-based momentum and for ventures with change-based momentum. Similarly, in addressing the "within and between" question, researchers will be able to determine whether change momentum and stasis momentum occur at different points in the new-venture creation process. Jansen suggests that both stasis momentum and change momentum are useful at different stages of the change life cycle, and perhaps the same is true for the new-venture creation process. Of course, in considering these questions, researchers will have to reconcile Jansen's conceptualization of change-based momentum as an organizational-level construct, tackling questions regarding whether the construct can operate at other levels of analysis and, if it can, how it is similar or different at the other levels of analysis.

In a similar vein, future work might consider how the first type of change in the new-venture process influences subsequent developments and processes. For example, are ventures that begin as extensions of the current trajectory of the founder more likely to experience stasis-based momentum? Some may argue that in the first phase, any entrepreneurial venture represents a change in trajectory (e.g., that stasis-based momentum at this stage is not even possible). Nevertheless, a number of engineers, for example, have worked in a field for their entire careers and then opened up their own consultancies – thereby following the same trajectory but just working for themselves. Contrasting that type of case with one where the venture represents a completely different field for the entrepreneur suggests that, because different types of momentum would characterize the change, very different enactment and effectuation processes would occur throughout the venture-emergence process for each case.

Thus, future research may consider questions such as "Is the sense-making process different at each level of analysis when a new venture comes to each level ready for transformation (with a change-based momentum) versus ready for just incremental change (with a stasis-based momentum)?" This type of inquiry would further our understanding regarding the implications for these two types of momentum in the entrepreneurial new venture emergence process.

The next section examines the processes that create the velocity and drive movement to other phases and/or levels of analysis. Because of the questions about whether we can be sure that escape velocity is actually occurring at all stages, the term "velocity" (rather than "escape velocity") is used to refer to either type of momentum in this situation.

Processes Creating the Velocity to Move From Phase to Phase at Each Level of Analysis

A number of opportunities exist for future studies to further Ford and Sullivan's model and investigate the processes that underlie velocity. First, the nature of the velocity at each level of analysis and the question of whether it is qualitatively different at each level of analysis (e.g., does the velocity for movement coming from an individual look the same as the velocity for movement coming from a team, and so on?) are wide-open topics for future research to explore. Similarly, future research might investigate the drivers of velocity at each level.

Consider, for example, that at the very beginning of the process something like entrepreneurial escape velocity exists (as in the preceding example) that drives an individual to consider an entrepreneurial venture and leave his or her current job. An interesting question for future research might build on Dobrev and Barnett's (2005) finding that organizational context and roles influence who exits to become an entrepreneur and examine the type of velocity created by these roles. It could ask, "*How* do organizational roles relate to whether founders pursue a stasis-momentum venture or a change-momentum venture?" Similarly, at other levels of analysis, future studies might examine what other kinds of cross-level drivers might create the particular type of velocity that occurs.

Another wide-open opportunity for future research stems from Ford and Sullivan's (this volume) statement: Proposals that fare well in these assessments gain traction (i.e., meet both aspiration and plausibility requirements) that can increase a proposal's momentum to a point when an "escape velocity" threshold is reached that motivates *organizing processes that create* the next higher level of analysis. For example, when a founder gets excited enough about a specific proposal, he or she might engage in forming a management team capable of launching the venture. Future research could explore the processes occurring under that excitement, along the way addressing a variety of questions: *How* does an idea excite the founder? Is it because of self-enhancement processes? Is it because of processes associated with satisfying needs? Or is it because of identification processes that the excitement occurs? Does entrepreneurial motivation (cf. Shane, Locke, & Collins, 2003) play a role in influencing excitement? Perhaps, factors such as family dynamics and family-related processes influence that excitement – visions of living up to a parent's expectations, for example.

Ford and Sullivan (this volume) also note that proposal momentum will be closely linked to the quality of narrative devices employed. What is the role of excitement in the "quality of narrative devices"? Does it influence the perception of quality? Does it add drama? Might it also stimulate quality, given the relationship between affect and creativity (cf. Amabile, Barsade, Mueller, & Staw, 2005)? And might that increased quality then drive the confidence that Ford and Sullivan also suggest creates the momentum to reach escape velocity?

While answering these types of questions will help scholars understand more about the processes that drive the velocity at a given level, more research is needed to then address how the individual-level confidence and the excitement noted earlier operate (potentially together) to drive social information processes that may justify the claim of a higher level of analysis. Jansen (2004) notes that social information conveying urgency, feasibility, and drama will prompt change-based momentum. Why? What are the processes underlying that transformation? Might emotional or social contagion be at work? Future research might address these questions in an effort to fully identify the processes that are occurring. Again, through the identification of processes, perhaps the appropriate levels of analysis will become more readily apparent.

To further complicate matters, at each level of analysis, there are bound to be cross-level antecedents and outcomes associated with the velocity of each level of analysis. For example, city-level variables (cf. Pennings, 1982) or national culture (cf. Busnitz, Gomez, & Spencer, 2000; Mitchell, Smith, Seawright, & Morse, 2000) may affect the processes underlying founder excitement about the opportunity, thereby resulting in escape velocity that will differ by country, or by the interaction of any of these variables. Again, many opportunities exist to build research agendas that address the processes associated with new-venture emergence at different levels of analysis and phases.

OTHER FUTURE RESEARCH

Ford and Sullivan's chapter provoked a great deal of thought for me regarding the relationship between the processes associated with different phases of new-venture emergence and the processes associated with levels of analysis issues associated with new-venture emergence. Through the process of writing this commentary, I hoped to make sense of some missing links and articulate my thoughts regarding potential avenues for further work in this area. My primary goal was to suggest ways that future research might investigate whether a direct relationship exists between the level of analysis at which a new venture should be considered and a corresponding phase of emergence. Perhaps, the two do not go directly hand in hand, and I look forward to future research that will help our field make further sense of the linkage between the two.

I am also moved to suggest a few final research ideas that involve linking the new-venture emergence process with areas of creativity and leadership that have started to tackle process-based approaches with levels of analysis implications. First, I agree wholeheartedly with Ford and Sullivan in their assertion that entrepreneurship and creativity are strongly related. They state: We argue that these previous process descriptions can be readily generalized to new-venture emergence processes because entrepreneurship is inherently a creative act. Given that the two are so closely related, I wonder about which level-specific processes suggested by creativity research might be relevant to each level of analysis for new-venture emergence. Questions such as "Which processes that drive creativity and innovation at the group and organizational levels also drive the construct of entrepreneurial action at the group and organizational levels?" would be rich avenues for future investigations. For those interested in considering such a research topic, a fruitful starting point might be Mumford and Hunter's (2005) multi-level perspective on creativity in organizations.

Ford and Sullivan's model also suggests possibilities for future research to link research on charismatic leadership and leader distance to the levels of analysis implications of this model of new-venture emergence. For example, scholars might consider the implications for the processes depicted in Ford and Sullivan's model when founders are perceived as "close" versus "distant" (Erskine, 2006). Another interesting research question might be whether members of the initial stages of a new venture conceptualize distance from the founder in the same dimensions (e.g., emotional, structural) as traditional subordinates see distance from their leader (cf. Antoinakas & Atwater, 2002). Yet another potential topic for exploration would be to consider levels of analysis and the direct versus indirect effects of the founder on the different phases of the new-venture emergence process. For example, are there cascading effects or bypass effects of the founder at different stages, similar to those associated with charismatic leaders (Chun, 2006; Waldman & Yammarino, 1999)? Research into these kinds of questions has yet to be conducted. Given the levels of analysis work that has already been done in these areas, we might potentially learn a great deal about the processes of new-venture emergence by considering these types of questions.

In conclusion, I thank Ford and Sullivan for stimulating me to think so intensely about these issues. I, too, am grateful for this opportunity for sense making, and I hope my comments help scholars build on their model and "see what they say" about the relationship between phases of new-venture emergence and levels of analysis from a process-based perspective.

REFERENCES

Amabile, T. M., Barsade, S. G., Mueller, J. S., & Staw, B. M. (2005). Affect and creativity at work. *Administrative Science Quarterly, 50*, 367–403.

Antoinakas, J., & Atwater, L. (2002). Leader distance: A review and a proposed theory. *Leadership Quarterly, 136,* 673–704.

Busnitz, L. W., Gomez, C., & Spencer, J. W. (2000). Country institutional profiles: Unlocking entrepreneurial phenomena. *Academy of Management Journal, 43,* 994–1003.

Chan, D. (1998). Functional relations among constructs in the same content domain at different levels of analysis: A typology of composition models. *Journal of Applied Psychology, 83,* 234–246.

Chun, J. U. (2006). *Close and distant charismatic and contingent reward leadership: Multiple levels-of-management and multiple levels-of-analysis perspectives.* Unpublished doctoral dissertation, Binghamton University (State University of New York), Binghamton, NY.

Dionne, S. D., Randel, A. E., Jaussi, K. S., & Chun, J. U. (2004). Diversity and demography in organizations: A levels of analysis review of the literature. In: F. Yammarino & F. Dansereau (Eds), *Research in multi-level issues* (Vol. 3, pp. 181–230). Oxford, UK: Elsevier Science.

Dobrev, S. D., & Barnett, W. P. (2005). Organizational roles and transition to entrepreneurship. *Academy of Management Journal, 42,* 433–449.

Elsbach, K. D., & Kramer, R. M. (2003). Assessing creativity in Hollywood pitch meetings: Evidence for a dual-process model of creativity judgments. *Academy of Management Journal, 46*(3), 283–301.

Erskine, L. (2006). A multidimensional understanding of relational distance in organizations. Proceedings of the Administrative Sciences Association of Canada Conference, Banff, Alberta, CA.

Ford, C. M., & Sullivan, D. M. (this volume). A multi-level process view of new venture emergence. In: M. D. Mumford, S. T. Hunter & K. E. Bedell-Avers (Eds), *Research in multi-level issue. Multi-level issues in creativity and innovation* (Vol.7). Oxford, UK: Elsevier.

Jansen, K. J. (2004). From persistence to pursuit: A longitudinal examination of momentum during the early stages of strategic change. *Organization Science, 15*(3), 276–294.

Lawrence, B. S. (1997). The black box of organizational demography. *Organizational Science, 8,* 1–22.

McMullen, J. S., & Shepherd, D. A. (2006). Entrepreneurial action and the role of uncertainty in the theory of the entrepreneur. *Academy of Management Review, 31*(1), 132–152.

Mitchell, R. K., Smith, B., Seawright, K. W., & Morse, E. A. (2000). Cross-cultural cognitions and the venture creation decision. *Academy of Management Journal, 43,* 974–993.

Mumford, M. D., & Hunter, S. T. (2005). Innovation in organizations: A multi-level perspective on creativity. In: F. J. Yammarino & F. Dansereau (Eds), *Research in multi-level issues* (Vol. 4, pp. 11–74). Oxford, UK: Elsevier Science.

Pennings, J. M. (1982). The urban quality of life and entrepreneurship. *Academy of Management Journal, 25,* 63–79.

Shane, S., Locke, E. A., & Collins, C. J. (2003). Entrepreneurial motivation. *Human Resource Management Review, 13,* 257–279.

Waldman, D. A., & Yammarino, F. J. (1999). CEO charismatic leadership: Levels of management and levels of analysis effects. *Academy of Management Review, 24,* 266–285.

RECURSIVE LINKS AFFECTING THE DYNAMICS OF NEW-VENTURE EMERGENCE

Cameron M. Ford and Diane M. Sullivan

ABSTRACT

Cogliser and Stambaugh (this volume) and Jaussi (this volume) provided valuable thoughts regarding the multi-level process view of new-venture emergence that we developed elsewhere in this volume. The current response to their suggestions focuses on two underlying themes that emerged from their commentaries. The first theme explores the existence of recursive links between the micro and macro levels of analysis during the new-venture emergence process. The second theme highlights the importance of understanding the underlying processes that may recursively affect venture organization at each level of analysis. Finally, this response reiterates our belief in the fruitful pursuit of studying new-venture emergence as an evolutionary process involving multiple levels of analysis.

INTRODUCTION

We begin our present essay much like we began our original chapter – with the motivation to investigate multiple levels of new-venture emergence

Multi-Level Issues in Creativity and Innovation
Research in Multi-Level Issues, Volume 7, 493–499
Copyright © 2008 by Elsevier Ltd.
ISSN: 1475-9144/doi:10.1016/S1475-9144(07)00020-3

processes as a means of adding coherence across the varied approaches to entrepreneurship research. Our motivation here, however, is enhanced as a result of the thoughtful commentaries provided by Cogliser and Stambaugh (this volume) and Jaussi (this volume). We are flattered and encouraged by the pieces that these authors contributed to this volume. Both commentaries have helped us to refine our thinking about the levels and processes associated with new-venture emergence and have provided encouraging advice for future research in this area. In the pages that follow, we discuss two underlying themes highlighted by both commentaries that are central to our thinking. We conclude with some thoughts intended to provoke future discussions on this research topic.

CONSISTENT THEMES

Mutually Exclusive and Nonrecursive Levels in New-Venture Emergence?

In considering the ideas presented in our chapter (Ford & Sullivan, this volume), both Jaussi and the duo of Cogliser and Stambaugh question the mutual exclusivity of the levels we discuss. Our original chapter identified three levels as being important in the new-venture emergence process: the individual/founder level, the team level, and the venture level. We described how enactment processes (cf. Weick, 1979; Weick, Sutcliffe, & Obstfeld, 2005) occurring at each level form the next higher level of new-venture organization. We further argued that each focal level corresponds, in general, to a different phase of entrepreneurial activity (e.g., opportunity discovery, opportunity evaluation, and opportunity exploitation). In our discussions of each phase of entrepreneurial activity, we argued that enactment processes of different focal actors, corresponding to the different levels of analysis, would be important. For example, founders' enactment processes are important during opportunity discovery, team enactment processes are important during opportunity evaluation, and venture enactment processes are important during opportunity exploitation.

In our original exploration of these topics, we seemingly – and inadvertently – implied that these levels, the focal actors primarily important for venture development activities occurring within these levels, and the enactment processes of the focal actors across these levels were mutually exclusive of one another. Although perhaps not clearly explicated, we intended to state that each subsequent level subsumes the prior level as thoughts, actions, and resources become more organized over time. This conclusion, therefore, requires that each level *not* be mutually exclusive of the others. Rather, we view levels as being nested, hierarchically organized categories of processes whose causal potency changes as an individual's vision evolves toward becoming a venture. For example, the team level is composed of a collective of interested parties who are organizing the venture for eventual economic exploitation (at which time the venture level becomes a more meaningful focus). As such, this level includes the founder along with others *within* the conditions imposed by the organization of the venture.

While we may not have made this point clear in our initial arguments, this idea should definitely not be taken lightly, because it has important implications for the enactment processes occurring at each level. The importance of this point is argued forcefully by Cogliser and Stambaugh (this volume), who note that within each level (e.g., individual, team, and venture levels), the macro states (e.g., the team or venture) are likely to influence the micro entities simultaneously existing at that macro level (e.g., individuals composing the team and the venture). More importantly, this process is recursive in nature – for example, the micro entities influence the simultaneously occurring macro states that they compose.

We agree with this interesting point. Its development made us consider another framework that might enhance our thinking regarding the enactment processes that occur at multiple levels during new-venture emergence. Specifically, we were struck by how closely these ideas conformed to processes of coevolution. In the case of coevolution, the goal is to explain how the populations of interest influence the evolutionary trajectory of each other through some bidirectional, causal, variation, selection, and/or retention (VSR) mechanisms (Lewin, Long, & Carroll, 1999; Murmann, 2003). Applying this concept to the levels of analysis view discussed here accounts for the non-mutually exclusive and recursive nature inherent in the levels and processes we describe.

Future work could consider expanding our thinking by applying coevolutionary logic and specifying the bidirectional, causal, VSR mechanisms at work at each level – certainly no easy task. Following the lead from Cogliser and Stambaugh, we might suggest that a good starting point would include the mechanisms discussed by Hedström and Swedberg (1998) – namely, the situational, action-formation, and transformation mechanisms. Initial inspection of these mechanisms suggests a correspondence to the VSR model mechanisms that are necessary for coevolution to occur. In particular, situational mechanisms are variation mechanisms, action-formation mechanisms are evaluation and selection mechanisms, and transformation mechanisms are retention mechanisms. While it is clearly speculative at this point in development, this idea surely presents some interesting possibilities for future work to consider going forward.

Which Underlying Processes Drive the Enactment Processes
at Multiple Levels?

To truly understand new-venture emergence, we must approach the study of this phenomenon by taking a process view. This notion, which we support strongly, has been advocated by many respected entrepreneurship and organizational researchers (cf. Shane, 2006; Mackenzie, 2004; Busenitz et al., 2003; Heath & Sitkin, 2001), including Jaussi and Cogliser and Stambaugh in this volume. This support is encouraging and suggests areas on which future work should concentrate to develop richer explanations for new-venture organization phenomena. Specifically, this consensus urges those exploring new-venture development and related phenomena to consciously approach their studies by taking a process view.

While our initial attempt to do so by applying enactment processes to explain new-venture emergence across multiple levels graciously met with approval from the authors of the commentaries, both sets of authors also suggested areas where future researchers might improve on this work. That is, Jaussi and Cogliser and Stambaugh suggested that future work should elaborate on the underlying processes driving the enactment processes we describe. While the speculative statements discussed in the previous section [e.g., Hedström and Swedberg's (1998) situational, action-formation, and transformation mechanisms] may begin to address this issue, at this point much uncertainty clouds this issue. Promising avenues for future efforts might include exploration of other underlying processes, which are likely to vary both across and within levels and stages of venture organization.

Jaussi poses useful questions to guide the investigation of some of these underlying processes. For example, in taking from our idea that visions are literally talked into becoming ventures through the creation of shared perceptions of a venture's concept across the various levels of analysis, Jaussi suggests that to fully understand how these shared perceptions are generated, we must delve into the processes creating these shared perceptions. Specifically, Jaussi suggests that research examining identity-related processes (e.g., individual-, team-, and organization-level identity) might prove helpful in uncovering how perceptions are formed that will potentially influence the ultimate form of and likelihood of reaching the next higher level of venture organization. This point is interesting, and it would clearly be useful to consider this and other underlying processes that may affect the likelihood of level formation and level content characteristics.

Another process that might be capable of expanding on the finer-grained details of our work, and that we employed only tangentially, is Sarasvathy's (2001) effectuation process. Sarasvathy describes effectuation as the decision process whereby entrepreneurs "take a set of means as given, and focus on selecting between possible effects that can be created with that set of means" (2001, p. 246). Analogical thinking aside, our initial application of effectuation does little to specify exactly how individual entrepreneurs', entrepreneurial teams', and new ventures' enactment processes might influence, or be influenced by, the corresponding level's focal actor's effectuation processes. Further, we do not explain how effectuation processes across levels might affect the likelihood of achieving each new-venture emergence level and/or the specific characteristics composing that level. In responding to the call from Jaussi and Cogliser and Stambaugh for a finer-grained explanation of the processes underlying enactment, studying effectuation processes at multiple levels might be a fruitful avenue for future work to explore.

CONCLUSION

Developing a comprehensive understanding of entrepreneurship phenomena inherently involves a theoretical perspective that integrates multiple levels and simultaneously explains the interplay between individual founders, founding management teams, new-venture organizations, and the necessary network partners (e.g., value networks) associated with each entity. We are encouraged by the responses to our initial attempts to develop a theoretical perspective capable of achieving these ends. As noted by Jaussi and Cogliser and Stambaugh, however, this is not an easy feat. Consequently, to become useful to our entrepreneurship theory, future research is charged with overcoming a difficult challenge.

Based on the work presented in this volume, a fruitful starting point for future work might entail more clearly delineating the components and interrelationships between the components of this multi-level perspective of new-venture emergence. The importance of pursuing a process view has been advocated not only in the broader organizational and entrepreneurship research (cf. Shane, 2006; Mackenzie, 2004; Busenitz et al., 2003; Heath & Sitkin, 2001), but also by Jaussi and Cogliser and Stambaugh as they have reviewed our work. This growing consensus suggests the need to apply process perspectives to phenomena like those investigated here and highlights the importance of clearly specifying the components and instigators of the process of new-venture emergence. We hope our effort has added momentum to this movement, and can guide further exploration of the processes that lead from visions to ventures.

ACKNOWLEDGMENTS

We are grateful to Michael Mumford for the opportunity to present our musings in a venue that has allowed us to expand our work in greater detail than we might have been unable to achieve elsewhere. We feel fortunate to be a part of a publication that encourages scholarly discussion of important topics such as those covered in this volume. We would also like to thank Kimberly Jaussi, Claudia Cogliser, and Jeffery Stambaugh for their considerate and constructive suggestions and commentaries on our work.

REFERENCES

Busenitz, L. W., West, G. P., Shepherd, D., Nelson, T., Chandler, G. N., & Zacharakis, A. (2003). Entrepreneurship research in emergence: Past trends and future directions. *Journal of Management, 29*(3), 285–308.
Cogliser, C., & Stambaugh, J. (this volume). A Multi-level process view of new-venture emergence: Impressive first steps toward a model. In: M. D. Mumford, S. T. Hunter & K. E. Bedell-Avers (Eds), *Research in multi-level issues: Multi-level issues in creativity and innovation* (Vol. 7). Oxford, UK: Elsevier.
Ford, C.M., & Sullivan, D.M. (this volume). A multi-level process view of new venture emergence. In: M. D. Mumford, S. T. Hunter & K. E. Bedell-Avers (Eds), *Research in multi-level issues: Multi-level issues in creativity and innovation* (Vol. 7). Oxford, UK: Elsevier.
Heath, C., & Sitkin, S. B. (2001). Big-B versus Big-O: What is *organizational* about organizational behavior? *Journal of Organizational Behavior, 22*, 43–58.
Hedström, P., & Swedberg, R. (1998). Social mechanisms: An introductory essay. In: P. Hedström & R. Swedberg (Eds), *Social mechanisms: An analytical approach to social theory* (pp. 1–30). Cambridge, UK: Cambridge University Press.
Jaussi, K. (this volume). Do levels and phases always happen together? Questions for considering the case of new-venture emergence. In: M. D. Mumford, S. T. Hunter & K. E. Bedell-Avers (Eds), *Research in multi-level issues: Multi-level issues in creativity and innovation* (Vol. 7). Oxford, UK: Elsevier.
Lewin, A. Y., Long, C. P., & Carroll, T. N. (1999). The coevolution of new organizational forms. *Organization Science, 10*(5), 535–550.

Mackenzie, K. D. (2004). The process approach to multi-level organizational behavior. In: F. Dansereau & F. J. Yammarino (Eds), *Multi-level issues in organizational behavior and processes* (pp. 347–417). Amsterdam: JAI Press.

Murmann, J. P. (2003). *Knowledge and competitive advantage*. Cambridge, UK: Cambridge University Press.

Sarasvathy, S. D. (2001). Causation and effectuation: Toward a theoretical shift from economic inevitability to entrepreneurial contingency. *Academy of Management Review, 26*(2), 243–263.

Shane, S. (2006). Introduction to the focused issue on entrepreneurship. *Management Science, 52*(2), 155–159.

Weick, K. E. (1979). *The social psychology of organizing* (2nd ed.). New York: McGraw Hill.

Weick, K. E., Sutcliffe, K. M., & Obstfeld, D. (2005). Organizing and the process of sensemaking. *Organization Science, 16*(4), 409–451.

PART VI:
ABOUT THE AUTHORS

ABOUT THE AUTHORS

Mark D. Agars is an associate professor of psychology at California State University, San Bernardino. He received his Ph.D. from the Pennsylvania State University in industrial and organizational psychology, where he worked with James L. Farr.

M. Ronald Buckley is the JC Penney Company Chair of Business Leadership and professor of management and professor of psychology in the Michael F. Price College of Business at the University of Oklahoma. He has published a myriad of research articles relating to human resources management and organizational behavior on the topics of performance appraisal, expectation-lowering procedures during organizational socialization, and ethics training programs. His research has appeared in *Academy of Management Review, Journal of Applied Psychology, Organizational Behavior and Human Decision Processes, Leadership Quarterly, Organizational Dynamics, Journal of Management*, and *Journal of Vocational Behavior*.

Claudia C. Cogliser is on the Faculty of Management at Texas Tech University. She received her Ph.D. from the University of Miami, with a focus on leadership and research methods, and served previously on the faculties of Oregon State University and the University of Oklahoma. Her research interests include leader–follower relationships, virtual team leadership, scale development, and multi-level analysis. Dr. Cogliser's research has been published in *Leadership Quarterly, Journal of Management, Journal of Organizational Behavior, Organizational Research Methods*, and *Educational and Psychological Measurement*. She serves on the editorial board of *Leadership Quarterly*. Dr. Cogliser is on the board of the Southern Management Association, and conducts numerous professional development workshops on multi-level analysis and scale development.

Jeremy F. Dawson is a research fellow in the Work and Organizational Psychology Group at Aston University, Birmingham, United Kingdom. He received an M.S. in statistics from the University of Sheffield in 1998, and his research focuses predominantly on statistical and methodological areas.

His research interests include measurement of group diversity, moderated multiple regression, missing data in team and group research, and the effects of aggregation on statistical inference.

Shelley D. Dionne is an associate professor of leadership and organizational behavior at Binghamton University's School of Management and a fellow in the Center for Leadership Studies. Her research interests include leadership, multiple levels of analysis, and creativity. She has published in *Journal of Applied Psychology*, *Leadership Quarterly*, *Organizational Dynamics*, and *Journal of Organizational Behavior*.

John E. Ettlie is the Madelon L. and Richard N. Rosett Professor of Business Administration and Director of the Technology Management Center at the Rochester Institute of Technology. He earned his Ph.D. at Northwestern University in 1975 and has held appointments since then at the University of Illinois Chicago, De Paul University, the Industrial Technology Institute, the University of Michigan Business School, the US Business School in Prague, and Catolica University in Lisbon, Portugal. Dr. Ettlie has published more than 70 refereed journal articles, 85 trade articles, and book chapters. He has also made more than 100 professional presentations worldwide, on the management of technological innovation. He has authored six books, including the second edition of his textbook *Managing Innovation* (Elsevier, 2006).

James L. Farr is professor of psychology at the Pennsylvania State University. He received his Ph.D. in industrial–organizational psychology at the University of Maryland. His research interests include employee selection, performance management, and workplace innovation. A former president of the Society for Industrial and Organizational Psychology, he was editor of *Human Performance* from 2001 to 2006.

Cameron M. Ford is the founding director of the UCF ʹTechnological Entrepreneurship Center and an associate professor of entrepreneurship at the University of Central Florida. He earned his Ph.D. in business administration in 1990 from Pennsylvania State University and served on the faculty of Rutgers University before joining UCF. His scholarly interests focus on creativity and entrepreneurship by describing how novel ideas evolve, gain legitimacy, and attract resources during the new-venture emergence process. Dr. Ford's research has appeared in more than 60 academic articles. He has also published numerous book chapters related to creativity and entrepreneurship, and edited the books *Creative Action in Organizations* and *The Handbook of Organizational Creativity*. Dr. Ford serves on the editorial boards of *Journal of Creative Behavior* and *Creativity and Innovation Management.*

Jonathon R. B. Halbesleben is an assistant professor in the Department of Management and Human Resources at the University of Wisconsin–Eau Claire. His current research interests include stress and burnout, work–family linkages, and health-care management. His research has appeared in such journals as the *Journal of Applied Psychology, Journal of Management, Leadership Quarterly,* and *Organizational Dynamics.*

Anne E. Herman is a Ph.D. candidate at the University of Nebraska at Omaha and a research consultant with Kenexa, Inc. She has focused her research and applied experiences on individual creativity, leadership, organizational effectiveness, group dynamics, problem solving, goal setting, organizational surveys, and measurement scale properties.

Kimberly S. Jaussi is an associate professor of organizational behavior and leadership in the School of Management at Binghamton University and a fellow in the Center for Leadership Studies. She received her Ph.D. from the Marshall School of Business at the University of Southern California. Her research interests include creativity and leadership, creativity and entrepreneurship, unconventional leader behavior, strategic leadership, organizational commitment, and identity issues in diverse groups.

James C. Kaufman is an associate professor at the California State University at San Bernardino, where he is also the director of the Learning Research Institute. He received his Ph.D. from Yale University in cognitive psychology, where he worked with Robert J. Sternberg. He is the co-editor of the Division 10 APA journal *Psychology of Aesthetics, Creativity, and the Arts,* and he has edited and authored nine books. Kaufman received the 2003 Daniel E. Berlyne Award from the APA for outstanding research by a junior scholar.

Tiffany R. Locke is a graduate student in the industrial and organizational psychology program at California State University, San Bernardino, where she is working with Mark D. Agars. Locke earned her B.S. in psychology from the University of Redlands.

Heather MacDonald is currently completing her Ph.D. in industrial/organizational psychology at the University of Waterloo. Her primary areas of research include leadership, cross-cultural psychology, and performance management.

Christine Miller is a Ph.D. candidate (anthropology and management) at Wayne State University. Her dissertation research incorporates an ethnographic study of the role of culture in mediating the relationship between formalization and innovation within the product development division of a Tier One automotive supplier. Ms. Miller's research interests include how sociality and culture influence the design of new products, and exploration of the human–computer interface in relation to technology-mediated communication within group, team, and network situations. She has served on the faculty of the Business School at Wayne State University and is currently involved in research for Motorola that focuses on sharing and communication practices within close social networks. Ms. Miller holds a position on the board of the National Association of Practicing Anthropologists (NAPA).

Richard N. Osborn is University Distinguished Professor of Management in the Department of Business, School of Business Administration, Wayne State University. His research focuses on strategic leadership, international alliance formation and performance, and the management of multinational firms using advanced technologies. Dr. Osborn is one of 33 charter members of the Academy of Management's Journals Hall of Fame. He currently serves on the editorial board of *Leadership Quarterly* and has served multiple terms on the editorial boards of *Academy of Management Journal, Academy of Management Review,* and *Journal of Management,* among others. He was also a guest editor for a special issue of *Academy of Management Journal,* and *Journal of World Business*'s editor for international strategy. His sponsored research totals some $8 million and includes contracts and grants from the National Science Foundation, the Nuclear Regulatory Commission, the Department of Energy, the Army Research Institute, the Department of Defense, and several private corporations.

Roni Reiter-Palmon is a professor and Director of the industrial/organizational psychology graduate program at the University of Nebraska at Omaha. She received her Ph.D. from George Mason University in industrial/organizational psychology. Dr. Reiter-Palmon has published and has applied experiences in the areas of individual creativity and innovation, leadership, personality in the workplace, and job analysis.

Mark A. Runco received his Ph.D. in cognitive psychology from the Claremont Graduate School. He has taught at the University of Hawaii, Hilo; California State University, Fullerton; and the Norwegian School of Economics and Business Administration. He is still on the faculty of the first two universities and holds an adjunct professorship with the Saybrook

Institute. Dr. Runco founded and edits the *Creativity Research Journal* and co-edited the *Encyclopedia of Creativity*. His latest book is *Creativity: Research, Development, and Practice*. He is past president and fellow of Division 10 of the American Psychological Association (APA) and recipient of the Early Scholar and E. Paul Torrance Awards from the National Association for Gifted Children.

Claudia A. Sacramento is a doctoral researcher at the Work and Organisational Psychology Group at Aston University, Birmingham, United Kingdom. Her research interests concern creativity and implementation of innovation, the impact of stressors on teams, and team regulation processes.

Christina E. Shalley is the NSF ADVANCE Professor for the College of Management and a professor of organizational behavior and human resource management at the Georgia Institute of Technology. She received her Ph.D. in business administration from the University of Illinois at Urbana–Champaign. Her current research interests focus on investigating the effects of various social and contextual factors in enhancing or stifling employee creativity and examining ways to structure jobs and the work environment to support creative work. She has published in such journals as *Academy of Management Journal, Academy of Management Review, Journal of Applied Psychology, Journal of Management,* and *Organizational Behavior and Human Decision Processes*. She also serves on the editorial board of *Journal of Management*.

Jeffrey E. Stambaugh is a Ph.D. student in the Area of Management at Texas Tech University. A graduate of the US Air Force Academy, he retired after 24 years of air force service flying high-performance jets and commanding various organizations. His research interests include the relationship between diversification and firm performance as well as the entrepreneurial exploitation phase. While still in the air force, he published in *Parameters*, the US Army's flagship journal.

Diane M. Sullivan is an assistant professor at the University of Dayton. She completed her Ph.D. in 2006 at the University of Central Florida. Her primary research interests include entrepreneurship, entrepreneurial networks, opportunity recognition, and organizational creativity. She has published research in journals such as the *Journal of Organizational Behavior* and the *Korean Journal of Thinking and Problem Solving*. She has also published book chapters related to creativity, entrepreneurship, and leadership; in addition, her work has appeared at a number of national and regional conferences.

Lorne Sulsky is a professor of management at Wilfred Laurier University. His primary areas of research are in the areas of performance management and work stress. He also serves as the editor of *Canadian Journal of Behavioral Science,* a quarterly journal published by the Canadian Psychological Association, and is a member of the editorial board for *Human Performance.*

Simon Taggar is an associate professor at Wilfrid Laurier University. His primary research interests lie in the areas of creativity, teams, and leadership. He has published in journals including the *Academy of Management Journal, Journal of Applied Psychology,* and *Personnel Psychology.*

Veronique Tran is assistant professor of organizational behavior at ESCP-EAP (European School of Management), Paris, France. She received her Ph.D. in psychology at the University of Geneva, Switzerland. Her research interests include emotion and decision making (both group decision making and strategic decision making), innovation and creativity as multi-level phenomena, team dynamics, team performance, top management teams, and organizational learning, linked to the issue of sharing information and knowledge.

Michael A. West is professor of organizational psychology and Head of Research at Aston Business School, Birmingham, United Kingdom. He graduated from the University of Wales in 1973 and received his Ph.D. in 1977 (the psychology of meditation). He then spent a year working in the coal mines of South Wales. He has authored 17 books and more than 150 scientific and practitioner articles and book chapters. He is a fellow of the British Psychological Society, the American Psychological Association (APA), the Chartered Institute of Personnel and Development, the International Association of Applied Psychology, and the Royal Society for the Encouragement of Arts, Manufactures, and Commerce. His areas of research interest are team and organizational innovation and effectiveness.

Anthony R. Wheeler is an assistant professor of human resources management in the Foster College of Business Administration at Bradley University. He holds a Ph.D. in industrial–organizational psychology from the University of Oklahoma, and he is a certified senior professional in human resources (SPHR). His research focuses on the influence of human resources on person–organization fit and focuses on alternative staffing strategies. He has published his research in management outlets such as *Research in Personnel and Human Resources Management, International Journal of Selection and Assessment, Journal of Business Logistics,* and *Journal of Business Ethics.*

SET UP A CONTINUATION ORDER TODAY!

Did you know that you can set up a continuation order on all Elsevier-JAI series and have each new volume sent directly to you upon publication? For details on how to set up a **continuation order**, contact your nearest regional sales office listed below.

To view related series in Business & Management, please visit:

www.elsevier.com/businessandmanagement

The Americas
Customer Service Department
11830 Westline Industrial Drive
St. Louis, MO 63146
USA
US customers:
Tel: +1 800 545 2522 (Toll-free number)
Fax: +1 800 535 9935
For Customers outside US:
Tel: +1 800 460 3110 (Toll-free number).
Fax: +1 314 453 7095
usbkinfo@elsevier.com

Europe, Middle East & Africa
Customer Service Department
Linacre House
Jordan Hill
Oxford OX2 8DP
UK
Tel: +44 (0) 1865 474140
Fax: +44 (0) 1865 474141
eurobkinfo@elsevier.com

Japan
Customer Service Department
2F Higashi Azabu, 1 Chome Bldg
1-9-15 Higashi Azabu, Minato-ku
Tokyo 106-0044
Japan
Tel: +81 3 3589 6370
Fax: +81 3 3589 6371
books@elsevierjapan.com

APAC
Customer Service Department
3 Killiney Road #08-01
Winsland House I
Singapore 239519
Tel: +65 6349 0222
Fax: +65 6733 1510
asiainfo@elsevier.com

Australia & New Zealand
Customer Service Department
30-52 Smidmore Street
Marrickville, New South Wales 2204
Australia
Tel: +61 (02) 9517 8999
Fax: +61 (02) 9517 2249
service@elsevier.com.au

30% Discount for Authors on All Books!

A 30% discount is available to Elsevier book and journal contributors on all books *(except multi-volume reference works)*.

To claim your discount, full payment is required with your order, which must be sent directly to the publisher at the nearest regional sales office above.